Build It Better Yourself

Editor: William H. Hylton

Assistant Editor: Steve Smyser

Copy Editor: Ann Snyder

Design: Terri Lepley

Shop Manager: Richard Weinsteiger

Copy:

Ken Bixby
William H. Hylton
Glenn Kranzley
Gene Logsdon
Jack Ruttle
Steve Smyser

Illustrations:

Steven DuPont
Erick Ingraham
David Onopa
Sally Onopa
David Purcell
Martin Remaly
David Traub
Pat Traub

Photos:

John Hamel
William H. Hylton
Gene Logsdon
Warner Tilsher

Special Assistance:

Hank Allison, Diana Branch, David Caccia, David Chase,
Roy Dycus, Harold Geiss, Judi Hylton, Karen Lalik, Drew
Langsner, Jim Schneck, Robert Sprague, Mike Stoner, Warner
Tilsher, Carole Turko, Billy R. Tyler, Dan Wallace, Al Wonch

Build It Better Yourself

*By the editors of
Organic Gardening
and Farming®*

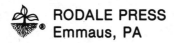 RODALE PRESS
Emmaus, PA

Library of Congress Cataloging in Publication Data
Main entry under title:

Build it better yourself.

    Includes index.
    1. Building—Amateurs' manuals. 2. Do-it-yourself work.
I. Organic gardening and farming.
TH148.B84   681'.763   76-55749
ISBN O-87857-133-7

Printed in the United States of America on recycled paper

4 6 8 10 9 7 5 3

Contents

Contents

PART II
Outdoor Gardening Projects

Contents

Contents

PART IV
Around the Homestead

Contents

Contents

PART I
Indoor Gardening Projects

PLANTING FLATS

One of the most basic woodworking projects for the gardener is the construction of planting flats.

It is a perfect project for the beginner. The construction of the flat is simple. The appearance of the flat isn't terribly important, so mistakes—imperfect joints, wood split by nails, and the like—are of little consequence. The most basic of hand tools—hammer, saw, and ruler—are all that are required. The materials are relatively inexpensive, and, even better, old crating and similar scrap materials make excellent flats.

Equally important for the gardener, planting flats are crucial to getting an early start in the garden. By planting seeds indoors in flats a month or two before the last frost, you'll be that much ahead when spring really does come.

A planting flat is nothing more than a shallow box with no lid. It can be any size you want it to be. If you buy new lumber to construct your flats, you can make them any size you want. If you use scrap materials, the materials may dictate the size of the finished product.

The most commonplace materials are suitable. Ordinary 1-inch pine board will do. Plywood will do, so long as it is an exterior grade (which means it is held together with a waterproof glue). You may want to treat your flats with a wood preservative; just make sure it is a copper naphthenate preparation, as most other kinds will injure plants. You could even paint your flats, with exterior house paint or a polyurethane varnish. For flats that will be in use continually—as opposed to the once-a-year use most flats are subjected to—you may want to spend the extra money for rot-resistant wood, such as redwood, cedar, or cypress.

MATERIALS

Wood

1 x 4 (length depends on the size of the flat you will make)

$\frac{3}{8}''$ or $\frac{1}{2}''$ ext. plywood (amount depends on the size of the flat you will make)

Hardware

4d box nails
Copper naphthenate wood preservative

If you've ever acquired a flat through purchase at a nursery or garden center, you'll probably find it made of ½-inch stock. And if you check with your local lumber dealer, you'll probably find ½-inch stock tough to come by. We'd suggest recycling a few wooden crates to make your flats. Or use 1-inch stock for the sides and strips of ⅜- or ½-inch exterior plywood for the bottom. Don't bother trying hardboard (Masonite) or interior plywood; your flats will self-destruct after only brief use.

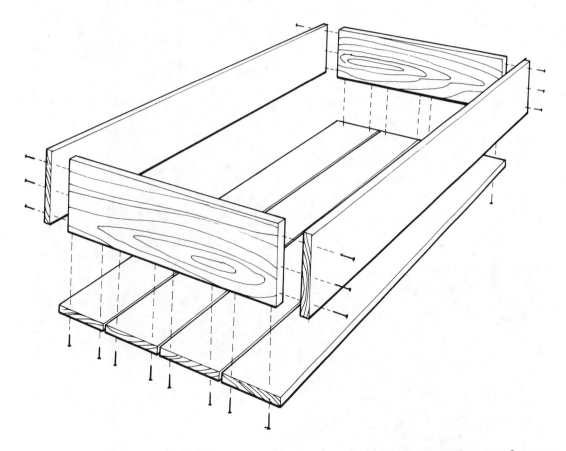

The exploded drawing clearly shows the construction procedure. Merely cut two sides of equal length, two ends of equal length, and nail them all together using common nails and the simple butt joint. Cut wood to cover the bottom and nail it in place. Voilà! A planting flat.

SPECIAL TOOLS

For the gardener who uses a lot of flats, early gardening can be speeded up with three simple tools.

Planting medium can be sifted right into the flats with a hand sifter. Nail together four pieces of 1 x 4 stock, just as though making a flat. But instead of bottom boards, nail or staple ¼-inch hardware cloth across the frame.

After the soil is sifted into the flat, tamp it with a float, made by nailing a 1 x 2, on edge, down the long center of a length of 1 x 8 or 1 x 10.

Next, using a board punctured with evenly spaced nails, make holes in the soil for seeds. Finally, after seeding the flat, tamp the surface once again with the float.

SEEDING SPACER

A more elaborate seeding spacer for flats was contrived by Warner Tilsher of California.

Tilsher cut a 9¾-inch square from ¾-inch exterior plywood and glued twenty-five nubbins to it with epoxy glue. The nubbins are ⅜-inch slices of 1 x 1, tapered with sandpaper or a file. They are glued to the plywood in a 2-inch grid, as shown. A handle was cut from plywood with a coping saw, finished with sandpaper, and attached to the board with ½-inch #6 screws. A standard door pull could just as easily be used.

MATERIALS

Wood

       1–2' sq. sht. ¾" ext. plywood or **Base:** 1 pc. 9¾" sq.

       1 pc. 1 x 1 x 2' or **Nubbins:** 25 pcs. 1 x 1 x ⅜"

Hardware

       Epoxy glue
       2–½" #6 screws
       Standard door pull

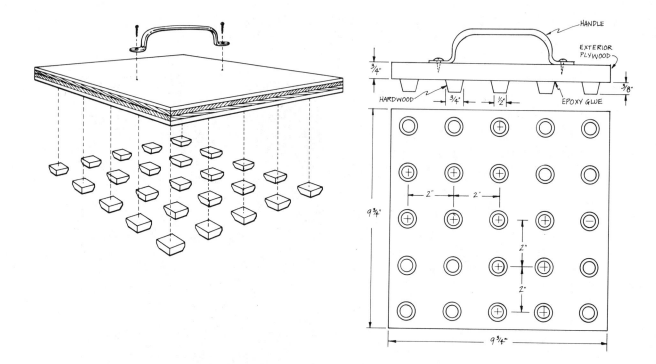

HANDLE

EXTERIOR PLYWOOD

HARDWOOD   3/4"   1/2"   EPOXY GLUE

3/4"   3/8"

2"   2"

9 3/4"

2"

2"

2"

9 3/4"

PEAT POT TRAY

Peat pots are popular with many gardeners. The idea is to start your plants indoors in little degradable pots that at the appropriate time you put in the ground along with the plant to eliminate any chance of transplanting shock. An added benefit is that you don't need flats. Or do you?

Wilmer Westbrook, an Alabamian, disliked handling each peat pot individually. His home climate allows for a double crop of most vegetables, if he cheats a little and starts them growing in flats and peat pots. So he uses a lot of peat pots regularly.

To eliminate the vexing piecework, he devised the pictured trays. The ends and bottom are cut from ⅜-inch exterior plywood. The bottom measures 12 inches by 16 inches. The ends are 3 inches by 12 inches and are butted against the bottom, with nails driven through into the bottom. Drill a ½-inch hole in each upper corner of the ends, an inch from the top and edge. Two lengths of 12-gauge electrical wire (with the insulation still on) are threaded through these holes in such a fashion as to provide a guard and a handle. The handgrip is a section of garden hose.

Each tray holds forty-eight of the 2-inch peat pots. The tray is home for the pots from the time they are seeded to the time they are transplanted into the garden.

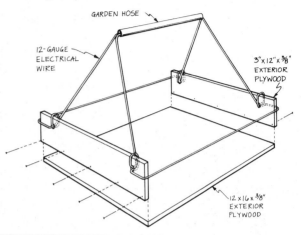

MATERIALS

Wood

    1–2′ x 4′ sht. ⅜″ ext. plywood   or   **Bottom:** 1 pc. 12″ x 16″

                                                          Ends: 2 pcs. 3″ x 12″

Hardware

    4d box nails

    Small roll 12-gauge electrical wire   or   **Handle and side guards:**

                                                                2 pcs. 5′ long

    12″ length of garden hose (handgrip)

PLANT BAND FLAT

Here's a low-cost wooden planting flat designed and constructed to take 3-inch-wide plant bands, which were cut from either pint- or quart-sized paper milk cartons. The project was the brainstorm of Montana gardener Al DeMangelaere.

The tray can be constructed of any scrap material; the one pictured was made from a 1 x 4 and ½-inch exterior plywood. It can be designed to hold any convenient number of planting bands—DeMangelaere made his to hold twenty-four. Consequently, the *inside* measurements are 17 inches by 11¼ inches by 3½ inches. One side is held in place by the planting bands on the inside and small cleats nailed to the ends on the outside, permitting the side to be removed. With the side removed, a flat trowel can easily be slipped under the plant and band to speed the transplanting process.

In transplanting, incidentally, the planting bands may be left around

the young seedlings to discourage cutworms.

The planting bands are easily accumulated, collapse conveniently for storage, and are durable enough, if treated with due care, to be reused several times. To make the bands, rinse out the empty paper container, then slice it into 3-inch bands with a sharp knife or single-edge razor blade. Fold them flat, put a rubber band around them, and store until needed.

CONSTRUCTION

1. Cut the 1 x 4 into two pieces measuring 17 inches long, two pieces measuring 13½ inches long and one piece measuring 3½ inches long. Rip two 1 x 1 cleats from the 3½-inch piece.
2. Nail the 1 x 1 cleats to the end pieces as shown.
3. Butt the ends to one 17-inch side and nail in place.
4. Nail the bottom in place.
5. Fill the tray with planting bands and slip the remaining side in place.

MATERIALS

Wood

    1 pc. 1 x 4 x 8′   or   **Sides:** 2 pcs. 1 x 4 x 17″
                                           2 pcs. 1 x 4 x 13½″

                                   Cleats: 2 pcs. 1 x 1″ x 3½″
                                         (rip from 1 x 4 scrap)

    1–2′ x 4′ sht. ½″ ext. plywood or **Bottom:** 1 pc. 18½″ x 12¾″

Hardware

    4d box nails

Miscellaneous

    24 milk carton bands

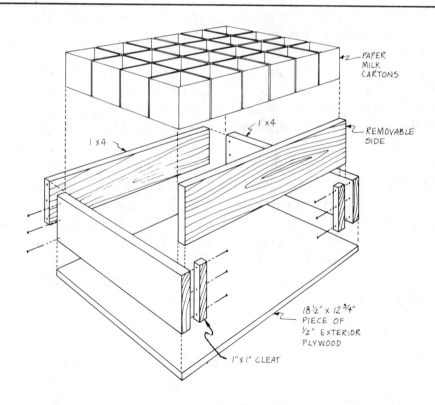

PAPER
MILK
CARTONS

1 x 4

1 x 4

REMOVABLE
SIDE

18½″ x 12¾″
PIECE OF
½″ EXTERIOR
PLYWOOD

1″ x 1″ CLEAT

PROPAGATION FLATS

An ordinary flat can be converted into an inexpensive propagation case with a single piece of glass. A more elaborate setup can be made with a flat and five pieces of glass.

A propagation case is good for reproducing favored plants from cuttings because they will stay true to variety and mature much earlier than plants grown from seed.

The successful rooting of cuttings is invariably aided by maintaining a warm moist environment for the entire cutting, not just the rooting area. The most primitive technique for doing this is to envelop a cutting-bearing pot or flat with clear plastic film (the sort dry cleaners use for packaging).

As shown, a pane of glass will convert a planting flat into a propagation case, but obviously it won't do for cuttings or for other than the barest of sprouts. So, use five panes of glass—four for the sides and one for the top, as shown. You may want to tape the panes that form the sides together,

leaving the top loose for access. The panes may not completely seal off the outside air, but you don't really want to do that anyway.

For the gardener-handyman who doesn't like to do things halfway, a wooden framework can be constructed to hold the panes and make a finished case.

But a fancy case isn't necessary for sprouting seeds and getting the gardening off to an early start. Steveson McDonald developed an inexpensive way to get seeds started indoors and to recycle egg cartons at the same time by creating a series of mini-greenhouses.

CONSTRUCTION

1. Form loops of the pieces of wire by bending them around a 1-pound-size coffee can. With pliers, bend ¾ inch of the end of the wire in at right angles.
2. Remove the lid of the carton, punch holes in the bottom of each egg compartment with a 6d nail, and attach the wire loops as shown. Tie

the wooden slat to the wire loops to hold them in place.

3. Lay the plastic out on a table and place the carton on top of it, with the 20-inch width parallel with the egg carton. Then lift one end of the plastic up over the wood slat, overlapping it about 2 inches, and staple the plastic to the wood at three points.

4. Next, fill the egg compartments with a good potting soil and firm each section, leveling and removing any excess. Lift the free end of the plastic sheet up over the top and secure with two pieces of masking tape. Twist each end and fasten about 1 inch back with rubber bands.

MATERIALS

Hardware

Small roll $\frac{3}{32}$" galvanized wire   or   **Loops:** 3 pcs. 20" long

Miscellaneous

Styrofoam egg carton
1 window shade slat   or   1 pc. $\frac{1}{4}$" x $\frac{3}{4}$" x 15"
String
1 roll 4-mil plastic, 36" wide   or   1 pc. 20" x 36"
Masking tape

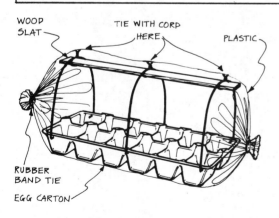

WOOD SLAT — TIE WITH CORD HERE — PLASTIC — RUBBER BAND TIE — EGG CARTON

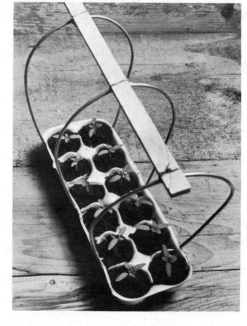

To use the miniature terrarium, carefully pull the masking tape off and pour an ounce or so of water onto the plastic being careful not to get water on the soil-filled sections. Don't add

13

too much water at first. Let it stand for a few hours and the holes in the bottom will allow the moisture to reach the soil by capillary action. When the soil appears moist on top, you're ready to plant the seeds.

Again, remove the masking tape carefully, reach through, and place the seed or seeds into each compartment, then cover lightly with some fine sand. Place in a warm, lighted window, and close up the top again to keep in the moisture, which will condense on the sides and run down again to be soaked up by the holes in the bottom.

Keep a close watch the first few days to make sure the top soil stays moist. Your miniature terrarium will need little attention until the seedlings get large enough to put in larger individual pots. At this time, the entire section can easily be lifted, as the sides are sloped, and placed into another pot of soil without shocking the root system in any way.

PLANT STANDS

If you have a lot of houseplants, finding a spot for all of them can be a trial. Table and furniture tops get crowded; windowsills are often too narrow. Hanging plants can block the light and restrict your view of the outdoors.

For the home handyman, it is just another opportunity to spend some time in the workshop. The following projects will undoubtedly start you thinking of ways to use them in your own home, or of ways to modify or improve them.

SINGLE-PLANT STAND

Perhaps the most simple plant stand is one that highlights a single, treasured plant. The one shown is ideal for the novice woodworker, since it is easily made in a single evening, using the most basic hand tools. It requires only one 8-foot piece of 1 x 12, some glue, a dozen 1¼-inch brads, and a dozen 8d finishing nails.

The design is very adaptable: the stand can easily be made shorter or taller or from a narrower board.

The finished product, which can be painted, stained, and/or varnished, is a handsome pedestal for your favorite houseplant.

MATERIALS

Wood

    1 pc. 1 x 12 x 8′ or **Sides:** 4 pcs. 1 x 12 x 20″

                                 Bottom: 1 pc. $\frac{3}{4}$″ x 10″ x 10″ (act. meas.)

                                 Cleats: 4 pcs. 1 x 1 x 6″ (rip from scrap)

Hardware

    $1\frac{1}{4}$″ brads
    8d finishing nails
    White glue

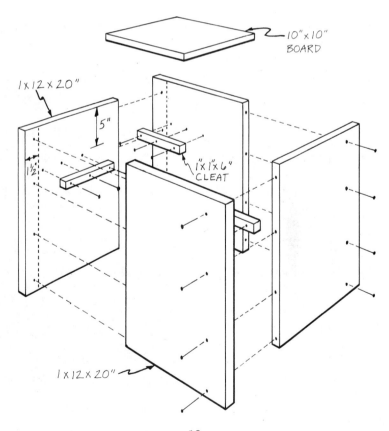

CONSTRUCTION

1. Cut four 20-inch lengths from the 1 x 12. Sand them well.
2. Cut a 10-inch-square piece from the remaining 1 x 12.
3. Rip the last scrap of 1 x 12 into 1 x 1 by 6-inch cleats. You'll need four.
4. Mark each of the four sides 1½ inches from the left-hand edge.
5. Fasten a cleat to each 20-inch board using glue and 1¼-inch brads. Locate the cleat 1½ inches from the left-hand edge of the board and 5 inches below the top (end-grain) of the board.
6. Glue and nail the sides together using 8d finishing nails. The pencil line will serve as a guideline and the cleat as a brace.
7. Drop the 10-inch-square piece into the top of the completed planter so it rests on the cleats. It can be glued and/or nailed in place.

INDOOR PLANT RACK

Here's an easily constructed indoor plant rack that you can use to hold houseplants against a glass patio door to make use of winter sunlight, or as a place for storing unused clay pots. When it's a seed-planting rack, the handholds allow you to turn it around. This way the seedlings will not become spindly as they twist toward the sun. Martin Burns, who designed and built this rack, notes it is economical to build from white pine shelving. Except for a saber or coping saw, all you need are common hand tools.

CONSTRUCTION

1. From the 1 x 10 cut two 30-inch lengths, to serve as the sides.
2. With a coping or saber saw cut the taper into the two sides, as shown, 8 inches at the bottom narrowing to 6 inches at the top. Round off the top.

17

MATERIALS

Wood

1 pc. 1 x 10 x 12' or **Sides:** 2 pcs. 1 x 10 x 30″

Shelves: 3 pcs. 1 x 10 x 24″
Lower shelf: 8″ wide
Middle shelf: 7″ wide
Top shelf: 6″ wide

Shelf strips: 6 pcs. 1 x 2 x 24″ (rip from scrap)

Hardware

4d finishing nails or 1¼″ brads
8d finishing nails
Wood glue

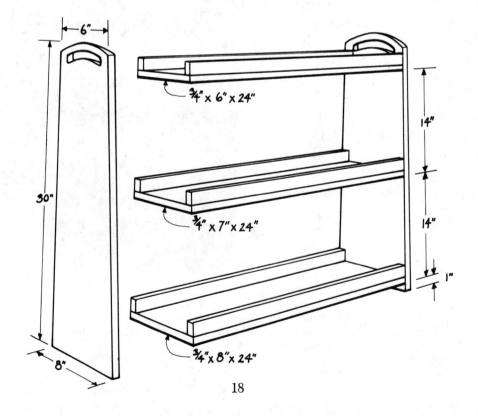

3. Cut handholds by drilling a ¾-inch hole at each end of the area to be cut, then saw between the holes.
4. Finish handholds with a round rasp, then sandpaper.
5. With a coping or handsaw rip three shelves to sizes shown, then rip six 1 x 2 by 24-inch outside shelf strips from 1 x 10 scrap.
6. Glue and nail strips to shelves using 4d finishing nails or 1¼-inch brads.
7. Position the 8-inch shelf 1 inch from the floor, then space the other shelves 14 inches apart. Glue and nail to the sides with 8d finishing nails.
8. Sand entire rack and finish.

MULTIPLE-PLANT STAND

A more complex project, but one still within the realm of possibility for the novice, is this stand for a variety of houseplants, large and small. It is essentially three boxes joined together, with a shelf hung on the front.

The project involves the use of basic hand tools, common board lumber, glue, and finishing nails. All the parts should be well sanded and finished before assembly. Moreover, the parts should be assembled in sequence, or assembly will be difficult indeed.

CONSTRUCTION

1. Cut the following pieces: three 1 x 8s, 24 inches long; two 1 x 12s, 24 inches long; six 1 x 12s, 18 inches long; one 1 x 4, 24 inches long; two 1 x 4s, 4¾ inches long. Sand them all well.
2. Cut a 6-inch by 4-inch corner from each of the 24-inch 1 x 12s. It is simplest to clamp the two boards together and cut both at one time. Leave them clamped together until the first set of cleats is installed.

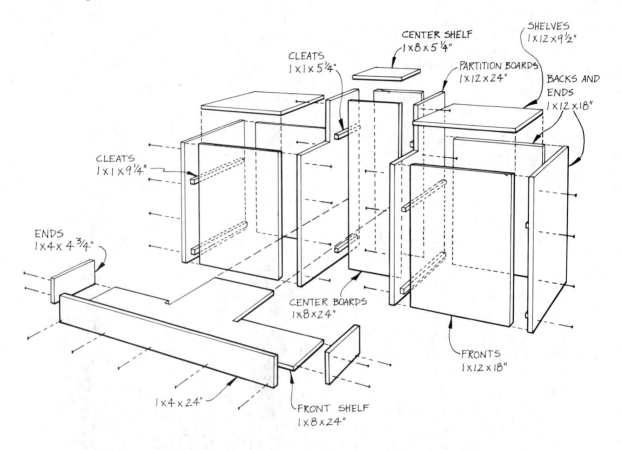

CENTER SHELF
1 x 8 x 5¼"

SHELVES
1 x 12 x 9½"

CLEATS
1 x 1 x 5¼"

PARTITION BOARDS
1 x 12 x 24"

BACKS AND
ENDS
1 x 12 x 18"

CLEATS
1 x 1 x 9¼"

ENDS
1 x 4 x 4¾"

CENTER BOARDS
1 x 8 x 24"

FRONTS
1 x 12 x 18"

1 x 4 x 24"

FRONT SHELF
1 x 8 x 24"

3. Using glue and 1¼-inch brads, install cleats to guide assembly and to support the plant shelves. There are quite a number of cleats to cut and install, and care extended here will make the final assembly that much easier.

    a. Do the ends—the 18-inch 1 x 12s—first. Cut four 9¼-inch lengths of 1 x 1. Fasten a cleat at the bottom of each end board, centering the cleat so that it is an inch from either edge. Fasten a cleat 6 inches below the top edge.

    b. The partition boards—the 24-inch 1 x 12s—have cleats fastened to both sides, and the proper cleats must be fastened to the proper sides, hence the admonition to leave the two boards clamped together. First cut four 9¼-inch lengths of 1 x 1. Then fasten a cleat at the bottom of each board, centering it so that it is an inch from each edge of the board. Fasten a cleat 12 inches below the very top of each board. Now unclamp the boards and lay them cleats-down on the workbench. Cut four 5¼-inch lengths of 1 x 1. Fasten a cleat to the bottom of each board, locating the cleat an

20

MATERIALS

Wood

1 pc. 1 x 8 x 8′ or	**Front shelf:**	1 pc. 1 x 8 x 24″
	Center boards:	2 pcs. 1 x 8 x 24″
	Center shelf:	1 pc. 1 x 8 x 5¼″
1 pc. 1 x 4 x 6′ or	**Front shelf box:**	1 pc. 1 x 4 x 24″
	Front shelf box ends:	2 pcs. 1 x 4 x 4¾″
1 pc. 1 x 12 x 16′ or	**Partition boards:**	2 pcs. 1 x 12 x 24″
	Fronts, backs, ends:	6 pcs. 1 x 12 x 18″
	Shelves:	2 pcs. 1 x 12 x 9½″
1 pc. 1 x 1 x 6′ or	**Cleats:**	8 pcs. 1 x 1 x 9¼″
		4 pcs. 1 x 1 x 5¼″

Hardware

Glue
1¼″ brads
8d finishing nails

inch from the back edge of the board. Fasten the remaining two cleats 5¾ inches below the very top of the boards and an inch from the back edge.

4. Begin assembly. Using a simple butt joint, glue and nail the 18-inch front pieces to the "inner" sides, countersinking the 8d finishing nails. The fronts merely need to be held against the cleats to get the proper alignment, which means the sides will overlap the fronts by ¼ inch.

5. Now join the two sections together by adding the 24-inch 1 x 8 front. Again, a simple butt joint is used, with the 1 x 8 being held against the cleats, the nails being hammered through the sides into the front piece. Attach the 1 x 8 back in similar fashion.

6. Attach the remaining two sections of the back, toenailing through the backs and into the sides.

7. Glue and nail the outer sides in place.

8. Cut the front shelf to fit from the remaining piece of 1 x 8. This will involve cutting a rectangle approximately 8⅝ inches by 4 inches from

either end of the board, leaving a T-shaped shelf. You will have to saw, chisel, or file two notches in the shelf to accommodate the ¼-inch overlap of the fronts by the inner sides. Getting the shelf to fit properly will probably be a trial and shave process.

9. Once the shelf fits, glue and nail it in place, driving the nails from inside the planter into the shelf. The shelf should be about 12 inches from the bottom.

10. Cut the sides for the shelf so that they will overlap the front by a ¼ inch. Glue and nail them in place, driving the nails from inside the planter into the 1 x 4s. It's best to have the front and sides overlap the bottom of the shelf by at least a ¼ inch.

11. Finally, attach the shelf front. Because of the proximity of the nails to the grain-end of the sides, it is best to drill pilot holes before driving these nails, or the side pieces may split.

12. Measure the interior dimensions of the three planter areas and cut shelves from your remaining scraps of 1 x 12 and 1 x 8.

A MOBILE FLOWER STAND

Here's a portable flower stand that costs about $25 and a few days' pleasant after-hours work, and will give your houseplants a happy home. Since the stand is on casters, it is readily moved from window to window as the seasons change.

The stand is actually made of two pieces of plywood. The 4 x 8 panel is ¾ inch thick. The 4-foot-square piece is ¼-inch material. The thicker wood is used for the sides and shelves, while the thinner forms the lower doors and the back.

According to Robert S. Tupper, who devised this plant stand, it is a good conversation piece when gardening friends call, and you probably will need a friend when you start using a portable saw on the plywood

MATERIALS

Wood

1 sht. ¾" int. plywood w/2 good sides or **Ends:** 2 pcs. 18" x 60"

Bottom: 1 pc. 18" x 45¼"

Top: 1 pc. 19½" x 45¼"

Bottom shelf: 1 pc. 10" x 45¼"

Top shelf: 1 pc. 6" x 45¼"

Base: 2 pcs. 1½" x 43"
2 pcs. 1½" x 16"

1–4' sq. sht. ¼" int. plywood w/1 good side or **Back:** 1 pc. 46" x 22"

Doors: 2 pcs. 23" x 21¼"

Hardware

Wood glue
8d finishing nails
Wood putty
1" brads
4 finger pulls
4 swivel *plate* casters

—the sheets will need solid and rigid support. At that, you'll probably have to finish off many of the cuts with a scroll saw, a band saw, and also a handsaw.

If plywood is used to construct the stand, the edges of each piece may be left a contrasting color, or stained to match the finished surface of the material. Staining should be completed before any glue is used on the stand. Stain will not color wood that has had any glue on it.

CONSTRUCTION

1. Cut the following pieces from the sheet of ¾-inch plywood: two pieces 18 inches by 60 inches (the ends), one piece 18 inches by 45¼ inches (the bottom), one piece 19½ inches by 45¼ inches (the top), one piece 10 inches by 45¼ inches (the bottom shelf), one piece 6 inches by

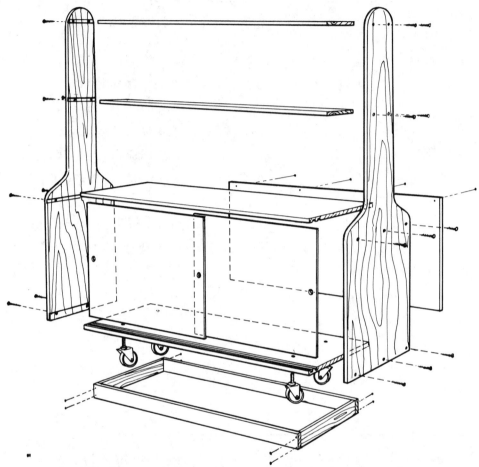

45¼ inches (the top shelf), two pieces 1½ inches by 43 inches and two pieces 1½ inches by 16 inches (the base). Cut the following pieces from the sheet of ¼-inch plywood: one piece 46 inches by 22 inches (the back), and two pieces 23 inches by 21¼ inches (the doors).

2. Clamp the two ends together, and cut them as indicated in the scale drawing.

3. Using a router, a dado on table or radial arm saw, or a handsaw and a chisel, make the rabbets and dadoes indicated on the scale drawing. The dadoes for the top and the shelves and the rabbet for the bottom are all ¾ inch wide and ⅛ inch deep. The rabbet for the back is ¼ inch wide and ½ inch deep.

4. Cut dadoes for the sliding doors and the rabbet for the back in the top. The two dadoes should be 2 inches from the front edge of the top. They should be $\frac{5}{16}$ inch wide, $\frac{5}{16}$ inch deep, and ⅛ inch apart. The rabbet should extend the length of the top, ¼ inch wide and ½ inch deep.

5. Cut dadoes for the sliding doors and the rabbet for the back in the bottom. The dadoes should be ½ inch from the front edge of the bottom. They should be $\frac{5}{16}$ inch wide, ⅛ inch deep, and ⅛ inch apart. The rabbet should be ¼ inch wide and ½ inch deep.

6. *An optional step.* The edges of the various pieces may be shaped as in the photo. All parts should be sanded well, and the finish may be applied. (Some woodworkers will prefer to apply the finish after the stand is assembled.)

7. Fit the top, bottom, and two shelves together with the sides. Fasten them using glue and finishing nails or screws. Countersink nails and fill over with wood putty; countersink screws and conceal them with bits of dowel.

8. Attach the back, using glue and brads.

9. Install the finger pulls in the doors and the doors in the stand. Insert the top of the door in the top groove; it will go in far enough to permit you to swing the bottom into position and drop it into its groove.

10. Assemble the base. You may use a simple butt joint, but a mitered joint will have a better appearance. Use glue and finishing nails.

11. Attach the base to the stand. Use glue and drive finishing nails through the bottom into the base.

12. Attach the casters to the *bottom* of the stand, inside the base.

13. Apply a finish, if you have not already done so.

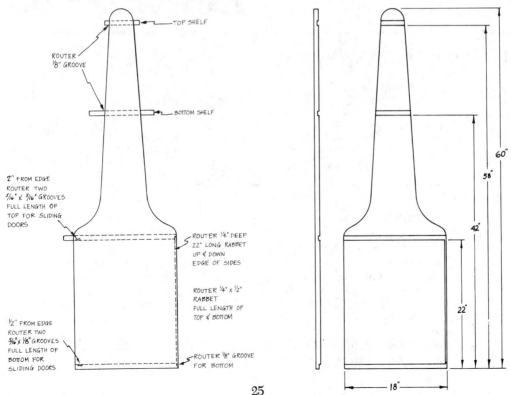

TOP SHELF

ROUTER ⅛" GROOVE

BOTTOM SHELF

2" FROM EDGE
ROUTER TWO
5/16" X 5/16" GROOVES
FULL LENGTH OF
TOP FOR SLIDING
DOORS

ROUTER ¼" DEEP
22" LONG RABBET
UP & DOWN
EDGE OF SIDES

ROUTER ¼" X ½"
RABBET
FULL LENGTH OF
TOP & BOTTOM

½" FROM EDGE
ROUTER TWO
5/16" X ⅛" GROOVES
FULL LENGTH OF
BOTTOM FOR
SLIDING DOORS

ROUTER ⅛" GROOVE
FOR BOTTOM

60"

58"

42"

22"

18"

HANGERS

A dozen feet of 1 x 1, some hardware, and some heavy twine can be the basis for a hanging garden. The materials can be used to make three hangers for potted plants, or they can be used to make a single hanging container for a plant.

MATERIALS (to make three)

Wood

> 1 pc. 1 x 1 x 12′ or 12 pcs. 1 x 1 x 12″ (4 per hanger)

Hardware

> 12–1″ eyebolts w/nuts and washers (4 per hanger)
> 6 yds. heavy twine or lightweight chain (2 yds./hanger)

CONSTRUCTION

1. Cut the 1 x 1 into 12-inch pieces.
2. Using a pencil and try square or a marking gauge, mark each piece for dadoing, as indicated. Two ¾-inch-wide by ⅜-inch-deep dadoes are cut in each piece, 1 inch from either end. Cut up to four pieces at a time, using a backsaw, and complete the dadoes with a chisel and wood rasp. If you have power equipment to cut the dadoes, you'll be done that much quicker.
3. Assemble each hanger. At each half-lap joint, drill a hole completely through the center of the joint to accept an eyebolt.

4. Glue each joint and install the eyebolts.
5. Attach the twine or chain for hanging each plant holder, and you are done.

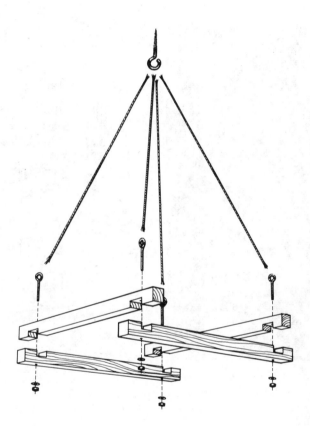

HANGING PLANT CONTAINER

Redwood, cedar, or other rot-resistant wood is generally recommended for such projects as this planter, but any wood, if treated with a copper naphthenate preservative, will do.

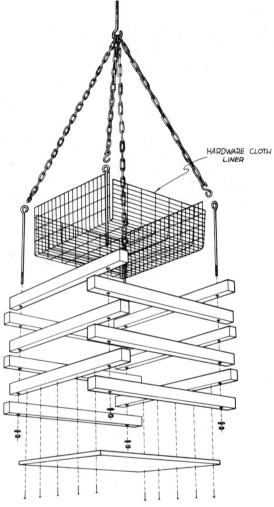

HARDWARE CLOTH
LINER

CONSTRUCTION

1. Cut the 1 x 1 into 12-inch lengths. Drill holes large enough for the eyebolts through each piece, $1\frac{3}{8}$ inches from either end.
2. Stack up the pieces as shown and fasten them with the eyebolts.
3. Rip or plane the 1 x 10 to a width of $8\frac{1}{2}$ inches, and nail it in place with 5d finishing nails.
4. Cut 3-inch by $3\frac{1}{2}$-inch rectangles from the corners of the hardware cloth, as shown. The 3-inch cuts should be into the $14\frac{1}{2}$-inch dimension, the $3\frac{1}{2}$-inch cuts into the 16-inch dimension. Fold the resulting shape into a basket, lace the corners with piano wire, and drop the basket into the hanging planter.
5. Attach the chain or rope to the eyebolts and your planter is finished.

MATERIALS

Wood

1 pc. 1 x 1 x 12'	or	**Sides:** 12 pcs. 1 x 1 x 12"
1 pc. 1 x 10 x 2'	or	**Bottom:** 1 pc. ¾" x 8½" x 10" (act. meas., rip from 1 x 10)

Hardware

4–4¼" eyebolts w/ nuts and washers
5d finishing nails
1 pc. 14½" x 16" hardware cloth, ¼" mesh
Piano wire
8'–12' lightweight chain or rope

HANGING PLANT POST

Hanging plants don't have to block your view or cut off the window light. Make this post for your hanging plants and have them grace your room without intruding on your life.

The idea can have a lot of variations. The arms can be arranged, as here, for a corner location. But they could project opposite each other, making your plant post not unlike a telephone pole. Given the proper environment, you could even combine the two approaches in a post with eight arms.

The hanging plant post doesn't even have to be confined to the indoors. Use an extra long post and sink it in the ground next to your patio or just about anywhere in your yard.

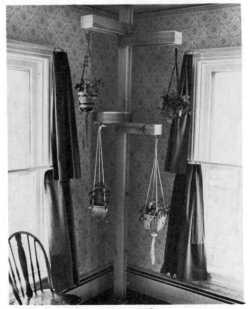

Hang your house number on it. Put a birdhouse on top. Or a lamp. Or a potted plant.

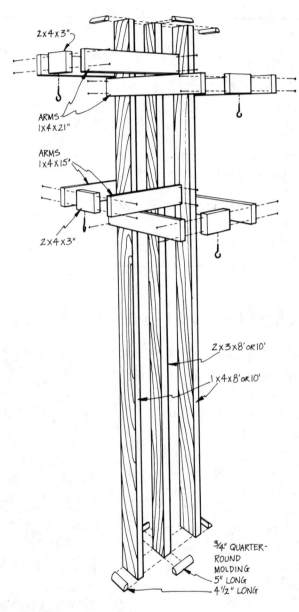

2x4x3"

ARMS
1x4x21"

ARMS
1x4x15"

2x4x3"

2x3x8'or10'

1x4x8'or10'

3/4" QUARTER-
ROUND
MOLDING
5" LONG
4½" LONG

CONSTRUCTION

1. Cut one piece of 2 x 3 to fit between floor and ceiling.
2. Cut two pieces of 1 x 4, the same length as the 2 x 3.
3. After sanding all three pieces well, sandwich the 2 x 3 between the 1 x 4s with glue and 8d finishing nails.

MATERIALS

Wood

1 pc. 2 x 3 x 8' or 10'   **Post:** Length depends on height of ceiling. It must reach from floor to ceiling.

2 pcs. 1 x 4 x 8' or 10' (same length as 2 x 3)

1 pc. 1 x 4 x 12' or **Arms:** 4 pcs. 1 x 4 x 21"
4 pcs. 1 x 4 x 15"

1 pc. 2 x 4 x 2' or   4 pcs. 2 x 4 x 3"

4'–¾" quarter-round molding or **Post trim:** 4 pcs. 5" long
4 pcs. 4½" long

Hardware

Glue
8d finishing nails
Wood putty
4 medium-sized threaded hooks
4d finishing nails

4. Cut four pieces of 1 x 4 to 21-inch lengths. Sand well.

5. Glue and nail (with 8d finishing nails) two pieces parallel to each other on opposite sides of the post, 6 inches from the top, forming the first of the four arms. It is advisable to drill pilot holes before driving the nails.

6. In the same manner, attach the remaining two pieces of 1 x 4 immediately below the first arm, extending perpendicularly to the first arm.

7. Complete the two arms by cutting scraps of 2 x 4 to fit between the elements of each arm, sanding each scrap well, and gluing and nailing it in place with 8d finishing nails.

8. Cut four pieces of 1 x 4 to 15-inch lengths. Sand well.

9. Glue and nail the first of the shorter arms 24 inches below the top of uppermost arm, followed by the second shorter arm immediately below it. Again, scraps of 2 x 4 are cut to fit and attached to complete the arms.

10. Countersink all nails and fill with wood putty. Turn a medium hook into each arm.

11. Install the post by toenailing into floor and ceiling. To finish off the installation, nail ¾-inch quarter-round molding around the base and the top of the post. For the best appearance, the molding should be cut to fit and mitered at the corners.

HANGING PLANT STAND

Still another hanging plant stand is this freestanding one. This project is especially nice for plant lovers who are also renters. It is a piece of furniture; no holes in walls, ceilings, or window frames are necessary to support your hanging plants.

We assembled this stand using ordinary 2 x 3 lumber. We used doweled half-lap joints in assembling the frames, but you could use blind- or open-doweled butt joints. Or you could cook up your own personal variation.

CONSTRUCTION

1. Cut the following pieces: four 6-foot 2 x 3s, six 18-inch 2 x 3s, four 18-inch 1 x 10s, and three 21-inch ¾-inch dowels. Plane the 2 x 3s carefully to give a good finish to the wood.

2. Notch both ends of all the 18-inch 2 x 3s for half-lap joints. The notches should be 2½ inches wide and ¾ inch deep.

3. Lay the 6-footers side-by-side and mark them in concert for the following half-lap joints: At one end and 4 inches and 15½ inches from the other end. The size of the notches are as in step 2.

4. Use ⅜-inch dowel to fasten the joints. Assemble one frame unit, and using a brace and bit, drill two ⅜-inch holes through each lap joint, twelve holes in all. Cut twelve 1½-inch lengths of ⅜-inch dowel and taper one end with sandpaper. Coat the inner faces of each joint with glue, and dab glue on each dowel before driving it into place. Assemble the second frame unit.

5. Clamp the two frame units together and drill three ¾-inch holes for the hanging plant support dowels. One hole should be centered in each frame upright, 5 inches from the top. The third hole is centered in the top crosspiece.

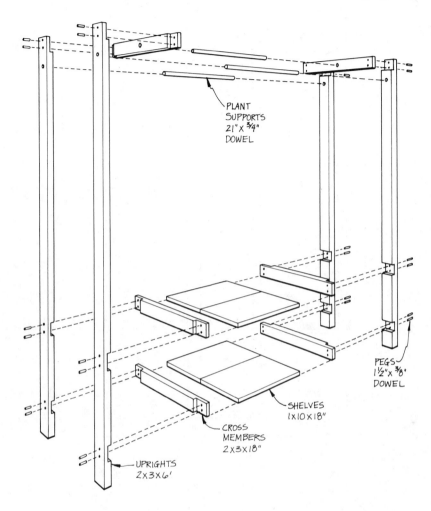

PLANT
SUPPORTS
21" x ¾"
DOWEL

PEGS
1½" x ⅜"
DOWEL

SHELVES
1x10x18"

CROSS
MEMBERS
2x3x18"

UPRIGHTS
2x3x6'

6. Assemble the shelves. We made our shelves by gluing up two lengths of 1 x 10, then planing the resulting panel to an 18-inch square. You could use ¾-inch plywood.

7. After sanding the frames carefully, drive the three plant support dowels into the holes in one frame unit. Then fasten the lower shelf in place, using glue and 8d finishing nails.

8. Lay the frame unit flat across sawhorses or on the floor so the dowels and the shelf project up into the air. Lay the second frame unit in place and work the dowels into their respective holes. Drive nails through the frame into the shelf. To secure the dowels, drive a 6d finishing nail through the frame into the dowel. Countersink all nails. Wood putty may be used to fill the nail holes.

9. Slip the upper shelf in place and glue and nail it fast.

10. Finish sand the stand and apply the finish of your choice.

Hanging Plant Stand

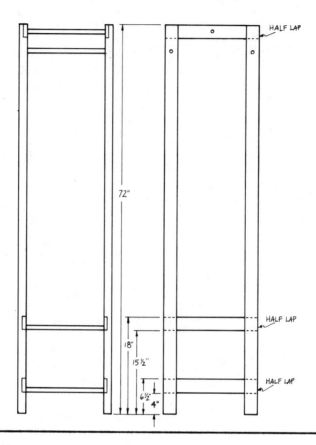

MATERIALS

Wood

      1 pc. 2 x 3 x 10'   or **Crossmembers:** 6 pcs. 2 x 3 x 18"

      2 pcs. 2 x 3 x 12'   or **Uprights:** 4 pcs. 2 x 3 x 6'

      1 pc. 36" x $\frac{3}{8}$" dowel   or **Pegs:** 24 pcs. 1$\frac{1}{2}$" x $\frac{3}{8}$" dowel

      3 pcs. 36" x $\frac{3}{4}$" dowel or **Plant supports:** 3 pcs. 21" x $\frac{3}{4}$" dowel

      1 pc. 1 x 10 x 6' or **Shelves:** 4 pcs. 1 x 10 x 18" (planed to fit)

Hardware

      White glue
      8d finishing nails
      6d finishing nails
      Wood putty

PLANTING TUBS

Plant stands and racks and posts are fine for the small houseplants, but what do you do with those big ones. As the plants get larger, you find them best suited to a position on the floor, and the handyman finds himself with another opportunity to make something useful for around the house. Begin with a tray to hold your most attractive pot and advance to tubs to replace those other big pottery plant containers.

THE TRAY

This redwood tray, constructed in the OGF Workshop, is about 2 inches deep and is covered inside with several coats of polyester resin to water-proof it. It's an attractive accent for that big potted plant, and it will keep your floor or carpet clean in the bargain.

CONSTRUCTION

1. Cut two 16-inch pieces and two 14½-inch pieces of redwood 2 x 4. Cut a 1½-inch by ¾-inch rabbet in the ends of the 16-inch pieces to form a half-lap joint.
2. Nail the sides together with 16d finishing nails to form a 16-inch square.
3. Cut three 13-inch pieces of redwood 2 x 6. Rip one to a width of 2 inches, and combine it with the other two pieces of 2 x 6 to form the tray bottom, nailing it inside the 2 x 4 frame with 16d finishing nails. The resulting tray should be 2 inches deep.
4. Rip redwood 2 x 4s into pieces measuring an actual ¾ inch by 2 inches by 17 inches. You will need four of these pieces for the cap. The corners should be mitered, and the cap nailed in place with 8d finishing nails.
5. Apply two heavy coats of polyester resin to the inside of the tray.

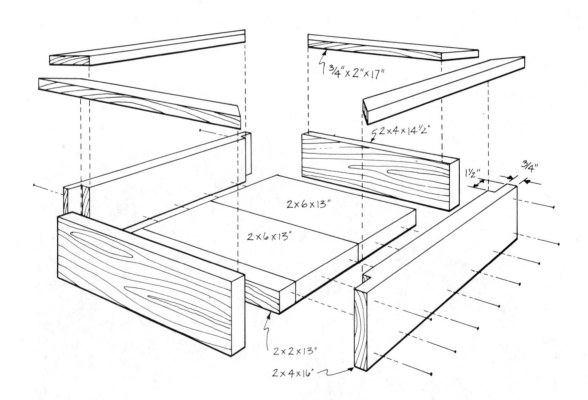

MATERIALS

Wood

1 pc. 2 x 4 x 8′ dressed redwood	or	**Sides:** 2 pcs. 2 x 4 x 16″ 2 pcs. 2 x 4 x 14½″
		Cap: 4 pcs. ¾″ x 2″ x 17″ (act. meas., rip from 2 x 4)
1 pc. 2 x 6 x 4′ dressed redwood	or	**Bottom:** 2 pcs. 2 x 6 x 13″ 1 pc. 2 x 2″ x 13″ (rip from 2 x 6 x 13″)

Hardware

16d finishing nails
8d finishing nails
1 qt. polyester resin

VARIATIONS

The tray can perhaps be more economically made by altering the dimensions to avoid the need for ripping stock. For example, the inside measurement could be enlarged to 14½ inches square to permit the use of two lengths of 2 x 8 for the bottom. Or it could be reduced to permit the use of two pieces of 2 x 6, making a tray with an inside measurement of 11 inches square. A third alternative is to use several pieces of 2 x 4 for the bottom; four pieces would make a 14-inch-square inside-dimension tray. Thus, the tray is a project that could easily be completed using only 2 x 4s, 16d finishing nails, and polyester resin.

The use of half-lap joints for the sides makes for a somewhat stronger assembly, as well as a slightly more polished appearance. But the joint can be time-consuming (and somewhat difficult) for the handyman with only hand tools to work with. A simple butt joint is the best alternative.

THE PLANTER

This planter, also constructed in the OGF Workshop, is made almost entirely of 2 x 12 redwood stock. It can be decorated with routered designs, as in the photo, or left plain. While conceived as an indoor planter, there's no reason why it can't be used as a porch or patio planter.

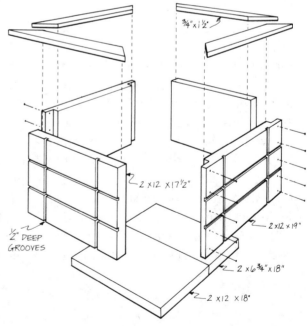

CONSTRUCTION

1. Cut two 19-inch lengths of redwood 2 x 12 and cut 1½-inch by ¾-inch rabbets in the ends (for a half-lap joint).
2. Cut two 17½-inch lengths of 2 x 12.
3. Mark these pieces for cutting the dadoed design as indicated. Use a ½-inch router bit or dado and cut the grooves ½ inch deep.
4. Assemble the sides, using 16d finishing nails.
5. Cut two 18-inch lengths of 2 x 12. Rip one to a 6¾-inch width, and combine it with the other piece to make the 18-inch square bottom.
6. Attach the bottom with 16d finishing nails, positioning it to leave a ½-inch recess around the circumference of the planter.
7. Cut a 19-inch length of redwood 2 x 4. Rip the 2 x 4 into four strips measuring an actual ¾ inch by 1½ inches. Miter the corners and nail with 8d finishing nails to the top to make the cap.
8. Finish the interior of the planter to waterproof it, using polyester resin, or other material.

MATERIALS

Wood

1 pc. 2 x 12 x 10' dressed redwood　or　**Sides:** 2 pcs. 2 x 12 x 19"
　　　　　　　　　　　　　　　　　　　　　　　2 pcs. 2 x 12 x 17½"

　　　　　　　　　　　　　　　　　　Bottom: 1 pc. 2 x 12 x 18"
　　　　　　　　　　　　　　　　　　　　　　　1 pc. 2 x 6¾" x 18" (rip
　　　　　　　　　　　　　　　　　　　　　　　　　from 2 x 12 x 18")

1 pc. 2 x 4 x 8' dressed redwood　or　**Cap:** 4 pcs. ¾" x 1½" x 19" (act.
　　　　　　　　　　　　　　　　　　　　　　　meas., rip from
　　　　　　　　　　　　　　　　　　　　　　　2 x 4 x 19")

Hardware

16d finishing nails
8d finishing nails
1 qt. polyester resin

VARIATIONS

With this planter, as with the tray, the dimensions can be altered to eliminate the need for ripping stock for the bottom.

The decorative grooves can be altered or eliminated. If you have a router, you are familiar with the variety of different-shaped grooves that can be cut using the tool.

Using a half-lap joint at the intersections of the sides is largely for the sake of appearance. If you wish to forego it, do so.

Finally, it isn't necessary to use redwood stock for this planter. If you do want to use a relatively rot-resistant stock, which was the basis for the selection of redwood for this planter initially, you could use cypress, cedar, or locust. Common pine stock could be used, too, but it should be treated with a copper naphthenate preservative (others will harm your plants).

HUGE-O PLANTER

This big planter is just the ticket for your enormous house tree, dwarf fruit tree, or ornamental shrub. Though designed and built for indoor use, it is ideal for outdoor use as well. That balled Christmas tree—the one you should have bought last Christmas, and will this Christmas if you have a planter like this—looks great in it.

As with the previous planter, the basic design lends itself to all sorts of personalizations. And just to prove those expensive "rot-resistant" materials aren't necessary for a project like this, the OGF workshoppers constructed it of ordinary pine stock.

MATERIALS

Wood

1 pc. 2 x 3 x 8′	or	**Base:** 4 pcs. 2 x 3 x 21¼″
1 pc. 2 x 12 x 4′	or	**Bottom:** 2 pcs. 2 x 12 x 24″
1 pc. 2 x 4 x 12′		1 pc. 2 x 1½″ x 24″ (rip from 2 x 4 x 24″)
		Cap: 4 pcs. 2 x 4 x 25″
1 pc. 2 x 2 x 12′	or	**Sides:** 4 pcs. 2 x 2 x 18″
		4 pcs. 2 x 2 x 15″
1 pc. 1 x 8 x 14′	or	4 pcs. 1 x 8 x 18″
		4 pcs. 1 x 8 x 19½″
1 pc. 1 x 4 x 8′	or	2 pcs. 1 x 4 x 18″
		2 pcs. 1 x 4 x 19½″
1 pc. 2 x 2 x 10′	or	**Side decorations:** 12 pcs. 2 x 2 x 18″
1 pc. 2 x 2 x 8′		
1 pc. 1 x 1 x 10′	or	12 pcs. 1 x 1 x 18″
1 pc. 1 x 1 x 8′		

Hardware

Glue
12d finishing nails
4d finishing nails
Polyester resin

CONSTRUCTION

1. Cut four 21¼-inch lengths of 2 x 3. Cut (miter) the ends at a 45-degree angle, and glue and nail (using 12d finishing nails) the four pieces, forming the planter base, as shown.
2. Cut two 24-inch lengths of 2 x 12 and a 24-inch length of 2 x 4. Rip the 2 x 4 to a 1½-inch width and combine it with the 2 x 12s to make a 24-inch-square bottom for the planter. Nail it to the base with 12d finishing nails.
3. Cut four 18-inch lengths of 2 x 2, cutting *one* end of each at a 45-degree angle. Cut four 15-inch lengths of 2 x 2. Nail the 15-inch lengths to the planter bottom as shown, using 12d finishing nails.
4. Next, nail the 18-inch lengths perpendicularly at the corners, as shown. Toenail through these uprights into the bottom.

Huge-O Planter

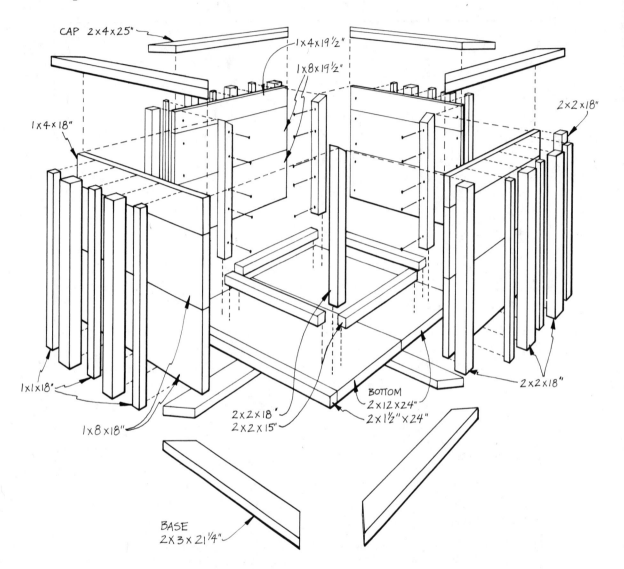

CAP 2x4x25"

1x4x19½"

1x8x19½"

2x2x18"

1x4x18"

1x1x18"

1x8x18"

2x2x18"
2x2x15"

BOTTOM
2x12x24"
2x1½"x24"

2x2x18"

BASE
2x3x21¼"

5. Cut four 18-inch lengths of 1 x 8, four 19½-inch lengths of 1 x 8, two 18-inch lengths of 1 x 4, and two 19½-inch lengths of 1 x 4. Glue and nail (use 4d finishing nails) the 18-inch lengths to the uprights, forming opposite sides of the planter. The 1 x 4 should be the topmost piece on each side. The edges should be flush with the sides of the uprights, to permit the 19½-inch sides to butt tightly against both the uprights and the edges of the short sides. For the sake of the appearance, nail through the uprights into the sides. Next, glue and nail the 19½-inch lengths to complete the planter box. Again, nail through the uprights into the sides.

42

6. Cut twelve 18-inch lengths of 2 x 2, twelve 18-inch lengths of 1 x 1, and four 25-inch lengths of 2 x 4. Cut 45-degree angles at the ends of the 2 x 4s to form a mitered-cornered cap for the planter. Attach the cap to the planter, gluing and nailing (with 4d finishing nails) the corners and nailing through the cap into the sides. Attach a 2 x 2 at each corner of the planter, with a corner of the 2 x 2 just touching the corner of the planter's sides, as shown. Nail through the cap and bottom into the 2 x 2.

7. Attach the remaining 2 x 2s and the 1 x 1s as decoration. The 2 x 2s should be centered on a line 6 inches from the corner, two to a side. The 1 x 1s should be placed between the 2 x 2s, three to a side. Drive 4d finishing nails from inside the box, through the sides into the 2 x 2s and 1 x 1s.

8. Waterproof the inside of the planter with polyester resin, roofing asphalt, or similar material.

VARIATIONS

Make the planter shorter. Make it taller. Run the decorative strips horizontally. Or diagonally.

The two planting tubs constructed in the OGF Workshop need not limit your imagination. Combine the construction concepts of the two planters we built.

For example, you could build a fairly deep planter of 2-inch stock. Use two lengths of 2 x 8 or 2 x 10 for each side, making a planter 15 or 19 inches deep.

And don't feel restricted to the square format. Make a rectangular planter and put two or more small trees or shrubs in it. Such a design would be particularly suited to a porch or patio location.

To construct such a planter, based on the two designs, picture a planter measuring 18 inches by 36 inches on the side, 12 inches deep, on a 2 x 3 base. You would need two 10-foot 2 x 12s and one 16-foot 2 x 3. From the 2 x 12s, cut two 41-inch lengths to be butted together for the bottom, two 18-inch ends to be butted against two 39-inch sides. For the base, cut two 21-inch and two 39-inch lengths of 2 x 3, miter the ends at 45 degrees, and glue and nail. From the remaining 2 x 3, cut a piece 38½ inches long and a piece 20½ inches long. Rip each of the two pieces of each length to a ¾-inch by 2½-inch dimension. Miter the corners at 45 degrees and nail in place as the cap.

There are many other variations and original designs. Use your imagination.

HOUSEPLANT CASES

American homes have been criticized in the past as being too warm and dry to provide a good environment for plants. Now, thanks to the energy crisis and the campaign to keep the thermostat at 68°F., these criticisms may be a thing of the past. This will come as good news to many overheated houseplants, but for tropical plants and tender varieties the prospect of cooler temperatures could be drastic, even deadly.

One answer to the problem is to pay the inflated fuel bills. A more economical solution is to put on another sweater and place the plants in their own separate environment. Since few of us can afford the space for a separate plant room, the alternatives are few: a terrarium or some sort of plant case. Terrariums are nice, but they suffer from space limitations, and if you're like most people, that sealed environment is like keeping the family dog in a zoo. Plant cases overcome both of these problems. They are larger, and if you want a close-up look at your favorites all you have to do is open the door.

When plant cases are mentioned, several objections always pop up: they are expensive, they don't fit the decor, they're the wrong size or the wrong shape. All valid points, to which we reply: build your own.

PLANT DISPLAY CASE

Building your own plant case doesn't require a cabinet shop. A few old windows or cabinet doors and some basic tools are all you need. David Warfield constructed two of the cabinets shown here and while he freely admits to using power tools, hand tools would work just as well, only a bit slower. The one thing you might not have around the house is a set of four-corner clamps. These useful and inexpensive items hold pieces of wood together at 90 degrees while you fasten them together.

Plant cases really are simple. The large horizontal one is simply a box. The three glass sides are old cabinet doors and the ends and bottom are exterior plywood. Add some hardware and cover with a coat of wood grain antiquing paint and you have a handsome addition to any home. The upright plant case may appear more complicated but really isn't. Here four windows were joined together with four posts and a top and bottom of plywood were added. The turned posts at the front are available, premade, at most hardware stores and lumberyards. In thinking about your own design, remember that many different shapes, sizes, and lengths of posts are available and that many

special touches can be easily made from preshaped moldings. Since we're dealing with plants, remember to use waterproof glues and finishes. One caution, however: provisions for special features such as fluorescent lights, heating cables, and shelves should be built in, not added later.

CONSTRUCTION

1. You can cut your work in half if you can scavenge some used window sashes about 19 inches by 29 inches. If not, you'll need the sash pieces listed in the materials list. In our model, the pieces were all ripped from a length of 1 x 6. You can use whatever common boards you have on hand, but the finished pieces must be of the measurements listed.

2. Cut a rabbet groove ⅜ inch deep and ⅜ inch wide along one edge of each of the eight 1¾-inch by 29-inch side pieces. Do the same with the eight pieces of 2¾ inches by 19 inches. Then make the same type of rabbet groove on both sides of the four pieces of 1⅛ inches by 19 inches and the four pieces of 1⅛ inches by 11¾ inches, as illustrated. These rabbet grooves are made easily with a dado attachment for your saw, but the same results can be obtained with repeated cuts of a table or radial arm saw.

3. All sash pieces are joined with half-lap joints (front and back members cut to the proper shape for joining). First cut ⅜-inch end half-laps on the front sides (same side as the rabbets) of the long pieces (A). Then cut ⅜-inch half-laps on the back sides of the 19-inch pieces marked B.

4. Make the ⅜-inch inlet cuts for the mullions on the back side of the sash frame.

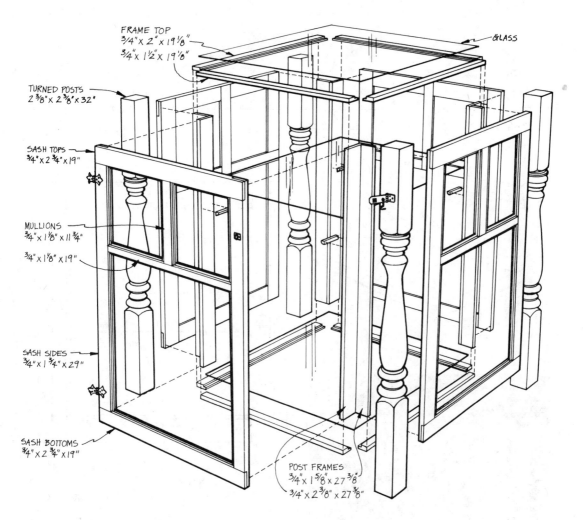

FRAME TOP
3/4" x 2" x 19 1/8"
3/4" x 1 1/2" x 19 1/8"

GLASS

TURNED POSTS
2 3/8" x 2 3/8" x 32"

SASH TOPS
3/4" x 2 3/4" x 19"

MULLIONS
3/4" x 1 1/8" x 11 3/4"

3/4" x 1 1/8" x 19"

SASH SIDES
3/4" x 1 3/4" x 29"

SASH BOTTOMS
3/4" x 2 3/4" x 19"

POST FRAMES
3/4" x 1 5/8" x 27 3/8"
3/4" x 2 3/8" x 27 3/8"

5. Assemble sash pieces and glue and clamp all joints. Sand and stain the sashes. Make cut-to-fit lengths of quarter-round molding to hold the glass in place, then sand and stain these pieces.

6. Insert appropriate size glass and fasten with $\frac{1}{4}$-inch quarter-round molding cut at 45-degree angles. Attach molding with $\frac{1}{2}$-inch brads.

7. The frame will require the pieces listed in the materials list. Our pieces were ripped from a 1 x 6 length. You can use whatever stock you have handy, but the finished pieces must be of the measurements listed.

8. Cut a $\frac{3}{8}$-inch by $\frac{3}{8}$-inch rabbet groove on one side of the top and bottom pieces of the frame to accommodate the glass.

9. Glue and nail (with 4d finishing nails) the $2\frac{3}{8}$-inch by $27\frac{3}{8}$-inch pieces to the $1\frac{5}{8}$-inch by $27\frac{3}{8}$-inch pieces to form a right angle, as illustrated.

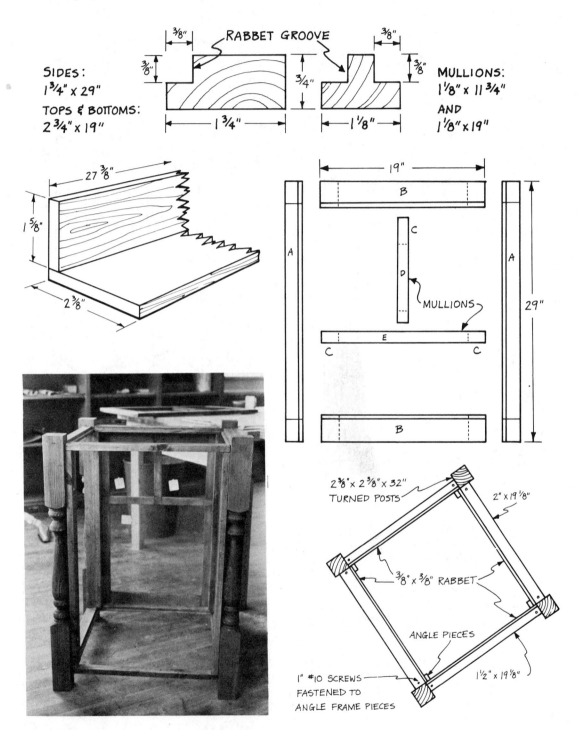

RABBET GROOVE

SIDES:
1 3/4" x 29"

TOPS & BOTTOMS:
2 3/4" x 19"

MULLIONS:
1 1/8" x 11 3/4"
AND
1 1/8" x 19"

3/8"
3/8"
3/4"
1 3/4"

3/8"
3/8"
1 1/8"

27 3/8"
1 5/8"
2 3/8"

19"
B
A
C
D
MULLIONS
C
E
C
A
29"
B

2 3/8" x 2 3/8" x 32"
TURNED POSTS
2" x 19 1/8"
3/8" x 3/8" RABBET
ANGLE PIECES
1" #10 SCREWS
FASTENED TO
ANGLE FRAME PIECES
1 1/2" x 19 1/8"

48

10. Install bottom of plant case (glass or plywood) and fasten the top and bottom frame members with 1-inch #10 screws. See illustration.
11. Sand and stain completed frame and the four turned posts.
12. Fasten posts to frame with two 1-inch screws on each post. Let posts protrude 1 inch above frame. Predrill and countersink all holes for screws and fill with wood putty.
13. Use quarter-round molding and $\frac{1}{2}$-inch brads to install glass in top.
14. Fasten three sashes to frame with 4d finishing nails.
15. Hinge the fourth sash to a turned post and fasten desired latch.

Option: A glass shelf can be installed even with the horizontal mullions by gluing and nailing four $2\frac{3}{8}$-inch pieces of $\frac{1}{4}$-inch quarter-round molding to the insides of the four turned posts. Use double-strength glass for this shelf.

MATERIALS

Wood

6 pcs. 1 x 6 x 8'   or   **Sashes** (act. meas.):

Sides: 8 pcs. $\frac{3}{4}''$ x $1\frac{3}{4}''$ x 29''

Tops and bottoms: 8 pcs. $\frac{3}{4}''$ x $2\frac{3}{4}''$ x 19''

Mullions: 4 pcs. $\frac{3}{4}''$ x $1\frac{1}{8}''$ x 19''

4 pcs. $\frac{3}{4}''$ x $1\frac{1}{8}''$ x $11\frac{3}{4}''$

Frame (act. meas.):

Post frames: 4 pcs. $\frac{3}{4}''$ x $2\frac{3}{8}''$ x $27\frac{3}{8}''$

4 pcs. $\frac{3}{4}''$ x $1\frac{5}{8}''$ x $27\frac{3}{8}''$

Tops and bottoms: 4 pcs. $\frac{3}{4}''$ x $1\frac{1}{2}''$ x $19\frac{1}{8}''$

4 pcs. $\frac{3}{4}''$ x 2'' x $19\frac{1}{8}''$

10'–$\frac{1}{4}''$ quarter-round molding

4 turned posts $2\frac{3}{8}''$ x $2\frac{3}{8}''$ x 32''

Hardware

Glue
Glass cut to fit
$\frac{1}{2}''$ brads
4d finishing nails
28–1'' #10 screws
Wood putty
1 pr. flush hinges
1 latch

GROWING CASE ON WHEELS

Year-round gardening plus an early start indoors to get things ready for the outdoor season—this is the ideal of the practiced gardener.

Lawrence Krumanocker of Allentown, Pennsylvania, has come close to achieving that goal painlessly by building an indoor growing case which can be moved along the porch or from window to window to keep step with the winter sun.

Over 7 feet high and securely em-

placed on sturdy casters, Krumanocker's case is covered with 4-mil clear plastic and holds a minimum of nine standard-sized flats, three on each of its three shelves.

Ventilation and damping-off are no problems. As the picture shows, the top of the case may be raised from ½ inch to as much as 9 inches to permit free passage of air.

The case is an ideal refuge for tender plants that have to come indoors when the days turn short and brisk. But its biggest bonus lies in the early start indoors it gives tomatoes, lettuce, and other tender crops. This early start permits second plantings in midsummer with extra yields coming in well ahead of the first killing frost.

Seeds are given their start in sphagnum moss and perlite to hold down fungus growth. All watering is from below, by capillary action. During the winter, the case is readily wheeled from window to window during the day and plants that require extra sun are easily favored.

Housewife-gardeners will particularly appreciate the movable growing case because it keeps the plants safe in a convenient unit, saving them extra steps and helping them keep things tidy indoors during the winter.

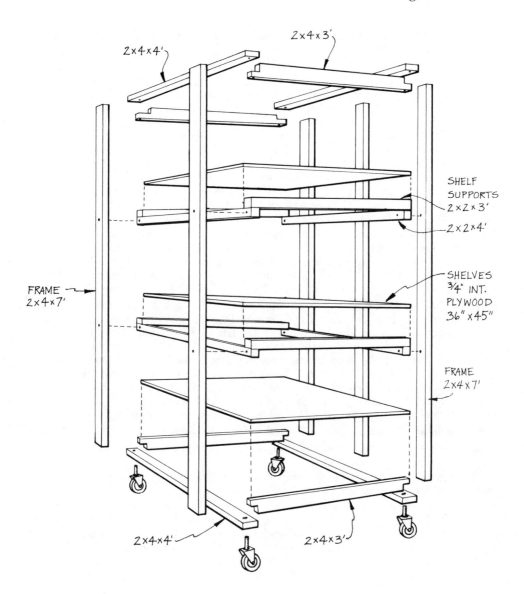

2x4x4'

2x4x3'

SHELF
SUPPORTS
2 x 2 x 3'

2x2x4'

SHELVES
3/4" INT.
PLYWOOD
36" x 45"

FRAME
2x4x7'

FRAME
2x4x7'

2x4x4'

2x4x3'

CONSTRUCTION

    1.   Make up top and bottom of frame.
        a.   Cut four 4-foot lengths of 2 x 4.
        b.   Cut four 3-foot lengths of 2 x 4.
        c.   Cut a 1½-inch by 2-inch rabbet from each end of the 3-foot 2 x 4s, as shown.

       d.   Glue and nail together, driving 8d nails as shown, making a top and a bottom.

2.   Cut five 7-foot lengths of 2 x 4. These are the posts of the case.

3.   Assemble the basic framework. The easiest way is to lay two of the posts on the shop floor, with the broad dimension down. Butt the top (or bottom) against the posts, so the posts align properly at the corners, and spike the top fast to the posts, using 12d nails, two to each post. Follow the same procedure to attach the bottom (or top). Next, roll the half-completed frame 180 degrees and attach the three back posts, one at each corner and one in the center of the back. Again, spike through top and bottom into the posts. As a finishing touch, you can drive a nail through each of the corner posts into the end of the half-topped side member. (The framework will probably seem a bit wobbly until the shelf-support assemblies are bolted into place.)

4.   Cut the shelf-supporting frame members: four 4-foot lengths of 2 x 2 and four 3-foot lengths of 2 x 2. To assemble, lay out two of the 4-footers, 3 feet apart; bridge the gap between the ends with two 3-footers. Drill a $\frac{3}{8}$-inch hole through each joint and bolt the assembly together with $3\frac{1}{2}$-inch by $\frac{3}{8}$-inch bolts. Assemble the second support.

5.   Install the shelf supports in the framework. The easiest way: Lay the framework front-down on the floor and slide the lower support assembly in place, aligning it carefully. Drill a $\frac{3}{8}$-inch hole through each post and on through the 4-foot support member. You'll probably want to clamp the support assembly in place, or have a helper hold it steady while you drill. Install $3\frac{1}{2}$-inch by $\frac{3}{8}$-inch bolts. Next, slide the upper support assembly into place, align, drill, and bolt. Then carefully roll the case over. Align the two support assemblies, drill through the front corner posts and support members, and install bolts.

6.   Drill holes in the corners of the bottom for the casters.

7.   Cut three shelves, 36 inches by 45 inches, from $\frac{3}{4}$-inch interior plywood, and slip them into place.

Note: If you plan to paint or otherwise finish the case, now is the time, before you attach doors and plastic.

8.   Cut and assemble the case-top door. Cut two 34-inch lengths of 1 x 4, two 40-inch lengths of 1 x 4, and a 27-inch length of 1 x 4. Lay out the four pieces of 1 x 4 to form a 34-inch by 47-inch rectangle, and fasten them together with a 1-inch-wide corner plate at each corner using $\frac{5}{8}$-inch #8 screws. Drop the 27-inch piece in place and attach with four corner plates and $\frac{5}{8}$-inch #8 screws. Paint or finish the door, if such is your want.

9.   Turn the case-top door over, and staple 4-mil clear plastic in place. First cut out a piece of plastic of the approximate dimensions and lay it over the doorframe. Lay a 46-inch length of lath along one edge and tack it and the plastic to the frame. (Paint or finish the lath before you tack it to the case.) Lay a like piece of lath along the opposite edge and, pulling the plastic tight, tack it and the plastic to the frame. Cut lath hold-down strips for the remaining sides and tack them and the plastic in place.

MATERIALS

Wood

4 pcs. 2 x 4 x 14′   or   **Top and bottom:** 4 pcs. 2 x 4 x 4′
1 pc. 2 x 4 x 8′   4 pcs. 2 x 4 x 3′

Frame: 5 pcs. 2 x 4 x 7′

2 pcs. 2 x 2 x 14′   or   **Shelf supports:** 4 pcs. 2 x 2 x 4′
                                               4 pcs. 2 x 2 x 3′

1 sht. $\frac{3}{4}$″ int. plywood   or   **Shelves:** 3 pcs. 36″ x 45″
1–4′ sq. sht. $\frac{3}{4}$″ int. plywood

1 pc. 1 x 4 x 8′   or   **Case-top door:** 2 pcs. 1 x 4 x 34″
1 pc. 1 x 4 x 10′   2 pcs. 1 x 4 x 40″
                                              1 pc. 1 x 4 x 27″

2 pcs. 1 x 3 x 14′   or   **Front doors:** 4 pcs. 1 x 3 x 7′
2 pcs. 1 x 3 x 8′   4 pcs. 1 x 3 x 15$\frac{1}{2}$″
                                            2 pcs. 1 x 4 x 15$\frac{1}{2}$″ (remainder of
                                               1 x 4)

Center post: 1 pc. 1 x 3 x 7′

2 bundles 8′ lath

Hardware

Glue
8d nails
12d nails
18–3$\frac{1}{2}$″ x $\frac{3}{8}$″ bolts
24–1″ corner plates
$\frac{5}{8}$″ #8 screws (number depends on total number
   of screw holes in corner plates)
4-mil plastic (cut to fit)
Tacks
2 dogleg hinges
2 standard door pulls
8 common hinges
4 casters

Growing Case on Wheels

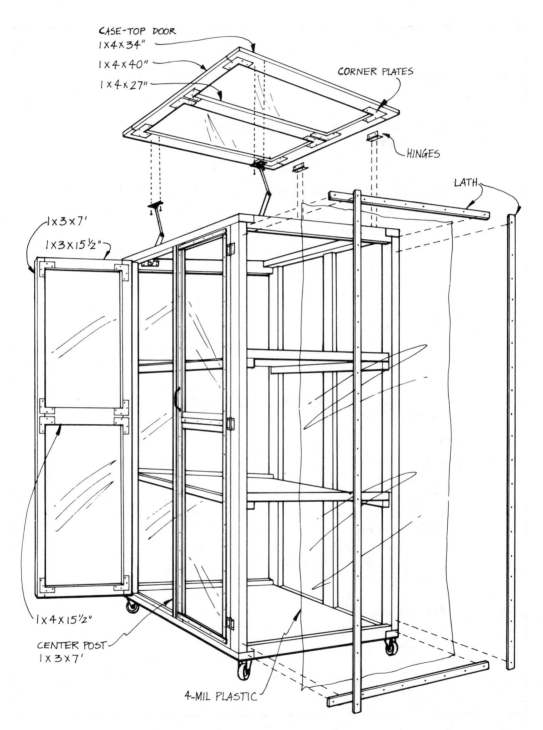

CASE-TOP DOOR
1 X 4 X 34"

1 X 4 X 40"

1 X 4 X 27"

CORNER PLATES

HINGES

LATH

1 X 3 X 7'

1 X 3 X 15½"

1 X 4 X 15½"

CENTER POST
1 X 3 X 7'

4-MIL PLASTIC

10. Install the door. Lay the door in place: centered left to right and flush with the front of the case. Mark the positions of the dogleg hinges on both the case and the door. Remove the door, install the hinges on the door, replace it, and fasten the hinges to the case.

11. Cut five 7-foot lengths of 1 x 3. Cut four 15½-inch pieces of 1 x 3 and two 15½-inch pieces of 1 x 4. Lay out one door using two 7-footers, two 15½-inch 1 x 3s, and one 15½-inch 1 x 4. Fasten the parts together using 1-inch corner plates and ⅜-inch #8 screws. Attach a standard door handle/pull as shown. Install 10-mil plastic on the door with wood lath, using the same procedure as with the case-top door. Assemble the second door and install the plastic.

12. Install the fifth 7-foot 1 x 3 in the case framework as a front center post/doorstop. Bolt, screw, or nail it to the top and bottom members and the shelf-support members.

13. Install the doors. Screw three common hinges to each door as shown. Place the doors in position in the case and screw the hinges to the case.

14. Install plastic on the back and the sides using wood lath hold-down strips.

15. Slip the casters into place.

GROWLIGHTS

Growlights are handy devices for every gardener. For the apartment gardener, the growlight is ofttimes the only light available. For the vegetable gardener, the growlight setup can help get seedlings growing indoors, so they will be ready for transplanting when spring truly arrives.

Most any electric light will serve as a growlight. The best, however, are the fluorescent lights. Incandescent lights generate a surprising amount of heat, and when you put the bulbs close enough to the plants for the light to do them some good, the heat does them some harm. Fluorescents, on the other hand, are cooler; only when the plants physically touch the fluorescent tubes will they be burned.

An added benefit is that fluorescents don't use as much electricity as incandescent lights do. Consider that your home is probably rife with 100-watt bulbs. Compare the light one of those 100-watt bulbs throws with the light created by a 4-foot-long, two-tube fluorescent light fixture. And consider that each of the tubes is rated at 40 watts; that's 80 watts for the two of them. The fluorescent tubes have a longer life, too.

Counterbalancing the inexpensive operation is the high initial cost. The purchase of one or two two-tubed fixtures will represent a significant purchase for most families. But many growlight users have acquired fixtures over a period of years, buying one fixture a year until they have enough to satisfy their needs.

Probably the very best growlight arrangement is the most simple to set up, but the least attractive. Hang the fixtures from ceiling hooks with lightweight chain, two hooks, and two lengths of chain for each light fixture. This is most flexible. The lights can be adjusted to hang very close to just-seeded flats, then progressively raised as the seedlings grow. One end of a light can be raised higher than the other, to accommodate a mixture of tall and short plants under one fixture. (Generally, the lights should be 4 to 6 inches above the plants.)

The vegetable grower probably will set up a growlight corner in the basement or a heated outbuilding. Turn hooks into the rafters or joists, or pound 12d or 10d finishing nails into the side of the rafter or joist. Use lightweight chain, wire, heavy twine, or whatever you have available to hang the light fixtures from the hooks or nails. Plug in the lights. Arrange your flats on the floor or on a table under the lights.

This setup is quite extemporaneous, very temporary, and very flexible. It need occupy a space for only a part of the year.

But such an arrangement can be adapted to be a part of your everday living quarters without being the home's most prominent eyesore. Do use hooks and chain. Use new or newly painted light fixtures. Hang them over an attractive table or cabinet. Or make a stand for your houseplants.

A HOUSEPLANT SINK

The low-slung model shown was constructed in the OGF Workshop. You can duplicate it, or you can use it as a jumping off point for your own design (and it need not be tied to a growlight; you could place it by a window, or roll it out on a patio or balcony). The idea is that it provides a waterproof "sink" for your houseplants, helping them maintain themselves in the properly humid conditions, while at the same time providing a floral focal point for your home.

We built ours to go with a double set of 4-foot fluorescent fixtures, thus making the sink 4 feet long. (There is light thrown beyond the ends of the fixtures—say a foot on either end—but

the quality of that light is strained. The light is strongest in the center of the tube and falls off at the ends.) The sink is sufficiently wide to take best advantage of the light the fixtures provide.

CONSTRUCTION

1. Cut a 12-foot 1 x 8 into two 48-inch-long pieces and two 24-inch-long pieces. With a router or power saw, cut a ¾-inch-wide and ⅜-inch-deep rabbet in the ends of the 48-inch lengths.
2. Cut four 21¾-inch lengths and four 46½-inch lengths of 1 x 1. These will be the cleats to support and seal the sink bottom.
3. Assemble the sides and fasten them using an open doweling technique. Using a brace and bit, drill three evenly spaced ¼-inch holes through the long side into the end of the short side; each hole should be about 2 inches deep. Cut three 2-inch pieces of ¼-inch dowel for each joint, and taper one end of each slightly with sandpaper. Apply glue to the joint and to the dowels, then drive the dowels into the holes.
4. Using glue and 3d nails, fasten the support cleat to the inside of the sink frame. The top edge of the cleat should be 3⅜ inches above the bottom edge of the frame.
5. Cut a 23¾-inch by 46½-inch panel from ½-inch exterior plywood. Slip it into place in the sink and glue and nail the sealing cleat in place.

6. Apply two or three liberal coats of polyester resin to the inside of the sink to waterproof it.

7. Attach the casters to the bottom of the sink.

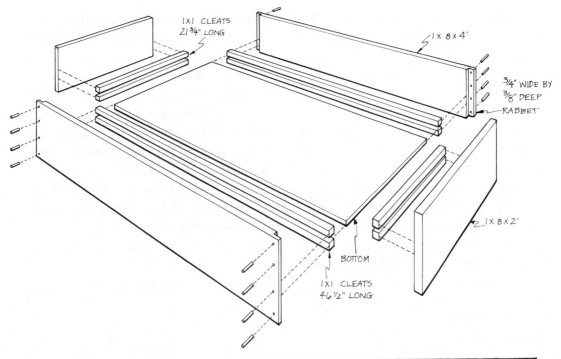

MATERIALS

Wood

1 pc. 1 x 8 x 12'   or   **Sides:** 2 pcs. 1 x 8 x 48"
2 pcs. 1 x 8 x 24"

2 pcs. 1 x 1 x 12'   or   **Cleats:** 4 pcs. 1 x 1 x 46½"
4 pcs. 1 x 1 x 21¾"

1–2' x 4' sht. ½" ext. plywood   or   **Bottom:** 1 pc. 23¼" x 46½"

1 pc. 36" x ¼" dowel   or   12 pcs. 2" x ¼" dowel

Hardware

Glue
3d nails
Polyester resin
4 swivel plate casters

VARIATIONS

Some simple alternatives first. You can use most any sort of waterproofing material in the bottom of the sink. Even roofing asphalt will do, provided you hide it from view with marble chips, pea gravel, or sand.

If you want to try your hand at some metal work, cut the sink lining from a sheet of galvanized steel, or for something flashier (and more expensive), a sheet of copper. Leave out the top set of cleats if you do this.

Start with a sheet large enough to cover the bottom, extend up the sides, overlap the top and extend down the outside about $\frac{3}{4}$ inch. For our planter sink, you will need a sheet $35\frac{1}{4}$ inches by $58\frac{1}{2}$ inches.

You can alter the sink by adopting it to a tabletop. Buy some ready-made legs at the lumber supply outlet and fasten them to the sink bottom, rather than the casters. Or fashion your own legs. Or use sawhorses. This will get the sink up off the floor, but it will also immobilize it.

MATERIALS

Wood

    1 pc. 1 x 8 x 12′ or **Sides:** 2 pcs. 1 x 8 x 48″
                                         2 pcs. 1 x 8 x 24″

    1 pc. 1 x 1 x 12′ or **Cleats:** 2 pcs. 1 x 1 x $46\frac{1}{2}$″
                                         2 pcs. 1 x 1 x $21\frac{3}{4}$″

    1–2′ x 4′ sht. $\frac{1}{2}$″ ext. plywood or **Bottom:** 1 pc. $23\frac{1}{4}$″ x $46\frac{1}{2}$″

    1 pc. 36″ x $\frac{1}{4}$″ dowel or 12 pcs. 2″ x $\frac{1}{4}$″ dowel

Hardware

    Glue
    3d nails
    4 swivel plate casters
    1 pc. $35\frac{1}{4}$″ x $58\frac{1}{2}$″, $\frac{1}{32}$″ sheet metal
    Roofing mastic
    Decorative brass nails
    1 pc. 4″ x 4″, $\frac{1}{32}$″ sheet metal

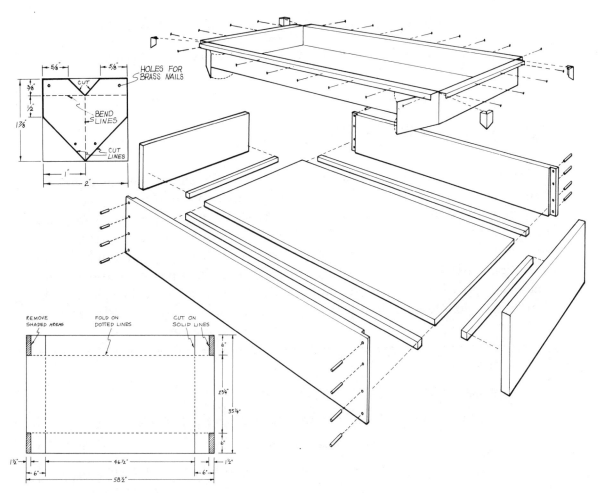

CONSTRUCTION

1. Lay out the sheet and scribe a line parallel to and 6 inches from each edge. This will result in the dimensions of the sink bottom being scribed in the center of the sheet, with a 6-inch square at each corner. Now scribe a line parallel to and 1½ inches from each of the 35¼-inch sides of the sheet.

2. With a pair of snips, cut away the 6-inch by 1½-inch rectangles indicated in the drawing, and make the 6-inch cuts indicated. Dull any rough edges with a file or emery cloth.

3. Make a 90-degree bend in the sheet along the scribe lines, except those 1½ inches from the short dimension. This will form the sheet into a box, as shown, which will slip inside the sink. The cuts you made will, when combined with the bending, form tabs that should underlap the sides of the metal sink lining. To waterproof the corner joints, smear roofing mastic on the tabs before you press the sides against them.

61

4. Bend the metal over the top of the wooden sides of the sink, down the sides, and nail in place with decorative brass nails.
5. From a second sheet of metal, cut four 2-inch squares, cut and bent as indicated in the detail drawing, and install at each corner.

BOOKCASE SINK

Build a bookcase topped with a plant sink.

Reduce the dimensions of the sink to, say, a nominal 1 foot by 2½ feet. Thus it will be wide enough to accommodate even larger pots, but still be small enough to accommodate standard dimension lumber in the construction.

Even this simple design is fodder for your own alterations. The bookcase shown here is open on both sides, but you could fasten a plywood or hardboard back to it. If you have the expertise, glue up stock and make the bookcase, and thus the plant sink, wider. Make the piece taller and install more shelves.

MATERIALS

Wood

1 pc. 1 x 12 x 14′	or	**Bookcase sides:** 2 pcs. 1 x 12 x 37½″
		Shelves: 2 pcs. 1 x 12 x 30″
		Sink bottom: 1 pc. ¾″ x 9¾″ x 30″ (act. meas., rip from 1 x 12 x 30″)
1 pc. 1 x 8 x 6′	or	**Sink sides:** 2 pcs. 1 x 8 x 31½″
1 pc. 1 x 4 x 6′	or	**Base:** 2 pcs. 1 x 4 x 30″
		Cleats: 2 pcs. 1 x 1″ x 9¾″ (rip from 1 x 4)

Hardware

Glue
6d finishing nails
8d finishing nails
1¼″ brads
Wood putty
Polyester resin

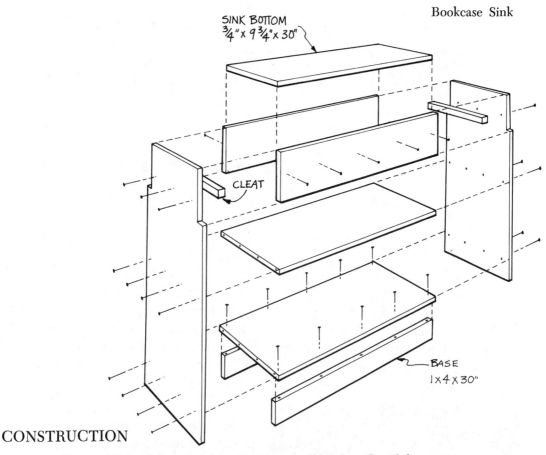

SINK BOTTOM
3/4" x 9 3/4" x 30"

CLEAT

BASE
1 x 4 x 30"

CONSTRUCTION

1. Cut two 37½-inch lengths of 1 x 12. These will be the sides of the bookcase. Cut three 30-inch lengths of 1 x 12 for shelves. Rip one of the shelves to a width of 9¾ inches to serve as the bottom of the sink. Cut two 31½-inch lengths of 1 x 8 to serve as the sides of the sink. Cut two 30-inch lengths of 1 x 4 for the base.

2. Clamp the bookcase sides together and cut ¾-inch by 7½-inch notches in either side at the top to accommodate the sink sides as shown.

3. Glue and nail the sink sides in place, using 6d finishing nails. Then nail the bases in place at the bottom of the sides. The baseboards should be inset about ¼ inch. Use 8d finishing nails here.

4. Slip the bottom shelf in place and nail it fast, driving 6d finishing nails through the sides into the edges of the shelf, and through the shelf into the baseboards.

5. Install the middle shelf, driving 8d finishing nails through the bookcase sides into the edges of the shelf, four nails to a side.

6. Cut two 1 x 1 by 9¾-inch cleats from scrap material and tack in place to locate and – to some degree, anyway – support the sink bottom. Make the sink 4 inches deep, so locate the cleats 4¼ inches below the top of the sink. Glue and nail (with 1¼-inch brads) the cleats to the sides inside the sink.

63

7. Drop the sink bottom in place and nail it fast, driving 8d finishing nails through the bookcase and sink sides into the edges of the sink bottom.
8. Countersink all nails, and fill with wood putty. Apply a finish of your choice, stain and varnish for example, to the almost-finished piece.
9. Waterproof the sink in a manner of your choice.

FLUORESCENT GROWING STAND

It isn't absolutely necessary to provide for adjustable light fixtures. It is just as reasonable to set up a fixture arrangement for the lights and plants.

Many growlight users, for example, set up shelves with a fixture above each one (usually fastened to the bottom of the shelf above). More than

one plant lover has a growlight room in the house, with plant benches and fluorescent fixtures above them.

A fairly simple arrangement was devised for a limited number of plants by Richard F. Krause. Krause uses his to start vegetables indoors, but it serves equally as well for housebound plants.

Krause used 1-inch pine throughout, but almost any lumber is suitable. The extent to which you wish your indoor garden to grow will determine the size of your stand. Yet it is important to remember that you must allow a distance of up to 25 inches from the base to fluorescent tubes so that there will be enough light for most plants.

CONSTRUCTION

1. Cut each 1 x 8 into one 54-inch length and one 30-inch length.
2. Make a 15-inch-wide base by joining the two 54-inch-long boards with glue.
3. Use 30-inch lengths to make T-shaped sides, as illustrated. Use your light fixture to guide you in shaping the tops of the supports. The sup-

ports do not need to be shaped as shown. Unmodified boards will serve as well to support the light. Drill a ¾-inch hole in one T for the light cord.

4. Cut four struts from the 1 x 3. Each is 17 inches long, tapered from a point at the top to 2½ inches at the base. Attach to the sides with glue and eight 1¼-inch #10 screws.

5. Attach sides and struts to base exactly the length of the light fixture, probably 48 inches. Use 1½-inch #10 screws.

6. Finish sides and base with oil stain, paint, or varnish. Install light fixture.

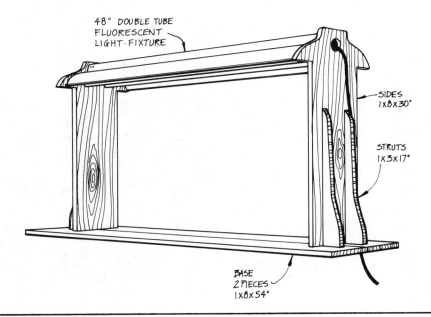

48" DOUBLE TUBE
FLUORESCENT
LIGHT·FIXTURE

SIDES
1x8x30"

STRUTS
1x3x17"

BASE
2 PIECES
1x8x54"

MATERIALS

Wood

        2 pcs. 1 x 8 x 8' or **Base:** 2 pcs. 1 x 8 x 54"

                               Sides: 2 pcs. 1 x 8 x 30"

        1 pc. 1 x 3 x 6' or **Struts:** 4 pcs. 1 x 3 x 17"

Hardware

    Glue
    8–1¼" #10 screws
    8–1½" #10 screws
    1–48" double-tube fluorescent light fixture

GROWLIGHT FURNITURE

If you like to grow houseplants for their beauty, it may seem anomalous to surround them with less-than-beautiful gizmos intended to make the plants grow and be beautiful. Gizmos like fluorescent lights.

But you can conceal the light fixtures in a carefully constructed growlight stand that will blend right in with the most costly furniture. Basically, the light fixture is concealed inside a finished wooden box, which is suspended over a matching box—into which you place your plants—by wooden supports.

Of course, you can use part of this design and not all of it. You can construct "lightboxes" to hang above your plants, wherever you locate them in your apartment or house. But this growlight plant stand was designed to be a self-contained plant display unit, and it looks best that way.

CONSTRUCTION

1. Cut the plywood into two pieces, each measuring 24 inches by $10\frac{5}{8}$ inches. Cut the 1 x 8 and the 1 x 4 each into two 24-inch lengths and two 12-inch lengths.

2. Construct the plant box from the 1 x 8s and one piece of plywood. The 12-inch ends should overlap the 24-inch sides in a simple butt joint. The bottom should be flush. Glue and nail using 8d finishing nails. Predrilling holes in the ends will prevent splitting. The best sequence is to nail the sides to the bottom, then the ends to the sides and bottom. Countersink the nails and fill with wood putty.

3. Make and attach the feet to the plant box. Cut the 1 x 2 into four 6-inch pieces and four 3-inch pieces. Scallop each piece as shown at

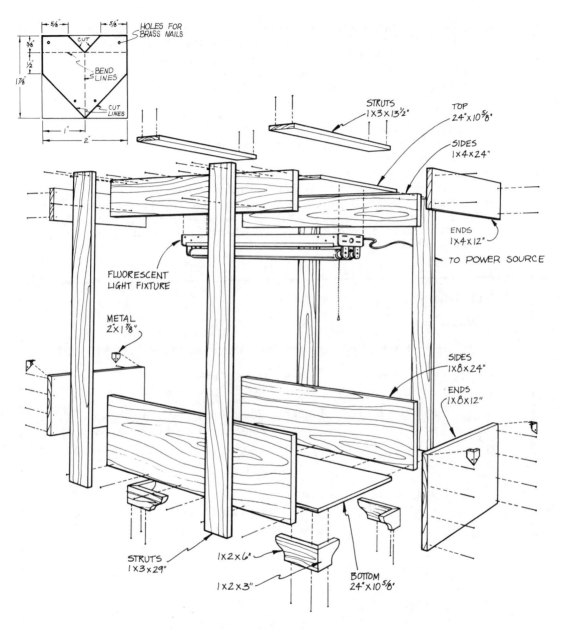

HOLES FOR
BRASS NAILS

CUT

BEND
LINES

CUT
LINES

STRUTS
1 X 3 X 13½"

TOP
24" X 10⅝"

SIDES
1 X 4 X 24"

ENDS
1 X 4 X 12"

TO POWER SOURCE

FLUORESCENT
LIGHT FIXTURE

METAL
2" X 1⅞"

SIDES
1 X 8 X 24"

ENDS
1 X 8 X 12"

STRUTS
1 X 3 X 29"

1 X 2 X 6"

1 X 2 X 3"

BOTTOM
24" X 10⅝"

one end, and bevel the other at a 45-degree angle. Attach the feet to
the bottom of the box as shown, the long pieces along the sides, the
short along the ends. Glue and nail, driving 8d finishing nails through
the feet and into the box.

4. Construct the light box in the same manner as the plant box, using the
    1 x 4 and the remaining piece of plywood.

67

5. Cut four 29-inch lengths from the 1 x 3. Glue and nail these support struts to the light box, as shown (two to a side, 3¾ inches from either end), driving 3d finishing nails through the side into the strut.

6. Measure for the remaining pieces of 1 x 3, which run across the top of the light box. They should be just about 13½ inches long. Glue and nail them in place.

7. Install the light fixture in the center of the light box.

8. Attach the light box to the plant box. The ends of the support struts should be flush with the bottom of the box, in line with the joint between the box and the feet.

9. Stain and/or varnish the stand. Apply a heavy coat (several coats would be best) of polyester resin to the inside of the plant box.

10. Attach the decorative corner pieces to the plant box (and to the light box, if you want). The corners are cut out of sheet metal and bent as shown. Paint them with flat paint, and when the paint has dried, nail them in place.

MATERIALS

Wood

1–2′ x 4′ sht. ¾″ int. plywood	or	**Bottom and top:** 2 pcs. 24″ x 10⅝″
1 pc. 1 x 8 x 8′	or	**Plant box sides:** 2 pcs. 1 x 8 x 24″
		ends: 2 pcs. 1 x 8 x 12″
1 pc. 1 x 4 x 8′	or	**Light box sides:** 2 pcs. 1 x 4 x 24″
		ends: 2 pcs. 1 x 4 x 12″
1 pc. 1 x 2 x 4′	or	**Feet:** 4 pcs. 1 x 2 x 6″
		4 pcs. 1 x 2 x 3″
1 pc. 1 x 3 x 12′	or	**Struts:** 4 pcs. 1 x 3 x 29″
		2 pcs. 1 x 3 x 13½″

Hardware

Glue
8d finishing nails
Wood putty
3d finishing nails
1–24″ double-tube fluorescent light fixture
Polyester resin
1 pc. 4″ x 4″, $\frac{1}{32}$″ sheet metal   or   4 pcs. 2″ x 1⅞″
Flat black paint
Decorative brass nails

VARIATIONS

Materials availability is almost always the biggest variable. You may have a longer fluorescent light fixture on hand. Alter the dimensions of the stand to accommodate the new fixture. If you have materials of slightly different dimensions, alter the stand as necessary to make use of them.

But you can also alter the stand to accommodate more plants. You might want to use a two-tubed 4-foot fixture. Thus, you'd want to make the sides of the plant box and the light box 4 feet long, rather than 2 feet long. And to completely conceal the fixture, you may have to use 1 x 6s, rather than 1 x 4s for the sides and ends on the light box.

Moreover, since plants respond best to the fluorescent light when they are but 4 to 6 inches from the light, you may want to reduce the length of the supporting struts. The length used in our design seems to be the best compromise, however, between providing adequate light and growing room.

HOUSEPLANT WORKTABLES

As people become more and more involved in houseplants, they usually find the need to set aside a special place for their houseplant work. All the potting soil ingredients, pots, organic fertilizers, tools, and miscellaneous items must be kept somewhere. A durable and spacious work surface is a must.

So why not meet that need with one of these houseplant worktables?

PLANT TABLE

David A. Caccia of Sewell, New Jersey, constructed this simple but durable plant table. It is useful wherever plants are kept—be it a greenhouse, a plant room, or in the backyard for summer sun.

CONSTRUCTION

1. Make two leg assemblies. Each has two legs, both a pair of 1 x 3 by 28-inch pieces separated at right angles by two 1 x 3 by 24-inch lengths. One of these separators is at top and one 5 inches up from the bottom. A third separator, cut from a 1 x 3 by 29-inch piece is placed diagonally between the other two, as shown.
2. Use twelve 6d galvanized nails to make each assembly. Make sure legs are square with 24-inch pieces. Nail from both sides.

3. Connect two leg assemblies with a 1 x 6 by 60-inch brace. It should rest atop two lower 24-inch pieces. Nail securely to all four pieces of back legs.

4. Nail six 1 x 3 by 72-inch boards to top members of leg assemblies. Space boards evenly.

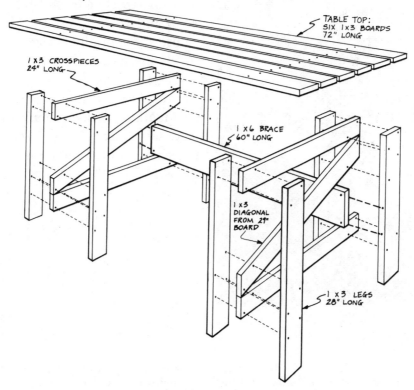

MATERIALS

Wood

1 pc. 1 x 3 x 8′	or	**Leg assemblies:** 4 pcs. 1 x 3 x 24″
5 pcs. 1 x 3 x 12′		8 pcs. 1 x 3 x 28″
		2 pcs. 1 x 3 x 29″

Top: 6 pcs. 1 x 3 x 72″

1 pc. 1 x 6 x 6′   or   **Brace:** 1 pc. 1 x 6 x 60″

Hardware

Galvanized 6d nails

POTTING BENCH

This potting bench was designed and constructed in the OGF Workshop and is being used in the greenhouse at the original Organic Gardening Experimental Farm.

The benchtop has a back and sides to prevent breakable pots from being accidentally pushed onto the floor. And deep bins below hold potting soil ingredients and other miscellaneous items.

CONSTRUCTION

1. From each of two 2 x 4s, cut two 21-inch lengths and a 38-inch length. From each of four more 2 x 4s, cut a 21-inch length and a 62-inch length. From the last 2 x 4, cut two 38-inch lengths. This will give you the required eight 21-inchers, four 62-inchers, and four 38-inchers and the least amount of scrap.

2. Take two 62-inch pieces and four 21-inch pieces and construct a frame as illustrated. Crossmembers should be placed about 20 inches apart and secured with two 16d box nails at each intersection with the longer 62-inch piece.

3. Construct another exactly the same.

4. Attach the 38-inch legs to the two frames using two 16d box nails, keeping the top frame flush with the ends of the 38-inch 2 x 4s and bottom frame 5 inches from the ground. See illustration.

5. From a sheet of ⅜-inch plywood cut two pieces 24 inches by 27 inches and nail them to ends of the bench using eight 4d nails. These pieces will fit between the legs and are nailed to the frames.

6. Next cut a piece 33 inches by 65 inches from the same piece and nail to the back also using 4d nails.

MATERIALS

Wood

7 pcs. 2 x 4 x 8′   or   **Frame crossmembers:** 8 pcs. 2 x 4 x 21″

Frame sides: 4 pcs. 2 x 4 x 62″

Legs: 4 pcs. 2 x 4 x 38″

3 shts. ⅜″ ext. plywood   or   **Sides:**
Ends: 2 pcs. 24″ x 27″
Back: 1 pc. 33″ x 65″
Front: 1 pc. 15″ x 65″
Bottom: 1 pc. 24″ x 62″
Partitions: 2 pcs. 24″ x 26½″

Top: 1 pc. 36″ x 72″

1 pc. 1 x 1 x 14′   or   **Partition cleats:**
Rear: 4 pcs. 1 x 1 x 26½″
Front: 4 pcs. 1 x 1 x 11½″

1 pc. 1 x 8 x 10′   or   **Benchtop sides:** 2 pcs. 1 x 8 x 24″

Backboard: 1 pc. 1 x 8 x 72″

Hardware

16d box nails
4d nails
1″ brads
Glue
Polyester resin
10–1½″ #10 screws
2–3″ door hinges and screws

7. Next cut a piece of plywood 15 inches by 65 inches from the remainder of the sheet and set aside.
8. Take another sheet of plywood and cut a piece 24 inches by 62 inches and nail to the top of the bottom frame using 4d nails.
9. To divide the bins cut two pieces of plywood according to the illustration.
10. Cut two pieces of 1 x 1 stock 26½ inches long and with 1-inch brads and glue, fasten them to the inside of the back plywood panel, spaced far enough apart to insert plywood dividers. Repeat for other divider —these slots should be about 20 inches apart.

Potting Bench

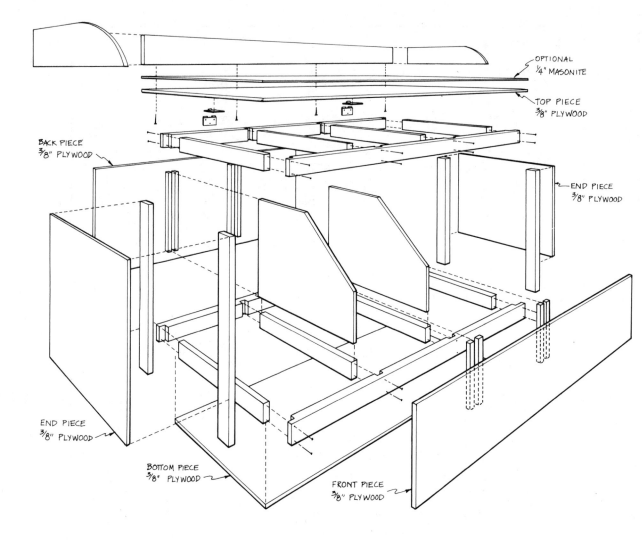

OPTIONAL
¼" MASONITE

TOP PIECE
⅜" PLYWOOD

BACK PIECE
⅜" PLYWOOD

END PIECE
⅜" PLYWOOD

END PIECE
⅜" PLYWOOD

BOTTOM PIECE
⅜" PLYWOOD

FRONT PIECE
⅜" PLYWOOD

11. Insert dividers and nail the 15-inch by 65-inch piece of plywood previously cut keeping it flush with the bottom of the 2 x 4s.

12. Attach 11½-inch lengths of 1 x 1 stock to the inside of the front as you did to the back. (Interior of the bins should be coated with a polyester resin or similar waterproofing material.)

13. Cut a piece of plywood 36 inches by 72 inches for the top of the bench. (As an option a similar piece of hardboard or Masonite can be glued to the top of the plywood. This will keep wood splinters from underneath fingernails.)

14. Cut the 10-foot 1 x 8 into three pieces, two pieces 24 inches long and one piece 72 inches long. Attach the 72-inch piece to the back of the

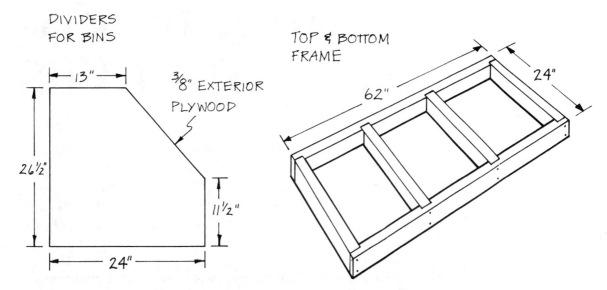

DIVIDERS FOR BINS

TOP & BOTTOM FRAME

13"

$\frac{3}{8}$" EXTERIOR PLYWOOD

26½"

11½"

24"

62"

24"

bench and the 24-inch sections to the sides (round one edge) with 1½-inch #10 screws. Drill pilot holes through plywood for screws.

15. The benchtop is fastened to the base using a pair of 3-inch door hinges spaced 2 feet apart. This will facilitate the loading of the bins. The top is mounted so that about 6 inches overhang on all sides.

MUSHROOM SHELVES

Mushrooms are *so* good. When the mushroom shelves—the ones you're about to learn about—were completed, Rudy Keller, a gardener at the original Organic Gardening Experimental Farm, volunteered to order some mushroom spawn and put them to the test. But he warned that few mushrooms would slip past his fast hand. "I love mushrooms."

And so do many other folks, people who have been buying mushrooms, when they could just as simply have been growing them. All that's needed is a dark, moist, cool place to locate trays or flats. A basement, a cold cellar, or root cellar would be ideal spots. A flat or two could suffice.

But for people with an insatiable appetite for mushrooms, people like Keller, something more elaborate is in order. Something like these mushroom shelves. You can build them in a short time. The space-saving tier-shelf beds are easy to fill, empty, clean, and disinfect.

Construct the uprights and crossbearers of rot-resisting cedar, redwood, cypress, or copper naphthenate-treated pine.

The bed-boards can be most any dimensions that are convenient for you to work with and that will fit the space you have for your mushroom shelves. In our model, the beds measure 36 inches by 18 inches and are just over 5 inches deep.

Place the bottom bed 6 to 8 inches away from the floor. Leave 18 inches between bed-boards, and allow for from 24 inches to 30 inches between the top shelf bed and ceiling. The air will circulate easily. Place away from drafts and sunlight.

Fill the beds with 5 inches of good-quality horse manure and wheat straw compost. The final fermentation (peak heat) will destroy insect and fungus enemies. You may encourage it with artificial heat.

When the beds cool below 80°F. and the pH is between 8.2 and 7.7, you are ready to plant the spawn. Purchase dry spawn of the prolific and disease-resistant brown variety from a commercial grower. Plant spawn the size of a walnut every 8 to 10 inches forming a diamond pattern 1 inch below the surface. Fill in the holes with compost.

From seven to fourteen days after spawning, check to be sure a blue grey color is "running" through the compost. Spread 1 inch of organically sterilized loam over the compost.

Keep the humidity between 70 and 80 percent and provide fans for good ventilation.

Pinheads will appear from ten to twenty days after casing. Spray the beds lightly with water, maintain the humidity at 95 percent, and regulate the temperature between 60° and 65°F.

Within six to eight weeks, mushroom clusters will appear. When the veils are stretched and they are ripe, harvest by grasping the stem and twisting. Cut out mushroom butts and fill the holes with ten parts casing soil to one part lime.

Rest periods and flushes will alternate for from two to five months before the medium is worn out.

CONSTRUCTION

1. Cut legs and framing members from 2 x 2, four legs 47½ inches long, six end pieces 15 inches long, and six side pieces 34½ inches long.
2. Lay out the legs for dadoes to accept the side (34½ inches long) framing members. The dadoes should be 1½ inches wide and ¾ inch deep. They should be 8¼ inches, 25¼ inches, and 42¼ inches from the foot of the legs.
3. Assemble the frame. Lay out two of the legs with three of the side pieces and nail them together. Repeat with the remaining legs and side pieces. Then nail the end pieces in place. Use 8d nails.

MATERIALS

Wood

3 pcs. 2 x 2 x 10' or **Legs:** 4 pcs. 2 x 2 x 47½"

2 pcs. 2 x 2 x 8' or **End supports:** 6 pcs. 2 x 2 x 15"

Side supports: 6 pcs. 2 x 2 x 34½"

2 pcs. 1 x 8 x 14' or **Sides:** 6 pcs. ¾" x 6" x 36" (act. meas.)

Ends: 6 pcs. ¾" x 6" x 19½" (act. meas.)

1 sht. ¾" ext. plywood or **Shelf bottoms:** 3 pcs. 18" x 36"

Hardware

8d nails
6d nails

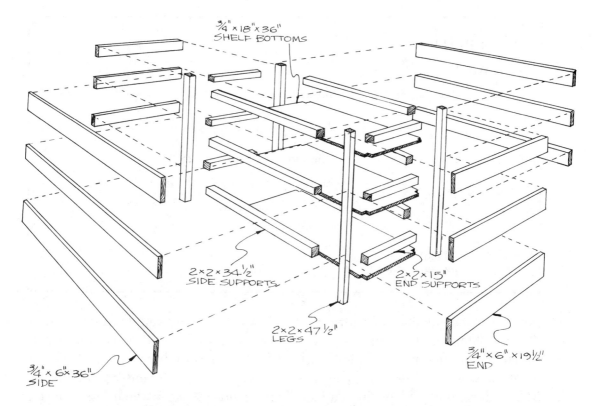

3/4" x 18" x 36"
SHELF BOTTOMS

2 x 2 x 34 1/2"
SIDE SUPPORTS

2 x 2 x 15"
END SUPPORTS

2 x 2 x 47 1/2"
LEGS

3/4" x 6" x 19 1/2"
END

3/4" x 6" x 36"
SIDE

4. Cut out the shelf bottom from ¾-inch exterior plywood. Each should measure 18 inches by 36 inches, with 1½-inch by 1½-inch notches at each corner. Nail the bottom in place, using 6d nails.

5. Rip the 1 x 8s to an actual width of 6 inches for the sides. You will need to rip 28 feet of material. Then cut six 36-inch-long pieces and six 19½-inch-long pieces. Nail the sides into place, using 6d nails. Nail through the sides into the bottoms, as well as into the support members, legs, and butting sides.

VARIATIONS

There are two clear variations to consider. One is to alter our model to make it easier to construct: eliminate the dadoes and use full-sized dimension lumber for the sides. The second is to alter the size to alter production: make larger beds for more mushrooms, smaller for fewer mushrooms.

If you want to make mushroom shelves like ours but don't have the

79

MATERIALS

Wood

2 pcs. 1 x 8 x 14' or **Sides:** 6 pcs. 1 x 8 x 36"
6 pcs. 1 x 8 x 19½"

2 pcs. 2 x 2 x 10' or **Legs:** 4 pcs. 2 x 2 x 51¼"

2 pcs. 2 x 2 x 12' or **Side supports:** 6 pcs. 2 x 2 x 33"

End supports: 6 pcs. 2 x 2 x 15"

1 sht. ¾" ext. plywood or **Shelf bottoms:** 3 pcs. 18" x 36"

Hardware

8d nails
6d nails

power equipment that makes ripping 28 feet of material a reasonable undertaking and that makes dadoes with a few passes, try this. Cut the legs 51¼ inches long. Skip the dadoes, merely mark the legs to position the framing members at 8¼ inches, 26½ inches, and 44¾ inches from the foot. Cut the side members 33 inches long and attach them to the legs with a simple butt joint. When it comes time to cut and attach the sides, use the full-size 1 x 8 lumber.

An even more simple design would be to construct the beds and attach the four legs to them.

If you want to enlarge the beds, remember to keep them less than an arm's length wide, unless you will locate them in a spot that allows access from either side. And remember as the bed-size increases, the weight of the compost-filled beds will be increasing. You may find it wise to use 2 x 3s or 2 x 4s and larger nails for framing.

WINDOW BOX

Window-box gardening isn't a year-round proposition, as is indoor gardening, unless you live in the very temperate sections of the world. But window-box gardening can be a form of indoor gardening, especially if you live in an apartment.

A window box is an excellent project for the fledgling woodworker, for a sturdy one can be constructed with elementary hand tools and a minimum of materials.

CONSTRUCTION

1. From 1 x 6, cut a 36-inch back, a 36-inch front, and a 19¼-inch piece for the sides. On the sides piece, measure 10 inches from one end along one edge, then 9¼ inches from the same end along the opposite edge, and scribe a line across the face of the board joining the two points. Cut along the line, and you will have two matching sides pieces. Cut a 34½-inch bottom board from 1 x 10 stock.

MATERIALS

Wood

1 pc. 1 x 6 x 8'   or   **Back and front:** 2 pcs. 1 x 6 x 36″

Sides: 1 pc. 1 x 6 x 19¼″

1 pc. 1 x 10 x 4'   or   **Bottom:** 1 pc. 1 x 10 x 34½″

Hardware

6d finishing nails
Paint
4–2″ #12 screws (or more, if necessary)

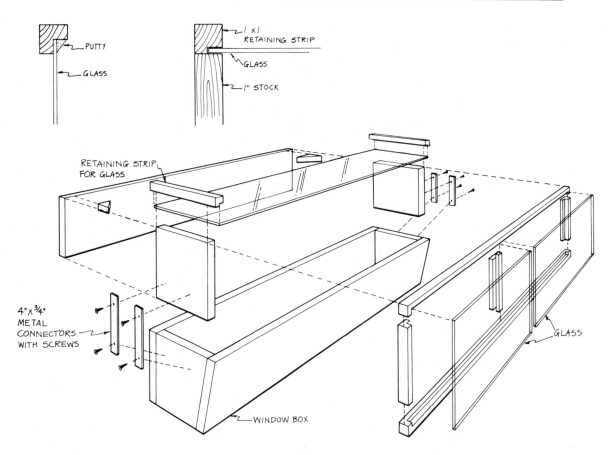

PUTTY

GLASS

1 x 1 RETAINING STRIP

GLASS

1″ STOCK

RETAINING STRIP FOR GLASS

4″ x ¾″ METAL CONNECTORS WITH SCREWS

GLASS

WINDOW BOX

2. Nail the back to the sides, then the bottom to the sides and back. Finally, nail the front in place. Use 6d finishing nails. Drilling pilot holes will prevent splitting.

3. Paint the window box inside and out to match the trim of the house.

4. The window box is attached to the windowsill with four (or more) 2-inch #12 screws. If the sill projects from the wall surface, it may be necessary to attach a filler strip to the back of the window box so it rests against the house but is level.

WINDOW BOX COLD FRAME

Window-box gardening doesn't need to be a summertime activity. With a little modification a wooden window box is easily turned into a miniature cold frame for starting summer's blooms in the early spring.

The cold frame shown was adapted to the window box described above. But since few window boxes are alike, you'll have to adapt the design to fit the window box you have. Or do what we did: build a window box and a matching cold frame.

CONSTRUCTION

1. From 1 x 6 lumber, cut a 36-inch back and two 10-inch sides. From 1 x 1 material, cut two 36-inch pieces, three 4-inch pieces, and two 11½-inch pieces.

2. The two 11½-inch pieces of 1 x 1 are the strips that will guide and retain the glass top of the cold frame. Cut a ⅛-inch by ¼-inch rabbet along one edge of each.

3. The remaining pieces of 1 x 1 compose the assembly that holds the two panes of glass on the front of the cold frame. Lay them out on your benchtop in their ultimate arrangement and mark them for rabbeting. You want an ⅛-inch-wide by ¼-inch-deep rabbet for the glass, as shown. Cut the rabbet.

4. Nail the front assembly together, using 4d finishing nails. Drilling pilot holes will prevent the nails from splitting these slender strips of wood.

5. Nail the back to the sides of the cold frame, driving 6d finishing nails through the back into the sides. Again, pilot holes are advisable. Nail the front assembly in place, again using 6d finishing nails, and again, drill pilot holes first.

6. Paint the unit, being especially careful to coat the rabbets on the front. Also paint the top glass retainers, then nail them in place.

7. Measure for the three panes of glass, and have it cut to fit (or cut it yourself). The panes on the front are each retained with four glazier's

points, then sealed in with glazing compound or putty. The top panel is merely slid into place (but best not before the cold frame is attached to the window box).

8. With a hacksaw, cut four 4-inch lengths of ¾-inch-wide metal. Drill a hole at either end of each strip. Attach the cold frame to the window box with these strips and ½-inch #6 screws, as shown.

MATERIALS

Wood

 1 pc. 1 x 6 x 6′ or **Back:** 1 pc. 1 x 6 x 36″

          Sides: 2 pcs. 1 x 6 x 10″

 1 pc. 1 x 1 x 10′ or **Front assembly:** 2 pcs. 1 x 1 x 36″
                 3 pcs. 1 x 1 x 4″

          Retaining strips: 2 pcs. 1 x 1 x 11½″

Hardware

 4d finishing nails
 6d finishing nails
 Paint
 Glass
 Glazier's points
 Glazing compound
 16″–¾″ metal strip or 4 pcs. 4″ x ¾″
 8–½″ #6 screws

VARIATIONS

The most difficult part of this project is the rabbeting. If you don't own the power equipment (or the rather exotic plane) necessary to cut rabbets, don't despair. You can alter the front and top assemblies. For example, use 1 x 2s for the top and bottom strips in the front assembly, and 2 x 2s for the short vertical posts as shown. Then cut 1 x 1 retaining strips to fit inside the assembled window frame to retain the glass. Install the glass with glazier's points and putty. (You'll want to make the 1 x 6 sides only 9¼ inches long, rather than 10 inches if you take this approach to the cold frame.)

WINDOW GREENHOUSES

You don't need a traditional greenhouse to dabble in greenhouse gardening. All you need is a window you are willing to devote to the endeavor. It should be one with a southern exposure, but in a pinch—and if you compensate by selecting plants carefully—any window will do.

A SIMPLE WINDOW GREENHOUSE

One of the most simple window greenhouses is designed around a storm window. Ruth Wendorff uses such a greenhouse; hers uses the storm window (and screen) made for

the particular window she uses. At the new Organic Gardening Experimental Farm, we constructed a similar greenhouse, but we used a storm window longer than the window we attached the greenhouse to. The difference is obvious in the photographs: Wendorff's greenhouse is built-up from the windowsill, while the greenhouse at the farm is flush with the windowsill.

Neither project is a difficult undertaking. There's no rabbeting for glass panes or complex framing to be done. Either one can be made with a single sheet of $\frac{3}{4}$-inch exterior plywood (and you'll undoubtedly have some left over, too).

Wendorff's greenhouse was made as follows.

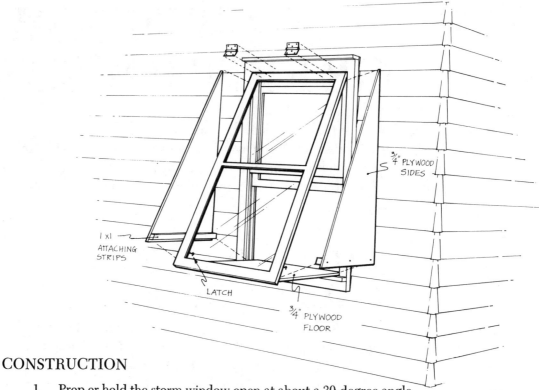

CONSTRUCTION

1. Prop or hold the storm window open at about a 30-degree angle. Measure the right triangle created by the storm window and the window casement (a, b, and c in the drawing), and the distance between the windowsill and the location of the floor of the greenhouse (d). Also measure the width of the window (e).

2. Lay out the measurements for four parts of the greenhouse on the sheet of plywood. There will be two triangles to fit between the window casement and the storm window (measurements a, b, and c). There will also be a shelf that is as deep as the baseline of the triangles (measurement a), and 1½ inches narrower than the width of the window (so the triangles can overlap the ends of the shelf). The fourth board is a baseboard to fill the gap between the shelf and the windowsill; it is as wide as the window (measurement e) and deep enough to fill the gap (measurement d).

3. Attach the shelf to the baseboard with glue and 6d finishing nails, putting the shelf atop the baseboard and driving the nails through it into the baseboard.

4. Attach a 1 x 1 or 1 x 2 cleat to both edges of the shelf with glue and 3d finishing nails.

5. Slip the baseboard-shelf assembly into position. The baseboard should fit snugly against the windowsill and the sides of the casement. Tack the assembly into place with 3d or 6d finishing nails.

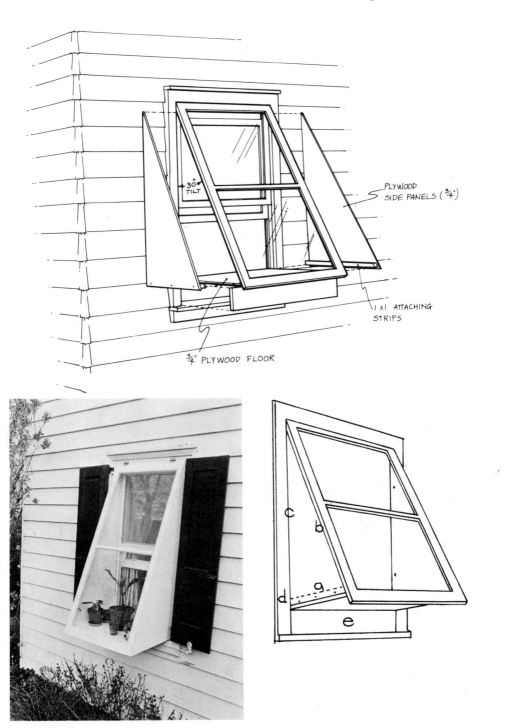

PLYWOOD
SIDE PANELS (¾")

30°
TILT

1 x 1 ATTACHING
STRIPS

¾" PLYWOOD FLOOR

c

b

g

d

e

6. Position one of the two triangles at the window and attach it to the window casement with four or five 2½-inch #10 screws. Position and attach the other triangle.

7. Drive three 2-inch #8 screws through the baseline of each triangle into the edge of the shelf.

8. Hang the storm window in place and secure it with a hook and eye at either side.

9. Caulk all the joints to seal out winter's cold. A coat of primer and house paint to match your home's trim will complete the project.

MATERIALS

Wood

1 sht. ¾″ ext. plywood (sides, bottom, baseboard)
1 pc. 1 x 1 x 8′ (cleats)

Hardware

Glue
6d finishing nails
3d finishing nails
8 to 10–2½″ #10 screws
6–2″ #8 screws
2 hooks and eyes
Caulking compound
Paint

A MORE ELABORATE WINDOW GREENHOUSE

This project is derived from a greenhouse used by Montanan Jane Stuwe.

Stuwe's greenhouse is located on the west side of the house and receives necessary sun from the south and west. It is attached to the window and can be removed easily. The enclosure is 4 feet high, 2½ feet wide, and 1½ feet deep, with two shelves on each side. There is room for plants and seedlings below, and more shelves can be added on the west as needed. Insulated and closed on the north and top, it is heated and ventilated from the house whose humidity plays an important part in the health of the plants. Geraniums especially respond to moisture absorbed through the leaves.

The inside window is movable for regulating and circulating heat—nighttime temperature is around 50°F. The Stuwes stretch clear plastic over the glass to provide storm-window protection.

It is important to construct the window as weathertight as possible by making it a part of the house. Here plants winter in a "warmer-day,

cooler-night" atmosphere. Since most of the sun can be picked up on the south and west, the top, bottom, and north sides of the window were insulated, then covered with plywood inside and siding and roofing outside.

For construction the Stuwes used three lengths of 1 x 8 lumber each 8 feet long, one 10-foot length, and six pieces of 10-foot 1 x 4s. A used window was placed on the west, while on the south glass was cut and fit in the casing. Scrap 2 x 4s formed the support where the window is attached to the house, while insulation and roofing were leftover material from a former project. They bought aluminum brackets, four lag screws, nails, and putty, but the inside shelves were cut from used 1 x 8s. This window structure can be adjusted to any size window.

Clearly, the Stuwes made good use of the materials available to them. Their greenhouse is unique, but provides a sound basic design concept for any woodworker to work from in building a window greenhouse. The construction directions below will help you construct a greenhouse very much like the Stuwe's. It is the same size and features windows on only two sides.

MATERIALS

Wood

1 pc. 2 x 4 x 10′ or		**Window units:**
(remainder used elsewhere)		Large sash sides: 2 pcs. 2 x 4 x 48″
2 pcs. 2 x 3 x 8′ or		Small sash sides: 2 pcs. 2 x 3 x 48″

1 pc. 2 x 4 x 10′   or
   (remainder used elsewhere)
2 pcs. 2 x 3 x 8′   or

Window units:
  Large sash sides: 2 pcs. 2 x 4 x 48″
  Small sash sides: 2 pcs. 2 x 3 x 48″
  Large sash top and bottom:
    2 pcs. 2 x 3 x 23″
  Small sash top and bottom:
    2 pcs. 2 x 3 x 13″

1 pc. 2 x 2 x 8′   or
   (remainder used elsewhere)
3 pcs. 36″ x $\frac{3}{8}$″ dowel   or
12′–$\frac{1}{2}$″ quarter-round molding   or

  Large sash mullion: 1 pc. 2 x 2 x 23″
  Small sash mullion: 1 pc. 2 x 2 x 13″
  24 pcs. 4$\frac{1}{2}$″ x $\frac{3}{8}$″ dowel
  Glass retainer, large sash:
    4 pcs. 20$\frac{3}{4}$″ long
    4 pcs. 23″ long

14′–$\frac{1}{2}$″ quarter-round molding   or
  Glass retainer, small sash:
    4 pcs. 20$\frac{3}{4}$″ long
    4 pcs. 13″ long

1 pc. 2 x 3 x 12′   or   **North wall frame:** 2 pcs. 2 x 3 x 48″
    2 pcs. 2 x 3 x 13″

1 pc. 36″ x $\frac{3}{8}$″ dowel   or   8 pcs. 4$\frac{1}{2}$″ x $\frac{3}{8}$″ dowel

1 pc. 2 x 4 x 10′   or   **Gable:** 1 pc. 2 x 4 x 18″ (ripped diagonally)
  (remainder used elsewhere)

1 pc. 2 x 2 x 8′   or   **Floor supports:** 2 pcs. 2 x 2 x 18″
  (remainder from above)

1 sht. $\frac{1}{4}$″ ext. plywood   or   **Int. wall:** 1 pc. 49$\frac{1}{4}$″ x 18″

                      Ext. wall: 1 pc. 51$\frac{1}{2}$″ x 18″

2 pcs. 1 x 8 x 8′   or   **Roof and bottom:** 4 pcs. 1 x 8 x 30″

                      Floor: 2 pcs. 1 x 8 x 27″

1 pc. 1 x 4 x 8′   or   **Roof and bottom:** 2 pcs. 1 x 4 x 30″

                      Floor: 1 pc. 1 x 4 x 27″

2 pcs. 2 x 4 (remainder from above)   or   **Braces:** 4 pcs. 2 x 4 x 18″
                                2 pcs. 2 x 4 x 22$\frac{1}{2}$″

                      Cleats: 4 pcs. (cut scrap to fit)

CONSTRUCTION

1. The first step is to construct the two window units.

    a. Cut two 48-inch lengths of 2 x 4 and two 23-inch lengths of 2 x 3 and a 23-inch length of 2 x 2. Assemble them into the frame for the window—the 2 x 3s at top and bottom, the 2 x 2 in the center, the 2 x 4s butting against them, and fasten them using the open doweling technique. Clamp each joint and bore two $\frac{3}{8}$-inch holes with a brace and bit through the upright and about an inch into the crosspiece. Drive a $4\frac{1}{2}$-inch length of $\frac{3}{8}$-inch dowel, tapered on the leading end, into each hole. The butting surface of the frame and the dowels should be glued.

    b. Cut four $20\frac{3}{4}$-inch and four 23-inch pieces of $\frac{1}{2}$-inch quarter-round molding. These will compose the permanent glass retainer. Miter the ends of the strips of molding at a 45-degree angle and nail in place as shown, using 4d finishing nails.

    c. At this point, you can measure the frame for the glass panes and have them cut to fit (or do it yourself). After the greenhouse is assembled and painted, the glass will be installed by pushing two glazier's points into each side of the window frame to retain the glass and sealing the joint with glazing compound or putty. Don't install the glass now!

Hardware

Glue
4d finishing nails
6d finishing nails
16d finishing nails
Paint
8–$1\frac{1}{2}$″ #10 screws
4–4″ lag bolts
2 pcs. glass $12\frac{7}{8}$″ x $20\frac{5}{8}$″
2 pcs. glass $22\frac{7}{8}$″ x $20\frac{5}{8}$″
Glazier's points
Glazing compound

Miscellaneous

1 pc. 43″ x 13″ fiberglass insulation
1 pc. 24″ x 18″ fiberglass insulation
Roofing felt 30″ x $18\frac{1}{2}$″
Metal flashing 30″ long
Roofing mastic
Asphalt roll roofing

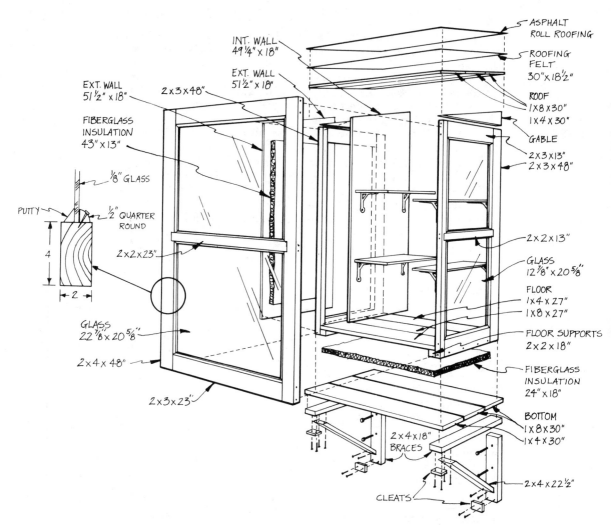

d. The side window is assembled basically in the same manner. The uprights are 48-inch lengths of 2 x 3, the top and bottom crosspieces are 13-inch lengths of 2 x 3, and the center crosspiece is a 13-inch length of 2 x 2. Cut the quarter-round molding glass retainer strips and the glass to fit (but don't install the glass).

2. One side of this greenhouse is blank; it is an insulated wall. Using 48-inch 2 x 3 uprights, 13-inch 2 x 3 top and bottom crosspieces, and the open doweling technique already described in step 1a, construct a perimeter frame for this wall.

3. Rip an 18-inch-long 2 x 4 in half on a diagonal. Fasten the resulting wedges atop the side window and the side wall by toenailing them with 6d finishing nails.

4. Cut two 18-inch lengths of 2 x 2. Nail (with 6d finishing nails) one to the inside bottom of the window and one to the inside bottom of the wall.

5. Cut two 27-inch and four 30-inch lengths of 1 x 8 and a 27-inch and two 30-inch lengths of 1 x 4. The 27-inchers will be the floor inside the greenhouse. The 30-inchers will be the roof and the bottom. Lay the 27-inchers in place, as shown, and nail fast. Nail the roof boards in place. Cut a piece of fiberglass mat insulation to fit between the floor and the bottom. After fastening it in place, nail the bottom on. Use 6d finishing nails.

6. Cut a piece of $\frac{1}{4}$-inch plywood to cover the inside of the side wall. It will measure $45\frac{3}{4}$ inches along the front edge and $49\frac{1}{4}$ inches along the back edge, being 18 inches wide. Nail it in place, using 4d nails. Then cut a similar, but slightly taller, panel to cover the outside of the wall. This panel will be 48 inches along the front edge, $51\frac{1}{2}$ inches along the back edge and be 18 inches wide. Before nailing this panel in place, cut a piece of fiberglass mat insulation to fill the air space in the wall, and fit it in place. Close up the wall.

7. Nail the front window in place, using 16d finishing nails.

8. Paint the greenhouse inside and out, being particularly careful to coat the insides of the window frames where the glass will seat.

9. Make the two brackets. Cut four 18-inch lengths and two $22\frac{1}{2}$-inch lengths of 2 x 4. Cut the ends of the two longer pieces at 45-degree angles, as shown. Assemble each bracket by butting one 18-inch piece against another and nailing it fast with 16d nails. Position the brace and fasten it with four $1\frac{1}{2}$-inch #10 screws. Finally, cut two small cleats to fit and fasten as shown with 4d nails.

10. Fasten the brackets below the window where the greenhouse will be installed, using two or more lag bolts at least 4 inches long. With a frame house, be sure the bolts seat in the studs; with a masonry house, drill holes in the wall with a masonry bit or star drill and insert expansion plugs for the bolts to seat in.

11. If there is no wooden window frame to nail the greenhouse to, you will have to fasten a 2 x 2 nailing frame for this purpose to the wall of the house. Install the nailing frame above and beside the window so the greenhouse will surround it, rather than butt against it.

12. Set the greenhouse in place on the brackets. Nail it to the nailing frame, or toenail it to the window frame.

13. Nail a sheet of roofing felt to the greenhouse roof. Then install a length of flashing between the house wall and the greenhouse roof, sealing it along the house with roofing mastic. Finally, nail on a length of roll roofing.

14. Install the glass, using glazier's points and glazing compound.

15. Install shelves inside the greenhouse to suit yourself.

VARIATIONS

Obviously, not everyone has a window suited to a greenhouse of this size. Make the greenhouse larger or smaller to suit your situation. Moreover, you can make your greenhouse with three windows, instead of only two.

And if you have suitable storm windows or other window units, use those and save yourself the bother of making window sashes.

PART II
Outdoor Gardening Projects

GARDENING TOOLS

Some of the best tools for gardening aren't for sale in the garden center. They are the tools conceived and tested in backyard gardens around the world. Some are just homemade varieties of commercially available tools. Others are personal answers to particular gardening problems. Whatever the case, however, a large measure of the pleasure that comes from their use is the knowledge that you made it yourself. So it's bound to be better.

"WHATZIT": Five-in-One Garden Tool

On his Kozy Korner homestead in Otis, Oregon, Bill Tyler asked himself: Why carry around a rake, hoe, hammer, and trowel when all you need is one garden tool? So he built a "whatzit." Simple to make from scrap materials, this handy item does a different job each time you turn it. The pictures show how.

CONSTRUCTION

1. Using a ¾-inch wooden dowel or a broomhandle, fashion a 24-inch long handle, tapering the last 2 inches on one end to a ¼-inch flat tip.
2. Cut a 4-inch by 3½-inch piece of ⅛-inch sheet metal for the hoe. Cut the hoe point as shown. Drill three $\frac{3}{16}$-inch holes along the 3½-inch end.
3. The head is a 6-inch length of 2 x 4. Drill a ¾-inch hole halfway through the face for the handle. Then drive six 16d nails, evenly spaced, into the side of the block. Remove the nail heads. Glue and nail (with ¾-inch

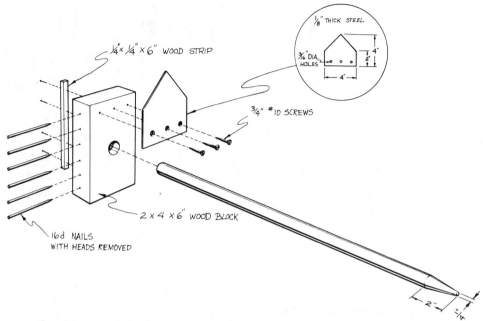

brads) a ¼-inch by ¼-inch by 6-inch wood strip to the side of the block opposite the handle.

4. Finally attach the hoe with ¾-inch #10 screws and the handle with glue, and an 8d nail driven through the edge of the head into the handle.

MATERIALS

Wood

1 pc. 36″ x ¾″ dowel or	**Handle:** 1 pc. 24″ x ¾″ dowel
1 pc. 2 x 4 x 2′ or	**Head:** 1 pc. 2 x 4 x 6″
1 pc. ¼″ x ¼″ x 2′ or	**Strip:** 1 pc. ¼″ x ¼″ x 6″

Hardware

1 pc. 4″ x 3½″, ⅛″ sheet metal (hoe)
16d nails
White glue
¾″ brads
3–¾″ #10 screws
8d nail

SOIL SAMPLER

A useful tool for taking core samples of soil for testing, this soil sampler is also easy to make. It is assembled from a length of electrical conduit and a length of ¾-inch dowel.

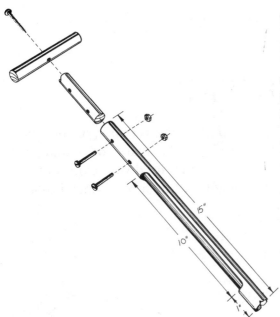

MATERIALS

Wood

1 pc. 36″ x ¾″ dowel   or   **Handle:** 1 pc. 5″ x ¾″ dowel
1 pc. 6″ x ¾″ dowel

Hardware

1 pc. 10′ x ⅞″ elec. conduit   or   **Tube:** 1 pc. 15″ long
1–1½″ #10 screw
2–1″ x ⅛″ roundhead stove bolts w/ nuts and washers

CONSTRUCTION

1. Start with a 15-inch piece of $\frac{7}{8}$-inch electrical conduit. One inch from one end, cut a section $\frac{3}{8}$ inch deep and 10 inches long from the pipe. This can be done with a hacksaw or a saber saw fitted with a metal-cutting blade. File four notches $\frac{3}{16}$ inch deep in the end of the pipe closest to the slot.

2. Make the handle. Cut a 6-inch and a 5-inch length of $\frac{3}{4}$-inch dowel. Notch one end of the 5-inch piece so the other piece fits snugly as shown. Fasten the two pieces together with a $1\frac{1}{2}$-inch #10 screw, drilling a pilot hole before driving the screw.

3. Slip the shaft of the handle into the pipe, drill two holes through the pipe and the dowel, and fasten the two together with two 1-inch by $\frac{1}{8}$-inch roundhead stove bolts.

SOIL SIFTER

A simple sifter for compost or potting soil can be made by nailing a piece of $\frac{1}{4}$-inch hardware cloth to the bottom of a 12-inch by 18-inch frame.

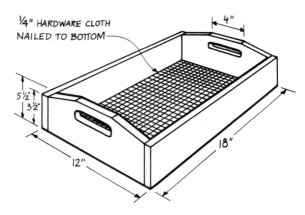

¼" HARDWARE CLOTH NAILED TO BOTTOM

CONSTRUCTION

1. Cut two 18-inch lengths of 1 x 4 and two 10½-inch lengths of 1 x 6.
2. Taper the ends and cut handholds into them. From a corner at each end of the boards, measure and mark 2 inches along the butt end and 3¼ inches along the edge. Draw a line connecting the two points and cut along the line. Then mark a 1-inch by 3½-inch rectangle in the upper middle of each end board, as shown. Cut out the rectangle with a keyhole or coping saw.
3. Butt the sides against the ends and nail the sifter frame together, using 6d nails.
4. Staple a 12-inch by 18-inch piece of ¼-inch hardware cloth to the bottom.

MATERIALS

Wood

1 pc. 1 x 4 x 4′	or	**Sides:** 2 pcs. 1 x 4 x 18″
1 pc. 1 x 6 x 2′	or	**Ends:** 2 pcs. 1 x 6 x 10½″

Hardware

6d nails
1 pc. 12″ x 18″ hardware cloth, ¼″ mesh
¾″ staples

LIME SPREADER

Here's a device to ease the chore of spreading lime and rock fertilizers on a large garden. The spreader is not difficult to make, and the hopper can be expanded or shrunk to serve the user or the materials at hand.

The model constructed in the OGF Workshop features homemade wooden wheels, similar to the one used on the wheelbarrow, but the plan could easily be modified to accommodate manufactured wheels.

CONSTRUCTION

1. The wheels are fabricated from 1 x 12 stock. Cut eight 20-inch lengths, four being used for each wheel. Select a scrap strip of wood at least 10 inches long and drive two nails through it 9 inches apart. This will be used to scribe the wheel. Lay out two of the 1 x 12 boards, their long dimensions abutting. Locate the center of the wheel 10 inches from either end and 1½ inches from the joint between the two boards. The idea is to avoid the weakness that would result from having the wheels' center hubs falling in the joint of the two boards. Using the homemade scriber, mark off the diameter of the wheel. After cutting out this first wheel with a coping saw or jigsaw, use it as a pattern for scribing and cutting the remaining four units. Glue and screw, using 1½ inch #10 screws, together two wheels, each comprising two of the wheel units. In doing this, have the joints between the board perpendicular to each other for additional strength.

2. The hopper is made of 1 x 10 stock. Cut two $30\frac{1}{2}$-inch lengths for the front and back, two $11\frac{1}{4}$-inch lengths for the ends, and a 32-inch length for the bottom. Clamp the end pieces together and along one edge measure $2\frac{1}{2}$ inches from one corner and mark, then along the same edge measure $2\frac{5}{8}$ inches from the other corner and mark. Draw a line from the marks to the nearest corners on the other edge of the board, then cut along the lines. This procedure will give the ends the appropriate shape, as shown. Drill a 1-inch diameter hole 2 inches from the bottom center of the end boards. Rip the bottom to an actual 6-inch width.

3. The axle is made from a 36-inch length of 1-inch dowel. Measure and mark 3 inches from each end of the dowel, then drill eight $\frac{1}{4}$-inch holes through the dowel, evenly spacing them *between* the marks and alternating the plane of the holes. Cut eight 3-inch lengths of $\frac{1}{4}$-inch dowel and drive a piece through each hole in the axle, leaving an inch protruding on each end of the hole. Make a saw kerf $1\frac{1}{2}$ inches deep in each end of the axle.

4. Cut two $9\frac{1}{4}$-inch lengths of 2 x 4 for the handle mounting. Measure $11\frac{7}{16}$ inches from each end of the hopper back and scribe a line across the board. Attach the two pieces of 2 x 4 to the back, one piece flush with each line. The lines should be $7\frac{5}{8}$ inches apart, and you want the two 2 x 4s that far apart. Use glue and three 2-inch #10 screws in each 2 x 4, driving the screws through the back into the 2 x 4s.

5. Assemble the hopper using glue and 8d nails. The ends overlap the front and back. Be sure to slip the ends over the axle as you butt them against the front and back, for you won't be able to install the axle after the hopper is fastened together. And be sure the bottom edges of the boards are flush, so you can seal off the bottom without leaks. You will probably find it desirable therefore to bevel the bottom edge of the back and front to give them a broader flat surface on the bottom. Use a sliding T bevel to duplicate the angle of the end pieces on the butt end of the front and back board, then join the butt-end marks across the faces of the boards and plane the edge to the line. Nail the bottom in place.

6. Make the handle assembly. Cut two 36-inch lengths and one 19-inch length of 2 x 3. Using a wood rasp or drawknife, round $4\frac{1}{2}$ inches at each end of the 19-inch 2 x 3 to form comfortable handgrips. Then cut two $1\frac{1}{2}$-inch-wide and $\frac{1}{2}$-inch-deep dadoes in each broad face of the 19-incher, locating them an equal distance—about $6\frac{5}{8}$ inches—from each end of the 2 x 3, the outer edges $7\frac{5}{8}$ inches apart. Fit the butt end of a 36-inch 2 x 3 into each dado and fasten with glue and two $1\frac{1}{2}$-inch #10 screws. Cut the free ends of the handle assembly on such an angle that the grips will be at a comfortable height when the spread is assembled. The angle must be fairly acute. Then slip the handle assembly between the mountings and drive two $1\frac{1}{2}$-inch #10 screws through each mounting member into the handle shaft. Fasten in place with a total of four $1\frac{1}{2}$-inch #10 screws.

7. The flow of lime is controlled by a sliding panel that covers or exposes holes drilled in the hopper bottom.

   a. Cut a $30\frac{1}{4}$-inch-long by 7-inch-wide piece of $\frac{1}{4}$-inch plywood. Cut two $6\frac{1}{2}$-inch lengths of 1 x 1 stock and cut a $\frac{5}{16}$-inch-wide by

103

$\frac{5}{16}$-inch-deep rabbet in each piece. Glue and nail these 1 x 1 guides to the bottom edges of the hopper end pieces, with the rabbet on the upper inside edge of the guide. Slide the plywood panel into the guides and fasten $\frac{1}{4}$-inch by $\frac{3}{4}$-inch strips 7 inches long to each end of the plywood, abutting the guide. These strips will hold the plywood panel in proper alignment, which makes it easier to slide back and forth, adjusting the lime flow. Attach a $\frac{1}{4}$-inch by $\frac{3}{4}$-inch strip $31\frac{3}{4}$ inches long to the lower front edge of the hopper, so it slightly overlaps the bottom edge and acts as a stop for the sliding panel.

b.   Now cut a 31-inch and a 12-inch piece of 1 x 1 hardwood stock for the control lever. Cut a 1-inch tenon at one end of the 12-incher and a $1\frac{1}{2}$-inch-deep notch in one end of the 31-incher; the width of the notch should be slightly greater than the thickness of the tenon. Slip the two together, forming a right angle, then drill a $\frac{1}{4}$-inch hole and fasten the two pieces together with a $1\frac{1}{2}$-inch-long $\frac{1}{4}$-inch bolt (with washers). Drill a similar hole 15 inches from the other end of the 31-incher. Measure 15 inches from the hopper end of one handle shaft and drill a $\frac{1}{4}$-inch hole in the handle. Fit a bolt through the handle and the lever, then position the short rod across the sliding panel. Mark the position and drive $\frac{3}{4}$-inch #6 screws through the plywood into the level rod. Use a 4-inch-long $\frac{1}{4}$-inch bolt to attach the control lever, placing washers between the bolt head and handle, handle and lever, lever and a spring, and spring and nut. Finally, drill $\frac{3}{8}$-inch holes in the hopper bottom (but not in the sliding panel). Drill them in several alternating rows so that you can vary the flow from slow to fast by uncovering more holes.

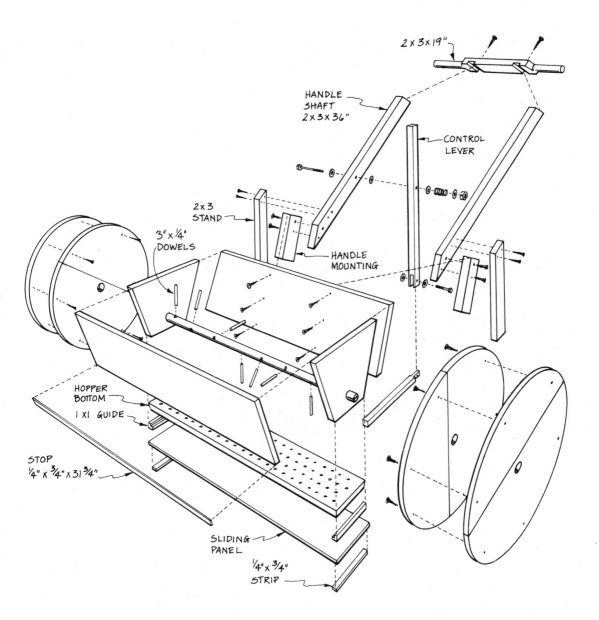

2 x 3 x 19"

HANDLE
SHAFT
2 x 3 x 36"

CONTROL
LEVER

2 x 3
STAND

3" x ¼"
DOWELS

HANDLE
MOUNTING

HOPPER
BOTTOM

1 x 1 GUIDE

STOP
¼" x ¾" x 31 ¾"

SLIDING
PANEL

¼" x ¾"
STRIP

8. Attach the wheels. Daub epoxy glue on the axle shaft and slip the wheels onto the axle. Drive a small wedge, cut from scrap, into the saw kerf in each end of the axle.

9. Hold the spreader in a standing position and measure from the handle shafts to the ground. Cut two lengths of 2 x 3 to this length and attach them to the handle shafts. They will be about 16½ inches long. Cut the corner that projects above the top of the handle shaft flush.

MATERIALS

Wood

1 pc. 1 x 12 x 14'   or   **Wheels:** 8 pcs. 1 x 12 x 20"

1 pc. 1 x 10 x 10'   or   **Hopper:**
         Front and back: 2 pcs. 1 x 10 x 30½"
         Ends: 2 pcs. 1 x 10 x 11⅛"
         Bottom: 1 pc. 1 x 10 x 32"

1 pc. 36" x 1" dowel (axle)

1 pc. 24" x ¼" dowel   or   **Pins:** 8 pcs. 3" x ¼" dowel

1 pc. 2 x 4 x 2'   or   **Handle mount:** 2 pcs. 2 x 4 x 9¼"

1 pc. 2 x 3 x 12'   or   **Handle:** 2 pcs. 2 x 3 x 36"
                                    1 pc. 2 x 3 x 19"
                                    2 pcs. 2 x 3 x 16½"

1–2' x 4' sht. ¼" ext. plywood   or   **Flow control board:** 1 pc. 30¼" x 7"

1 pc. 1 x 1 x 6' hardwood   or   **Flow control board tracks:**
         2 pcs. 1 x 1 x 6½"

         Control lever: 1 pc. 1 x 1 x 31"
                            1 pc. 1 x 1 x 12"

1 pc. ¼" x ¾" x 48"   or   **Stop:** 2 pcs. ¼" x ¾" x 7"
                                  1 pc. ¼" x ¾" x 31¾"

Hardware

8d nails
White glue
24–1½" #10 screws
3–2" #10 screws
1–1½" x ¼" bolt w/ nut and washers
4–¾" #6 screws
1–4" x ¼" bolt w/ nut and washers
1–2" coil spring
Epoxy glue

STRAIGHT-ROW MARKER

The most common way to lay out straight garden rows is to stretch a cord between two stakes, one at either end of the row. This quickly and easily made row marker keeps stakes and cord together for easy use and storage.

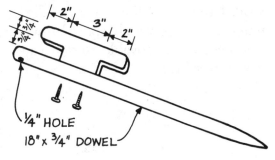

¼" HOLE

18" x ¾" DOWEL

CONSTRUCTION

1. Cut a 36-inch length of ¾-inch dowel in half and sharpen one end of each piece. Then drill a ¼-inch hole through the unsharpened end of each piece.
2. Cut a 7-inch length of 1 x 2 and shape it as shown. Attach this cleat to one of the dowels with two 1¼-inch #10 screws.
3. Tie the cord to the cleat, then run the free end through the hole in the stake and tie it to the second stake. Loop the excess around the cleat as shown.

MATERIALS

Wood

    1 pc. 36″ x ¾″ dowel or **Stakes:** 2 pcs. 18″ x ¾″ dowel

    1 pc. 1 x 2 x 2′   or **Cleat:** 1 pc. 1 x 2 x 7″

Hardware

    2–1¼″ #10 screws
    Cord

ROW MAKER

Once your seedbed is tilled and raked out, you can save the trouble of lining out individual rows with this simple row maker. Just drag it across the garden like a big rake, and it will excavate little trenches for your seeds. You can prepare five closely spaced rows at a time, or a smaller number of more widely spaced rows. The pegs are removable so you can vary row spacing.

CONSTRUCTION

1. Select a knot-free, 6-foot length of 2 x 2 and round off 4 feet of one end, using a drawknife, block plane, or rasp, to form a handle that's comfortable to the hand. If you are unable to purchase a 2 x 2—some lumberyards don't stock it—rip a 2 x 4 or a 2 x 3.

2. Next, rip a 36-inch length of 1 x 6 into a piece 2 inches wide (the crosspiece) and two pieces ¾ inch wide (the braces).

3. Cut a notch ¾ inch deep by 2 inches wide into the square end of the handle. Remove the wood with a coping saw or a chisel.

4. Starting 2 inches from each end of the crosspiece, drill five ¾-inch diameter holes through the center of the broad face, locating them 8 inches apart on center. These are for the pegs. Since you want to be able to adjust the pegs, and since the center hole will be obstructed by the handle, you will have to extend the hole through the handle after it is secured in place. Drill a pilot hole for a screw eye, which will serve as a setscrew for each peg, through the narrow face of the crosspiece into each peg hole.

5. Join the handle and the crosspiece, using glue and a 1-inch #10 screw. The crosspiece will fit into the notch in the handle, and the handle will be at the center of the crosspiece. Extend the center peg hole through the handle.

6. Lay the braces in place as shown, mark the ends for the appropriate angle cuts, and make the cuts. Then secure the braces in place with glue and 1-inch #10 screws.

7. Saw a ¾-inch dowel into five 6-inch pieces. Sharpen or round one end of each peg, then insert in the peg holes. Turn a screw eye into each pilot hole far enough that it holds the peg in place. A light coat of linseed oil will help preserve the finished row maker.

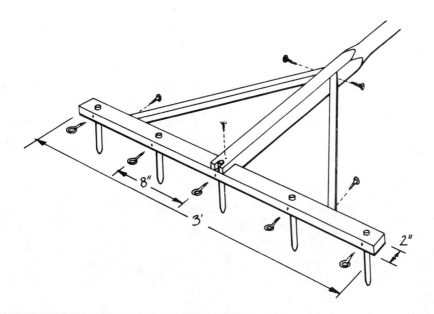

MATERIALS

Wood

      1 pc. 2 x 2 x 6′ (handle)

      1 pc. 1 x 6 x 4′   or **Crosspiece:** 1 pc. ¾″ x 2″ x 36″ (act. meas.)

                             Braces: 2 pcs. ¾″ x ¾″ x 36″ (act. meas.)

      1 pc. 36″ x ¾″ dowel or **Pegs:** 5 pcs. 6″ x ¾″ dowel

Hardware

      Glue
      5–1″ #10 screws
      5 screw eyes
      Linseed oil

HAND FURROW TOOL

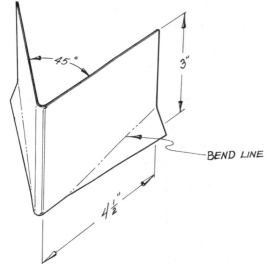

45°

3"

BEND LINE

4½"

This easily made tool does a fine job on small beds of lettuce, carrots, or other plants in closely spaced rows. It pushes the soil up against the plants and makes a nice furrow for irrigating.

It is fashioned from a 3-inch by 9-inch piece of ⅛-inch sheet metal. Simply bend the metal into a **V**-shape. Then, with a pair of pliers, bend a slight flare into the lower trailing ends, as shown.

SEEDING TOOL

Rather than sow seeds thickly along a row, Warner Tilsher of Rosemead, California, prefers to space them in little hills 2 inches apart, with two or more seeds to a hill. This gives nice even stands of plants and cuts down on thinning. As the plants grow and interfere with adjacent ones, they can be quickly thinned. But for most plants, the 2-inch spacing seems to be the best compromise for final spacing.

To speed the spacing, Tilsher devised this simple seeding tool. It is much like the seeding spacer he made for planting his flats, using bits of dowel to make the holes for the seeds.

MATERIALS

Wood

1 pc. 36″ x ⅞″ dowel	or	**Handle:** 1 pc. 5″ x ⅞″ dowel
1 pc. 1 x 2 x 2′	or	**Base:** 1 pc. 1 x 2 x 10″
1 pcs. 1 x 1 x 2′	or	**Spacers:** 5 pcs. 1 x 1 x ⅜″

Hardware

1–1½″ #6 screw
Epoxy glue

Seeding Tool

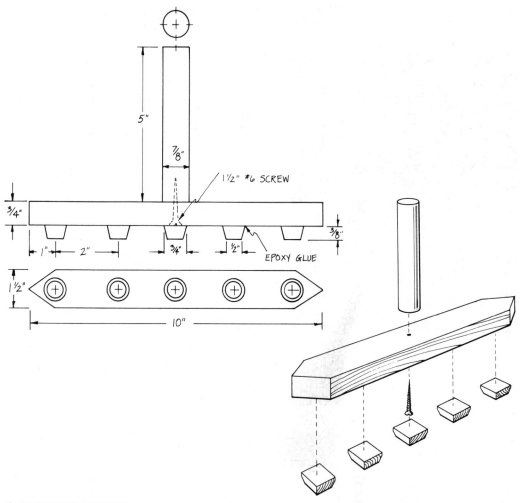

CONSTRUCTION

1. Attach the piece of $\frac{7}{8}$-inch dowel to the center of the 1 x 2 piece with the #6 screw.
2. Cut five $\frac{3}{8}$- to $\frac{1}{2}$-inch pieces of the 1 x 1 or $\frac{3}{4}$-inch dowel. Using epoxy glue, fasten them to the bottom of the 1 x 2 as shown.
3. With a file or sandpaper, taper the bits of dowel.

SEED FUNNEL

After hours of back-bending labor, Don Green, a Michigan gardener, decided there was an easier way to put his seeds in place—make an extension of his hand. Using the top part of a ½-gallon distilled water container and a plastic tube used in a golf bag to protect the club shafts, he created a planter. Total cost was 10 cents, and his device can be used to place rock fertilizers on shrubs or garden plants too.

SEED ROW COMPACTOR

Another easily made garden tool devised by Tilsher is the seed row compactor. This tool can ensure good germination. How? It keeps seeds moist by compacting the soil around them; thus soil particles draw moisture from below as upper layers dry out. The tool should be made of hardwood, but any scrap wood could provide the two main pieces. The only hardware needed is a small carriage bolt.

113

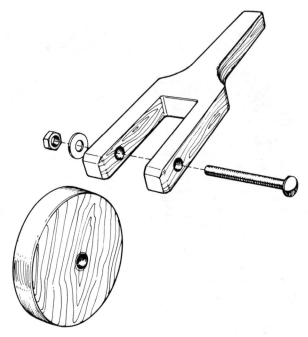

CONSTRUCTION

1. From a length of 1 x 3 hardwood cut a piece measuring an actual $\frac{3}{4}$ inch by $1\frac{3}{4}$ inches by $9\frac{3}{8}$ inches. Cut the handle according to the following directions (using a coping saw, saber saw, or jigsaw): Taper two sides as shown $3\frac{7}{8}$ inches from one end until width is $1\frac{1}{2}$ inches. Cut a $1\frac{1}{2}$-inch by $3\frac{5}{8}$-inch "mouth" in the wide end.

2. From a piece of 2 x 6 hardwood, saw the compactor wheel, measuring $4\frac{1}{2}$ inches in diameter and $1\frac{1}{8}$ inches thick. Sandpaper all edges.

3. Drill $\frac{1}{2}$-inch holes in the wheel center as well as in the handle $1\frac{1}{8}$ inches from the wide end.

4. Assemble with a 3-inch by $\frac{1}{2}$-inch carriage bolt and a $\frac{1}{2}$-inch washer.

MATERIALS

Wood

1 pc. 1 x 3 x 2' hardwood   or   **Handle:** 1 pc. $\frac{3}{4}''$ x $1\frac{3}{4}''$ x $9\frac{3}{8}''$ (act. meas.)

1 pc. 2 x 6 x 2' hardwood   or   **Wheel:** 1 pc. $1\frac{1}{8}''$ x $4\frac{1}{2}''$ dia. (act. meas.)

Hardware

1–3'' x $\frac{1}{2}''$ carriage bolt w/ nut and washer

SEED PLANTER

On a medium-sized garden plot, planting can be one of the most physically demanding tasks to be faced. If your plot is too big for hands-and-knees work, a homemade seed planter like this can give many years of labor-saving service.

Plans for this seeder first appeared in *Countryside and Small Stock Journal*. With the approval of *Countryside*, we constructed one in the OGF Workshop and put it to the test. And we recommend it for anyone with a large garden to plant.

A variety of seeds and grains can be planted. By consulting the accompanying tables, you can determine what size holes to drill in the planter drum and at what interval to space them. By taping over every other hole or two holes in every three, you can get different spacings using one drum. You will need a different drum for each different *size* of seed, however.

The planter works in this way: As you walk, the 20-inch wheel drives the seed drum. Gravity causes seeds to drop through the drum's holes. They drop through the drill tube into the ground. A length of heavy chain could be attached to the rear of the

planter to drag soil over the trench and save you the trouble of closing up the seed trench.

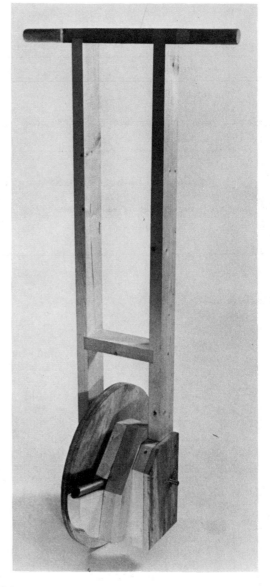

Hole Size and Spacing on Seed Container for Various Seeds

As a Garden Seeder	Hole Size (in inches)	Hole Spacing (in inches)
Beans	1/2 to 9/16	1
Beets, Spinach, Swiss Chard	1/4	3/4
Cabbage	1/8	3-1/2 to 6
Lettuce, Turnips, Carrots, Onions	1/8	3/4
Peas	1/2	3/4
Okra	5/16	6
Corn	1/2	3
As a Grain Drill		
Wheat, Oats, Rye	5/16	1/8
Milo, Sorghum	5/16	1/2

Relationship Between Hole Spacing On Seed Container and Spacing in Row

Space Between Holes on Seed Container	¾"	1"	1½"	2½"	3"	4½"	6"	9"
Spacing of Seed in Row	3"	4"	6"	10"	12"	18"	24"	36"

CONSTRUCTION

1. For the handle assembly, cut the 2 x 4 into two pieces 54 inches long; one piece 25 inches long; and one piece 9 inches long. Using a saw, wood rasp, or drawknife, and sandpaper, fashion a handle out of the 25-inch piece as illustrated.

2. On both of the 54-inch pieces, cut grooves to snugly hold the 9-inch crosspiece. The grooves should be about ½ inch deep, 32 inches from the handle end. From the other end, measure 7 inches and drill a ½-inch hole, centered in each piece. Assemble the four pieces using 2-inch #10 screws and glue.

3. For the wheel, cut two 20-inch diameter circles from ¾-inch exterior plywood. Glue and clamp the circles together, so that their grains are perpendicular to each other. When the glue is dry, drill a ½-inch hole exactly in the center.

4. Out of 1 x 10 stock, cut four 6-inch diameter discs and one 3-inch diameter disc. Drill a ½-inch hole in the center of each.

5. To make the seed holder, you will use two of the 6-inch discs for the drum, and another for the drive attachment to the wheel. Mark these discs 1, 2, and 3. In the first, drill a 1-inch hole completely through.

116

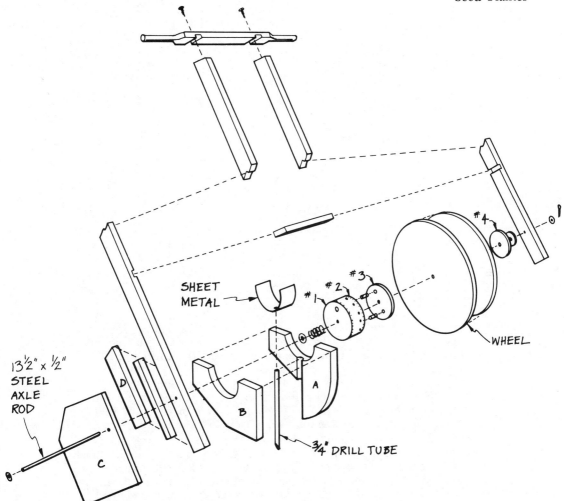

This will be the filling hole and will be stopped up with a snug cork or wooden plug. Draw a diameter line on the second disc. One inch in from each end, drive in a 1-inch brad, leaving about ½ inch protruding. Snip off the heads, leaving points which will be used to mark and align the third disc, which will be attached to the 20-inch wheel later. Mark the third disc by placing the 13½-inch by ½-inch rod into the second, sliding the third down and pressing firmly. Separate the discs and remove the rod and the brads. Drill a ½-inch hole ½ inch deep at each brad mark in both discs.

6. Drill holes of the size and interval you want in the center of the 3-inch by 19½-inch piece of sheet metal (see the charts for size and spacing of holes for different seeds). Punch a series of holes ⅜ inch in from each edge of the metal for the brads you will use to fasten the sheet metal to the first and second discs. The ends of the metal strip should overlap each other by about a ½ inch when wrapped around the discs.

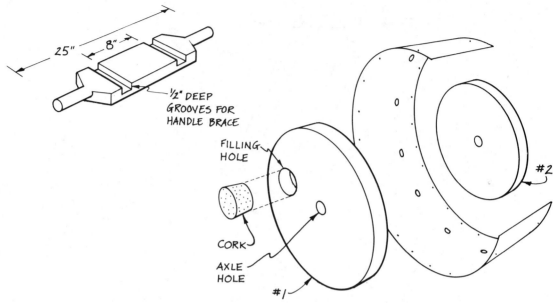

25" 8"

½" DEEP
GROOVES FOR
HANDLE BRACE

FILLING
HOLE

CORK

AXLE
HOLE

#1

#2

7. Assemble the wheel and drive. Lay the 20-inch wheel flat on the work-bench and insert the axle to assure alignment. Place the fourth 6-inch disc over the axle and fasten it to the wheel with two 1½-inch #10 screws. Flip the wheel over and in like manner fasten the third disc to the wheel. As the wheel is mounted with the seed drum, two 1-inch-long pieces of ½-inch dowel will be slipped into the holes in the third disc; the matching holes in the second disc will fit on the projecting ends of the dowel, and the drum will turn with the wheel.

8. Cut out and assemble parts A, B, and C. Part A is cut from a nominal 2 x 14, 12 inches long, made by gluing up a 12-inch 2 x 10 and a 12-inch 2 x 4. Shape and groove the part as shown. Part B is cut from a nominal 3 x 10, 12 inches long, made by gluing a 12-inch 2 x 10 and a 12-inch 1 x 10 together. Shape the part as shown. Part C is shaped, as shown, from an 11-inch length of 1 x 10. Drill the ½-inch axle hole as shown. The 2¼-inch-wide strip ripped from the 1 x 10 used for Part C can be planed down for use as the 1 x 2 spacer between Part D and the handle assembly. Part D, as shown, is an 11-inch length of 2 x 4.

9. Fasten parts A and B together with three 2-inch #10 screws. Cut a piece of sheet metal to fit the semicircular cut-out for the seed drum. Mark the metal for the location of the seed drill tube and drill the hole. Punch small holes in the edges of the metal for brads, which you will use to fasten the metal in place. Cut a 9¼-inch length of ¾-inch galvanized pipe, cutting a 45-degree angle on what will be the bottom end. Slip the drill tube into place, put the sheet metal piece atop it, and solder the two together. Fasten the metal in place with 1-inch brads.

10. Glue up the handle assembly, the 1 x 2 spacer, and Part D, as shown. When the glue has dried, attach parts A and B with four 3-inch #10 screws and glue. Attach Part C using four 2-inch #10 screws and glue.

MATERIALS

Wood

1 pc. 2 x 4 x 14'   or   **Handle shafts:** 2 pcs. 2 x 4 x 54"

Handle grip: 1 pc. 2 x 4 x 25"

Handle brace: 1 pc. 2 x 4 x 9"

Part D: 1 pc. 2 x 4 x 11"

1–2' x 4' sht. $\frac{3}{4}$" ext. plywood   or   **Wheel:** 2 pcs. 20" dia.

1 pc. 1 x 10 x 6'   or   **Discs:** 4 pcs. 6" dia.

Disc: 1 pc. 3" dia.

Part B (pcs. glued up):
1 pc. $\frac{3}{4}$" x $7\frac{1}{2}$" x 12" (act. meas.)
1 pc. $1\frac{1}{2}$" x $7\frac{1}{2}$" x 12" (act. meas., ripped from 2 x 10)

Part C: 1 pc. $\frac{3}{4}$" x 7" x 11" (act. meas.)

Spacer: 1 pc. $\frac{3}{4}$" x $1\frac{1}{2}$" x 11" (act. meas.)

1 pc. 36" x $\frac{1}{2}$" dowel   or   **Drive pins:** 2 pcs. 1" x $\frac{1}{2}$" dowel

1 pc. 2 x 10 x 2'   or   **Part A** (pcs. glued up): 1 pc. 2 x 10 x 12"
1 pc. 2 x 4 x 12"

Hardware

11–2" #10 screws
White glue
1" brads
1 pc. $13\frac{1}{2}$" x $\frac{1}{2}$" steel rod (axle)
1 pc. 4" x 30", $\frac{1}{16}$" sheet metal   or   **Seed drum:** 1 pc. 3" x $19\frac{1}{2}$"
Drill plate: 1 pc. $3\frac{3}{4}$" x 10"
4–$1\frac{1}{2}$" #10 screws
1 pc. $9\frac{1}{4}$" x $\frac{3}{4}$" galvanized pipe (drill tube)
4–3" #10 screws
1" compression spring
4–$\frac{1}{2}$" ID flat washers
2 hitch pins
1" dia. cork
Linseed oil

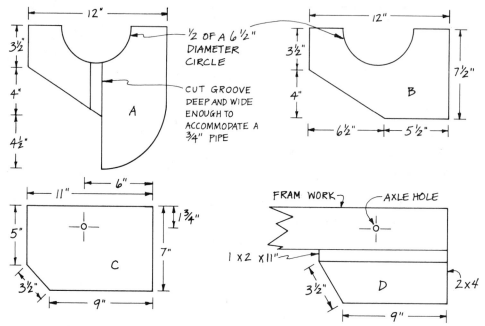

½ OF A 6½"
DIAMETER
CIRCLE

CUT GROOVE
DEEP AND WIDE
ENOUGH TO
ACCOMMODATE A
¾" PIPE

11. Before assembling the planter on the axle, drill holes through each end of the axle for hitch pins. Starting from the inside of the frame with pieces C and D attached, place a compression spring (about 1 inch long) with a flat washer on each end, the seed drum, the 20-inch wheel (with drive attachment inside), the 3-inch circle, and the other half of the handle onto the axle. A flat washer goes on the inside of each hitch pin.

12. Give your planter a light coat of linseed oil to protect it from weathering.

SEED HOLDER

Many garden plants produce seeds that are easily collected at the end of the growing season. With a fixture

such as this to keep the seeds sorted, clean, and safe over the winter, gardeners can start off the following season with an inexpensive supply of seeds that are as good as those bought in the store. Moreover, this seed holder is good for storing excess seed you paid for but didn't use.

The most important part of this seed holder is jars. David Caccia, who designed the device, used junior size baby food jars, but if you have a supply of another size, adjust these measurements to accommodate them.

Because the jars are fairly airtight, make sure the seeds are well dried. Put a slip of paper in each jar identifying the seed and the date.

CONSTRUCTION

1. Cut the wood into five pieces; two 8-inch lengths, one 12-inch length, and two pieces just $\frac{1}{16}$ inch less than 12 inches. Lightly sand the ends.

2. To form the square spindle part of the seed holder, fasten the two pieces that are just under 12 inches back to back, using four $2\frac{1}{4}$-inch #10 screws. Keep the screws at least 2 inches from the ends so they don't interfere with the spindle-mounting screws later.

3. Fasten the sixteen jar lids, four to a side, evenly spaced, with nails or tacks.

4. Drill two holes in the 12-inch piece, centered and about 4 inches from each end. This will be the part of the bracket that is mounted to the wall. For the other two pieces, drill two holes in one end, about $1\frac{1}{2}$ inches apart and $\frac{9}{16}$ inch from the end of the wood. (These are for fastening the 8-inch pieces to each end of the 12-inch piece.) You can

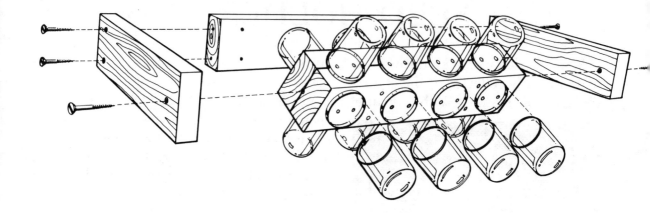

also drill small pilot holes in the ends of the 12-inch piece. On the opposite end of each of the 8-inch pieces, drill a $\frac{5}{16}$-inch hole centered in $1\frac{1}{4}$ inches from the end for attaching the spindle.

5. Assemble the U-shaped frame using $2\frac{1}{2}$-inch #10 screws. Drill small pilot holes into the ends of the spindle. Using two $2\frac{1}{2}$-inch #12 round-head screws, with a washer under each head, attach the spindle. Don't tighten these screws too much or the spindle will not turn.

6. Screw the jars into the lids, and your seed holder is ready for the seeds.

MATERIALS

Wood

1 pc. 2 x 3 x 6′   or   **Top and bottom plates:** 2 pcs. 2 x 3 x 8″

Wall bracket: 1 pc. 2 x 3 x 12″

Spindle: 2 pcs. 2 x 3 x $11\frac{15}{16}$″

Hardware

4–$2\frac{1}{4}$″ #10 screws
Small nails or tacks
4–$2\frac{1}{2}$″ #10 screws
2–$2\frac{1}{2}$″ #12 roundhead screws
2–$\frac{1}{4}$″ ID flat washers

Miscellaneous

16 junior size baby food jars w/lids

WEEDER

You can take an old bucksaw blade and make it into a fine weeder.

Carve a piece of hardwood for the handle, making it wide at the business end, narrow and rounded at the handle end. Make the handle as long as you like. But remember, you can always shorten an overlong handle, but one that's too short can't be stretched.

Bend the bucksaw blade and attach the ends to either side of the handle. Use two screws in each end.

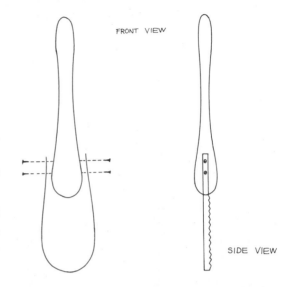

FRONT VIEW

SIDE VIEW

"FLO-HOE" CULTIVATOR

One way to create a thin layer of mulch, slice off weeds, and gently cultivate garden soil without turning your earth is to swing a "Flo-Hoe." Designed by Tilsher, the tool cuts off weeds just below the ground surface and cultivates without moving the soil, creating a loose, fluffy and effective dust mulch.

The hoe can have either a stainless or ordinary steel "bite." The regular hoe-length handle is suggested for backyard gardeners. You can scale it down for box beds or plantings with

narrow spaces by shortening the handle and fashioning a 4-inch blade. This homemade tool goes the ordinary open-ended weed-cutter one better—it does more than just shorten weeds; it tears them out at the roots.

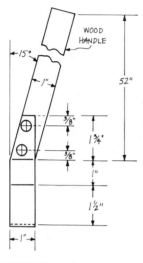

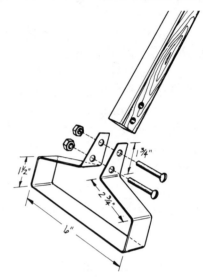

CONSTRUCTION

1. Bend a 1-inch by 18-inch sheet metal strip into the shape illustrated. Provide a 6-inch blade, 1½-inch sides, 2¾-inch tapered backs, and 1¾-inch collars.
2. Cut a 15-degree angle from the collar bottoms. Drill two $\frac{3}{16}$-inch holes in each collar, making them $\frac{5}{8}$ inch apart or $\frac{3}{8}$ inch from each end of the collars. Center the holes to allow for a 15-degree angle at the point where the handle will be connected.
3. Drill two $\frac{3}{16}$-inch holes at one end of the 1 x 1 by 52-inch wood handle. Connect handle and cultivator using two 1½-inch by $\frac{3}{16}$-inch roundhead stove bolts.
4. Sharpen the edge of the 6-inch blade on the same side as the handle is slanted.

MATERIALS

Wood

> 1 pc. 1 x 1 x 6′   or   **Handle:** 1 pc. 1 x 1 x 52″

Hardware

> 1 pc. 1″ x 18″, $\frac{1}{16}$″ sheet metal (blade)
> 2–1½″ x $\frac{3}{16}$″ roundhead stove bolts w/ nuts

WHEEL HOE

One of the oldest and best of cultivation tools, the wheel hoe has become difficult to find in commercial outlets in recent years. If you can find or make the plow blade or cultivator attachments, you can put together a homemade version that works as well as the best of them.

The wheel hoe should not be viewed as a tool for breaking ground. It is, rather, a cultivating tool, the usefulness of which is greatest in fairly large gardens, with long rows to be cultivated.

There are two basic styles of wheel hoe—the low wheeler (10 to 12 inches in diameter) and the high wheeler (18 to 24 inches). The high wheeler shown here is easier to push. If you substitute a metal wheel for the wooden version, avoid anything so heavy as to pack the soil. An old bicycle wheel, on the other hand, would probably be too light.

CONSTRUCTION

1. To construct the wheel, cut two 20-inch discs out of ¾-inch exterior plywood. (Drive two nails through a scrap strip of wood, 10 inches **apart.** Press one nail into the plywood at what will be the center of the wheel and swing the other nail around to scribe the outer circumference of the wheel.) Use a saber saw, band saw, or coping saw to cut out the discs. Cut out two 2¼-inch-square pieces of the plywood. Using a waterproof glue and six 1-inch #10 screws, join the two wheel discs together. Then nail a plywood square to the center of each side of the wheel—the centers of the squares to the center of the wheel—and drill a ¾-inch-diameter hole through the center of the wheel assembly.
2. The handle assembly is constructed next. Cut two 54-inch lengths of 2 x 2. Cut off one butt edge at a 9-degree bevel, as shown, to provide additional wheel clearance. Lay them out on the workbench or shop

125

Wheel Hoe

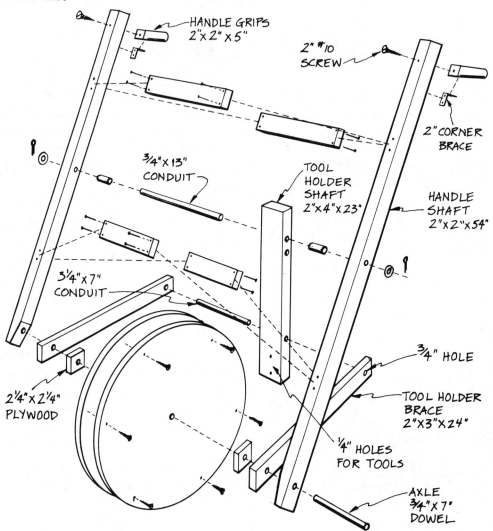

HANDLE GRIPS
2"x 2" x 5"

2" #10
SCREW

2" CORNER
BRACE

3/4"X 13"
CONDUIT

TOOL
HOLDER
SHAFT
2"x4"x 23"

HANDLE
SHAFT
2"x2"x54"

3/4"x 7"
CONDUIT

3/4" HOLE

2 1/4"x 2 1/4"
PLYWOOD

TOOL HOLDER
BRACE
2"x3"x24"

1/4" HOLES
FOR TOOLS

AXLE
3/4"X 7"
DOWEL

floor, using a chalk line or length of wood as a center line. The wheel
ends of the handle shafts should be 4½ inches apart, and the handle ends
12½ inches apart. Measure 14½ inches from the wheel end of each shaft
and mark, then measure from mark to mark—it should be about 10
inches—and cut a 1 x 3 brace to fit, nailing it in place with 4d nails.
Measure 12 inches from the handle end of each shaft, measure from
mark to mark—it should be about 14 inches. Cut a 1 x 3 brace to fit and
nail it in place. Turn the assembly over, cut two more braces and nail
them in place, as shown.

3. For the handle grips, cut two pieces of 2 x 2, each approximately
5 inches long. Cut the end that is to join the handle at a 24-degree
angle, and round off the gripping end with a rasp or drawknife. Fasten
the grips to the handle assembly with 2-inch #10 screws (driven
through the shaft into the grip butt) and 2-inch corner braces.

4. Fashion the tool holder assembly. Cut a 23-inch length of 2 x 4 and two 24-inch lengths of 1 x 3. Drill a ¾-inch hole 1½ inches in from each end of both 1 x 3s. (One hole is for the axle, the other is for the piece of ¾-inch conduit that positions the tool holder shaft.) Drill three ¾-inch holes through the narrow face of the 2 x 4, one 4½ inches and one 6½ inches from the top (for adjusting the depth of cultivation) and the third 6 inches from the bottom. Lastly, drill two ¼-inch holes through the tool holder shaft, one 1½ inches and another 4 inches from the bottom of the shaft. Install a 3½-inch by ¼-inch machine bolt with a nut and washer in each hole. These bolts will secure any tools that you make for your cultivator, so in making the tools, make them so that these two bolts will attach them.

5. The tool holder is held in place by the axle and by two pieces of ¾-inch conduit, one a piece about 13 inches long that attaches the holder shaft to the handle assembly and the second a piece about 7 inches long that holds the shaft and the support braces together.

   a. First, cut the two lengths of conduit, leaving them slightly long. Then measure 27 inches along the handle shafts from the grip ends. Lay a scrap of wood or a ruler across the handle shafts, connecting the two points, and scribe a line along this straightedge on each shaft. Drill a ¾-inch hole through the side of each handle shaft so that it is parallel to the line you have just scribed. Slip the conduit through one handle shaft, through the holder shaft, then through the second handle shaft. Slide a large washer over each end of the conduit, then drill a small hole through each end of the tube for a hitch pin clip or a cotter pin. A hitch pin clip will make it easier to reposition the holder assembly up or down.

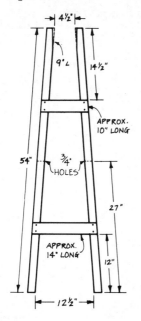

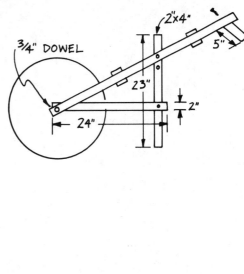

b. To further stabilize this segment of the assembly, cut two short (approximately 2½-inch) lengths of 1-inch conduit to slip over the longer, smaller diameter conduit between the handle shafts and the holder shaft. Install the second length of conduit in the same fashion, running it through the bottom hole in the holder shaft, with a 1 x 3 brace, cut previously, secured on each side of the shaft.

6. Install the wheel, using a 7-inch length of ¾-inch dowel. Slide the dowel, in sequence, through a handle shaft, a tool holder brace, the wheel, another brace, and finally the other handle shaft. If the dowel is loose, or if it works loose after some use, secure it by driving a 1-inch brad through the handle shaft into the dowel.

MATERIALS

Wood

1–2' x 4' sht. ¾" ext. plywood	or	**Wheel:** 2 pcs. 20" dia.
		Reinforcements: 2 pcs. 2¼" sq.
1 pc. 2 x 2 x 10'	or	**Handle:** 2 pcs. 2 x 2 x 54"
		Grips: 2 pcs. 2 x 2 x 5"
1 pc. 1 x 3 x 8'	or	**Braces:** 2 pcs. 1 x 3 x 10"
		2 pcs. 1 x 3 x 14"
		Tool holder: 2 pcs. 1 x 3 x 24"
1 pc. 2 x 4 x 2'	or	**Tool holder:** 1 pc. 2 x 4 x 23"
1 pc. 36" x ¾" dowel	or	**Axle:** 1 pc. 7" x ¾" dowel

Hardware

6d nails
Waterproof glue
6–1" #10 screws
4d nails
2–2" #10 screws
2–2" corner braces
2–3½" x ¼" machine bolts w/nuts and washers
1 pc. 10' x ¾" elec. conduit   or   1 pc. 13" long
                                              1 pc. 7" long
4–¾" ID washers
4 hitch pin clips or cotter pins
1 pc. 10' x 1" elec. conduit   or   2 pcs. 2½" long

CULTIVATOR ATTACHMENT

An excellent cultivator attachment can be made from a weed cutter share from a farm cultivator mounted on a piece of 2 x 2. Lacking a premade share, you may be able to cut one from $\frac{1}{4}$-inch steel. A shovel or spade head could also be used.

TINED CULTIVATOR ATTACHMENT

This attachment is made from a 5-inch by $4\frac{1}{2}$-inch piece of right angle steel that mounts to the tool holder with two $2\frac{1}{2}$-inch by $\frac{1}{4}$-inch bolts. Cut two 6-inch pieces of 1 x 1 oak. In one piece, drill a $\frac{9}{32}$-inch hole every $1\frac{1}{4}$ inches to accommodate the four 60d spikes. Drill $\frac{1}{4}$-inch holes $1\frac{3}{4}$ inches in from each end of both pieces of 1 x 1 and corresponding holes in the piece of right angle steel.

Place the nails through the lower piece of 1 x 1 and join the two pieces of 1 x 1 to the right angle steel with $2\frac{1}{2}$-inch by $\frac{1}{4}$-inch bolts.

129

MULCH PLATE FOR ROTARY MOWERS

The mulch plates furnished with rotary mowers seldom do a good job. They either clog up or don't throw the material where you want it. But making your own plate is not difficult.

The plate shown is made of a piece of galvanized sheet metal, which is easily cut and bent, yet is sturdy enough to stand up to the blast of shredded material.

Since mowers aren't standardized, you must shape your mulch plate to fit your mower. Use whatever holes exist or drill new ones. Using galvanized bolts with wing nuts makes it easy to remove the mulch plate for ordinary grass cutting. In forming the plate, the guiding objective is to deflect the shredded material downward and in the particular direction that suits your setup (most likely directly to the side).

One good system is to drive several 4-foot stakes about a foot into the ground, then lean a sheet of plywood against them. Pile up the material to be shredded about 3 feet opposite the panel. Run the mower over the material so the discharge is directed at the panel.

HARVEST KNIFE

This harvesting tool was created by Don Green from two small scraps of steel. "It fits my hand for any hand pull cutting I have to do," he says. Shaped to fit one's own hand and created to do a particular job, this well-designed tool cuts down on blisters as well as time.

LONG-HANDLED KNIFE

Do your arms ever seem too short? Don Green added reach to his by making knives with extra-long handles. By using blades of existing knives and scrap wood to fashion handles for them, he has made cucumber and other vine vegetable picking a much easier job.

TOOL CLEANER

A good way to keep your garden tools both clean and rust free is to build an oiling/cleaning pit. All you

need do is dig a hole near the entrance to your toolshed, build a wood or metal framework inside the hole, and fill it with sand. Next time you change the oil in your car, tractor, or mower, just pour the old oil into the sand and mix it up. You can get old oil from gas stations if you don't have any around. Try to maintain a sandy texture without too much oil; if you put your hand in, it should just pick up a trace of oil, not be dripping wet. With the oil and sand mixed, just work your tools in the mix for a few seconds, and they should be clean, oiled, and ready to be put away.

Cut four 12-inch-long pieces of 1 x 12. Using a simple butt joint and 8d nails, fasten the pieces together into a square frame. Dig a hole large enough to accommodate the frame so that it will project about 2 inches above the ground. Fill the frame with

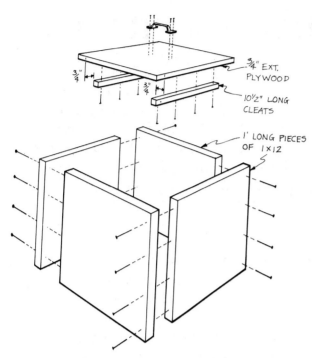

3/4" EXT. PLYWOOD

3/4"

3/4"

10½" LONG CLEATS

1' LONG PIECES OF 1×12

builder's sand, then backfill with soil around the outside of the frame. Pour that old oil in with the sand and work it with a shovel.

If you are a bit fussy, you could fashion a lid for the tool cleaning pit. Cut an 11¼-inch-square piece of ¾-inch exterior plywood. To one side fasten a common door pull handle. To the other fasten two 10½-inch cleats with brads to help keep the lid in place.

For the sake of longevity, it would be good to use the well-known rot-resistant materials or wood treated with a wood preservative.

MATERIALS

Wood

1 pc. 1 x 12 x 6'	or	**Walls:** 4 pcs. 1 x 12 x 12"
		Lid: 1 pc. 1 x 12 x 11¼" (or 1–11¼" sq. sht. ¾" ext. plywood)
1 pc. 1 x 1 x 2'	or	**Cleats:** 2 pcs. 1 x 1 x 10½"

Hardware

8d nails
1¼" brads
1 door pull
Wood preservative

HAY RAKES

Farmers have used wooden rakes to help harvest hay and other herbage for many generations. Various crops, topography, and cultural preferences have resulted in the evolution of different rake styles. But hay rakes are always lightweight, strong, easy to handle, and smoothly finished.

According to Drew Langsner of Marshall, North Carolina, one can knock together a functional hay rake before the morning dew dries, or one

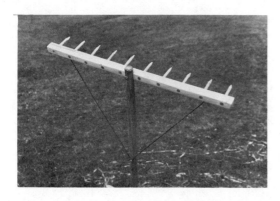

can take extra care and produce something of exceptional craftsmanship. Both rakes will function equally well, although the latter might outlast the "cobbled up" version. And there is an additional aesthetic value to consider.

Dimension your rake to suit expected needs. For windrowing hay a wide rake head is desirable, but somewhat tiring to use. Thirty inches is a good size. For smaller jobs, such as lawns or around obstacles, 22 to 25 inches is adequate. Use stout hardwood.

For most work, a handle 66 to 78 inches is fine; a large windrowing rake might be 80 inches or more. The wood should be lightweight, but strong. Ash is excellent. However, Langsner has even used a seasoned poplar sapling.

Rake tines can be handmade or cut from commercial dowel. To make your own, choose a tough wood, such as locust or heart of oak. Be sure to season before fitting to the rake head. We have used $\frac{3}{8}$-inch dowel, mainly because it's convenient and easy to get a snug fit. In planning a rake be sure to have an even number of teeth, so that the center of the head will be free for the handle.

Tines can be spaced $2\frac{1}{2}$ to $3\frac{1}{2}$ inches apart. For raking lush herbage they should extend *through* the head 3 to $3\frac{1}{2}$ inches. For tough going, shorter tines are called for. In Langsner's experience, breakage has only occurred when a rake was stepped on.

Throughout the years, farmers have devised various ways to fasten rake heads to their handles. Langsner has experimented with several traditional styles and has concluded that for utility, simple wire braces work best. (Wooden struts are not usually replaceable, so if one should break, the entire rake becomes useless.) These braces can be made of any heavy wire, such as from coat hangers. On a large rake of 30 inches or more, the use of two pairs of braces for extra strength is recommended.

Langsner offers plans for two well-tested designs: He has developed one rake that is easy to make, and yet is quite elegant in its *simplicity*. The second rake involves making a *traditional* mortise and shouldered tenon joint, and a somewhat fancier rake head. *Simplicity* has the advantage that it could be disassembled. *Traditional* is somewhat stouter.

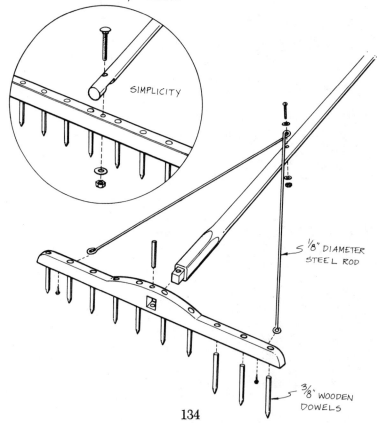

SIMPLICITY

$\frac{1}{8}$" DIAMETER STEEL ROD

$\frac{3}{8}$" WOODEN DOWELS

CONSTRUCTION

1. Cut a 30-inch length of 1 x 3 hardwood, then shape the head.
   a. *Simplicity:* Rip the head to an actual width of $1\frac{1}{8}$ inches.
   b. *Traditional:* Using a drawknife or coping saw, shape the head like a flattened bell, with a width of $1\frac{7}{8}$ inches in the center and $1\frac{1}{16}$ inches along the flanks. Bevel the upper edges. Cut out a $\frac{3}{4}$-inch-square mortise in the center.
2. Drill tine holes, $\frac{3}{8}$ inch in diameter. (It is Langsner's opinion that drilling straight through is satisfactory; "blind" tine holes cause more problems than advantage.)
3. Cut out and point the tines. Do not sharpen them excessively. (For *Traditional*, be sure to allow extra length for the bell-shaped head.)
4. Apply a small dab of waterproof glue to the dowel ends and drive them into the head with a mallet.
5. Make the handle from a 1-inch hardwood dowel cut to the desired length.
   a. *Simplicity:* Make a notch 1 inch from one end halfway through the handle and the exact width of the rake head. Drill a $\frac{1}{4}$-inch hole through the handle and rake head and secure with a 2-inch stove bolt.
   b. *Traditional:* Saw and chisel a $\frac{3}{4}$-inch square-shouldered tenon to fit snugly in the rake head mortise. Glue. Drill a $\frac{1}{4}$-inch hole through head and handle and secure with glued $\frac{1}{4}$-inch dowel pin.

MATERIALS

Wood

1 pc. 1 x 3 x 4′ hardwood	or	**Head:** 1 pc. 1 x 3 x 30″
1 pc. 36″ x $\frac{3}{8}$″ hardwood dowel	or	**Tines:** 10 pcs. $3\frac{1}{2}$″ x $\frac{3}{8}$″ dowel
1 pc. 6′ x 1″ hardwood dowel	or	**Handle:** 1″ dowel cut to desired length
1 pc. 36″ x $\frac{1}{4}$″ hardwood dowel	or	**Pin:** 1 pc. 2″ x $\frac{1}{4}$″ dowel (*Traditional*)

Hardware

Waterproof glue
1–2″ x $\frac{1}{4}$″ stove bolt w/ nut and washer (*Simplicity*)
36″ x $\frac{1}{8}$″ steel wire (to brace head)
2–$\frac{3}{4}$″ #8 screws
1–$1\frac{1}{2}$″ x $\frac{1}{4}$″ stove bolt w/ nut and washers

6. Cut wire to length to make brace for either rake. Wires must be straight. Bend and flatten ends so that they wrap around screws being used. Heating heavy wire red hot (with propane) simplifies this process. Locate stove bolt on handle approximately one-and-a-half times further from the joint as are screws on rake head. Running braces from the lower side of the head to the upper surface of the handle gives some additional triangulation.

7. Sand nicely. Finish with a mixture of two parts linseed oil to one part turpentine.

WHEELBARROW

Every gardener needs a good wheelbarrow. The wheelbarrow is one of those perfect tools: highly functional, beautiful in its simplicity, incapable of being improved.

This wheelbarrow, constructed in the OGF Workshop, is our version of the classic all-wood wheelbarrow. While you may not save a significant amount over the cost of a production-line wheelbarrow, you will have the satisfaction of knowing that yours is sturdy and versatile. And a product of your own hands.

While we constructed a wooden wheel for our wheelbarrow, you could substitute a pneumatic-tired wheel if you are willing to purchase one, or if you have one to recycle.

CONSTRUCTION

1. From 2-inch hardwood stock, cut two 58-inch lengths of 2 x 2 for handles. Using a drawknife, rasp, or block plane, round off 8 inches of one end of each handle so it is comfortable to the hand. Finish these grips with sandpaper.

2. From the remaining hardwood 2 x 2, cut two 14½-inch legs and four 24-inch-long supports. The supports must be planed to an actual measurement of 1¾ inches by 1¼ inches by 24 inches. From a piece of 1 x 2 hardwood, cut four 13-inch side supports.

3. Lay out the handles as shown, together with the supports, so you can mark the pieces for half-lap joints. The supports must also be short-

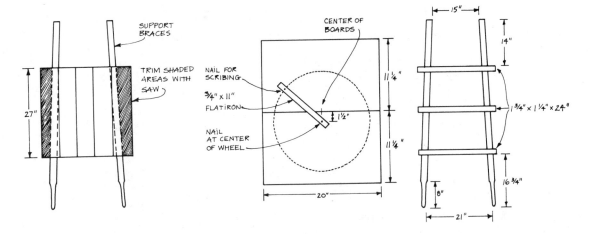

ened, and by laying out the assembly, you will be able to get an exact fit. The dadoes and rabbets for the joints should be cut $\frac{5}{8}$ inch deep, as shown.

4. Assemble the handles and support pieces, using glue and a 1½-inch #10 screw at each joint. Cut a 1½-inch-wide and ¾-inch-deep rabbet in one end of each leg and secure it to the assembly, just in front of the support nearest to the handle grips, using a 4-inch-long ⅜-inch carriage bolt (with washers) in each leg.

5. Cut five 27-inch lengths of 6-inch roofers (tongue and groove boards). Secure them to the handle assembly, as shown, using 1-inch #10 screws to fasten each board to the front and rear supports. There will be some overhang, which you should trim off.

6. Cut two 22¾-inch lengths and one 35-inch length of the ¾-inch-wide flatiron. Drill a ½-inch hole through each end of the 22¾-inchers, then bend about an inch of each end, as shown, in a vise. Then attach them to the feet of the legs and the handles with 1½-inch #10 screws. Bend the 35-inch piece at its middle, forming a V-shape. Then, with the help of a vise and a pair of vise-grip pliers, twist each extender of this brace, as shown. Drill a hole at each end and in the center of the bend, then fasten it to the legs and rear support with 1½-inch #10 screws.

7. Fabricate the wheel. Cut six 20-inch lengths of 1 x 12 and a single 11-inch piece of the ¾-inch-wide flatiron. Drill two holes in the flatiron, 9½ inches apart. This, together with two nails, will be the scriber used to lay out the wheel.

   a. Place two of the 20-inch 1 x 12s side by side and scribe a circle with the flatiron scriber, as shown. To avoid the weakness that would result from having the wheel's hub at the joint between the two pieces of wood, locate the center of the wheel 1½ inches in from the center of one edge of one board. Tap a nail into the center point, slip the flatiron over it, and swing the free end around, marking the boards with a second nail in the other hole in the flatiron. After you've cut out these two boards, use them as a pattern in marking the other four boards.

137

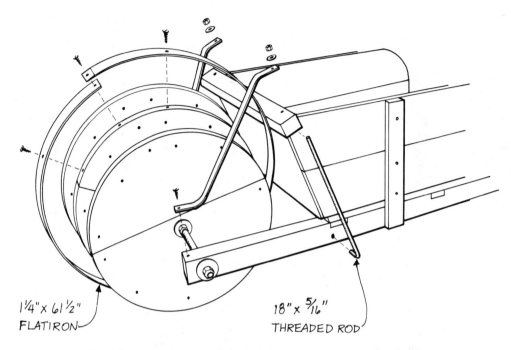

1¼" × 61½"
FLATIRON

18" × 5/16"
THREADED ROD

b. Glue the finished wheel pieces together, and drive 1½-inch #10 screws into each side of the assembled wheel. The joints between the two boards forming each ply should *not* be congruent. Moreover, you should have the center-hole mark visible, so you can easily and accurately drill the 1-inch hub of the wheel.

c. Finally, cut a 61½-inch length of 1¼-inch-wide flatiron. Bend it around the wheel, as shown, securing it in place with six 1½-inch #10 screws. The ends of the flatiron should be filed to a taper so they can overlap smoothly.

8. Drill a ¾-inch hole in the wheel-end of the handles, making sure to get the proper angle for the axle. Cut a 2¼-inch piece of 1-inch OD pipe and drive it into the hole to serve as the hub of the wheel. Cut a 22-inch length of ¾-inch threaded rod, the axle, and mount the wheel in place, using four flat washers and four nuts.

9. Assemble the front of the wheelbarrow's bed.

a. Cut a 19-inch length of 1 x 12. Trim the remaining hardwood support to a 22-inch length and fasten it to one edge of the 1 x 12 with glue and two deeply countersunk 1½-inch #10 screws, as shown. Plane the bottom edge of this assembly so it will lean forward at an angle 20 degrees from vertical. Drill two $\frac{5}{16}$-inch holes in the support, locating one $\frac{9}{16}$ inch in from each butt end of the piece and ⅜ inch from the inside edge.

b. Cut an 11-inch length of the ¾-inch-wide flatiron, drill two ¼-inch holes through it, and fasten it to one butt end of the 1 x 12, using 1-inch #10 screws. Fasten the piece of flatiron used to scribe the wheel to the other butt end of the 1 x 12.

138

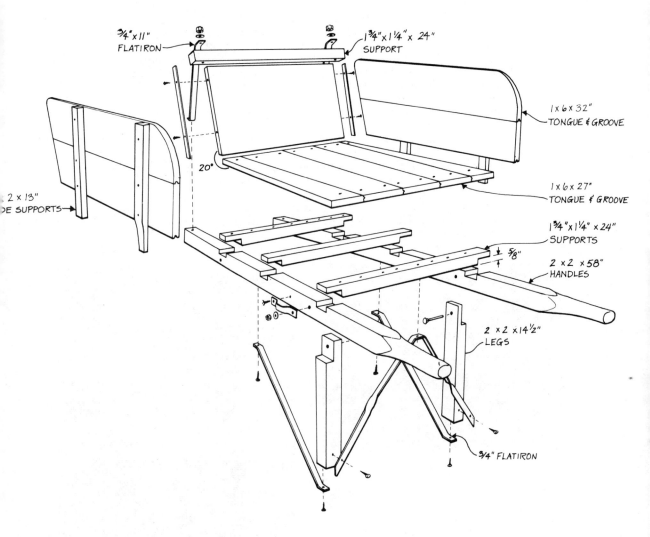

c. Cut a 36-inch length of $\frac{5}{16}$-inch threaded rod in half and put a 90-degree bend in each piece, about 1 inch from one end. Drill a $\frac{5}{16}$-inch hole in the center of the side of each handle shaft, immediately below the point where the bed front abuts the shafts. Slip the bent ends of the threaded rods into these holes and the straight ends through the holes in the bed front support.

d. Cut two 16$\frac{3}{4}$-inch lengths of the $\frac{3}{4}$-inch-wide flatiron. Drill a $\frac{5}{16}$-inch hole in one end of each piece, and a $\frac{1}{4}$-inch hole in the other end of each piece. Bend the ends as shown. Take one, slip one end over the threaded rod, and attach the other end to the handle shaft, using a 1$\frac{1}{2}$-inch #10 screw. Put a washer and nut on the threaded rod and turn it down. Repeat on the other side.

10. Assemble the bed sides. Cut four 32-inch lengths of the tongue and groove roofers. Place two of the roofers together, pushing them forward into the opening between the bed front and the threaded rod hold-down until they are flush with the back end of the bed floor. Scribe a line on them along the front edge of the bed front. Fasten a 13-inch hardwood side support, cut earlier, to the roofers near the front, as shown, using 1-inch #10 screws. This will hold the roofers together while you trim them. Now cut two 6-inch lengths of the $\frac{3}{4}$-inch-wide flatiron and drill a $\frac{3}{8}$-inch hole through one end of each and a $\frac{1}{4}$-inch hole through the other end. Put a rough 90-degree bend on the end with the larger hole and attach one iron to the handle assembly on each side using the bolt that secures the leg. Put the side in place, locate the second side support, screw it in place, bend the flatiron around it, and fasten the free end to the handle shaft, as shown, with a 1-inch #10 screw. Repeat this process, using the remaining materials, to assemble the second side. The rear ends of the sides may be rounded off, as shown, or left square.

MATERIALS

Wood

1 pc. 2 x 2 x 14' hardwood   or   **Handles:** 2 pcs. 2 x 2 x 58″

                                               Legs: 2 pcs. 2 x 2 x 14½″

1 pc. 2 x 2 x 8' hardwood   or   **Supports:** 4 pcs. 1¾″ x 1¼″ x 24″
(act. meas.)

1 pc. 1 x 2 x 6' hardwood   or   **Side supports:** 4 pcs. 1 x 2 x 13″

2 pcs. 1 x 6 x 12' t & g roofers   or   **Bottom:** 5 pcs. 1 x 6 x 27″

                                            Sides: 4 pcs. 1 x 6 x 32″

1 pc. 1 x 12 x 12'   or   **Wheel:** 6 pcs. 1 x 12 x 20″

                                        Front: 1 pc. 1 x 12 x 19″

Hardware

Glue
28–1½″ #10 screws
2–4″ x ⅜″ carriage bolts w/ nuts and washers
40– 1″ #10 screws
5 pcs. $\frac{1}{16}$″ x ¾″ x 36″ flatiron   or   **Leg braces:** 2 pcs. 22¾″ long
                                             Leg brace: 1 pc. 35″ long
                                             Reinforcements: 2 pcs. 11″ long
                                             Front braces: 2 pcs. 16¾″ long
                                           Side mounting brackets:
                                                    2 pcs. 6″ long

1 pc. $\frac{1}{16}$″ x 1¼″ x 72″ flatiron   or   **Wheel rim:** 1 pc. 61½″ long
1 pc. 2¼″ x 1″ galvanized pipe (hub)

1 pc. 36″ x ¾″ all thread rod   or   **Axle:** 1 pc. 22″ long
4–¾″ ID flat washers
4–¾″ nuts
1 pc. 36″ x $\frac{5}{16}$″ all thread rod   or   **Reinforcers:** 2 pcs. 18″ long
2–$\frac{5}{16}$″ ID flat washers
2–$\frac{5}{16}$″ nuts

GARDEN CART

You've seen them in advertise-
ments. You've wanted one. But you
didn't want to mortgage the house to
get it, so you didn't. Here's your
chance to build your own garden
cart.

CONSTRUCTION

1. From ¾-inch plywood, cut pieces as follows: a 39-inch by 30-inch
   bottom, two 39-inch by 15-inch sides, and a 15½-inch by 30-inch front.

2. Cut diagonals at rear of sides from point at top 31½ inches from front
   to bottom, as shown.

3. Fasten sides to bottom using two 2-inch-square corner braces with
   screws on each side. Cut 1 x 6 stock 31½ inches long and fasten to
   underside of cart bed 13 inches from front with several 1-inch #10
   screws, placed so they will not interfere with wheel braces.

4. Cut a 4-foot piece of angle iron in half and drill eight holes in each
   piece side to accommodate 1-inch #10 screws. Fasten to inside corners
   of cart bed 4 inches from handle end of cart as shown. Each piece will
   have four screws into the bottom and four into the side.

5. From 1 x 6 stock rip two pieces 1¼ inches by 14¼ inches, two pieces
   1¼ inches by 15 inches, and one 1¼-inch by 30-inch piece. An optional
   embellishment is on the 14¼-inchers, to cut a 45-degree angle the length
   of one side, and on the 30-inch piece, to cut 45-degree angles on either
   end. Round all corners with sandpaper.

6. Fasten 1¼-inch by 30-inch piece to top of 15½-inch by 30-inch plywood
   front with five 1½-inch #10 screws after predrilling all screw holes.

7. Attach 1¼-inch by 15-inch pieces to front edge of side pieces with four
   1½-inch #10 screws on each, making sure to mount flush with outside.

8. Insert plywood front piece and scribe line on each side piece. Fasten
   the two 1¼-inch by 14¼-inch pieces on either side using 1-inch #10
   screws. Leave about $\frac{1}{16}$ inch from scribe line.

9. Turn cart upside down and fasten large 1¼-inch by 8½-inch corner
   braces in the center of either end of the 1 x 6 mounted to cart underside. Use 2-inch by ⅜-inch round stove bolts to fasten corner braces,
   four on each side. Bend a ¾-inch by 36-inch piece of flatiron to fit
   corner braces as shown. Use a 1½-inch #10 screw in the center of the
   flatiron brace and 1-inch by ¼-inch machine bolts on the ends.

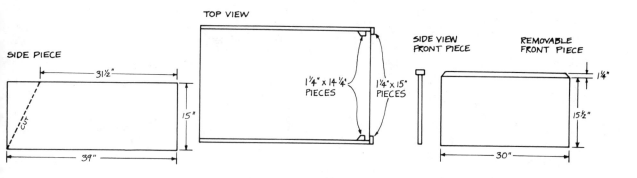

MATERIALS

Wood

1 sht. $\frac{3}{4}''$ ext. plywood	or	**Bottom:** 1 pc. 39″ x 30″
		Sides: 2 pcs. 39″ x 15″
		Front: 1 pc. $15\frac{1}{2}''$ x 30″
1 pc. 1 x 6 x 6′	or	**Wheel mounting:** 1 pc. 1 x 6 x $31\frac{1}{2}''$
		Cleats: 2 pcs. $\frac{3}{4}''$ x $1\frac{1}{4}''$ x $14\frac{1}{4}''$ (act. meas.)
		2 pcs. $\frac{3}{4}''$ x $1\frac{1}{4}''$ x 15″ (act. meas.)
		1 pc. $\frac{3}{4}''$ x $1\frac{1}{4}''$ x 30″ (act. meas.)
1 pc. 2 x 4 x 6′	or	**Legs:** 2 pcs. 2 x 4 x $28\frac{1}{2}''$
1 pc. 2 x 2 x 6′	or	**Handles:** 2 pcs. 2 x 2 x 34″
1 pc. 36″ x 1″ dowel	or	**Handle:** 1 pc. 31″ x 1″ dowel

Hardware

4–2″ x 2″ corner braces
34–1″ #10 screws
1 pc. $\frac{1}{4}''$ x $\frac{1}{4}''$ x 4′ angle iron
24–$1\frac{1}{2}''$ #10 screws
2–$1\frac{1}{4}''$ x $8\frac{1}{2}''$ corner braces
8–2″ x $\frac{3}{8}''$ round stove bolts w/ nuts and washers
1 pc. $\frac{1}{16}''$ x $\frac{3}{4}''$ x 36″ flatiron
2–1″ x $\frac{1}{4}''$ machine bolts w/ nuts
2–24″ bicycle wheels (rims, tires) w/ axles
4–3″ x $\frac{1}{4}''$ stove bolts w/ nuts and washers

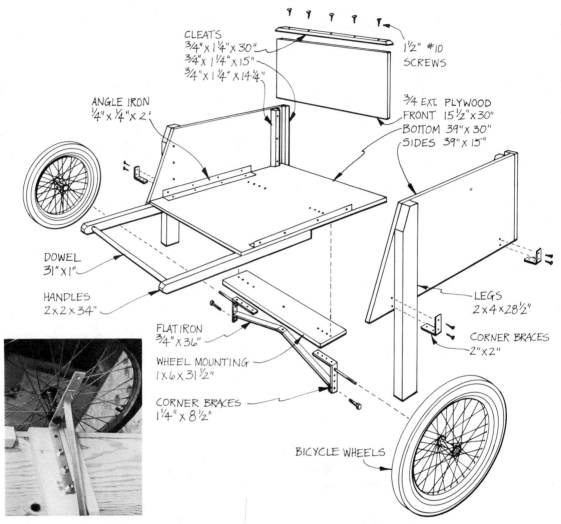

CLEATS
3/4" x 1 1/4" x 30"
3/4" x 1 1/4" x 15"
3/4" x 1 1/4" x 14-1/4"

1 1/2" #10 SCREWS

ANGLE IRON
1/4" x 1/4" x 2'

3/4 EXT. PLYWOOD
FRONT 15 1/2" x 30"
BOTTOM 39" x 30"
SIDES 39" x 15"

DOWEL
31" x 1"

HANDLES
2 x 2 x 34"

FLAT IRON
3/4" x 36"

WHEEL MOUNTING
1 x 6 x 31 1/2"

CORNER BRACES
1 1/4" x 8 1/2"

LEGS
2 x 4 x 28 1/2"

CORNER BRACES
2" x 2"

BICYCLE WHEELS

10. Attach bicycle wheels to corner braces about 1½ inches from cart underside. Corner braces are usually predrilled but might have to be enlarged for ⅜-inch bolts and bicycle axle.

11. Cut two 28½-inch 2 x 4 legs. Sand corners and fasten to outside of cart with several 1½-inch #10 screws, driven from inside the cart. Drill pilot holes before driving the screws.

12. For handles, cut two 34-inch 2 x 2s, round corners on one end, and drill 1-inch holes about ½ inch deep on rounded ends to secure a 1-inch wooden dowel or pipe. Attach to underside of cart with four 3-inch by ¼-inch stove bolts with washers, leaving about 16 inches of handle assembly protruding.

13. A final option is to fasten two pieces of flatiron along top edges of sides to prevent wood from splintering.

144

LIGHT-DUTY TRAILER

This light-duty trailer for a lawn tractor was designed and built by P. G. Howerton of Carterville, Illinois.

Howerton designed the trailer around four 8-inch wheels off an old rotary lawn mower, but any similar size can be used. By using four wheels, larger loads can be handled with relatively small wheels. (If you use larger than 8-inch wheels, you will have to enlarge the carriers.)

Standard lumber and hardware is used throughout. The dimensions can easily be changed to make your wagon larger or smaller, but the clearances required for dumping must be considered. The pivot point should be about 2 inches to the rear of the bed's center. This maintains weight on the tongue and increases the dump angle.

The owner rates his wagon at a 350-pound capacity, so care is exercised when hauling sand, stones, or other heavy materials. Howerton uses it primarily for carting grass clippings, leaves, garden tools, and the like. While the low load capacity is sometimes a disadvantage, the potential cost savings in building your own trailer will undoubtedly offset it.

CONSTRUCTION

1. Fabricate the carriers first. Cut two 12-inch lengths of 2 x 6. Clamp the pieces together and drill a 1-inch hole, its center 1 inch from the top and 6 inches from either end. Then drill two axle holes, the size determined by the axles you are using, located 1½ inches from the back and 1 inch from the bottom and 1½ inches from the front and 1 inch from the bottom. Drill two ¼-inch holes, 6 inches from either end, one an inch from the bottom, the other 2½ inches from the bottom. Finally mark each piece for two holes to be drilled only half through each piece; one hole is 2 inches from the front and 2 inches from the bottom, the other is 2 inches from the back and 2½ inches from the bottom. After drilling these holes, cut the corners off. Measure 4 inches from each end at the top and 3½ inches down the ends from the top, connect the two points with a diagonal line and cut along the line. Round the corners with a rasp.

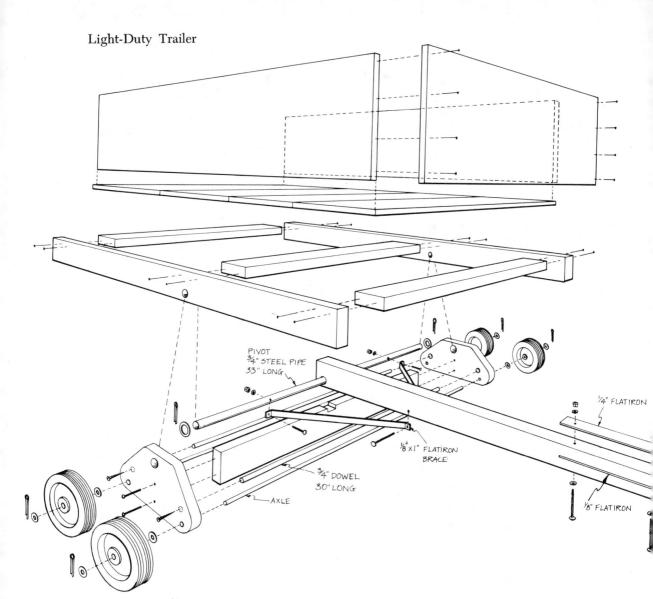

PIVOT
¾" STEEL PIPE
33" LONG

⅛"x1" FLATIRON
BRACE

¾" DOWEL
30" LONG

AXLE

¼" FLATIRON

⅛" FLATIRON

2. Cut two 30-inch lengths of ¾-inch dowel and a 28½-inch length of 2 x 4. Cut a 1-inch-deep by 2-inch-wide notch in the center of one narrow face of the 2 x 4. Insert the dowels in the holes drilled only half-through the carriers; secure each with a 2½-inch #10 screw. The 2 x 4 is centered between the carriers, broad face upright, notch up, flush with the bottom of the carriers, and secured with two 5-inch by ¼-inch lag bolts turned into it from each carrier.

3. Fabricate the tongue. Cut a 45-inch length of 2 x 4. Drill a 1-inch hole through the broad face, 1 inch from one edge and 1½ inches from one end. Cut a 10-inch kerf into the center of the broad face at the other end. Drill ¼-inch holes through the narrow face of the tongue, 1 inch and 9 inches from the front. Drill matching holes through a 12-inch

MATERIALS

Wood

1 pc. 2 x 6 x 10'	or	**Carriage sides:** 2 pcs. 2 x 6 x 12"
		Side members: 2 pcs. 2 x 6 x 45"

2 pcs. 36" x $\frac{3}{4}$" dowel   or   2 pcs. 30" x $\frac{3}{4}$" dowel

1 pc. 2 x 4 x 14'	or	**Carriage crossmember:** 1 pc. 2 x 4 x 28$\frac{1}{2}$"
		Tongue: 1 pc. 2 x 4 x 45"
		Crossmembers: 3 pcs. 2 x 4 x 25"

2 pcs. 1 x 12 x 12'	or	**Floor:** 4 pcs. 1 x 12 x 30$\frac{1}{2}$"
		Front/tailgate: 2 pcs. 1 x 12 x 30$\frac{1}{2}$"
		Sides: 2 pcs. 1 x 12 x 46$\frac{1}{2}$"

Hardware

4–2$\frac{1}{2}$" #10 screws
4–5" x $\frac{1}{4}$" lag bolts
1 pc. $\frac{1}{8}$" x 1$\frac{1}{2}$" x 12" flatiron (hitch)
1 pc. $\frac{1}{4}$" x 1$\frac{1}{2}$" x 12" flatiron (hitch)
2–4" x $\frac{1}{4}$" bolts w/ nuts and washers (tongue)
12d nails
1 pc. 33" x $\frac{3}{4}$" steel pipe (pivot)
2–$\frac{3}{4}$" ID flat washers
6 cotter pins
1 pc. $\frac{1}{8}$" x 1" x 36" flatiron   or   2 pcs. $\frac{1}{8}$" x 1" x 18" flatiron (braces)
2–1" x $\frac{3}{16}$" bolts w/ nuts and washers
1–2$\frac{1}{2}$" x $\frac{1}{4}$" machine bolt w/ nut and washers
8d nails
2 pcs. $\frac{1}{16}$" x $\frac{3}{4}$" x 8" steel strap
2 pcs. 4" flatiron inside corner brace
8–1" x $\frac{1}{4}$" carriage bolts w/ nuts and washers
2–$\frac{3}{4}$" x $\frac{1}{4}$" machine bolts w/ nuts and washers
1 barrel bolt
Paint
2 pcs. 34" steel rod, diameter matched to wheel hub,
    w/ 4 washers (axles)
4 wheels

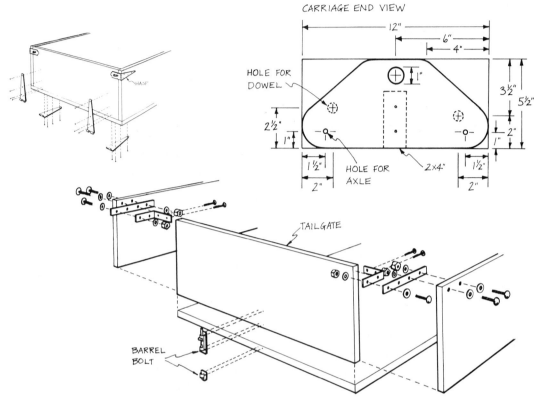

CARRIAGE END VIEW

HOLE FOR DOWEL

HOLE FOR AXLE

TAILGATE

BARREL BOLT

length of ⅛-inch by 1½-inch flatiron and a 12-inch length of ¼-inch by 1½-inch flatiron. Slip the ⅛-inch thick flatiron into the saw kerf and line up the holes. Lay the ¼-inch flatiron on top of the tongue and line up the holes. Insert 4-inch by ¼-inch bolts in the holes, washers top and bottom, and tighten them up.

4. Frame the bed. From 2 x 6 stock, cut two 45-inch side members and three 25-inch crossmembers from 2 x 4 stock. Clamp the side members together and drill a 1-inch hole through them, locating the center 20½ inches from one end and 1 inch from one edge. Lay out the frame so the crossmembers rest on a broad face, the side members on a narrow face. Be sure the holes are directly opposite each other and are above the crossmembers, or you won't be able to assemble the pivot. Using 12d nails, spike the frame together, a crossmember flush with the ends of the side members, one centered.

5. Assemble the three components at the pivot. Set the carriage on your shop's floor. Lay the tongue in the notch, the hole roughly lined up with those in the carrier tops. Set the bed frame atop the carriage, again roughly lining up the holes in the components. You will use a 33-inch length of ¾-inch steel pipe for the pivot. Before sliding it in place, locate the mid-point of the length, then drill $\frac{3}{16}$-inch holes through the pipe 8½ inches on each side of that point, keeping the holes parallel. Slip the

pipe through the holes. Place a washer over each end of the pipe. Secure the pipe in place by drilling a hole for a large cotter pin in each end and installing the pin.

6. Install the flatiron braces between the pivot and the tongue. Cut two 18-inch lengths of $\frac{1}{8}''$ by 1″ flatiron. Drill a $\frac{1}{4}$-inch hole through one end of each strap, $\frac{1}{2}$ inch from the end. Drill a $\frac{3}{16}$-inch hole through the other ends, $\frac{1}{2}$ inch from the end. Bend 1 inch of each end up. Bolt the braces to the pivot pipe with 1-inch by $\frac{3}{16}$-inch bolts. Mark the tongue where the braces meet it, drill a $\frac{1}{4}$-inch hole, and bolt the braces to the tongue, using a single $2\frac{1}{2}$-inch by $\frac{1}{4}$-inch bolt.

7. Construct the bed. Cut six $30\frac{1}{2}$-inch 1 x 12s and nail four of them to the bed frame, using 8d nails. Nail the fifth to the front edge of the floor. Cut two $46\frac{1}{2}$-inch 1 x 12 sides and nail them to the edge of the floor and front. Cut two 8-inch lengths of $\frac{3}{4}$-inch-wide steel strap, drill four holes in each. Attach a flatiron inside corner brace to each end of the remaining $30\frac{1}{2}$-inch 1 x 12 at the top, as shown, using two 1-inch by $\frac{1}{4}$-inch bolts. Set this tailgate in place, locate the position of the $\frac{3}{4}$-inch steel strap hinge pieces, and attach the steel straps to the sides with 1-inch by $\frac{1}{4}$-inch bolts. Bolt the tailgate in place using two $\frac{3}{4}$-inch by $\frac{1}{4}$-inch bolts. Attach a barrel bolt to the bottom center of the tailgate to hold it closed. (To make a tailgate that hinges at the bottom, use two 6-inch strap hinges, as shown.)

8. Paint the trailer.

9. Install the axles and wheels. Locate washers between the carriers and the wheels and the wheels and the cotter pins which retain the wheels on the axles.

GARDEN-TRACTOR TRAILER

Another trailer designed to be used with a garden tractor is this one, constructed by Robert Branch of Waterbury, Connecticut. Branch was lucky enough to scrounge the wheel assembly for his trailer from a neighbor's old wagon. The large tires and the great strength of the axle and springs are important. The wagon has been through constant rugged use for more

than twelve years and is still going strong. Branch believes a good wheel assembly with large balloon tires is the key.

It is unlikely that you'll have easy access to a similar wheel assembly, but the box and the tool carrier are easily adaptable to most any carriage setup. You could adapt the setup from Howerton's trailer, described earlier, for example, or you could design your own.

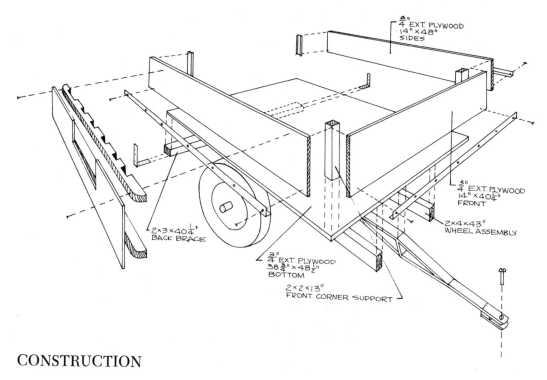

CONSTRUCTION

1. From ¾-inch exterior plywood, cut two 14-inch by 48-inch sides, a 38¾-inch by 48½-inch bottom, a 14-inch by 40¼-inch front, and a 13¼-inch by 38½-inch tailgate. With white glue and 2-inch #12 screws, attach the sides and front to the bottom. The sides butt against the bottom, and the front against the bottom and sides.

2. The two 13-inch 2 x 2 front corner supports go in next. Drive 2-inch #12 screws through the plywood into the 2 x 2s.

3. Cut two 4-inch by 48-inch pieces and one 4-inch by 40-inch piece of sheet metal. Bend all three pieces to a 90-degree angle, drill or punch screw holes in them, and screw them in place along the bottom edges of the trailer, as shown, with ½-inch #12 sheet metal screws.

4. Glue and screw the back brace underneath the bottom of the trailer at the back edge through the trailer bottom. Use six 1½-inch #10 screws.

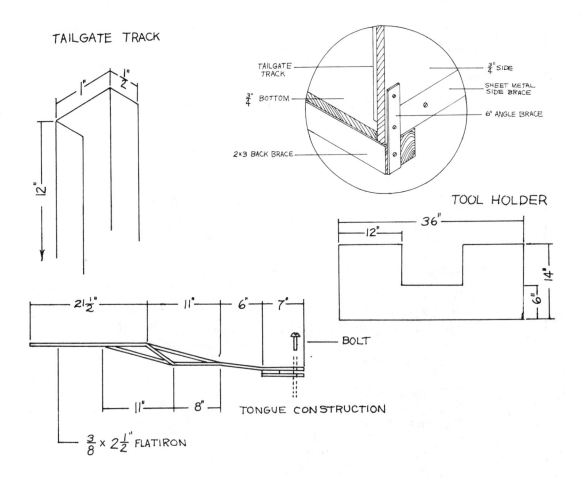

TAILGATE TRACK

1" 1/2" 1"

12"

TAILGATE TRACK

3/4" BOTTOM

2×3 BACK BRACE

3/4" SIDE

SHEET METAL SIDE BRACE

6" ANGLE BRACE

TOOL HOLDER

36"

12"

14"

6"

21 1/2" 11" 6" 7"

BOLT

11" 8"

TONGUE CONSTRUCTION

3/8 × 2 1/2" FLATIRON

5. Attach the two 6-inch angle braces on the outside of the trailer at the back corners, driving 3/4-inch #6 screws through the brace first, then into the side and bottom brace.

6. The tailgate track can go on next, on the inside of the two sides at the rear. Screw through the track into the plywood side with 1/2-inch #6 screws.

7. The tongue is welded up of 3/8-inch by 2 1/2-inch flatiron, as shown. You may want to change the design to fit your tractor. The trailer tongue on Branch's tractor was considerably lower than the bottom of the trailer—thus the gradual braced downward slope of the tongue.

8. Two 43-inch lengths of 2 x 4 are attached to the bottom of the trailer to act as mountings for the running gear. The 2 x 4s extend from front to rear and have a narrow face against the trailer bottom. Three-inch #12 screws driven through the trailer floor into the 2 x 4s secure them in place.

151

MATERIALS

Wood

1–2' x 4' sht. ¾" ext. plywood	or	**Sides:** 2 pcs. 14" x 48"
		Bottom: 1 pc. 38¾" x 48½"
1 sht. ¾" ext. plywood		**Front:** 1 pc. 14" x 40¼"
		Tailgate: 1 pc. 13¼" x 38½"
1 pc. 2 x 2 x 4'	or	**Front corner supports:** 2 pcs. 2 x 2 x 13"
1 pc. 2 x 3 x 4'	or	**Back brace:** 1 pc. 2 x 3 x 40¼"
1 pc. 2 x 4 x 8'	or	**Wheel assembly:** 2 pcs. 2 x 4 x 43"

Hardware

White glue
24–2" #12 screws
1 pc. 2' x 4', $\frac{1}{16}$" sheet metal   or   **Side braces:** 2 pcs. 4" x 48"
Front brace: 1 pc. 4" x 40"
40–½" #12 sheet metal screws
6–1½" #10 screws
2–6" angle braces
12–¾" #6 screws
2–12" tracks for tailgate
10–½" #6 screws
⅜" x 2½" flatiron as needed for tongue
10–3" #12 screws

TOOL HOLDER

A unique feature of Branch's trailer is the side-mounted tool rack. You should build yours to accommodate the tools you have and use the most. Branch usually takes along a rake, a log roller, a sickle, some rope, wedges, grass clippers, rose clippers, a brush cutter, a hatchet, a trowel, a bow saw, and a hooking tool. And he still has room for a trailer load!

CONSTRUCTION

1. Round the front and rear edges of the two 2 x 3s so you don't catch the corner on a tree or your leg.

MATERIALS

  Wood

      1 pc. 2 x 3 x 8'   or   **Top and bottom:** 2 pcs. 2 x 3 x 40"

      1–2' x 4' sht. ¼" ext. plywood   or   **Side piece:** 1 pc. 14" x 36"

  Hardware

      12–1¼" #10 screws
      4d nails

---

2. Drill holes or cut notches in the top 2 x 3 to fit the tools you plan to carry.
3. Screw the 2-inch edge of the two 2 x 3s to the side of the trailer from the inside, making sure the custom cut one is on top.
4. Nail the side piece on.

UTILITY WAGON

If you can round up some iron wagon hardware and a discarded tongue and wheel assembly from the front of a horse-drawn wagon, you can construct a useful two-wheel wagon rugged enough for just about any job, from hauling manure or picking rocks to bringing in logs from the woodlot. Not everyone will be able to obtain the same type of axle and wheels, but the basic design here is highly adaptable.

CONSTRUCTION

1. The framework is constructed of six pieces of rough-sawn oak 2 x 4s. The bed is 72 inches long and 53 inches wide (just 4 inches narrower than the distance between the wheels) to allow maximum load space. The two 72-inch 2 x 4s are spaced 26 inches apart, and the four crossmembers

153

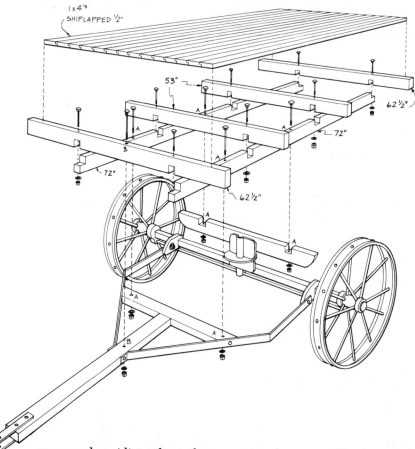

are spaced equidistantly on these, on 24-inch centers. The front and rear crossmembers should be aligned flush with the ends of the 72-inchers, and the two 53-inch pieces should be marked to overlap the longitudinal members equally on both sides.

2. Mark all six members where they touch and notch them out to half their depth with saw and chisel (sixteen notches) so that when assembled they form a strong, flat platform. Now you're ready to bolt the sections together at the joints with eight 6-inch by $\frac{3}{8}$-inch carriage bolts with lock washers. Recess holes for the bolt heads so as not to interfere with flooring. It may be necessary to modify the wheel assembly slightly to make the floor level with the wagon tongue. Next, using 8-inch by $\frac{1}{2}$-inch carriage bolts, secure the new frame to the wooden crossmembers of the original assembly at the four points indicated (A). Then bolt the front member of the framework (B) to the tongue for added strength.

3. The sides are constructed of four 72-inch-long by 1-inch-thick boards attached to the frame with four iron wagon side braces bolted to the extensions of the front and rear crossmembers (see illustration). In this case, the bolts on the brace ends weren't long enough to penetrate the

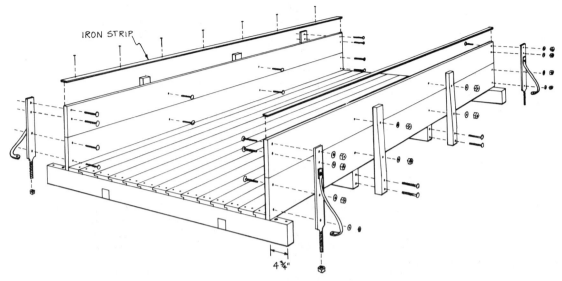

IRON STRIP

4¾"

2 x 4, so it was necessary to drill holes large enough to accommodate the nut into the end crossmembers. The braces are then turned in tight and bolted to the side boards with 2½-inch by ¼-inch carriage bolts. The final step in this sequence is to secure the outside braces to the front and rear crossmembers with 2-inch lag bolts.

4. In most cases, the height of your wagon's sides will be dictated by the height of whatever side braces you can obtain. Our braces were 15 inches, so two boards, a 1 x 6 and a 1 x 10, were used on each side. Take care to see that the sides are flush with the ends of the two 53-inch center crossmembers.

5. After attaching the metal side braces, you're ready to add the four 2 x 2 oak braces. Each brace is attached to the crossmember with a pair of 3-inch lag bolts. For a more graceful appearance, these braces can be tapered gradually from 2 x 2 at their bottoms to 2 x 1 at the tops. The edges of the ends of the frame extensions can be leveled similarly.

6. To protect the top edges of the sides from splintering, it's a good idea to attach iron strips—either nailed or screwed down. These can sometimes be salvaged from disused horse wagons.

7. The floor is made of 1 x 4 oak boards shiplapped ½ inch. The lapped 1 x 4s can either be purchased or cut with a router or table saw and dado attachment. The boards are nailed to the crosspieces with 8d cut nails.

8. Tailgates and side extensions are also desirable, and can be constructed using wagon hardware and a little ingenuity (see illustration).

    a. For hauling manure, gravel, or other loose material, you'll want to add some removable front and rear gates. If possible, use the kind of side braces that have small 1- or 2-inch extensions projecting outward at right angles.

    b. Make the gates from 1-inch oak boards, like the sides. Bolt these to two wooden stakes that can slide in and out of metal stake pockets attached to the outside frame members.

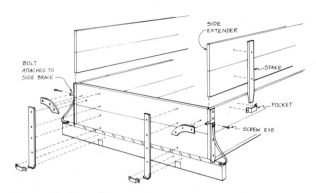

c. To attach the tailgate to the rear side braces (i.e., to close the gate), attach a pair of "ears" with holes large enough to accommodate bolts extending from the rear side braces. Drill holes in bolts so that the gate can be closed with pins. Large screw eyes would serve the same purpose.

MATERIALS

Wood

1 pc. 2 x 4 x 12′ hardwood	or	**Frame:** 2 pcs. 2 x 4 x 72″
2 pcs. 2 x 4 x 10′ hardwood	or	**Frame crossmembers:** 2 pcs. 2 x 4 x 53″ 2 pcs. 2 x 4 x 62½″
1 pc. 1 x 6 x 12′ hardwood	or	**Sides:** 2 pcs. 1 x 6 x 72″
1 pc. 1 x 10 x 12′ hardwood	or	**Sides:** 2 pcs. 1 x 10 x 72″
1 pc. 2 x 2 x 8′ hardwood	or	**Braces:** 4 pcs. 2 x 2 x 18½″
7 pcs. 1 x 4 x 12′ hardwood	or	**Floor:** 14 pcs. 1 x 4 x 72″

Hardware

8–6″ x ⅜″ carriage bolts w/ lock washers
5–8″ x ½″ carriage bolts w/ lock washers
4 iron wagon braces
26–2½″x ¼″ carriage bolts w/ nuts and washers
4–2″ lag bolts
8–3″ lag bolts
8d cut nails
2–6′ strips of strap iron

COMPOST BINS

Compost can be made on open ground just by heaping up layers of organic matter and natural mineral fertilizers in a corner of the backyard or on the edge of the vegetable plot. Many gardeners, however, prefer to make their compost in bins or cages. These easy-to-build constructions keep compost piles neat, discourage rodents, pets, and children from exploring them, protect the compost from washing rains and baking sun, and make covering the piles during the cold winter months simple.

The type of container you select depends on your personal taste, the amount of labor you wish to expend, and the materials you have on hand.

CAGE-TYPE BIN

Most composting methods are aerobic. That is, they rely upon a supply of oxygen to enable bacteria to quickly and thoroughly break down organic materials into rich, black, soil-lightening humus. Un-

fortunately, the oxygen must be brought to the bacteria and this usually involves periodically turning the pile. Anything that can make this task easier is welcomed by the busy gardener.

This easily constructed compost "cage" makes turning simpler and more methodic than the usual random procedure. In addition, a good deal of the pile is constantly exposed to the air.

The cage is set up with a building as a fourth wall. The front panel is held in place with four hooks and eyes, thus being easily removed for access to the compost or for turning the pile.

CONSTRUCTION

1. Cut the 2 x 4s in half to create the uprights and front panel cross-members. Cut the four 26-inch 2 x 3 side panel crossmembers and the 41-inch 2 x 2 upright for the front panel. For the gussets, cut six 12-inch-square panels from the ¼-inch exterior plywood, then cut the squares diagonally. From the remaining plywood, cut two 4-inch by 5-inch gussets to secure the center upright in the front panel. You can cut two of the corners off, as shown, if you like.

2. Construct the side panels by laying out the crossmembers, then butting the uprights against them. Toenail the pieces together with 12d nails. Place a triangular gusset over each corner, square up the panel's frame with a framing square, then nail the gussets fast with 6d nails.

3. Construct the front panel in much the same fashion, toenailing the outer uprights and the crossmembers together, squaring the frame, then nailing the corner gussets in place. Locate the central upright, then fasten with the gussets.

4. Paint the compost cage framework.

5. Cut the two sheets of metal lath in half. The lath is stapled to the side of the frame that is not gusseted.

6. Select the location for the compost cage and position the two wall mounts, about a foot from the ground and 18 inches apart. Secure them to the wall with 12d nails or masonry nails. Place the side panels against the ends of the wall mounts, drill ¼-inch holes through the side into the ends of the mounts, then turn in the 4-inch by ¼-inch lag bolts with washers.

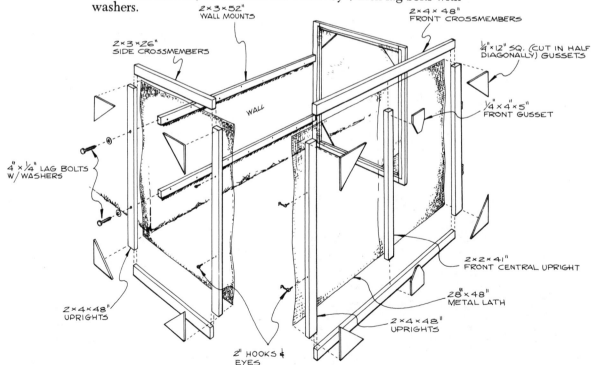

2×3×52"
WALL MOUNTS

2×4×48"
FRONT CROSSMEMBERS

2×3×26"
SIDE CROSSMEMBERS

¼"×12" SQ. (CUT IN HALF
DIAGONALLY) GUSSETS

WALL

¼"×4"×5"
FRONT GUSSET

4"×¼" LAG BOLTS
W/WASHERS

2×2×41"
FRONT CENTRAL UPRIGHT

28"×48"
METAL LATH

2×4×48"
UPRIGHTS

2×4×48"
UPRIGHTS

2" HOOKS &
EYES

MATERIALS

Wood

4 pcs. 2 x 4 x 8'	or	**Uprights:** 6 pcs. 2 x 4 x 48"
		Front crossmembers: 2 pcs. 2 x 4 x 48"
2 pcs. 2 x 3 x 10'	or	**Side crossmembers:** 4 pcs. 2 x 3 x 26"
		Wall mounts: 2 pcs. 2 x 3 x 52"
1 pc. 2 x 2 x 4'	or	**Front central upright:** 1 pc. 2 x 2 x 41"
1–2' x 4' sht. ¼" ext. plywood	or	**Corner gussets:** 6 pcs. 12" sq. (cut diagonally)
		Front gussets: 2 pcs. 4" x 5"

Hardware

12d nails
6d nails
1 gal. ext. paint
2 pcs. 28" x 96" metal lath
Staples
4–4" x ¼" lag bolts w/ washers
4–2" hooks and eyes

---

7. Position the front panel against the edges of the side panels, mark for the locations of the hooks and eyes. Install these latching devices and hook your cage together.

VARIATIONS

A slightly different bin can be made by constructing four panels, as described, but using eight hooks and eyes to hitch them together. Or one could be made of two **L**-shaped sections lying on their sides and held together with four hooks and eyes. Size is not critical, but a 3-foot by 3-foot by 3-foot model is very convenient to handle and has the capacity to put out 18 to 24 cubic feet of finished compost per batch after shrinkage.

Such a cage could be constructed of 2 x 2s, lined with chicken wire or other material. The corners of each section should be braced with 2 x 2s. In use, the two sections are fastened together (no top or bottom neces-

right next to the square-sided pile. Finally, peel the layers off the old pile with a fork and toss them into the empty cage. It's best at this point to peel the drier material from the sides and top of the heap into the bottom of the cage to ensure complete composting. During this turning opera-

sary) and filled with the material for composting.

When you are ready to turn the pile, the hooks at the sides of the cage are unfastened; then the two **L**-shaped sections are separated from the pile, reassembled, and fastened

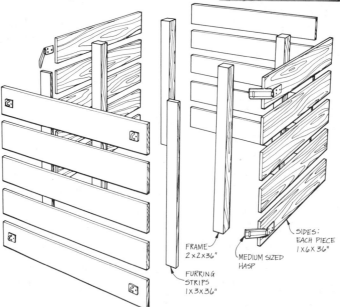

FRAME
2 x 2 x 36"

FURRING
STRIPS
1 x 3 x 36"

MEDIUM SIZED
HASP

SIDES:
EACH PIECE
1 x 6 x 36"

MATERIALS

Wood

1 pc. 2 x 2 x 12'	or	**Frame:** 4 pcs. 2 x 2 x 36"
5 pcs. 1 x 6 x 12'	or	**Sides:** 20 pcs. 1 x 6 x 36"
1 pc. 1 x 3 x 6'	or	**Furring strips:** 2 pcs. 1 x 3 x 36"

Hardware

6d nails
3d nails
4 medium-sized hasps

tion, keep a hose handy to wet down the new heap as the material is transferred.

Another version of the cage-type bin has three permanent sides and a removable front. The cage is constructed of 1 x 6s nailed front and rear to four 2 x 2 posts. When nailing the front 2 x 2s, allow space for the vertical furring strips that connect the removable front piece.

Attach four hasps to the front piece for easy access and turning of compost.

LEHIGH-TYPE BIN

The Lehigh-style bin is easy to erect and disassemble; it's adjustable in size, attractive, portable, long lasting, and is ideal for proper ventilation and protection.

Construction is of alternating 2 x 4s, with the corners drilled out and held together with $\frac{3}{8}$-inch rods. Use five 36-inch-long 2 x 4s to a side to make a bin that will produce approximately 1 cubic yard of compost per batch.

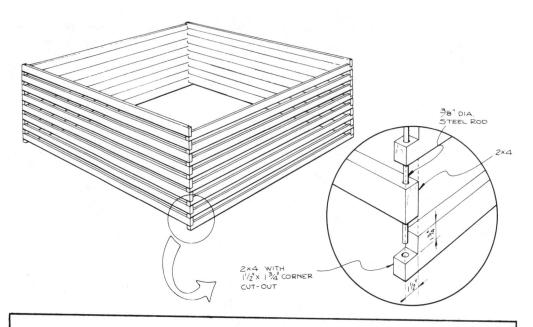

3/8" DIA.
STEEL ROD

2×4

2×4 WITH
1½" x 1¾" CORNER
CUT-OUT

MATERIALS

Wood

5 pcs. 2 x 4 x 12'   or   **Side slats:** 20 pcs. 2 x 4 x 36"

Hardware

4 pcs. 36" x ⅜" steel rod

VARIATION

A variation of the Lehigh bin, these log bins adjoining the truck garden of Eliot and Sue Coleman, Harborside, Maine, assume a plentiful supply of trees. Open construction allows maximum amount of air to get into the pile, where Coleman experiments with various combinations of materials available to him—kelp, grass clippings, pine needles, manure, etc.

A BLOCK OR BRICK BIN

The block or brick bin is easily constructed; it is made from concrete block or bricks, laid with or without mortar. Usually, the blocks are laid to permit plenty of open spaces for air circulation which is essential for the proper decomposition of the composted materials. But the blocks or bricks can be closely stacked, set into the ground and mortared together, or formed into a circle with an access gate at the bottom.

163

LEAF MOLD BIN

The leaf mold bin was developed by Warner Tilsher of Rosemead, California, who describes his bin as "the most practical for gardeners with small plots." He advises having two, for rotation.

A 30-inch-wide piece of 1 x 2-inch-mesh woven-wire fencing is formed into a circle with a 30-inch diameter. Then, 30-inch lengths of roll roofing are cut, slipped inside the fencing, and wired to it. Vent holes are punched in the roofing. The roofing is durable and prevents small bits and pieces of composting materials from falling out of the bin.

After the bin is full, it is covered with a layer of 6-mil plastic and the heap is left to rot. Because he doesn't take the time to regularly turn the compost heap, Tilsher gives the material additional time to compost and

is very careful about what he tries to compost.

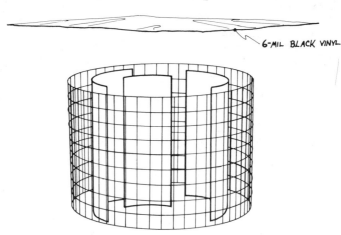

6-MIL BLACK VINYL

MOVABLE BIN

Here's a movable model that requires no screws or nails and can be adapted to fit even the tiniest city lot. To make it, Bette Wahlfeldt cut 10-foot-long 1 x 10 boards into 60-inch lengths, slotting each board 4 inches in from the end, and then $4\frac{5}{8}$ inches across its width so they can be nested. When finished, the bin is $50\frac{1}{4}$ inches square and $18\frac{1}{2}$ inches high inside.

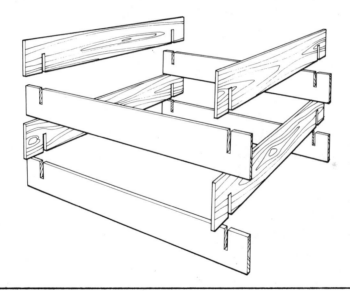

MATERIALS

Wood

    4 pcs. 1 x 10 x 10'   or   **Sides:** 8 pcs. 1 x 10 x 60"

STEEL DRUM COMPOSTER

This novel approach to composting, designed by John Meeker of Gilroy, California, utilizes a 50-gallon steel drum raised 6 inches off the ground by means of a circular metal frame with legs.

After removing both ends from the drum, a 3-inch-wide, 6-foot-long hoop of metal was spot-welded to the outside bottom rim of the barrel. A ½-inch lip was welded to the bottom of this hoop, and a circular grate rests on the lip. Four pieces of 8-inch-long, ¾-inch pipe were then welded on for

legs, to allow air to circulate up from the bottom of the pile. The 6-inch space permits easy removal of finished compost with a hoe or shovel.

To get air to the middle of the mass, the user punches a hole from top to bottom of the crushed bulk with a broomhandle or bean pole. A perforated pipe would work as well.

The size and shape of this unit make it ideal for the small garden. Despite its compactness, a surprising quantity of high-grade compost can be obtained from it. Since there's

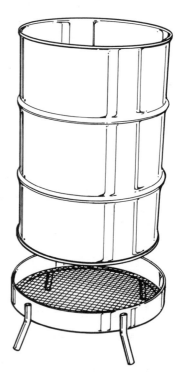

always at least some material undergoing decomposition, there is usually a bushel or two ready once the compost cycle has begun. Summer grass cuttings and garden gleanings are composted by the time one is ready to lay down a winter mulch; autumn leaves and dead garden wastes go in as the summer's material comes out; and the autumn compost is ready in time for spring planting.

To avoid odor problems, the dampened pile should be sprinkled with ground limestone and a thick layer of dried steer manure whenever sizable amounts of fresh vegetable wastes (lettuce leaves, beet tops, grass cuttings, kitchen wastes) are added. The limestone helps neutralize any odor and decreases the acidity of the green refuse and garbage.

Another virtue is that the barrel is easily movable by walking it on its four legs. When it is kept full, the compactness and weight of the mass force the loose finished material at the bottom to stay behind when the barrel is moved.

COMPOST SIFTER

In about two hours of your time you can build a sturdy compost sifter for just a few dollars. You can keep it beside your compost pile or move it right into your garden for working right over beds you're preparing; or you can move it quickly to various compost areas in your yard. It will fold flat for easy carrying or for storing in your cellar, garage, or under the porch to keep it from the rigors of winter weather. This will help to preserve its durability, so that it is good for a lifetime.

From your local lumberyard purchase five 2 x 3 boards, 6 feet long (they'll have to be cut from 12-foot lengths). From your hardware man you'll need two yards of 36-inch galvanized, $\frac{1}{2}$-inch wire screening (some may prefer $\frac{1}{4}$-inch screening), a box of fence staples, two 5-inch by $\frac{3}{8}$-inch carriage bolts with three washers for each, and some 8d nails. Handy folks will have the makings of this already around the house, making the cost of their sifters practically nil.

167

Using two 72-inchers as side pieces, make a frame by cutting two end pieces 33 inches long from another 2 x 3. This will give you a 6-foot-long frame that is slightly wider than 3 feet. Use the 8d nails to join the corners by pounding them in at angles.

Now tack your wire screening to your frame starting at one end and going along one side. Space the staples about 3 inches apart and keep the screening taut. Then finish the

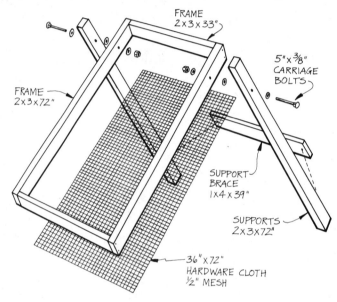

FRAME
2 x 3 x 33"

5" x ⅜"
CARRIAGE
BOLTS

FRAME
2 x 3 x 72"

SUPPORT
BRACE
1 x 4 x 39"

SUPPORTS
2 x 3 x 72"

36" x 72"
HARDWARE CLOTH
½" MESH

MATERIALS

Wood

5 pcs. 2 x 3 x 6'	or	**Frame:**	2 pcs. 2 x 3 x 72"
			2 pcs. 2 x 3 x 33"
		Supports: 2 pcs. 2 x 3 x 72"	
1 pc. 1 x 4 x 4'	or	**Support brace:** 1 pc. 1 x 4 x 39"	

Hardware

8d nails
1 pc. 36" x 72" hardware cloth, ½" mesh
Fence staples
2–5" x ⅜" carriage bolts w/ nuts and 3 washers ea.

other side. If your hardware man was generous in his cutting of the screening, trim off the excess after it has been nailed down.

Next, measure 11 inches from the top of each side of your frame and drill holes to take the diameter of your bolts, on center, through these side pieces. Measure 11 inches down, on center, on the remaining 72-inch 2 x 3s and drill same size holes through the narrow dimension.

Secure these supports to the frame with the carriage bolts, placing washers on both sides of the joists. Keep threaded ends and nuts inside frame for trim-looking outer edges. Using 8d nails, secure a 39-inch length of 1 x 4 across the supports, as shown.

Set your screen up to the angle that works best for you and throw compost up high on the frame to let it slide down and sift through.

WHEELBARROW-SIZED SIFTER

Here's another version of the compost sifter designed especially to be propped up in a wheelbarrow. The sifter in this case is propped up with an adjustable 28-inch-long 1 x 3 brace. Nail together a 36-inch by 48-inch frame of 1 x 3s and attach either ½-inch or ¼-inch wire screening. Brace each frame corner with a 2½-inch block of 2 x 2. Drill holes for, glue, and attach three ½-inch dowel pins, 2 inches long and 2 inches apart, to one end of the support, and hinge the other end to the sifter frame. Pegs allow screen to be slanted at different angles for composting materials of varying consistencies and moisture levels. You could merely drive several 12d nails through the support, as

shown in the photo, rather than using the pegs.

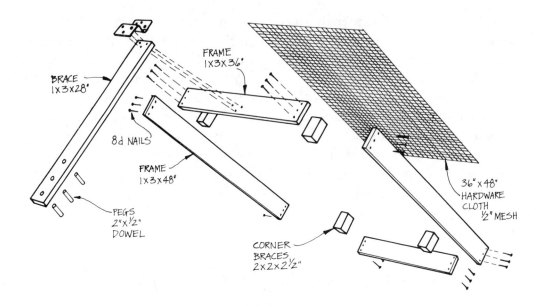

BRACE
1X3X28"

FRAME
1X3X36"

8d NAILS

FRAME
1X3X48"

PEGS
2"X½"
DOWEL

CORNER
BRACES
2x2x2½"

36"x48"
HARDWARE
CLOTH
½" MESH

MATERIALS

Wood

1 pc. 1 x 3 x 8′	or	**Frame:**	2 pcs. 1 x 3 x 36″
1 pc. 1 x 3 x 10′	or	**Frame:**	2 pcs. 1 x 3 x 48″
		Brace:	1 pc. 1 x 3 x 28″
1 pc. 2 x 2 x 2′	or	**Corner braces:**	4 pcs. 2 x 2 x 2½″
1 pc. 36″ x ½″ dowel	or	**Pegs:**	3 pcs. 2″ x ½″ dowel

Hardware

8d nails
1 pc. 36″ x 48″ hardware cloth, ½″ mesh
Glue
1 hinge

COLD FRAMES

For most people their cold frame quickly becomes more than the perfect place to start seedlings for the garden. First you will be tempted to stretch spring and fall into winter a bit with cold-hardy plants. It is easy to grow vegetables for extra early salads right next to the space reserved for garden seedlings. Later on the humidity in a frame makes an ideal environment for rooting cuttings over summer if the bed is slightly shaded. A cold frame can be a low-cost, reach-in greenhouse, with many of the virtues of a full-sized one at a fraction of the cost.

The cold frame has to make the most of short-day sunlight. So it does best in a location that faces directly south. The spot should also be sheltered (see "Attached Cold Frames," below). Don't hesitate to set the windows at a fairly steep angle (up to 45 degrees). Of course water won't drain well from panes which lie flat or nearly so. Moreover, a flat angle will reflect a sizable share of the sun's rays during the cool months, just when you want as much light as you can get.

THE WINDOWS

Glass panes are durable and provide the best lighting. Most people say they have found enough used window sash at auctions or wrecking sales to make cold frame construction fairly inexpensive. But if you can't find enough used windows, carefully compare material costs and construction time to the cost of new sash before you embark on building your own. With old windows, make sure the caulking and paint are sound; a lot of water will lie along the seams.

The width of the sash and the number of units you buy determine how long your frame will be. As a rough estimate in buying lumber, figure the width of the frame to be equivalent to the length of your windows.

Though not as good as glass, a clear rigid plastic (any fiberglass reinforced plastic) will make a fine inexpensive and long-lasting cold frame. Don't bother to use polyethylene sheets. For all the work you'll put into the frame, the plastic will only last two years in the sunlight, at best. Here are plans for a plastic window.

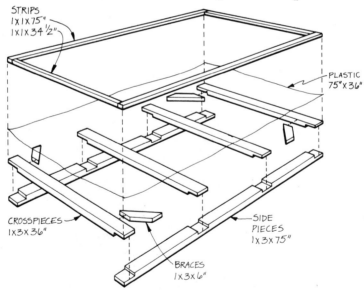

STRIPS
1 X 1 X 75"
1 X 1 X 34 1/2"

PLASTIC
75" X 36"

CROSSPIECES
1 X 3 X 36"

SIDE
PIECES
1 X 3 X 75"

BRACES
1 X 3 X 6"

CONSTRUCTION

1. Cut two 75-inch and four 36-inch lengths of 1 x 3 (or furring, which is less expensive but of a rougher finish). Cut a lap joint at each end of the 36-inch crosspieces. Cut four lap joints in each side piece, one at each end and one 25 inches from each end. Assemble the window frame, using glue and two screws at each joint.

172

2. Cut four 6-inch braces from 1 x 3, cutting the ends at 45-degree angles, as shown. Fasten the braces in the four corners of the frame, driving 6d or 8d finishing nails through the ends of the brace into the frame members. Drilling pilot holes will prevent splitting.

3. Stretch your glazing sheet over the frame and tack it fast using 1 x 1 strips or lath, as shown, and 3d nails.

MATERIALS

Wood

1 pc. 1 x 3 x 12′	or	**Crosspieces:** 4 pcs. 1 x 3 x 36″
1 pc. 1 x 3 x 16′	or	**Braces:** 4 pcs. 1 x 3 x 6″
		Side pieces: 2 pcs. 1 x 3 x 75″
2 pcs. 1 x 1 x 10′	or	**Strips:** 2 pcs. 1 x 1 x 75″
		2 pcs. 1 x 1 x 34½″

Hardware

White glue
16–⅝″ #10 screws
6d finishing nails
75″ x 36″ sht. plastic glazing
3d nails

A DIFFERENT APPROACH

Another relatively easy way to construct your own sashes is to join frame elements cut from 2 x 4 or 2 x 3 with open-doweled joints and to form a ledge for the glass with quarter-round molding or 1 x 1.

There are a couple of variations in approach that are possible. For example, you can use a blind-doweling technique to join the members of the frame. Or you could use half-lap joints or mortise and tenon joints. These joints are somewhat more diffi- cult and time-consuming to make without power equipment. The retaining strips for the glass panes could be lath or quarter-round molding. Or, if you have the appropriate power equipment, you could cut a rabbet in the 2 x 4 frame to accept the panes.

In terms of material, you can easily use 2 x 3, 2 x 2, ¾-inch or 1-inch stock.

And don't be limited to our suggested dimensions. Make them whatever size you want. Just remember that the care with which you cut and finish the various parts of the sash will in large measure determine the tightness of the finished product. A window sash like this is quite a simple assembly. Here's how to make a 2-foot by 4-foot window with two glass panes.

CONSTRUCTION

1. Cut two 48-inch lengths and three 17-inch lengths of good-quality 2 x 4.
2. Lay out the pieces as shown. At each of the six joints, you must drill two $\frac{3}{8}$-inch holes through the 48-inch piece into the end-grain of the 17-inch piece. Each hole should penetrate about 2 inches into the 17-inch piece.
3. Cut twelve 3½-inch lengths of $\frac{3}{8}$-inch dowel. With a file or coarse sandpaper, taper one end of each piece.
4. Put a little glue on a dowel and drive it, tapered end first, into the first hole of the first joint. Repeat the process until all twelve dowels are in place.
5. Measure the inside dimensions of the frame and cut 1 x 1 strips to serve as a retainer for the glass panes. Fasten the retainer strips in place with glue and 4d finishing nails. The strips should be dead-center, so there is a $\frac{3}{8}$-inch-deep groove formed around the inside of the frame on either side.
6. Paint the frame, being careful to coat the groove for the glass panes.
7. Cut glass panes to fit and install them using glazier's points. Seal the panes with glazing compound or putty.

MATERIALS

Wood

1 pc. 2 x 4 x 14'	or	**Frame:**	2 pcs. 2 x 4 x 48"
			3 pcs. 2 x 4 x 17"
2 pcs. 36" x $\frac{3}{8}$" dowel	or	**Pegs:**	12 pcs. 3½" x $\frac{3}{8}$" dowel
1 pc. 1 x 1 x 12'	or	**Retainers:**	4 pcs. 1 x 1 x 17"
			4 pcs. 1 x 1 x 18¾"

Hardware

Glue
4d finishing nails
Paint
2 panes of glass 16$\frac{3}{8}$" x 18$\frac{5}{8}$"
Glazier's points
Glazing compound

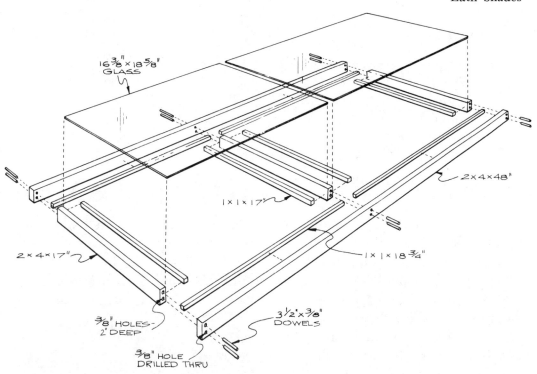

16 3/8" × 18 5/8" GLASS

2 × 4 × 48"

1 × 1 × 17"

2 × 4 × 17"

1 × 1 × 18 3/4"

3/8" HOLES— 2" DEEP

3 1/2"× 3/8" DOWELS

3/8" HOLE DRILLED THRU

LATH SHADES

Even in cool weather, midday temperatures in an airtight cold frame can rise too high for tender seedlings. So the windows must be movable for ventilation. Since there also must be some way to secure them in the wind, using hinges to fasten them along the top provides a way to build in both features.

For any late seedlings or summertime propagation, a lath shade is an indispensible accessory. The shade will reduce both the demand for water on weak root systems and the temperatures in the frame. Then in cold weather, the lattice can serve as a framework for burlap insulation blankets to reduce heat losses at night. Here's how to make a shade out of lath for one window.

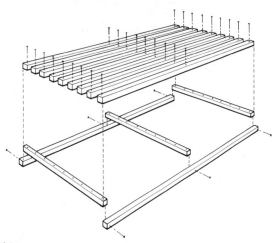

175

CONSTRUCTION

1. Cut three 1 x 1 crosspieces the width of the window and two 1 x 1 sides the length of the window.
2. Lay out the five pieces as shown, forming a frame the size of the window. Nail through the sides into the butt ends of the crosspieces using 6d nails.
3. Cut 1 x 1 laths the length of the sides and cover the frame, as shown, leaving about an inch between lath strips. Use 4d nails.

PERMANENT COLD FRAMES

The main advantage to sinking the cold frame into the ground is that it is the easiest way to eliminate drafts, which quickly drive out whatever heat is gained in the day. Lowering the bed also allows you to benefit from the temperature moderating effects of the earth during the changes of season. But remember that when the ground is colder than the air inside, the earth absorbs heat from the frame. The depth to which you sink it depends on your location. You can also bank soil up around the sides to seal out drafts. The plans here assume the surface of the bed lies 5 inches below the soil surface.

Drainage in the frame, especially when the bed lies below the ground level, should be excellent. You can remedy poor draining soils by digging out an extra foot and a half, then laying a 6-inch gravel bed. Amend the soil you removed with sand, then fill into the bed as needed. Last, add 6 to 8 inches of the soil you want to plant into.

Wood that is unpainted when you start construction, especially any wood which will be in contact with the soil, should be treated to retard decay. Be sure to use a wood pre-

servative (like Cuprinol) which releases no fumes toxic to plants. To find one, try firms that deal in supplies for wholesale greenhouses. It also helps to use a wood with a long life (cypress, redwood, or cedar) if you can get it.

Two-inch planks are expensive, but they will have a longer life; more than twice the life of 1-inch lumber, for example. The plans here are for 2-inch planks; if you use thinner wood, be sure to nail into 2 x 2 strips in the corners.

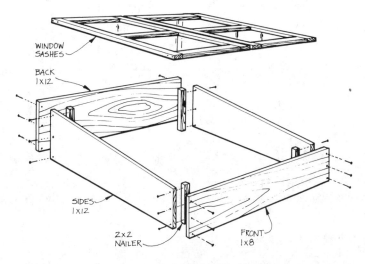

MASONRY COLD FRAME

Perhaps the most durable cold frame is one constructed of masonry. You can construct forms and pour a concrete frame. Stone is often available free, and a well-constructed stone cold frame would look nice. But bricks or cement blocks may be the easiest masonry materials to work with. Moreover, they are inexpensive and are often available used (thus even more cheaply). For the fledgling mason, a cold frame is a good project to bolster confidence and hone skills.

The first step is to determine the size of the cold frame, and the size is very much a function of the window size. If you are using old storm windows or old window sashes, these will obviously determine the size of the cold frame. If you are going to construct windows specifically for your cold frame, you can make the frame any size you desire.

To determine the precise width of your cold frame, lay out the two slanted end pieces for the frame. Use 2 x 10 planks; the 10-inch width ensures ample pitch when using ordinary window sash. First, take the section of the plank reserved for these end pieces (it is as long as the window sash), and draw a diagonal from one corner, which is exactly as long as the window. Where this line meets the bottom of the plank, mark a perpendicular line and cut off the little excess wood. Then cut the plank, dividing it along the diagonal.

These are the two end pieces. The length of one of these, then, gives you the *inside* width of the cold frame, minus 1 inch. You must subtract the inch because the tip of this piece should extend 1 inch onto the front wall so that the window overlaps and rests on the wall.

In the following construction sequence, it is assumed that you have done your initial planning, that you know just how big your frame must be. For specific information about working with masonry, see the masonry chapter in this book.

CONSTRUCTION

1. Using stakes and string, lay out the dimensions of your cold frame. Dig below the frost line and pour a footing. The footing should be somewhat wider than the block. When it is cured, lay the 4-inch block walls of the frame. The wall should rise high enough above the depth of the planting bed to allow at least a 6-inch clearance between the bed and the glass. This should be enough even if you start seedlings in flats on top of the bed. As shown, the top surface of the wall is flat.

2. Secure at least two anchor bolts in each of the four walls. To do this, at each location for the bolts fill in the cavity in the block with gravel or sand to within a few inches of the top. Position a bolt so that it protrudes about 1¼ inches over the top of the wall, and set the bolt with concrete.

3. Cut 2 x 4s to make the plates, and drill holes to receive the anchor bolts. Then drill enough of a recess at each hole so that the nut which secures the plate will lie flush with the surface. Fasten the plates after the bolts have firmly set. If you have not already done so, cut out the two end pieces in accordance with the instructions above. Attach them to the two end walls. These should be aligned so they are flush with the inside of the wall. The narrow point should extend 1 inch onto the plate on the front wall, and the heel should be in line with the inside of the back wall. Toenail these two pieces into position, with nails on either side of the board.

4. Measure the distance between the outside edges of the end pieces, and cut a piece of 2 x 10 that length. To secure it, nail through the back into the end pieces. Drill pilot holes to prevent splitting.

5. Now you can position the 1 x 2 lip across the back wall. Cut the strip so that it fits snugly between the end walls. Again, you may want to drill holes for the nails to prevent splitting. Position the lip so that its outer edge is just flush with the slanted face of the end wall, and nail it on.

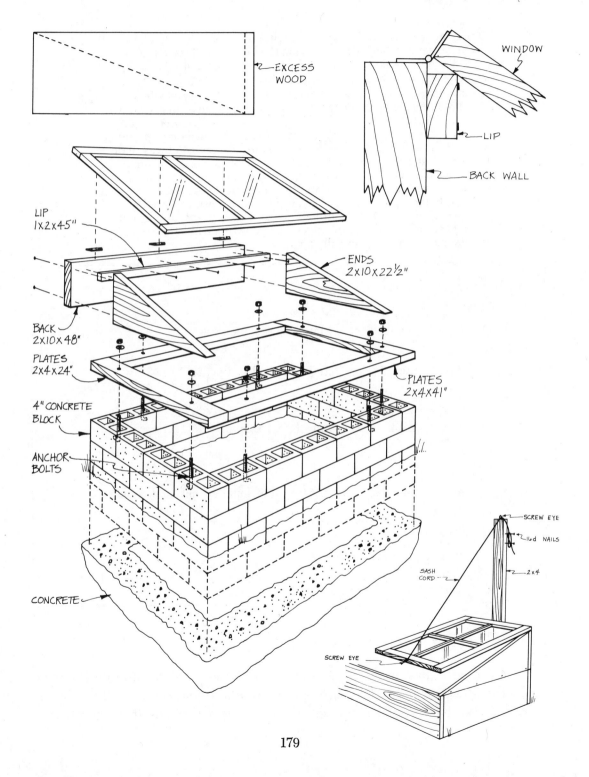

EXCESS WOOD

WINDOW

LIP

BACK WALL

LIP
1x2x45"

ENDS
2x10x22½"

BACK
2x10x48"

PLATES
2x4x24"

PLATES
2x4x41"

4" CONCRETE BLOCK

ANCHOR BOLTS

CONCRETE

SCREW EYE

16d NAILS

2x4

SASH CORD

SCREW EYE

179

6. Attach the windows. The top of the windows should lie right next to the inside edge of the back wall. Position the hinges, drill starter holes, and screw the hinges onto the tops of the windows, then onto the back wall.

7. For the final touches, you can add handles to the windows (either metal or just wooden blocks). If wind might blow a propped-open window shut, you should rig a way to secure them so you won't have your windows shattered or the seedlings steamed by the caprice of Mother Nature. Certainly you will need to devise a way to keep the windows propped open safely while you work with your plants. A very good way to do this is to attach a 2 x 4 behind each window, as shown, so the top of the 2 x 4 is flush to the window when it is fully open. Turn a screw eye into the bottom end of the window and the top of the 2 x 4, and drive a nail or two into the side of each 2 x 4. Tie a length of sash cord to the window's screw eye, run it through the 2 x 4's screw eye, and loop it around the nail. With this arrangement, you will be able to secure the windows part way open or fully open.

MATERIALS

Wood

1 pc. 2 x 4 x 12′	or	**Plates:** 2 pcs. 2 x 4 x 24″
		2 pcs. 2 x 4 x 41″
1 pc. 2 x 10 x 6′	or	**Ends and backs:** 1 pc. 2 x 10 x 48″
		1 pc. 2 x 10 x 22½″ (cut according to instructions)
1 pc. 1 x 2 x 4′	or	**Lip:** 1 pc. 1 x 2 x 45″

Hardware

12d nails
8–⅝″ all thread anchor bolts (about 8″ long) w/ nuts and washers
3 hinges

Miscellaneous

4″ concrete block
Concrete
Sand

HOT BED

To start seedlings early in extra cold climates, an electric heating cable can be used to warm the soil. It is an easy modification on the concrete block cold frame. All that is required is a thermostat, some electric heating cable (from a garden or greenhouse supplier), a nearby out- let, and a little extra preparation of the bed.

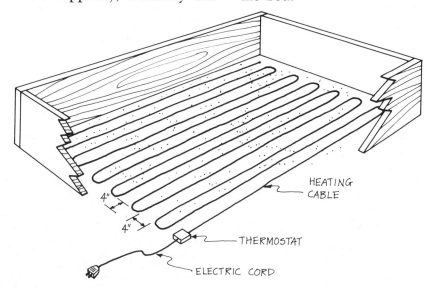

HEATING CABLE

4"

4"

THERMOSTAT

ELECTRIC CORD

CONSTRUCTION

1. Excavate the bed deep enough to lay down 1 foot of gravel or cinders mixed with sand. On top of this, lay $\frac{1}{2}$ inch of sand.
2. Outline the pattern for the cable, as in the diagram, with 20d nails every 6 inches. Lay the cable next to them and cover it with 2 inches of soil.
3. Attach a preset thermostat at the junction of the cable and the electric cord, and lay the instrument on the soil. Remove the nails and fill with about 4 inches more of the planting soil.

WOODEN COLD FRAME

This frame is made just like the concrete block frame, substituting 2 x 10 planks for the base. A wooden frame isn't set so deep; it can rest on the ground at the same level as the surface of the planting bed. This leaves 10-inch clearance for the plants. How deep you set it depends on local weather. If the frost line is shallow, you can put your bed below it. If not, you may just as well keep out the wind by piling up a berm around a frame which is set fairly shallow.

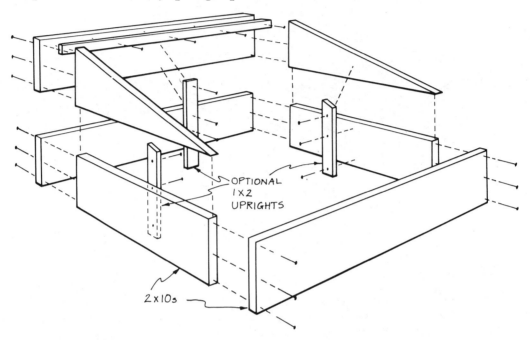

OPTIONAL
1 X 2
UPRIGHTS

2 x 10s

CONSTRUCTION

1. Dig the pit down to the level of the planting bed, and construct the frame.

2. In joining the 2 x 10s for the four walls, drill starter holes in the longer pieces before nailing them to the end walls, as described for the top segment of the block cold frame.

3. Again as for the top segment of the block frame, attach each level of this frame to the one below it by toenailing. You can use 1 x 2 uprights for reinforcement, but they shouldn't be necessary with 2-inch lumber for the walls.

4. When the frame is situated as you want it, carefully fill in the pit around the outside of the frame. Then excavate enough soil from the bottom of the frame in order to establish a well-drained planting bed. Be sure to leave a ledge (about 2 inches) of the original earth around the edges as a foundation for the walls. Finally fill in your planting medium.

5. Attach the windows as directed for the block frame.

ATTACHED COLD FRAMES

If your home has a south wall free from shading trees (primarily evergreens) and shrubs—and these should be far enough away so that their roots won't invade the planting area—building the cold frame onto the wall yields advantages. The heat from the home that the wall transmits steadily will help to heat the frame. And the ground all along that wall will be warmer than ground out in the yard. A south wall of a garage or any large building is the next best thing.

The cold frames described in this section can easily be built onto a building by attaching plates to the wall wherever wooden parts of the frame meet the wall.

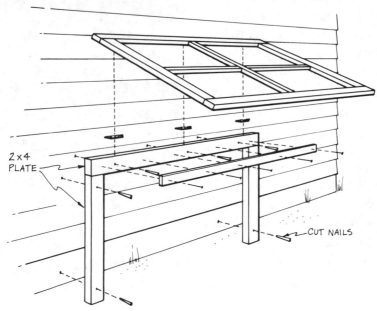

CONSTRUCTION

1. Build a masonry frame right up to the wall.
2. Attach 2 x 4 plates to the wall as shown. Use cut nails or masonry nails. Or, with a star drill, punch holes in the foundation, put expanding plugs in the holes and screw the plates to the wall. The broadest face is parallel to the wall.
3. Toenail wooden parts of the frame to the plates, attach the lip to the plate across the top plate, and fasten the windows as has been described.

COLLAPSIBLE COLD FRAME

Following the model of the wooden cold frame, you can construct a frame that can be taken apart and stored when your seedlings are grown, by joining the lumber with screws. This frame would rest on top of the ground. Not only does all this greatly increase the life of the frame, but it also requires much less material. You can seal it by banking a little soil around the bottom. Put it over a flower bed and plant directly into the soil or in flats.

Since the wood comes in little contact with the soil and is out of the weather most of the year, you can save more money by using 1-inch lumber for the walls. Similarly, you should consider using narrower planks, especially in the top assembly. The only effect of this will be the shallower pitch produced by dividing a narrower board.

Construction techniques are identical to the permanent wooden cold frame, except that you use screws instead of nails.

PORTABLE COLD FRAME

This is a variation with manifold advantages. Start cold-hardy plants in thick beds directly in the garden, and transplant them in succession for a steady harvest. When the weather warms, move the frame to harden off flats of more tender plants. In summer it can cover a propagation bed in a shady spot.

CONSTRUCTION

1. Measure 6 inches up along one side of the plywood, as illustrated. At this point mark a 45-degree angle and draw a line the height of the window sash. Repeat on the other side of the plywood.
2. Cut out the two plywood end pieces exactly the same size.
3. To determine the length of the frame, measure the width of your window, multiply by two, and add ¼ inch.

MATERIALS

Wood

1 sht. ½″ ext. plywood	or	**Ends:** 2 pcs. 24″ x 31″ (cut as illus.)
1 pc. 2 x 4 x 8′	or	**Spine:** 1 pc. 2 x 4 x 50¼″
		Gluing blocks: 4 pcs. 1½″ x 1½″ x 6″ (act. meas.)
2 pcs. 1 x 6 x 8′	or	**Fronts:** 2 pcs. 1 x 6 x 50¼″
		Handles: 4 pcs. ¾″ x 2″ x 15″ (act. meas.)

Hardware

4–31″ x 25″ window sashes
4 pr. hinges w/ screws
6d nails
White glue
Paint

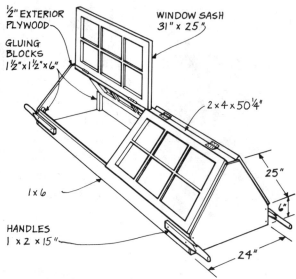

½" EXTERIOR PLYWOOD

WINDOW SASH 31" x 25"

GLUING BLOCKS 1½" x 1½" x 6"

2 x 4 x 50¼"

25"

6"

1 x 6

HANDLES 1 x 2 x 15"

24"

4. Then, cut two pieces of 1 x 6 and one piece of 2 x 4 to this length.
5. Cut four gluing blocks 1½ inches by 1½ inches by 6 inches out of the leftover 2 x 4 and assemble.
6. Attach window sashes to the 2 x 4 spine with hinges.
7. From the remaining 1 x 6, cut four pieces 2 inches wide by 15 inches long for handles. Round off 5 inches on one end of each handle and fasten to the sides with 6d nails and glue. Sand lightly and paint.

WINDOW-SCREEN COLD FRAME

If nothing else, this project demonstrates that there are no absolutes in constructing cold frames. Not only is the arrangement of the window units contrary to traditional cold frame design, but the window units are screens, rather than storm windows.

This particular cold frame was constructed of scrap materials and is set up for off-season gardening, being

disassembled and stored during the summer growing months. Since it is set against the house, it has no back panel.

You can easily make a similar cold frame using ¾-inch exterior plywood. Or you can adapt some of the ideas to a cold frame of your own design. Use plastic-covered screens, for ex-ample, rather than storm windows. Or arrange the window units differ-ently. In the sequence below, the frame is constructed around screens measuring 62 inches by 28 inches. Unless you have window units of that size, you will have to revise the di-mensions given to accommodate the units you use.

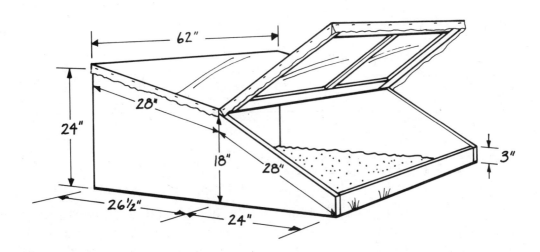

CONSTRUCTION

1. From ¾-inch exterior plywood, cut two side panels of the dimensions indicated. Perhaps the easiest way is to cut two 24-inch by 50½-inch panels, then mark them for the two tapering cuts indicated. Then cut a 24-inch by 60½-inch panel for the back (unless you will be locating the frame against a house; in that case, cut two 3-inch by 60½-inch strips to brace the back) and a 3-inch by 60½-inch front brace.

2. Nail the two sides to the front brace and to the back panel or back braces (one at the top, one at the bottom). Use 8d nails, driving them through the sides into the front and back boards. If you intend to dismantle the frame, use screws.

3. Nail or screw the top screen in place. With three butt hinges, attach the lower screen to the top screen.

4. Paint the cold frame, then cover the screens with heavyweight clear plastic film. You wrap the plastic over the sides of the screen and staple it along the edges, or you can tack it in place with lath strips.

MATERIALS

Wood

1 sht. ¾″ ext. plywood	or	**Sides:** 2 pcs. 24″ x 50½″
		Back braces: 2 pcs. 3″ x 60½″
		Front brace: 1 pc. 3″ x 60½″

Hardware

8d nails
2–28″ x 62″ window screens
3 butt hinges
Paint
Heavyweight plastic film
Staples

YOUR COLD FRAME

Don't let these few plans limit your imagination. We know that no one thing can put a gardener on the way to real expertise and a rich gardening experience like the ability to grow whatever he wants from seed. Cold frame construction is easy, and in case all these seem too elaborate for your schedule, we offer one more idea that works as well as any.

Take bales of the spoiled hay that you'll be needing for mulch after the weather turns hot, arrange them to fit the windows you have, then prop up two planks between the bales for end walls. The windows rest neatly on the planks, and you'll have plenty of room to start your own plants from seed—another example of the no-work gardening properties of mulch!

PLANTING BEDS

Gardeners seem never to tire of finding new ways of showing their plants to their best advantage. The means they have used have long taken a variety of practical as well as ornamental forms. Typical of their inventiveness is the lady at a Maine summer resort who once assembled a series of old-fashioned bathtubs; instead of filling them with water, she filled them to the brim with flowering plants.

Planting containers may be as small as a humble window box or as large as a full-scale elevated garden. The wooden variety is usually made of rot-resistant lumber such as heartwood of redwood, cedar, or cypress. There are those composed of red brick or cinder block. Inventive gardeners can fashion discarded railroad ties or broken concrete to form raised bed containers.

The ornamental aim of the raised planting bed is to place your plants on stage. There they can run through their seasonal performances as part of your entire home landscape scheme. There is a specific practical advantage, too. People with arthritis or back problems find that they can still garden if the planting area is raised. Besides, raised beds drain freely if they are built with a coarse gravel base below the topsoil and so help a gardener overcome a soggy yard. In addition, should your planting area slope, don't go to the trouble of grading—build a cheap but strong raised planting area. A 24-inch-high brick planter can be built to help conceal a house foundation.

Since the style of planter you choose depends upon the specific shape your garden or homescape demands, there are few hard and fast rules for building raised plant beds. For the most part, they ought to be no more than 2 feet high, made from weather-resistant materials, and anchored firmly, preferably below the frost line. Once your raised planting bed is finished, though, it will not succeed unless it is carefully "made." Generally, that involves the following mix: two parts fertile soil, one part fine compost, and one part sand. This is usually placed over thoroughly broken up subsoil and 6 inches of gravel. The exceptions to these guidelines are spelled out in the following examples.

STRAWBERRY BARREL

What's good about "scraping the bottom of the barrel"? Easy—that way your backyard barrel is emptied and ready to fill with soil for growing strawberries or other plants. Like Virgil Talbot, of Arkansas, you can use a traditional vinegar barrel, complete with wooden bung and some vinegar sloshing around. Smaller containers, like an empty nail keg, work just as well for building a strawberry barrel.

If your barrel is about ready to fall apart, soak it a few days in water.

Clean the inside of any barrel thoroughly, using a neutralizer such as a soda water solution to remove acid. Carefully select the spot where you want your barrel to rest. The hot summer sun shouldn't scorch it. It shouldn't be hidden away either—its overflowing vines and leaves make it an attractive addition to your yard. If you want a movable feast, put castors on smaller barrels. Large barrels take thirty plants. The variety of berry is your pick.

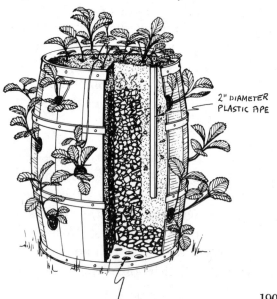

2" DIAMETER PLASTIC PIPE

DRAIN HOLES

CONSTRUCTION

1. For large barrels cut six evenly spaced 2-inch holes 10 inches from the bottom. Cut four holes per row for kegs. A power saber saw makes cutting holes easier.
2. Repeat 10 or 12 inches higher but offset from first row. For large barrels eighteen holes in three rows are enough.
3. In the bottom of the barrel drill several small drainage holes.
4. Paint according to your taste or leave natural wood surface.
5. Place large barrel in yard. Line bottom with 6 inches of gravel or small stones.
6. Mix soil, compost, well-rotted manure, and sand. Pack the mixture around the inner circumference of the barrel, leaving an empty column 6 inches in diameter in the center of the barrel. While doing this, bury several lengths of 2-inch perforated plastic pipe in the mixture, as shown.
7. Pour cinders, gravel, or small stones into the center column. Save enough loam mixture for growing layer of 6 inches at barrel's very top.

SPOT PLANTERS

There are other approaches to spotting plants around the house and yard besides the strawberry barrel. The two planters we made and described in the chapter on indoor planting tubs are ideally suited to outdoor use. The window box is as much an outdoor planter as it is an indoor gardening project.

The planters pictured here are all portable. They are all easily made. And they all suggest what you can do if you think about it.

Cut a keg or barrel in half to make two planters. Or nail together several planter boxes from 1 x 6 or 1 x 8 material. Use a rot-resistant wood and galvanized or aluminum nails.

Attractive planters can also be

191

made from 1- to 5-gallon metal cans by wrapping building paper or roofing around them and holding it in place with galvanized wire or metal bands. Adequate drainage holes should of course be provided.

BEATING HARD SOIL

Some gardeners have compacted, hardpan soil that is almost as difficult to work with as concrete. Raised planters can overcome hardpan, and solve drainage difficulties besides.

Betty R. Armenta of Huntington Beach, California, tempered her hardpan woes by building redwood planters—with nonsplinter seats—around the edges of her backyard, amid a brick patio, and next to her home. Her 20-feet by 24-inch garden is on a raised bed, but most of her garden space encompasses trees—orange, lemon, and loquat. When you go beyond vegetables, the size of your planter must be geared to the specific plant for which it is intended. A pine tree, for example, needs more space than a dwarf apple tree. Dwarf deciduous fruit trees such as apple or pear should be planted 6 feet apart. Make sure your redwood seats are well sanded to prevent splinters. And, too, the addition of earthworms to your soil-compost mix helps loosen hardpan.

Although Armenta used redwood for her planters, yours could just as well be made of cypress, cedar, lo-

cust, oak, or other rot-resistant wood. It's wise, too, to liberally treat all wood that will be in contact with the soil with a wood preservative. Be sure to use one that won't harm plants.

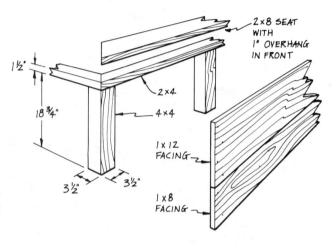

CONSTRUCTION

1. Using stakes and string, outline the area to be enclosed by the planter. Dig post holes and set 4 x 4 posts at the corners and spaced at least every 4 feet between corners. Use a level to ensure that the posts are plumb and that the tops are level. The posts should be sunk about 18 inches into the ground and have 18½ inches projecting above the ground.

2. Cut 1 x 8 to fit around the outside of the planter and, using galvanized 8d nails, fasten it to the outside of the posts, against the ground. Cut 1 x 12 to fit around the planter and nail these boards in place, above the 1 x 8s, as shown.

3. Cut lengths of 2 x 8 to form seats. Nail, using galvanized 10d nails, to the tops of the posts. Miter the seat boards at corners. Bevel the edges and sand them well.

4. An optional treatment is to cut trim pieces to cover, and to some degree protect, outside corners of the siding boards. Cut lengths of 1 x 4 to extend from ground level to seat level, bevel one edge, and nail to the corners, as shown in photo. Another optional treatment is to set the posts, then nail 2 x 3s or 2 x 4s across the tops. Attach the siding boards, then the seat boards.

RAISED BEDS FOR INTENSIVE GARDENING

One of the oldest and most successful styles of gardening to make use of the raised bed technique is that known as the Bio-Dynamic–French intensive method.

Basically the idea behind intensive gardening is to get maximum production with minimum inputs. All soil conditioners are used in planting beds, not on areas that will be used for paths, thus enabling your plants to benefit directly from all the material you put on your garden.

The method relies on raised or rounded planting beds from 3 to 5 feet wide. These beds are prepared by working the soil to a depth of about 2 feet, and adding generous amounts of compost and manure. When the soil has been properly prepared, you can either surround the seedbeds with 2 x 6s or simply leave them mounded. The mounded beds produce a soil that warms quickly, drains well, and takes in air easily. With beds you never walk on, or carry equipment across, soil compaction is no problem.

In the mounded beds, plants are spaced as close as possible in triangular patterns covering an entire bed. This close spacing encourages improved growth, conserves moisture, and greatly helps to control weeds.

Although the intensive system is great for those with limited space, it was not designed with them in mind. Most gardeners who use the system have more than enough gardening space. They use the system because of its increased yields, improved quality, and efficiency.

The key to intensive gardening is the construction of a raised bed. Once you have prepared the bed, you do your weeding, watering, and harvesting from the sides. For this reason beds should not be made more than 4 to 5 feet wide. For items to be staked such as tomatoes, the bed can be as narrow as 1½ feet. Whenever possible, beds should be laid out for maximum sun exposure. The length of the bed is entirely up to you.

Because of the number of plants the bed will be supporting, the soil must be almost hand built to ensure an ample supply of nutrients to all the plants. A high organic matter content is a must and some intensive gardeners lay claim to over 20 percent organic matter in their beds.

Add soil conditioners to the upper layers of the bed only, as is done in nature. When leaves fall, they lay on top of the ground, not 15 inches under it. By working manure and compost into the topsoil layers you protect

these layers from nutrient leaching, drying, and other ills they are exposed to at the surface.

The primary tool for preparing a raised bed is a technique known as double digging. The prescribed method is to dig a trench the width of your bed, removing soil one shovel deep and wide. Set it aside, and use your spade to break up the next level of soil until it is loose and crumbly to a depth of almost 24 inches. After you have removed one shovel depth of soil and worked the lower layer in your first trench, move the top layer of soil from the next trench back into the first trench, filling it and exposing subsoil in the new trench. You continue this digging of a trench and filling it in until the entire bed is dug. Soil removed from the first trench is then used to fill the last trench.

Let the bed set for a few days before working it again. This time, again remove the top layer of soil and loosen the bottom layer. As you return the topsoil to each trench, you add nutrients at different levels. For example, add rock fertilizers and bone meal first, then a little topsoil, some compost, more topsoil, rotted manure, some more topsoil, a small amount of wood ashes, and the final layer of topsoil. Rake the top surface well.

When planning an intensive garden, remember that plants do not grow in rows in nature and should not in your garden. Row planting is an invention of man to make it easier to cultivate large areas at one time. In an intensive raised bed, the plants are grown so that their leaves just touch, thus providing a very effective form of living mulch, much like a mature pine forest.

Where planning and planting really get fun is when you start interplanting. You may have a fast-growing crop at 6-inch intervals, with a later-maturing crop on 12-inch spacings, using the centers of the hexagons. When you really get good, you may find yourself with a bed having four or more different items growing in it. The ideal, however, is to have one bed for carrots, one for lettuce, maybe one for a combination of peppers and onions, and so on.

The old French market gardeners would strive to have an entire bed of plants ready to be harvested at the same time. This would enable them to re-dig their beds and get in another crop almost immediately. When you interplant long-season and short-season plants you cannot do this. It is therefore more productive to have individual beds for each vegetable, and plant herbs and flowers at the ends of the beds.

BOXED BEDS

For the practitioner of intensive gardening, framed-in beds, as exemplified by the ones constructed and cultivated by Warner Tilsher in California and Chet Nielson in Florida, may be the solution to the need for raised beds.

Neither Tilsher nor Nielson practice intensive gardening in the strictest sense, so the use of boxed beds is obviously not restricted. For their own reasons, both have turned to the boxed bed.

TILSHER'S BOX BEDS

Tilsher considers box beds the ultimate in intensive gardening especially where space is limited.

Plants can be spaced in both directions as closely as their growth habits allow and a bed can often produce twice as much as regular methods for a given area, he says. They require a minimum of labor to prepare, cultivate, and control weeds and pests. They are easy to irrigate and fertilize. They are ideal for crop rotation and succession planting. Furthermore, says Tilsher, they can be used as cold frames, and it is easy to install shades for cool-weather crops when it turns warm. They can be readily covered to provide protection from early frosts. Trellises are easily installed.

The Tilshers have used box beds for over twenty-five years; some of them have lasted twenty years. They are, of course, not particularly suited for such crops as corn, melons, vining winter squash, etc. The Tilshers have ten such beds in use most of the year. They run the beds north and south for the best light condition.

Having experimented with various sizes, they settled for 3-feet by 6-feet beds. This size works out well for standard lumber, plant spacing, and ease of working. The space between

the beds can be a mere footpath, or you can space them so that a hand edger-mower can be run between them.

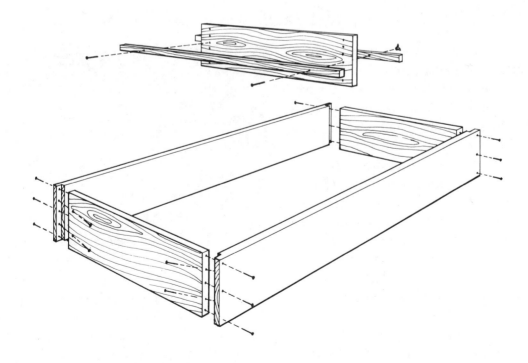

SOIL LEVELER

To level the soil in his box beds, Tilsher concocted a special tool. He cut a 32-inch length of 1 x 8, then attached a 48-inch length of 1 x 2 to each side of it as shown in the illustration. Using bolts and wing nuts in conjunction with rows of holes enables you to raise or lower the leveling board, thus altering the depth of soil in the bed.

MATERIALS

Wood

1 pc. 1 x 8 x 4′	or	**Leveler:** 1 pc. 1 x 8 x 32″
1 pc. 1 x 2 x 8′	or	**Supports:** 2 pcs. 1 x 2 x 48″

Hardware

2–3″ x ¼″ bolts w/ wing nuts

NIELSON'S UNITIZED GARDEN

If you demand neat rows for your carrots or beans, but have trouble keeping weeds trimmed once it's well into summer, then you may want to try Nielson units. Chet Nielson, a retired Army officer, brought military symmetry to his backyard vegetable plot in Florida by designing what he calls a "unitized" garden. The idea is pretty simple: All you need are 1 x 4 cypress (or other rot-resistant) boards nailed into frames to accommodate each kind of plant. Then put down wood shavings about 4 inches deep for footpaths.

Such an arrangement helps slow down weed growth inside the units

and effectively prevents stray weeds on paths. At the same time, unitizing allows crop rotation planning a season or two ahead. In addition, applying compost either in the off-season or during the growing season is accomplished easily. According to Nielson, the biggest advantage may be a psychological one. Instead of casting worried looks from your back porch as you submit to the determined creep of growing weeds, you can beat them back a bit at a time by hoeing a few units a day.

CONSTRUCTION

1. Use full dimension lumber, selecting the heartwood of redwood, cypress, cedar, or the like. Thoroughly treat the boards with wood preservative. Cut two 72-inch lengths of 1 x 8 for the sides and two 34½-inch lengths for the ends. Cut 1-inch-wide by ⅜-inch-deep rabbets in the ends of each side board, as shown.
2. Using galvanized 10d nails, nail the frame together.
3. Set the frame into the ground, so that at least 3 inches projects above ground level. Level the frame.

MATERIALS

Wood

1 pc. 1 x 8 x 12′	or	**Sides:** 2 pcs. 1 x 8 x 72″
1 pc. 1 x 8 x 6′	or	**Ends:** 2 pcs. 1 x 8 x 34½″

Hardware

Galvanized 10d nails
Wood preservative (copper naphthenate)

LOGGED-IN GARDEN

When Harry and June Griswold migrated from Oregon to British Columbia, they built a log house that kept them warm. But they had trouble keeping their garden warm because of killing frosts in May and September. Using "early" seed varieties and a large planting box with a plastic cover, the Griswolds have found an answer to their problem.

One of the unique things about their answer is that it is made of logs.

Near the fiftieth parallel on Lake Kootenay and in sight of snowcapped peaks, a raised garden extends the growing season, particularly when the log frame is covered with plastic. If moles and gophers are a problem, screens can be built into the frame before adding your soil-compost mix. By the third week in May the Griswolds were pulling lettuce and radishes. Their log box garden was filled with manure, wood chips, bone meal, rock phosphate, and a foot of good soil.

You don't need to live in the northern woods, however, to use a logged-in garden bed. There are a lot of applications for the basic idea expressed here. A single level of logs would enclose a raised bed intensive garden. Or logs could be used to enclose a terraced garden, or to highlight a wild garden.

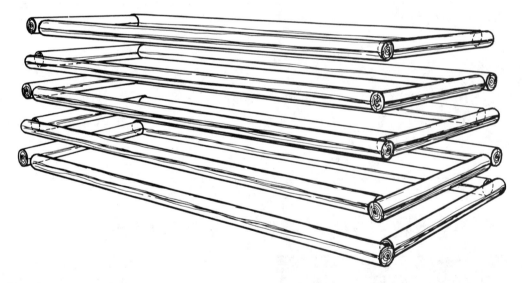

CONSTRUCTION

1. Hew five sets of logs to build a box measuring approximately 3 feet by 4 feet by 14 feet.
2. Position the logs, as shown, so that they do not sit one just above the other. Cut logs so that, when piled, top dimensions are slightly smaller than base dimensions. *Optional:* Notch logs for tighter construction.
3. Drive stakes around the base, if necessary, to hold the foundation logs in place.

GROWING ON CONCRETE

There's no need to let asphalt or concrete deter you from an active gardening program. If, like Mrs. Tony Mertz of Malibu, California, you haven't a single square foot of real earth to plant, just build a raised planting bed.

Faced with solid asphalt in front of her new home, Mertz took cinder blocks and laid out eighteen growing beds. Each was two blocks deep; the total bed depth was 24 inches. Then she shoveled in several tons of horse manure and bedding, mixed it with 10 percent good earth, and filled her beds to a depth of 18 inches. Four months after adding thousands of earthworms, she had ready-to-plant compost. To keep birds and rabbits out, she covered her bed with light wire mesh.

GARDENS IN THE AIR

Aching joints can keep you out of the garden, but not if you raise the planting bed so you don't have to bend over. That's what Californians Howard Knapp and Vollie Tripp did. Both tell the same story—adjust a raised bed according to your height and you can garden in boxes situated right next to the house or in the middle of the backyard.

A raised garden puts you eye-level with plants, enabling you to search and destroy pests and weeds with ease. Folks who walk on crutches and cannot use a wheelbarrow can substitute a child's wagon with a spring attachment to keep the handle within reach. Instead of sitting at a window dreaming of the garden that might have been you can get outside and garden in a raised planter located just below that window.

Knapp's six boxes were built from redwood, each 2 feet wide and 4 feet long. They were set on 2 x 4 legs, hip high. Some of the beds are 8 inches deep, some 12 inches. Half-inch holes were drilled in the box bottoms and covered with copper screening for drainage. The handyman can assemble these boxes easily without detailed plans. Requiring a step-by-step approach is Tripp's design.

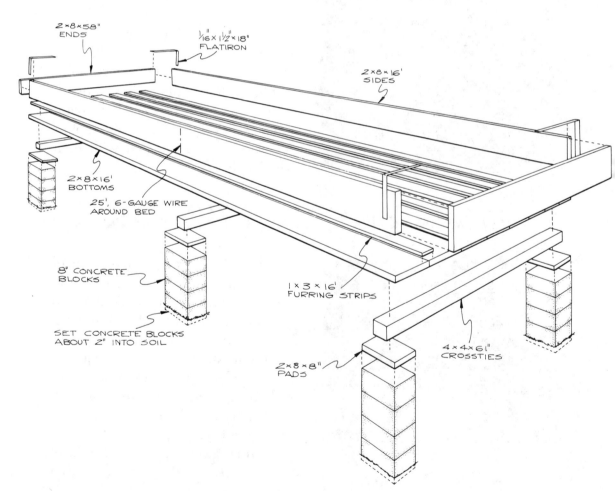

2×8×58"
ENDS

1/16 × 1 1/2 × 18"
FLATIRON

2×8×16'
SIDES

2×8×16'
BOTTOMS

25', 6-GAUGE WIRE
AROUND BED

8" CONCRETE
BLOCKS

1 × 3 × 16'
FURRING STRIPS

SET CONCRETE BLOCKS
ABOUT 2" INTO SOIL

2×8×8"
PADS

4 × 4 × 61"
CROSSTIES

CONSTRUCTION

1. Arrange six columns of cinder blocks to support a box 61 inches wide by 16 feet long. Set the blocks 2 inches or more into the ground, and stack them to a height comfortable for the gardener.
2. Cut six pads from scrap lumber 2 inches thick and 8 inches wide, and place them on the blocks.
3. Cut three 4 x 4 crossties to 61-inch lengths and nail lightly into pads. Make sure this foundation is level before proceeding.
4. Spread seven 16-foot 2 x 8 floor planks across the crossties and nail them in place with 16d nails.
5. Toenail two 16-foot 2 x 8 sides to the tops of floor planks to give extra soil depth. Cover exposed joints in the flooring with battens.
6. Cut 2 x 8 ends to fit and nail in place.
7. To prevent spreading at corners, nail flatiron strips there. To prevent swelling when wood gets wet, run a double set of 6-gauge wire across middle and twist tight.

MATERIALS

Wood

10 pcs. 2 x 8 x 16' or	**Pads:** 6 pcs. 2 x 8 x 8"	
	Bottom: 7 pcs. 2 x 8 x 16'	
	Sides: 2 pcs. 2 x 8 x 16'	
	Ends: 2 pcs. 2 x 8 x 58"	

1 pc. 4 x 4 x 16' or **Crossties:** 3 pcs. 4 x 4 x 61"

6 pcs. 1 x 3 x 16' furring (battens)

Hardware

16d nails
6d nails
1 pc. $\frac{1}{16}$" x 1$\frac{1}{2}$" x 6' flatiron or **Corner braces:** 4 pcs. 18" flatiron
25' 6-gauge wire

Miscellaneous

30–8" concrete blocks

PLANT PROTECTORS

Every garden needs occasional protection, whether it be from the vagaries of the weather or the depredations of insects and varmints. Not every protective technique is fully successful, but there are measures you can take to safeguard your plants.

The projects that follow have been conceived and built by practicing gardeners. Inevitably they are home-brewed, rough-edged, and highly personal. But equally inevitably, they work.

PLASTIC-PANEL ROW-COVERS

Sweet corn is such a delight, the Gene Logsdon family hates to wait until July to enjoy it. So they decided to do something about changing that —egged on in part by a friendly contest with neighbors over who could raise the earliest corn.

Logsdon's winning technique involved a really early-maturing variety and a stack of corrugated clear-plastic panels. Logsdon bent the panels to make covers over the rows of his early corn. The plastic makes a sort of miniature greenhouse over the plants, keeping out cold air but letting sunlight flood into warm the soil. Furthermore, the panels keep out pesky crows, blackbirds, and rabbits.

The idea works like a charm. He merely bent the panels to the desired form, tied them in that shape with two loops of string to keep them from springing back flat, then set them over the row with stakes on both sides so the wind couldn't blow them away.

The row-caps are, in practice, not unlike cloches or hot caps. They can easily be used to protect seedlings or transplants, regardless of the plant variety.

Moreover, Logsdon presses them into service later in the year to protect endive from fall's frosts. By doing so, he is, in some years, able to have garden-fresh endive on the table when there's snow on the ground.

Incidentally, plastic row-covers aren't an original idea by any means. Southern California has whole acres planted under them, and both Rutgers and Cornell have experimented with the idea, especially for tomatoes and other tender vegetables. But in these cases, growers use plastic film rather than semirigid panels, stretching it over various kinds of wire frames. Panels are considered too expensive for large-scale commercial projects. But for the home gardener —who needs only a few panels—it's worth trying if you like early corn and late endive, or if you are having a particularly difficult problem with birds or rabbits.

PATIO FROST SHIELD

Do you have a patio loaded with potted plants and small shrubs? Then a forecast for frost must set you scurrying like it did Airi Kulpa until she devised this easily assembled protector. Now she no longer needs to upset her living room on the occasional cold night. And it doubles as a place to root cuttings or start bedding plants.

She chose redwood since it's easy to maintain and there's no need to finish it. This one is scaled (10 feet by 3 feet by 3 feet) to fit against a handy south wall of her home, but it can easily be enlarged by adding sections.

MATERIALS

Wood

18 pcs. 1 x 1 x 8' rough-sawn redwood	or	**Front and top panels:**

Front and top panels:
Sides: 8 pcs. 1 x 1 x 60"
Crosspieces: 12 pcs. 1 x 1 x 34½"
Braces: 16 pcs. 1 x 1 x 12"

End panels:
Sides: 4 pcs. 1 x 1 x 36"
Crosspieces: 4 pcs. 1 x 1 x 34½"
Braces: 8 pcs. 1 x 1 x 12"

Brace: 1 pc. 1 x 1 x 33"

15 pcs. 1½" x ¼" x 8'   or   **Front and top panels:**
redwood lath   8 pcs. 1½" x ¼" x 60"
                                            12 pcs. 1½" x ¼" x 33½"

End panels: 4 pcs. 1½" x ¼" x 36"
                            4 pcs. 1½" x ¼" x 33½"

3 pcs. 2 x 2 x 8' redwood   or   **Posts:** 6 pcs. 2 x 2 x 48"

1 pc. 1 x 2 x 10' redwood (hinge mount)

Hardware

Galvanized 6d nails
24–1" inside corner irons
48–¾" #6 screws
4d nails
25' roll 4-mil wire-reinforced translucent plastic, 36" wide
Staples
8d nails
16–2" x ¼" lag bolts
4–2" butt hinges w/ screws
2 hooks and eyes

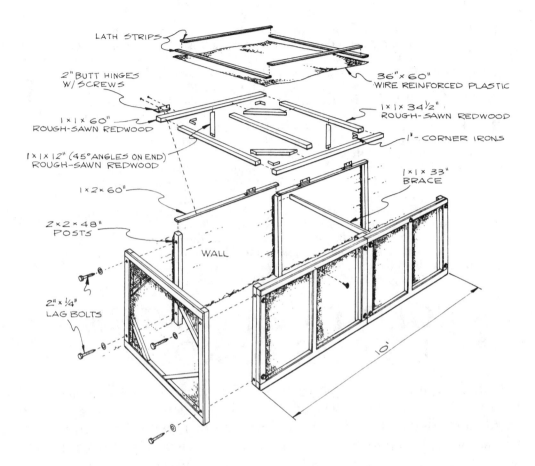

LATH STRIPS

2" BUTT HINGES W/ SCREWS

36" x 60" WIRE REINFORCED PLASTIC

1 x 1 x 60" ROUGH-SAWN REDWOOD

1 x 1 x 34½" ROUGH-SAWN REDWOOD

1 x 1 x 12" (45° ANGLES ON END) ROUGH-SAWN REDWOOD

1" - CORNER IRONS

1 x 2 x 60"

1 x 1 x 33" BRACE

2 x 2 x 48" POSTS

WALL

2" x ¼" LAG BOLTS

10'

CONSTRUCTION

1. The panels are framed with rough-sawn redwood 1 x 1s, which measure much closer to an actual 1-inch by 1-inch than dressed stock. (If you haven't access to rough-sawn stock and if the dressed 1 x 1 stock seems too flimsy to you, try using "five-quarters" stock.) Cut the 1 x 1 into the pieces listed in the materials list. Each top and front panel is framed with two 60-inch lengths, three 34½-inch lengths, and four 12-inch corner brace pieces. The end panels are framed with two 36-inch 1 x 1 sides, two 34½-inch 1 x 1 crosspieces, and four 12-inch 1 x 1 braces each. Drive 6d nails through the sides into the butt ends of the crosspieces in assembling the panel frames. Then attach a 1-inch inside corner iron at each of the four corners of the panels with ¾-inch #6 screws. Finally, cut 45-degree angles on the ends of the 12-inch braces and nail them in place—four to a panel— with 4d nails.

2. Cut sheets of wire-reinforced translucent plastic and staple them to the frame, wire over plastic. The top and front panels take 36-inch by

60-inch sheets, the end panels 36-inch-square sheets. For a finished look, cut lath strips, as indicated in the materials list, to nail to the frame over the plastic and wire.

3. Cut six 48-inch 2 x 2 posts. Three of them will be set next to the house or garage. Sink these about a foot into the ground. The outside posts should be 10 feet apart, outside edge to outside edge. The third post should be exactly halfway between them. Lay the 1 x 2 across the top of the three posts and make sure all three are level. When they are, fasten them to the building with nails or masonry nails, and fasten the 1 x 2 to the posts with 8d nails. Set the other three posts in the ground the width of the end panels from the building, one at each end and one in the center. Cut a 33-inch 1 x 1 brace and toenail it between the two center posts.

4. Set the panels in place against the posts, then drill ¼-inch holes through the panels and into the posts, one hole in the corner of each panel. Turn 2-inch by ¼-inch lag bolts into the holes. Attach the two top panels to the 1 x 2 with 2-inch hinges, two per panel. Use hooks and eyes, one per panel, to hold the top panels closed.

COLD FRAMING THE ENTIRE GARDEN

In the extreme northern parts of the United States and in Canada, where late spring and summer frosts play havoc with garden planning, a giant cold frame of easily unrolled plastic film can make an enormous contribution to one's peace of mind.

Minnesotans Pamela Thompson and her husband rely on this system to provide them with their entire year's supply of vegetables from a 25-foot by 40-foot garden. Their basic approach is to plant all the hardy vegetables—lettuce, radishes, spinach, peas, carrots, kale—at one end of the garden, and all the other things that can't stand a frost on the other end—summer and winter squash, tomatoes, peppers, melons, beans—leaving a 2-foot space between the two gardens. Then the Thompsons rigged up an oversize cold frame for the tender side.

On evenings when frost looks likely, they unroll the plastic film out over the supports. In the morning, it's important to go out early and roll the plastic back off, because a great deal of heat builds up underneath as the sun strikes the plastic. Keeping it rolled up during the day also prolongs the cover's usefulness.

The Thompsons put their giant cold frame together in the following sequence.

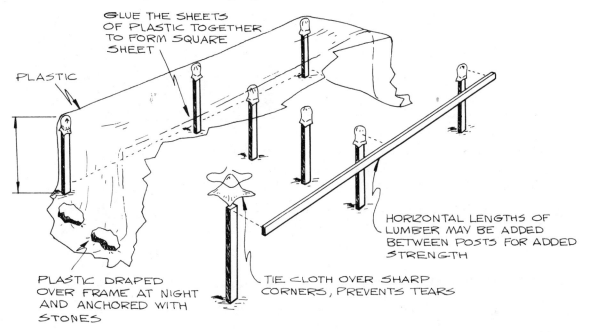

GLUE THE SHEETS OF PLASTIC TOGETHER TO FORM SQUARE SHEET

PLASTIC

HORIZONTAL LENGTHS OF LUMBER MAY BE ADDED BETWEEN POSTS FOR ADDED STRENGTH

PLASTIC DRAPED OVER FRAME AT NIGHT AND ANCHORED WITH STONES

TIE CLOTH OVER SHARP CORNERS, PREVENTS TEARS

CONSTRUCTION

1. Pound in 2 x 4 posts around the garden perimeter so that they stand about 4 feet above ground level. Place a post in each corner and four down the middle for support.
2. Cut lengths of lumber to fit and nail horizontally from post to post. Brace where necessary with extra posts. Tie pieces of old cloth around any sharp corners to prevent the plastic roof from tearing.
3. Cover the entire frame with 4-mil transparent plastic. To make a square piece of plastic, unroll the plastic in the yard, cut it in half, and carefully glue the two pieces together with contact cement. In this manner, a 16-foot by 65-foot roll of plastic can make a square cover approximately 32 feet square.
4. Lift the rolled plastic up onto the frame and unroll it all the way across. Plan on having enough plastic to allow for a 4- or 5-inch "skirt" all the way around. This allows you to anchor the sheet on the ground with rocks or blocks in windy weather. It also prevents frost from creeping into any areas where the plastic doesn't touch the ground.

SUNSHADING PEAS

To anyone familiar with the disappointment of returning from summer vacation to find their pea vines withered from the heat or knocked down by a hard rain, a pea plant shade could come as a real blessing. Beside protecting peas from the sun during extended hot spells, a shade like this one in the garden of Marjorie Dee in southern Wisconsin makes possible a second, late crop in areas where it would be otherwise impossible.

As the sun moves across the sky, the slats of snow fence produce stripes of shadow across the garden, breaking up the heat. On those days when even the "filtered" sunlight is too much for seedlings, a couple of old bedsheets stretched over the top will help keep the peas cool and moist.

CONSTRUCTION

1. Sink nine 4-foot-long 2 x 2 posts in the ground, as illustrated. Steel fence posts may be substituted, if desired.
2. Stretch three 12-foot lengths of chicken wire from post to post and attach with ½-inch staples.

MATERIALS

Wood

6 pcs. 2 x 2 x 12'	or	**Posts:** 9 pcs. 2 x 2 x 4'
		Horizontals: 3 pcs. 2 x 2 x 12'

Hardware

1 roll 36″ x 50′ chicken wire	or	3 pcs. 12′ long
½″ staples		
25′ roll of snow fence	or	2 pcs. 12′ long
4d duplex nails		

3. Nail three 12-foot lengths of 2 x 2 to tops of posts.
4. Lay two 12-foot lengths of snow fence side by side (overlapping slightly) on top of the 2 x 2s, as illustrated. (Use 4d duplex nails, if available.)
5. Tack a bedsheet on top of the snow fence.

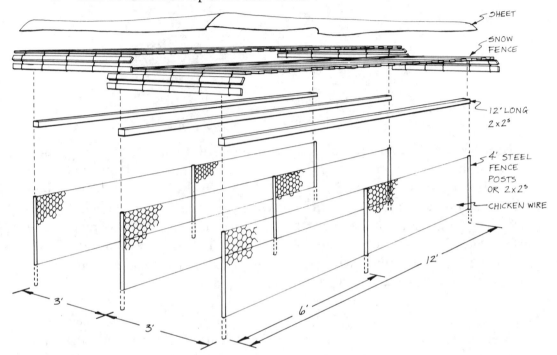

WIRE RACKS TO PROTECT YOUR PLANTS

You will rack up one success after another in the garden if you use lightweight, movable wire frames to achieve top results in both quality and quantity.

Handled properly, they soon become indispensable to any gardening program. They can be used for the following purposes:

- Keeping all wildlife away from the young, tender plants;
- Protecting the plants from early and late frosts, also from the midsummer sun by draping plastic or

light muslin over the racks;

● Training young plants by using the frames for scaffolding.

You can build them yourself quite easily, working out in the garden where they will be used. A pair of gardeners, equipped with wire nippers and pliers, can make and set up a 30-foot wire rack in as many minutes.

As the pictures show, they are simple tentlike frames made of 14-gauge galvanized wire. Two people can carry a finished 30-foot frame easily, setting it in place or moving it readily from one row to the next.

The cost is not low, but you can count on using them at least ten years. Moreover, if your garden's large enough, each rack will pay for itself yearly in rescued lettuce, peas, spinach, and beans.

But wire racks will do more than merely protect your garden from predatory vegetarians. Covered with lengths of plastic, they have served as effective, if temporary, greenhouses, protecting sensitive plants from both late and early frosts. And, sheathed with light muslin or cheesecloth, they have cast cooling shadows over entire rows of midsummer plantings.

Placed on each side of a row of young tomato plants or bush beans, a pair of frames offers excellent growing support. Keeping the foliage and fruit clear of the ground, they improve circulation of air and light and hold insect infestation to a minimum. When necessary, spread an extra layer of hay between the rows before setting the frames in place on top of the bedded-down mulch.

The wire comes in 25-, 50-, and 100-foot rolls, 3 or 4 feet wide, and with a variety of mesh sizes. The width is important because you will fold along the length to make your tent. A 4-foot width will make a tent with 2-foot sides that is 18 inches high. A 3-foot width makes a tent with 18-inch sides that is 13 inches high. Check the amount of growing room needed inside the frame before buying.

Properly made and used, these frames will last for years. They store quite easily over the winter, nesting one atop the other, making a neat stack and taking little room.

This is how you build the wire frames.

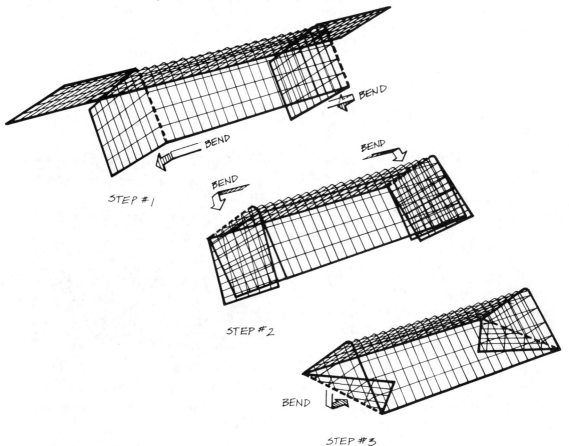

STEP #1

STEP #2

STEP #3

CONSTRUCTION

1. Bring the roll of wire to the site and check all measurements carefully, particularly the width of the rows.
2. Measure off the length of wire needed for one rack, adding 6 feet to the width of the row to allow for end flaps, plus clearance at each end of the row, and then cut. (A 20-foot row takes 26 feet of wire, a 30-foot row takes 36 feet, etc.)
3. Fold the length of wire down its middle, using a heavy straightedge

213

board or plank for a guide. Take your time and make an accurate, even fold with a 90-degree angle.

4. Using wire nippers, cut down the center fold to make end flaps. The flaps should be square. If the sides of the tent are 2 feet wide, cut 2 feet down the fold from each end. If the sides are 18 inches, cut 18 inches.

5. Fold down each end flap, using a thick, short board for template. Start at the end of the center cut and bend straight across to the edge. Each square flap should fit snugly over its mate when folded into position.

6. Bend the bottom of the flaps to make an even edge and an entrance-proof end which will keep small animals out. The entire frame should sit evenly and securely on the ground so that no intruder can work its way under it.

CABBAGE TENT

The way all those white moths were fluttering around his small garden, Elmer Holman of Denver, Colorado, knew he'd never get a 10-pound head of cabbage. Pesticides were out, so he built a simple nylon mini-tent. It protected his patch so well that he harvested 9- to 10-pound heads, as well as twenty varieties of vegetables.

He chose nylon because it has more body than cotton and has better staying power against the elements. The miniature tent was Holman's answer for protecting the postage-stamp-sized vegetable plot that he was al-

lowed as an apartment dweller. Those wanting to adapt his tent to a larger garden should sew together several widths of nylon.

CONSTRUCTION

1. Drive 2 x 2 wooden stakes 3 feet long at each end of the bed you wish to cover.

2. Nail a 2 x 2 board across the top of the stakes. To the top of each stake, extending to the ground, nail two 36-inch 1 x 1s to form a tent frame. Across the base of these, nail a 2 x 2.

3. Tack nylon mesh to the frame on all sides.

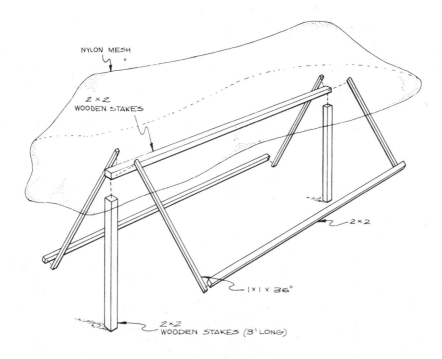

NYLON MESH

2 × 2
WOODEN STAKES

2 × 2

1 × 1 × 36"

2 × 2
WOODEN STAKES (3' LONG)

CHERRY TREE CAGES

You don't have to sit back and watch a customarily welcome flock of birds pick your cherry trees for you. Do like Californians Elmer A. Kulsar and his wife—build cheesecloth cages around your smaller cherry trees. That solution allows sufficient sunlight in and keeps hungry birds out, assuring a batch of cherry pies. It has been far more successful than the sometimes humorous attempts the Kulsars first made to protect their harvest. These included pie tins tied to trees, imitation owls, scarecrows, as well as rattling tin cans fastened to a slowly rotating motor. They even considered hanging a radio on a limb —presumably turned to a station that had very low ratings among cherry-snatching birds.

But with a good two weekends of

215

work and shelling out a surprisingly small amount of money, the couple was able to encase their 15-foot trees in cheesecloth. Through a mail-order catalog they secured enough cheesecloth to cover two Bing cherry trees: two bolts, each 90 feet long and 3 feet wide. When it comes time to install your frame and roll out the cheesecloth, wait for a windless day. Later on in the summer you'll find, as you eat cherry pie, that your attitude toward backyard birds has improved.

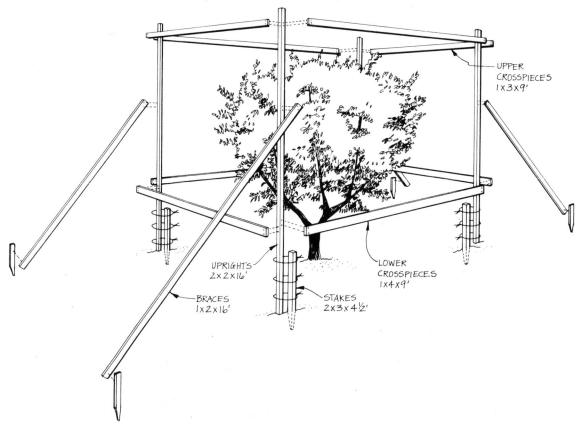

UPPER CROSSPIECES 1 x 3 x 9'

LOWER CROSSPIECES 1 x 4 x 9'

UPRIGHTS 2 x 2 x 16'

BRACES 1 x 2 x 16'

STAKES 2 x 3 x 4½'

CONSTRUCTION

1. To build a cage for one 15-foot tree, cut each of two 3-foot by 90-foot bolts of cheesecloth into thirds. Sew 3-foot widths together to make two sheets, each 9 feet wide by 30 feet long. Rip an old sheet into 6-inch strips and sew along edges of sheets.

2. Cut four 2 x 3 stakes each 4½ feet long. Drive the stakes into the ground at the corners of a square, 9 feet on a side, measured off around the tree. Some 3 feet of stake should be exposed.

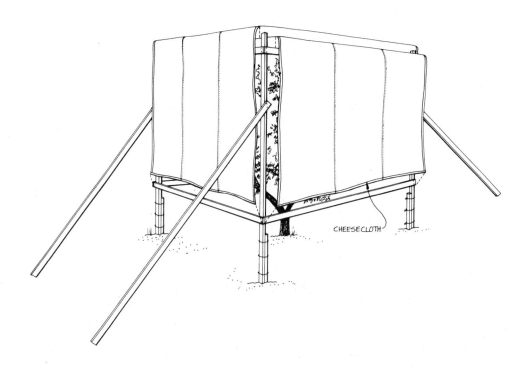

CHEESECLOTH

MATERIALS

Wood

2 pcs. 2 x 3 x 10'	or	**Stakes:** 4 pcs. 2 x 3 x 4½'
4 pcs. 2 x 2 x 16'	or	**Uprights:** 4 pcs. 2 x 2 x 16'
4 pcs. 1 x 3 x 10'	or	**Upper crosspieces:** 4 pcs. 1 x 3 x 9'
4 pcs. 1 x 4 x 10'	or	**Lower crosspieces:** 4 pcs. 1 x 4 x 9'
4 pcs. 1 x 2 x 16'	or	**Braces:** 4 pcs. 1 x 2 x 16'

Hardware

4d nails
72" of baling wire
½" staples

Miscellaneous

2 bolts of cheesecloth 3' x 90'

3. Lay out two 16-foot 2 x 2 uprights 9 feet apart. Lay a 9-foot 1 x 3 across one end of them and nail in place. Repeat the process to make the second side. Then erect the uprights tying each upright to a stake with several lengths of wire. Then nail two more 1 x 3s in place to complete the framing at the top of the cage.

4. Roll the cheesecloth sheets around a 10-foot length of pipe, gutter pipe, or wood. Then unroll it atop the erected frame and draw it into place so the ends are an equal distance from the ground. Staple the sides to the uprights. One sheet goes up one side, across the top, and down the opposite side. The second sheet encloses the two remaining sides, and makes a second layer on top.

5. Nail four 1 x 4s, cut to fit, to the 2 x 2s at the bottom of the cheesecloth, then staple the cheesecloth sheets to the 1 x 4. If necessary, enclose the remaining gap with chicken wire.

6. You will probably find it wise to brace each cage. Nail four 1 x 2s to the cage and to stakes driven into the ground.

A VARMINT FENCE

When Lesley and Marion Blanchard moved to their eight-acre homestead near Sedona, Arizona, they found that although their heavily mulched garden produced prodigiously all summer, they were able to harvest only a scant amount. The problem was predators: "Deer, porcupines, rock squirrels, chipmunks, trade rats, skunks, gray foxes, jackrabbits, range cattle, and birds," Mrs. Blanchard relates. "You name it, we have it."

The Blanchards live in "open range" country, which means that it's legally up to the homeowner to fence in his property against cattle, not up to the cattleman to keep his roaming herd within bounds. The cattle, porcupines, and squirrels were particularly destructive.

Refusing to surrender, the Blanchards designed a colossal cage 20 feet wide by 100 feet long to keep out the marauders. In this space Les planted sixteen dwarf fruit trees—peaches, pears, apples, apricots, plums, cherries, and prunes—all of which would mature at less than the 8-foot height of the cage. The trees were planted 10 feet apart, with vegetables occupying the rows between the trees.

Within two years, the apricot, peach, and apple trees were bearing heavily. Thanks to the cage, the fruit now belongs exclusively to the Blanchards, who no longer need battle the beasts and the birds for their tree-ripened harvest.

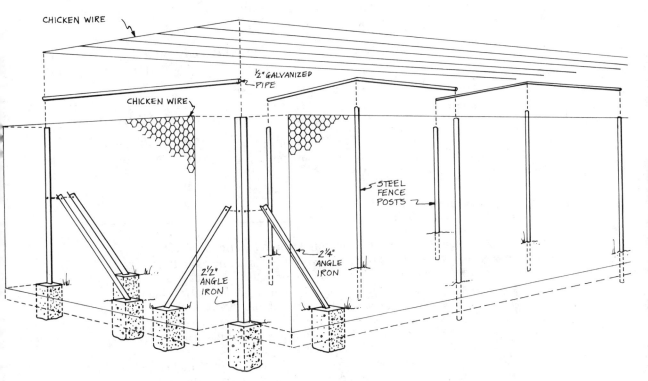

CONSTRUCTION

1. Measure the garden perimeter (keeping width 10 feet), mark the corners with stakes, and stretch a string between the stakes.
2. Stretch a string lengthwise down the center.
3. Space the outer posts 12 to 15 feet apart.
4. Use the center string to mark the position of the center posts. They should be in line with the outer posts.
5. At each mark and the corners dig a hole about 12 inches deep.
6. Between holes dig a narrow trench about 6 inches deep.

MATERIALS

Hardware

2 pcs. 18′ x 2½″ angle iron   or   **Corner posts:** 4 pcs. 9′ x 2½″

6 pcs. 18′ x 2″ steel posts   or   **Side post:** 12 pcs. 9′ long

6 pcs. 10′ x 2″ steel posts (center posts)

4 pcs. 12′ x 2¼″ angle iron   or   **Corner braces:** 8 pcs. 6′ x 2¼″

8–1″ x ¼″ bolts w/ nuts and washers

6 pcs. 12′ x ½″ ID galvanized pipe   or   **Overhead crosspieces:**
        6 pcs. 10′6″ x ½″ ID

2 pcs. 10′ x ½″ ID galvanized pipe (end crosspieces)

100′ 10-gauge galvanized wire

11 rolls 36″ x 100′ chicken wire

1 pc. 8′ x 2″ steel post   or   **Gate post:** 1 pc. 7′ long

Miscellaneous

Masonry concrete mix

7. Cut four pieces of 2½-inch angle iron 9 feet long for corner posts.
8. Mix cement. Place the 9-foot corner posts in corner holes and cement in place. Posts can be tied in vertical position until cement sets.
9. Assemble as many side uprights as needed, using 9-foot-long 2-inch steel posts. Place in holes and fill with dirt, tamping down well.
10. Set steel fence posts 10 feet long for center uprights in holes and fill with dirt, tamping down well. Then brace with dirt packed to a height of 12 inches around base of posts.
11. After corners are set, brace each corner with two 2¼-inch angle irons set in concrete. Fasten the braces to the uprights with 1-inch by ¼-inch bolts.
12. Overhead crosspieces are of ½-inch galvanized pipe cut 10½ feet long and bent to arch over taller center uprights.
13. End crosspieces are 10-foot sections of ½-inch galvanized pipe. The end crosspieces are not bent.
14. To fasten the crosspieces to the center posts to keep them from moving, run a length of 10-gauge galvanized wire down the center of the plot from one end to the other.
15. Starting at the center of the top, unroll 1-inch wire netting the length of the plot. Work your way down to the sides wiring each new row together.

16. Before beginning sides, decide where you want the gate. The best spot is next to an upright. Measure 3 feet from an upright and dig a 12-inch hole. Sink a 7-foot length of fence post into hole and fill with dirt. The 6-inch trench which runs between these posts (under the gate) should be filled with concrete.

17. Continue covering sides with 1-inch wire netting, but leave the gate opening uncovered.

18. The gate can be as plain or fancy as you like. Its purpose is to keep the varmints out.

ANOTHER VERSION OF THE CAGED GARDEN

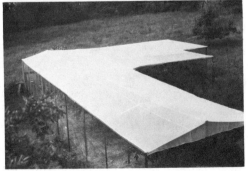

Another version of the caged garden, this one designed specifically to keep the birds away from Harold Norton's prize blueberry bushes in southern Connecticut, utilizes a 7½-foot-high framework of 1-inch, secondhand galvanized pipe. Side walls consist of 1-inch-mesh galvanized wire. To give the berries the diffused sunlight they like, Norton spreads tobacco canvas (heavy cheesecloth) over the top. The cloth is attached to the top sides of the framework by basting with sail twine and a large sail needle.

In this unit, the 1 x 2 crossmembers are joined at the center poles with two 4-inch pieces of 1 x 2. One inch from the top of the center poles, drill two ¼-inch holes 2 inches apart. Drill corresponding holes in the 1 x 2s and join the assembly with 3-inch stove bolts. Crossmembers are attached to outer poles by nailing them to 4-inch pieces of 1 x 2.

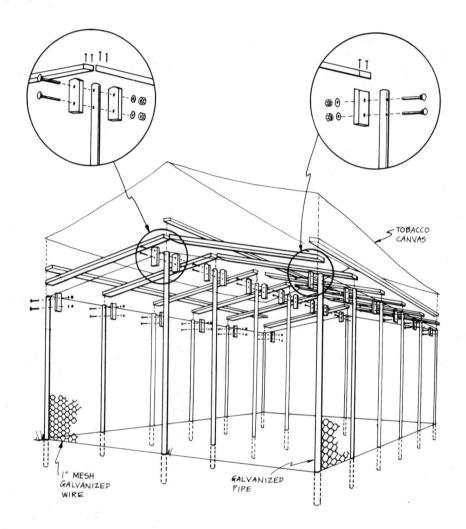

TOBACCO CANVAS

1" MESH GALVANIZED WIRE

GALVANIZED PIPE

TRAPS

The insect or varmint that never gets into the garden never harms the plants in it. For that reason, we've included the following trap projects, despite the fact that they weren't designed as plant protectors. They just happen to offer that benefit as a by-product.

DICK'S BUG MACHINE

Right now you're chuckling to yourself, imagining a machine that makes bugs. Go on and chuckle, but that's just about what this gizmo does.

When Gladys Geddes of Winsted, Connecticut, made up her mind to begin raising chickens, she was provoked enough by the high cost of feed to seek a new protein source for her poultry. Her husband Dick suggested insects, but collecting the quantity needed seemed more outrageous than the cost of the commercial feed. So he devised a machine that, although it's collecting them, seems to be manufacturing insects.

In brief, the machine works this way: Flying insects, attracted to a light, are sucked through a fan located next to the light, and are exhausted into a collection bag. Dick Geddes used materials he had on hand, and the machine didn't cost him anything. The fan is the biggest expense, and if you don't have one kicking around—and you probably don't—scout out a used or surplus one, since a new model will be expensive. The remaining materials are commonplace. Geddes used wood scraps, a peanut can, and a nylon stocking.

The nice thing about Dick's Bug Machine is that it doesn't really produce bugs and insects. It actually depletes the insect population. Mrs. Geddes noticed a marked reduction of green cabbageworms in her garden after the machine went into use. In fact, she has prodded her husband into making several more of the devices, not to produce more chicken feed, but to protect her garden plants.

The bug machine is operated at night, being turned on at sunset and off at dawn. The overnight collection is usually sufficient to satisfy the poultry. Blacklight bulbs were tried for daylight operation, but the catch was very poor.

Dick's Bug Machine

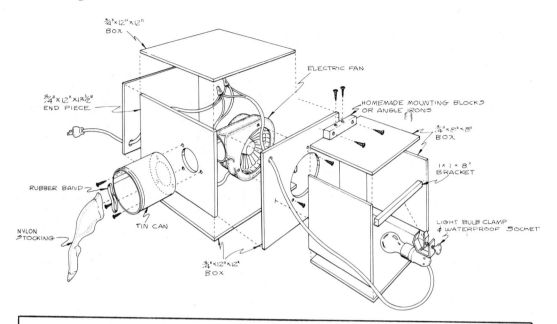

MATERIALS

Wood

1–2′ x 4′ sht. ¾″ ext. plywood	or	**Sides:** 4 pcs. 12″ sq.	
		End: 1 pc. 12″ x 13½″	
		Sides: 4 pcs. 8″ sq.	
1 pc. 1 x 1 x 2′	or	**Brace:** 1 pc. 1 x 1 x 8″	
		Mounting block: 1 pc. 1 x 1 x 4″	

Hardware

6d nails
3–½″ #6 screws
1 light bulb clamp and waterproof socket
1–40-watt light bulb
4–1″ #6 screws

Miscellaneous

1 electric fan, approx. 4½″ intake
1 tin can
1 nylon stocking
1 heavy rubber band

CONSTRUCTION

1. From ¾-inch plywood, cut four 12-inch-square pieces and a piece 12 inches by 13½ inches. Nail the square pieces together, forming an open-ended box, using 6d nails.

2. Measure the diameter of the fan intake and cut a hole that size in the center of one side of the box. Mount the fan in the box, intake against the hole cut for it, exhaust directed out one of the open ends of the box.

3. Place the remaining piece of plywood against the open end through which the fan exhausts. Mark the location and size of the exhaust on the plywood, then remove the plywood and cut out the exhaust hole. Cut a similar-sized hole in the bottom of the peanut can and secure it over the exhaust hole with three ½-inch #6 screws. Finally, nail the plywood to the box, using 6d nails.

4. Cut four 8-inch-square pieces of ¾-inch plywood. Nail them together, forming another open-ended box. Cut an 8-inch length of 1 x 1. Nail it across one open end of this box, so the light socket can be clamped to it, with the bulb inside the box.

5. Secure the light box to the fan box, using small corner irons or a home-made mounting, as shown in the photo.

6. Slip a nylon stocking over the exhaust pipe and secure it with a stout rubber band.

7. Plug in the light and fan. A 40-watt bulb will provide adequate light.

BOX TRAP FOR GREENHEAD FLIES

The salt marsh greenhead fly, *Tabanus nigrovittatus,* is an abundant and bothersome summertime pest along eastern coastal marshes. Because the female greenhead bites during daylight, and because of its high numbers, long flight range, and persistent attacks, these pests can limit one's enjoyment of gardening, picnics, and other outdoor activities throughout much of the summer.

Conventional methods of biting-fly control such as those used for mosquitoes, are either environmentally dangerous or economically impractical. Both adults and larvae of greenhead flies are large by comparison to other, nontarget organisms. In general, the larger the insect, the heavier the dose of insecticide needed to control it.

The box trap design was tested by Elton J. Hansens of Rutgers University and E. P. Catts of the University of Delaware in East Coast salt marsh areas. Their results indicate that it does capture greenhead flies in sufficient numbers (about 3,000 flies per day) to noticeably decrease the problem. The trap provides an ecologically safe, inexpensive, effective means of control. Traps should be set out during the last week in June and kept operational through August. Maintenance is simple. Tears or holes in the screens or sides should be patched or plugged. Trapped flies usually die in less than twenty-four hours. Removal of dead flies is unnecessary because they dry and decompose rapidly.

Trap location is quite important; success varies greatly between sites.

In general, traps should be placed on the marsh edge near the upland or along the open edge of wooded or shrubby areas. The best locations are at breaks, or openings of low vegetation in screening stands of trees or tall brush near the marsh. Clusters of two or three traps in a fly-path tend to capture more flies than the combined totals of isolated traps.

Vegetation beneath and around the trap should be kept low, 4 to 6 inches high, for about a 12-foot radius.

The trap is basically a black, four-sided box on legs, having a screen top and inverted **V**-shaped bottom. Flies enter the trap from below through an entry slot at the top of the **V**. The sides of the box can be made of nearly any kind of paneling, including plywood, cardboard, or plastic sheeting tacked to wooden framing.

The trap dimensions have been developed through experimental trial and error, and the builder should try to stick to the 16-inch by 32-inch dimensions—larger and smaller box traps were found to be less efficient. These dimensions allow five sides to be cut from a standard 4 x 8 panel with minimal waste, which is good to know if you are making more than one trap.

Following the guidelines established by Hansens and Catts, a box trap was constructed in the OGF Workshop. Here's how it was done.

CONSTRUCTION

1. Cut four 16-inch by 32-inch pieces of ½-inch exterior plywood. Form a box frame by butting two end pieces against two side pieces and nail it together using 6d nails. Cut two 2-inch-square pieces of 1-inch stock, then cut each in half on a diagonal, producing four triangular braces. Attach one in each corner of the box frame, at the top, using two 1-inch #6 screws.

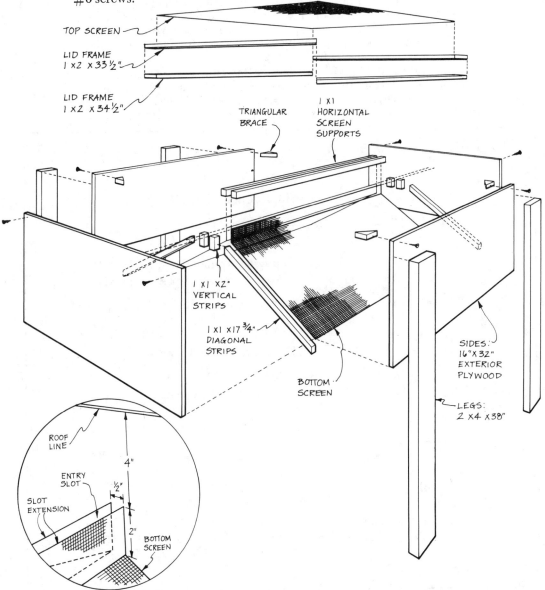

TOP SCREEN

LID FRAME
1 x 2 x 33½"

LID FRAME
1 x 2 x 34½"

TRIANGULAR BRACE

1 x 1 HORIZONTAL SCREEN SUPPORTS

1 x 1 x 2" VERTICAL STRIPS

1 x 1 x 17¾" DIAGONAL STRIPS

BOTTOM SCREEN

SIDES: 16" x 32" EXTERIOR PLYWOOD

LEGS: 2 x 4 x 38"

ROOF LINE

ENTRY SLOT

SLOT EXTENSION

4"

½"

2"

BOTTOM SCREEN

2. Working inside the frame, locate the vertical center line of the ends. Cut four 2-inch lengths of 1 x 1 stock. Using 1-inch brads, fasten two inside each end of the frame, locating them, as shown, 4 inches below the top and $\frac{1}{2}$ inch apart, parallel to the center line (one a $\frac{1}{4}$ inch to each side of the center line). Now measure from each vertical strip to the closest corner, as shown, and cut a strip of 1 x 1 to fit, mitering the butt ends to ensure a snug fit against the side of the vertical strip and in the frame corner. Each of these strips should be about 17$\frac{3}{4}$ inches long. Fasten in place with 1-inch brads. Finally, measure from vertical strip to vertical strip, across the box, and cut two horizontal screen supports from 1 x 1 and fasten in place, using the 1-inch brads. Each horizontal support should be about 31 inches long.

3. From 2 x 4 stock, cut four 38-inch legs. Attach them to the trap box, locating them 2 inches shy of the top edge of the box and positioning them with a broad face against the side of the box and flush with the corners. Drive several 4d nails through the box into each leg.

MATERIALS

Wood

1 sht. $\frac{1}{2}$″ ext. plywood	or	**Sides:** 4 pcs. 16″ x 32″
1 pc. 1 x 2 x 12′	or	**Corner braces:** 2 pcs. 1 x 2″ sq. (cut as indicated)
		Top screen frame: 2 pcs. 1 x 2 x 34$\frac{1}{2}$″ 2 pcs. 1 x 2 x 33$\frac{1}{2}$″
1 pc. 1 x 1 x 12′	or	**Vertical screen supports:** 4 pcs. 1 x 1 x 2″
		Side screen supports: 4 pcs. 1 x 1 x 17$\frac{3}{4}$″
		Horizontal screen supports: 2 pcs. 1 x 1 x 31″
1 pc. 2 x 4 x 14′	or	**Legs:** 4 pcs. 2 x 4 x 38″

Hardware

6d nails
8–1″ #6 screws
1″ brads
4d nails
Glue
Glossy black paint

1 pc. 36″ x 84″ metal insect screen	or	**Bottom:** 2 pcs. 32″ x 20″ **Top:** 1 pc. 34$\frac{1}{2}$″ x 33$\frac{1}{2}$″

Staples

4. Construct a frame to hold the top screening. Cut two 34½-inch lengths and two 33½-inch lengths of 1 x 2, making the cuts through the broad face of the stock on a 45-degree angle. Assemble the slightly over-square frame, using mitered corners, with glue and 4d nails.

5. Paint the trap inside and out with glossy black paint.

6. Once the paint has dried, cut metal (not plastic) insert screen to fit and staple it to the bottom edge of the 1 x 1 supports inside the trap. The screen should extend down the vertical strips and along the descending diagonals to the bottom edge of the frame. The two horizontal braces will hold the screen the proper ½-inch distance apart. Cut screen to fit over the top frame and staple it in place. Then carefully fit this screened lid over the open top of the box trap.

VARMINT TRAP

Some of the most destructive garden pests are the varmints: raccoons, groundhogs, rabbits, and their ilk. The night before you are going to harvest your sweet corn, the raccoons will do it for you. As your peas come up, the rabbits will nibble them to the ground. And the groundhog will move right into your bean patch.

Perhaps the best remedy is to shoot the varmints. But that's unsavory to many gardeners, who would prefer to trap the animal and free it far from the garden. For those people, here's an easily constructed trap, designed in the traditional style by Roy Dycus of Blue Ridge, Georgia.

The trap is a box with one end seemingly—to the varmint—open. When the victim enters the trap, enticed by the bait, it hits the trigger, releasing a sliding door, which closes, trapping the animal.

Dycus has made and used hundreds of these traps. He suggests that the bait be placed at the wire screen, so that the animal cannot avoid bumping the trigger if it is to get the bait. The following baits are recommended: for chipmunks, use peanuts or any other nuts; for squirrels, use dried corn or cracked hickory nuts; for other small rodents—including rats—use dried, shelled corn. Raccoons are drawn to fresh sweet corn. Skunks and opossums are baited using any meat. Use an apple slice for rabbits. And for any animal, use the food it is destroying as bait.

Dycus further recommends making the trap setting as natural as possible. Don't locate it in the open fields or in the garden, but rather place it in tall weeds, shrubbery, or trees at the edge of a woods. Rabbits particularly cannot be trapped in the garden. And Dycus says they are impossible to trap in summer.

CONSTRUCTION

1. From a 1 x 6 board, cut a 25-inch bottom, two 24-inch sides, and a 22-inch top. Using 6d nails, attach the bottom to the sides, making sure

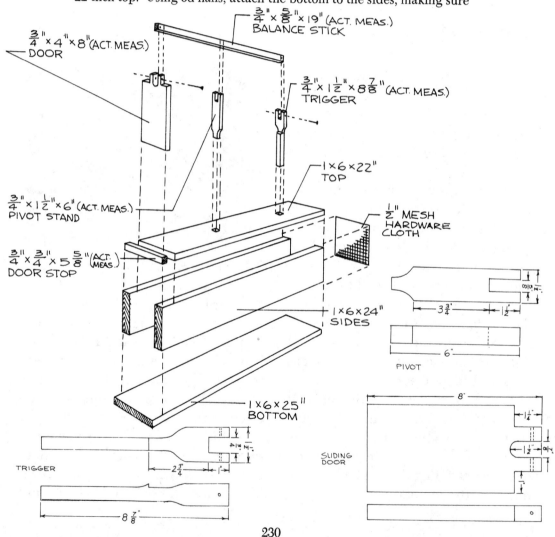

all three line up flush at one end of the box (to be the back). Nail the top in place.

2. Cut a 5-inch by 6½-inch piece of ½-inch mesh hardware cloth, and nail or staple it over the back opening of the box.

3. Drill a ¾-inch-diameter hole in the center of the top, 9 inches from the door end, for the pivot stand. Drill a ¾-inch-diameter hole in the center of the top, 4½ inches from the screened end, for the trigger.

4. Cut an 8-inch length of 1 x 6. Rip it into pieces 4 inches wide and 1½ inches wide. The 4-inch-wide piece is the door. Mark and cut the top of the door, as illustrated, using a backsaw, chisel, and file. The 1½-inch-wide piece is the pivot stand, which is shortened to a 6-inch length, tapered and rounded on one end, and notched on the other, as illustrated.

5. From the remaining length of 1 x 6, rip a 19-inch-long strip $\frac{5}{8}$ inch wide for the balance stick, a 5⅝-inch-long strip ¾ inch wide for the doorstop, and an 8⅞-inch-long strip 1½ inches wide for the trigger. Nail the doorstop in place across the tops of the sides, leaving sufficient clearance between the top and the stop for the door to slide very freely. Shape the trigger as illustrated, using saw, chisel, and rasp. Be sure to file the notch in the trigger shaft to hold it in the "cocked" position. Drill a small hole about a ⅛ inch in from the butt of each end of the balance stick. Drill matching holes through the notched ends of the door and trigger and fasten the three pieces together with small nails slipped through the holes.

MATERIALS

Wood

1 pc. 1 x 6 x 12'   or   **Bottom:** 1 pc. 1 x 6 x 25"

Sides: 2 pcs. 1 x 6 x 24"

Top: 1 pc. 1 x 6 x 22"

Door: 1 pc. ¾" x 4" x 8" (act. meas.)

Pivot stand: 1 pc. ¾" x 1½" x 6" (act. meas.)

Balance stick: 1 pc. ¾" x ⅝" x 19" (act. meas.)

Doorstop: 1 pc. ¾" x ¾" x 5⅝" (act. meas.)

Trigger: 1 pc. ¾" x 1½" x 8⅞" (act. meas.)

Hardware

6d nails
1 pc. 12" x 36" hardware cloth, ½" mesh   or   1 pc. 5" x 6½"

ARBORS

When the sun is too bright, you shade your eyes with your hand. A homemade arbor does the same—and more—for a sunburned gardener. A simply built wood and pipe arbor offers viny plants a place to wind, and it adorns in a natural way your backyard landscape. Figuratively speaking, you could call an arbor an "architectural tree." Literally, "arbor" is derived from the Latin word for tree. Practically, it provides shade for people and climbing places for vines. But technically, it is not a trellis nor a pergola. The former is a latticework used to support climbing plants; it may compose part of an arbor. The latter is actually an elaborate arbor; it usually consists of parallel collonades supporting an open roof of cross rafters. In all, the arbor offers the handy landscaper the easiest access into shading with plants.

232

With a hand shading your eyes, then, survey your property and decide where your arbor ought to be situated. Before planning construction, though, remember these secrets of backyard shading: Keep it light. Make it strong. Let the air blow through. The three arbors discussed in detail in this chapter present increasing levels of difficulty. But each should just outline a possibility, one adaptable to your terrain. Arbors are most often successful when they are combined with other architectural features. They can cover a walk, gate, garden bench, or terrace paving. New gardens particularly welcome an arbor to shield direct spring sun. Many arbors double as roofs for toolsheds, porches, or patios.

WEEPING MULBERRY ARBOR

There is a way to grow a living room in your backyard. All you need do is plant a weeping mulberry one year and build a simple "umbrella" arbor the next. The dense foliage and May-blooming berries, if properly trained and tied, will take the shape of the double **T**-shaped frame you've built, providing a shady outdoor retreat. When your arbor is overrun with mulberry vines, you can escape a hot gardening sun, eat a berry yourself, or watch birds pick away overhead, diverted from your cherry trees. The prodigious crop is spread over two-and-a-half months and begins the second year, so there will be plenty of berries left for pies and time for taking it easy outdoors. Make the arbor strong enough and you'll be able to enjoy your backyard living room for years.

Start your "room" by planting the tree correctly. If there is hard subsoil, drill through it with a 6-inch soil auger to allow the taproot to reach more deeply. Fill that hole with compost to give the mulberry a fighting chance even in concretelike soil. The first year an 8-foot stake is enough to train one or two of the strongest

mulberry canes upward. Weaker branches should be pinched back, then removed in the fall. Here's what you do in the second year.

CONSTRUCTION

1. Drive two 9-foot lengths of 1¼-inch outside diameter pipe into the ground 30 inches on either side of tree, leaving 6½ feet above ground.
2. Two feet from top of pipes drill ¼-inch holes clear through each.
3. Build two main horizontal arbor supports from 2 x 2 lumber, both 60 inches long.
4. Fashion an 8-inch-long dowel from a piece of 2 x 2, whittling it down so it will slip into the pipe. Nail the dowel to the support by driving a 16d nail through the support into the end of the dowel. Position the dowel in the middle of the support.
5. Brace each horizontal support with two 1 x 3 boards 36 inches long. Nail one brace to one side of the support, the other to the opposite side, as shown. Drill a hole through the braces and pipe, then insert a 16d nail through the hole.

6. Position five 2 x 2 by 72-inch crossmembers across the supports, spacing them evenly. Then nail them to the supports with 8d nails.

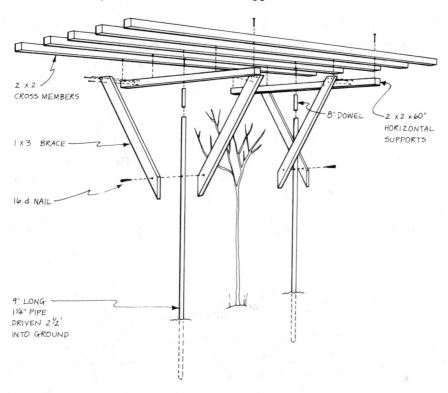

2 x 2 CROSS MEMBERS

1 X 3 BRACE

16 d NAIL

8" DOWEL

2 X 2 x 60" HORIZONTAL SUPPORTS

9' LONG 1¼" PIPE DRIVEN 2½' INTO GROUND

MATERIALS

Wood

3 pcs. 2 x 2 x 12'	or	**Horizontal supports:** 2 pcs. 2 x 2 x 60"
1 pc. 2 x 2 x 6'		**Dowels:** 2 pcs. 2 x 2 x 8" rounded
		Crossmembers: 5 pcs. 2 x 2 x 72"
1 pc. 1 x 3 x 12'	or	**Braces:** 4 pcs. 1 x 3 x 36"

Hardware

1 pc. 18' x 1¼" OD steel pipe   or   2 pcs. 9' long
16d nails
8d nails

WISTERIA ARBOR

The arbor pictured here is rectangular, but the shape—octagonal or round—is up to you. We have called this one a wisteria arbor, but you can grow roses, melons, or grapes on it. The name merely points up the fact that this arbor is more durably constructed than the one we have described for the weeping mulberry. If you are thinking about wisteria, you'll have to make sure your arbor is ready for the onslaughts of its twisting, powerful vines.

It is likely you will choose to make your arbor out of wood. If you do, then it's best to use redwood or cedar. If you use pine or fir, it should be treated with wood preservative. Creosote post bottoms only, or it will injure the vines. Any wood used for posts other than rot-resistant varieties should not be placed in the ground but be supported atop concrete footings.

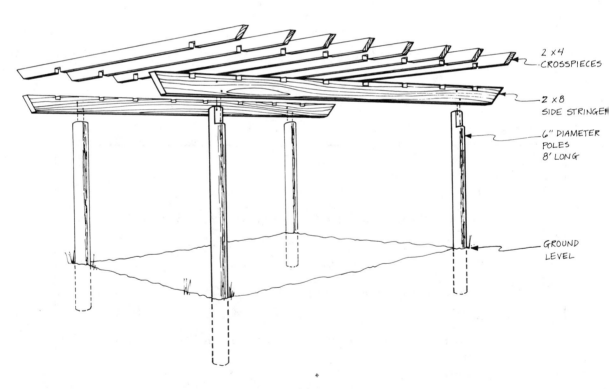

2 x 4
CROSSPIECES

2 x 8
SIDE STRINGER

6" DIAMETER
POLES
8' LONG

GROUND
LEVEL

CONSTRUCTION

1. Strip bark from four 6-inch-diameter cedar poles 8 feet long. This will discourage boring insects.
2. Cut a flat face, as shown, at top of each pole to receive 2 x 8 side stringers. Bevel the top of the post to aid it in shedding rain. Then erect the posts, sinking them 2 feet in the ground.
3. Cut off the ends of the 16-foot 2 x 8 stringers on a 45-degree angle, as shown. Cut eight dadoes on each stringer locating them on 18-inch centers, beginning 9 inches from either end. Each dado will be $1\frac{3}{4}$ inches deep by $1\frac{1}{2}$ inches wide. Spike the stringers to the posts with 16d nails.
4. Cut off the ends of the 2 x 4 crosspieces on 45-degree angles, as shown. Then lay the crosspieces in place, so they are in the dadoes and projecting equally on the outsides of the stringer. Mark the crosspieces for dadoes similar to those in the stringers; when completed, these dadoes will permit the crosspieces to rest flush with the top of the stringers. Cut the dadoes, then nail the crosspieces in place with 12d nails.

MATERIALS

Wood

    4 pcs. 6″ dia. x 8′ cedar posts

    2 pcs. 2 x 8 x 16′ (side stringers)

    8 pcs. 2 x 4 x 8′ (crosspieces)

Hardware

    16d nails
    12d nails

VARIATIONS

Your version of this arbor need not be quite as elaborately constructed. You could use 2 x 6 for the stringers and 2 x 3 for the crosspieces. Moreover, the dadoes aren't entirely necessary. If you don't have the power equipment to cut them, the alternative of cutting them with a saw and chisel is very time-consuming.

The arbor can be any size you desire or have room for. Modify the dimensions accordingly.

HIDEAWAY GARDEN ARBOR

A handy backyard homescaper can put together a cedar pole arbor in a weekend. A bit more sophisticated but only a little more expensive is a hideaway garden arbor. Two or three weekends of work will give your vines a place to climb and will give you a more formal retreat than the weeping mulberry arbor, described previously. Built large enough and against your home, it makes an airy addition that can accommodate a barbecue, book table, and easy chairs—as well as some sunlight.

Measurements are readily adaptable to the needs of your location. To give some of the boundaries in which your imagination can range, consider

the following construction plan. Then consider modifying it. Plant ivy for a shady corner. Temporary annual climbers with which you can adorn your garden arbor include red scarlet bean runners, sweet pea, moonflower, or pole beans.

CONSTRUCTION

1. With stakes and string, lay out a 6-foot by 14-foot area next to a house or other appropriate structure. Excavate a trench along two sides of the area, about 8 inches wide (or more) and 6 inches deep. Cover the bottom of the trench with 2 inches of sand.

2. Starting at the corner, lay blocks in a line toward the building, making a mortared joint between the blocks. Then lay blocks parallel to the building, butting the first block against the corner block of the other course, and again using a mortared joint. Backfill the trench around the blocks, so they project 3 or 4 inches above the ground line.

3. Position an 8-foot 4 x 4 post at each end of the longer course of block, and one in the center on the course. Slip the post into the hole in the block at the appropriate location, plumb it up, and fix it in place with temporary braces running from the post to stakes driven in the ground. Mix a small batch of concrete and pour it in the blocks around the posts.

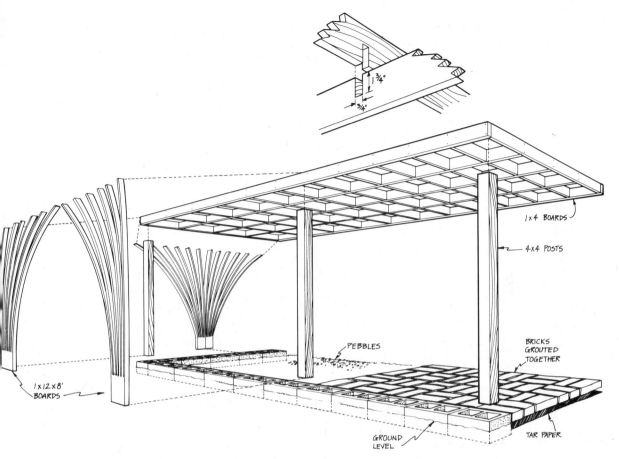

1 x 4 BOARDS

4 x 4 POSTS

PEBBLES

BRICKS
GROUTED
TOGETHER

1 x 12 x 8'
BOARDS

TAR PAPER

GROUND
LEVEL

4. \ Assemble the overhead framework. From 1 x 4s, cut eight 69-inch
lengths, two 14-foot lengths, and three 166½-inch lengths (1½ inches
less than 14 feet). Clamp the 69-inchers together and mark a line across
their collective edges 23¼ inches from each end and in the center
(34½ inches from either end). Lay two of these boards aside, as they will
be the end pieces in the frame. The others must be cut for a cross-lap
joint. The marks locate the centers of the cuts, which are ¾ inch wide
(⅜ inch on either side of the mark) and 1¾ inches deep, as shown. Hold
the boards together in alignment on edge and make the vertical cuts in
all at once, then knock the waste out of each board individually with a
hammer and chisel. Nail the 69-inchers between the 14-footers,
locating them on 2-foot centers. Slip the 166½-inchers into the notches
and mark them for the location of the similar notches that must be cut in
them. Pull these boards out, cut the notches, slip them back into place,
and nail them fast. Use 6d nails throughout this assembly.

5. Nail the completed framework to the top of the posts and to the side of
the building (using masonry nails if the building is of masonry construction). Make fan-shaped trellises from 8-foot 1 x 12 boards. Rip ½-inch-

wide strips from three boards, as shown. When cutting strips, saw lengthwise evenly but stop 1 foot from the bottom. Nail the trellis to post bottoms. Spread out the strips at top and nail each to overhead framework.

6. Cover floor area with tar paper to retard weeds. Lay bricks over part or all of the floor. Fill in remaining area with white river bottom stones or colored paving stones.

7. Give all wood surfaces two coats of paint.

MATERIALS

Wood

3 pcs. 4 x 4 x 8' pressure-treated posts

4 pcs. 1 x 4 x 12'	or	**Overhead framework:** 8 pcs. 1 x 4 x 69"
5 pcs. 1 x 4 x 14'	or	2 pcs. 1 x 4 x 14'
		3 pcs. 1 x 4 x 166½"

3 pcs. 1 x 12 x 8' (trellises)

Hardware

6d nails
6d masonry nails
1 roll (100 sq. ft.) tar paper or 2 pcs. 3' x 14' (enough to cover 6' x 14')
Paint

Miscellaneous

Sand
15–8" concrete blocks
Cement
Bricks
1 yd. white river stone

TRELLISES

A trellis is any support for a climbing plant. Trellises can be plain or fancy, permanent or movable.

For most organic gardeners, the trellis is a device to support tomato plants, heavy with fruit, or for bean vines to wind around. These gardeners are most interested in practical, durable trellises. And they've come up with quite a few different varieties.

For tomatoes, you can erect a cage of 1-inch by 2-inch or 2-inch by 4-inch turkey wire. Another trick is to lash pairs of furring strips together and set up whole batteries of tomato—or bean—trellises. Drop scrap poles of some sort into the small **V**'s that form when you spread the strips to straddle the rows to tie the pairs of strips together.

241

TOMATO-CUCUMBER TOWER

Most trellises leave something to be desired and after building all kinds, Warner Tilsher has settled on the simple permanent design shown. It can be used for tomatoes, cucumbers, or other fruiting climbers and vines.

Designed for three plants or three hills it can be set up or stored in a few minutes. Loose pins in the butt hinges allow the trellis to be put up and taken down quickly. An alternate method is to thread wire through the holes as shown in the detail illustration.

Plants or hills should be set on a 45-inch-diameter circle and located as indicated; this allows the plants on the south side to shade the ones in the rear. During the frequent hot spells in the California locale, the Tilshers protect the fruit on the south-facing plants from sunscald with a nylon net.

Usually they plant marigolds between the hills to minimize damage by nematodes, which occur in warm

climates and especially in lighter soils.

Irrigation is easily accomplished by making a circular depression and ponding until the water penetrates at least 42 inches.

Slats may be nailed to the trellis to help support the plants, but the Tilshers usually wind nursery twine around the tower as the plants grow.

CONSTRUCTION

1. Cut six 72-inch lengths and six 40-inch lengths from stock that measures a full (rather than a nominal) 1 inch by 1 inch. From ⅛-inch tempered Masonite, cut twelve 4-inch squares, then recut the squares so they taper evenly from a 4-inch width to a 1-inch width, as shown.
2. Assemble the three subunits of the trellis. Attach the lower crosspiece

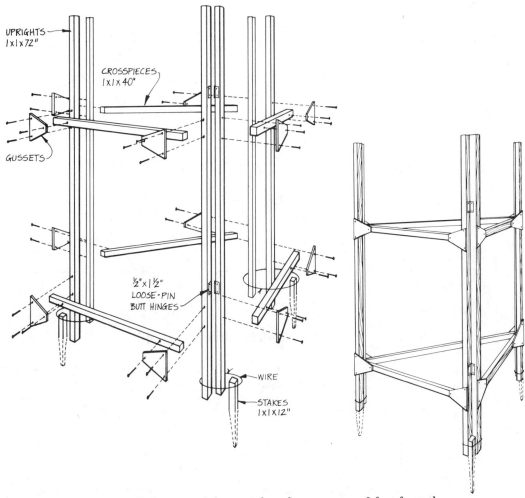

1 foot from the bottom of the uprights, the upper one 2 feet from the top of the uprights. Use a waterproof glue and 2d nails or 1-inch brads to fasten the Masonite gussets in place.

3. Attach loose-pin butt hinges to the subunits. The hinges are 18 inches from each end of the uprights. It's a good idea to lay out the subunits side by side in installing the hinges so the assembled units are in proper alignment.

4. To set up the tower, set the subunits together and slip the hinge-pins into place. Drive 12-inch stakes into the ground, leaving about 3 inches above the surface, at each foot of the tower, and loop a wire around the uprights and the stake.

5. *Optional:* Nail six sharpened 42-inch slats to poles, two on each side nailed 10 inches above one another beginning 10 inches above the lower cross stick.

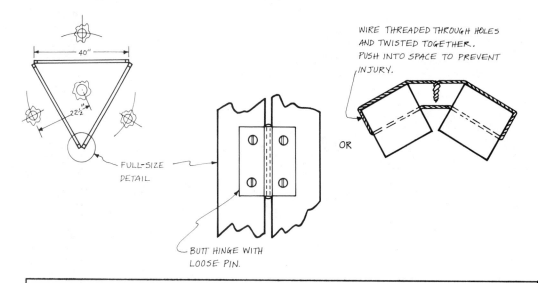

WIRE THREADED THROUGH HOLES AND TWISTED TOGETHER. PUSH INTO SPACE TO PREVENT INJURY.

OR

FULL-SIZE DETAIL

BUTT HINGE WITH LOOSE PIN.

MATERIALS

Wood

4 pcs. 1 x 1 x 12'	or	**Uprights:** 6 pcs. 1 x 1 x 72"	
1 pc. 1 x 1 x 10'	or	**Crosspieces:** 6 pcs. 1 x 1 x 40"	
		Stakes: 3 pcs. 1 x 1 x 12"	
1–2' x 4' sht. $\frac{1}{8}$" tempered Masonite	or	**Gussets:** 12 pcs. 4" sq.	

Hardware

Waterproof glue
2d nails
6–$\frac{1}{2}$" x 1$\frac{1}{2}$" loose-pin butt hinges
Wire

WIGWAM TRELLIS

Still another project from Tilsher's productive organic garden is this wigwam trellis. Actually a simpler version of the tomato tower already described, the wigwam provides 6 feet of climbing space for cucumbers or other kinds of plants such as luffas. Instead of three hinged parts, two units are fastened with wire. They spread to suit your bed width and dismantle for off-season storage.

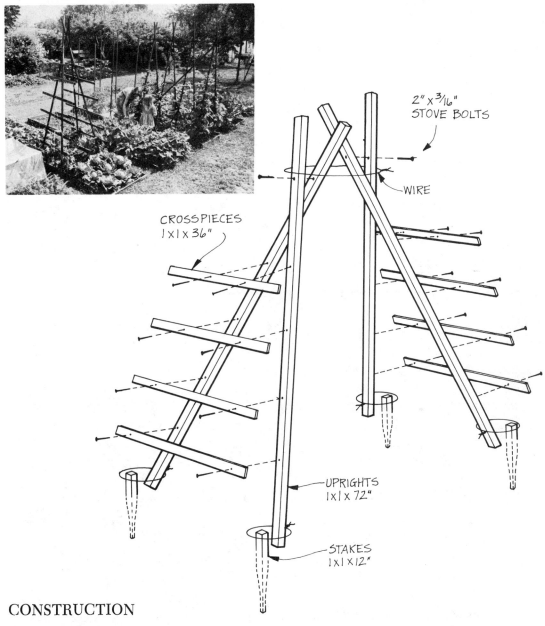

CONSTRUCTION

1. Make each wigwam unit, as shown, by connecting two 1 x 1 by 72-inch poles with a $\frac{3}{16}$-inch stove bolt 5 feet from pole bottoms.

2. With brads nail four 1 x 1 by 36-inch crosspieces to each wigwam as follows: nail the first 1 foot from base; make next three 10 inches apart. Make sure base is 3 feet wide.

245

3. Connect two wigwams at apex with wire.
4. Pound 1 x 1 by 12-inch sharpened stakes into ground and attach to poles with wire.

MATERIALS

Wood

2 pcs. 1 x 1 x 12′	or	**Uprights:** 4 pcs. 1 x 1 x 72″
2 pcs. 1 x 1 x 12′	or	**Crosspieces:** 8 pcs. 1 x 1 x 36″
1 pc. 1 x 1 x 4′	or	**Stakes:** 4 pcs. 1 x 1 x 12″

Hardware

2–2″ x $\frac{3}{16}$″ stove bolts w/ nuts and washers
$1\frac{1}{4}$″ brads
Wire

TENT TRELLIS

You can get your pole beans to "camp out" happily in your garden by building a tent trellis. This simple framework is not a permanent backyard fixture. The $\frac{3}{16}$-inch bolts act as hinges which allow easy set up and storage.

Tilsher designed this trellis especially for his box beds, but it serves just as well on ordinary planting beds. Dimensions are, of course, adaptable to the climbers you choose to plant. The Tilshers use it primarily for pole varieties such as Kentucky Wonders and climbing limas. Horizontal slats can be added. When using a small 3-foot by 6-foot box bed, space beans 20 inches apart. Construction suggestions that follow are outlined according to a bed of that size.

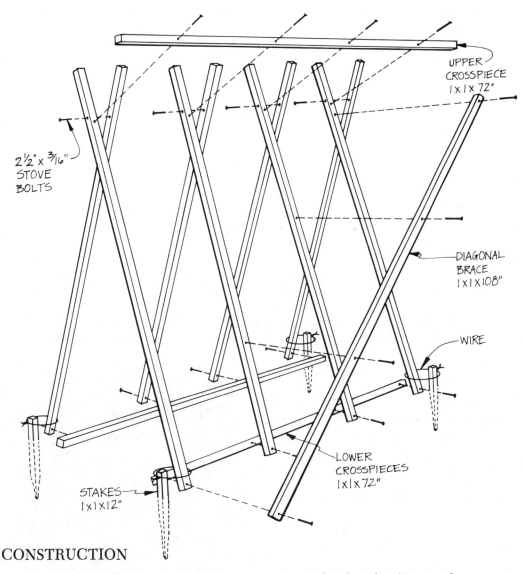

UPPER
CROSSPIECE
1 x 1 x 72"

2½" x ³⁄₁₆"
STOVE
BOLTS

DIAGONAL
BRACE
1 x 1 x 108"

WIRE

LOWER
CROSSPIECES
1 x 1 x 72"

STAKES
1 x 1 x 12"

CONSTRUCTION

1. Make each of four "tents" by connecting two 8-foot lengths of 1 x 1 with $\frac{3}{16}$-inch stove bolts 7 feet from the base, as shown.

2. Set up the four tents, spacing them 20 inches apart. Nail with brads a 1 x 1 by 72-inch crosspiece at the hinge point to brace the tents and to tie them together. Do the same with two other crosspieces to inside of poles at their base. Leave 6 inches on either end of the crosspieces.

3. Nail on a 1 x 1 by 108-inch diagonal brace, as shown.

4. Anchor trellis with four 1 x 1 by 12-inch sharpened stakes attached at corners with wire.

MATERIALS

Wood

8 pcs. 1 x 1 x 8' (tents)

2 pcs. 1 x 1 x 10'   or   **Upper crosspiece:** 1 pc. 1 x 1 x 72"

Diagonal brace: 1 pc. 1 x 1 x 108"

Stakes: 4 pcs. 1 x 1 x 12"

1 pc. 1 x 1 x 12'   or   **Lower crosspieces:** 2 pcs. 1 x 1 x 72"

Hardware

4–2$\frac{1}{2}$" x $\frac{3}{16}$" stove bolts w/ nuts and washers
1$\frac{1}{4}$" brads
Wire

A HOUSE-SIDE TRELLIS

After two summers of gardening on their small city lot, Al and Jane Wonch began to discuss putting a trellis on the south side of the house. They thought the trellis would increase their gardening yield. Also the vines on the trellis would shade the south wall from the searing summer sun.

At first they were thinking along the lines of a rose trellis attached to the exterior of the house, but a carpenter friend, Don Franz, suggested that they run the support most of the way across the wall and use chain link fence for the trellis. After some measuring, they decided they could have a trellis about 18 feet long by 10 feet high.

To avoid possible structural damage to the house or trellis, Franz recommended that they hang the fence from 4 x 4s run into the attic and anchored to the ceiling joists.

Based on one year's experience, Wonch says the design is good. "Though we often have 35- to 40-mile-per-hour winds—and occasionally 60 miles per hour or more—we've had no wind damage to the trellis, even when it was carrying a full load of vines," he said. "We also achieved the desired shading which markedly reduced the temperature in the two south bedrooms."

CONSTRUCTION

1. The first construction step is determining the position for the two 4 x 4s. Cut 3½-inch-square holes on 6½-foot centers through the wall of the house. The holes are cut so their bottoms align with the top of the ceiling joists.

2. After cutting these holes, push the 8-foot 4 x 4s through the holes, positioning them to allow a 36-inch clearance after a 2 x 4 is bolted to the ends.

3. The 4 x 4s are anchored to the ceiling joists with truss anchors. These anchors have prepunched nail holes and are preformed to fit around the 4 x 4 and over the ceiling joist. Each 4 x 4 is anchored to three ceiling joists.

4. After anchoring the 4 x 4s, position an 18-foot 2 x 4 to the ends of the 4 x 4s, and nail it in place. Using a ⅜-inch spade bit and a variable speed drill, bore two pilot holes in through the 2 x 4 and into the end of each 4 x 4 for 6-inch by ½-inch lag bolts. Countersink the lag bolts into the 2 x 4 so the bolt heads won't interfere with the fence or a second 2 x 4, which will help anchor the fence. A ½-inch washer prevents the lag bolt from digging into the wood. With the lag bolts tightened, the support structure for the trellis is complete.

5. Install the fencing. A 12-foot by 18-foot piece of 11-gauge, 2-inch-mesh galvanized chain link fence makes a roll about 18 inches in diameter, weighing about 75 pounds. You will need at least two people to position the fence against the 2 x 4, while a third person staples it to the 2 x 4. When the fence is stapled to the 2 x 4, drill holes and, using ten

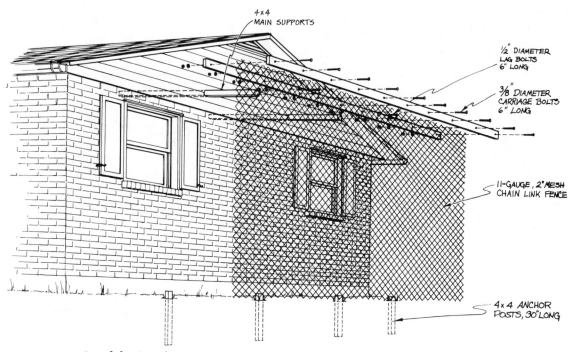

6-inch by $\frac{3}{8}$-inch carriage bolts, fasten a second 2 x 4 against the fence and to the 2 x 4 which is attached to the 4 x 4s.

6.   If necessary, use bolt cutters to remove excess mesh from the bottom of the fence. This is a tedious task requiring care to assure that the same

MATERIALS

Wood

2 pcs. 4 x 4 x 8' (main supports)

2 pcs. 2 x 4 x 18' (fence supports)

1 pc. 4 x 4 x 10'   or   **Ground anchors:** 4 pcs. 4 x 4 x 30"

Hardware

6 truss anchors
12d nails
4–6" x $\frac{1}{2}$" lag bolts
4–$\frac{1}{2}$" ID flat washers
1 pc. 12'x 18' 11-gauge 2" mesh galvanized chain link fence
Staples
10–6" x $\frac{3}{8}$" carriage bolts w/ nuts and 2 washers ea.
Exterior sealing caulk

mesh is cut. The cut ends should be bent double to prevent unraveling of the fence.

7. To secure the bottom of the fence, dig holes and position four 30-inch 4 x 4s below the fence. After the 4 x 4s are firmly tamped in, staple the fence to the outside of the 4 x 4s. This is stronger than stapling to the tops.

8. To complete the job, use exterior sealing caulk to seal the opening between the house siding and the 4 x 4s.

GRAPE TRELLIS FOR THE SMALL VINEYARD

If you're planning on grapes you'll soon have to design and build a trellis. This trellis consists of two 9-gauge wires stretched between posts set 9 feet apart, with a grape plant between each post. The bottom wire is 30 inches above the ground with the top wire 24 inches above the bottom wire.

CONSTRUCTION

1. Set four 8-foot redwood 4 x 4s in 3-foot holes, located 9 feet apart. Use a level to keep the posts straight and a line level to align the post tops. (Eyeball leveling the post tops in relation to the bed's topography would be adequate and much easier.)

2. After the posts are straight, backfill around the posts, adding a small amount of water to settle the soil. (Use caution—don't add so much water you form mud. Mud won't support the post and you'll have a long wait until the mud dries.)

3. Measure out the points where the trellis wires attach. Measure from the soil line up 30 inches to the bottom wire, then up another 24 inches to the top wire. Drill a $\frac{5}{16}$-inch hole.

4. Place a 1½-inch outside diameter washer with a ¼-inch hole over a 5-inch by ¼-inch eyebolt. Tap an eyebolt through both holes in both end posts. Put on a second washer and secure the eyebolt with a ¼-inch nut.

251

Grape Trellis

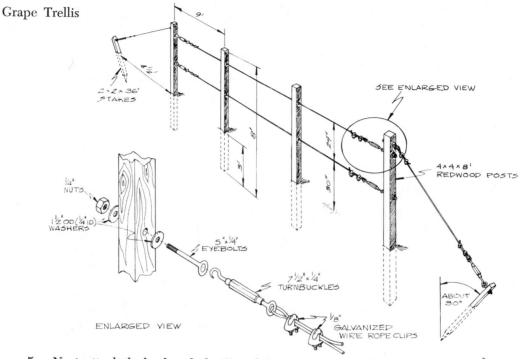

ENLARGED VIEW

5. Next, attach the hook end of a $7\frac{1}{2}$-inch by $\frac{1}{4}$-inch turnbuckle to the eyebolt in the post. Then thread 9-gauge galvanized steel wire through the eyebolt end of the turnbuckle and secure it with two $\frac{1}{8}$-inch galvanized wire rope clips.

6. Drive a 36-inch 2 x 2 stake into the ground about 4 feet beyond the end posts. To increase the stake's holding capacity, angle the stake toward the post. Run a strand of the steel wire between the end post and a turnbuckle attached to the stake. Twist the turnbuckle until the end post is securely braced. Adjust the turnbuckle to take up the slack in the trellis wire.

MATERIALS

Wood

4 pcs. 4 x 4 x 8' redwood (posts)

1 pc. 2 x 2 x 6' redwood   or   **Stakes:** 2 pcs. 2 x 2 x 36"

Hardware

16–$1\frac{1}{2}$" OD ($\frac{1}{4}$" ID) washers
8–5" x $\frac{1}{4}$" eyebolts w/ nuts
6–$7\frac{1}{2}$" x $\frac{1}{4}$" turnbuckles
75' 9-gauge galvanized steel wire
16–$\frac{1}{8}$" galvanized wire rope clips

ORCHARD AND WOODLOT AIDS

The ideal homestead has a few fruit trees, maybe a nut tree or two, and a woodlot. Caring for these trees can be eased with some handy aids that you can make yourself.

A fruit picker will speed harvesting those standard-sized trees. A truss ladder will be a help anytime you need to get up into the branches, whether it be to prune or to harvest. The sawbuck, the log holder, and the log cart will serve those with fireplaces and wood-burning stoves to feed.

In each case, the problem solving is an opportunity for the homestead handyman to show off his skills.

FRUIT PICKER

When your fruit trees are ready for picking, don't get a stiff neck staring up at the crop. Don't break your neck climbing up to pick apples or pears. And don't settle for bruised or over-ripe fruit because you waited until it hit the ground. Try this old-time remedy—make your own fruit picker. Once you get the knack of operating this homemade gadget, you may out-strip a champion hand-picker. The key to quickly snipped, unspoiled fruit is the length of your pole and sleeve.

Fruit Picker

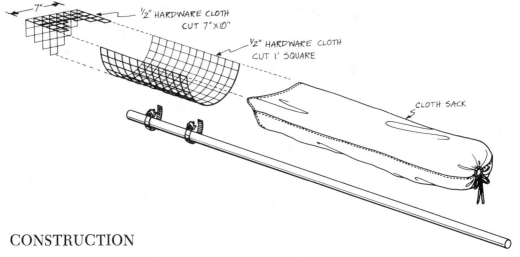

CONSTRUCTION

1. Cut a 1-foot-square piece of $\frac{1}{2}$-inch hardware cloth, and a 7-inch by 10-inch piece of $\frac{1}{2}$-inch hardware cloth.

2. Cut the smaller piece into an "arrow" shape with a notch on one 7-inch end and a tapered point on the other.

3. Form the square piece into a **U**-shaped trough. Using thin wire, fasten the smaller piece to the top of the trough, folding the "point" to enclose one end.

4. Using 1-inch hose clamps, fasten the resulting hardware cloth basket to an 8- to 10-foot pole.

5. Cut the muslin in half, forming a sleeve of each piece, then sew the two together to form one long sleeve. Hem one end and attach to the hardware cloth basket. Sew a large hem in the bottom, with drawstrings. This will permit you to collect in the sleeve.

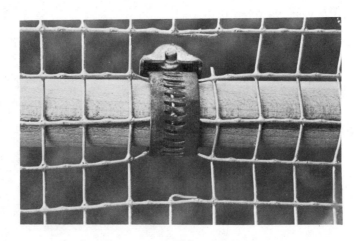

MATERIALS

Wood

    1 pc. 8' to 10' x ½" dowel (pole)

Hardware

    1 pc. 24" x 36" hardware cloth, ½" mesh   or **Basket:** 1 pc. 12" sq.

                                                              1 pc. 7" x 10"

    Wire

    2–1" hose clamps

Miscellaneous

    2 yds. muslin

TRUSS LADDER

A sturdy ladder is an invaluable orchard and woodlot tool, but it is also a fairly expensive tool. This truss ladder will not only shave that expense, it will be a challenging woodworking project for any homestead handyman. And its use doesn't need to be restricted to the orchard and woodlot.

This ladder was constructed, following an old design, using 1 x 2 material. The rungs should be hardwood; the uprights can be either hardwood or softwood. Ours was made 10 feet tall; but the design is adaptable for any length, 8 feet or 14 feet.

Just be sure to keep the bolts tight.

Truss Ladder

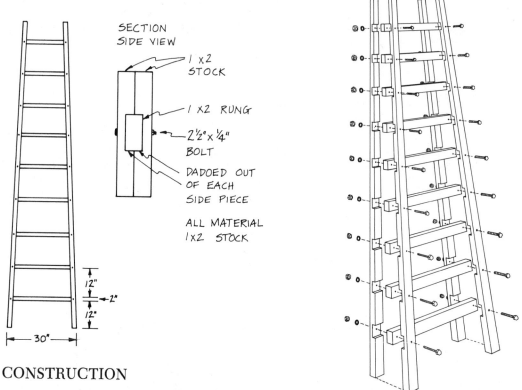

SECTION
SIDE VIEW

1 x 2
STOCK

1 x 2 RUNG

2½" x ¼"
BOLT

DADOED OUT
OF EACH
SIDE PIECE

ALL MATERIAL
1 x 2 STOCK

12"

2"

12"

30"

CONSTRUCTION

1. Rough cut the rungs from 1 x 2 hardwood. You will need two 18 inches long, two 20 inches long, two 24 inches long, one 27 inches long, and two 30 inches long. If you are using 12-foot lengths of hardwood to construct the ladder, cut 2 feet off each of four boards, making four rungs and the uprights. A fifth 12-footer will yield the remainder of the necessary rungs.

MATERIALS

Wood

5 pcs. 1 x 2 x 12′ hardwood   or   **Uprights:** 4 pcs. 1 x 2 x 10′

Rungs: 2 pcs. 1 x 2 x 18″
2 pcs. 1 x 2 x 20″
2 pcs. 1 x 2 x 24″
1 pc. 1 x 2 x 27″
2 pcs. 1 x 2 x 30″

Hardware

18–2½″ x ¼″ machine bolts w/ nuts and 2 washers ea.

2. Layout is half the battle in this project. Since the uprights are converging, the dadoes for the rungs must be cut on a slight angle. To determine the angle, lay out two of the uprights on your shop floor, the bottom ends 30 inches apart, the tops 12 inches apart. To ensure that all is level and plumb, you should lay out the uprights in relation to a center line, whether it be an imaginary one or an actual chalk line drawn on the shop floor, and a bottom line—one perpendicular to the center line. Measure up 12 inches along the center line and lay the first rung (a piece of 1 x 2) across the two uprights, making sure—through the use of a framing square—that it is perpendicular to the center line. Mark the uprights above and below the rung for the dado. Measure 12 inches up along the center line from the top of that first rung to the bottom of the second rung. Lay it in place and mark the uprights for dadoing. Keep repeating the process until the uprights are marked for all nine rungs. Since you need four uprights altogether, mark a second pair, using the first pair as patterns. If you think about it, you'll see that the uprights are not exactly alike. Rather they are mirror images, so don't lay out one upright and use it as a pattern for the other three.

3. Cut all the dadoes, making them $\frac{3}{8}$ inch deep.

4. Lay out the uprights again, this time across sawhorses. Put the rungs in place and lay the second pair of uprights atop them. Now drill a $\frac{1}{4}$-inch hole through each joint of rung and uprights. Fasten the joints with $2\frac{1}{2}$-inch by $\frac{1}{4}$-inch machine bolts, each with two washers.

5. After the ladder is completely assembled, trim off the excess rung material.

SAWBUCK

Here's an extra set of hands to use while cutting firewood. Most sawbucks take up too much room in the toolshed. Some have a metal bar in the center for support, which always seems to dull your saw. But this one is great! No metal parts exposed which can dull your saw; and it helps conserve space in the shed by folding to a nice compact size.

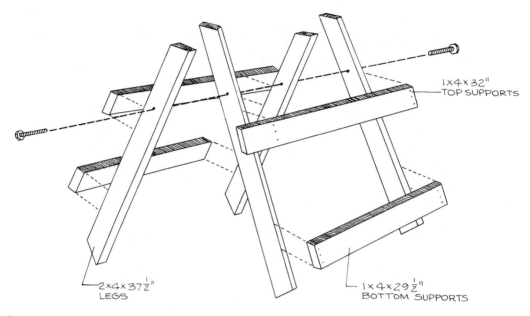

1×4×32"
—TOP SUPPORTS

2×4×37½"
LEGS

1×4×29½"
BOTTOM SUPPORTS

CONSTRUCTION

1. The legs, or crosspieces, should first have an angle cut in the base so the buck will stand squarely on the ground.
2. Nail the pieces together for the two frames as shown. Two 2 x 4s are positioned 29½ inches apart, the full length of the bottom supports. Notice that the top support extends beyond one crosspiece by 2½ inches. This overhang is where the crosspiece from the other side will rest. It is important that the top of the top support be 10½ inches from the top of the crosspieces.
3. Stand the two frames 30 to 36 inches apart at the base and tip the tops inward until they meet. The crosspiece should rest on the top support

MATERIALS

Wood

1 pc. 2 x 4 x 14′	or	**Legs** (crosspieces): 4 pcs. 2 x 4 x 37½″
1 pc. 1 x 4 x 12′	or	**Bottom supports:** 2 pcs. 1 x 4 x 29½″
		Top supports: 2 pcs. 1 x 4 x 32″
		Cover blocks: 2 pcs. 1 x 4 x 2½″

Hardware

6d nails
2–3″ x ¼″ carriage bolts w/ nuts and washers

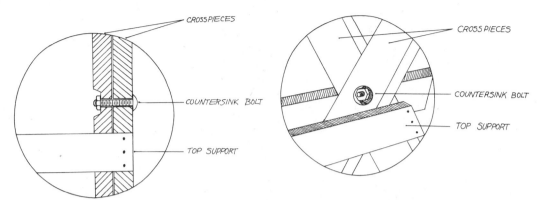

CROSSPIECES

CROSS PIECES

COUNTERSINK BOLT

COUNTERSINK BOLT

TOP SUPPORT

TOP SUPPORT

of the opposite frame and be flush against the opposite crosspieces. Drill a hole for a carriage bolt to join the crosspieces of the two frames and bolt. This fitting should be slightly loose so the sawbuck can fold on this joint.

4. To keep from dulling your saw on the carriage bolts, cut two small 2½-inch blocks out of 1 x 4-inch scrap. Drill a hole in the center of each block big enough to fit over the protruding nut and bolt, but don't go all the way through. Nail the block in place so no metal is exposed.

HANDY WOOD-SPLITTING STAND

While splitting wood is always good exercise, it is also tough work. This easily constructed log-holding device can make wood splitting a mite easier.

To use the wood-splitting stand most effectively, cut chunks upside down (in the opposite direction from which it grew). Split slabs by hitting wood chunks near the edge rather than cleaving through the center. By following these hints, you will be able to cut wood more easily. All that is needed to make an old-fashioned wood-splitting stand on which chunks are placed is one 8-foot piece of 2 x 8 and some nails.

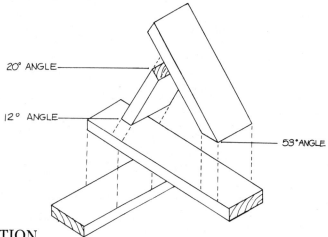

20° ANGLE

12° ANGLE

53° ANGLE

CONSTRUCTION

1. Cut the 8-foot 2 x 8 as follows: one 36-inch piece, one 12-inch piece, one 28-inch piece, and one 20-inch piece.

2. On one end of the 12-inch piece cut a 20-degree angle; cut a 12-degree angle on the other. Then cut a 53-degree angle on one end of the 28-inch piece. This is most easily done with a power saw, but it can be done with hand tools. Using a combination square or a sliding **T** bevel and a protractor, mark the angle on both edges of the board; then mark across the face of the board with a try square. A scrap of wood can be clamped or nailed (temporarily) to the face of the board to help guide the saw at the proper angle.

3. Assemble using the 12-inch piece as the upright and the 36-inch piece for the base. The 28-inch piece is the upright brace and the 20-inch piece is the cross brace. Nail all pieces with 8d nails.

4. Drive 20d nails in the upright brace and base until about 1 inch is showing. Cut off heads and file to dull points.

MATERIALS

Wood

1 pc. 2 x 8 x 8'   or   Base: 1 pc. 2 x 8 x 36"

Cross brace: 1 pc. 2 x 8 x 20"

Upright brace: 1 pc. 2 x 8 x 28"

Upright: 1 pc. 2 x 8 x 12"

Hardware

8d nails
20d nails

FIREWOOD CART

The Robert Branch family of Waterford, Connecticut, uses a lot of wood in the course of a winter. To ease the chore of getting out and bringing in a load of wood when the weather's just right, Branch built the firewood cart. It carries enough wood for a full day's supply and is so neatly balanced that even a small child can pull it. With balloon tires, it pulls especially well up stairways too. This may be just the thing you've been looking for to get wood up to the up- stairs bedroom fireplace or stove for those chilly winter nights.

The Branches like to stack the first logs upright in the bottom of the cart for easy unloading. It saves some bending. Otherwise, just fill the re- maining space with logs on their side and hoist away!

Branch scrounged all his materials, but you can change these plans to fit what you have available.

CONSTRUCTION

1. Once you have cut all pieces to size as listed, cut a $\frac{5}{16}$-inch-deep dado into the inside of the two side pieces of plywood, 1 inch from the bot- tom and parallel to it. The cut should be $\frac{5}{8}$ inch wide, the thickness of the bottom panel. Now slip the bottom into the grooves you have just made for them and glue and screw with $1\frac{1}{4}$-inch #10 screws.

2. Tack and glue the front in place, keeping the top edges flush, with either 4d nails spaced 4 inches apart or 1-inch #10 screws 6 inches apart. Notice that the sides are 1 inch longer at the bottom than the front and back. It's meant to be that way as a place to attach the axle.

3. So the handle braces will fit snugly to the cart, cut a rabbet $\frac{1}{4}$ inch deep by 1 inch wide halfway up the brace. If you use a table saw or radial arm saw for this, you will have to square off the cut with a chisel. Drill a hole an inch or two from the top of the handle braces just the right size for the broomstick handle to fit snugly into; drill both holes at the same time. Screw the glued handle braces in place with $1\frac{1}{4}$-inch #10

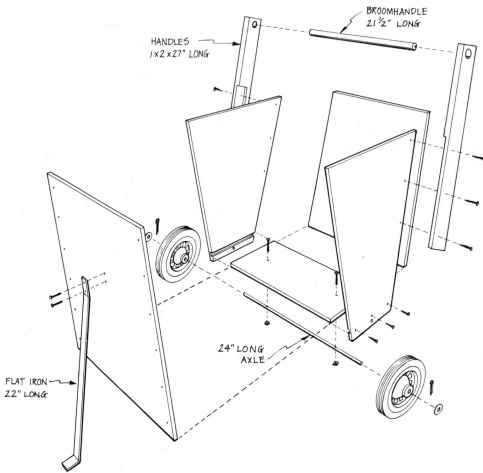

BROOMHANDLE
21½" LONG

HANDLES
1 x 2 x 27" LONG

24" LONG
AXLE

FLAT IRON
22" LONG

screws. Place the broomstick in the handle braces and tack through the edge of the braces into the handle with 1¼-inch brads.

4. Installing the wheels is a simple task. Drill a hole the diameter of your axle through the 1-inch side overlap extending beyond the bottom of the cart. Drill it as close to the bottom as possible so that the axle will fit snugly next to the bottom of the cart for support once it has been inserted through the holes just drilled. Place the axle through these holes and, leaving adequate room on either end for the wheels, fix the axle in place with two nuts and bolts. To do this, drill a hole through the bottom of the cart and through the axle. Slip a bolt through from the inside, and secure with a nut. To attach the wheel, first put a washer on the axle, then the wheel and finally another washer. Drill a small hole through the axle right next to the last washer. A cotter pin fits in here to keep the wheel from sliding off. Now do the other wheel. Don't forget to bend the cotter pins open.

5. Prebend a 22-inch piece of flatiron 2 inches from either end (see diagram). Drill two holes through one 2-inch bend for the bolts which

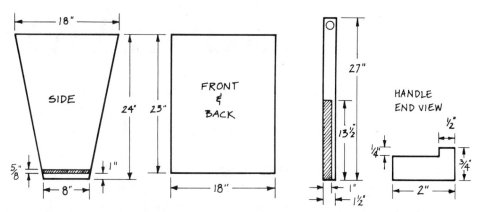

will secure the brace to the cart. Tilt the cart slightly off square toward the front (away from handles). Put the brace in place and mark. Drill holes through the front of the cart as if continuing drilling through the bar. Place bolts through the holes from the outside and secure on the inside with appropriate nuts.

MATERIALS

Wood

1–4' x 4' sht. ⅝" ext. plywood	or	**Sides:** 2 pcs. 18" x 24" (see dia.)
		Front and back: 2 pcs. 18" x 23"
		Bottom: 1 pc. 8¼" x 17⅜"
1 pc. 1 x 2 x 6'	or	**Handle braces:** 2 pcs. 1 x 2 x 27"
1 pc. 36" x ¾" dowel	or	**Handle:** 1 pc. 21½" x ¾" dowel (or broomhandle)

Hardware

Glue
12–1¼" #10 screws
4d nails
1¼" brads
1 axle (dia. to fit wheels) 24" long
2–8" to 10" wheels (ball bearings recommended)
2 bolts to secure axle (size depends on axle size) w/
    nuts and 2 washers ea.
2 cotter pins
1 pc. ¼" x 1" x 22" flatiron
2–1¼" x ¼" bolts w/ nuts

IRRIGATION

Irrigation can work for the organic gardener, insuring him against total crop loss and helping him build the land on which he lives. However, irrigation, except in cases of real distress or emergency where complete failure threatens, has certain drawbacks which do not recommend it to the thoughtful gardener. Excessive and continual irrigation must inevitably cause the soil to lose some nitrogen and mineral content through steady leaching. Also, continual watering of the soil overstimulates it into hyperactivity so that, despite a sound composting program, the soil can actually be depleted.

But neither of these considerations is valid when a real drought strikes and the prospect of total crop loss threatens. Irrigation, under such circumstances, means saving the crop and should be used where possible.

Now the soil is a reservoir, but it isn't a blotter.

This little dictum will help you understand what's happening in the soil when you irrigate. The water goes straight down; it doesn't spread out sideways as it would if it acted like a blotter. And so, to get the right amount of water to your crops, irrigation has to put the water right to the roots of the plants, not to the leaves or the area surrounding the crop.

Throwing a nice spray of cool water with a garden hose after a nerve-wracking day may relax you—but it's hard on the garden.

First, it's practically impossible to put down water evenly by hand sprinkling. Second, it would take hours to fill the root zone of even shallow-rooted plants. If sprinkled late in the day, plants don't have time to dry off; this gives mildew and other diseases a chance to start. Worse yet, irrigation water contains salts; shallow watering doesn't wash these deep into the soil out of the reach of crops' roots, and they gradually build up to trouble-making concentrations. And leaves can absorb quite a bit of salt through overhead watering and actually poison plants. This is particularly true of tree crops such as citrus, peaches, plums, and other stone fruits.

Of course, hand sprinkling can be important when planting. Sun and dry winds can parch the surface quickly and prevent the seeds from germinating. Sprinkling keeps up the moisture level until the seedlings have a chance to send their roots down into moister soil.

There is another place for hand sprinkling. Since the food-making efficiency of leaves depends in part on the amount of light and carbon dioxide available to them, it helps to wash off the dust periodically. Near cities and industrial areas this dust is usually contaminated with chemicals and other air pollutants which can damage plants and trees.

OVERHEAD SPRINKLER

There are a few legitimate uses for overhead sprinkling. It is usually the best method of watering lawns, pastures, and grasses. One of the most useful irrigators for lawns and other large areas is this high stand made of ½-inch pipe by Warner Tilsher.

Tilsher made his years ago using galvanized pipe. Galvanized pipe isn't cheap; you could successfully substitute rigid plastic pipe, but you'd probably have to add some ballast to the base to prevent it from tipping over (since plastic is considerably lighter than galvanized pipe).

Assembly is quite simple. All the pipe is threaded on both ends; use plumber's paste or tape (joint compound) on the threads before assembly to prevent leakage.

Screw a 36-inch-long upright, two 10-inch legs, and a 15-inch inlet into an elbow fitting with three side outlets. Screw caps on the open ends of the legs, a hose adapter on the inlet, and a standard square pattern head on the top of the upright.

With the fittings shown, you can adapt the stand to accept a 90-degree pattern head.

After determining the best place for a sprinkler in a lawn or in other areas, cut out a section of sod and drive in a small can flush with the ground. The grass soon grows over it, mowers ride over it, and it is easily found, saving set-up time.

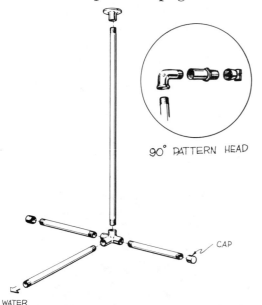

90° PATTERN HEAD

CAP

WATER SOURCE

MATERIALS

Hardware

Joint compound
1 pc. 36″ x ½″ ID galvanized pipe (upright)
2 pcs. 10″ x ½″ ID galvanized pipe (legs)
1 pc. 15″ x ½″ ID galvanized pipe (inlet)
1–½″ ID elbow w/ 3 side outlets
2–½″ ID galvanized caps
1 hose adapter
1 standard square pattern head

SPRINKLER SLED

If you *do* have reason to use a sprinkler, but you are tired of getting wet clothes and muddy feet when relocating the sprinkler, build a sled like this one, devised by Don Green of Kalamazoo, Michigan.

Green constructed his sleds of scrap materials he had in his workshop. He attached a mist sprayer to each sled. The rope hitched to the end of the sled allows him to reposition the sprinkler from the edge of the garden; he starts at the far boundary and periodically pulls it a little closer to him, until the entire garden row has been watered.

MATERIALS

Wood

1 pc. 1″ x 1″ x 14′ (act. meas.) (if unavailable, use 1 x 2)	or	**Runners:** 2 pcs. 1″ x 1″ x 36″ (act. meas.)
		Legs: 4 pcs. 1″ x 1″ x 18″ (act. meas.)
		Cross braces: 2 pcs. 1″ x 1″ x 8″ (act. meas.)
1 pc. 1 x 3 x 4′ (furring)	or	**Side braces:** 2 pcs. 1 x 3 x 12″
		Cross braces: 2 pcs. 1 x 3 x 8″
1 pc. 1 x 8 x 2′	or	**Seat:** 1 pc. 1 x 8 x 12″

Hardware

4d nails
Paint

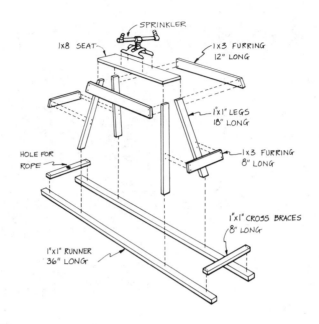

CONSTRUCTION

1. Cut the following lengths from the 1 x 1 stock: two 36-inch runners, four 18-inch legs (cut on parallel 60-degree biases), two 8-inch cross braces. Nominal 1 x 1 stock will be too flimsy for this sled, so if you cannot locate material measuring a full 1 inch by 1 inch, use 1 x 2 stock. Cut the furring into two 12-inch side braces and two 8-inch cross braces.
2. Nail the legs to the 1 x 8 sprinkler seat as indicated. Fasten a side brace to each side of the seat, nailing into the legs as well as the seat.
3. Lay out the runners 8 inches apart and fasten the cross braces to them. Drill a hole through what will be the front brace, to tie a rope through.
4. Center the seat and leg assembly on the runners and nail them fast. Nail the furring cross braces to the legs.
5. After painting the sled, attach your sprinkler to the seat.

FURROW IRRIGATOR

Irrigating by means of furrows between crops has so many advantages that most vegetables, strawberries, cane berries, and many orchards are irrigated in this way in California and other dry areas. This method saves water, reduces the danger of mildew, and allows easier weed control.

In commercial operations, rows are spaced to allow machine cultivation that produces a dust mulch and gets rid of most of the weeds. Home gardeners can space their rows closer together and use mulches. Planting can be done on the flat—but raised beds provide better aeration and drainage in rainy weather, which normally overlaps the beginning and end of the summer dry season.

On level land the irrigation furrows shouldn't be more than 40 feet long. Longer furrows must be graded so the water flows along them. In sandy soil, the maximum allowable drop is about 1 foot in 100 feet; loam and clay, half a foot. Steeper grades will give problems in getting the water down deep enough in a reasonable time and they'll waste water. They may also cause flooding and salt buildup in the lower areas. Shallow-rooted crops should be wetted to 18 to 24 inches; medium rooted, down 30 to 36 inches. Be sure to check with a rod. Furrow irrigation should be watched so that the running water

doesn't break through the edge of the ditch and gopher holes can be promptly repaired.

To speed up the furrow and hill watering he does in his garden, Tilsher developed this irrigator. It can water up to three rows spaced 2 feet apart at one time, and the design is such that you can keep adding until you water all your furrows at one time. The individually controlled valves permit adjustment to insure an even flow of water to each hose. The 12-inch height prevents backflow.

CONSTRUCTION

1. Wrap plumber's tape (or apply plumber's paste) to the threads on the several pieces of pipe. Assemble the plumbing as shown. Screw the 8-inch length of pipe in a **T**-fitting and screw a valve on the other end of the pipe. Screw a 26-inch pipe into the **T**-fitting, and screw the second **T**-fitting onto the growing assemblage. Screw on the second 26-inch length of pipe and complete the run of plumbing with the elbow. Screw valves onto the two **T**-fittings and the elbow.
2. Cut the tubing—electrical conduit is excellent material for this use—into two 26-inch-long pieces. Hammer the center 4 inches of each piece flat. Bend the flat part of the tubing as shown. Drill ¼-inch holes

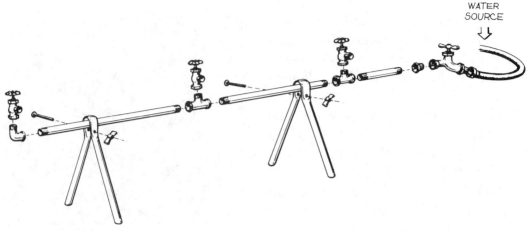

WATER SOURCE

through each side of the leg units, so the bolts will pass under the pipe and clamp the pipe tightly.

MATERIALS

Hardware

Joint compound
1 pc. 8″ x ½″ ID galvanized pipe (both ends threaded)
2 pcs. 26″ x ½″ ID galvanized pipe (both ends threaded)
2–½″ **T** fittings
4 valves
1–½″ 90° elbow
1 pc. 10′ x ½″ elec. conduit   or   **Legs:** 2 pcs. 26″ long
2–1″ x ¼″ bolts w/ wing nuts

SOIL SOAKER SYSTEMS

One of the best methods of watering vegetables is to get the water into the soil around their plants, where it will do the plants the most good. Many gardeners rely on porous canvas hose (soil soaker), laying it right alongside the plants. The water goes straight down into the root zone evenly, with practically no waste or evaporation loss. Mulches don't interfere and you don't have to worry about unseen holes or a breakthrough.

Soil soakers come in lengths up to 50 feet, are inexpensive, and last many seasons with reasonable care. It pays to have two; one can be running while you set up the other one.

While some plants may show signs of water shortage before wilting, it takes a lot of experience to be sure of this, and it is best to depend on more positive evidence. Weather greatly influences water needs, so timetables are only approximate. There is simply no substitute for physical inspection of the soil. Home gardeners can dig down 6 or 8 inches. When the soil appears to be dry, it is time to water. Commercial farmers usually use a soil auger or tensiometer.

In home gardens, considering the advisability of rotating crops, it may be best to treat all crops as shallow rooted, but wet the soil to 2 or 3 feet. One danger of underwatering is that it encourages plants that are normally deeper rooting to develop shallow root systems. Comes a hot, windy spell, their root system simply can't deliver enough water to keep up with the accelerated rate of transpiration of the leaf system. Under these conditions the plants wilt. No matter how much water you apply, they may suffer a serious setback and even die.

Too much water is almost as bad as too little. Plants must have air in their root zone—overwatering drives out the air and the plants may literally drown. When you irrigate, wet the

soil to the needed depth, then allow the plants to use up the water to nearly the point of beginning to wilt —then irrigate again right away.

The simplest way of checking how far irrigation water has penetrated is by pushing a pointed $\frac{1}{4}$-inch or $\frac{3}{8}$-inch metal rod into the ground, while the *water is running*. For trees the rod should be at least 6 inches long, with marking notches filed in at 1-foot intervals.

TIN CAN RESERVOIRS

Here's another way of getting the water to the roots of your garden plants. Irrigate your garden this year by the "tin can" method. If your garden space is limited, the tin can reservoirs will allow you to plant everything closer together—which will actually give you three times as much garden in the same area. The idea is not entirely new—fifty years ago farm papers were telling about punching holes in tin cans, sinking them in the ground, and then planting around them.

If the holes clog with mud, cut out both tops and bottoms, getting a simple cylinder which works perfectly when sunk into the soil and filled with water—a small but effective reservoir!

There are a lot of sources for tin cans. The best are the gallon-size food cans, #10. Restaurants and churches that buy foods in large quantities are the best sources for this size. If you buy fruit juices in the large 46-ounce tin can, save them; the 2-pound coffee can is good, though not quite as deep.

Set cans in rows the length of your garden, planting in the rows between them. Stretch a line to keep them straight, and set them in about 3 feet apart, leaving the top rim about 1 inch above ground level to keep the soil out. Stuff a wad of hay, straw, or lawn clippings into the can. This material can be spaded under the following spring when it is well composted, using a trowel to dig it out and filling the can with a wad of new hay.

You can improve on this system by digging a little larger hole, filling it partially with compost, setting in the tin cylinder, and then filling it up with good garden soil. This way the hole gives off liquid fertilizer every time you fill the can with water, enriching the surrounding area.

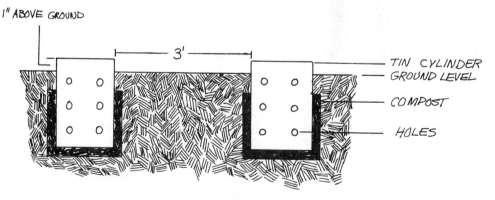

1" ABOVE GROUND

3'

TIN CYLINDER
GROUND LEVEL
COMPOST
HOLES

When the rainfall is adequate, the tin can watering holes might seem superfluous. But in the summer heat, or during seasonal droughts, they are literally lifesavers. Take your hose without the nozzle and walk down each row and back, filling each can as you go. In dry weather you may have to fill each hole two, three, four, and even five times to saturate the soil.

Because soil needs air as well as water, do not water every day, but give the soil a good soaking once each week. If you try this method, and especially if you fill each hole with compost to begin with, you will have a lush and luxuriant growth such as you have never seen before. When the foliage gets so thick you cannot see the tin cans, use laths as markers, putting one in each hole so you know where to aim the hose.

DRAINPIPE IRRIGATION

An interesting method of deep watering uses drain spouting. Use corrugated metal spouting, with elbows hooked onto the spouts so they stick up out of the ground where you feed them with the garden hose.

A ¼-inch drill is used to make holes in the bottom of the spouts 8 inches apart and staggered from side to side. An electric drill does a good job, especially when you first use a sharp-marking punch, but a hand drill will also get results.

After sliding lengths of spouting together, seal the joint with asphalt cement (putty or caulking compound can also be used) and wind a strip of cloth over the joint.

You can have your irrigation pipe open and above ground at both ends. Or you can seal up one end before joining the spouts by standing one length in a #10 tin can which you fill with cement and let harden. Again, putty or caulking compound may be

used—whichever is cheap and available.

The spouts are placed in a trench 5 inches or more deep.

A variation, producing a more durable installation, is to use drain tile or perforated septic system lead pipes.

Installation of the rows of tile may seem expensive in time, money, and labor, but it should be stressed that this is a permanent project which should produce extra yields for years without further maintenance.

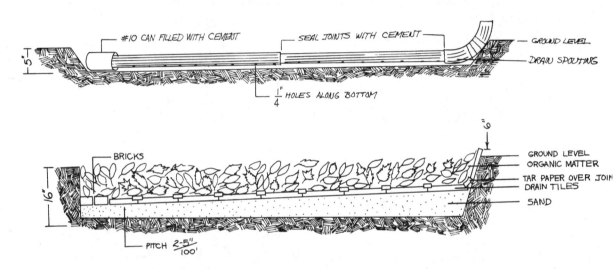

CONSTRUCTION

1. Stretch a line the length of the proposed row of tiles and, using a narrow spade, dig a trench about 16 inches deep.
2. Cover the bottom of the trench with sand. Using a yardstick, measure the distance between the string, which is a fixed distance above the soil surface, and the bottom of the trench. You must have pitch—about 2 to 5 inches per 100 feet—or the water won't flow properly through the system.
3. Lay the tiles, wrapping each joint with a band of tar paper. Block the lower end with a couple of bricks.
4. Before filling in the trench, put down a lot of leaves, hay, and other organic matter to act as a sponge in holding water.
5. When you reach the upper end of the line, bring the tile up to the surface with an elbow or angle joint with the top tile protruding about 6 inches above ground level. If you have curious or mischievous kids in your neighborhood, it's a good idea to camouflage the top tile and cover it with something that will prevent them from dropping earth into the system. When you want to irrigate, insert the hose in the vertical end and let it run until the system is full—about a half hour.

SEEDLINGS SOAKER

Flats filled with seedlings should also be watered from underneath. That way you can prevent washouts, insure strong healthy root systems, and water your plants less frequently. To do all of those things, Tilsher has designed the next best thing to an upside down watering can—the seedlings soakers.

CONSTRUCTION

1. To accommodate most flats, nail together a 23½-inch soaker container using 1 x 6 boards for the sides and a ¼-inch plywood bottom. Cut two sides 22 inches long and two sides 23½ inches long. The bottom should measure 23½ inches square. Nail with 6d nails.
2. Line the bottom and sides of the container with 6-mil black polyethylene. Secure the film by nailing four ¼-inch by ¾-inch by 22-inch strips to top edges of container.
3. Place three flat stone supports in container base to hold flat level.

MATERIALS

Wood

1 pc. 1 x 6 x 8′	or	**Sides:** 2 pcs. 1 x 6 x 22″ 2 pcs. 1 x 6 x 23½″
1–2′ x 4′ sht. ¼″ ext. plywood	or	**Bottom:** 1 pc. 23½″ sq.
1 pc. ¼″ x ¾″ x 8′ (lath)	or	**Holding strips:** 4 pcs. ¼″ x ¾″ x 22″

Hardware

6d nails
1″ brads

Miscellaneous

1 roll 6-mil black polyethylene, 36″ wide	or	**Lining:** 1 pc. 35″ sq.
3 flat stones		

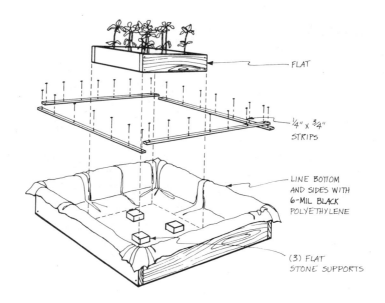

FLAT

¼" x ¾" STRIPS

LINE BOTTOM AND SIDES WITH 6-MIL BLACK POLYETHYLENE

(3) FLAT STONE SUPPORTS

FLOODING IRRIGATOR

Flooding is a good method of irrigating small level plots. The area must be walled in so that a pond is formed. Penetration should be checked at various points. Flooding saves water and is ideal for flushing out salts.

An old chicken feed trough or gutter with holes punched through the bottom makes a good irrigator for box beds, ponded beds, or closely spaced crops with furrows between the rows. It can also be used to break the force of water when flooding an area to leach out irrigation water salts or pre-

irrigating before planting. Fasten wooden blocks to the ends of the trough to hold it up off the ground.

TREE IRRIGATOR

If you have a tree, shrub, or bush that needs water, you can simply run the hose out back and point it in the appropriate direction. But even with an adjustable nozzle, there is no assurance you'll get even water distribution or penetration. And if you have mulched the parched area heavily, there may be a hidden groundhog hole that will act like a drain. For more than twenty-five years Tilsher has used a device he built that turns a simple garden hose into a tree irrigator. The design is adaptable to any size tree, shrub, or berry bush. It employs a couple of 360-degree sprinklers and requires you to do some basic plumbing.

MATERIALS

Wood

1 pc. 1 x 3 x 6′ redwood	or	**Arms:** 2 pcs. 1 x 3 x 28½″
		Blocks: 4 pcs. 1 x 3 x 2½″
1 pc. 2 x 2 x 4′ redwood	or	**Crosspiece:** 1 pc. 2 x 2 x 36″

Hardware

3d nails
2–3½″ x $\frac{5}{16}$″ carriage bolts w/ wing nuts and washers
2–½″ 90° elbows
1 standard **Y** hose adapter
2–360° sprinkler heads
2 hose adapters

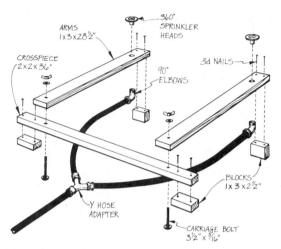

CONSTRUCTION

1. Cut two 28½-inch lengths and four 2½-inch lengths of redwood 1 x 3. Cut a 36-inch length of redwood 2 x 2.
2. Drill a $\frac{5}{16}$-inch hole 1¼ inches from one end of each 28½-inch length, and a 1⅛-inch hole 2⅛ inches from the opposite ends. At the end with the larger hole, nail a 2½-inch block.
3. Drill $\frac{5}{16}$-inch holes 4¾ inches from the ends of the 2 x 2. Nail the remaining 2½-inch blocks to the ends of the 2 x 2.
4. Connect frame parts with two 3½-inch by $\frac{5}{16}$-inch carriage bolts, $\frac{5}{16}$-inch washers, and $\frac{5}{16}$-inch wing nuts.
5. Attach sprinklers and hose adapters to elbows. Use standard **Y** to provide two spray sources.

WATER SPIKE

Here is a tree-watering device that is able to put water down into the ground where the tree's feeder roots can get at it—all of it.

All you have to do is hook it onto the garden hose, turn it on, and in a few seconds the point is down 4 feet. Now reduce the water flow; if your soil is reasonably friable, workable, and growth producing, you can saturate a large underground area right where it will reach the thirsty mass of fine feeder roots. There it will do the most good in the shortest time, and with a very minimum of worry about water bills, evaporation, waste, or depth of penetration.

A few minutes study of the water spike will show any reasonable handyman how easy it is to make. Reading from the top of the spike down we give the list of parts that are required. All pipe fittings are standard ½-inch galvanized or black pipe. Black pipe is usually cheaper, but both kinds work very well. Plumber's paste or tape should be used when joining all parts to prevent leakage. When the spike is assembled, cut the bottom off on a 60-degree angle to make it easier to push in the ground.

This is the sort of project that should utilize salvaged materials. New materials are not cheap; the cost of new pipe and fittings will probably make you think twice about whether or not you really need such a watering device.

But if you have a genuine need, this water spike is very durable and well worth the expense.

MATERIALS

Hardware

Joint compound
1 double female standard hose connection
1 standard ½″ to ¾″ brass connection
1–4″ x ½″ nipple
1–½″ 90° elbow
1–½″ female thread shut-off valve
1–1½″ x ½″ pipe nipple
2–8″ x ½″ nipples
2–½″ pipe caps
1–½″ pipe cross
1 pc. 48″ x ½″ pipe

DRIP IRRIGATION THE HOMEMADE WAY

A drip irrigation system is a good way to get moisture to your plants without wasting a drop of water or a second of your time.

Such a system can be constructed easily at home because most of the parts can usually be found either in the kitchen, basement, or home workshop. What can't be scrounged up around the house can be found no farther away than the local hardware store. Drip systems are practical because they have no moving parts to wear out and a drive system that never fails: gravity. Most importantly, this type of watering system can bring nourishment to your plants while you tend to other gardening chores.

Here are three systems that typify what homemade drip irrigation is all about.

The photo shows the basic parts of this drip system. A widemouthed plastic jug is best to use because it allows you to get your hand inside to tighten the nut on that side of the hose fitting. If you do use a small-mouthed jug, rig up an adjustable wrench to a longer handle and use that to secure the nut inside the bottle as you tighten the hose fitting from the outside. The rest of the parts are

the same regardless of the jug you use: pieces of small garden hose, wooden or metal plugs for the ends of the hose, an Aeroquip hose fitting, a metal washer and nut to fit the inside of the hose fitting, a rubber grommet, and a cotter pin. This equipment will make one outlet from the container. Any size can be used, but because the volume of water is not of primary importance—it really is a drip system —$\frac{1}{4}$-inch and smaller parts are best. Often more than one outlet per container is desirable.

CONSTRUCTION

1. Cut a hole the size of the hose fitting very close to the bottom of the container. Insert the grommet and hose fitting into the opening.
2. After putting the metal washer on the part of the hose fitting on the inside of the jug use your hand or a wrench to hold the nut as you turn and tighten it into place. This connection will eliminate any wasteful leaks.
3. After jamming the hose over the outside portion of the hose fitting, stop up the end of the hose with a wooden or metal plug.
4. About 1 inch from the end of the hose make a small slit and insert the cotter pin. The pin can be opened and closed to regulate the flow of water, and it keeps the opening from clogging.
5. Punch holes in the top of the lid or place screening over the opening, especially on smallmouthed jars, to allow air to enter the container. Remember more than one hose outlet is often preferable.

VARIATIONS

A variation of this same irrigation system that will supply water to a whole row of crops is just as simple to construct.

The water container in this case should be larger; a 25- or 50-gallon drum is best. After putting the hose fitting into the drum—use the same method as with the smaller plastic jug —a simple on/off valve can be added to allow control over the amount of water released to the crops during any one watering period.

Attach a two-hose connector to the on/off valve and place the lengths of hose onto the connector and run them down the row of crops. By attaching the hose to a wire or pole just off the ground the hose will remain free of soil and prevent the clogging of the drip points. At each plant insert a cotter pin into the hose and a steady

supply of water will nourish your plants while you tend to other gardening chores.

A second variation uses a 1-gallon paint bucket, small pieces of $\frac{1}{4}$-inch rigid vinyl tubing (this depends on how many outlets you want), a number of feet of $\frac{1}{4}$-inch flexible vinyl tubing (cut into a desired length for each of the outlets), wooden or metal plugs for the tube ends, and some window screen.

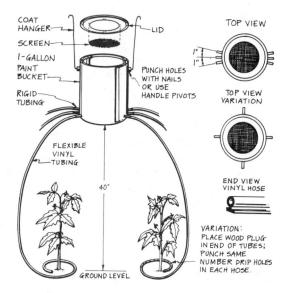

An important thing to remember is if you plug up one of the outlets you should plug up all the others from that can in order to equalize the pres-

sure and allow an equal flow to each plant.

If you can't find what you need to make one of these proven systems, use what you've got and, while keeping the principles that make these work in mind, put your own system together.

CONSTRUCTION

1. Drill holes into the sides of the bucket—four to six seems to be the ideal number. Insert the rigid 1-inch pieces of vinyl tubing into these holes—they should make a tight fit. Copper tubing can be a good substitute for the vinyl tubing.

2. Now force the flexible vinyl tubing or a small diameter rubber hose over the tubing. It's important that each of the pieces of tubing or hose you attach to a single can are the same length. If they vary in length the amount of water delivered to the plants will also vary.

3. Stop up the ends of the tubes or hoses with wooden plugs and poke holes in the hose—if you want to make the water come slowly from drip holes. Always make the same number of holes in each outlet. If you want a more rapid flow just allow the water to come out the unimpeded end of the hose.

4. Next, cut a large hole in the paint can top and fit a cover of window screen over it. Attach by punching holes in remaining ring of metal and threading extra wire through holes to secure the screen. This will allow air to enter but will keep leaves and twigs out.

THE RAIN BARREL

Build up your water supply by placing rain barrels under the downspouts to catch and direct the run-off from the roof. To avoid providing a breeding place for mosquitoes, the downspout goes through a smooth-fitting hole in the cover of the barrel.

Two 1-inch pipes are inserted in the side. The one at the top is for overflow during rainy weather. It is fitted with a **T** connection for a hose which takes the water to the thirstiest plants, instead of letting it all fall around the barrel. This hose can have a double **Y** connection at the end so the water can flow through two hoses to different spots.

In cloudbursts, water also runs from the end of the overflow pipe. A dry brook—easily made of tile covered with various sizes of stones—can direct this water to nearby plants.

The bottom pipe is fitted with a faucet to which a hose is connected so the barrel can be emptied to the desired areas during dry spells. It can be emptied a little at a time or all at once. This is a 55-gallon barrel, but with the overflow pipe where it is set, it probably holds about 50 gallons. It must, of course, be emptied before hard winter, or the water could freeze and burst the barrel.

WELLS

If irrigation is a must, you will probably need more than rain barrels to augment your domestic water supply. If you live near a stream or a pond, you can, perhaps, use them for irrigation water.

Or you can try your hand at well digging. At least two OGF contributors have successfully tried their hands at it in years past. One dug a shaft, while the other used a posthole auger to drill a shallow well.

Considering the great savings involved, any physically able gardener who has the time should try the shallow-well method. Having a well on the property cuts down appreciably on water bills and proves invaluable during a drought, especially when all lawn watering is banned.

DIGGING A WELL FOR IRRIGATION

There is no reason why you can't dig a well on a farm or homestead where the soil is fairly loose and free of stones, and blasting will not be needed. You can go down to about 50 feet. Some sort of pump will be necessary to get a good "stand" of water.

Obviously, you'll want to work a spot that is sure to yield water within 30 to 50 feet of the surface. It's too much work to produce only a dry hole. The water table tends to follow the contours of the land, sloping down from the hills to the low spots. There are two basic types of water-bearing formations: sand or a mixture of sand and gravel, and deeper down, rock interlaced with fissures.

Forget about the second category, because you're going to work with hand tools.

Work with a 4-foot diameter—it's easier to move around inside the pipe or tube. Start with 30 feet of 4-foot pipe, which serves as a well-liner.

First dig a round hole 3 feet deep and 4½ feet wide, and shove a section

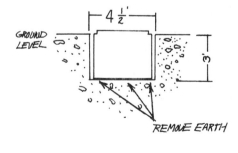

(1) DIG 4½'x3'deep hole
Insert 3'section of pipe + level

(2) Fit a 3'section of pipe on Top of 1st
section - fit flanged ends
Dig earth from around bottom of 1st section
causing entire unit to settle as earth is
removed

of upended pipe into it. Use a carpenter's level to true it up vertically and make sure the flanged or female end is down. When the top of the first section is even with the ground, move a 3-foot section on top of it, fit the flanged ends, and make sure that the pipes are trued up vertically. Then get into the tube and, using a short-handled shovel, dig and scrap the earth from under the edge of the upended pipe, which will settle into the ground as the gravel is removed.

When the second section of pipe is even with the ground, a third section is placed upon it. It will become difficult to throw the sand and dirt out of the tube at about this point, due to a lack of room to swing a shovel. When the third pipe is even with the ground, rig a tripod over the "well."

The tripod can be constructed of three sound 2 x 4s each 10 feet long, and tied together, tepee-fashion, at the top to hold a pulley wheel. Using ½-inch rope and a stout iron pail, haul the sand to the surface.

As each section of the pipe settles down, come to the surface, rest a bit, and help set another section on the lengthening liner. Keep working until signs of water are struck.

As more and more of the pipe liner is added, the increased weight helps to force the tube into the earth. There is never a chance of a cave-in or of a loose stone letting go and hurting the

digger—the two chief dangers in digging a well.

Vollie Tripp of Palm Springs, California, who has dug at least one good well with this technique, swears it works to near perfection. Of his experience he says, "We never had any trouble keeping the well true and vertical because we took care not to dig too much at any one place, but instead nibbled our way clear around the pipe flange."

The last section of the pipe Tripp allowed to project 2 feet above the ground. He worked a thin but rich concrete around the crack to seal off surface water. Later he poured a concrete pad several feet all around the well to prevent contamination, made a sturdy wooden cover for the top, and installed a small pump.

Where the "lift" is not too great, about 24 to 26 feet, a small centrifugal pump is about the least costly and most satisfactory type. Where the lift is greater, the pump should be located down in the well. However, there is a variety of ways of getting water out of a well, and each case should be considered on its merits.

In sections where septic tanks and cesspools are widely used, the water may be unfit for drinking or domestic purposes, though safe for irrigation. In all cases, the water should be tested by the public health authorities before being used for the home.

③ After 3 sections construct tripod + pulley system to hoist earth

④ the last section should project 2' above ground level. Fill in section with concrete, add wooden case + pump

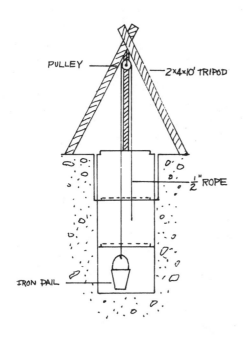

PULLEY

2×4×10' TRIPOD

½" ROPE

IRON PAIL

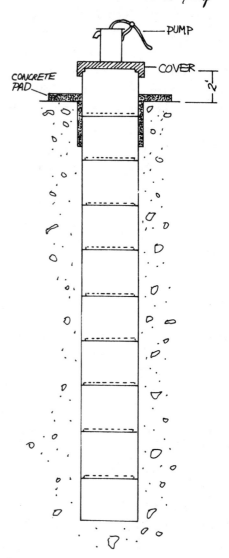

PUMP

COVER

CONCRETE PAD

2'

DIG YOUR OWN SHALLOW WELL

Another way to dig a shallow well for irrigation involves the use of a posthole digger and auger from a plumbing supply or hardware dealer.

Assuming that the well will be 20 feet deep, this is what you'll need: three or four lengths of 1¼-inch galvanized pipe, 5 feet long, with couplings and a well point. While it may be cumbersome, one 20-foot-long pipe may be used to reduce chances of breakage and the number of couplings. Be sure to select a site close to an electrical outlet so it will be easy to hook up your pump. And, before you start digging, make sure you know all about the local licensing requirements in your area, and be careful to choose a site free of old foundations, boulders, sewer lines, or other obstacles. Try to make it as easy for yourself as possible.

But before using the posthole digger and auger, dig down a few feet with pick and shovel until you pass all tree roots and other encumbrances. The posthole digger and auger is then inserted into the soil, leaned on, and turned in a circle. When the shovel is full, it is lifted gently so it misses the sides of the hole, and emptied into a wheelbarrow or a pile.

As the hole sinks deeper, the extensions of old pipe that will be supplied with the posthole digger and auger must be coupled securely onto the device. At first, the operation is easy, but by the time you hit wet sand at 13 feet or more, you'll be lifting heavy earth out of the hole, hand over hand at a height that will tower

over your head. Here another pair of hands is called for, and the assistance of a friend or neighbor will save a lot of trouble.

Once you hit really wet sand or a small glimmering puddle of water at 13 to 20 feet, and the sand is too slippery to lift, put the posthole digger and auger aside. It is important to stop digging at this stage; eager homeowners all too often bore down past the water table.

The next step is to drive the 4-foot well point all the way into the water-bearing stratum. The well point should have a brass filter screen built inside so that it will be protected by the steel skeleton during driving.

Couple your well point with your 1¼-inch lengths of pipe, using plenty of good pipe compound so the connections are tight. Otherwise you may lose the well point in the sand. Then lower the piping and well point into the hole, working carefully and gently. If you want to spend the extra money, you can first insert a larger-diameter pipe and use it as a casing, slipping the smaller pipe down through it.

When the pipe is set in place, attach a driving coupling or cap, and sledge the well point down 4 feet or so, hitting the coupling squarely. A heavy wooden maul may be used in place of the sledgehammer, but a sledge does a better job. Be sure, however, to use a driving coupling, or the pipe will have to be rethreaded. Also stop driving and begin elsewhere if your well point strikes a rock or solid object.

Next, prime the sunken pipe with water, using the garden hose, and attach a hand pump, priming this in turn. You should have sandy water as soon as the pump is primed, and after a half hour of pumping, the water will be clear and ready to be tested. If you intend to install an electric pump, make certain that there is about 5 feet of water in the pipe, measuring carefully by lowering a tape measure and weight down the pipe. If there is 5 feet or more of water present, the electric pump will operate efficiently and you can fill in the hole around the pipe.

Where surface water contamination is a problem, especially in low-lying areas with no natural drainage, fill the space between the over-size borehole and pipe with cement grout to a depth of 15 feet, or lay a 2-foot-square concrete slab around the pipe.

If you haven't reached a steady supply of water, you can go deeper, adding another length of pipe. But it's not advisable to go further than 25 feet unless you're ready to work a lot harder and spend more money on an electric pump powerful enough to handle a deep well adequately.

The practical limit for all shallow-well pumps is a lift of 25 feet. Although water theoretically can be drawn up 34 feet, it is not possible because the pump cannot create a perfect vacuum, and there is friction loss in the suction pipe. The only alternative when no water is reached at about 25 feet is to take up the pipe and begin the process all over again at another site. Most people generally find water at 13 to 20 feet, but you may have to dig two or three times before you're successful.

CHOOSING A PUMP FOR YOUR WELL

Pumping the water out is the next problem, once your well is dug or drilled. While many types of pumps have been used, three basic kinds are now available.

A shallow-well pump is used when the well is 25 feet or less. It can be piston driven or centrifugal. The setup is simple—one pipe leads from the well to the pump inlet, and one pipe from the pump outlet to the storage tank.

If the well is over 25 feet deep, the

water can't be lifted by the suction of the pump, but must be pushed up. This can be accomplished in two ways. One is to use a submersible pump. With this installation, the pump is actually lowered to the bottom of the well, and a single pipe goes from the pump to the storage tank.

The other deep-well pump is a jet pump. This is similar to the shallow-well centrifugal pump, but the hookup is different. The pump has one inlet and two outlets. The inlet pipe comes from the well while one outlet goes into the well and the other to the storage tank. Part of the water brought up from the well is sent back down again.

The jet or ejector at the bottom of the well is actually a pump working on the Venturi principle. The water that is pumped back enters the jet and creates a suction that pulls more water from the well. Both the water that was pumped down, plus that drawn in from the well is forced back up to the pump. The extra water then goes into the storage tank, and the rest is sent back to the jet.

For depths to about 100 feet, a submersible or jet pump can be used. To 200 feet, the choice is between a submersible or a multistage jet pump. From 200 feet to about 700 feet, a submersible is a "must."

Submersibles are more efficient, since all the water pumped is used, and none is recirculated. Piping is also simpler with the submersible, with only one pipe the depth of the well instead of two as with the jet pump. Also, the submersible is quieter than the jet. One other advantage of the submersible is that the pump can't freeze in winter, while a jet may if used in an unheated building. However, it is more expensive and less accessible if repairs are needed.

The higher a pump must lift water, and the farther it must push, the less water it delivers. Choose a pump with enough capacity to give you the water you need. Total head means total load—feet of suction lift, plus feet beyond pump water must be pushed and raised, plus pressure; one pound equals 2.31 feet of head.

You don't need a storage tank if you're only irrigating, since you can take water directly from the pump. Otherwise, you'll need a storage tank, regardless of the type of pump used. The air is compressed in the tank as the water is pumped in, shutting off the pump when the water pressure reaches 40 pounds to the square inch (PSI). As the water is taken from the tank, the air expands, water pressure drops, and at about 20 PSI the pump goes on again to refill the tank. Care should be taken not to restrict the flow of the water—excess pressure can harm the pump.

BIRDHOUSES

One way you can attract birds to your homestead is to set out houses for them. The best houses are those that you build yourself, even though a great variety of birdhouses can be bought from stores and mail-order houses. If you succeed in attracting resident birds, the benefits are twofold. First, birds such as swallows eat several times their weight in mosquitoes and other insects, including garden pests. Second, your family will have the pleasant and educational experience of observing bird families go through their seasonal cycle.

Start planning your birdhouses by determining what species are most likely to become residents. The birds you are able to observe yourself is a start, but don't assume that they are the extent of the local bird population. Check with your local Audubon Society or wildlife club for a rundown of birds you may attract and information on what dates they arrive from their seasonal migrations.

Certain types of houses are suited to certain species of birds. Factors such as the size of the entrance hole, the height of the hole from the bottom of the house, the dimensions of the house, and the location and height at which the house is mounted all vary from species to species. The accompanying chart and details listed below for specific houses will tell you what you need once you have determined what birds to expect. With these specifics in mind, you can design your own houses, or adapt one of the designs described here to suit your needs.

Birdhouses must be located in safe places. If it does not look safe to the birds, they will not move in. Squirrels or cats will smash eggs and kill young birds, so they must be thwarted. One safe place is atop a metal pole or pipe, far enough from buildings and trees so cats cannot jump onto them. A wooden pole or a tree can be fitted with antipredator devices. These include an 18-inch-wide tin sleeve around the trunk, or a horizontal, circular baffle.

BIRDHOUSE DIMENSIONS

Dimensions of nesting boxes for various species of birds that regularly use them, and the height at which they should be placed above the ground.

Species	Floor of Cavity	Depth of Cavity	Entrance above Floor	Diameter of Entrance	Height above Ground [1]
	Inches	Inches	Inches	Inches	Feet
Bluebird	5 x 5	8	6	1½	5–10
Robin	6 x 8	8	([2])	([2])	6–15
Chickadee	4 x 4	8–10	6–8	1⅛	6–15
Titmouse	4 x 4	8–10	6–8	1¼	6–15
Nuthatch	4 x 4	8–10	6–8	1¼	12–20
House wren	4 x 4	6–8	1–6	1–1¼	6–10
Bewick's wren	4 x 4	6–8	1–6	1–1¼	6–10
Carolina wren	4 x 4	6–8	1–6	1½	6–10
Violet green swallow	5 x 5	6	1–5	1½	10–15
Tree swallow	5 x 5	6	1–5	1½	10–15
Barn swallow	6 x 6	6	([2])	([2])	8–12
Purple martin	6 x 6	6	1	2½	15–20
Prothonotary warbler	6 x 6	6	4	1½	2–4
Starling	6 x 6	16–18	14–16	2	10–25
Phoebe	6 x 6	6	([2])	([2])	8–12
Crested flycatcher	6 x 6	8–10	6–8	2	8–20
Flicker	7 x 7	16–18	14–16	2½	6–20
Golden-fronted woodpecker	6 x 6	12–15	9–12	2	12–20
Redheaded woodpecker	6 x 6	12–15	9–12	2	12–20
Downy woodpecker	4 x 4	9–12	6–8	1¼	6–20
Hairy woodpecker	6 x 6	12–15	9–12	1½	12–20
Screech owl	8 x 8	12–15	9–12	3	10–30
Saw-whet owl	6 x 6	10–12	8–10	2½	12–20
Barn owl	10 x 18	15–18	4	6	12–18
Sparrow hawk	8 x 8	12–15	9–12	3	10–30
Wood duck	10 x 18	10–24	12–16	4	10–20

[1] Many experiments show that boxes at moderate heights mostly within reach of a man on the ground are readily accepted by many birds.

[2] One or more sides open.

Some houses can be hung from a horizontal tree limb, if you use two wires to keep it from spinning in the wind. Birds such as robins and phoebes and some sparrows will make nests on simple shelves nailed under the eaves or roof overhang of buildings.

Don't crowd the birdhouses, because birds are territorial creatures. That is, they do not like to live in colonies, with the exception of purple martins. Tree swallows may tolerate several houses placed close to each other. If you are planning for less than an acre, don't put up more than a few houses, and no more than two of the same type, since bird competition is sharpest among members of the same species.

Mount birdhouses with the hole facing away from the prevailing winds, to keep as much rain out as is possible. Likewise, don't mount the house tilted forward, causing rain to run toward the hole.

The height at which you mount your houses depends somewhat on what bird they are intended for. Consult the chart for the species you have in mind. Unless you are hoping for a sparrow hawk with a house atop a 25-foot pole, it makes sense to mount the houses no higher than you can easily reach.

It is necessary to reach the houses because they must be cleaned out after every season. Remove old nesting material, dirt, shell fragments, and dead nestlings. Inspect for, and remove any eggs laid by the gypsy moth, tussock moth, or other insects. Birds are subject to lice, and if any are present, dust the house with pyrethrum powder.

Put your houses out early in spring, before the birds have arrived for the summer. If you put them out after birds already have begun building nests, the houses are likely to be ignored. Some people bring their birdhouses in for repairs and repainting in the winter. However, it also is a good idea to leave houses out, because on cold nights, birds will seek them out, and some birds even pile on top of each other for warmth. (You can adapt a birdhouse specifically for this purpose by installing extra perches on the inside of a house, making a winter roosting box.)

Birdhouses can be built out of almost any kind of wood, including exterior plywood. Bark slabs are an inexpensive and attractive choice. Birds do not shun knotted, chipped, or what otherwise might become scrap wood. Redwood, cedar, and cypress are durable and need no protective finish, but are relatively expensive. If you paint or stain your birdhouse, do it well before it is time to place the house outside.

The basic shape of a birdhouse is simple; sides, floor, and a slanted or peaked roof. The entrance hole should be cut exactly the size specified, or it will not be used by the birds for which it was intended. Perches on the outside actually are not necessary and may be more an aid to the birds' enemies than a convenience to the birds themselves. Install the perch inside the hole, or roughen the inside surface beneath the hole to make it easier for fledgling birds to climb out.

To protect the house from the rain, the roof should overhang the entrance by about 3 inches. To keep rain from running back under the roof, cut a crosswise groove near the front edge. You can tack a shingle on top for a really waterproof roof.

You should bore a few holes in the bottom of the house to drain any rain that gets blown in. Also, bore two small holes no bigger than $\frac{1}{4}$ inch, near the top of the walls, to provide ventilation on hot summer days.

Some of the designs here provide for cleaning out the box. If you design your own house, make the bottom or one of the sides removable for this purpose.

When you build the house, make sure its construction will not injure the birds. Make sure there are no protruding nail points. Make sure there are no cracks or crevices that can jam and break off a claw.

Keep in mind this house is for the birds. You can paint and decorate it to look like a Swiss chalet, a Frank Lloyd Wright home, or a log cabin, but birds do not care, and may even be repelled by such gaudiness. The simpler, the better. Choose dull or at least subdued colors of paint.

GOURD HOUSE

A really natural style birdhouse can be made from a gourd. It is suitable for wrens, chickadees, tree swallows, downy woodpeckers, titmice, and even bluebirds. The best variety of gourd to use is the Lagenaria, known as the dipper or bottle gourd.

Catherine Hanley of Minnesota recommends the following approach as the best method for making a gourd house.

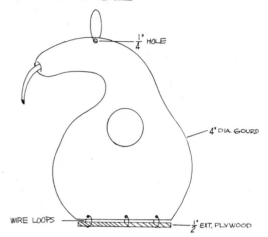

CONSTRUCTION

1. Leave the ripe fruit on the vine until the first frost warnings are out. Then, cut it off, leaving a few inches of vine attached for easier handling.
2. Wash the gourd in warm, soapy water. Rinse and dry it and place it on layers of newspaper in a warm spot. Darkness will keep the colors bright, but bright colors are not necessary. Turn the gourd every other day or so.
3. After about a week, the surface moisture should be evaporated, and you can cut the hole. Place the hole well above the bottom of the gourd to allow nesting room. You can use an expansion bit or keyhole saw to cut the hole.
4. If you can't clean out the gourd through the hole, cut off a slice from the bottom to do so. You can use loops of light wire to fasten the piece back on, or cut a piece of ¼-inch or ⅜-inch plywood to fit, and wire it on.
5. Drill a ¼-inch hole through the neck of the gourd, near the top, for stringing the gourd to a tree limb.

WREN HOUSE

Wrens are industrious insect eaters. They are not fastidious in their choice of houses, but a partly sunlit spot about 6 feet off the ground is best. The entrance hole should be either a 1-inch-diameter circle, or a 1-inch-

high, 3-inch-wide horizontal slot, which will allow the wrens to carry in the twigs they favor for nesting material more easily.

This wren house is made from ½-inch board, but you could use exterior plywood. The shape of pieces you will need are illustrated; it may be easier if you make templates to trace onto the wood.

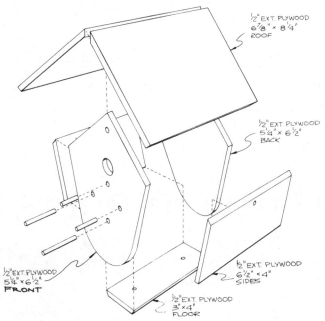

½" EXT. PLYWOOD
6⅞" × 8¼"
ROOF

½" EXT. PLYWOOD
5¼" × 6½"
BACK

½" EXT. PLYWOOD
5¼" × 6½"
FRONT

½" EXT. PLYWOOD
6½" × 4"
SIDES

½" EXT. PLYWOOD
3" × 4"
FLOOR

CONSTRUCTION

1. First, cut two pieces, 5¼ inches on the short sides, 6½ inches on the long sides, for the front and back.

2. Measure 3½ inches from the top point of the front piece to center the 1-inch-diameter entrance hole. Cut the hole with an expansion bit or a keyhole saw.

3. Next, cut two 6½-inch by 4-inch side panels and bevel the upper edges for a better fit with the roof. Drill a ¼-inch hole near the top of each for ventilation.

4. Cut two 6⅞-inch by 8¼-inch roof pieces and bevel one edge of each so they fit tightly at the peak.

295

5. Cut one 3-inch by 4-inch floor piece and bevel both 4-inch sides to fit the sloping side walls. Drill two ¼-inch drain holes.

6. Assemble using 4d finishing nails. First nail the sides to both front and back, then the roof pieces, and then the floor.

7. Drill ⅛-inch starter holes into the peak of the roof where it is supported by the front and back. Use screw eyes to hang the house with loops of wire.

MATERIALS

Wood

1–2' x 4' sht. ½" ext. plywood   or   **Front and back:** 2 pcs. 5¼" x 6½"

Sides: 2 pcs. 6½" x 4"

Roof: 2 pcs. 6⅞" x 8¼"

Floor: 1 pc. 3" x 4"

Hardware

4d finishing nails
2 small screw eyes
Wire

BLUEBIRD HOUSES

Bluebirds are valuable because three-quarters of their diet consists of crop-destroying insects. This includes grasshoppers, all kinds of caterpillars, beetles, corn borers, and other pests. As tenants, bluebirds are not very particular about the houses they settle into.

Bluebirds like abandoned orchards and will use houses placed in trees, as well as posts. If you use a tree, install predator guards first. An open, sunny spot is best, and the houses can be

placed as low as 5 feet off the ground. Some people have observed that if you place the house 3 feet off the ground, bluebirds still will use them, but sparrows will not.

The bluebird houses described here have in common simple design and an entrance hole that is 1½ inches in diameter.

One good design was developed by Stiles Thomas of Allendale, New Jersey, who observed that as natural nesting places disappeared, so did the bluebirds. He placed these houses on pipes or posts, 3 to 6 feet off the ground. Thomas suggests placing the houses 300 feet apart to avoid crowding. He also observed that although some houses were not occupied until June, bluebirds sometimes bred twice in one summer.

This house is made from any soft wood, ½ inch to ¾ inch thick.

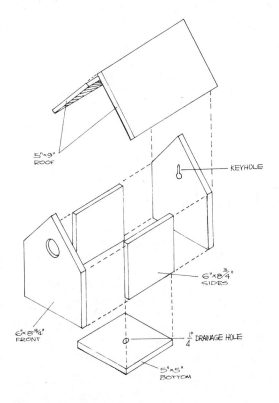

CONSTRUCTION

1. Cut two pieces 9 inches by 5 inches for the roof.
2. Cut three pieces 5 inches square for the sides and bottom.
3. Cut two pieces 6 inches by 8¾ inches for the front and back. Cut a peak at one end, leaving 5-inch sides, as shown.
4. For the front, measure 6 inches from the bottom to center the 1½-inch-diameter entrance hole. Measure to the same spot on the back piece to cut a keyhole which will be used in hanging the house from a post.
5. Drill a ¼-inch hole in the bottom piece for a drain. Note that the tops of the sides are not beveled, which allows a ventilation space between the sides and the roof.
6. Assemble the house with 4d finishing nails, except for one side, where you use a 1¼-inch #6 screw in the center, into the bottom piece. This will allow you to remove the side.
7. Mount on a post, using a 10d or similar-sized nail or screw.

MATERIALS

Wood

    1–2′ x 4′ sht. ½″ ext. plywood or **Roof:** 2 pcs. 9″ x 5″

                                        Sides and bottom: 3 pcs. 5″ sq.

                                        Front and back: 2 pcs. 6″ x 8¾″

Hardware

    4d finishing nails
    1–1¼″ #6 screw

AN ALTERNATIVE STYLE

Massachusetts gardener Walter Masson reports that New Jersey isn't the only state where the bluebird needs friends. Masson said bluebirds were becoming scarce in his state because suburban developments were crowding the reclusive birds. He placed his houses on 6-foot poles, about 50 feet from the house.

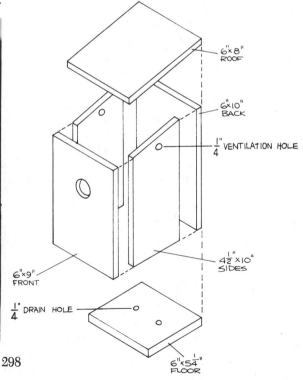

CONSTRUCTION

1. This house uses six pieces cut from almost any stock, ranging from ½-inch plywood to 1-inch pine. Cut one piece 6 inches by 9 inches for the front.
2. Cut one piece 6 inches by 10 inches for the back.
3. Cut two side pieces 4½ inches by 10 inches, but tapered to 9 inches in the front to accommodate the slanted roof.
4. Cut one piece 6 inches by 8 inches for the roof, and one piece 6 inches by 5¼ inches for the floor.
5. Drill two ¼-inch drain holes in the bottom. Drill a ¼-inch ventilation hole near the top of each side. On the front piece, measure 6 inches from the bottom to center the 1½-inch entrance hole.
6. Assemble the house using 4d nails.

MATERIALS

Wood

1–2' x 4' sht. ½" ext. plywood or **Front:** 1 pc. 6" x 9"

Back: 1 pc. 6" x 10"

Sides: 2 pcs. 4½" x 10"

Roof: 1 pc. 6" x 8"

Floor: 1 pc. 6" x 5¼"

Hardware

4d finishing nails

SWALLOW HOUSE

Tree swallows are another species whose eating habits should make them welcome in any garden. A good simple box can be made from any stock.

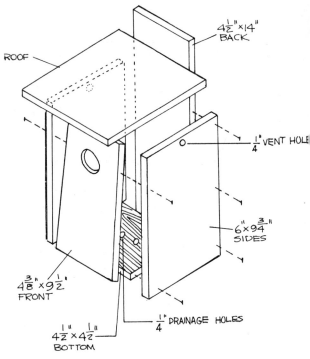

CONSTRUCTION

1. Cut a piece 4½ inches square for the bottom.
2. Cut one piece 8 inches by 7 inches for the roof.
3. Cut two pieces 6 inches by 9¾ inches for the sides.

MATERIALS

Wood

    1–2′ x 4′ sht. ½″ ext. plywood or **Bottom:** 1 pc. 4½″ sq.

    Roof: 1 pc. 8″ x 7″

    Sides: 2 pcs. 6″ x 9¾″

    Front: 1 pc. 4⅜″ x 9½″

    Back: 1 pc. 4½″ x 14″

Hardware

    4d finishing nails

4. Cut one piece 4⅜ inches by 9½ inches for the front.
5. Cut one piece 4½ inches by 14 inches for the back.
6. Measure 2 inches down from the top edge of the front piece to center the 1⅝-inch-diameter entrance hole. Drill two ¼-inch drainage holes in the bottom and ¼-inch ventilation holes near the top of the sides.
7. Nail the house together with 4d finishing nails. Put the front on last by using only two nails, placed directly opposite each other about a third of the way down from the top. They will act as pivots so the front will open. A third, temporary nail at the bottom will keep the "hinged" front shut.
8. Mount the swallow house in any sunny spot, 3 to 6 feet off the ground. Put them no less than 90 to 100 feet apart. Note that the long back piece is used to nail the house to a post.

ROBIN AND PHOEBE HOUSE

Robins and phoebes favor simple ledges, or three-sided boxes to build their nests. Robins do not mind being close to houses, so you can mount the nesting ledge under eaves, on a ledge, or in a tree. It should be mounted 6 to 15 feet high, and it is important that it face away from prevailing winds.

This nesting box uses ¾-inch or 1-inch stock and 1 x 2 strips.

CONSTRUCTION

1. Cut two pieces 9 inches by 8 inches for the roof. One piece is reduced on the 8-inch edge in size by the thickness of the back.
2. Cut three pieces 9 inches by 8 inches for the floor and sides. Bevel one 8-inch edge of each side piece on a 45-degree angle.
3. Cut one piece 8 inches by 13 inches for the back. Cut a peak by measuring 4 inches from one end along both 13-inch edges and cut a 45-degree angle from both corners.
4. Cut one piece of the 1 x 2 stock 17 inches long and another piece 9 inches long.

301

5. Drill two ¼-inch drainage holes in the floor.
6. Assemble, using 4d nails or 1½-inch #6 screws.
7. Use the 17-inch strip on the back of the nesting box to mount the box to the building or tree.

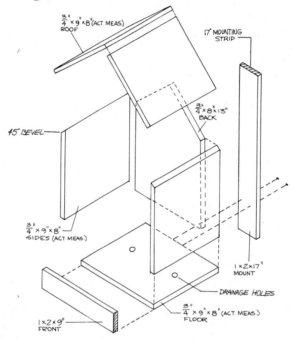

MATERIALS

Wood

1 pc. 1 x 10 x 6′	or	**Roof:** 2 pcs. ¾″ x 9″ x 8″ (act. meas.)
		Floor and sides: 3 pcs. ¾″ x 9″ x 8″ (act. meas.)
		Back: 1 pc. ¾″ x 8″ x 13″ (act. meas.)
1 pc. 1 x 2 x 4′	or	**Front:** 1 pc. 1 x 2 x 9″
		Mount: 1 pc. 1 x 2 x 17″

Hardware

4d nails

THE "ADD-ON" MARTIN HOUSE

You can provide for some backyard martins by making a birdhouse having stories that come in attachable sections. A one-floor house will have eight ventilated rooms, but more uniform sections can be added to house an expanding colony of martins. The roof, built to the same lateral dimensions, attaches to the top story. All sections are held together with hooks and screw eyes. To clean, just take the house apart and dump out the debris.

One advantage this house has is ventilation. A central shaft and vents under the eaves and in the gable walls permit air to circulate.

Such houses should be situated in open spaces. Like other swallows, these birds are attracted by water and so there is a better chance you'll attract a colony if there is a pond or stream nearby.

The suggested construction plan is for a two-story house. Follow the same dimensions for adding other floors.

CONSTRUCTION

1. Cut pieces for roof as follows: two 16-inch by 29½-inch pieces and a 22¼-inch-square floor from ½-inch exterior plywood, and two 6-inch by 20½-inch gable walls from ¾-inch exterior plywood (tapered to make pitched roof from peak to point 1 inch up from each end).

2. Cut a 2-inch-diameter hole in the center of each gable wall and cover it with window screen. Cut a 6-inch-square air shaft hole in the center of the roof floor. Glue and nail (with 4d nails) the gable walls to the floor. Place screening along the 1-inch-high vent under eaves, stapling it first to the floor, then to the roof panels as they are attached.

303

The "Add-On" Martin House

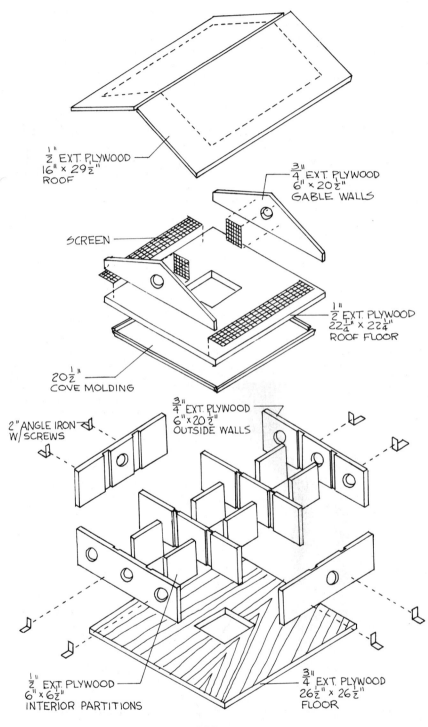

$\frac{1}{2}$" EXT. PLYWOOD
16" × 29$\frac{1}{2}$"
ROOF

$\frac{3}{4}$" EXT. PLYWOOD
6" × 20$\frac{1}{2}$"
GABLE WALLS

SCREEN

$\frac{1}{2}$" EXT. PLYWOOD
22$\frac{1}{4}$" × 22$\frac{1}{4}$"
ROOF FLOOR

20$\frac{1}{2}$"
COVE MOLDING

2" ANGLE IRON
W/ SCREWS

$\frac{3}{4}$" EXT. PLYWOOD
6" × 20$\frac{1}{2}$"
OUTSIDE WALLS

$\frac{1}{2}$" EXT. PLYWOOD
6" × 6$\frac{1}{2}$"
INTERIOR PARTITIONS

$\frac{3}{4}$" EXT. PLYWOOD
26$\frac{1}{2}$" × 26$\frac{1}{2}$"
FLOOR

304

Assemble roof with glue and nails. Cut lightweight roofing paper and fasten to roof.

3. For one story cut pieces of $\frac{3}{4}$-inch exterior plywood as follows: one 26$\frac{1}{2}$-inch-square floor, two 6-inch by 20$\frac{1}{2}$-inch walls, two 6-inch by 19-inch walls, two 6-inch by 19$\frac{1}{2}$-inch interior partitions. Cut six 6-inch by 6$\frac{1}{2}$-inch interior partitions from $\frac{1}{2}$-inch exterior plywood.

4. Cut 2$\frac{1}{2}$-inch entrance holes and dadoes for the partitions. In the 20$\frac{1}{2}$-inch-long outside walls, cut three entrance holes, the first in the center of the wall, and one 6 inches to each side of the first. Cut a single hole in each of the 19-inch outside walls. Measure 7 inches from each end of the 20$\frac{1}{2}$-inch walls and mark the center line for $\frac{3}{4}$-inch-wide by $\frac{1}{4}$-inch-deep dadoes. Measure 6$\frac{1}{4}$ inches from each end of the 19-inch walls and mark the center line for a $\frac{1}{2}$-inch-wide by $\frac{1}{4}$-inch-deep dado. Measure 6$\frac{1}{2}$ inches from each end of the 19$\frac{1}{2}$-inch partitions and mark the center line for $\frac{1}{2}$-inch-wide by $\frac{1}{4}$-inch-deep dadoes; mark both sides of the partitions, since dadoes must be cut in both sides; cut all the dadoes. Lay out and cut out a 6-inch-square air shaft hole in the center of the floor panel.

5. Assemble the walls with glue, using nails where possible. Center the wall assembly on the floor panel, leaving a 3-inch-wide porch around the outside of the walls, and attach it with two small angle irons on each wall. (These two steps must be duplicated for each additional story that will be added to the house.)

6. A cove molding around the underside of the roof and each story holds the parts in alignment. Set up the house and cut molding to size. Then nail it below each porch and below the roof.

7.   Connect the sections with one hook and eye on each of two sides on each section.

8.   Make foundation as follows: build central cross with double thickness of 1 x 3 oak. Cut four pieces 19 inches long, and dado each in the center for a half-lap joint. Assemble two crosses, then glue them together. The frame should be 1 x 3 pine 20½ inches square, assembled

---

MATERIALS

Wood

1–4' x 4' sht. ½" ext. plywood or	**Roof:** 2 pcs. 16" x 29½"
	Roof floor: 1 pc. 22¼" sq.
	Interior partitions: 12 pcs. 6" x 6½"
1 sht. ¾" ext. plywood or	**Gable walls:** 2 pcs. 6" x 20½"
	Floors: 2 pcs. 26½" sq.
	Outside walls: 4 pcs. 6" x 20½" 4 pcs. 6" x 19"
	Interior partitions: 4 pcs. 6" x 19½"
1 pc. cove molding 10' long or 1 pc. cove molding 12' long	**Alignment pieces:** 12 pcs. 20½" long
1 pc. 1 x 3 x 8' oak or	**Central crosses:** 4 pcs. 1 x 3 x 19" (in foundation)
1 pc. 1 x 3 x 8' pine or	**Foundation frame:** 2 pcs. 1 x 3 x 20½" 2 pcs. 1 x 3 x 19"
1 pc. 36" x ½" dowel or	**Rail posts:** 16 pcs. 1½" x ½" dowel
8 pcs. 36" x ¼" dowel or	**Railing:** 8 pcs. 26" x ¼" dowel
1 pc. 4 x 4 x 16' cedar (post)	

Hardware

1 pc. 12" x 36" window screen
Staples
Glue
4d nails
Roofing paper (36" x 36")
16–2" angle irons w/ screws
6 hooks and eyes
4–4" angle irons w/ screws

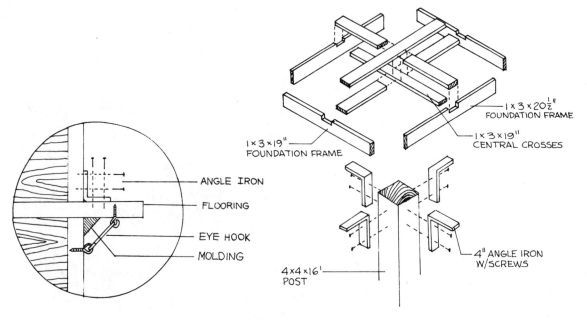

ANGLE IRON

FLOORING

EYE HOOK

MOLDING

1 × 3 × 20½"
FOUNDATION FRAME

1 × 3 × 19"
CENTRAL CROSSES

1 × 3 × 19"
FOUNDATION FRAME

4" ANGLE IRON
W/SCREWS

4 × 4 × 16'
POST

from two 20½-inch and two 19-inch lengths, as shown. Attach four heavy angle irons to the cross pieces for fastening to the supporting pole.

9. A guardrail around each porch may prevent young martins from falling and provide a secure perch for all the birds. Construct a rail as shown, to fit, using ½-inch and ¼-inch dowel.

10. The house is erected on a 16-foot 4 x 4 cedar post, cemented into a 4-foot-deep hole. Weighing more than 50 pounds, a two-story house is too heavy to mount atop a hinged post. Instead, use a ladder for the annual cleanout, carrying the roof to the ground, then the top story, and finally the lower story.

BIRD FEEDER

Some of the best projects are the most rudimentary. A bird feeder, for example, need not be fancy to suit the birds. It merely needs to hold a supply of food and be located in a safe, for the birds, spot.

This particular feeder was nailed together using scrap materials, in less than an hour.

307

Bird Feeder

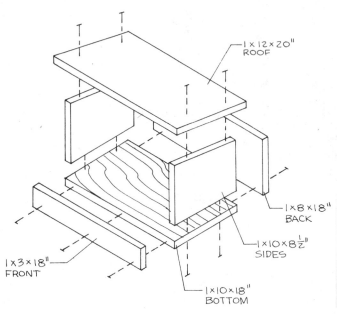

1 x 12 x 20"
ROOF

1 x 8 x 18"
BACK

1 x 10 x 8½"
SIDES

1 x 3 x 18"
FRONT

1 x 10 x 18"
BOTTOM

CONSTRUCTION

1. From a length of 1 x 10, cut two 8½-inch-long side pieces and an 18-inch-long bottom. Cut an 18-inch-long back from a piece of 1 x 8. Cut an 18-inch-long front board from a 1 x 3. Cut a 20-inch length of 1 x 12 for the roof.

2. Clamp the two sides together and crosscut a slope at one end. The ends

MATERIALS

Wood

1 pc. 1 x 10 x 4'	or	**Sides:** 2 pcs. 1 x 10 x 8½"
		Bottom: 1 pc. 1 x 10 x 18"
1 pc. 1 x 8 x 2'	or	**Back:** 1 pc. 1 x 8 x 18"
1 pc. 1 x 3 x 2'	or	**Front:** 1 pc. 1 x 3 x 18"
1 pc. 1 x 12 x 2'	or	**Roof:** 1 pc. 1 x 12 x 20"

Hardware

6d nails
2 screw eyes
12-gauge wire

should be 8½ inches high at the front of the feeder and 6½ inches high at the back.

3. Nail the bottom on the sides. Nail the back in place, then the top and the front. Use 6d nails. Two screw eyes or eyebolts and a length of 12-gauge wire can be used to fasten the feeder in a tree. Or corner irons can be used to mount atop a post. In any case, locate the feeder in an accessible spot to ease the chore of replenishing the feed supply.

GLASS-SIDED BIRD FEEDER

This attractive glass-sided bird feeder was constructed by OGF reader James MacMahon. He made his from ⅜-inch stock redwood, but any similar stock or exterior plywood also can be used. Its best feature is the sliding tin lid which allows the feeder to be loaded with seed without disassembling it as so many other feeders of this type require.

The finished feeder should be placed away from heavy traffic areas, on a post or suspended from a tree limb. Place it where predators will not get to feeding birds.

CONSTRUCTION

1. Cut two 5½-inch by 12-inch pieces for the roof pieces. Cut a 2-inch-wide by 3-inch-long notch for the filler hole near the center along the top edge of one piece.

2. Cut two ends. Start with 5½-inch by 8-inch rectangles and taper the bottom end to 3¼ inches, by beginning your cuts 2 inches below the top edge. Make the top peak shape by cutting from the same point to the center of the top edge.

3. Cut two pieces 2¼ inches by 7¾ inches, with a 20-degree bevel cut on one long edge of each, because the floor is peaked so the seeds empty by themselves.

4. Cut two pieces 1 inch by 7¾ inches for supports under the floor. Drill two ⅜-inch holes 4¼ inches apart for the perches.

5. Cut two pieces of glass 5 inches by 8 inches.

6. Cut two 8-inch lengths of ⅜-inch dowel.

7. Cut from ⅜-inch redwood strips six pieces for around the floor (two pieces 7¾ inches, four pieces 2¼ inches); four pieces to use as guides for the glass (four pieces 6 inches). Glue these strips into place as illustrated. The glass guides should be close enough together to hold the glass snugly.

8. Assemble the bird feeder using 1-inch brads, in combination with glue, if you like. Before attaching the roof pieces, remember to slide the glass into place.

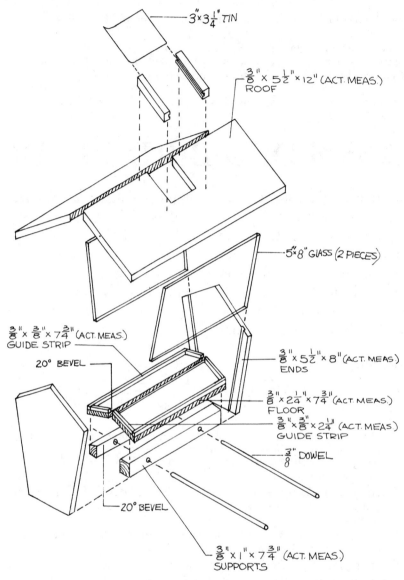

$3'' \times 3\frac{1}{4}''$ TIN

$\frac{3}{8}'' \times 5\frac{1}{2}'' \times 12''$ (ACT. MEAS.)
ROOF

$5'' \times 8''$ GLASS (2 PIECES)

$\frac{3}{8}'' \times \frac{3}{8}'' \times 7\frac{3}{4}''$ (ACT. MEAS.)
GUIDE STRIP

20° BEVEL

$\frac{3}{8}'' \times 5\frac{1}{2}'' \times 8''$ (ACT. MEAS.)
ENDS

$\frac{3}{8}'' \times 2\frac{1}{4}'' \times 7\frac{3}{4}''$ (ACT. MEAS.)
FLOOR

$\frac{3}{8}'' \times \frac{3}{8}'' \times 2\frac{1}{4}''$ (ACT. MEAS.)
GUIDE STRIP

$\frac{3}{8}''$ DOWEL

20° BEVEL

$\frac{3}{8}'' \times 1'' \times 7\frac{3}{4}''$ (ACT. MEAS.)
SUPPORTS

9. Glue two grooved 3-inch by $\frac{3}{8}$-inch strips about a $\frac{1}{4}$ inch from the edges of the filler slot of the roof.
10. Cut a piece of tin 3 inches by $3\frac{1}{4}$ inches for the filler cover. Bend one edge (about $\frac{3}{8}$ inch) to lap over the roof peak.
11. Glue the two dowel perches into place.

MATERIALS

Wood

1 pc. $\frac{3}{8}$″ x $5\frac{1}{2}$″ x 6′ redwood or **Roof:** 2 pcs. $\frac{3}{8}$″ x $5\frac{1}{2}$″ x 12″ (act. meas.)
(act. meas.)

Ends: 2 pcs. $\frac{3}{8}$″ x $5\frac{1}{2}$″ x 8″ (act. meas.)

Floor: 2 pcs. $\frac{3}{8}$″ x $2\frac{1}{4}$″ x $7\frac{3}{4}$″
(act. meas.)

Supports: 2 pcs. $\frac{3}{8}$″ x 1″ x $7\frac{3}{4}$″
(act. meas.)

Guide strips: 2 pcs. $\frac{3}{8}$″ x $\frac{3}{8}$″ x $7\frac{3}{4}$″
(act. meas.)
4 pcs. $\frac{3}{8}$″ x $\frac{3}{8}$″ x $2\frac{1}{4}$″
(act. meas.)
4 pcs. $\frac{3}{8}$″ x $\frac{3}{8}$″ x 6″
(act. meas.)

Filler guides: 2 pcs. $\frac{3}{8}$″ x $\frac{3}{8}$″ x 3″
(act. meas.)

1 pc. 36″ x $\frac{3}{8}$″ dowel or **Perches:** 2 pcs. 8″ x $\frac{3}{8}$″ dowel

Hardware

Glue
1″ brads
2 pcs. glass, 5″ x 8″
1 pc. tin, 3″ x $3\frac{1}{4}$″ (filler cover)

PART III
Food Storage Projects

FOOD PROCESSING

Food storage problems provide ample opportunities for the homestead handyman to practice his avocation. There are storage bins to be built, a cold cellar smokehouse to be constructed.

Even the gardener/handyman who cans or freezes his garden's produce will find woodworking projects that can ease the harvest season activities: knife racks, stools, juice presses, and the like.

KRAUTER

This handy gadget designed by Bill Tyler of Otis, Oregon, is no magic way to make sauerkraut. But it is an easy way to kraut cabbages at stocking-up time. The krauter is different from most, in that it is designed to use a knife to slice the cabbage; no special blade). The knife can be removed for modify the krauter to use a built-in blade). The knife can be removed for cleaning and other slicing chores.

CONSTRUCTION

1. Nail and glue slide from 1-inch hardwood cut as follows: two 3-inch by 8-inch sides and two 4-inch by 5¾-inch ends.
2. Nail and glue cutter channel from 1-inch hardwood as follows: two 2-inch by 18-inch sides and a 6-inch by 18-inch base.
3. Make slots in the channel sides 2 inches from the end on one side and 6 inches from the same end on the opposite side. Locate the bottom of the slots ⅛ inch from the channel base. Mark the length and location,

then drill out the slots with a series of overlapping $\frac{1}{8}$-inch holes.

4. To make the krauter extra fancy, cut $\frac{1}{8}$-inch by $\frac{3}{8}$-inch rabbets along the inside edges of the channel sides and the outside bottom edges of the slide.

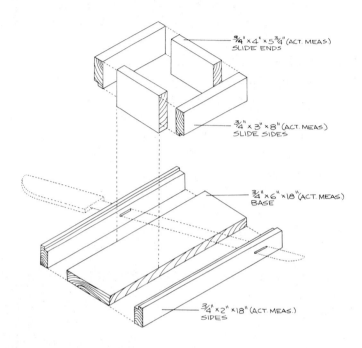

MATERIALS

Wood

    1 pc. 1 x 4 x 2' hardwood   or **Slide sides:** 2 pcs. $\frac{3}{4}''$ x 3" x 8" (act. meas.)

    1 pc. 1 x 6 x 2' hardwood   or **Slide ends:** 2 pcs. $\frac{3}{4}''$ x 4" x $5\frac{3}{4}''$ (act. meas.)

    1 pc. 1 x 3 x 4' hardwood   or **Sides:** 2 pcs. $\frac{3}{4}''$ x 2" x 18" (act. meas.)

    1 pc. 1 x 8 x 2' hardwood   or **Base:** 1 pc. $\frac{3}{4}''$ x 6" x 18" (act. meas.)

Hardware

    4d finishing nails
    Glue
    1–8" knife

TAMPER

To pack the sliced cabbage into a crock or bowl for fermenting, use this handy tamper. Shape it from a 33-inch length of 2 x 4 as shown. Taper the body beginning 6 inches from head to 3 inches from tail; cut two ¾-inch-deep notches, ¾ inch wide and 2 inches apart, at the bottom end.

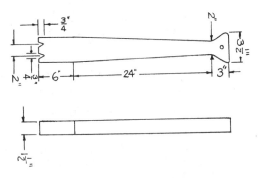

VARIATION

A more interesting variation on the traditional krauter was devised by Richard Weinsteiger, manager of the OGF Workshop. He constructed one with a slot in the base next to the blade. In use, the krauter is positioned atop a crock or other container; the slices of cabbage drop through the slot into the crock as they are cut.

The krauter is made the same way that Tyler's krauter was, except for the bottom of the cutter channel and the blade. The bottom is a 16-inch length of 6-inch-wide hardwood. From one end of the board, measure 6 inches along one side and 2 inches along the other. Draw a diagonal line joining the two points and saw the board into two pieces along the line. Glue and nail the longer piece of the bottom to the two sides, making it

flush with the butt ends and the bottom edges of the two side boards. The shorter piece of the bottom is glued and nailed flush with the butt ends, but ⅛ inch above the bottom edges of the side boards. When completed the cutter channel should have a 2-inch-wide slot in the bottom, with the back portion of the bottom slightly above the front portion.

The blade is made from an old hacksaw blade. It is cut to fit along the edge of the slot, then sharpened and mounted in place with two ½-inch #6 screws. Mount it so the sharpened edge just juts out over the slot a fraction of an inch.

MATERIALS

Wood

1 pc. 1 x 4 x 2′ hardwood	or	**Slide sides:** 2 pcs. ¾″ x 3″ x 8″ (act. meas.)
1 pc. 1 x 6 x 2′ hardwood	or	**Slide ends:** 2 pcs. ¾″ x 4″ x 5¾″ (act. meas.)
1 pc. 1 x 3 x 4′ hardwood	or	**Sides:** 2 pcs. ¾″ x 2″ x 18″ (act. meas.)
1 pc. 1 x 8 x 2′ hardwood	or	**Base:** 1 pc. ¾″ x 6″ x 16″ (act. meas.)

Hardware

Glue
4d finishing nails
Hacksaw blade
2–½″ #6 screws

CHEESE PRESSES

For the homesteader with a milk animal, an excess of milk can be a problem. However, with one of these easily made presses and some cheesecloth, that milk can be turned into cheese.

The idea of any cheese press, of course, is to mechanically squeeze the excess moisture out of the curd, a process that takes hours. Either of these presses can put a variable amount of pressure on the curd.

Either press should be washed and sterilized in boiling water after each use. This will help prevent spoilage of future pressings because of contamination.

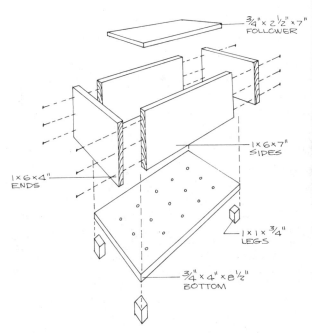

¾" x 2½" x 7"
FOLLOWER

1 x 6 x 7"
SIDES

1 x 6 x 4"
ENDS

1 x 1 x ¾"
LEGS

¾" x 4" x 8½"
BOTTOM

BOX PRESS CONSTRUCTION

1. From a piece of 1 x 6 hardwood, cut two 7-inch sides, two 4-inch ends, one 8½-inch bottom, and a 7-inch follower. The latter piece should be ripped to an actual 2½-inch width. From the scraps can be cut four ¾-inch 1 x 1 legs.

2. Butt the ends against the sides and nail together with 4d finishing nails. You'll probably need pilot holes in hardwood.

3. Drill ⅛-inch holes in the bottom piece in a grid, then butt it against the frame and secure with the 4d finishing nails.

4. Each leg can be secured, one to a corner, with two nails.

5. In use, the curd should be drained, then covered with several layers of cheesecloth, and dropped into the box. Put the follower on top and pile a brick or two on it.

MATERIALS

Wood

    1 pc. 1 x 6 x 4' hardwood   or   **Sides:** 2 pcs. 1 x 6 x 7"

                                      Ends: 2 pcs. 1 x 6 x 4"

                                        Bottom: 1 pc. $\frac{3}{4}$" x 4" x $8\frac{1}{2}$" (act. meas.)

                                        Follower: 1 pc. $\frac{3}{4}$" x $2\frac{1}{2}$" x 7" (act. meas.)

                                        Legs: 4 pcs. 1 x 1 x $\frac{3}{4}$"

Hardware

    4d finishing nails

TIN CAN PRESS CONSTRUCTION

1. Cut both ends out of a 16-ounce can.
2. Cut two discs from wood scraps—$\frac{1}{4}$-inch exterior plywood in the press shown—to just fit the can. Drill $\frac{1}{4}$-inch holes in the centers of the discs. Drill several other holes, for drainage, in one disc.
3. Cut a length of $\frac{1}{4}$-inch threaded rod about 3 inches longer than the can. Turn a wing nut on one end. Then add a fender washer, one disc, the can, the second disc, another fender washer, and another wing nut.
4. In use, wrap the curd in at least three layers of cheesecloth and work it into the can, forming it around the rod with your fingers. Turn both wing nuts at the same time, trying to press the curd into the can from both ends, rather than in one end and out the other.

MATERIALS

Wood

    Wood scraps to fashion 2 discs to diameter of can

Hardware

    1 pc. 24" x $\frac{1}{4}$" threaded rod
    2-$\frac{1}{4}$" wing nuts
    2-$\frac{1}{4}$" fender washers

Miscellaneous

    1-16-oz. can

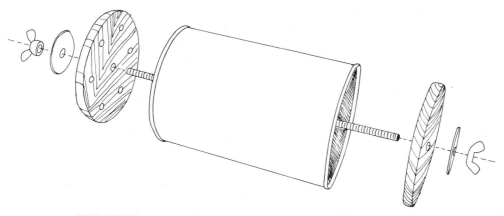

CUTTING BOARD

This cutting board is very easy to make. Any 1-inch stock of hardwood such as maple, oak, or birch is fine.

The design shown is very common and easy to make. But the board can be made in any design which you desire, keeping in mind to keep the main body of the board solid to prevent splintering and possible splitting.

KNIFE RACK

Every homestead kitchen needs a place to keep knives so they will stay sharp and clean. And to prevent accidental cuts. This rack is quickly made, provided you have a power circular saw.

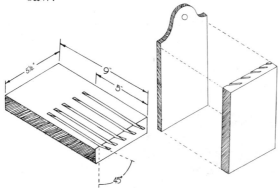

CONSTRUCTION

1. Cut the rack backing from a 12-inch length of 1 x 6, shaping the top as shown. Drill a small hole in the center of the top for hanging the rack on the wall.

2. Cut a 9-inch length of 2 x 6. Saw 1¼-inch-deep and 5-inch-long slots for knives at a 45-degree angle. (This is where the power saw is needed. Not only is making these cuts by hand difficult, but the kerf of a handsaw won't be wide enough to comfortably accommodate a knife.)

3. Glue block to backing, slots inward. Round all edges, sand, and varnish or apply oil finish.

MATERIALS

Wood

1 pc. 1 x 6 x 2′	or	**Backing:** 1 pc. 1 x 6 x 12″
1 pc. 2 x 6 x 2′	or	**Block:** 1 pc. 2 x 6 x 9″

Hardware

Glue

STEP STOOL

This handy little step stool can be made in an hour's time from a single board less than 5 feet long. Elwood Brown of Ballinger, Texas, who made the stool pictured, uses fence board, which measures an actual 1 inch by 6 inches.

MATERIALS

Wood

    1 pc. 1″ x 6″ x 6′ (act. meas.)   or   **Legs:** 2 pcs. 1″ x 6″ x 10″ (act. meas.)

    Top: 2 pcs. 1″ x 4″ x 18″ (act. meas.)

    Side braces: 2 pcs. 1″ x 2″ x 14″ (act. meas.)

    Cross braces: 2 pcs. 1″ x 2″ x 4″ (act. meas.)

Hardware

    5d finishing nails

CONSTRUCTION

1. Cut the board into two 10-inch pieces and two 18-inch pieces.
2. Rip each of the 18-inch pieces into a 4-inch-wide piece and a 2-inch-wide piece.
3. Cut each 2-inch-wide piece into a 14-inch length and a 4-inch length.
4. Clamp the two 10-inch-long leg pieces together. Cut a 1-inch by 2-inch rectangle from each side at one end (as shown) and cut a **V**-notch in

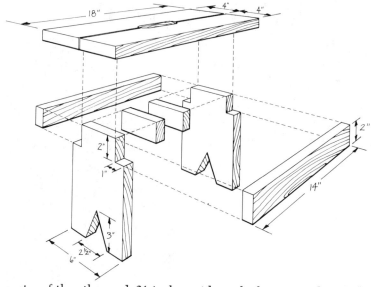

the center of the other end, 2½ inches wide at the bottom and extending 3 inches into the board.

5. Assemble the stool. Nail the shortest pieces to the legs along the top, between the 1-inch by 2-inch notches. Nail the 14-inch-long pieces in place, joining the two legs. Finally, nail on the top.

6. Cut the hand hole in the center of the top, as indicated. Drill two 1-inch-diameter holes, with centers 3 inches apart, with a brace and bit. Using a keyhole saw, cut out the wood between the holes. Smooth rough edges with a wood rasp.

TALL KITCHEN STOOL

Nothing's so handy as a kitchen stool that permits you to work at the sink or countertop while sitting. Especially so at stocking-up time.

This stool was concocted in the OGF Workshop. And after being tested and posed in the Fitness House kitchen, the stool was returned to the shop, where casters were added. It's now a dandy shop stool. (The casters would make it a better kitchen stool, too.)

324

MATERIALS

Wood

1–2' x 4' sht. $\frac{3}{4}$" int. plywood   or   **Seat:** 1 pc. 13" dia.

1 pc. 1 x 2 x 6'   or   **Top leg brace:** 4 pcs. 1 x 2 x $6\frac{5}{8}$"

                               Bottom leg braces: 4 pcs. 1 x 2 x $8\frac{1}{4}$"

1 pc. 2 x 2 x 10'   or   **Legs:** 4 pcs. 2 x 2 x 27"

Hardware

6d finishing nails
8–$1\frac{1}{2}$" #10 screws
8–$\frac{3}{4}$" #10 screws

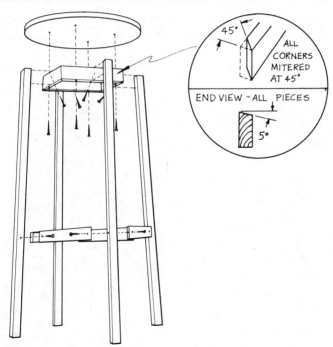

CONSTRUCTION

1. Cut a 13-inch-diameter disc from the plywood (or glue up 1-inch stock and cut the disc from that).
2. Cut four $6\frac{5}{8}$-inch lengths of 1 x 2 for the top leg brace. The ends should be mitered at a 45-degree angle and the tops should be beveled to a

5-degree angle. When assembled and fitted properly, the sides of this frame should splay out slightly. You will have to sand, file, or plane material from the tops of the miter cuts until the brace frame fits together tightly and seats securely against the seat. Fasten the frame together with 6d finishing nails (countersink them). Then drill a hole for a #10 screw in each side of the frame, penetrating the narrow face of the stock; countersink the hole quite deeply, about ½ inch. Finally, fasten the brace frame to the seat with four 1½-inch #10 screws.

3. Cut four 27-inch lengths of 2 x 2. Cut a 5-degree angle on each end, so the top and bottom faces are parallel. Secure one leg to the center of each side of the brace frame with a 1½-inch #10 screw, driven through the frame into the leg.

4. Cut four 8¼-inch lengths of 1 x 2, with 45-degree miters on each end. Using ¾-inch #10 screws, attach the braces to the legs as shown, 10 inches above the bottom of the legs.

5. If you desire a "wheeled" stool, install casters with 1½-inch by 1½-inch swivel plates to the bottom of each leg.

SMALL JUICE PRESS

This small juice press is just the right size for the gardener or homesteader with a half-dozen or so fruit trees. In short order, it will turn the culls into minor floods of fresh, natural fruit juice.

Although this press seems rather small, it is also inexpensive to construct, easy to store, and simple to use. It was devised by Dick Ott, of Rodale Press's Research and Development Group (R & D), and constructed and tested in the OGF Workshop.

The press is designed around an ordinary automobile bumper jack. The jack is modified so that it will press pulped apples, or other stone-free fruit, against a sturdy bench surface. The juice runs out through holes drilled through the bench.

The secret with this press, as with all juice presses, is the chopping of the apples or other fruit. The idea is to bruise, if possible, every cell in the fruit. The better the chopping, the greater the yield of juice. Pulp the apples in a food grinder or using some technique of your own devising. Wrap about three pounds of the pulp in cheesecloth, place it in the juice box on the press, and start jacking. Use a pan under the bench to collect the juice.

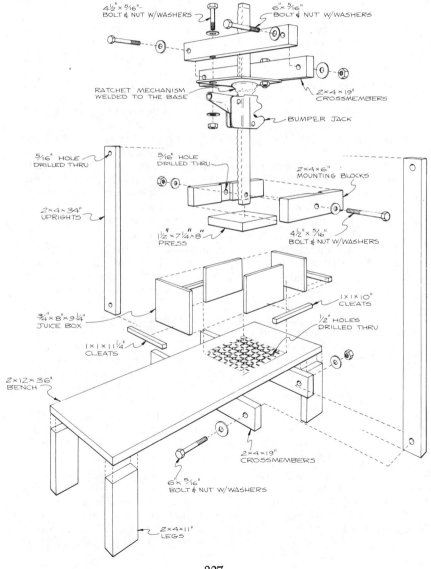

4½" × 5/16"- BOLT & NUT W/WASHERS

6" × 5/16" BOLT & NUT W/WASHERS

RATCHET MECHANISM WELDED TO THE BASE

2×4×19" CROSSMEMBERS

BUMPER JACK

5/16" HOLE DRILLED THRU

5/16" HOLE DRILLED THRU

2×4×6" MOUNTING BLOCKS

2×4×34" UPRIGHTS

1½" × 7¼" × 8" PRESS

4½" × 5/16" BOLT & NUT W/WASHERS

1×1×10" CLEATS

½" HOLES DRILLED THRU

¾" × 8" × 9¼" JUICE BOX

1×1×11¼" CLEATS

2×12×36" BENCH

2×4×19" CROSSMEMBERS

6" × 5/16" BOLT & NUT W/WASHERS

2×4×11" LEGS

327

CONSTRUCTION

1. Cut a 36-inch length of 2 x 12 and four 11-inch lengths of 2 x 4. Using 16d nails and glue, fasten the 2 x 4 legs to the bench, as shown.

2. Cut four 19-inch lengths of 2 x 4 for jack support crossmembers. Fasten one to the bottom of the bench, against the front legs. A narrow face of the 2 x 4 should be against the bench bottom, a broad face against the legs. Use glue and 16d nails, driving the nails through the support into the legs, and through the bench into the support. Using a short 2 x 4 as a temporary spacer, locate the second lower support crossmember and glue and nail it in place, as shown. Then remove the spacer.

3. Construct the box. The R & D press has a plywood box, but you can construct yours of 1 x 10 material. Cut four 8-inch by $9\frac{1}{4}$-inch pieces of $\frac{3}{4}$-inch plywood, then glue and nail them together, using 8d nails, forming the juice box, as shown.

4. Place the box in position, centered on the bench between the supports. Scribe a line on the benchtop around the inside of the box. Remove the box, then drill three rows of $\frac{1}{2}$-inch holes through the bench. You must locate the rows of holes so they penetrate the bench in front of, between, and behind the supports. The juice will run out of the box through these holes. To speed that process, a crosshatch pattern of grooves should be routed into the bench within the confines of the box. In doing this, be sure not to damage your router bit on the nails you've driven into the bench to secure the jack support crossmembers. Now replace the box and toenail it in place with 6d nails. Cut two $11\frac{1}{4}$-inch and two 10-inch lengths of 1 x 1 stock and using 6d nails, fasten them to the bench around the outside of the box.

5. Modify the bumper jack. The jack shaft socket in the base must be cut off, so the shaft will pass through the base. Then the ratchet mechanism must be welded to the base, as shown, so the base moves up and down the shaft with the ratchet mechanism. A welding shop can do this work quickly and inexpensively.

6. Cut two 6-inch lengths of 2 x 4. With a backsaw and chisel, cut a groove across the center of a broad face of each to accommodate half the thickness of the jack shaft. The two blocks are then sandwiched with the end of the shaft between them, as shown. Drill a $\frac{5}{16}$-inch hole through the three-piece assemblage and fasten it together with a $4\frac{1}{2}$-inch by $\frac{5}{16}$-inch bolt. Use fender washers on each side of the assemblage.

7. Cut an 8-inch length of 2 x 12, then rip it to the width of a nominal 2 x 8, that is, an actual $7\frac{1}{4}$ inches. Nail this piece to the 2 x 4s fastened to the end of the jack shaft, being sure to position the wood grains of the two parts perpendicular to each other. Use 16d nails.

8. Cut two 34-inch lengths of 2 x 4, for the jack support uprights. Slip one between the two crossmembers on each side of the bench, drill a $\frac{5}{16}$-inch hole through crossmembers and upright, then bolt them together with a 6-inch by $\frac{5}{16}$-inch bolt and nut with fender washers. Set the jack in place, then take the two remaining upper jack support crossmembers (cut at the outset of the project) and, after drilling the

MATERIALS

Wood

1 pc. 2 x 12 x 4'	or	**Bench:** 1 pc. 2 x 12 x 36"
		Press: 1 pc. $1\frac{1}{2}$" x $7\frac{1}{4}$" x 8" (act. meas.)
1 pc. 2 x 4 x 10'	or	**Legs:** 4 pcs. 2 x 4 x 11"
		Uprights: 2 pcs. 2 x 4 x 34"
1 pc. 2 x 4 x 8'	or	**Crossmembers:** 4 pcs. 2 x 4 x 19"
		Mounting blocks: 2 pcs. 2 x 4 x 6"
1–2' x 4' sht. $\frac{3}{4}$" ext. plywood	or	**Juice box:** 4 pcs. 8" x $9\frac{1}{4}$"
1 pc. 1 x 1 x 2'	or	**Cleats:** 2 pcs. 1 x 1 x $11\frac{1}{4}$"
		2 pcs. 1 x 1 x 10"

Hardware

16d nails
Glue
8d nails
6d nails
3–$4\frac{1}{2}$" x $\frac{5}{16}$" bolts w/ nuts
8–$\frac{5}{16}$" ID fender washers
4–6" x $\frac{5}{16}$" bolts w/ nuts
Enamel paint

Miscellaneous

1 bumper jack

appropriate holes, bolt them to the support uprights, as shown. Use 6-inch by $\frac{5}{16}$-inch bolts and nuts with fender washers.

9. Slide the jack-base/ratchet mechanism up the shaft until it seats firmly against the upper crossmembers. Drill a $\frac{5}{16}$-inch hole through the metal base and each crossmember. Then secure the metal jacking mechanism to the crossmembers with $4\frac{1}{2}$-inch by $\frac{5}{16}$-inch bolts and nuts, with a fender washer included against the wood surface.

10. Paint the entire press with a high-quality nonleaded enamel paint.

LARGE JUICE PRESS

This fruit press has a far greater capacity than our bumper-jack press, but it is far more difficult to construct and uses more materials. It is a reasonable project, nonetheless, for a homesteader with a lot of apple trees or a food-buyers cooperative whose members want to produce their own cider.

The fruit press is primarily designed for apples but it can be used for pressing any pulped fruit. The grater can be used for any fruit free of large stones. With apples, the fruit press will handle from one to five boxes yielding two to ten gallons at one pressing.

The original design is from the Canadian Department of Agriculture. But in building our own press in the OGF Workshop, we noted a few shortcomings and made several changes to correct them.

The essential parts consist of the frame, drainboard, rack, trays, platform, grater, and hopper.

Apples are placed in the hopper. A piece of unbleached cheesecloth, 36 inches square, is placed on the slatted rack with the corners of the cloth in the middle of the sides of the rack. The apples are grated until the resulting pulp forms a layer 2 to 3 inches thick and 18 inches square. The corners of the cloth are then

folded over the pulp, completely en-
closing the mass. A lath tray is then
placed on top of this apple pulp and
cloth, and the operation is repeated.
If a short jack is used, five layers can
be pressed at one time, yielding approximately ten gallons of juice. The
pressure platform is placed on top of
the last layer and the jack worked between this and the shaft.

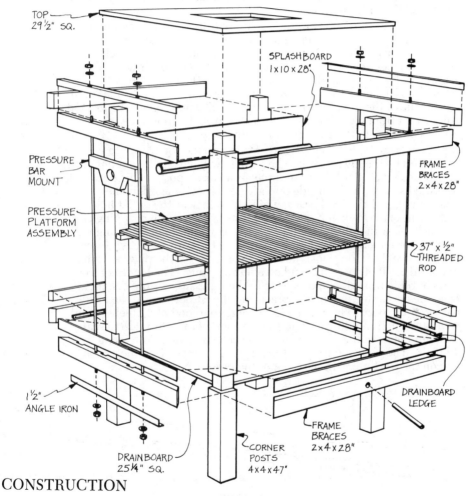

CONSTRUCTION

1. The four corner posts are made of 4 x 4 cedar 47 inches long. These
   posts are joined together with 2 x 4 braces, placed 12 inches from the
   bottom and across the top, using 16d nails. These are set into the
   corner posts sufficiently so that their outer surface will be flush with
   the piece of 1 x 3 nailed to the posts immediately above the lower
   braces, using 6d nails. The 2 x 4 braces and the 1 x 3 are cut at
   45-degree angles at the corners. The length of these pieces is 28 inches.

2. The top 2 x 4 braces on both sides of the press are strengthened by
1½-inch angle iron 28 inches long. Holes large enough for ½-inch rods
are drilled 9⅜ inches (measured to the center of the hole) from each
end. Two pieces of 1½-inch angle iron 19¾ inches long, with similar
holes 5⅜ inches from each end, reinforce the lower side braces. Holes
are bored in the 2 x 4 braces to correspond with the holes in the angle
iron. The 37-inch by ½-inch rods are put in place and the nuts tightened until the rods are firm.

3. The same 2 x 4s in the lower group that are drilled to accommodate
the ½-inch rods are also notched in four places to take care of the
reinforcements on the rack, as shown. These notches are 1½ inches
wide, 1¾ inches deep, and ¾ inch into the 2 x 4. Two of these notches
are situated ⅛ inch from the corner post, while the near side of the
other two is 6 inches from the corner post. Finally, drill a 1-inch drain
hole in one of the unnotched frame braces. The hole should be located
equidistant from either end, and 1½ inches from the bottom edge.
Force a 6-inch length of 1-inch pipe in the hole.

4. A piece of ¾-inch plywood is tightly fitted into the square space
developed by the lower 2 x 4s. The corners will have to be cut out of the
plywood, so that it will fit around the 4 x 4 corner posts. This plywood
is located so that the high side opposite the drain hole is 2 inches
below the top of the 2 x 4 brace, while the side near the outlet hole
is 2½ inches below the top of the 2 x 4 brace. Any rough stripping can
be used below the plywood to form a ledge, while small right-angled
triangles of ¾-inch material can be nailed in the corners for reinforcement. Since the corner posts cut into the corners of the plywood, you
will need eight of these triangular reinforcements. The length of the
sides of these triangles on each side of the right angle is the distance
from the corner formed by the brace and the corner post to the inside
corner of the post. This will be in the neighborhood of 2½ inches. Nail
½-inch chamfer molding around the perimeter of the top side to seal
the joint between the plywood, the braces, and corner post, using
4d nails. The plywood catches the juice and delivers it to the 1-inch
hole in the 2 x 4 brace in the front of the press.

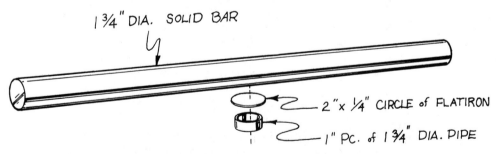

1¾" DIA. SOLID BAR

2"x ¼" CIRCLE of FLATIRON

1" PC. of 1¾" DIA. PIPE

5. The pressure bar is installed next. Use a 28-inch length of 1¾-inch
steel shaft (solid metal, not a pipe) for the pressure bar. To provide
a firm seat for the jack during the pressing operations, a flat pad must
be welded to the center of the shaft. Cut a 2-inch circle of ¼-inch
flatiron, then weld a 1-inch piece of 1¾-inch pipe to it; this is the pad,

which you weld to the pressure bar. The pressure bar is mounted using two 8-inch pieces of 2 x 6. Drill a 1¾-inch hole in the middle of each piece, 2⅝ inches from one edge. Shape the mountings roughly as shown, then attach to the upper frame braces between the threaded rod supports, using two 3½-inch #12 screws in each.

6. Because the finished grater will have a tendency to throw bits of grated apple out the front of the press, it is wise to nail, using 6d nails, a 28-inch length of 1 x 10 (or like-sized piece of plywood) into the inside of the corner posts at the front of the press, to serve as a splashboard.

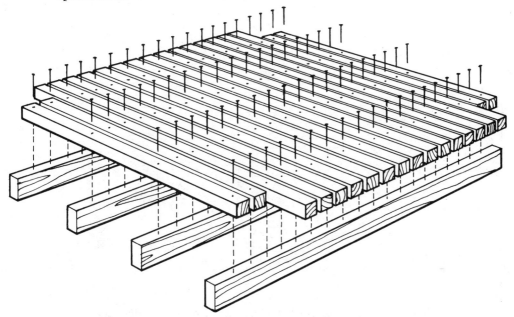

7. The rack is made of nineteen pieces of 1 x 1 nailed to four stringers measuring 1¼ inches by 1⅞ inches. The stringers will have to be ripped from a 2 x 4. The stringers are spaced so that they will fit into the notches previously described in the side braces. The stringers and the 1 x 1 pieces should be made of the strongest wood available as the rack has to withstand the full pressure of the jack. The two 1 x 1 pieces on each side of the rack are cut off flush with the first stringer to allow room for the corner posts. The rack is removable to ease cleaning.

8. Five lath trays are next assembled using ⅜-inch by 1½-inch wooden strips, cut to a length of 19 inches. If you can't buy the proper-sized material, rip 19-inch lengths of 2 x 8 into ⅜-inch strips. Each length should yield fourteen strips, enough for one tray; an 8-foot 2 x 8 should thus yield enough strips for the five trays needed. A tray is 19 inches square and consists of a single layer of laths placed parallel to one another and the thickness of a lath apart. These laths are crossed at each end (above and below) with laths that hold the rack together.

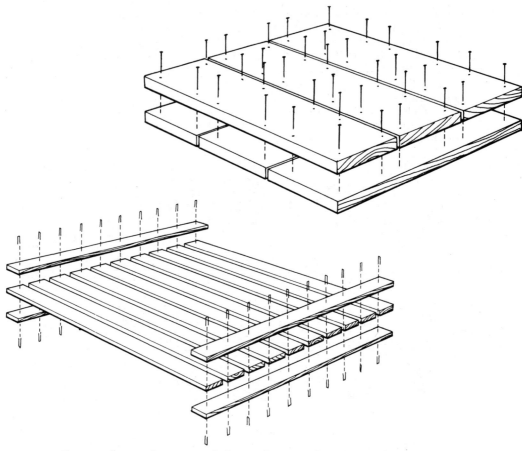

Copper clout nails, one to a lath, are driven in from both sides. No more than five lath trays can be used at a time.

9. The pressure platform is made of 2 x 6s. Cut seven 19-inch lengths and rip one in half. Lay out three full-width pieces and one of the halves, then lay the remaining pieces on top, at right angles to the first layer, and nail them together. As this platform is subjected to considerable strain it is wise to nail it thoroughly with nails long enough to clinch (20d).

10. The grater drum can be made in either of two ways. The easiest, if you have the equipment and know-how, is to turn down a solid block of wood on a lathe. The second method, which is the one we used, is to cut a number of discs from standard 1- or 2-inch stock, then fasten them together. The drum must be about 8 inches long and 8 inches in diameter. We cut eleven 8-inch-diameter discs from 1 x 10 material. Drill a 1-inch-diameter hole through the center of each disc and four ¼-inch-diameter holes, evenly spaced around the disc, midway between the center hole and the outer edge, but in exactly the same spots in each disc. When all are finished, deeply countersink the four

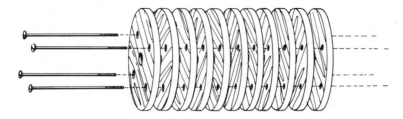

¼-inch holes in two of the discs, then bolt all eleven together with those two as the outermost layer. Use four 7½-inch machine bolts. A little waterproof glue between layers wouldn't hurt.

11. The circumference of the drum is marked into eights and lines are drawn lengthwise on its surface. On each line a saw cut is made into which saw blades will be fitted. The depth of these cuts will depend on the size of blades being used. In the cuts, pieces of a coarse saw blade (such as a bucksaw or pruning saw) are placed with $\frac{3}{16}$ inch of teeth protruding from the drum.

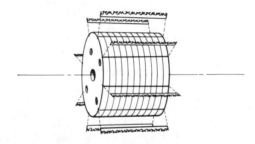

12. We used a 23-inch piece of ¾-inch steel pipe as a shaft. We used a scrap crank handle. The shaft and handle could be created from ¾-inch pipe and two elbows: Use a 23-inch piece for the shaft; turn an elbow on the end, screw a 12-inch length of pipe into the elbow, add another elbow and a 6-inch length of pipe. At each end of the drum, ¼-inch holes are drilled so that pins may be inserted to keep the drum from turning on the shaft. You can use a nail with the head cut off for a pin. Collars are also used on the shaft to keep the drum properly spaced between the bearings. These collars are ¾-inch lengths of 1-inch pipe with a setscrew through one side.

13. The top of the press is covered with a piece of ¾-inch plywood. In the center of the 29½-inch-square panel, cut a hole measuring 8½ inches by 9½ inches. The grater mounting will be constructed to surround this hole. The top is screwed in place using twelve 1½-inch #12 screws.

14. To construct the grater mounting, take two pieces of 2 x 4, 12½ inches long, and rip them to 2¾ inches. In the middle of these two pieces (6¼ inches) drill a 1-inch hole, 1 inch in from the edge. Rip the 12½-inch pieces so that the saw cut is precisely in the center of the hole. From 2-inch stock cut two pieces, one 2¾ inches by 8½ inches and one 1¾ inches by 8½ inches. The higher of these pieces must have the inner

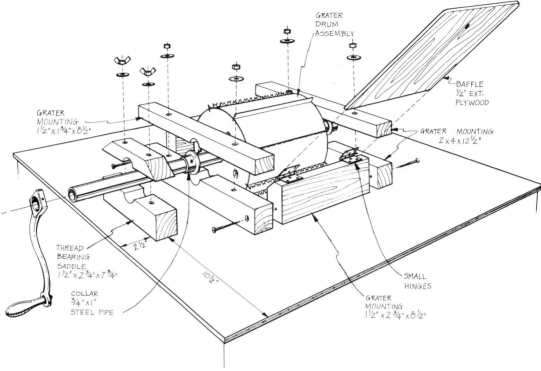

edge beveled off so the baffle board that will be hinged to it will operate freely. Lay out the four parts to form a rectangle measuring $12\frac{1}{2}$ inches by $11\frac{1}{2}$ inches. After drilling a pilot hole and countersinking, drive a $2\frac{1}{2}$-inch #10 screw through the side of the longer pieces into the butt end of the shorter pieces.

15. A third bearing saddle—the grater mounting has two—is made for the grater shaft by ripping a $7\frac{3}{4}$-inch length of 2 x 6 down to $2\frac{3}{4}$ inches. Drill a 1-inch hole in the middle of the piece, 1 inch from the edge, then rip the piece through the center of the hole.

16. Lay the mounting assembly over the hole in the plywood top and drill four $\frac{1}{4}$-inch holes through the assembly and the top, locating a hole on each side of the saddles for the grater shaft. Remove the upper portion of the grater mounting and lay the grater in place. Slip the lower portion of the third bearing saddle in position beneath the portion of the shaft that extends beyond the edge of the plywood. It should be about $4\frac{1}{2}$ inches shy of the edge of the top. Lay the bearing cap in place and drill a $\frac{1}{4}$-inch hole through the bearing saddle block and the top on either side of the shaft. Secure the assembly with two 5-inch by $\frac{1}{4}$-inch machine bolts with fender washers and wing nuts. Replace the grater mounting bearing caps and secure them in place with $4\frac{1}{2}$-inch by $\frac{1}{4}$-inch machine bolts with fender washers and nuts.

17. Cut a 10-inch by $11\frac{1}{2}$-inch panel of $\frac{1}{2}$-inch exterior plywood, to serve as the movable baffle board inside the hopper. It is attached to the taller crossmember of the grater mounting assembly with two small hinges.

336

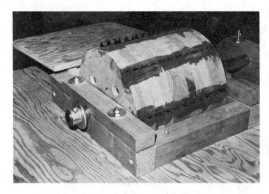

18. The hopper is constructed of ½-inch exterior plywood. Cut out two 11½-inch by 13¾-inch pieces for the front and back panels, two 26-inch by 13-inch pieces, from which the side panels will be cut, and a piece 11½ inches by 20 inches for the inner panel. Cut an 8½-inch-wide by 6½-inch-deep notch in the center of one end of the inner panel, so that it will fit around the grater drum. The side panels are cut as follows: along one 26-inch edge, measure 6¾ inches from each end. Draw ¾-inch perpendicular lines from those points, then extend the lines to the corners of the opposite side of the panel, forming the **V**-shaped hopper sides. Cut along the lines. Hold each side panel in place against the grater mounting and mark for the **U**-shaped cut that must be made to accommodate the grater shaft. The hopper is glued together. For a finished appearance, the top edges of the front and back panels should be beveled flush with the top edges of the sides.

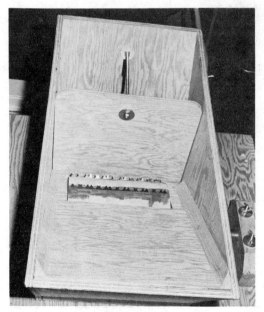
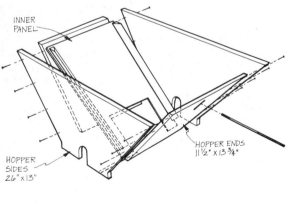

INNER PANEL

HOPPER ENDS
11 ½" x 13 ¾"

HOPPER SIDES
26" x 13"

To fit properly against the front, the inner panel must be beveled at the upper edge. It must be fitted to clear both the grater and the movable inner baffle. The bottom edges of both the front and back panels must be beveled so the hopper fits securely over the grater mounting. Finally, to prevent apples from hanging up between the grater and the hopper sides, nail, with 6d nails, two 16-inch lengths of 2 x 4 inside the hopper, as shown. The ends must be cut on an angle—determined by fit so the baffle board can be moved freely.

19. Drill a ¼-inch hole in the upper center of the baffle board. Create a ¼-inch-wide by 3-inch-long slot in the upper center of the back panel by drilling a series of overlapping ¼-inch holes, then filing the edges smooth. By trial and error, bend a 12-inch length of ¼-inch threaded rod so that it will extend through both holes. Secure it in the movable baffle board with two fender washers and two nuts. Use a nut and fender washer on the inner side of the back panel, and a fender washer and wing nut on the outer side. By jockeying the baffle back and forth, you will be able to adjust the feed of apples to the grater.

20. The press should be painted, primarily to ease the post-pressing cleanup.

MATERIALS

Wood

2 pcs. 4 x 4 x 8' cedar	or	**Corner posts:** 4 pcs. 4 x 4 x 47"
2 pcs. 2 x 4 x 12'	or	**Frame braces:** 8 pcs. 2 x 4 x 28"
		Grater mounting: 2 pcs. 2 x 4 x 12½"
		Hopper: 2 pcs. 2 x 4 x 16"
1 pc. 1 x 3 x 12'	or	**Frame braces:** 4 pcs. 1 x 3 x 28"

Triangular braces: 4 pcs. 1 x 3 x 2¾″
(cut each
diagonally to
make 8 triangles)

1 sht. ¾″ ext. plywood   or   **Drainboard:** 1 pc. 25¼″ sq.
(good one side)

Top: 1 pc. 29½″ sq.

1 pc. 1 x 1 x 8′   or   **Drainboard ledge:** 2 pcs. 1 x 1 x 14¾″

Drainboard ledge: 2 pcs. 1 x 1 x 15″

10′–½″ chamfer molding (cut to fit)

1 pc. 2 x 6 x 4′   or   **Pressure bar mount:** 2 pcs. 2 x 6 x 8″

Grater mounting: 1 pc. 1½″ x 2¾″ x 8½″
(act. meas.)
1 pc. 1½″ x 1¾″ x 8½″
(act. meas.)

Third bearing saddle: 1 pc. 1½″ x 2¾″ x 7¾″
(act. meas.)

1 pc. 1 x 10 x 10′   or   **Splashboard:** 1 pc. 1 x 10 x 28″

Grater drum: 11 pcs. 1 x 10 x 8″

4 pcs. 1 x 1 x 12′ oak   or   **Rack:** 15 pcs. 1 x 1 x 26¾″
4 pcs. 1 x 1 x 19¾″

1 pc. 2 x 4 x 12′ oak   or   **Stringers:** 4 pcs. 1¼″ x 1⅞″ x 26¾″ (act. meas.)

1 pc. 2 x 8 x 8′   or   **Trays** (5): 5 pcs. 2 x 8 x 19″ (rip each into
14 pcs. ⅜″ x 1½″ x 19″)

1 pc. 2 x 6 x 12′   or   **Pressure platform:** 7 pcs. 2 x 6 x 19″

1–4′ sq. sht. ½″ ext. plywood   or   **Baffle:** 1 pc. 10″ x 11½″
(good both sides)

Hopper ends: 2 pcs. 11½″ x 13¾″

Hopper sides: 2 pcs. 26″ x 13″

Inner panel: 1 pc. 11½″ x 20″

Hardware

 16d nails
 6d nails
 1 pc. 8' x 1½" angle iron or 2 pcs. 28" x 1½"
              2 pcs. 19¾" x 1½"
 2 pcs. 8' x ½" threaded rod or 4 pcs. 37" x ½"
 8–½" nuts
 8–½" flat washers
 1 pc. 6" x 1" steel pipe (drainpipe)
 4d nails
 1 pc. 28" x 1¾" steel shaft (pressure bar)
 1 pc. ¼" x 2" x 2" flatiron
 1 pc. 1" x 1¾" steel pipe
 4–3½" #12 screws
 Copper clout nails
 20d nails
 Waterproof glue
 4–7½" x ¼" machine bolts w/ nuts and washers (drum)
 1 pc. 23" x ¾" steel pipe (shaft)
 2–¾" 90° elbows
 1 pc. 12" x ¾" steel pipe
 1 pc. 6" x ¾" steel pipe
 2 pcs. ¾" x 1" steel pipe (collars)
 2 small setscrews
 12–1½" #12 screws
 4–2½" #10 screws
 2–5" x ¼" machine bolts w/ wing nuts and
  fender washers (handle bearing)
 4–4½" x ¼" machine bolts w/ nuts and fender washers (grater bearings)
 2 small hinges
 1–12" x ¼" threaded rod w/ 3 nuts, 1 wing nut, and 4 fender washers
 Paint–white enamel

Miscellaneous

 4 pruning saw blades or 8 pcs. 8¼" long

HOT BOX

The hot box is a homemade device with which you can make casserole and soup-type dishes with a fraction of the energy you would use in traditional stove-top or oven-cooking techniques. The box works on this principle: food is brought to boiling, 212°F. and above, and quickly placed in the insulated box. Its own heat is retained and finishes the cooking.

You should have a reliable kitchen thermometer to use with the hot box. Experience with the hot box in Rodale Press's Fitness House kitchen showed that after four or five hours in the hot box, the temperature of food dropped to between 140° and 160°F., depending on the ingredients and how full the pot was.

According to the U.S. Department of Agriculture, the danger with slow-cooking methods is when the warming time to high temperatures, the 200°-plus range, is long. This allows bacteria to multiply before they are killed, leaving behind toxins that can make you just as sick as the live bacteria.

The USDA say that between 140° and 165°F., bacteria *growth* is prevented, but live bacteria may survive. The key, therefore, is to bring the food to the boiling temperature to kill these bacteria first.

Hot Box

There are directions here for two hot boxes. One is easier to make, and the other is more efficient, requiring shorter "cooking time."

The simpler box uses 2-inch-thick Styrofoam and is lined with aluminum foil. The box itself is made from $\frac{1}{4}$-inch plywood. You will have to know what size pot you will be using, because the box must be built to fit it.

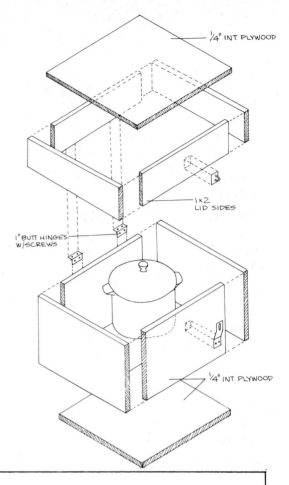

MATERIALS

Wood

      1–4′ x 4′ sht. $\frac{1}{4}$″ int. plywood cut to fit your pot

      1 x 2 stock cut in 4 pcs. to form sides of lid

Hardware

      $\frac{3}{4}$″ brads
      Wood glue
      White glue
      2–1″ butt hinges w/ screws
      1 hasp and staple

Miscellaneous

      2″ x 2′ x 9′ Styrofoam cut to fit inside of box
      Aluminum foil

CONSTRUCTION

1. Construct a square box 4 inches larger than the outside diameter of your pot. It should be 2 inches taller than the pot with its lid in place. Use ¾-inch brads and wood glue to assemble the box.

2. To make the lid, start with a square of plywood with dimensions 1½ inches greater than the outside dimensions of the box. Cut 1 x 2 stock to fit the edges, and nail and glue the pieces in place to make a tight fit.

3. Before you cut your Styrofoam sheet, cover it with aluminum foil, shiny side up. Use white glue to fasten it. After it has dried, cut the Styrofoam to fit first the bottom, the sides, and inside the lid of the box. Again, use glue to hold it in place.

4. Use two 1-inch butt hinges to attach the lid. Install a light hasp to the front edge of the lid and a staple to the front of the box.

VARIATION

The second hot box is harder to make only because you must work with urethane insulation. You buy two separate resin compounds and mix them in equal proportions to start a chemical reaction which forms the foam.

CONSTRUCTION

1. Construct a box exactly the way you did the other box, but leave off the bottom. Build the lid frame in the same manner, but do not fasten the top piece of plywood yet.

2. The urethane will mold to the shape of the pan, so to leave room to grasp the pot handles, cut wooden blocks, about 2 inches by 2 inches with a notch for the handles, to fit around them.

3. Lay a sheet of aluminum foil, shiny side down, on the workbench and invert the pot, with handle blocks in place on top of the foil. Cover the pot and handles with aluminum foil, always keeping the shiny side out. Leave several inches of foil extending from around the top of the pot. Then, carefully center and place the four-sided box on top and mold the foil flat on the table and then up a few inches on the sides of the box. Get the bottom, nails, and hammer ready.

4. Mix one pint of each resin in a can or bucket that you can discard. When it begins to foam, or when you can feel the mixture getting warm through the container, dump the urethane around the pot. As it swells, you will be able to see when you have enough to fill the box.

343

5. Before it reaches the top, quickly nail the bottom in place and hold it in position. An alternative method is to allow the foam to overflow and trim it off flush with a saw after it has hardened, and then nail the bottom on. Allow 30 minutes for the urethane to cure.

6. Stand the box right-side up, and hinge the lid frame into place. Put the lid on the pot and cover it and the exposed surfaces of the box with aluminum foil, again, shiny side down. Use a sheet big enough to extend up to cover the sides of the lid.

7. Mix one cup of each of the resins. Mix and pour it onto the center of the pot lid so it expands outward. Quickly nail the top of the lid in place. Or, allow the urethane to overflow, trim it off flush, and nail the lid top in place. Attach the hasp and staple and your hot box is ready for cooking.

MATERIALS

Wood

1–4' x 4' sht. ¼" int. plywood cut to fit your pot

1 x 2 stock cut in 4 pcs. to form sides of lid and wood blocks (step 2)

Hardware

¾" brads
Wood glue
4d nails
2–1" butt hinges w/ screws
1 hasp and staple

Miscellaneous

Aluminum foil
3 cups each type urethane resin

EARTH BOX SPROUTER

Whether you are an old hand at sprouting seeds to eat or not, you're going to be surprised by a great "new" method for sprouting that the Chinese have used for thousands of years. The technique has tremendous advan-tages. It makes sprouting very simple, cuts out a lot of fuss and bother, and produces a finished product of much improved nutritional value.

Production cost of sprouts made by this method is low, and anybody can do it in his own yard. In fact, you can also use this method to make high-nutrient sprouts indoors.

The Chinese earth box method of sprouting simply involves placing the soaked seeds on soil inside a wooden box partly buried in the earth. The bottom is first covered with a layer of fine soil, and over it are spread beans with a thickness not surpassing two beans. The pit is again covered with a layer of fine soil. No watering is needed. You can go away for a few days and come back to harvest your sprouts.

We tried the earth box technique at the new Organic Gardening Experimental Farm and found that the Chinese claims are not exaggerated. Sprouting is easily accomplished, with very little fuss and bother. In very hot and moist weather some mold can grow, but that can be prevented by keeping the cover of the sprouting box open, to improve ventilation.

To use the sprouter, first soak a ¼ pound of seeds for twelve hours before sowing. Then scatter the seeds evenly over the soil surface, cover them lightly with soil, and put the lid in place. That's all there is to it! (Wetting down the soil before planting hastens sprouting by a half-day, but creates a slight mold problem. The natural moisture in most soil is all that's needed.)

VARIATION

The earth box system works just as well indoors by adding a bottom (another piece of plywood the size of the lid will work fine). Fill the box with 3 inches of loose soil, sow your seeds, and cover them lightly. Leave them undisturbed in the dark for four days. Should mold appear, prop the lid open several inches to admit fresh air. When sprouting alfalfa shoots by this method, remove the lid when the first leaves begin to form to allow photosynthesis to create peak nutritional value.

MATERIALS

Wood

1 pc. 1 x 10 x 6'	or	**Sides:**	2 pcs. 1 x 10 x 16"
		Ends:	2 pcs. 1 x 10 x 12"
1 pc. 1 x 1 x 2'	or	**Cleats:**	4 pcs. 1 x 1 x 6"
1–2' x 4' sht. ½" ext. plywood	or	**Top:**	1 pc. 17½" x 12"
		Bottom (optional):	1 pc. 17½" x 12"

Hardware

8d nails
1¼" brads

CONSTRUCTION

1. From a 1 x 10, cut two 16-inch sides and two 12-inch ends.
2. Assemble the box with the ends overlapping the sides in a simple butt joint. Nail using 8d nails.
3. Using 1¼-inch brads, attach four 6-inch-long 1 x 1 cleats to the 17½-inch by 12-inch panel of ½-inch exterior plywood.
4. Work the frame into fine, loose soil to a depth of 3 inches.

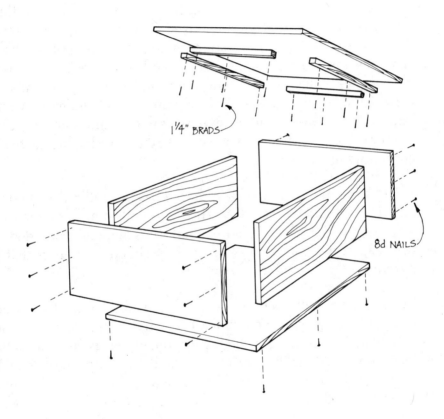

1¼" BRADS

8d NAILS

FOOD DRYERS

With the advent of canning and freezing, drying foods has almost become a lost means of preservation. Drying, however, is an excellent natural method of preserving fruit and vegetables. Nothing is added and only the water is removed. The drying process removes 80 to 90 percent of the moisture content so that spoilage bacteria can't develop during storage. Dried food conserves storage space—five pounds of fresh fruit will yield approximately one pound of dried fruit. With the exception of some loss of vitamins A and C, both fruits and vegetables contain the same vitamins and minerals as fresh produce. Dried fruit is sweeter than fresh, due to the high concentration of fruit sugar.

Unlike canning and freezing, drying has no "set" rules. Food may be dried in a number of ways. The important thing is to remove that 80 to 90 percent of the water content, thus allowing the dried foods to be stored without spoilage in tightly closed containers that keep moisture out.

Apples, apricots, berries, cherries, coconut, dates, figs, peaches, pears, plums, prunes, and rhubarb are fruits that dry well. Select only blemish-free fruit of the highest quality at its peak of maturity. Small fruit like strawberries, cherries, and plums may be dried whole. Larger fruit, like pears and apples, should be cut into wedges or slices of a uniform size so that they complete the drying process at the same time. For better nutrition leave those vitamin- and mineral-laden skins on the fruit.

Some vegetables that dry well are beans, cabbage, carrots, corn, mushrooms, okra, onions, peas, peppers, spinach, squash, and tomatoes. Potatoes and most other root vegetables store well under fruit cellar conditions, so should be stored whole instead of dried. Celery doesn't dry well, although celery leaves do.

The same methods and preparations for drying vegetables are used as in drying fruit. Select only high-quality, blemish-free vegetables at the peak of their maturity for drying.

Fruit is sufficiently dehydrated when it becomes leathery—dry and shriveled on the outside and only slightly soft inside. If the fruit isn't dry enough, it will mold in storage. On the other hand, over-dried fruit becomes hard and brittle with the loss of flavor. Once you begin drying fruit, you'll learn when it is just dry enough.

Conditioning is important to guarantee proper storage of your dried fruits and vegetables. Pour cooled, dried food in large, open-mouthed containers (gallon glass jars, crocks, or enamelware). Store the open vessels in a warm, dry room for ten to fourteen days, stirring the contents daily. Once you're sure no mold is forming, and the contents are storing well, pasteurize to ensure that no insect eggs or harmful spoilage will develop. Spread dried produce 1 inch thick on cookie sheets or trays. Process for ten to fifteen minutes in a 175°F. oven, then cool thoroughly before storing.

To revitalize dried produce, add three cups of liquid for each cup of dried fruit or vegetable. Allow to soak for several hours until swollen and the liquid is returned to the food. Then cook or otherwise use as you normally would.

Drying is probably the best technique for storing herbs. The delicate flavors of herbs add new dimensions to old recipes. Growing, collecting, and drying your own herbs is a pleasant hobby and can give you a wide variety of the freshest herbs possible. But regardless of whether you grow your own herbs or gather them from the wild, it is important to dry and store them correctly in order to preserve their oils and flavor. Collect your herbs after the dew dries, using a sharp knife or scissors to cut the stems. Cut perennials and biennials only halfway to the ground, while cutting annuals to the ground. Harvest the herbs before they begin to flower, as the blossoms of many impart a bitter taste. Moreover, when herbs set their flowers, they begin to pull all their energy into the buds, and so the leaves begin to lose their prime quality. Most herbs are harvested in August and September.

To test for dryness, see if they crumble into small pieces between your fingers. If not crumbly dry, allow them more drying time. In humid weather, herbs sometimes must be spread on cookie sheets placed for two to ten minutes in a warm oven to completely dry them. Then remove leaves from the stems and crumble them as fine as you wish. A simple way to remove leaves is to hold the stem in one hand and with the other, strip off the leaves, starting at the base of the stem. (Save those stems! They give off a fragrant aroma when tossed into a wood fire.) Store crumbled herbs in tightly covered glass jars in a dark place. Herbs stored in plastic or paper will lose their flavor. Never store herbs in metal containers because the metal will impart an off-flavor.

When gathering bark herbs, do so either in the winter or fall when the sap isn't running. Cut off the bark in small pieces and dry in a single layer in a dark place. When dry, crumble the bark or run it through a food grinder and store in glass bottles with snug-fitting lids.

Roots of some herbs may also be dried. After digging the roots, scrub them well. Place on a cookie sheet in a 325°F. oven for two to three hours until they are browned and crumble easily.

Gather seeds when they are fully mature but before they begin to shatter and fall off the plant. Dry in shallow layers in a dark, dry place. Be sure to store them in glass bottles.

Store all your carefully grown, harvested, dried, and processed herbs in a cool, dry place away from light. A cabinet or closet is a good place. Dark glass bottles may also be used to keep the dried herbs in darkness.

In selecting a food dryer to construct, several specific criteria should guide your design. Naturally you want to make the initial cost as low as possible. But you also want the dryer to operate as efficiently—and as inexpensively—as possible.

You also want a heat retention capability built into the dryer; in other words, you must insulate it. A thermostat is also a useful feature, since it allows you to select temperatures according to the food being dried. It helps you avoid over- and under-heating the dryer.

Equally important is the selection of materials. You want to avoid materials that might taint the flavor of the dried foods. You don't want materials that retain odors or that are difficult to clean.

A final consideration is size. You want a dryer that is large enough to process everything you want to dry while the foods are still fresh from the garden, but you don't want a monster, difficult to store (since your dryer will probably be stored ten months of the year).

A LOW-COST INDOOR FOOD DRYER

Interested in an indoor food dryer that you can put together in ten minutes for as little as six dollars? One that uses about one-sixteenth of the energy consumed by an electric oven at its lowest setting and costs well under three cents to run per drying session? One that works at a temperature well below 150°F., thereby keeping loss of vitamins and other nutrients at an absolute minimum?

If you just nodded three times, you'll want to build this food dryer, developed by Rodale Press's Research and Development Group. The simple materials you'll need are a topless cardboard or wooden box at least 8 inches deep; a socket, base, and cord (such as Bell's Deluxe Floodlighting Kit); a 60-watt bulb; a cookie sheet or piece of sheet metal cut to fit the box; some aluminum foil; and a few brushfuls of black paint.

Start by painting the bottom of the cookie sheet or metal sheet black for maximum heat absorption. While it's drying, line your box with the aluminum foil, shiny side up. Then place your bulb setup in the center of the box, angling the bulb at 45 degrees. (To help diffuse heat evenly, you might also put a little foil on the top of the bulb, as shown.)

After notching the top corner of the box so the cord can exit, place the tray over the box (black side down) so it is suspended a few inches over the light bulb. Then fill the tray with a layer of sliced fruit or vegetables, and plug it in. In about twelve hours (more time on a high-humidity day; much less time for herbs and foods cut into fairly small pieces), you'll have a trayful of dried goodies for storage or snacking.

R & D's prototype dryer features a cardboard box 12 inches by 18 inches and 8¼ inches deep. The 1-inch-deep cookie sheet, which fits the top exactly, will hold about 1½ pounds of raw prepared food.

To dry larger amounts at one time, simply increase the size of your box and tray, figuring that every square foot of tray surface will accommodate about one pound of raw prepared food. For every two to three square feet of tray you add, use one additional 60-watt bulb setup, taking care to space the bulbs carefully for even heating. This should keep your surface tray temperature at about 125° to 130°F.—"cool" enough so you can just bear to touch it, but hot enough to dry your harvest slowly and surely without scorching or the kind of nutrient loss that begins at around 150°F.

For savings in energy and fuel bills, our dryer compares very favorably with an electric oven. Assuming a cost-per-kilowatt-hour of 3 cents, a one-bulb dryer will process a batch of apples in twelve hours, at a total cost of 2¼ cents, while an electric oven at 200°F. with the door slightly ajar takes about four-and-a-half hours, or a total cost of 13½ cents.

MATERIALS

Miscellaneous

1–12″ x 18″ x 1″ cookie sheet	Aluminum foil
Black paint	1 socket, base, and cord assembly
Cardboard box–12″ x 18″ x 8¼″	1–60-watt bulb

ANOTHER BOX-AND-BULB DRYER

Here's another simple food dryer that can be used right in the kitchen without occupying too much space. It too consists of a cardboard box with a light bulb for heat.

For drying pumpkin, squash, apple, or anything that can be cut into strips or rings, simply hang the fruit over the dowels. For smaller-sized fruit pieces, place a baking sheet atop a layer of dowels and spread the fruit on it.

MATERIALS

Wood

3 pcs. 36″ x ¾″ dowel   or   6 pcs. 18″ x ¾″ dowel

Miscellaneous

1 cardboard box, preferably double-walled
1 light socket and cord
1 light bulb
Aluminum foil
White glue

CONSTRUCTION

1. Start with a sturdy box, preferably a double-walled type as is sometimes used to ship appliances. You can use any size box you want, but a convenient size is about 12 inches by 16 inches, which will allow you to use standard-sized cookie sheets for shelves.

2. Mark each side for six holes, three in a row about 2 inches from the top and three more about halfway down the box.

3. Insert ¾-inch dowels through the holes. They should extend 1 inch on each side.

4. Cut a hole in one side of the box and fit the light bulb. You may want to install a collar of aluminum foil (or a foil pie plate) around the bulb to protect the cardboard.

5. Your dryer will be more efficient if you line the inside with aluminum foil, shiny side out. Use white glue.

RACK DRYER

What is described here is a versatile dryer that can be used with almost any type of heat source. It is constructed of ¼-inch exterior plywood or Masonite nailed to a 2 x 2 frame. The trays can be made from 1 x 2 wood frames with either cheesecloth or light screening tacked on.

This dryer uses almost any type heater that supplies a steady flow of heat. The object should be to maintain a temperature of somewhere between 110° and 170°F. The heat will be better distributed if you hang a horizontal tin baffle about midway between the top of the heater and the bottom shelf.

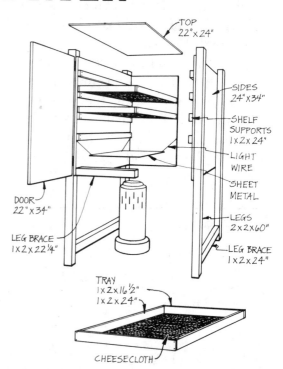

CONSTRUCTION

1. Cut four pieces of 2 x 2s 60 inches long for the legs.

2. Cut two pieces of ¼-inch plywood 24 inches by 34 inches and nail to the 2 x 2s leaving 2 inches of the legs exposed at the top, which will provide for a ventilation space after the top is in place. The 2 x 2s will be on the outside of the dryer.

3. Cut eight pieces of 1 x 2s 24 inches long. Nail these 6 inches apart on the sides, measuring carefully to set them level and matched side to side. Start with the supports for the bottom shelf about 10 inches from the bottom of the sides, and leave about 6-inch spaces between the rest of the shelves.

4. Cut a piece of plywood 22 inches by 34 inches for the back, and another piece 22 inches by 24 inches for the top. Nail the back on, again allow-

354

ing for a 2-inch air space at the top, and then nail on the top.

5. Cut another piece of plywood 22 inches by 34 inches for a door. Use two 1-inch butt hinges to hang the door. Install a hasp and staple or pivot-block to hold the door shut.

6. Cut four pieces of 1 x 2, two 22$\frac{1}{4}$ inches and two 24 inches long. Nail them to the legs as braces.

7. Cut a piece of sheet metal 12 inches by 18 inches. Punch holes in all four corners. Attach light wire and suspend it from tacks at four corners inside the dryer, below the bottom shelf.

8. Construct four trays 18 inches by 24 inches using 1 x 2 wood and cheese-cloth. Cut two 24-inch 1 x 2s and two 16$\frac{1}{2}$-inch 1 x 2s for each tray. Nail the four pieces together to form a 1$\frac{1}{2}$-inch-deep frame. Cut a piece of cheesecloth to fit each frame. Use a $\frac{1}{4}$-inch tacking strip to fasten the cheesecloth in place.

MATERIALS

Wood

2 pcs. 2 x 2 x 10'	or	**Legs:** 4 pcs. 2 x 2 x 60"
1 sht. $\frac{1}{4}$" ext. plywood	or	**Sides:** 2 pcs. 24" x 34"
		Back and door: 2 pcs. 22" x 34"
		Top: 1 pc. 22" x 24"
5 pcs. 1 x 2 x 8'	or	**Shelf supports:** 8 pcs. 1 x 2 x 24"
		Leg braces: 2 pcs. 1 x 2 x 22$\frac{1}{4}$"
		2 pcs. 1 x 2 x 24"
		Trays: 8 pcs. 1 x 2 x 24"
1 pc. 1 x 2 x 12'	or	**Trays:** 8 pcs. 1 x 2 x 16$\frac{1}{2}$"

Hardware

6d nails
2–1" butt hinges w/ screws
1 hasp and staple
1 pc. 12" x 18", $\frac{1}{16}$" sheet metal
24" light wire
$\frac{3}{4}$" tacks
12' x $\frac{1}{4}$" tacking strip

Miscellaneous

3 yds. cheesecloth

SOLAR DRYER

The beauty of a solar dryer is that it is so efficient and consumes no energy. The model described here was built and used on the new Organic Gardening Experimental Farm. The design is based on one developed by the Brace Research Institute in Canada. Its construction is fairly simple, and you can design your own if you provide plenty of ventilation holes, a top that gives unobstructed exposure to the sun's rays, and an easy means of removing the trays of fruit or vegetables.

The solar box has 2 inches of insulation in the bottom and sides, double panes in the sash top, and the inside is painted black. With holes in the top edge and in the bottom, the box is ventilated by natural convection action as the sun warms the interior.

To avoid too much of your fruit being in the shade as the sun moves,

make the box three times as long as it is wide. The one made in the OGF Workshop measures about 6 feet by 2 feet.

CONSTRUCTION

1. To construct the base unit, cut two pieces of ⅜-inch exterior plywood 76¼ inches by 24¼ inches. Drill three rows of ½-inch holes spaced 3 inches apart in each piece. Locate these rows of holes at 9, 36, and 63 inches from one end. Staple narrow strips of screening to cover rows of holes on one side of the plywood to keep insects from entering the dryer.

2. If ¾-inch by 2-inch material is not available from your local lumber company you will have to rip 2-inch strips from wider boards. With this stock build a frame 2 inches thick and the exact dimensions of the pieces of plywood. Nail one piece of plywood to the frame using 4d nails; also cut and nail pieces of the ¾-inch by 2-inch wood on either

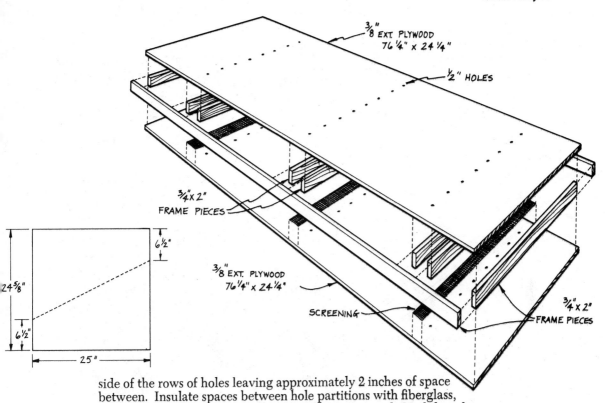

side of the rows of holes leaving approximately 2 inches of space between. Insulate spaces between hole partitions with fiberglass, Styrofoam, sawdust, or some other insulating material. Nail the other piece of plywood to the top, as shown.

3. From the ⅜-inch plywood cut the two side pieces, as shown. Perhaps the easiest way to do this is to cut one 25-inch by 24⅝-inch piece, then cut it in half on a slant, to yield two pieces of the indicated dimensions. Nail these side pieces to the ends of the base panel, flush with the bottom.

4. Cut one piece of ⅜-inch plywood 76¼ inches by 18 inches. Cut a slot 4¼ inches wide and 69¼ inches long, 3½ inches from bottom of plywood and 3½ inches from each end edge. With ¾-inch by 2-inch material, construct a frame as shown, with a 69¼-inch length above the slot cut in the back and two 15¼-inch pieces attached to the ends. Cut the proper top slope on the ends of the 15¼-inch pieces and nail them in place. Then nail a 69¼-inch length between the uprights at the appropriate angle. After framing is finished and fastened to the back piece, slip it against the base, between sides, and measure for the inside piece of plywood, which will be smaller than the outer piece. It must be notched at the bottom to duplicate the outer panel's access slot. The top surface of the frame will also have to be planed for proper fit. Cut the piece, install insulation, and nail the plywood to the framing.

5. Make the front in the same fashion as back. The outside panel should measure 76¼ inches by 6½ inches, while the inner panel will again be smaller (determine the exact dimensions by fit).

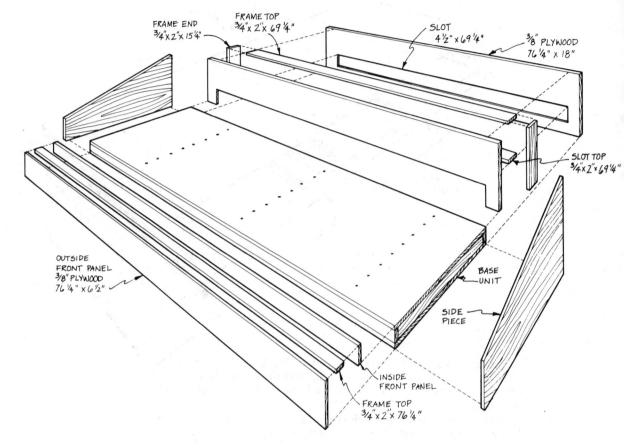

FRAME END
3/4"x 2"x 15 1/4"

FRAME TOP
3/4" x 2" x 69 1/4"

SLOT
4 1/2" x 69 1/4"

3/8 " PLYWOOD
76 1/4" X 18"

SLOT TOP
3/4 x 2"x 69 1/4"

OUTSIDE
FRONT PANEL
3/8" PLYWOOD
76 1/4" x 6 1/2"

BASE
UNIT

SIDE
PIECE

INSIDE
FRONT PANEL

FRAME TOP
3/4"x 2" x 76 1/4"

6. Nail the sides and ends permanently to each other and the base with 10d nails.

7. Construct a frame for each of the side pieces from the ¾-inch by 2-inch material and insulate it. Cut an inner panel from the ⅜-inch plywood and secure to the frame.

8. Three drying trays are made with dimensions 22½ inches by 19½ inches. Use ¾-inch by 2-inch material to construct the frames. Attach ¼-inch hardware cloth or screening (fiberglass is recommended as it does not react with acids in fruit) to one side of each frame.

9. To give better air circulation a ¾-inch by 2-inch tray support strip is attached to base along back (inside of opening) and along both sides.

10. A door is fashioned from ¾-inch by 2-inch material and plywood, as it is also insulated. The outside piece of plywood should overlap approximately 1 inch along entire perimeter. Use a standard door pull as a handle.

11. Paint the interior and exterior of the dryer black.

12. If you have no ready-made window sashes to use for the top of the dryer, you can construct your own, but it is not a simple project.

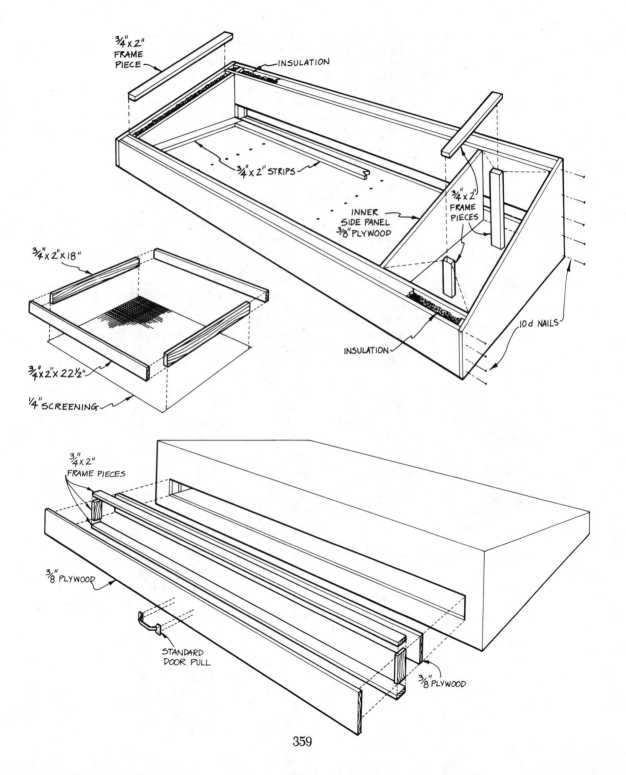

3/4" x 2" FRAME PIECE

INSULATION

3/4" x 2" STRIPS

INNER SIDE PANEL 3/8" PLYWOOD

3/4" x 2" FRAME PIECES

10d NAILS

INSULATION

3/4" x 2" x 18"

3/4" x 2" x 22 1/2"

1/4" SCREENING

3/4" x 2" FRAME PIECES

3/8" PLYWOOD

STANDARD DOOR PULL

3/8" PLYWOOD

359

a. The window sash is constructed from ¾-inch stock. Cut the following pieces: one piece 5 inches by 77 inches, one piece 2¾ inches by 77 inches, and three pieces 2 inches by 27 inches. Cut a double rabbet; the first $\frac{3}{16}$ inch wide and to a depth of exactly one-half the thickness of the ¾-inch stock, the second being $\frac{3}{16}$ inch wide and ¼ inch deep. These rabbets will be cut on one entire edge of both long pieces. Rabbeting the 27-inch pieces is trickier. One piece—the center piece—is rabbeted along both edges. One is rabbeted on the right edge, the last on the left edge. In all cases, the first rabbet starts $4\frac{13}{16}$ inches from one end and stops $2\frac{9}{16}$ inches from the other end. The second rabbet starts $4\frac{5}{8}$ inches from the same end as you started the first rabbet and stops $2\frac{3}{8}$ inches from the other end.

b. Use half-lap joints at the corners and for the center piece. (There are two important points to remember for halved joints—always work from working face when gauging for depth and obtain joint measurements by superimposition, that is, placing one piece on top of another to obtain the proper width.) Use glue and ¾-inch #8 screws to fasten. The top or 5-inch-wide side has ⅝-inch vent holes drilled horizontally at 5-inch intervals to a depth of 3½ inches with holes drilled at right angles to intersect from the underside along entire back edge. Paint the sash frame black. Take measurements for double panes of single-strength glass, cut, and insert the glass, glazier's points, and glaze. Fasten the window sashes to the top of the drying unit with 1½-inch #10 screws.

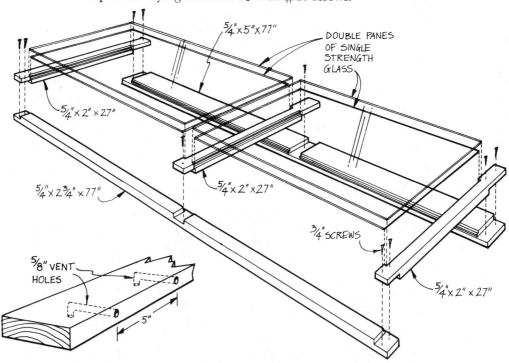

MATERIALS
Wood

3 pcs. 1 x 12 x 8′   or   **Base frame sides:** 2 pcs. ¾″ x 2″ x 76¼″ (act. meas.)

Base frame crossmembers: 8 pcs. ¾″ x 2″ x 22¾″ (act. meas.)

Back frame horizontals: 2 pcs. ¾″ x 2″ x 69¼″ (act. meas.)

Back frame uprights: 2 pcs. ¾″ x 2″ x 15¼″ (act. meas.)

Front frame horizontal: 1 pc. ¾″ x 2″ x 76¼″ (act. meas.)

Side rear uprights: 2 pcs. ¾″ x 2″ x 14½″ (act. meas.)

Side front uprights: 2 pcs. ¾″ x 2″ x 4¼″ (act. meas.)

Side tops: 2 pcs. ¾″ x 2″ x 21¾″ (act. meas.)

Tray ends: 6 pcs. ¾″ x 2″ x 18″ (act. meas.)

Tray sides: 6 pcs. ¾″ x 2″ x 22½″ (act. meas.)

Tray support strips: 2 pcs. ¾″ x 2″ x 19½″ (act. meas.)
1 pc. ¾″ x 2″ x 67½″ (act. meas.)

Door frame horizontals: 2 pcs. ¾″ x 2″ x 69⅛″ (act. meas.)

Door frame uprights: 2 pcs. ¾″ x 2″ x 2⅝″ (act. meas.)

1 pc. ¾ x 12 x 8′   or   **Sash upper side:** 1 pc. ¾″ x 5″ x 77″ (act. meas.)

Sash lower side: 1 pc. ¾″ x 2¾″ x 77″ (act. meas.)

Sash crosspieces: 3 pcs. ¾″ x 2″ x 27″ (act. meas.)

3 shts. $\frac{3}{8}$" ext. plywood or **Base:** 2 pcs. $76\frac{1}{4}$" x $24\frac{1}{4}$"

Outer sides: 1 pc. 25" x $24\frac{5}{8}$" (cut as indicated)

Outer back: 1 pc. $76\frac{1}{4}$" x 18"

Inner back: 1 pc. $76\frac{1}{4}$" x $15\frac{1}{4}$"

Outer front: 1 pc. $76\frac{1}{4}$" x $6\frac{1}{2}$"

Inner front: 1 pc. $76\frac{1}{4}$" x 5"

Inner sides: 1 pc. $19\frac{1}{2}$" sq. (cut as indicated)

Outer door: 1 pc. $6\frac{1}{8}$" x $71\frac{1}{8}$"

Inner door: 1 pc. $4\frac{1}{8}$" x $69\frac{1}{8}$"

Hardware

1 pc. 24" x 96" insect screen   or   3 pcs. 1" x $22\frac{3}{4}$"
3 pcs. $22\frac{1}{2}$" x $19\frac{1}{2}$"

Staples
4d nails
Insulation
10d nails
Door pull w/ screws
Black exterior paint
Waterproof glue
12–$\frac{3}{4}$" #8 screws
4 pcs. single-strength glass, cut to fit
Glazier's points
Glazier's compound
10–$1\frac{1}{2}$" #10 screws

SMOKEHOUSE

If you do your own butchering, you may want to do your own smoking. Or, you may want to try your hand at smoking just to produce meats that have a better taste than the production line hams sold in most markets.

To do your own smoking, you will need a smokehouse. It can be a simple, temporary structure made from a packing crate, barrel, or metal drum. Or it can be a bigger, more elaborate wooden or block building, capable of smoking several hogs at once.

An intermediate model was built from scrap wooden shipping pallets in the OGF Workshop. An old refrigerator would provide a similar-sized smokehouse, but if you use a refrigerator, make sure there is no danger of children locking themselves in. In many communities, it is illegal to leave refrigerators with their doors and locks intact lying around.

If you can get shipping pallets, you probably also will need a power saw to rip the pallet lumber into the dimensions specified here. If you don't have power tools, you can buy the lumber in the proper size, or compromise by using the pallets for 1-inch boards and buying the heavier pieces. The materials list for this smokehouse will tell you what you need whatever your source of lumber is.

No matter what kind of smokehouse you build, it must have four things: a source of smoke (use hardwoods only); an area to confine the smoke; racks to hold the meat; and a draft.

The draft is essential. If you do not have a draft the meat will have a sooty taste, caused by stagnant smoke.

Before you build a smokehouse, you should consider the argument against eating smoked meats. Meats get their smoky flavor by absorbing smoke. Smoke contains coal tars, which have been linked to a variety of cancers, if they are ingested in sufficient concentration.

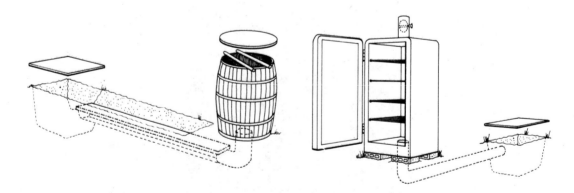

CONSTRUCTION

1. Dismantle several pallets. Each will yield a quantity of random width 1-inch boards and two pieces 2¼ inches by 8 inches by 4 feet. Rip (cut with the grain) these pieces into lighter ones measuring 2¼ inches by 1½ inches by 4 feet. You will need thirteen of these for the smokehouse framework.
2. To make the top and bottom rectangular frames, cut four pieces 36 inches long and four pieces 42 inches long. Nail together with 10d

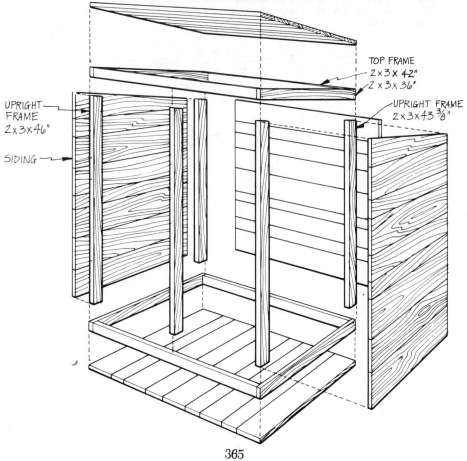

TOP FRAME
2 x 3 x 42"
2 x 3 x 36"

UPRIGHT
FRAME
2 x 3 x 46"

SIDING

UPRIGHT FRAME
2 x 3 x 43 3/8"

nails. If your pallet wood is very hard and knotty, you may want to drill holes first.

3. The five remaining pieces will form the upright parts of the frame. Cut a 5-degree angle on one end of each, which will give the roof of the smokehouse a pitch. Measuring on the longest side, cut three pieces 46 inches long and two pieces 43⅜ inches.

4. To assemble the smokehouse frame, toenail four of the five angled pieces to the bottom rectangle. The angled ends should be up, with all the angles sloping in the same direction. In the center of the 42-inch piece with the taller uprights, nail the third 46-inch upright. This will be the front of the smokehouse.

5. Fasten the top rectangle in the same manner. Use the angle you cut into the ends of the uprights as a guide in positioning the rectangle.

6. Cut the random width 1-inch boards to fit the bottom, back, sides, and half the front. The top will be done later. Leave a 3-inch-wide opening at the top of the front panel for a hinged vent. Use a 1½-inch by 1¼-inch butt hinge or a similar small hinge to attach the vent.

7. The first step in making the door is to cut three pieces from the random width boards and fasten them around the doorframe. Measure the height and width of the door opening, and subtract ¼ inch from each measurement.

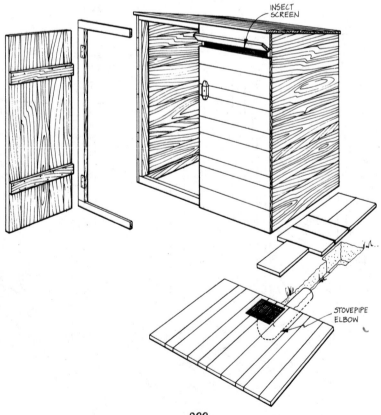

INSECT SCREEN

STOVEPIPE ELBOW

8. Cut and lay out boards to fit your measurements. Use two horizontal battens to hold the door pieces together, fastening them with 1-inch #10 screws.

9. Hang the door using 2½-inch butt hinges, about 5 inches from the top and bottom. If you put a piece of cardboard or several thicknesses of newspaper under the door (between the door and threshold), the door will not bind when opening and closing.

10. Make a latch for the door using a piece of wood scrap about 1½ inches by 3 inches. Drill a hole in the center, big enough so the latch can turn when nailed to the doorframe with an 8d nail.

11. Cut a 6-inch-diameter hole in the floor to accommodate your smoke flue pipe. Cover the hole and the draft vent with insect screen.

12. On the inside, make a rack for hanging meat. Rip two narrow pieces from the 1-inch boards you are using for siding, and cut them to 36-inch lengths. After drilling 1-inch holes in the pieces, mount one on each side wall. A galvanized pipe then fits into the holes.

13. Attach your top. Cut lengths of the siding to span from side to side, fitting flush with the sides. There should be about a 1- or 2-inch over-hang at the front and back.

14. Choose a spot for your smokehouse. It should be downwind of dwellings and out of the way of children and livestock. Dig a 6-inch-square trench about 10 to 12 feet long, connecting the fire pit and an elbow section of pipe. Put the smokehouse on bricks and attach the elbow. (The fire pit should be upwind from the smokehouse.) ·

15. Place the pipe in the trench and cover with dirt or tiles.

MATERIALS

Wood

3 pcs. 2 x 3 x 8'	or	**Top and bottom frames:** 4 pcs. 2 x 3 x 42″
		4 pcs. 2 x 3 x 36″

2 pcs. 2 x 3 x 12'   **Upright frame:** 3 pcs. 2 x 3 x 46″

2 pcs. 2 x 3 x 43$\frac{3}{8}$″

18 pcs. 1 x 6 x 8' cut to fit (siding)

Hardware

10d nails
1–1$\frac{1}{2}$″ x 1$\frac{1}{4}$″ butt hinge
10–1″ #10 screws
2–2$\frac{1}{2}$″ butt hinges
8d nails
1 pc. 24″ x 36″ insect screen
1 pc. 42″ x 1″ galvanized pipe
1 stovepipe elbow
12' of 6″ stovepipe

UNDERGROUND STORAGE

Underground storage is perhaps the easiest method for storing large amounts of food crops, for once the storage area is constructed, there is little effort and expense involved in storing large quantities of fruits and most vegetables.

Into the category "underground storage" can be lumped cold cellars (specially designed and constructed basement rooms), root cellars (an underground outbuilding designed for food storage), and variations on these, including barrels and chests of food buried in the ground and the cold box (a freezerlike cold storage device). None is particularly difficult to construct, yet all provide an interesting challenge for the homestead handyman.

BASEMENT FOOD STORAGE

A cold cellar, in our terminology here, is an improved area of a cellar in a house to be used for keeping fruits or vegetables. One prerequisite is a window above grade into which an air vent can be installed. Another vent will be installed in the door in the partition with the interior of the cellar, to assure air circulation. You should install 3½-inch sheets of insulation in the partitions and between the ceiling joists to maintain a temperature of about 50°F. inside.

It does not matter if your cellar has a dirt floor, in fact, such an unfinished floor probably will keep cool better. The cellars in old houses didn't have dirt floors just because they were cheap and easy to construct. These dirt floors made cellars excellent food storage areas; they helped keep food cool and moist. These old root cellars have long been used for storage in the colder parts of our country, and some houses without central heating on farms and homesteads are now being built with dirt floor cellars for just this reason.

With few exceptions, the most desirable temperature is at or very near 32°F.—the freezing point of water. Except for potatoes, vegetables are not injured at this temperature. It is difficult, however, to keep the temperature as low as 32°F. without danger of it going low enough to cause actual freezing during exceedingly cold weather. It is suggested, therefore, that the storage room temperature be kept between 35° and 40°F. Such temperatures cannot be reached and kept except in a room separated from the rest of the basement, reasonably well insulated, and having adequate ventilation.

The size of the basement storage room will vary with the space available and the family needs; 8 feet by 10 feet is suggested for most families who plan to store both vegetables and other foods in the same room; a room this size will hold sixty bushels of produce. A storage room, if properly constructed and managed, will be suitable for nearly all foods commonly preserved. Where practical, the storage room should be located either in the northeast or northwest corner of the basement and away from the chimney and heating pipes.

At least one wall having outside exposure should be used, preferably the one with the least sunlight, on the north side and with a window that is easily reached. The other walls can be made of wood which will do a good job of keeping the storage area cool—providing their construction is tight.

Three types of insulating material can be used: board, flexible batts or blankets, or loose fill. It is important to keep them dry or their insulating properties will be reduced. So moisture-vapor barriers, such as damp-proof paper, tar, asphalt, are used, inside and out.

Board insulation can be nailed to the walls and ceiling. Two thicknesses should be used to prevent leakage through joints.

Flexible batts are most commonly used for home insulation, since they are easily installed and are sufficiently effective. This is the most likely choice for the cold cellar.

Loose-fill insulation includes planer shavings, cork dust, and minerals. It is much more difficult to work with. You must stagger the studs so they are exposed on one surface only. Sheathing and dampproofing should be done when the wall space is being filled. And filling the wall can be troublesome.

The temperature of the surrounding basement will determine the thickness of the walls. The insulation dealer will undoubtedly have information on the effectiveness of his particular product. Ask him.

The walls to close off a corner of the basement are easily constructed with a 2 x 4 framework, sheathing on both sides, and 3-inch insulation batts between the studding. Leave an opening in one wall for a door. The door may be framed with 2 x 3 studs, faced on each side with ¼-inch plywood, and the center filled with insulation. Fit the door tightly and secure it with a type of latch that holds it firmly closed.

To insulate the ceiling of the storage space, sheathe underneath the ceiling joists and apply 4 inches or more of insulation between the joists, extending the insulation out over the walls of the storage space.

The ability to maintain a desirable temperature range of 35° to 40°F. in the basement storage room depends largely on the outside weather conditions. In both early fall and late spring, day temperatures are likely to be higher than those desired in the storage area. Therefore, it is important during these times to keep windows closed. As a general rule, windows should be opened whenever the outside temperature is lower than that in the storage room and the inside temperature is above 40°F. When the temperature in the storage room drops to 35°F., windows should be closed. Place one reliable thermometer inside and another outside a window for guidance, or use a combination indoor-outdoor thermometer.

Light must be excluded from stored vegetables and fruits, so cover the windows with opaque material. Wide, wooden louvres fitted to the outside of the window frame aid in excluding light if the window is opened for ventilation in the daytime. Cover louvres, or open windows if louvres are not used, with copper screening to keep out insects and animals.

For the handyman two other approaches offer opportunities to design and build a completely unique food storage chamber.

A small, but simple and inexpensive storage area can be made by utilizing the cellar steps of an outside cellar entrance. Install an inside door to keep out basement heat at the bottom of the steps. If you want to create an even larger storage area, build inward into the basement, but take care to insulate extra wall space. Temperatures in the stairwell will go down as you go up the steps, and a little experimenting will help you determine the best levels for the different crops you are storing. If the air is too dry, set pans of water at the warmest level for extra humidity.

In a pinch, window area wells can hold bushels of food over part or all of the winter. Because they are adjacent to the house and below ground level, the temperatures inside them should remain fairly constant throughout the winter. Cover the wells with screening and wood. To raise the temperature in very cold weather, open basement window and allow some house heat to enter. When the temperature in the window well gets too high, remove wood from the top of the well to permit the cold, outside air to cool the area. If basement windows open inward or are the sliding type, access can be convenient and simple during the cold winter months.

A COLD CLOSET

Raymond W. Dyer, an architect living in New England, designed a closet-sized cold cellar when he became his own client and was to design himself a new small house out in the country. For years he and his family had been living in a large, gracious house of the 1850s in the center of town. Vegetable storage was no problem there. The cellar was damp and cool, with a dirt floor and enormous granite stone walls with open joints. It was the size of the full house and plenty of distance could be found from the heater for a cool spot for the squashes, potatoes, and onions.

But the new house was to have a basement with a tight concrete floor and insulated walls, too warm for vegetable storage. What to do?

Well, on the north wall of the cellar, which had earth up to the bottoms of the wood sill on the outside, Dyer located a large closet 3 feet deep and 6 feet long. The closet was framed with wood studs, covered with gypsum board on both sides. These walls, and likewise the ceiling, were insulated with 4-inch-thick fiberglass

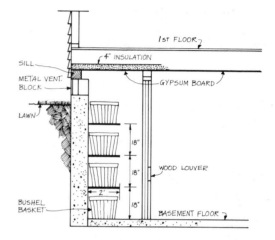

blankets. Thus the closet was cut off from the cellar warmth.

To make sure enough cold air was coming in to cool the closet, a metal ventilating block was installed high up in the concrete wall. This ventilating block is common to most lumberyards and generally is used to ventilate crawl spaces in houses. It is about 8 inches high and 12 inches long. It has open slots in it that can be closed or opened to allow air in from the outside by means of a sliding shutter operated from the exterior of the house. Thus cold, fresh air was provided to the closet.

To insure the Dyers could moderate the severe cold of winter with warm air, they placed in the doors of the closet a small wood louver that could be open or shut. These closet doors were of ample size—a pair, 2 feet 6 inches wide and 6 feet 8 inches high, normal house doors.

Inside the closet four heavy wood shelves, 2 feet deep, were arranged to take bushel baskets. The wood boards of these shelves were installed with a ½-inch space between them for air

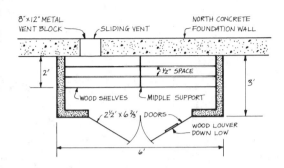

circulation over the vegetables, which is a must for their keeping.

A COLD CELLAR

A full-sized cold cellar was constructed by Richard Weinsteiger and Harold Geiss of the OGF Workshop, following the guidelines already stated. The cold cellar measures 7 feet by 8 feet outside and provides enough storage room to serve the biggest family. Specific information on stud-wall construction is in the chapter "Building, From the Ground Up."

CONSTRUCTION

1. Start by framing the walls, one 7 feet long, the other 8 feet long with 2 x 4s. Use a 2 x 4 for a sill on the floor. Vertical studs are toenailed on 16-inch centers and can be nailed to your floor joists or a 2 x 4 plate. Use 12d nails.

2. The door opening is 32 inches by 76 inches. The door is near the center of the 7-foot side.

3. Staple insulation batts between the joists, and then nail up insulation

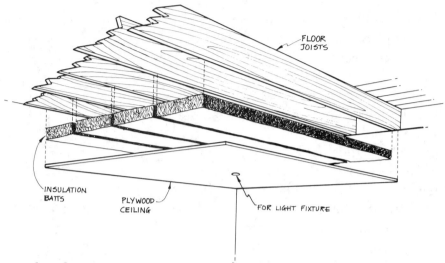

FLOOR
JOISTS

INSULATION
BATTS

PLYWOOD
CEILING

FOR LIGHT FIXTURE

board or plywood for the ceiling, using 4d nails. Rough-in electrical
work at this time for a light inside the storage cellar.

4. Nail the insulation board or plywood to the outside of the frame. Then
    staple insulation batts between the studs. Finally, nail on the interior
    wall.

5. You will need two 12-inch by 14-inch metal, louver-type vents, a

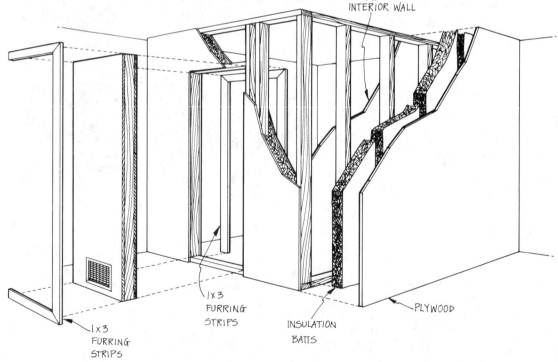

INTERIOR WALL

1x3
FURRING
STRIPS

1x3
FURRING
STRIPS

INSULATION
BATTS

PLYWOOD

standard item available in hardware stores. Construct frame to adapt one vent to your existing window frame. Depending on the size of window you start with, you can do this with common boards.

6. For the door, construct a frame of 2 x 4s with simple butt joints at the corners. The door should be $\frac{3}{8}$ inch smaller in height and width than the opening in the wall. Cut another piece of 2 x 4 for a diagonal brace. Using 2 x 4s frame in an opening for the 12-inch by 14-inch vent. Center and toenail it on the bottom of the doorframe. Cut plywood to fit, including a cut-out for around the vent, and nail it in place. Staple insulation inside the door and nail on the inside sheet of plywood or insulation board.

7. Use three 3-inch butt hinges to hang the door. Nail furring strips to the outside door edge so they overlap the doorframe by 1½ inches. Notch the furring strips for the hinges, and miter the corners. On the inside, nail strips to the doorframe so they overlap the door when it is closed.

MATERIALS

Wood

18 pcs. 2 x 4 x 8' or	**Studs:** 13 pcs. cut to fit ceiling to floor	

Sill: 1 pc. 2 x 4 x 7'
 1 pc. 2 x 4 x 8'

Door headers: 2 pcs. 2 x 4 x 35"

Door trimmers: 2 pcs. 2 x 4 x 76"

Door: 2 pcs. 2 x 4 x 75⅛"
 2 pcs. 2 x 4 x 31⅛"

Brace: 1 pc. 2 x 4 x 8'

Vent frame: 1 pc. 2 x 4 x 17"
 2 pcs. 2 x 4 x 12"

12 shts. ½" ext. plywood (wall sheathing)

1" board (length and width depend on size of window)

5 pcs. 1 x 3 x 8' furring   or   **Door sealing strips:** 2 pcs. 1 x 3 x 34"
 4 pcs. 1 x 3 x 77"

Hardware

12d nails
Insulation
Staples
4d nails
2–12" x 14" metal louver-type vents
3–3" butt hinges w/ screws

ROOT CELLARS

Root cellars are underground rooms for storing fruits and vegetables. The cellar is dug either below grade or into a hillside. All root cellars should be designed to provide protection from excessive moisture and from freezing. They must be ventilated.

The best way to keep out seeping

connected to a French drain. (To make a French drain, sink an oil drum without a bottom into the ground. Fill the drum with gravel and connect it to the floor drain with a 2- or 3-inch soil pipe.)

In very cold climates food may freeze if air temperatures drop well below zero for several days. Having a double door between the outside and the main storage area can help insulate the root cellar. The inner door should be fitted with sheet insulation. It also will help to lay out the cellar so the door faces away from prevailing winds.

water is by waterproofing the outside of the walls and laying drain tile along the cellar's footings. You also should install a floor drain, even if it is only

The use of a heater isn't advisable in such situations, since heaters gen-

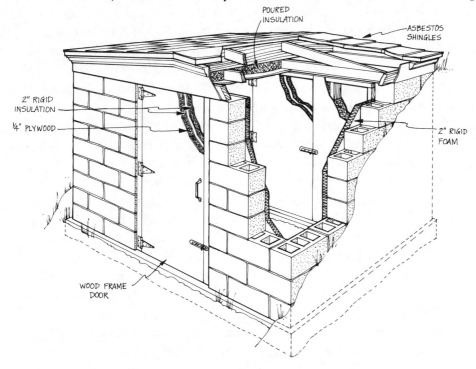

erate too much heat. But a kerosene lantern or a low-wattage electric light bulb gives off just enough heat to break the frost without affecting storage. (The lights should be shrouded somehow to protect the stored foods.)

If you have an above-ground roof, you can install louvered vents that can be opened or closed as the weather changes. For an underground cellar, install a flue extending above the surface of the ground. You should have a hinged damper door on the bottom to close during cold weather.

The dimensions of your excavation can vary. You may have to duck to get through the doorway, but the interior roof should be anywhere from 6½ to 8 feet high. A cellar whose floor measures 6 feet by 8 feet will provide enough storage space for an average family.

Perhaps the easiest root cellar to construct is a small wood-frame roofed, concrete block building with earth graded up around the walls to the height of the eaves. This root cellar is most successful if it is built into a hillside, has a double-doored entrance, and has its entrance facing away from the prevailing winds.

Howard Strenn of Greenleaf, Wisconsin, constructed such a root cellar in a hillside of their farmyard. The 8-foot by 10-foot concrete block structure is banked with earth on three sides, while the roof and the entrance-way are exposed. The concrete block structure has a wood frame roof with asbestos shingles. Not an impressive building at first glance, the root cellar serves its purpose exceedingly well.

The interior of the cellar is insulated with 2-inch rigid foam, while the ceiling has an additional 6 inches of poured insulation. The wood frame doors contain 2-inch rigid insulation faced on each side with ¼-inch plywood. Divided into two rooms, the root cellar is wired for electricity.

The partition between the two rooms is insulated to keep the inner room from freezing in the coldest weather. The compact inner room holds thirty bushels of produce. With the partition and two doors, the inner room's temperature remains stable, even though the outdoor temperature varies. The outer room is used to hang the family's smoked hams, bacons, and sausage.

Since temperature is extremely important in a root cellar, it is checked every day during the winter. When the temperature drops to minus 20°F. some small amount of heat must be supplied, and Strenn uses an old-fashioned kerosene lantern. Moreover, on "really cold" days, the door to the root cellar simply is not opened.

The earthen floor of the root cellar is laced with concrete slats and wire mesh to prevent rats and chipmunks from tunneling in.

Ventilation is extremely important. A good root cellar needs an air intake and an outlet to allow an exchange of air. The produce should be stored in slatted apple boxes located off the floor to allow good air circulation.

While Strenn believes anyone can build a root cellar, not everyone will be able to give it the consistent attention it needs. Strenn checks his once every day during the winter. Each summer he empties the cellar out and lets it air good. He gives it a thorough cleaning, fumigating it and all the containers he will be using. This kills any mold or fungus picked up in the past year.

Each year he seals all the cracks in the concrete blocks. The ground around the outside has to be filled in as it settles.

More specific information, helpful in designing and constructing such a root cellar, may be found in the chapters on masonry, walls, and outbuilding construction.

STORAGE CONTAINERS

An efficient way of storing food in your cellar will lessen spoilage and give food an extra margin of freshness by protecting fruit and vegetables from bruises and moisture.

Wooden boxes, which were originally designed to store and ship apples and other fruits, make ideal storage units for root cellars or larger storage areas. Interior packing for stuffing between food may be leaves (dry and crisp), hay, straw, string-sphagnum moss, or crumpled burlap.

Pails, baskets, and watertight barrels are used just as boxes are. Layer packing material and produce alternately, finishing with 2 inches or more of packing at the top. These containers are used in pit storage areas as well as in larger units.

Metal tins are adaptable for storage, providing you patch-paint raw metal or use galvanized metal to keep rusting at a minimum. Leave them open topped or cover produce with leaves, sphagnum moss, or straw.

Bins are used primarily in larger storage units. They should be constructed for permanent use 4 inches

off the floor. They are good for potato and other root crops.

Orange crates and mesh bags are excellent for onion storage and other foods that need good air circulation.

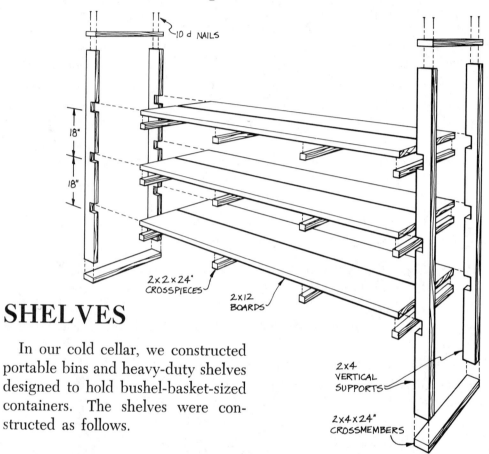

SHELVES

In our cold cellar, we constructed portable bins and heavy-duty shelves designed to hold bushel-basket-sized containers. The shelves were constructed as follows.

CONSTRUCTION

1. Use two 2 x 4s for the vertical supports and two 2 x 4 pieces 24 inches long for the support crossmembers. Use a backsaw and chisel to cut three notches 1½ inches deep and 3 inches wide into the vertical supports. Space the notches 18 inches apart, measured from bottom edge to bottom edge. Nail the frame together with 10d nails.
2. Make an identical frame to be placed against the opposite wall.
3. To make the shelves, use 2 x 12 boards. The length obviously must be tailored to your cold cellar's dimensions. To fit our cold cellar, previously described, the shelf boards were cut 90 inches long. Use four 24-inch-long 2 x 2s as crosspieces to tie two 2 x 12s together to form each shelf. These shelves then will slide into the notched uprights.

MATERIALS

Wood

5 pcs. 2 x 4 x 8'	or	**Uprights:** 4 pcs. 2 x 4 x 8'
		Crossmembers: 4 pcs. 2 x 4 x 24"
4 pcs. 2 x 12 x 8'	or	**Shelves:** 4 pcs. 2 x 12 x 90"
2 pcs. 2 x 2 x 8'	or	**Crosspieces:** 8 pcs. 2 x 2 x 24"

Hardware

10d nails

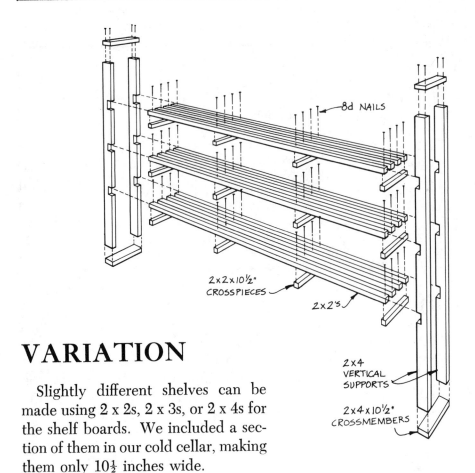

8d NAILS

2x2x10½"
CROSSPIECES

2x2's

2x4
VERTICAL
SUPPORTS

2x4x10½"
CROSSMEMBERS

VARIATION

Slightly different shelves can be made using 2 x 2s, 2 x 3s, or 2 x 4s for the shelf boards. We included a section of them in our cold cellar, making them only 10½ inches wide.

CONSTRUCTION

1. The shelf supports are constructed as in the previous shelving system. Use 2 x 4 uprights, two for each end of the shelf setup. Cut two 10½-inch crosspieces for each end and nail to the tops and bottoms of the uprights as shown. Cut the notches in the supports as previously described.

2. For each shelf, cut four pieces of 2 x 2 the length of the shelf setup, probably the length of the cold cellar minus 4 inches (the combined thicknesses of the two uprights after the notches have been cut). For our cold cellar, each 2 x 2 was 90 inches long. Cut four 10½-inch lengths of 2 x 2 to be used to join the shelf boards.

3. Lay the shelf pieces on the crosspieces and nail them together, using 8d nails. There should be a gap the thickness of a 2 x 2 between each board in the shelf; an extra 2 x 2 could be cut and used to lay out the shelves.

4. As with the previous setup, the upright support units are held in position against opposite walls while the shelf units are slid into place.

MATERIALS

Wood

2 pcs. 2 x 4 x 10'	or	**Uprights:** 4 pcs. 2 x 4 x 8'
2 pcs. 2 x 4 x 8'		**Crossmembers:** 4 pcs. 2 x 4 x 10½"
9 pcs. 2 x 2 x 8'	or	**Shelves:** 8 pcs. 2 x 2 x 90"
		Crosspieces: 8 pcs. 2 x 2 x 10½"

Hardware

10d nails
8d nails

FOOD BINS

Another good way to provide storage is with wooden storage bins of the sort designed by Billy R. Tyler, an Oregon homesteader. Each bin takes up 4½ square feet in floor space, and each bin has three compartments that will together hold about 75 pounds of fruit or vegetables. The bins can be stacked and can be carried into the kitchen or other areas for storage.

CONSTRUCTION

1. Cut four 18-inch pieces of 1 x 12 and mark 12 inches along one long edge and 6 inches along one butt end, scribe a line between the two points, and cut off one corner, as shown. Drill four $\frac{3}{4}$-inch-diameter ventilation holes evenly spaced about 1 inch above the long, or bottom edge.

2. Cut two 36-inch pieces of 1 x 12, one each for top and back. Nail in place with 6d nails.

3. Cut a 36-inch piece of 1 x 6 for the front, and nail it in place.

4. Cut a piece of $\frac{1}{4}$-inch plywood 19$\frac{1}{2}$ inches by 36 inches for the bottom, and nail it in place.

MATERIALS

Wood

1 pc. 1 x 12 x 12′	or	**Uprights:** 4 pcs. 1 x 12 x 18″
		Top and back: 2 pcs. 1 x 12 x 36″
1 pc. 1 x 6 x 4′	or	**Front:** 1 pc. 1 x 6 x 36″
1–2′ x 4′ sht. $\frac{1}{4}$″ ext. plywood	or	**Bottom:** 1 pc. 19$\frac{1}{2}$″ x 36″

Hardware

6d nails

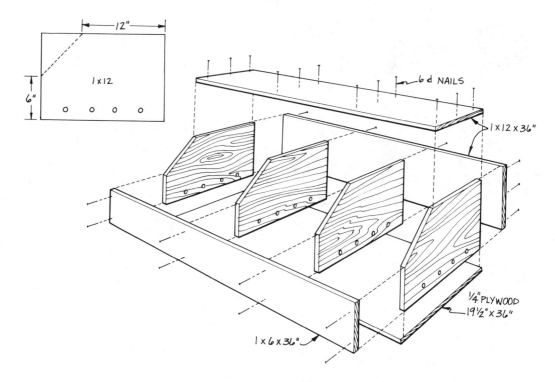

12"

1 x 12

6"

6 d NAILS

1 X 12 X 36"

¼" PLYWOOD
19½" X 36"

1 X 6 X 36"

COLD BOX

Before you dig a root cellar to store your winter squash, apples, root vegetables, or cabbages, take a look at this alternative the Rodale Press's Research and Development Group has come up with. If you have your own well, this cold box can tap all the cooling effects of a deep root cellar or springhouse by using incoming water to carry off any heat in excess of underground water temperatures in your area.

Well water temperatures don't fluctuate with the seasons, but they must be 55°F. or lower to retard

spoilage, according to R & D's experiences. Remember, town water pipes run parallel to the surface, usually just below the frost line. While that water may get very cold in winter, it may be too warm to preserve vegetables in late summer and fall.

This cold box provides no-energy cold storage, conveniently located in the basement. It is essentially an insulated closet or chest built near the incoming water pipe, which keeps the cooling effect from dissipating around the basement.

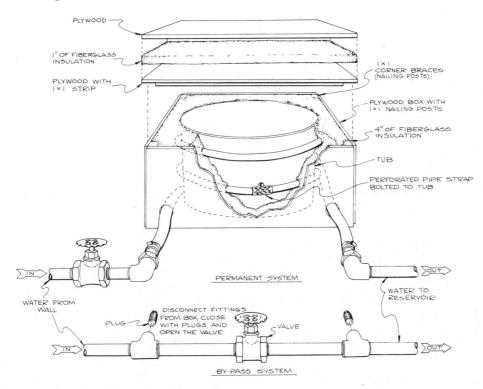

CONSTRUCTION

1. Construct a square box about 8 inches longer along its sides than the diameter of the tub and 4 inches deeper than the tub. The box needs no bottom. Cut nailing posts from the 1 x 1 for the corners. Since plywood does not hold nails well, put glue along the side of the post before nailing into it.

2. Remove the handles from the tub. Beginning at the bottom, you will wrap the tubing around it. Leave enough extra tubing at each end so it can extend out the side of the box. First, wrap some of the perforated pipe strap around the tubing about where it will meet the bottom of the tub. Drill a hole in the tub there, and bolt on the tubing. Then wrap the tubing around it in a spiral. At the top, put on more of the strap, drill through the tub, and bolt the tubing in place.

MATERIALS

Wood

$\frac{5}{8}''$ ext. plywood (sides and top)

1 x 1 (corner posts and side of the lid)

Hardware

Glue
4d nails
1–20- or 30-gallon galvanized tub
$\frac{1}{2}''$ plastic tubing for the coil and pipe
1' perforated metal strap
2–$\frac{3}{4}''$ x $\frac{1}{4}''$ machine bolts w/ nuts and washers
Fiberglass insulation
Valves and fittings to hook into the water system (see diagram
for options)

---

3. Drill holes in the side of the box for the inlet and outlet of the coil.
4. Make the lid so it rests on top of the box. Cut two squares of plywood to size, and nail and glue strips of 1 x 1 around the perimeter of one of them. Lay down 1 inch of fiberglass, then fasten the second square of plywood on top. If you've never worked with fiberglass, you will appreciate the warning to wear gloves and long sleeves.
5. Put the box in place and lay 4 inches of fiberglass in the bottom. Next center the tub in the box and run the tubing through the sides. Fill in with insulation evenly around the sides.
6. Hook your coil into the water system. This should be as close to the inlet to the house as possible, but it must be behind a cut-off valve. If your home has a storage tank for the well water, connect the cold box between the inlet and the tank. Every plumbing system is a little different, so here are a few options to consider.
   a. As the diagram shows, you can make the circuit that you build around the cold box "permanent" or you can build in valves that allow you to disconnect it easily. Of course, the "permanent" arrangement can easily be reversed with some minor plumbing.
   b. The diagram shows two kinds of joint fittings. There are many different kinds of these, as well as valves, to suit your situation. A visit to a building or plumbing supply house will acquaint you with the options. Plastic fittings are the most easy to work with, and adapters are available to join plastic elements to a metal-pipe system.

VARIATIONS

It is simple to convert this design to a unit which can hold large amounts of squash, root crops, and fruit. Use stud wall construction to make a chest or upright closet. The chest is better, since the cold air won't flow out every time it's opened. If there is no space to get into the water line between the inlet and the water tank, enclose the whole tank in the "box."

In a deep basement the floors and walls are often cold enough so that the box will need no floor. If the cellar is very warm it's better to insulate all facets. On larger cold boxes we suggest making the lid 2 inches deep and attaching it with hinges.

ROOT STORAGE BARREL

A root cellar or cold cellar are not the lone underground storage facilities. A homesteader or gardener who doesn't have a lot of food to store can use a barrel or chest, buried in the ground for storage.

At the new Organic Gardening Experimental Farm, we installed a storage barrel next to one of the residences. The method has proven satisfactory. Although we used a wooden barrel, a metal container—like a 55-

gallon drum or a metal trash can—would work just as well.

What you store depends on what you grow, but a few basic rules are important. Don't store vegetables and fruit in the same container. (Apples release gases which cause potatoes to sprout. Cabbage and turnips can transmit their odor to apples and pears.) Season fruits and vegetables by keeping them in the shade for a week or so. (This allows some surface dehydration.) Finally, start the storage as late in the season as possible.

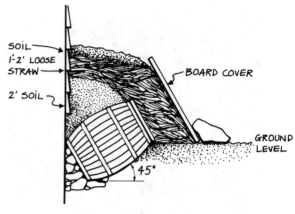

CONSTRUCTION

1. Start by finding a well-drained place to dig a hole, big enough to hold your barrel and about 3 feet deep. If you want to put it next to a building, choose a north exposure.
2. Put the rocks in the bottom of the hole, and work the barrel in so it rests on a 45-degree angle, with its lower lip just at ground level.
3. Fill in the hole and mound about 2 feet of earth on top of the barrel. Pile a foot or two of loose straw on top.
4. After the barrel is loaded with produce, put the lid on, and pack a foot or two of straw in front. Another layer of soil on top, and boards to keep everything in place, and the storage barrel is ready for the winter.

A footnote on packing the barrel: Your vegetables or fruit need low temperature and fairly high humidity. A good way to assure this, and needed ventilation, is to alternate layers of produce with loose layers of burlap, straw, or string sphagnum moss. The top layer may be sprinkled with water from time to time if it has dried out.

VARIATIONS

Pennsylvania homesteader Jane Preston devised a pit-storage setup similar to the storage barrel.

Her pit is neatly cut out, 3 feet wide, 6 feet long, and 2 feet deep. It is on sloping ground, so that excess water promptly drains away. She and her husband lined the inside entirely with ¼-inch hardware cloth, carefully kept tight—as it must be—to keep out rodents. The top is finished with a frame of 2 x 4s and a neat wooden lid.

Four bales of straw can be laid on the cover, and this then is covered with a plastic sheet to keep off snow. The insulation provided by the straw bales not only helps keep things "warm" in winter (avoiding freezing), but also cool in the warm days

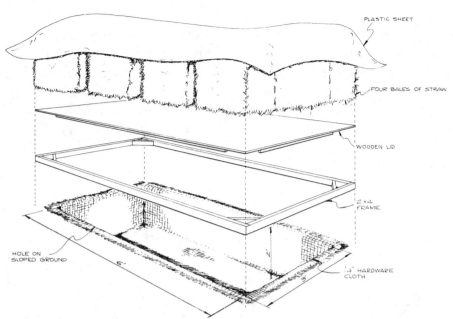

PLASTIC SHEET

FOUR BALES OF STRAW

WOODEN LID

2 x 4 FRAME

HOLE ON SLOPED GROUND

½" HARDWARE CLOTH

of early spring. Good-quality vegetables have been taken from the pit as late as May—even early June. Then it is time to clean everything out and let in sunshine and ventilation over the summer.

The Preston's pit has been in steady use for over ten years. They have had to replace the wooden parts and mend the wire on occasion, but that's about all. And they've been able to maintain a supply of good home-grown varieties of all root vegetables, plus cabbage and celery as well.

Gardener Elmer L. Onstott, of St. Louis, Missouri, solved a good part of his storage problem when he discovered that 10-gallon garbage pails can be converted into storage bins by burying them in 16-inch holes, leaving their rims above ground. In addi-

tion to being inexpensive and readily accessible, the garbage-pail storage bins are water- and rodent-proof and store easily over the summer as a compact stack of pails.

Onstott harvests his carrots, beets, and turnips and places them in cans without washing them. He then puts the lids on the cans and covers everything with 6 inches of straw, adding more when the ground freezes.

Instead of emptying one pail at a time, Onstott takes a little from each in turn, so that the level in each can is lowered as the winter progresses. The lower the contents are, the less chance of damage from frost. If the vegetables are 6 to 8 inches below the bin cover, with even a little straw, it will take a very severe freezing to cause frost damage because the heat from the earth below the frost line will feed into the bins.

While these storage containers do not equal the airtight, atmospherically controlled and refrigerated rooms that large, commercial operations boast of, these simple, inexpensive garden storage containers give results. All through the winter months and into early spring, long after the average gardener has all but forgotten his garden, you can bring in those garden-fresh, organically grown vegetables from the storage bins of your garden.

PART IV
Around the Homestead

CONCRETE

Mixing and working with concrete is a useful skill that can save lots of money for the homesteader. Concrete can be used to make footings, slabs for outbuildings, corncribs and the like, sidewalks, floors, steps, and walls. You also can cast paving slabs or flagstones and building blocks. A successful concrete project requires three things: careful planning, meticulous adherence to instructions (meaning no shortcuts), and some brute strength.

Some nomenclature must be discussed first. Cement and concrete are words which often are used interchangeably, but they are not the same thing. Cement, usually Portland cement, is a manufactured product. It is a mixture of limestone, clay, chalk, and other materials, which is roasted and ground to a fine consistency.

Concrete is a mixture of cement, sand, and pebbles or gravel. Depending on the job, different proportions of these ingredients, and water, are called for.

MIXING CONCRETE

In almost all cases, your concrete mixture will begin with Portland cement. This comes in standard 94-pound bags referred to as sacks. It must be kept dry, because it absorbs moisture readily, and when it does, it lumps up. If there are lumps which do not crush easily between your fingers, the cement has been ruined.

When you add water to cement, it forms a paste which binds the aggregates—sand and gravel—into concrete. An important ingredient in Portland cement is an air-entraining chemical. This gives home-mixed concrete the same characteristic as ready-mixed concrete: a saturation of tiny air bubbles. These bubbles are important in climates with winter freezes, because they protect against scaling and cracking damage during the freeze-thaw cycle.

Aggregates include sand and gravel, which actually are discussed as separate ingredients. The sand must be clean, for if it is not, the concrete will not bind. *Do not* use seashore sand. Mortar sand is another, finer variety, and it should not be used for mixing concrete.

When buying gravel, you can specify the maximum size you want, or you can order what is known as "bank run," which includes gravel of all sizes and some sand.

Obviously, the water you use must be clean. It should not contain any oil or organic waste. Potable tap water is clean enough. Seawater should not be used.

Before you order your materials, you will have to determine the proper mix for your job. Generally speaking, the more wear and weathering the

CONCRETE MIX

Here are recommended proportions for common home projects.

	Cement (Bags)	Sand (Cubic Feet)	Gravel (Cubic Feet)
Floor	1	2	3
Sidewalk (light traffic)	1	2	4
Sidewalk (heavy traffic)	1	1½	3
Driveway	1	2½	3½
Stairs	1	2	4
Footings	1	2	4
Foundation wall	1	2	4
Posts, cast forms	1	1½	3

concrete must endure, the greater the percentage of cement you will use. (Consult the accompanying chart.)

The amount of water you use depends on how wet the sand you started with is. Damp sand will not form a ball when you squeeze it. Wet, or average sand, forms a ball, but will leave no noticeable moisture on your hand. Very wet sand drips water. With damp sand, deduct one quart of water from the amount specified per sack of cement in the accompanying chart. For average sand, deduct two quarts. For very wet sand, deduct a gallon.

WATER-CEMENT RATIO

Use the specified number of gallons of water for each sack of cement in the following home projects.

Basement or interior floor	5½	Driveway	5
Patio exterior floor	5	Stairs	5
Sidewalk (light traffic)	5	Footings	5½
Sidewalk (heavy traffic)	4½	Foundation wall	5

To estimate how much concrete your job calls for, first compute the area you are covering. Multiply this by its thickness, which will give you a figure in cubic feet. To get cubic yards, divide this figure by 27, for the 27 cubic feet in each cubic yard.

Mix your concrete only after all your forms and other equipment are ready and in place. If you are using only a few cubic yards of concrete, it can be mixed by hand. For bigger jobs, you may want to consider having premixed or ready-mixed concrete delivered to the job. More on how to order ready-mixed later.

A wheelbarrow is ideal for mixing small batches of concrete. You also can use a washtub or a mixing trough, or mix on a piece of plywood or a concrete floor. A hoe or square-ended shovel are the best mixing tools.

MORTAR BOX

There are many times around the homestead when it is necessary to mix small batches of concrete: for planters, posts, or repair jobs; for mortar work. This mixing box is easily made of common board lumber.

CONSTRUCTION

1. Cut a 19-inch-long piece of 1 x 12. Shape the board as shown. The hand slot is made by drilling holes at either end of the area to be removed and then cutting out the rest (using a keyhole saw).
2. Cut a 9¾-inch piece of 1 x 12. Cut two 43-inch lengths of 1 x 10.
3. Measure 3 inches in from each bottom edge of the 43-inchers and scribe a line from there to the corner. Cut these corners off.
4. Using 4d nails, fasten these side pieces to the back board (with hand slot), locating the back piece between the sides.
5. Take the 9¾-inch piece, fit between the sides, and nail to front end of box. Top and bottom may have to be trimmed to make an even joint.
6. The ends of the bottom piece must be beveled at an angle of about 10 degrees to conform with the slope of the ends of the box. From a 1 x 12 cut a piece 36 inches long. Set your circular saw at a 10-degree angle and cutting so the longer side measures 36½ inches and the shorter side 36 inches with bevels sloping toward each other. This bevel can also be made with a wood rasp or a block plane. Fit this board on the bottom and secure with 4d nails.
7. Cut two 4-inch lengths of 2 x 2. In the center of each piece, drill a ¾-inch hole. With 10d nails secure them to the bottom edge of each side 31 inches from the intersection with the back.
8. Insert a 17-inch length of ½-inch steel pipe through holes.

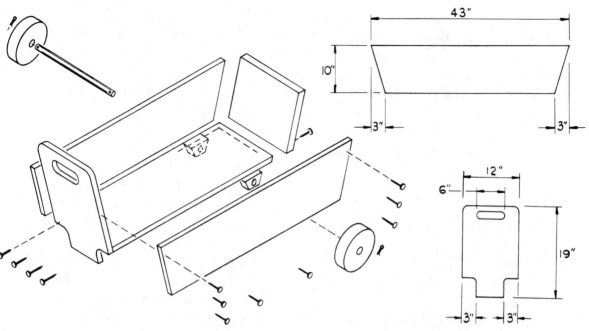

9. Wheels may be cut from 2-inch stock or by nailing 1-inch stock together. In the center, drill a ¾-inch hole and secure the wheels on the pipe with cotter pins.

MATERIALS

Wood

1 pc. 1 x 12 x 8'	or	**Back end:** 1 pc. 1 x 12 x 19″
		Front end: 1 pc. 1 x 12 x 9¾″
		Bottom: 1 pc. 1 x 12 x 36″
1 pc. 1 x 10 x 8'	or	**Sides:** 2 pcs. 1 x 10 x 43″
1 pc. 2 x 2 x 2'	or	**Wheel axle supports:** 2 pcs. 2 x 2 x 4″
1 pc. 2 x 10 x 2'	or	**Wheels:** 2 pcs. 2 x 10 x 8″

Hardware

4d nails
10d nails
1 pc. 17″ x ½″ steel pipe (axle)
2 cotter pins

When it comes right down to mixing your ingredients, just keep the proportions and the relative consistency of the product you want in mind. The charts really reflect the proportions to use: one quantity of cement to two like quantities of sand and three like quantities of gravel. You can use a can or bucket to measure your quantities. Or even measure in shovelfuls.

First, mix the cement, sand, and gravel. They must be thoroughly blended and should have a uniform color, showing neither light nor dark streaks.

Add the water, little by little, until the entire mixture is evenly moist. To test the blend, draw the back of the shovel over the concrete, in a poking motion to create a series of ridges. If the mix is too wet, the ridges will sink back into the pile. If it is too dry, the ridges will be indistinct.

If your mixture is too wet, add small amounts of cement, sand, and gravel, in the same proportions you used in the original mix. If it is too dry, sprinkle only small amounts of water across the heap.

If you use a mixer, first measure the ingredients to the proportions you need. With the mixer stopped, load in the gravel and half the water. If your cement calls for an air-entraining agent you add yourself, add it at this time.

Start the mixer, and while it is running, add the sand, cement, and the rest of the water. Keep the mixer running for at least three minutes, or until the mixture is of uniform color. Use the concrete as quickly as possible.

If you have a distance to wheel the concrete, take the time to make a decent road. If the dirt is soft, lay down some planks or boards. Mixing and wheeling concrete is hard work but it doesn't have to be difficult.

When you get done working with concrete, clean up everything. Once the concrete hardens on tools it's all but impossible to get it off. A stiff fiber brush is a big help in cleaning up and unless you're looking forward to swinging a two-hundred-pound shovel someday, what little time it takes is worth the trouble. A good hard stream of water will do a pretty good job on the mixer but throw five or six shovelfuls of gravel in, add water until it's really sloppy, and just let it thrash around for a while. Then rinse it out with the hose until the water runs clean. It's surprising, but some people will spend a couple hundred dollars on a mixer and then let it become thoroughly encrusted with hardened concrete. Once a little concrete hardens on the inside it gets harder and harder to clean each time.

When concrete has obtained its initial set, usually in about twenty-four hours, you can remove the forms. At this time, however, the concrete is still "green" and while it won't fall apart it isn't very strong, either. To obtain maximum strength, assuming everything else has gone right, concrete must be cured. Curing is nothing more than making sure that the water you added so carefully when you mixed the concrete stays in long enough to complete hydration. Concrete continues to cure and gain strength for twenty-eight days after its initial set. This is what concrete people refer to as the 28-day strength when they're dealing with structural concrete. All you really need to be concerned with is keeping the concrete damp for about a week. One way is to leave the forms on. Another is to carefully strip the forms and cover the green concrete with a sheet of plastic. Concrete will get hard anyway, but it will get a lot harder and stronger if it's cured properly.

Freshly poured concrete should be protected from freezing, too. Concrete that freezes before it reaches its initial set is ruined and will never be very strong. Concrete can freeze *after* its initial set without too much harm but the curing time will be lengthened considerably. Take a few precautions. If the weather is cold and below freezing at night, pour the concrete early in the day while the temperature is rising. If you think there's a chance the concrete might freeze before it sets, cover it with plastic or felt paper and some loose hay. Concrete generates heat while it sets and cures, and this will help hold in the heat.

TOOLS

Working with concrete requires some special tools. Fortunately, you can make many of them yourself.

Striking-off, or screeding, is one of the first smoothing operations. It can be performed with a 2 x 4 cut a few inches longer than your job is wide. If you will be working with a helper, you may want to add handles on each end, as shown, so you both can do the striking-off.

A float, or leveling trowel, can be made from workshop scraps. Cut a 14-inch piece of 1 x 6 for the bottom. Cut a handle in the shape shown from a 14-inch-long 2 x 3. After sanding the handle and the trowel base, fasten the handle to the trowel base with glue and two 1½-inch #10 screws.

A bull float is used for sidewalks and other large area jobs. Make one

Tools

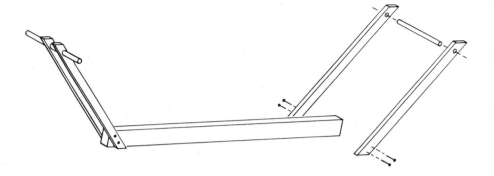

MATERIALS

Wood

1 pc. 2 x 4 x 4′ (screed board)

2 pcs. 1 x 4 x 8′   or   **Handle supports:** 4 pcs. 1 x 4 x 48″

1 pc. 36″ x ¾″ dowel   or   **Handles:** 2 pcs. 18″ x ¾″ dowel

Hardware

6d nails

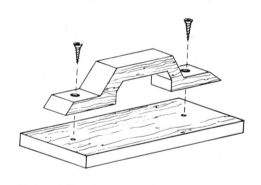

MATERIALS

Wood

1 pc. 1 x 6 x 2′   or   **Bottom:** 1 pc. 1 x 6 x 14″

1 pc. 2 x 3 x 2′   or   **Handle:** 1 pc. 2 x 3 x 14″

Hardware

2–1½″ #10 screws
Glue

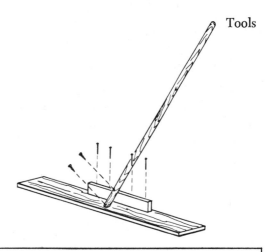

using a 48-inch length of 1 x 8 for the bottom. Nail an 18-inch strip of 1 x 3 along one edge of the board. Then, using 1¼-inch #8 screws, attach a broomhandle, as shown, to the bottom board and the 1 x 3 brace.

An edging trowel, or edger, is for finishing the edges of your sidewalk.

MATERIALS

Wood

1 pc. 1 x 8 x 4′	or	**Bottom:** 1 pc. 1 x 8 x 48″
1 pc. 1 x 3 x 2′	or	**Brace:** 1 pc. 1 x 3 x 18″

Hardware

8d nails
2–1¼″ #8 screws

Miscellaneous

1 broomhandle

You can make one from a piece of sheet metal, as shown.

Make the base from a 4-inch by 8¼-inch piece of $\frac{1}{16}$-inch-thick sheet metal cut, as shown, with 1⅛-inch-square tabs in the center of the 4-inch ends, reducing the long sides to 6 inches. Drill a small hole in each tab for a screw.

Cut the wooden handle from a 6-inch length of 2 x 3. Shape it into an inverted **U** of 1-inch thickness by cutting out a 2-inch by 4-inch rec-

tangle from the side. Round all corners and sand.

Bend the tabs and connect the handle to the base with 1-inch #10 screws. Bend the metal around a $\frac{3}{4}$-inch pipe so one side points down, the other up.

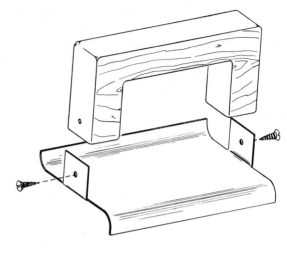

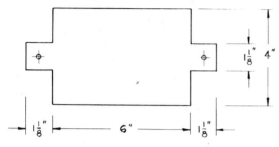

MATERIALS

Wood

    1 pc. 2 x 3 x 2'   or   **Handle:** 1 pc. 2 x 3 x 6"

Hardware

    1 pc. $\frac{1}{16}$" x 4" x 8$\frac{1}{4}$" sheet metal (base)
    2–1" #10 screws

A finishing trowel is usually made of metal. It will put a smooth, dense finish on your concrete, though that isn't necessary for all jobs.

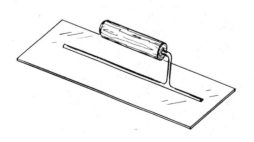

You could make a finishing trowel from a piece of sheet metal, but you'll probably get better results if you buy a finishing trowel. A good one won't be cheap either.

A standard mason's trowel will also be handy for many concrete projects.

You'll also need at least one shovel.

Kneeboards are useful for distributing your weight over a broader position on the concrete than your feet and are used in floating and troweling broad expanses of concrete. Use 1- or 2-foot-square pieces of plywood.

ORDERING READY-MIX

Ready-mix concrete, delivered by truck and poured right into your forms, is a convenience. Concrete contractors are eager to sell their product and will offer advice and information to potential customers. But if you know exactly what you want, that knowledge will ensure that you get the material your job calls for.

Tell the ready-mix contractor what you are building and its dimensions. Then specify the maximum coarse aggregate size, which should be no greater than one-third of the thickness of the slab you are making.

Some contractors also will give you options on minimum cement content, which should usually be six bags per cubic yard.

Maximum slump refers to the mix's workability. Specify that this should not exceed 4 inches.

The load-bearing capacity of ready-mix should be at least 3,500 pounds per square inch after twenty-eight days.

Also ask about entrained air content. It should be about 6 percent by volume.

THE BASIC PROCEDURES

With any concrete project, some careful planning is necessary.

First, develop your specifications. Measure the area to be paved or the volume of the form to be filled, and compute how much material you will need.

You will need forms. If you are

casting a planter or post, you must construct a "mold." If you are pouring a wall or slab, you must construct a form to run around the perimeter.

Forms can be constructed of common boards or dimension lumber. The very best forms are constructed of green wood (wood that hasn't been

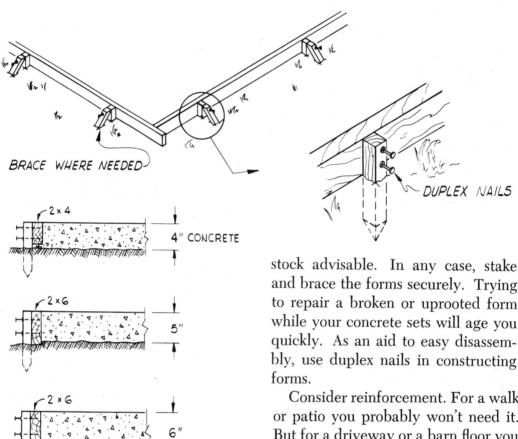

BRACE WHERE NEEDED

2 x 4

4" CONCRETE

2 x 6

5"

2 x 6

6"

CONCRETE UNDER FORM

DUPLEX NAILS

dried). If you will be buying wood specifically to build your forms and you can buy directly from a sawmill, by all means buy and use green lumber. It'll be less expensive, too.

In constructing forms, consider the weight of the concrete. For a sidewalk, 1-inch stock will be adequate. For a large patio or wall, you may decide the extra strength of 2-inch

stock advisable. In any case, stake and brace the forms securely. Trying to repair a broken or uprooted form while your concrete sets will age you quickly. As an aid to easy disassembly, use duplex nails in constructing forms.

Consider reinforcement. For a walk or patio you probably won't need it. But for a driveway or a barn floor you probably will.

There are two types of reinforcement: wire mesh and steel rods. There are specific products marketed for reinforcing concrete, but you can improvise, using pipes, rods, flat and angle iron, wire, and various types of woven wire fencing.

The purpose of the reinforcement is to prevent the loads that the concrete will be subjected to from pulling it apart. Ordinarily, the reinforcement is located in the center of the concrete mass, either by pulling it from

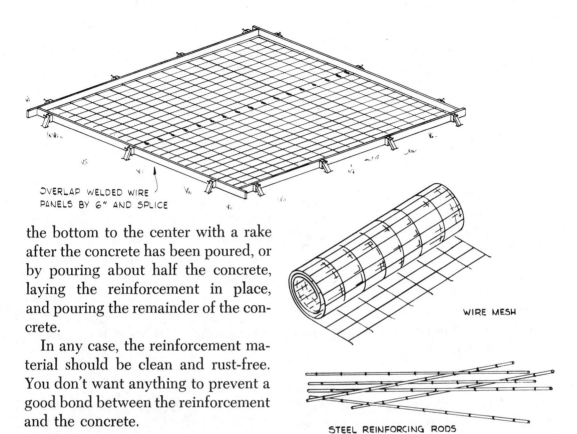

OVERLAP WELDED WIRE
PANELS BY 6" AND SPLICE

WIRE MESH

STEEL REINFORCING RODS

the bottom to the center with a rake after the concrete has been poured, or by pouring about half the concrete, laying the reinforcement in place, and pouring the remainder of the concrete.

In any case, the reinforcement material should be clean and rust-free. You don't want anything to prevent a good bond between the reinforcement and the concrete.

THE BASE

A firm foundation will immeasurably lengthen the life of any concrete slab, small or large. It will provide the support and ensure the drainage it needs. And the foundation necessary will depend on the soil conditions and the use you'll put the concrete slab to.

First, you will need a crushed stone base on any filled soil. The soil should be rolled or tamped and topped with at least 6 inches of stone.

On clay or any other poorly drained soil, use about 2 inches of stone.

On sandy or other well-drained soil, a stone base won't be needed.

When excavating for your concrete slab, be sure to make allowance for the thickness of whatever base is required.

Second, if you want to ensure that hydrostatic pressure won't force water through the slab, you will want to cover the base with building paper or heavy plastic sheets. This is stan-

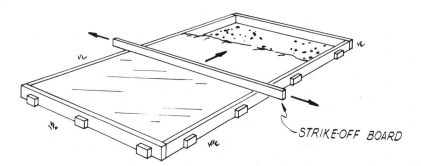

STRIKE-OFF BOARD

dard practice in homebuilding, but isn't necessary for sidewalks or patios.

After all these preparations are completed, set up your forms.

Oil the surfaces of all the form boards where they will touch the concrete, to avoid sticking. You can use used crankcase oil, which you usually can get free at a garage or gas station.

Mix the concrete and pour it into the forms as quickly as possible. Work quickly but carefully, placing the concrete as accurately as you can with a shovel or hoe, leaving it about an inch above the top of the form.

Strike off the concrete using the strike-off board. The board rests on the top of the forms. Your object is to skim off the excess concrete so the surface is flush with the top of the form boards.

Next you bull-float the concrete. Hold the surface of the bull float level, and work it as if you were using a sponge mop. This step will level bumps and fill holes, pushing pieces of gravel below the surface.

After bull-floating you must wait as the water rises to the surface and evaporates. The amount of time it takes can range from one hour to eight hours.

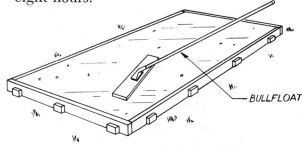

BULLFLOAT

Check the concrete periodically. After the sheen of water has disappeared, run a trowel along the edges of the forms. If the concrete has set enough to hold the shape of the trowel, you can proceed with the floating. This further smooths the surface. Work the float flat on the concrete, in wide, arc motions. But *don't press too hard*. It is hard to erase gouges made at this point.

Troweling isn't absolutely necessary. But it will increase the smoothness of the surface and make it more dense. The first troweling is done

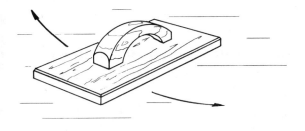

FLOAT IN WIDE ARC MOTIONS

a skid-resistant surface, use a stiff-bristled brush on the concrete after the last troweling.

Curing takes five to seven days, depending on the weather. The object is for the concrete to dry slowly, so you must keep it moist by covering it with damp burlap or straw or by sprinkling it periodically.

immediately after floating. Hold the trowel flat against the concrete. The second troweling should be done later, when your hand leaves only a slight impression in the concrete. For

After several days of curing, the forms can be removed. But for best results, allow your concrete to cure several days after removing the forms and before subjecting it to use.

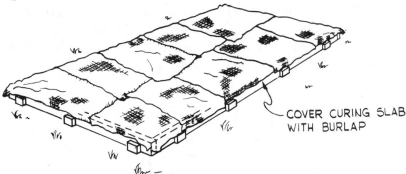

COVER CURING SLAB
WITH BURLAP

FOOTINGS

Concrete footings, slabs or columns of poured concrete, are a preliminary and important step in many construction projects. Whether you are building a barn, a greenhouse, or steps for the back porch, footings will give the solid support the job needs. Footings must always be set below the frost line so they can protect the structures built upon them from frost-heaving damage. Many specifics on how deep,

how wide, how thick, and other details about the footings for your area are spelled out in local building codes. Do not fail to check your local codes, if they exist, because some footings require a building permit, and the finished job may have to be inspected before your community will issue a "certificate of use" or "certificate of occupancy."

LAYOUT

If you are building a house or other project that requires some excavation before you set the footings, you first must lay out the building lines. The first step is to determine the front line, which is the outside face of the foundation beneath the front wall. Measure from a property line, or from existing buildings, to locate this line. (Check local zoning codes on what is required for front and side yard setbacks, if applicable.)

Drive in at least two temporary stakes to define this first line, and stretch a line between them. Working from your plans, locate first one front corner and then the other. Drive a stake exactly at each corner, and drive a nail into the exact center of each stake.

Working from these nail heads, set up the other two corners in the same manner. To check your work (on a rectangle or square structure) measure the diagonals in both directions: they must be the same.

Since these stakes and lines obviously will be in the way of further digging, the next step is to set up batter boards. The purpose of batter boards is to preserve the building lines without hampering digging and other work.

BATTER BOARD CONSTRUCTION

1. For each corner you will need three lengths of 2 x 4 for stakes, each 2 to 3 feet long. You will need two lengths of 1 x 6 or similar stock for the crosspieces, and each of these should be 3 or 4 feet long.
2. Set the three stakes an equal distance from the corner stake already in place. They should be arranged so that when connected, they form a right angle which repeats the shape of the building's intersecting

---

MATERIALS

Wood

| 1 pc. 2 x 4 x 10′ | or | Stakes: 3 pcs. 2 x 4 x 2′ to 3′ |
| 1 pc. 1 x 6 x 8′ | or | Crosspieces: 2 pcs. 1 x 6 x 3′ to 4′ |

Hardware

String
8d nails

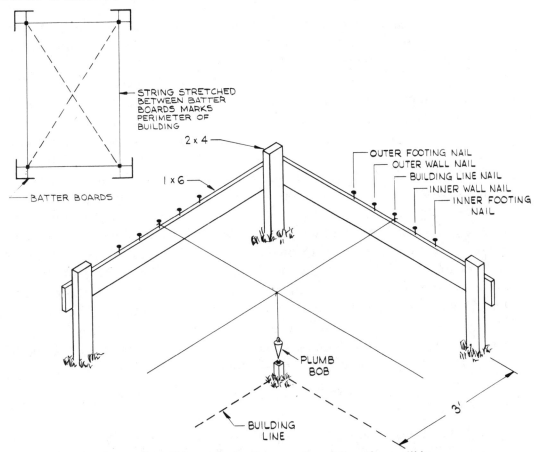

WHEN THE CORNERS ARE SQUARE THE DIAGONALS WILL BE EQUAL.

BATTER BOARDS

STRING STRETCHED BETWEEN BATTER BOARDS MARKS PERIMETER OF BUILDING

2 x 4

1 x 6

OUTER FOOTING NAIL

OUTER WALL NAIL

BUILDING LINE NAIL

INNER WALL NAIL

INNER FOOTING NAIL

PLUMB BOB

BUILDING LINE

3'

corners. One stake will be opposite the corner, and the others will be about 3 feet along each building line. Repeat this for all four corners.

3. Then, loop string around each horizontal batter board crosspiece, and stretch it along the building lines to the corresponding batter board on the next corner. When all four lines are in place, two will cross at each corner. The object is to adjust the lines by sliding them back and forth to get them to intersect directly over the stake with the nail in its top.

4. This accomplished, drive a nail into the top edge of each batter board crosspiece to mark the proper line location. With these nails in place at each corner, you can remove the first set of stakes and the strings. By using the batter boards with their nails, it will be an easy matter to re-establish the lines later.

5. To carry this process one step further, you can add other nails to the top of the batter board crosspieces to mark the inner edge of your footings and the front and back lines of each wall.

411

SLAB FOOTING

As a rule of thumb, the thickness of the slab is twice the width of the wall or other structure it is supporting. The footing should be twice the width of the wall it supports. If it is supporting a retaining wall, increase the width by at least one-third.

Part of your preplanning also should include determining if a particular location and type of reinforcement is required by any local codes. Usually, a minimum of three horizontal rods are placed in the lower third of the footing's thickness. Also, some walls require vertical reinforcing bars, which actually must be anchored in the footing. Usually, they are placed no closer than 24 inches. A useful feature is a keyway in the foot-ing, which is a groove in the top surface of the footing to help locate and align the wall.

To make a keyway, prepare a 2 x 4 ahead of time. It must be as long as your footing. Plane the 2 x 4 so the edges taper, as shown, and drill holes to fit the spacing interval of the vertical reinforcers. Then, rip the 2 x 4 into two equal strips.

Finally, under the category of preplanning, determine the necessary depth of footings. The object is to set the footing below the frost line. In Bangor, Maine, for instance, that is 48 inches. In Tampa, Florida, which has no real frost line, it is 6 inches.

The steps for making a slab footing follow.

CONSTRUCTION

1. Level the ground along the inside of your front line, a strip as wide as your footing is to be. Lay about 2 inches of smooth sand.
2. Build your forms from 1-inch stock, or ¾-inch exterior plywood cut to match the thickness of your slab. Use 2 x 4s for supporting stakes on the outside of the form, and nail it together. If your footing is more than 1 foot thick, it is a good idea to add diagonal braces, perpendicular to the side of the footing. Oil the inside of the forms.
3. Mix and pour the concrete. The horizontal reinforcing rods should be evenly spaced in the lower third of the footing.
4. When the concrete is 1 inch from the top of the form, you will put in the keyway form. To locate the keyway, refer to the batter board nails marking the front and back faces of the wall itself, and center it between them. You also can simply center it on the footing. The 2 x 4 should be placed with its wide edge up. Insert the vertical reinforcing bars through the holes in the keyway form.
5. Finish pouring. Strike off and bull-float the footing. It must cure for at least one week before the forms are removed and the footing is used.

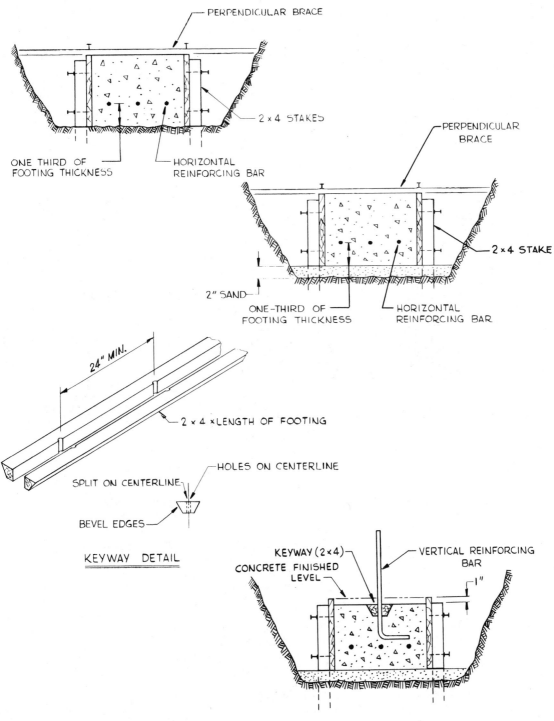

PERPENDICULAR BRACE

2 x 4 STAKES

ONE THIRD OF
FOOTING THICKNESS

HORIZONTAL
REINFORCING BAR

PERPENDICULAR
BRACE

2 x 4 STAKE

2" SAND

ONE-THIRD OF
FOOTING THICKNESS

HORIZONTAL
REINFORCING BAR

24" MIN.

2 x 4 x LENGTH OF FOOTING

HOLES ON CENTERLINE

SPLIT ON CENTERLINE

BEVEL EDGES

KEYWAY DETAIL

KEYWAY (2 x 4)
CONCRETE FINISHED
LEVEL

VERTICAL REINFORCING
BAR

1"

413

FLOORS

The most difficult slab to pour is a floor, especially the floor of an existing building. The basic principles are the same as any concrete project: you make a form and pour the concrete. In a building, the walls will generally serve as the form, but they won't provide a surface for the strike-off board to rest on in leveling the concrete. The explanation below tells you how to handle that problem.

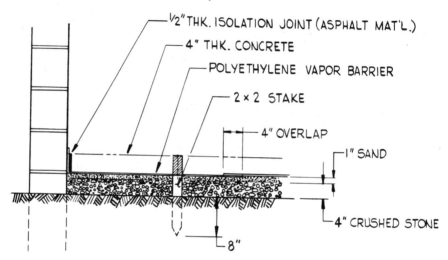

CONSTRUCTION

1. If the subbase is compact and well drained, lay the concrete directly on top of it. If it is wet or uneven, dig down 4 more inches and lay 4 inches of crushed stone or gravel.

2. The floor must be sloped to drain. In a garage or barn, slope the floor toward the door. So slope the subbase to keep the thickness for the concrete uniform. If you need floor drains, install them now, as well as any other conduits or pipes to go under the slab.

3. Drive 2 x 2 stakes about 8 inches long into the ground so the tops are just about flush with the surface. They should be no closer than 2 feet to the wall, and placed 2 feet apart in parallel rows. You will work your strike-off board in a direction perpendicular to these stake rows. If you will have a corner to get out of the room when the floor is done, arrange a second set of stakes to work in that direction. Check the stakes in both directions with a level.

4. Install a vapor barrier on the ground using heavy plastic sheeting.

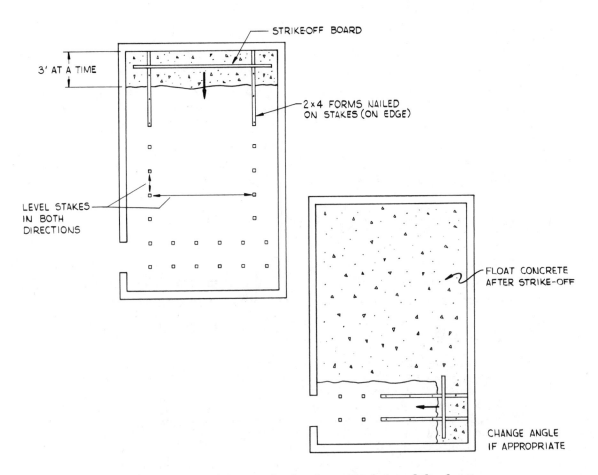

Pieces of sheeting should overlap by about 4 inches, and the sheeting should run up the wall past the level of the finished floor.

5. Use 6-foot lengths of 2 x 4s to gauge the thickness of the slab and to support the strike-off board. They are tacked temporarily to the stakes, as shown. The strike-off board you use here should be a foot or two shorter than the width of the floor.

6. Pour enough concrete for a 3-foot strip along the farthest wall from the door. Begin striking off, working backward. Lift the side tracks and retack them as you go, a strip of 3 feet at a time. Note that you will have to reach back to repair the grooves left by the side forms after you lift and move them. Cut joints every 10 feet, making them about one-fourth as deep as the floor. Do the bull floating as you go. Allow the concrete to set for several hours, until the sheen of water has evaporated. (If your floor is in an enclosed area, it will help to set up a fan to hasten evaporation.) Then float and trowel it.

7. Cover the floor with plastic sheeting and allow it to cure for six or seven days before walking on it.

415

SLABS

The pouring of a slab, such as a patio or the floor of a building that is just being constructed, involves a combination of the procedures explained above. The perimeter of the slab is established using batter boards, then sturdy forms are constructed. In the actual pouring process, the top edge of the form serves as a level surface to guide the striking off. If the area of the slab is so large as to make striking off unwieldy, use the stakes as you would in pouring a floor in an existing building.

EXPANSION JOINTS

A professional touch you can add to a variety of projects such as the floor just described, is an expansion joint where the new concrete meets an existing structure. There is a choice of methods you can use.

CONSTRUCTION

1. If a new slab is to abut an existing wall, install a ⅜-inch thickness of wood instead of the regular form board along the wall. Leave the wood in place after the concrete is poured.
2. Building supply stores sell asphalt-impregnated material in rolls, for just this purpose. Install it in place of form boards where the new concrete abuts an existing structure. For appearance's sake, trim it to fit your new pouring.
3. Cut the form board that will go along the existing structure in half, along the diagonal. After the concrete has been poured and cures, remove the top half of the wood and fill the groove with hot tar.

CONCRETE PROJECTS

You can use concrete to make a large variety of very durable items. Fence posts. Birdbaths. Troughs for watering or feeding livestock. Planters. Slabs and blocks for walls, walks, or patios.

For whatever you want to make from concrete, you must first make a mold or form. This is the most difficult part of the process, in most cases. But the form can be used again and again, suggesting that you could even make several birdbaths, or whatever it is you need, and sell the extras.

CONCRETE POSTS

Properly made concrete posts will outlast almost any type of wood post. You can cast posts to accommodate woven wire, barbwire, welded panels, or wooden rails. You also can cast post bases directly in the ground or anchor a length of angle iron or other upright to support the fence itself.

For some basic information on what types of fencing are available, and specifics on what size posts are needed, consult the chapter on fences.

Posts can be cast in wood forms. Another simple possibility is to use metal rain gutter, cut to the proper length and blocked at both ends with

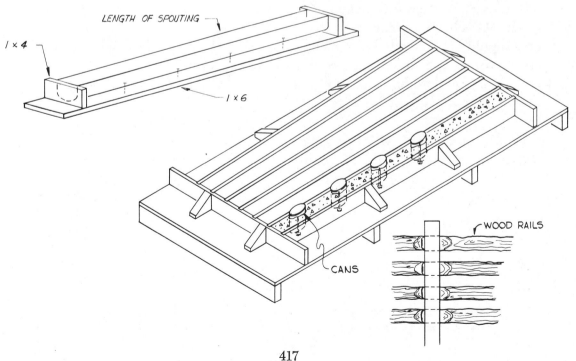

pieces of wood. You also can fashion your own out of common board lumber, using a shipping pallet as a base. Such posts should be at least 6 inches in diameter at the bottom, and they can be tapered to no less than 3 inches at the top of an 8-foot post. This size will support a fence that is about 5½ feet high.

Concrete posts for a rail fence should be about 8 feet long, 7 inches square at the base, and 5 inches at the top. You will have to cast holes in the post to accommodate the rails. Blocks of wood or tin cans pressed into an oval shape can be set on guide spikes in the bottom of your form for this purpose.

If you have chosen posts that are 6 feet long or longer, it is a good idea to add ¼-inch reinforcing rods. The rods should be embedded in the concrete as soon as it has been poured, but make sure that the mix is not too thin or the rods will sink to the bottom.

If you are using wire fencing, U-shaped clips are available in hard-ware stores for fastening the fencing to plain concrete posts. You can fashion your own clips from 9-gauge wire. Cut a piece that is long enough to wrap all the way around the post, plus a few inches extra to twist the clip tight.

To cast small holes through which to run single strands of wire, insert

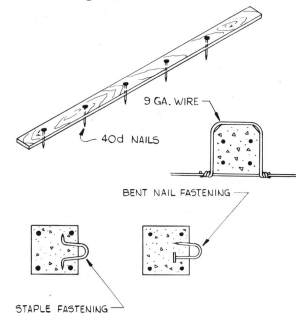

9 GA. WIRE

40d NAILS

BENT NAIL FASTENING

STAPLE FASTENING

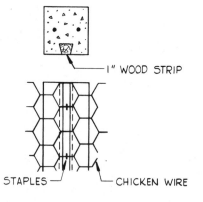

1" WOOD STRIP

STAPLES

CHICKEN WIRE

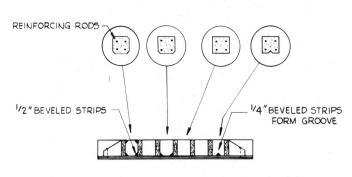

REINFORCING RODS

½" BEVELED STRIPS

¼" BEVELED STRIPS FORM GROOVE

40d nails in the concrete, and then in five or seven hours, after the initial set has taken place, remove them. To set all the wire holes at the same intervals in all the posts, drive your 40d nails through a board and use this device over and over.

Barbwire and woven wire will have to be hung from staples. To embed regular fencing staples in the concrete, flare the ends out a bit for better holding. Or, you can make your own staple mounts by bending a 10d nail into the needed **U** shape.

CONCRETE FENCE POST FORM

This easily constructed form will enable you to pour all the fence posts you need. The model built in the OGF Workshop yields posts just under 6 feet long. They have squared corners and measure 3½ inches square at the base and 3 inches square at the top.

By changing the size and length of the form boards you use, you can change the thickness and length of the posts your form will yield. If you want posts with beveled edges, nail chamfer molding to the platform and to the top edges of the divider boards.

When working with turkey or chicken wire, it may be easier to embed a 1-inch strip of wood into the concrete. Trim the wood to a slight wedge shape, with the narrow side out for a strong hold. Set the wood right after the concrete has been poured, and position it so the wood is flush with the surface of the concrete, and you will have a good place to staple your fencing. *Note:* It is a good idea to treat any wood pieces in fencing with a preservative. Check the chapter on fences for details.

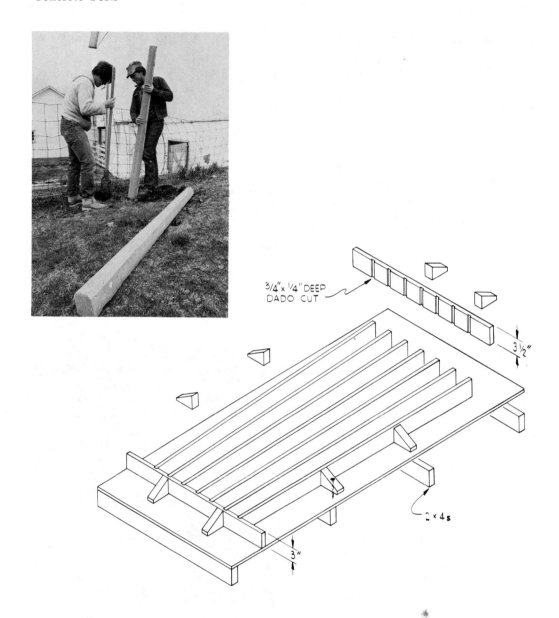

3/4" x 1/4" DEEP DADO CUT

3½"

2 x 4s

3"

CONSTRUCTION

1. Cut a 36-inch by 78-inch panel of ½-inch exterior plywood. Cut four 36-inch lengths of 2 x 4. Cut seven 72-inch lengths and two 36-inch lengths of 1 x 4.

2. Nail the 2 x 4s to the plywood to brace it, locating one 2 x 4 along each end and spacing the remaining two evenly between. Use 8d nails.

MATERIALS

Wood

1 sht. $\frac{1}{2}''$ ext. plywood	or	**Bottom:** 1 pc. 36″ x 78″
1 pc. 2 x 4 x 12′	or	**Braces:** 4 pcs. 2 x 4 x 36″
4 pcs. 1 x 4 x 12′	or	**Sides:** 7 pcs. 1 x 4 x 72″
		Ends: 2 pcs. 1 x 4 x 36″
1 pc. 2 x 4 x 4′	or	**Blocks:** 8 pcs. 2 x 4 x $3\frac{1}{2}''$

Hardware

8d nails
16d nails

3. The 6-foot 1 x 4s must be tapered from their actual $3\frac{1}{2}$-inch width at one end to an actual 3-inch width at the other end. Mark them for the taper, taking an equal amount of material from each edge. Use a plane to remove the excess material.

4. Cut one 36-inch 1 x 4 down to an actual width of 3 inches, using a ripsaw or plane.

5. Cut seven $\frac{1}{4}$-inch-deep by $\frac{3}{4}$-inch-wide dadoes in both 36-inch 1 x 4s. The wider board should have the dadoes $3\frac{1}{2}$ inches apart (or $4\frac{1}{4}$ inches from the center of one dado to the center of the next dado), while the narrower board should have them 3 inches apart (or $3\frac{3}{4}$ inches center to center). The easiest way to lay out the dadoes is to locate the center of each board. That will be the center of the middle dado. From that point, mark the centers of three dadoes on either side. Then lay out the dadoes themselves, marking $\frac{3}{8}$ inch to each side of each center line.

6. After cutting the dadoes, assemble the form and roughly locate it on the plywood platform, as shown. Cut eight blocks from scraps of 2 x 4, cutting off a corner of each so the blocks are roughly triangular. Then attach two blocks along each outer face of the form, using one 16d nail in each block. You want the nail to penetrate the 2 x 4 platform braces, and you want the block to swivel on the nail, so that you can knock the blocks aside and disassemble the form. (A more elaborate setup would use permanent blocks and wedges. Nail the blocks securely to the platform, locating them about an inch shy of the face of the form. Use a wedge at each block to hold the form tightly together. Remove the completed posts by knocking the wedges out.)

POURING THE POSTS

Here—step-by-step—is how to pour fence posts.

1. Oil the interior faces of the forms and prepare all the material you will embed such as reinforcing rods and staples.

2. Mix and pour the concrete into the forms. Your mix should be one part cement, two parts sand, and 2½ parts gravel. Use no more than four gallons of water per sack of cement for average damp sand. The maximum size of the gravel should be about ¾ inch.

3. Set the reinforcing bars, staples, or wood strips.

4. Using a trowel, scrape off any excess concrete, and make sure all the inserts still are where they should be.

5. Allow the posts to set for several hours. Then, try removing any objects you are using for casting holes. If the concrete holds its shape, you can proceed.

6. Cover the posts with damp burlap or straw and allow them to cure for six or seven days before removing the forms.

CONCRETE HOG TROUGH

Hogs are pretty tough to deal with. You need a tight, strong fence to confine them. And you need a practically indestructable trough for feeding them (a hog can chew up a wooden trough in short order).

This concrete hog trough is just the ticket. It is fairly easily made. It is practically indestructable.

The form made in the OGF Workshop yields a trough that's 3½ feet long. It won't serve too many hogs,

but it isn't too difficult to move either. You can easily stretch the length of the form you make, but remember that the weight will increase along with the size.

But you don't need to be a hog raiser to make use of such a trough. Although designed as a hog feeder, it will serve as well as a planter (drive a few 20d nails into the bottom of the core to make drainage holes; pull the nails, then remove the core from the finished product) or as a feeding and/ or watering trough for a variety of homestead livestock.

MATERIALS

Wood

1 sht. ½" ext. plywood or	**Bottom:** 1 pc. 15¾" x 54"
1 pc. 2 x 2 x 6' or	**Bottom braces:** 4 pcs. 2 x 2 x 15¾"
1 pc. 1 x 10 x 10' or	**Sides:** 2 pcs. 1 x 10 x 41"
	Ends: 2 pcs. 1 x 10 x 12½"
2 pcs. 1 x 2 x 10' or	**Cleats:** 4 pcs. 1 x 2 x 9¼"
	Outside braces: 6 pcs. 1 x 2 x 15¾"
	Long clamp piece: 4 pcs. 1 x 2 x 18"
	Short clamp piece: 8 pcs. 1 x 2 x 3"
12'–½" chamfer molding or	**Bevel trim:** 4 pcs. 9¼" long 2 pcs. 12½" long 2 pcs. 38" long
1 pc. 1 x 8 x 12' or	**Inner core:** 3 pcs. 1 x 8 x 37"
	Inner core ends: 2 pcs. 1 x 8 x 5"

Hardware

4d nails

Concrete Hog Trough

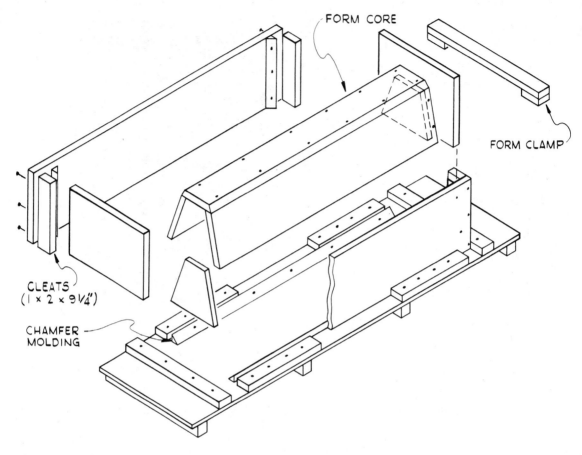

FORM CORE

FORM CLAMP

CLEATS
(1 x 2 x 9 1/4")

CHAMFER
MOLDING

CONSTRUCTION

1. Cut a 15¾-inch by 54-inch panel of ½-inch exterior plywood. Cut four 15¾-inch lengths of 2 x 2 and locate them at each end of the plywood, spacing the remaining two evenly between the ends. Nail them to the plywood with 4d nails (driven through the plywood into the 2 x 2s).

2. Cut two 41-inch lengths and two 12½-inch lengths of 1 x 10. Cut four 9¼-inch cleats from 1 x 2 and fasten one to each end of both 41-inch 1 x 10s, positioning the narrow edge against the 1 x 10.

3. Set up this initial portion of the form on the platform. Nail 9¼-inch lengths of chamfer molding inside the form, nailing into the sides (so the ends are free to be slipped out from between the cleat and the molding). Cut several pieces of 1 x 2, and nail them to the platform, as shown, around the outside of the form, to hold the form in position on the platform. Also nail lengths of the molding to the platform around the inside edge of the form (so the outside edge of the trough will be beveled).

4. From 1 x 2, cut four 18-inch lengths and eight 3-inch lengths. Nail two

short pieces to a long piece, so these clamps will slip over the top of the form, as shown, and hold it tightly together.

5. The inner core is made of 1 x 8s. Cut three 37-inch lengths, and rip one to a 5-inch width. On this narrowed board, plane slight bevels (about 5 degrees). Nail the sides to the bottom (the narrowed board). Cut ends to fit, and nail them to the core, between the sides and the bottom. Position them so they slope out from the bottom slightly, as should the sides. This slight taper of the core will ease its removal from the completed concrete trough. With a rasp, round the corners of the core. Then nail it to the platform.

WATERING TROUGH

A concrete watering trough is not difficult to cast. It will give many years of service, and its most attractive feature is its ease of keeping clean. Such a trough will give your livestock a consistently clean supply of water.

The trough is fitted with an overflow pipe, which can be removed to use the same pipe connection for a drain. Use 1-inch pipe, of which you will need one piece 19 inches long, one piece 15 inches, and another for as long a horizontal drain as you want. You also will need one coupling and one elbow. These pipes must be placed in the ground before the trough's foundation is prepared.

To reinforce the trough, you will need a sheet of poultry netting, about 72 inches by 55 inches, and enough $\frac{3}{8}$-inch reinforcing rod to go around the top rim, about 16 feet total.

Build the wooden forms first. The hardest part of the whole project is the interior form, a box with sloping sides and a flat bottom.

CONSTRUCTION

1. Cut 1-inch boards, or $\frac{1}{2}$-inch or $\frac{5}{8}$-inch exterior plywood, for the sides (two pieces 62 inches by 19 inches); bottom (one piece 62 inches by 16 inches); and ends (two pieces 19 inches tall, 20 inches wide at the top, 16 inches wide at the bottom).

2. Cut six pieces of 2 x 3 stock 24 inches long and three pieces 12 inches long. Use these pieces as a frame to assemble the main part of the interior frame, as illustrated. Cut a 2-inch hole in the bottom to accommodate the overflow pipe.

3. Cut three pieces of 1 x 2 or similar stock, 32 inches long. Nail these across the sets of 2 x 3 uprights, as shown. Later, when the interior form is in place, these pieces also will be nailed to the exterior wall stakes.

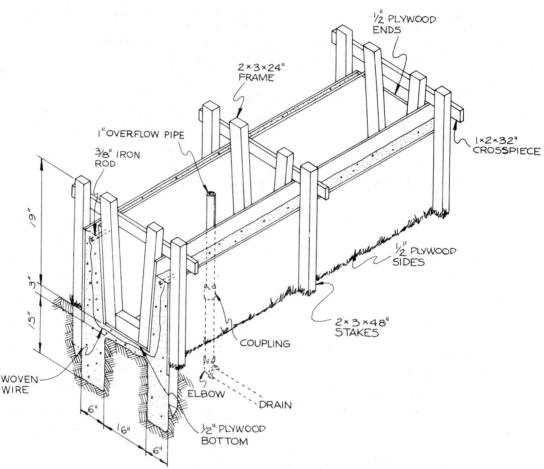

½" PLYWOOD
ENDS

2 × 3 × 24"
FRAME

1"OVERFLOW PIPE

⅜" IRON
ROD

1 × 2 × 32"
CROSSPIECE

19"

½" PLYWOOD
SIDES

3"

15"

2 × 3 × 48"
STAKES

COUPLING

WOVEN
WIRE

6"

ELBOW

DRAIN

6"

½" PLYWOOD
BOTTOM

6"

4. Start the exterior form by choosing a level spot in a convenient place, near a water supply. Cut six stakes, 48 inches long, from 2 x 3 stock. Sharpen one end of each, and drive them 18 inches into the ground. The stakes should be about 3 feet apart, for the 6-foot-long trough made here. The inside edges of the two rows should be 28 inches apart.

5. Working with a square spade, dig the foundation trenches as shown. Dig down about 3 inches for the entire bottom area of the trough. Then, dig the two long trenches about 15 inches deeper. Each should be 6 inches wide.

6. Nail your exterior wall to the insides of the six stakes. It should be 19 inches tall, so cut your boards an inch or two bigger so they can be embedded into the ground. These boards should be 6 feet long. Cut the end boards and nail them to the stakes also.

7. Oil all the faces of the forms which will contact the concrete. Put the pipes, elbow, and coupling in place.

426

MATERIALS

Wood

2 shts. ½" or ⅝" ext. plywood	or	**Sides:** 2 pcs. 62" x 19"
		Bottom: 1 pc. 62" x 16"
		Ends: 2 pcs. 19" tall, 20" wide at top, 16" wide at bottom
3 pcs. 2 x 3 x 12'	or	**Interior frame:** 6 pcs. 2 x 3 x 24"
1 pc. 2 x 3 x 4'	or	**Interior frame:** 3 pcs. 2 x 3 x 12"
		Stakes: 6 pcs. 2 x 3 x 48"
1 pc. 1 x 2 x 4'	or	**Crosspieces:** 3 pcs. 1 x 2 x 32"

Hardware

6d nails
1 pc. 1" pipe 19" long (drainage pipe)
1 pc. 1" pipe 15" long (drainage pipe)
1 pc. 1" pipe (size depends on length of horizontal drain needed)
1 elbow
1 coupling
1 roll 36" x 25', 2" chicken wire   or   **Reinforcement:** 2 pcs. 55" long
1–16' x ⅜" reinforcing rod

8. Mix the concrete, and with the interior form still set aside, begin to pour, working the concrete first into the foundation trenches.

9. When the concrete reaches about half the thickness of the bottom, embed the wire mesh, centering it so you can stand the sides up the sides of the form. At this time, pour more concrete to give the bottom a thickness of about 3 inches, and put the interior form in place.

10. Continue pouring, working the concrete into the corners. Before the sides are filled, push down a bit on the pipe end of the trough to give it the needed pitch for drainage.

11. As you pour the sides, make sure the woven wire is embedded. When the concrete is 3 inches from the top, embed the ⅜-inch rod all the way around. At this point, snip off the remaining ends of the wire mesh.

12. Continue pouring to the top of the form. Trowel the top edge smooth. Allow a day for the concrete to set, and then remove the forms. Keep the trough moist, covering it with either burlap or straw. Do not use the trough for about two weeks. Care must be taken for the next six months to a year to allow the concrete to fully cure. If it receives a sharp blow before that time, it may shatter.

PAVING BLOCKS

Cast paving blocks are useful for making your own patio or garden walk. They are fairly easy to make in basic square, rectangular, triangular, or round shapes. For more decorative blocks, texture and design can be added with pebble and sand casting techniques.

The basic slabs, which also are known as flagstones, can be made 2 to 4 inches thick. Choose form boards, therefore, that match the thickness you desire.

One technique for making the blocks is to pour a slab and cut it into blocks. A simple perimeter form several feet in each dimension is constructed. Nail your side pieces to each other, and reinforce the corners or other joints with 2 x 2 or similar stock stakes, about 8 inches long. They

should be driven into the ground so they are flush with the top of the form. Your form should be placed in a smooth, level place. Allow a $\frac{1}{2}$ inch below the bottom of the form to lay a layer of sand. Smooth the sand, and it will make the finished slabs easier to lift.

A variation is to cast your blocks in individual forms. You can construct these from 1 x 2s or 2 x 4s to give the size blocks you want.

Hinge three corners using either one or two butt hinges fastened with 1-inch #8 screws to the face of one board and the end of the adjoining board. You also could use strap hinges screwed to both faces, with the ends of each board cut on a 45-degree angle for the necessary interior joint. No matter what type of hinges you

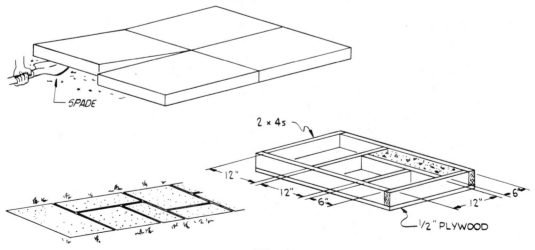

SPADE

2 x 4s

12"

12"

6"

6"

12"

12"

1/2" PLYWOOD

use, install a hasp instead of a hinge on the fourth corner to close the form while casting.

Here are the steps for making paving blocks or flagstones.

1 x 2, OR 2 x 4

OIL INSIDE SURFACES

HINGE (2 CORNERS)

PEG OR BOLT

HASP

45° BEVEL

STRAP HINGE

ALTERNATE METHOD

CONSTRUCTION

1. Set the form in place and oil the inside faces. Lay and smooth the sand bed.

2. Mix the concrete and pour it into the forms. Using a strike-off board, bring the concrete even with the top of the forms.

3. After about four hours, cut the concrete into the size blocks you want. Use a long board or your strike-off board as a straightedge, and cut all the way through the concrete with the tip of a trowel. It may appear that the cuts close back up, but as you will see later, they have not done so.

4. After two or three days, remove the form boards. You will be able to lift the blocks by sliding the tip of a spade under them. Note how they crack apart where you made the cuts earlier.

5. Stand the blocks on edge for two to three weeks for complete curing. Cover them with moist sacks and protect from direct sun and freezing.

VARIATIONS

With a single block form, the procedure is the same, except that you do not make any cuts. Remove the form after four days and stand the blocks on edge to cure.

For round paving stones, you can make a form by cutting a disk from 1-inch plywood in whatever diameter you want, say 18 inches. Then, cut from heavy sheet metal a strip about 2½ inches wide and about 4 inches longer then the circumference of the disk. Bend 2 inches of each end up. Wrap the strip around the edge of the circle, and hold the ends together with a **C**-clamp. You also can use the same strip placed on a bed of sand on the ground. The procedure for casting in these round forms is exactly the same as the single block form discussed above.

Pebble-cast blocks use smooth, river

rock to give the paving blocks a decorative, textured surface. These blocks are ideal for a more formal flower or herb garden, or for a patio, but your taste can dictate that they go anywhere else. Here is the method you should use.

CONSTRUCTION

1. Spread a layer of sand, and smooth it (about ½ inch thick) with a straight board.
2. Press your pebbles halfway into the sand. These pebbles should be clean, with no oil or organic matter that will keep the pebbles from adhering to the concrete. Place your pebbles either in a pattern, or randomly.
3. Mix the concrete and carefully pour it over the pebbles so you do not disturb their placement. Strike off the concrete, being careful to work it into all the edges of the form. Leave a ½ inch of space in the form.
4. Cut a piece of chicken wire to fit the form, and embed it into the concrete. Fill the form, and strike off.
5. Cover the block with wet sacks or straw, and allow the blocks to cure for about one week.

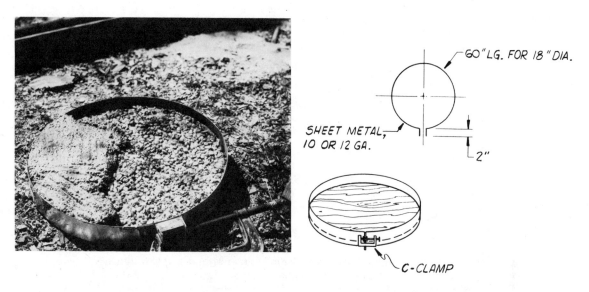

6. Remove the forms and gently turn the slab over, so it is pebble-side up. Brush away the loose sand, and you will be able to see the embedded pebbles.

7. Flood the surface with water and scrub the pebbles to bring out the pattern. *Note:* If the pebbles seem to have been swallowed by the concrete, it means your concrete mixture was too thin. Reduce the water or increase the cement and sand in your next batch.

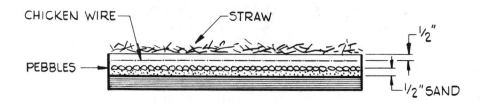

BRICKS

Bricks that can be used for garden dividers and walls also can be made by the homesteader. Use a mixture of one part cement and three parts sand. This mixture should only be made damp, never soft and sloppy. For forms, use boards that are 5 or 6 inches wide. The procedure for making these bricks is exactly the same as in making concrete slabs, up to when they have been stricken off and allowed to set for an hour or so.

431

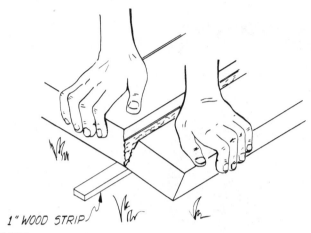

1" WOOD STRIP

CONSTRUCTION

1. Test for a crust on the bricks. If one is present, cut one-third through the brick slab with a trowel, using a board as a straightedge to cut the size bricks you want.

2. Allow the bricks to set for twenty-four hours. Then, knock the form away. Slide a spade under the slab and lift. The bricks should break apart where the trowel cut was made. If they do not, place a 1-inch strip of wood under the slot and press down to separate the bricks.

3. The rough edges probably can be left as is for garden use. If you want to smooth it, use a rasp plane or a Surform tool. Then stack the bricks in a cool place to cure for four weeks.

SOIL CEMENT

The practice of building with soil bricks is ancient. The soil cement described here is a mixture of Portland cement and soil. It is a technique best practiced by those who have experimented with the soil in their area. Because soil varies so much from place to place, it is almost impossible to advise exactly what mix to use, how much water to add, and how long to cure the bricks. But, some general guidelines can be useful. If you take the trouble to make some trial bricks before taking on any major project, you can build at a fraction of the cost for purchased bricks.

First, you must determine what type of soil you have on your land. Suitable types are classified as sandy, silt, or clay soils. Sandy soil is stable only when wet. It does not contract when dry, and it is easily compressed. Silt soil is difficult to work with because it has little cohesion and is difficult to compact. Clay soil has high plasticity and easily takes the desired shape.

The easiest and most reliable way

to determine what soil you have is through your local farm agent or state university extension office. When you have the results, you are ready to begin work. You can form the bricks one by one in individual molds, as with cast concrete, or you can compress them in a patented device called a Cinva-Ram. A third alternative is to build forms for a wall, and compact the soil mixture into it in what is known as a monolithic wall.

The recommended mixture of cement to soil is, for sandy soil, 4.75 to 9.1 percent; silt soil, 8.3 to 12.5 percent; and clay, 12.5 to 14.4 percent. These percentages may see unwieldy, but if you mix your batches using ten of any measure, such as a bucket, it will be easier. (For instance, each bucket is 10 percent, half a bucket 5 percent, etc.)

The advantage of working with a machine press is that blocks can be made quickly, and they will be of uniform size and compression. This machine is operated by hand, requiring no electricity or other fuel. For more information on the Cinva-Ram machine, which costs about $250, contact the Bellows-Valvair International Co., 200 West Exchange Street, Akron, Ohio 44309.

CONSTRUCTION

1. Choose a level, nonabsorbent surface on which to mix. Spread the soil in a layer no thicker than 3 inches.
2. Sprinkle the cement evenly on top, and mix until a uniform color is achieved.
3. Spread the mixture out again, and slowly add the water. In order to determine the proper amount of water ahead of time, make some tests. The water is right if the mixture retains the shape of your hand and can be pulled apart without disintegrating into a loose pile resembling the original mixture. If there is too much water, you will not be able to form it into bricks.
4. Put the mixture into the forms or molds. It should sit for two hours.
5. The curing of blocks differs from that of walls. For walls, keep the forms in place for three days. Then, remove the forms and cover the wall with moist sacks for five more days. Blocks should be stored out of the sun and protected from rain. Water the blocks for twenty-four hours. Remove them from the forms. After forty-eight more hours, the blocks should be stacked and sprayed for five more days. They can be used for construction after twenty-one days.

WALKS AND PATIOS

A variety of walks can be made for the garden or elsewhere around your homestead. Walks can be made from bricks, cast concrete slabs, flagstones, blocks of heavy stone such as granite, or even a poured concrete walk of the type familiar in cities. A walk also can be a simple gravel path.

THE FOUNDATION

A good foundation and efficient drainage are essential to any of these. If the area through which you plan to run the walk is sloped, you will have to dig a foundation that is essentially level and at the same time allow for drainage. Later, when laying the walk itself, you will have to construct its surface to allow runoff from its surface. If your walk is well drained, water will not collect along its edges, and the walk will last longer.

One method for building a good foundation with built-in drainage is as follows.

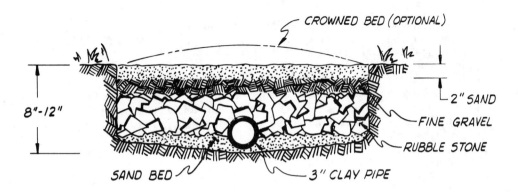

CROWNED BED (OPTIONAL)

8"-12"

2" SAND
FINE GRAVEL
RUBBLE STONE

SAND BED

3" CLAY PIPE

CONSTRUCTION

1. Dig down 8 to 12 inches for the length and width of the path. The foundation should follow the slope of the land, and the base also should slope gently on both sides toward the center.
2. Cover the soil bed with a thin layer of sand. In the center, place sections of 3-inch clay pipe, end-to-end, but not mortared together. These will gather water from beneath the walk, and because they run down the slope of your land, will carry it away.
3. Cover the sand base with broken rubble stone, and pack the stone around the clay pipe. Ram the stones into the bed, but do not disturb the clay pipes.
4. Cover the stone with finer gravel, and allow for a 2-inch bed of sand on top.

THE CROWNED BED

This type of foundation will support any walk, except, perhaps, solid poured concrete. The sand bed can be leveled, and you have two choices for providing surface drainage to the walk itself. One way is to build one edge of the bed higher than the other side so the water runs off the lower side. Or, you can build a crowned

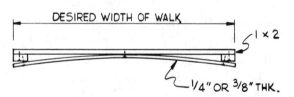

DESIRED WIDTH OF WALK

1 x 2

1/4" OR 3/8" THK.

bed so water drains off both sides. Keep in mind that you want to drain water away from buildings.

CONSTRUCTION

1. Figure your slope, with ⅛-inch drop per foot of width. The walk will slope both ways from the center, so each side will have the same drop. If, for instance, the walk is 4 feet wide, it will drop ¼ inch on both sides.

435

2. To accurately crown the sand bed, make a wooden template. Start with a piece of 1 x 2 as long as the walk is wide. On each end, nail a block of wood equal in thickness to the drop you want. Then, nail another length of ¼-inch or ⅜-inch wood (it must be flexible) to the two end blocks. Finally, bow the ¼-inch wood and nail it to the 1 x 2 exactly in the middle to give the needed crown shape.

3. Spread sand 4 to 5 inches thick. Press the template, curved face down, onto the sand and draw it along to form the needed crowned bed. To avoid disturbing the bed as you work, use a kneeboard for leaning or kneeling as you work along. The bed now is ready for your sidewalk material.

A BRICK WALK

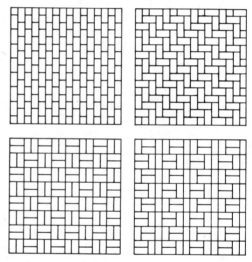

BRICK PAVING PATTERNS

Any walk will be far more durable with edging or a curb. You can use bricks, laid as stretchers as edging for a brick walk. You can use 2 x 4, set on edge and treated with preservative. You also can make forms and pour concrete for a curb.

In this case, you will use bricks set in mortar as edging. You should determine beforehand the pattern in which you intend to set your walk. Basket-weave patterns, which have sets of two or three bricks placed in alternate directions to suggest weaving, are one popular choice. A herringbone pattern requires some brick cutting, but the results are attractive. Many walks also are set in a simple running brick wall pattern. You can set the bricks either flat or on edge.

CONSTRUCTION

1. Lay one of the edgings. Spread a strip of mortar (one part masonry cement and three parts sand) about ¾ inch thick along one edge. Place the bricks end-to-end, pressing them into the mortar and tapping them level.

2. Next, mix a thin mortar of one part masonry cement and one part sand, with enough water to make it smooth. Pour this mixture over the sand and spread it about ⅜ inch to ¾ inch thick.

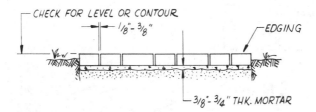

CHECK FOR LEVEL OR CONTOUR

1/8" - 3/8"

EDGING

3/8" - 3/4" THK. MORTAR

3. Working quickly, place the bricks in the mortar, leaving a space of $\frac{1}{8}$ inch to $\frac{3}{8}$ inch between them. Work across the walk and leave space to lay the opposite curb line.

4. After both edgings and the rest of the walk are in place, check the shape of the finished walk with the wood template. If you have to tap any bricks into the bed, hold a block of wood against them and use the hammer. When the mortar has set for a day or two, scatter loose sand on top and brush it into the cracks.

VARIATIONS

The method for building a walk with paving stones, flagstone, or slate is essentially the same. You will have to vary the depth you dig for foundations to suit the thickness of whatever you are working with. An attractive walk can be made using a combination of blocks and bricks. Start by laying bricks down the middle of the path, spacing them about $\frac{1}{4}$ inch apart. Then, lay the blocks along both sides of the bricks.

All these walks also can be laid on sand, without mortar. Lay a 2-inch bed of sand and tamp it down. If the sand is dust-dry, sprinkle it with water to aid in settling. The sand should dry again before bricks are placed. Allow about a $\frac{1}{4}$ inch between bricks, and when the walk is in place, dump loose sand on top and sweep it into the cracks. Wet everything down

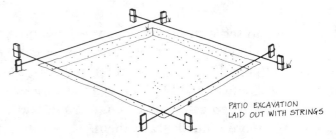

PATIO EXCAVATION LAID OUT WITH STRINGS

A LEVELING BOARD CAN BE MADE EASILY TO LEVEL BOTH THE SAND BASE AND THE BRICK SURFACE.

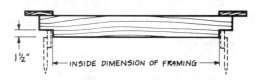

1½"

INSIDE DIMENSION OF FRAMING

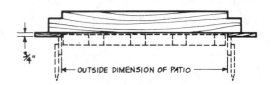

¾"

OUTSIDE DIMENSION OF PATIO

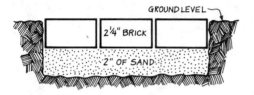

PATIO CROSS SECTION

WALKWAY CROSS SECTION

to settle the sand and sweep in more sand. If any bricks are protruding, pound them down with a mallet or a hammer and block of wood. If bricks are depressed, pry them out and add more sand beneath them.

Another possibility is to mix dry mortar and sweep it into the brick cracks. Then, spray the walk with water and allow it to dry for a more rigid surface.

A gravel walk is easily constructed. Start with a stone and sand foundation as described above. You will have to install curbing along the length of the walk. Different types of gravel are available, and which kind best suits you depends largely upon where you live. Limestone chips, sandstone, and smooth river pebbles all make attractive walks, but you may want to choose what best suits the environment where you live. Naturally, if the source of your gravel is nearby, its cost will be lower.

Once the gravel is in place, it simply is raked smooth. It can then be hosed down to help it settle. It's a good idea to keep a little extra gravel on hand, because over the years, as the walk settles and gravel gets scattered, you can add more to fill in depressions. Maintenance also is simple. Raking the gravel gives it a new appearance. Weeds may have to be pulled from time to time.

A CONCRETE WALK

Pouring a concrete sidewalk or driveway is somewhat more work than constructing one of stone or brick, but if you prefer concrete, here's how to do it. As with any concrete project, some careful planning is necessary. First, check to determine if there are local building specifications governing for thickness and width of walks or driveways. Usually, sidewalks and drives are 4 inches thick. If the driveway has to take heavy wear, from trucks or farm machinery, 6 inches is a better thickness.

Measure the area to be paved, and compute how much material you will need. You also will need 2 x 4s or 2 x 6s for forms, enough to run around the perimeter of your walk, plus temporary crosspieces every 4 or 5 feet in a sidewalk, 10 feet in a drive. If you want to install wooden joints, you will need ⅜-inch stock, as wide as the walk is thick, and as long as the walk is wide. They are placed at the same intervals as the temporary crosspieces mentioned above.

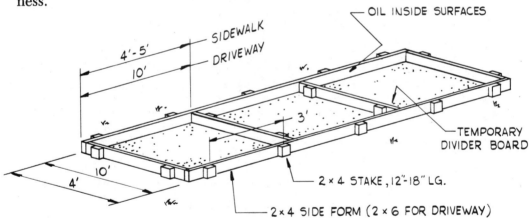

CONSTRUCTION

1. Prepare the ground for the walk by leveling bumps and pulling out any grass or weeds. If the soil is well compacted and well drained, you can pour the concrete directly onto it. If the ground is dust-dry, sprinkling it with water just before you pour the concrete will keep the ground from absorbing too much water. If the ground is not well drained, dig down and lay a subbase 4 to 6 inches thick, using crushed gravel or stone, and compact it well. If you are laying the walk on top

of an existing cracked sidewalk, break the old surface up with a sledgehammer and compact the rubble.

2. Install the forms by placing them on edge, with 2 x 4 stakes driven in along the outside of the forms, flush with the top edge of the forms. Nail the forms to the stakes, which should be placed every 3 feet, and also at each joint between form boards. There should be no cracks between the form boards. At this point, you must provide for a pitch in the walk for drainage. Always drain away from buildings. You can raise the form boards on one side, or slope the subbase as well. Figure on ⅛-inch pitch per foot of width from the center line. You also can make a crown in the middle of the walk by using a more concave strike-off board.

3. Oil the surfaces of all the form boards where they will touch the concrete, to avoid sticking. You can use used crankcase oil, which you usually can get free at a garage or gas station.

4. Mix the concrete (see the concrete chapter for specifics) and pour it into the forms as quickly as possible. Place it as accurately as you can to avoid excessive handling. Work quickly but carefully with a shovel or hoe to spread the concrete around the form. You should leave it about an inch above the top of the form.

5. Strike off the concrete using the strike-off board. Start at one end of the form and inch the board along, working back and forth with a sawing motion. The board rests on the forms on both sides, and your object is to lower the concrete so it is flush with the top of the form boards.

6. Insert the ⅜-inch joints if you are using them. Work them between the crosspieces and the concrete. You can remove the crosspieces after the dividers are in place.

7. Bull-float the concrete. This step will further level bumps and fill holes, and will push pieces of gravel below the surface. Hold the surface of the bull float level, and work it as if you were using a sponge mop.

8. Next, you must wait. As the concrete sets, the water will rise to the surface and evaporate. When the sheen of water has disappeared, you can proceed with finishing. The amount of time it takes to reach this point depends a good deal on the weather; it could take anywhere from one to eight or nine hours. You should not attempt to pour side-

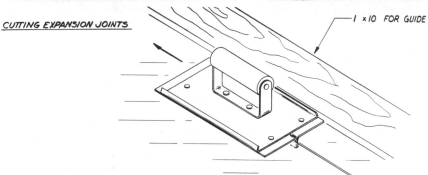

CUTTING EXPANSION JOINTS

1 x10 FOR GUIDE

walks or any other concrete project if there is danger of freezing weather.

9. Run a trowel along the edges of the forms. If the concrete has set enough to hold the shape of the trowel, you can proceed. Using the edging tool, smooth all the outside edges.

10. If you have not installed wooden joints, use a jointing tool to cut joints every 4 or 5 feet, or 10 feet for drives. Use your strike-off board as a straightedge when cutting joints. The joints will prevent the surface from cracking as the concrete curves.

11. Floating is the next step, and it further smooths the surface and pushes large gravel pieces below the surface. Work the float flat on the concrete, in wide, arc motions.

12. The first troweling is done immediately after floating. Hold the trowel flat against the concrete. The second troweling should be done later, when your hand leaves only a slight impression in the concrete. For a skid-resistant surface, use a stiff bristled brush on the concrete after the last troweling.

13. Curing takes five to seven days, depending on the weather. The object is for the concrete to dry slowly. Keep it covered with burlap or straw, which must be kept moist. Or, frequently spray the surface with a hose or lawn sprinkler. Stay off the walk for six days. After that, you can remove the forms, but keep heavy traffic, such as vehicles, off for another six days.

STEPS

Steps should be made on footings that are 6 inches below the frost line, or 2 feet below grade in no-frost areas. Plan the steps to be as wide as the walk leading up to them. To figure how many steps to make, figure on one step for every 7½ inches in drop from door to sidewalk. For instance, if the drop is 36 inches, four 7½-inch risers and one 6-inch, five steps in all, will do the job. You should make the steps no less than 11 inches wide.

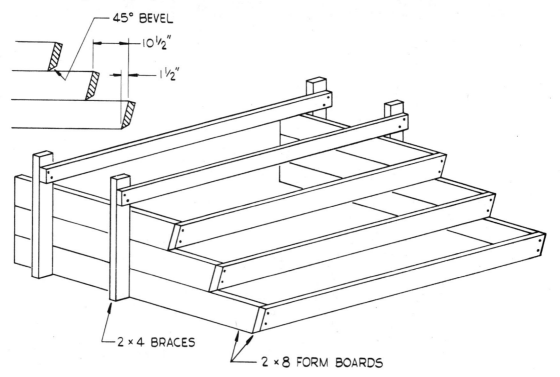

CONSTRUCTION

1. Dig and pour the footings. Check locally for the depth necessary in your area.
2. Make your forms using 2 x 8 boards for the sides and riser faces. Use 2 x 4s spaced no more than 36 inches apart as supporting stakes outside the forms. The stakes must be long enough to support the top step, and these stakes should have a diagonal 2-inch by 4-inch brace for strength. On the riser faces, you will place a diagonal 2 x 4 reaching

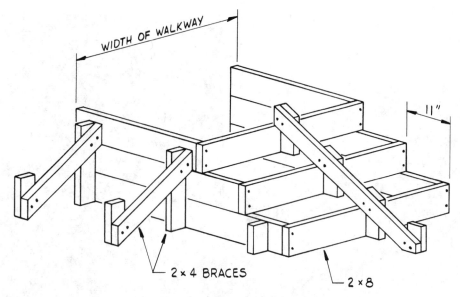

WIDTH OF WALKWAY

11"

2 x 4 BRACES

2 x 8

from sidewalk to top step. To support the riser faces, nail 10-inch lengths of 2 x 4 to the front diagonal so they butt against the riser boards. Check your form with a level, and oil all the inside surfaces.

3. You can save on concrete by filling part of your form with stone, covered with a well-tamped layer of sand. Allow about 4 inches to the top of the form on each step.

4. Mix your concrete and pour, working from bottom to top. Work the concrete into the corners, and tap the form boards from time to time to loosen bubbles.

5. Strike off all the surfaces, and float them. Remember to give a pitch of about a ¼ inch toward the edge of each step for drainage.

6. Let the concrete stand for several hours, and then work the edges with an edger. Go over the surfaces with a stiff brush to give a nonskid surface.

7. Cover the steps with sacks or straw, kept moist. Allow the steps to cure for six days with the forms in place. After that, remove the forms and allow them to further cure for six days.

PATIOS

A patio, strictly speaking, first was a feature of Spanish-style architecture. It provided an outdoor, yet protected or enclosed space for eating, relaxing, or other activities. A more modern definition includes any outdoor area that has a floor, maybe a roof, and maybe partial or whole walls.

Floors can be poured concrete, or

any of the surfaces described in the section on walks. This would include bricks, blocks, or flagstones, set in either mortar or sand. Or, it can be a combination of any of these. The method of construction is just the same as for the walks, with a few special points to consider.

The foundation should allow for a drainage slope of ⅛ inch per foot of width, always away from buildings. If you plan to install electric outlets or water taps on the far side of the patio, you must first install pipes or conduits in the foundation before you lay the patio floor.

If you are installing walls and/or a roof, you should pour concrete footings to support them before you lay the foundation. Locate the footings around the perimeter of the patio where walls or roof supports are to be placed. Consult the section on concrete for details of making footings.

ROOFING THE PATIO

For almost any kind of roof you choose, the basic upright support and rafter construction is the same. Generally, 4 x 4 wooden posts are heavy enough. They can be planted in concrete, as if they were extra-long fence posts. In such a case, they should be treated with preservative.

An alternative to setting the posts in concrete is to place them on metal rods set in the concrete footings. Allow 3 to 4 inches of a ½-inch rod to protrude above the surface of the concrete, and make sure it is plumb. Then, drill a ½-inch hole to the same depth in the bottom of the post. The post then should fit snugly on the supporting rod.

If you are using metal posts, the most common size is 2 inches, usually galvanized pipe. Have it threaded on one end, the top. This will accept a flat flange, a stock hardware item designed to support the rafters. This pipe can be set directly in the concrete footing, about 24 inches deep.

To determine the height of these uprights, first measure the height of the building wall that will support the other side of the roof. Figure on anywhere from $\frac{1}{8}$-inch to $1\frac{3}{4}$-inch drop per foot of width.

There are two common ways of supporting the roof against the house. If the construction of the building allows it, the best way to insure a watertight junction is to fit the patio roof under the eave, or roof overhang of the building. Fasten a 2 x 4 stringer, as long as the roof is to be wide, along the house. Measure from your upright posts and the corners of the patio to set the location. Use lag bolts to attach the 2 x 4 stringer to the studs or the top plate of the house wall. The patio roof rafters then are butted onto the stringer.

The other method is to nail or bolt the rafters directly onto the house rafters, one patio rafter to each house rafter. You can do this only if your rafters extend past the wall. Use 2 x 6 for these rafter extensions. For the crossbeam joining the posts at the far side of the patio, you can use a 4 x 4 or two 2 x 4s face-nailed together.

When joining the rafters to the crossbeam, you can simply toenail them, or notch their ends to fit. Use 16d or 20d nails for the roof rafter construction.

You have a wide variety of roofs to choose from. Fiberglass sheets, flat or corrugated, make a good, raintight roof, but they create somewhat of a greenhouse effect if your patio is exposed to hot, afternoon sunshine. Likewise, aluminum sheets make a good roof, but are not best suited to an area that gets a lot of direct sunlight. A good roof can be made with sheets of $\frac{1}{2}$-inch or $\frac{5}{8}$-inch plywood, covered with rolled tar paper or shingles.

Walls for the patio can be designed to provide privacy, a windbreak, or a place to decorate with plants. If you want to make poured concrete walls, stone, block, or brick walls, consult the sections of the book that deal with their construction in detail. You also can erect studding, or have your roof supports 4 feet apart, to accommodate prefabricated screen and storm window-type panels.

A kitchen-area patio is a perfect place for an herb garden, either along the edges of the patio surface or in boxes or planters. Green plants, summering houseplants, bulbs, flowering shrubs, and roses all go a long way in making your patio a bit more pleasant.

WALLS

Erecting a wall, whether a low, unmortared garden wall or a carefully constructed brick building wall, need not be intimidating. There's nothing particularly difficult about building walls, so long as you plan the work carefully. The physical labor, however, can be considered both taxing and tedious.

Wall construction is a logical extension of the concrete work discussed in previous chapters, and it is an important skill for anyone contemplating repairing or constructing an outbuilding.

For the homesteader, potential projects range from low garden or retaining walls that are as much aesthetic as practical to foundations for frame buildings and complete masonry buildings. It is good, in any case, for the beginner to get a simple project under his belt before tackling a major project. And it is good to consider the alternatives before tackling any project. Consider, for example, that a wall may be constructed of stone, brick, concrete, soil cement blocks cast at the construction site, or concrete blocks purchased from a building materials supplier. The homesteader has to decide the materials best suited, for whatever reasons, to his particular needs.

447

Most any wall construction will begin with concrete work, since a sound masonry wall should be erected upon a concrete footing poured below the frost line. Details on working with concrete, including information on constructing forms and pouring footings, is found in the chapter, "Concrete." The chapter will also be helpful for the homesteader considering a poured concrete wall. Such walls are strong and durable, but the construction of them doesn't lend itself to spare-moments work. Once the forms are erected and the pouring is begun, the pouring must continue until the wall is completed. With blocks, bricks, and stones, the fledgling mason can work a-batch-of-mortar-at-a-time, spreading the wall building over a long time.

BLOCKS

Precast concrete blocks with hollow cores are a popular building material. Full-size blocks weigh about 30 pounds each, and the standard size is 8 inches wide, 8 inches high, and 16 inches long. Actually, the dimension are $7\frac{5}{8}$ inches by $7\frac{5}{8}$ inches by $15\frac{5}{8}$ inches but the nominal dimensions allow for a $\frac{3}{8}$-inch mortar joint along each dimension in the finished wall. Specialized blocks are available for corners, solid top courses, and building door and window openings and the vertical seams that are known as control points. Also available are

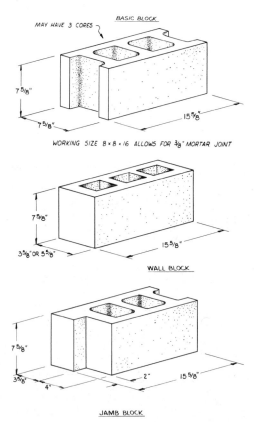

BASIC BLOCK

MAY HAVE 3 CORES

$7\frac{5}{8}''$

$7\frac{5}{8}''$

$15\frac{5}{8}''$

WORKING SIZE 8 × 8 × 16 ALLOWS FOR $\frac{3}{8}''$ MORTAR JOINT

$7\frac{5}{8}''$

$15\frac{5}{8}''$

$3\frac{5}{8}''$ OR $5\frac{5}{8}''$

WALL BLOCK

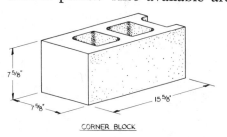

$7\frac{5}{8}''$

$7\frac{5}{8}''$

$15\frac{5}{8}''$

CORNER BLOCK

$7\frac{5}{8}''$

$3\frac{5}{8}''$

$4''$

$2''$

$15\frac{5}{8}''$

JAMB BLOCK

4-inch-wide blocks to be used in partition and other nonload-bearing walls.

Tools you will need start with the same mixing equipment used in concrete work: shovel or hoe, mixer or wheelbarrow, or trough. Also very handy is a mortar board—a 12-inch-square piece of plywood is fine—which you use to carry mortar as you work along the wall.

To apply mortar to the blocks, you will use a trowel. Choose one with a substantial wooden handle because you will use that end to tap the blocks into place on the mortar bed. (If you use the metal trowel blade, the blocks or bricks can crack.)

You also may want a mason's jointer to finish the mortar joints, but a length of ⅜-inch rod with a curve in it also will do the job.

If you have to cut holes in the blocks for wiring or pipes, you also will need a hammer and cold chisel.

You will need plenty of string to mark guidelines. Masons use a handy device, called a line stretcher, which fits in pairs over blocks at each end of a course to hold a string as a guideline for the blocks being placed in between.

You should make yourself a storyboard. This simply is a straight length of wood, longer than the wall is to be high, carefully marked at 8-inch intervals. It is held against the wall as

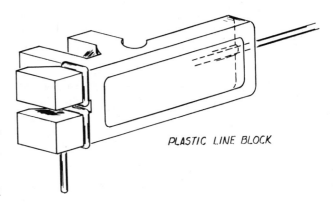

PLASTIC LINE BLOCK

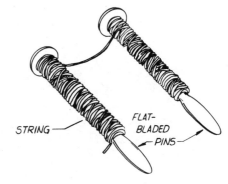

STRING

FLAT-
BLADED
PINS

MASON'S LINE PINS

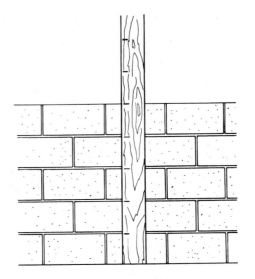

STORYBOARD

449

you work to check that the top surfaces of each course are level at all points along the wall.

Perhaps the most important tool is a mason's level. It should be long enough to span two blocks. It will be used to check both horizontal level and vertical plumb. As you work, be sure to keep the level clean, because

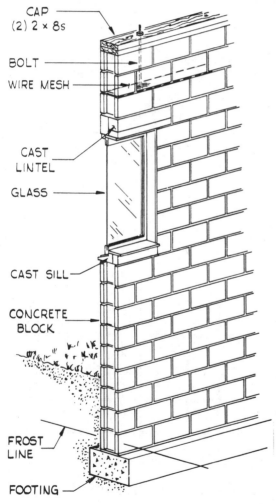

CAP
(2) 2 × 8s

BOLT

WIRE MESH

CAST LINTEL

GLASS

CAST SILL

CONCRETE BLOCK

FROST LINE

FOOTING

even a small dab of mortar can cause inaccurate readings.

To make the job a bit easier, you should plan your walls with dimensions that are evenly divisible by 8 inches. This will avoid any tricky block cutting.

When your building plans are on paper, use this formula to figure how many blocks and how much mortar to buy. Multiply the height of the wall in feet by $1\frac{1}{2}$ to give the number of levels, or courses. Multiply the length of the wall in feet by $\frac{3}{4}$ to give the number of blocks in a course. Multiply the two figures to get the total number of blocks. Figure on one 70-pound bag of cement and 3 cubic feet of sand for each hundred blocks.

Your plans should tell you how many lintels you will have to buy or make; how many corner blocks you need; how many solid blocks for the top course; how many jamb blocks for control joints; and how many metal tie bars or how much hardware cloth you need for tying walls together.

Before you begin laying blocks you should know that "stretchers" refer to blocks laid with their long dimension parallel to the wall line. "Headers" are blocks laid with their longest dimension across the wall.

You also should know how to make control joints and lintels, how to tie walls together, and how and where to use grout.

Control joints are vertical seams which will control cracks in the wall's mortar. Local codes specify where they are to be placed; usually, they go above doors and windows, where walls intersect at other than a corner, and no more than 20 feet apart on long walls. Control joints can be made using jamb blocks, regular stretcher blocks, or special control joint blocks which fit together in tongue-and-groove fashion.

If you use jamb or stretcher blocks, you will have to add a piece of hardware known as a **Z** bar, which is embedded horizontally in the mortar across the joint. **Z** bars are placed in every other course. If you are using regular stretcher blocks, line one side of the cavity between two blocks with building paper and fill the cavity with grout.

After the wall is up and the mortar has begun to harden, you can remove

mortar from control joints down to a depth of $\frac{3}{4}$ inch using the jointer. If the wall is exposed to weather, or if you want to hide the control joint, you can fill in with caulking compound. *Note:* Some caulking compounds require that a primer be applied to the blocks first.

If you are installing precast lintels you will have to install a noncorroding metal plate on top of the jamb block to evenly distribute the weight of the lintel on the whole block. Cover the plate with a $\frac{3}{4}$-inch mortar bed to hold the lintel in place, and check the lintel with your level for horizontal level and vertical plumb.

To make you own lintels using stretcher blocks, start with a length of noncorroding angle iron, whose one leg is 8 inches wide to support the blocks. The other (vertical) leg need be only 2 or 3 inches wide. Use a full mortar bed to seat the stretchers across the angle.

A lintel made from header bricks

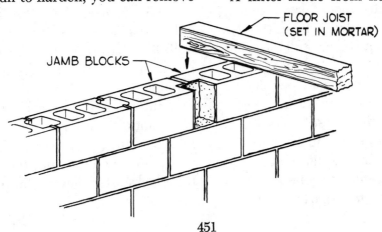

FLOOR JOIST
(SET IN MORTAR)

JAMB BLOCKS

also starts with a metal angle. This piece is installed on the inside of the wall, facing in. Another angle iron is installed back to back, facing out, which supports a header row of bricks. A full mortar bed must be used.

When joining two load-bearing walls, a steel strap $\frac{1}{4}$ inch by $1\frac{1}{2}$ inches by 28 inches, with 2-inch right angles bent in alternate directions at both ends, is used. Place the tie bars no farther apart vertically than 4 feet. You must sink the bent ends of the tie bar into grouted block cores. No mortar joint is needed where the two walls meet, but you may fill the spaces with caulking.

Nonbearing walls may be joined in essentially the same fashion using hardware cloth. These joints should be installed in every other course.

Grout is a thin mortar, comparable to concrete, calling for one part Portland cement, two parts sand, and three parts pea-sized gravel. You also can make your mortar mix on the thin side and use that as grout. Grouting is loaded into the blocks' cores to install tie bars, to install anchor bolts in the top course or to close the cores in the top course, and to secure reinforcing bars. Building codes will say specifically what your grouting requirements are. If the cores are to be filled from top to bottom of the wall (as with reinforcing bars) you can fill them as each course is built, after the entire wall is built, or at any interval in between. If you are grouting only specific blocks (as for anchor bolts) use hardware cloth beneath the block to keep the grout from falling through.

Reinforcing bars are anchored in your footing. Be sure they are placed in accordance with your local code, and that they align with the cores of the blocks after they are in place.

BUILDING THE WALL

Before you start, remember that you should use your mortar in less than two hours after it is mixed. Some on-the-job experience will show how big a batch suits your work pace.

The mortar you use for these blocks must be mixed quite stiff. Use one part masonry cement to three parts sand. Mix the dry ingredients first and add only enough water to make it workable. Also, the blocks must be kept absolutely dry. When you stop working for the day, protect them from the weather.

With the foundation, reinforcing rods, and batter boards in place, you are ready to lay the important first course. You should lay the first course all the way around the walls you are building to be sure the walls fit together as planned.

You also will note that the blocks are thicker on one side than the other, and the thicker edges always go up.

CONSTRUCTION

1. Make a dry run of the first course. Lay out the corners first, working *without* concrete. Then place all the stretcher blocks along the footing, leaving ⅜-inch space between them for mortar. You can use a ⅜-inch piece of wood as a guide for these spaces.

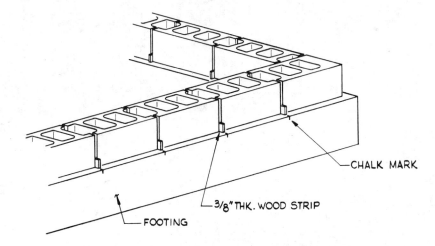

CHALK MARK

3/8"THK. WOOD STRIP

FOOTING

2. Keep in mind the position of control joints as you work. With the first course sitting in position without mortar, install a course string, stretching from batter board to batter board, ½ inch away from the outside edges of the blocks, to define the top edge of the first course. Remove all the blocks, and stand them on end along the footing.

453

3. Spread a 1-inch-thick bed of mortar, 8 inches wide and long enough for about three blocks on the footing. Place one of the corner blocks, or the end block of a freestanding wall, into place on the mortar bed and tap it into place. Check that it is in line with the guide string, is horizontally level, and is plumb.

4. Put mortar about ¾ inch thick on the end of the first stretcher block that is to abut the corner block. Place this block on the mortar bed, and tap it into place. With this and each other stretcher block, check for vertical plumb, horizontal level, and proper alignment with the guide string and the other blocks. As you work, scrape excess mortar off the joints and use it on the next block you place.

5. To install the last block, or closure block, in the first course, spread mortar on both ends, and a layer on each exposed end of the blocks in the course. Carefully ease the block into position, and check it for plumb, horizontal level, and alignment with the guide string and the other blocks. If you end up with a mortar joint ¾ inch or less in thickness, the course is properly set.

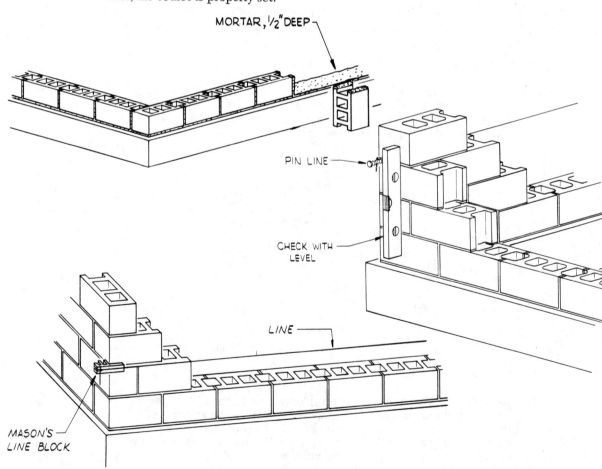

MORTAR, ½" DEEP

PIN LINE

CHECK WITH LEVEL

LINE

MASON'S LINE BLOCK

The key from here on is the corners. Build up your corners two or three courses, making sure the blocks are level and plumb. To complete the next full course, you use the line blocks to run a string—the mason's line—from one corner to another, the line carefully aligned against the upper edge of the corner blocks. As long as every block you lay between the corners aligns with the line, the course should be level and plumb. If you had to check each block with a level, you'd never finish.

6. So, corners and ends are built up next. For an end, use half-blocks every other course so the vertical mortar joints are staggered. Likewise, alternate the corner blocks from one wall to the other in each course so as to stagger the vertical joints. Check your work frequently with the storyboard, and for plumb and horizontal level. Make sure all the block faces align with the other blocks in the wall, even if it actually is the end of a corner block from the adjoining wall.

7. With corners and ends built up, you can fill in the walls. Spread mortar about ¾ inch thick on the top of the preceding course, and spread mortar about ¾ inch thick on the end of the previous blocks in the course you are building. When you get to the last block in the course, place mortar on both ends of the last block and on both exposed ends of the blocks it is being placed between. Ease it into place. When the course is finished, take the time to check for plumb, horizontal level, and alignment with guidelines and the rest of the wall. This may seem time-consuming at first, but as you gain experience—and confidence—it will go more quickly.

8. When all the walls have been built, you can finish with the top course. There are special solid blocks sold for this purpose, or you can use cap blocks, laid as headers. You also can grout the cores shut in regular stretcher blocks. If a wooden sill or top plate is to be attached, you will embed 18-inch by ½-inch anchor bolts about halfway into grouted cores.

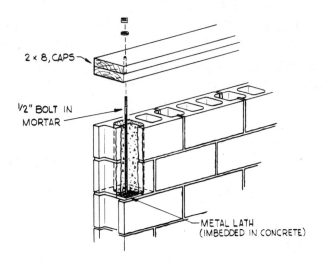

2 × 8, CAPS

½" BOLT IN MORTAR

METAL LATH (IMBEDDED IN CONCRETE)

BRICKS

Brick walls can be made of single, double, or triple thickness, and there is a variety of ways of arranging or bonding bricks. There is a variety of grades of bricks available, and they are made with various finishes and in various colors. Finish and color are matters of personal taste, but the grade of the brick depends on the job it is to do.

Severe weathering bricks (**SW**) are for wherever the bricks come in contact with the ground, such as with retaining walls, foundations, patios, and garden walls. Medium weathering (**MW**) are used where the bricks will be exposed to freezing temperatures, and they can be used for any above-ground exterior work. No weathering bricks (**NW**) are for interior work.

Most bricks measure 8 inches by $2\frac{1}{4}$ inches by $3\frac{3}{4}$ inches. When calculating the number of bricks that you need, however, use nominal dimensions which take into account a $\frac{1}{2}$-inch mortar joint between the

bricks. This would give you dimensions of $8\frac{1}{2}$ inches by $2\frac{3}{4}$ inches by $3\frac{3}{4}$ inches. To figure how many bricks you need, first figure the area you are covering in square feet. Subtract the area of any windows and doors. Then figure 6.16 bricks per square foot. For each 100 square feet, figure 21 cubic feet of mortar (seven bags of masonry cement and 21 cubic feet of sand).

The pattern of bricks, half-bricks, bricks placed as headers or as stretchers, is called the bond. The simplest, and in the United States by far the most common, is the running bond. It has all bricks laid as stretchers, except on ends and corners. Corners use half-bricks, or half-bats, set as headers. A stronger bond, because it has more transverse strength, is the American bond. In it, every sixth course is a header course. English, English garden, Flemish, and Dutch bonds are for 8-inch-thick walls. English uses alternate courses of all headers and all stretchers, with half-header bricks

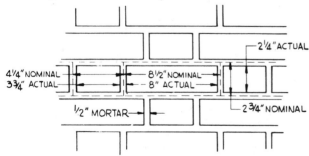

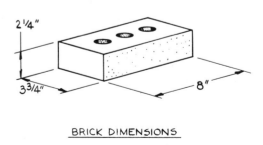

BRICK DIMENSIONS

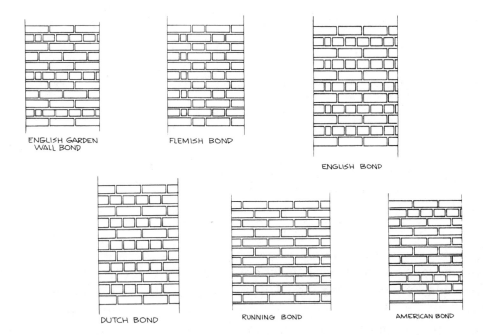

ENGLISH GARDEN WALL BOND

FLEMISH BOND

ENGLISH BOND

DUTCH BOND

RUNNING BOND

AMERICAN BOND

used on the header courses to properly stagger the vertical joints. English garden bond is three courses of stretchers for every course of headers. In Flemish bond, all the courses are the same, with two stretchers alternating with headers. Again, vertical joints are staggered by using half-headers. Dutch bond is similar to English bond's alternating courses of stretchers and headers, except that coinciding vertical joints are separated by two header courses and a stretcher course.

For corners, ends, and junctions, you will use quarter, half, and three-quarter bats. In running bond, you alternate courses at the corners so the ends of the bricks are seen only in alternate courses in either wall. For ends, you use half bats in alternate courses. For junctions, you use two three-quarter bats which meet in the center of the header bricks in the abutting wall.

In English bond, use quarter bats in alternate courses in each wall for corners. Ends use quarter bats in alternate courses placed one header brick from the end. For junctions, use two quarter bats centered against the adjoining wall.

Flemish bond uses quarter bats in exactly the same way as does English bond.

Note that in double thickness or

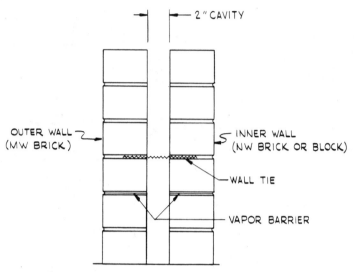

8-inch walls, the stretcher courses are laid side by side, so the wall is two bricks thick. Header courses, since they are laid the long way, are one brick thick.

Your brick construction must offer protection against moisture from both the soil and through the air. To stop moisture from being absorbed from the soil, you will install a vapor barrier in the horizontal mortar bed between the second and third courses.

Vapor barriers should be placed at breaks in walls and between bricks used to close cavities between brick veneer and other walls. To install the vapor barrier in this manner, use either waterproof building paper or plastic sheeting. Lay about a ¼ inch of mortar on top of the second course of bricks. Cover the course with the sheeting, and then top it with another ¼ inch of mortar. Wherever sheets of vapor barrier meet, they must be overlapped by several inches.

To stop moisture from the air from penetrating a brick wall, one method is to build a 2-inch cavity between two parallel walls. The walls are tied together with noncorroding metal hardware. They can be **Z**-shaped or corrugated ties. Build the two parallel walls simultaneously so you can install the ties as you go. Because water that penetrates the outside wall falls into the cavity, some means of draining it off must be provided. These are called weep holes. To make them you either leave the mortar out of a vertical joint every two feet or so, or you insert ⅜-inch tubes through the mortar under the first course of bricks. Place the tubes every 24 inches to 36 inches apart, and make sure they slope to the outside.

If you are installing a brick veneer

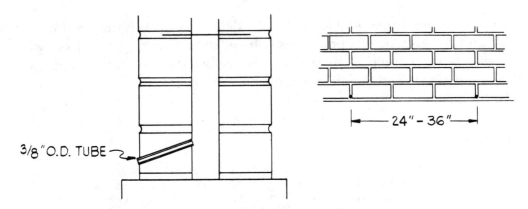

3/8" O.D. TUBE

24" – 36"

wall next to sheathing or other building material, allow for a 1-inch air space. This construction also uses metal ties between the interior wall and the brick veneer.

A technique you will have to learn for almost any kind of brick work is cutting bricks. Use a heavy hammer and a wide chisel. Score both sides of the brick and lay it on a bed of sand. Tilt the chisel handle toward the waste end, and give it a strong, sharp rap. Clean the ragged end with the edge of a trowel. This will help you understand the popularity of the running bond: you don't have to cut many bricks. Mix no more mortar than you can use in about two hours. If the mortar gets stiff within that time, you can add more water.

Bricks are different from blocks in that they must be wet when you build

CUTTING A BRICK

with them. This helps the mortar to stick, and because the wet brick does not absorb water from the mortar, it cures more slowly and therefore gives a better bond.

Before you start laying bricks, your foundation should be in place, with batter boards or stakes marking your building line.

CONSTRUCTION

1. Lay a thin layer of mortar on the foundation beneath the strings from the batter boards. You start working at the corners. Use the thin mortar bed for marking guidelines for the first course of bricks. Use a plumb bob or suspend the level next to the guide string to mark a spot directly

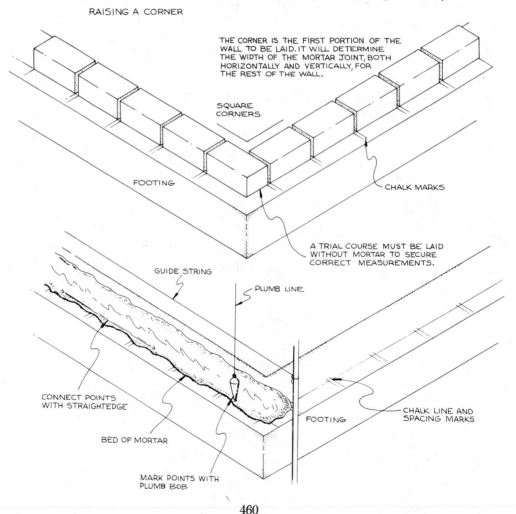

RAISING A CORNER

THE CORNER IS THE FIRST PORTION OF THE WALL TO BE LAID. IT WILL DETERMINE THE WIDTH OF THE MORTAR JOINT, BOTH HORIZONTALLY AND VERTICALLY, FOR THE REST OF THE WALL.

SQUARE CORNERS

FOOTING

CHALK MARKS

A TRIAL COURSE MUST BE LAID WITHOUT MORTAR TO SECURE CORRECT MEASUREMENTS.

GUIDE STRING

PLUMB LINE

CONNECT POINTS WITH STRAIGHTEDGE

FOOTING

CHALK LINE AND SPACING MARKS

BED OF MORTAR

MARK POINTS WITH PLUMB BOB

below it in the mortar. Locate similar points about 2 feet away and connect the two with a straightedge. Repeat the process for the adjoining wall, and you can remove the strings.

2. Lay about a ½ inch of mortar from the corner down one wall line, but be careful not to cover the lines in your first mortar. Place the first brick in the mortar against the line. Check it for horizontal level, both lengthwise and crosswise. Take the next brick and put about a ½ inch of mortar on one end. Place that end against the first brick, and place it into the mortar bed. Check for level and alignment with the guideline. Repeat the process for a half-dozen bricks or so along both walls.

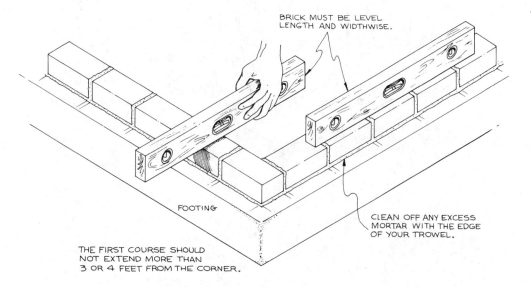

BRICK MUST BE LEVEL LENGTH AND WIDTHWISE.

FOOTING

CLEAN OFF ANY EXCESS MORTAR WITH THE EDGE OF YOUR TROWEL.

THE FIRST COURSE SHOULD NOT EXTEND MORE THAN 3 OR 4 FEET FROM THE CORNER.

3. Go back to the corner and start the second course. Check frequently with the level, and use the storyboard. The top of this course will be the base for the vapor barrier.

4. Install the vapor barrier, and you can then build up the corner for several courses. Repeat the first four steps for each corner. Check frequently for level, plumb, and alignment with the building lines.

5. Using pins or bricklayer's line stretchers, string a line between corners and begin laying up the walls, lining up the bricks with the string. Remember to follow your plans to achieve the desired bond. When you get to the last brick in a course, put mortar on both ends, and ease it into place.

6. Before the mortar hardens, use the trowel to scrape off any excess mortar on the bricks. Then, using a jointer, point the bricks by rubbing it along first the vertical joints, then the horizontal. Brush off any excess mortar.

7. The technique is basically the same for double-thickness walls. Place mortar between the parallel courses of bricks, as well as the bottom and ends as in single thickness walls.

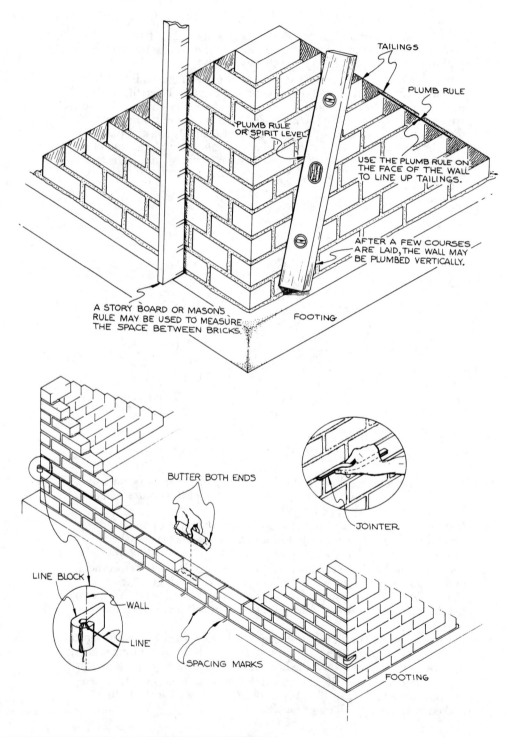

TAILINGS

PLUMB RULE

PLUMB RULE OR SPIRIT LEVEL

USE THE PLUMB RULE ON THE FACE OF THE WALL TO LINE UP TAILINGS.

AFTER A FEW COURSES ARE LAID, THE WALL MAY BE PLUMBED VERTICALLY.

A STORY BOARD OR MASON'S RULE MAY BE USED TO MEASURE THE SPACE BETWEEN BRICKS.

FOOTING

BUTTER BOTH ENDS

JOINTER

LINE BLOCK

WALL

LINE

SPACING MARKS

FOOTING

STONE

Stone is probably the most overlooked building material available today. It's strong, extremely attractive, usually almost cost free, and best of all, it's easy to work with. All you need to build with stone is time, determination, cement, and stone. For some stonework, you don't even need cement.

The art of stonemasonry is usually shrouded in mystery, for the stonemason is a person who literally builds structures out of the bare earth. Stonemasonry need not be thought of as some sort of archaic art; it's a basic construction method, easily adaptable to those with limited experience or ability.

For many reasons, stone is a better medium for the beginner than wood, brick, or concrete block. Because of the very nature of stonework, there is room for error. In laying bricks or blocks, you must have your mortar spread evenly, the bricks level, and all spacings the same. With stone, all you need worry about is that the face of your wall remains plumb.

To build a stone wall, an obvious prerequisite is a good supply of stone. In the old days, the growth of stone walls was almost organic; as the farmer cleared stones from his field, he lined the edges of his cropland with them and later built them into

walls. If you do not have a lot of stone on your property, you may have to seek out some twentieth century sources.

There may be abandoned or ruined stone buildings in your area. Seek out the owner and bargain. Construction crews often consider the stones they had to excavate a nuisance. Offer to take them off their hands. Abandoned quarries never are picked clean, so check at the bottom of slopes for usable rubble.

If you have to buy stone from a working quarry, keep in mind that unless the quarry is close to your home, hauling costs may exceed the cost of the stone itself.

To find quarries, start with the Yellow Pages of your telephone directory. If there are any cement plants in your area, inquire whether you can buy stone from their limestone pits. Most states have a geological service, which is roughly akin to the cooperative farm office. The geological service offers information, maps, and advice as to what is available in your area. Many colleges have departments of geology, where students and faculty members are full of useful information.

When buying stone, you will order by the cubic yard. Measure the length of your wall in feet, multiply by the height and width. Divide this total by 27 to get the cubic yards needed. Add 5 percent or so for waste.

Once you have the stones at the building site, you must sort them. A word on stone-handling safety is in order. Regardless of your age, remember that the age of a stone wall is measured in decades, so if you become fatigued while working, it is of no consequence at all should you decide to leave the next stone for tomorrow. Unless you are used to this heavy labor, your body will do only so much work at first, but each day, your strength will build.

Remember that the way to lift is by making your legs do the work, not your back. Always keep the stone close to your body. Always be careful of your footing. It also is worthwhile to purchase tough-skinned mason's gloves.

Separate your pile of rocks. In one pile, put the flattest, squarest, and most regular pieces. These will be needed for ends, corners, and top. Put long stones whose length is equal to the wall's width in another pile. These will be the "tie" stones. Also, make a pile of small, wedge-shaped stones.

Drywall, and other cement construction work, may require from time to time that you cut stones. This is done with a chisel and sledgehammer. To cut a slab, score a groove about a $\frac{1}{2}$ inch deep where the stone is to be cut. Make the cut in one of three methods; lift one end of the slab and strike along the groove with a hand sledge; lay the slab on a bed of sand and strike along the groove; or place an angle iron beneath the slab and strike it from the top with the sledge.

Building should follow the standard

USE YOUR HEAD WHEN HANDLING STONES. NEVER LIFT MORE THAN YOU MUST. USING ROLLERS, RAMPS, AND LEVERS CAN HELP GET THE JOB DONE SAFELY.

procedures of laying a foundation. The only difference between stone and brick is that a stone wall should be thicker, usually from 18 to 24 inches at the base.

There are several techniques for building with stone. You can leave the stones in their natural form, known as rubble masonry, or you can shape each individual stone, known as

465

ashlar masonry. Either rubble or ashlar style stone can be laid up in coursed or random fashion. In coursed fashion the stones are laid in layers, giving the final wall distinct horizontal layers of stone.

Random rubble would be the crudest (and easiest) form of all, with stones in their natural form simply being placed atop one another to form a wall with mortar binding the stones together. The most intricate form of construction would be ashlar coursed, with individually shaped stones laid in layers, as usually seen in older church construction.

The tools needed for stone construction can be very simple, or rather intricate. You can mix your cement in a wheelbarrow, use a pick to dig the foundation, a trowel to

apply the mortar. You'll need too a stone hammer, a level, a shovel, and a plumb line. A small electric cement

mixer could be added as well as tucking trowels for the finish work. That's about it.

Once the foundation is started, you build from the corners first, and fill in the middle. For the bottom layer of stone, a layer of mortar up to 2 inches thick should be spread, and stones laid in this. Each stone in the entire wall should always be laid on its broadest face. With a layer of stone in place, smaller stones should be used to fill in the gaps behind the face of the wall, to both add strength and save mortar.

To lay the second layer of stone, spread mortar about 2 inches thick along an area 4 to 5 feet. Place stones so they intercept joints between stones below. This will greatly add strength to the wall, as there will be no channels of mortar running straight for any distance. For beginners, it is better to find a stone to

fit an area than to shape a stone to fit.

When you are laying up a wall, run a string from one corner to the other, directly along the face of the wall. As you prepare to put a stone in place, look over the top of the wall, down the string and the face of the wall, line up the face of the new stone with this plane, and gently rest it on the bed of mortar, gently pushing it down to ensure good contact. If a stone must be moved after it has been set in the mortar bed, it should be lifted out entirely and reset to ensure good bond.

With the front stones in place, the back of the wall may be filled with a cheaper class of masonry or poured concrete known as backing, to save cost. Every few feet you should place a stone that runs entirely through the width of the wall, to tie the different layers together and add strength.

Due to the weight of the stones, you should not add more than about 2 feet in height to the wall at a time. Allow the mortar to dry completely before adding another layer. On a small project, this will greatly add to the time of the project, but in a larger project, you can simply work your way around the building, and by the time you get completely around, the starting layer should be dry.

If you are going to build from stone, you should remember a few design restraints. Once a wall is up, it's up, so don't plan on knocking many walls down to redesign your place. Try to keep your project to one story, for when you start lifting stone up two or three floors, any cost savings are quickly lost. Corners are the hardest area of a stone building, so you may want to keep your design simple.

A stone building tends to be damp during cold periods, but this can be overcome by insulation. The combination of stone walls with insulation in the inside and good windows installed, will give you a building that requires very little heating in the win-

ter and little cooling in the summer.

If you can find a free source of stone, you should give thought to building with it. A stone building will require more cement than brick or block, but with free stone it should be

about a third to a half cheaper than conventional buildings, and will last more than a lifetime, in addition to giving its builder a feeling of satisfaction matched by few other enterprises.

SLIPFORMING

A method of stone and concrete wall construction that seems perfectly suited for a do-it-yourself project is slipforming. Long, narrow wooden forms allow you to place stone and mortar layer by layer, up the wall. As one layer is setting inside the form, the next layer is begun inside a second, separate form right on top of the first. After it has cured for three days, the first form is removed and is used again on top of the second form, and so on. This is a process that uses materials economically.

Make your slip forms yourself. They are used in matching pairs. You can start with 1 x 6 boards for the faces

of the two forms. You also can use ½-inch exterior plywood, cut from 16 inches to 20 inches in width and whatever length you choose. The dimensions of your form can be determined from your building plans. The height of the walls should be evenly divided by the width of the forms. Eight feet is a good length if your walls are to be in multiples of 8 feet, but you also may have to build 4-foot forms, or any other length.

Use 2 x 4 stock to assemble the forms. Cut two pieces equal to the length of the form, say 8 feet. Cut four pieces to fit between these as vertical studs. (If your form is 20

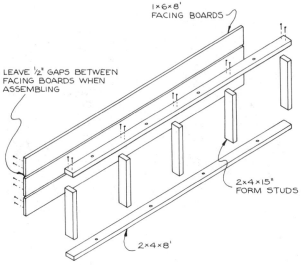

1×6×8'
FACING BOARDS

LEAVE ½" GAPS BETWEEN
FACING BOARDS WHEN
ASSEMBLING

2×4×15"
FORM STUDS

2×4×8'

provide for this, drill four ½-inch holes 24 inches apart on each lengthwise 2 x 4, and two on each of the end studs, 4 inches from the ends. You also will be using loops of wire to hold the forms together as you fill them with stones. To provide for this, drill ¼-inch holes in the face boards on either side of the vertical 2 x 4s so you can loop the wire through them and around the studs.

The absolute minimum number of forms you can get away with on even a small project is four pairs, because when doing corners, you have to build both walls up together. Each wall line would necessarily have two forms in use at once. (One is holding the previous day's work, and you are loading the other.)

A normal thickness for a one-story wall is 14 inches or 16 inches. With your footing already in place, with a keyway but no vertical reinforcer bars, you are ready to start.

inches wide, subtract the thickness of two 2 x 4s to get this size, in this case, 17 inches.) Nail the forms together as illustrated, using 16d nails. When you nail the facing boards or plywood on, use 10d nails. Be sure that the perimeter of 2 x 4s is flush with the edges of the facing boards, or else the forms will not fit together snugly.

During the slipforming process, you will bolt adjoining forms together. To

CONSTRUCTION

1. Draw chalk lines on the foundation to mark the thickness of the wall and set up your first pair of forms so that their inside faces are along the chalk lines.

2. Using 1 x 2 or other similar wood, temporarily nail two or three horizontal cross braces across the top of the form pair. Next, insert the light wire through the ¼-inch holes and loop it around the 2 x 4. Use a nail or other rigid object to twist it tight. It should not be twisted so tight so as to bow the frame, however. A good way to regulate this is to keep a supply of 1 x 1 pieces on hand, cut in lengths equal to the wall's thickness. Insert them between the form faces as you go.

3. Next, check that the forms are plumb by holding a level against the

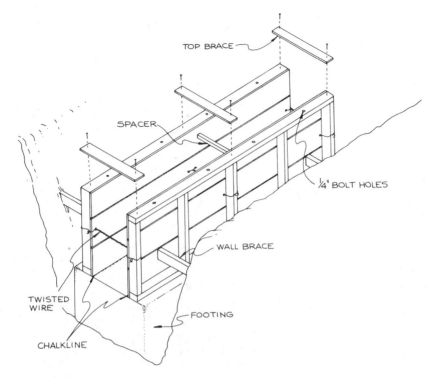

TOP BRACE

SPACER

¼" BOLT HOLES

WALL BRACE

TWISTED
WIRE

FOOTING

CHALKLINE

outside edges. Loosen the top horizontal brace and tap the forms this way or that to get them plumb, and then replace the brace. At this point, you also can prop the forms as additional bracing.

4. Before you begin loading stones and mortar into the forms, prepare a thin paste of concrete and water to bind the wall to the footing. Prepare the mixture and coat the footing and keyway with it just before placing the stones.

5. For the wall mixture, proportions of one part cement, three parts sand, and four parts gravel are recommended. Keep the mixture on the dry side, using no more than five gallons of water.

6. Pour about 2 inches of concrete into the form and start setting your stones. These stones should have at least one flat face, which should go against the outside face of the wall. The stones should not touch each other, but should have 1 inch to 2 inches of concrete between them. The placement of your stones should not be entirely random. The rule of "one over two, two over one" should be followed. Use the biggest rocks at the bottom of the wall.

7. As you place the stones, keep in mind that the style of this wall is for the inside face to show only concrete. Keep the stones at least 4 inches away from the inside face. Because you must place your stones blind, and cannot in fact see the pattern until at least three days later when you remove the forms, the going may be difficult at first. After some practice, however, you will develop a sense for "seeing" the pattern through the forms and you will be able to work with more confidence.

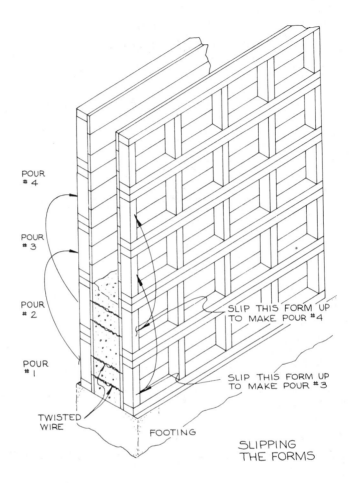

POUR
4

POUR
3

POUR
2

SLIP THIS FORM UP
TO MAKE POUR #4

POUR
1

SLIP THIS FORM UP
TO MAKE POUR #3

TWISTED
WIRE

FOOTING

SLIPPING
THE FORMS

8. As you work, use the trowel, hoe, and your hands to work the concrete around the stones. Rap the forms with a hammer from time to time to release bubbles in the concrete.

9. When you get to the top of the form, do not finish with a layer of concrete, or your wall will have horizontal strips of concrete every 20 inches. Instead, leave stones protruding at the top, either flush with the top of the form or extending slightly above it. Between pours of concrete, slope the top of the old pour down toward the outside so no wind-driven rain can seep through the wall.

10. The next slip form is placed directly on top of the first. Use the holes in the horizontal 2 x 4 to bolt the forms together. (Likewise, the holes in the vertical studs can be used to bolt forms end-to-end on the same level.) Repeat the process of plumbing and bracing the form.

11. After three days, remove the first form. Cut the wires flush with the stone surface.

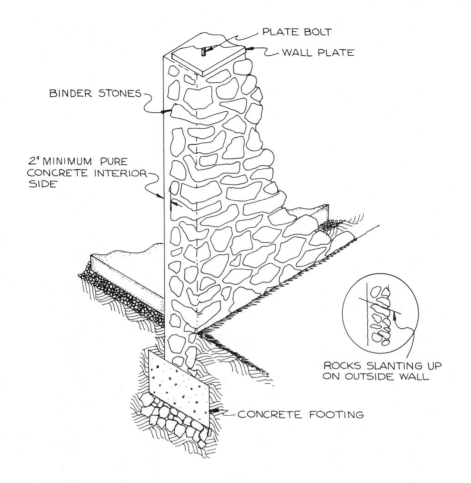

PLATE BOLT

WALL PLATE

BINDER STONES

2" MINIMUM PURE
CONCRETE INTERIOR
SIDE

ROCKS SLANTING UP
ON OUTSIDE WALL

CONCRETE FOOTING

SLIPFORMING A BUILDING

To make windows, doors, or frames for ventilators, construct the entire frame first, and place it against the inside face of the form. Good, heavy frames for doors and windows look best in stone walls like these, so use anything up to 8-inch-square stock. Construct the frames with lap, mortise and tenon, or rabbeted joints. Install a temporary diagonal brace to keep the frame rigid while working. To give the frame a better hold with the concrete, "porcupine" the outside surfaces by driving waste and bent nails partway in. You will notice that when the frame is placed against the inside face, there is space between the frame and the outside face. This must be blocked off for the length of the frame with 2 x 4 or other wood. Allow

473

an inch or two of concrete beneath the frame.

When you reach the top of your wall, fill the last 2 inches of your top forms with a smooth layer of concrete. Embed 6-inch by ½-inch bolts halfway into the concrete about 24 inches apart. These will be used to anchor a 2 x 8 top plate.

Working with slip forms is a job for at least two persons. It takes two people to get the long forms into place, and a good work routine calls for one person to be mixing concrete and hauling supplies while the other pours concrete and packs stones into the forms.

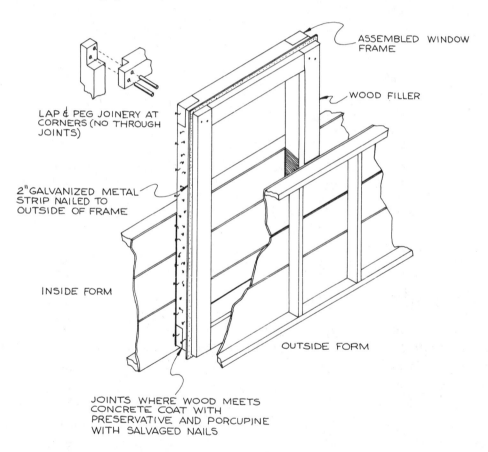

LAP & PEG JOINERY AT CORNERS (NO THROUGH JOINTS)

ASSEMBLED WINDOW FRAME

WOOD FILLER

2" GALVANIZED METAL STRIP NAILED TO OUTSIDE OF FRAME

INSIDE FORM

OUTSIDE FORM

JOINTS WHERE WOOD MEETS CONCRETE COAT WITH PRESERVATIVE AND PORCUPINE WITH SALVAGED NAILS

DRYWALLS

Cultures all around the world have built walls without mortar. Here in North America it is mostly a rural tradition, but a well-laid drywall will beautify a garden or home landscape anywhere.

The first step in the actual construction is to lay out the wall. The techniques are similar to laying out building lines. Working with your property line or existing buildings as a starting point, measure to the front, or outside face of the wall. Stake the two front corners, and then the back two corners.

The width of a drywall is not altogether arbitrary. For a wall 3 feet or less in height, the minimum width is 24 inches. For each 6 inches higher than 3 feet, add 4 inches to the bottom width. A real journeyman wall builder lays up low and medium height walls with both faces plumb. The taller the wall, the stronger the argument for building it with a bit of taper, or batter. A good guideline is that the top should be one-fifth narrower than the bottom. It will be easier for you to achieve this if you make a wooden frame from three pieces of light stock. The shorter, horizontal top piece should equal the top width of the wall. The two side legs should equal the height, and the distance between the bottom ends

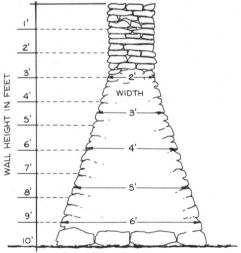

should equal the wall's bottom width.

At this point you also should plan for any gates, steps, or stiles. If you are building on a slope, you must step

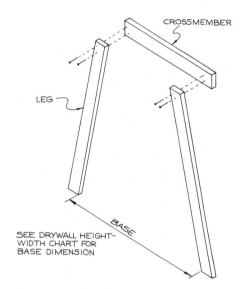

CROSSMEMBER

LEG

BASE

SEE DRYWALL HEIGHT–
WIDTH CHART FOR
BASE DIMENSION

course of stones will settle into the ground anyway. For taller walls, it will be a stronger construction if you dig down a foot or so and flatten the bottom of the trench.

One natural force that can ruin your wall fairly quickly is the draining of surface water. If your wall is along, or at the bottom of a hill, you should dig a parallel drainage ditch on the uphill side to carry water away. You also can lay a terra cotta or metal pipe through the wall as you build. Its uphill end can be placed to collect water from an uphill drainage ditch.

up the wall, rather than follow the contours as with a split rail fence.

When these planning steps are complete, prepare your foundation. Walls 3 feet high and less generally can be built right on the ground, without any digging besides leveling a strip equal in size to the wall's bottom dimensions. As time passes, the bottom

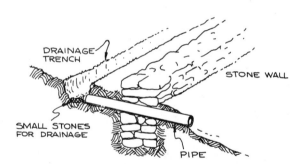

DRAINAGE
TRENCH

STONE WALL

SMALL STONES
FOR DRAINAGE

PIPE

CONSTRUCTION

1. The first layer of stone must be a sound, level base. Instead of using valuable slablike rocks below ground, you can achieve the same effect by digging holes to fit rocks with only one flat face so the flat face is up. These faces need not be exactly level but should dip slightly toward the inside of the wall. This will turn the force of gravity in your favor by having all the pieces of the wall pull inward. Place all the stones that are below ground level a few inches apart, and fill in the spaces with smaller rocks and gravel for drainage purposes.

2. For the first above-ground course, use the biggest rocks you have so you don't have to lift them off the ground. At this point you will begin to apply the basic principle in drywall construction: "one over two, two over one." This is exactly the way a brick wall is laid, and it provides that there be no vertical fissure where the wall can separate. So, position your stones so that the one going on top always covers the space between at least two stones beneath it.

476

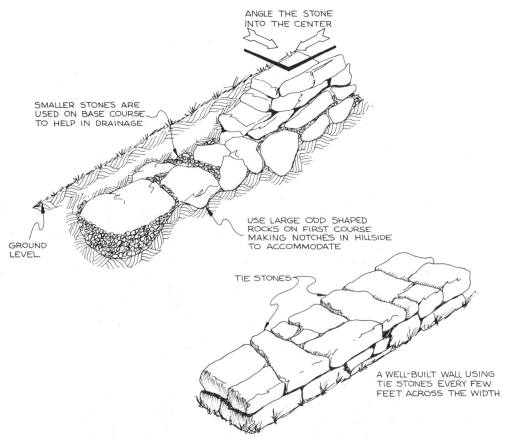

ANGLE THE STONE INTO THE CENTER

SMALLER STONES ARE USED ON BASE COURSE TO HELP IN DRAINAGE

USE LARGE ODD SHAPED ROCKS ON FIRST COURSE MAKING NOTCHES IN HILLSIDE TO ACCOMMODATE

GROUND LEVEL

TIE STONES

A WELL-BUILT WALL USING TIE STONES EVERY FEW FEET ACROSS THE WIDTH.

3.   Check the stones with a level as you go. If a rock wobbles, see if you can knock off a knob or point to make it fit more solidly. If not, use the small wedge-shaped stones to shim it up. These shims should always be placed toward the inside of the wall, pointed end out. If they are placed near the outside, they tend to work themselves out.

4.   As you work, place your stones with the flattest sides as top and bottom. The next flattest side, or the next largest flat dimension, should go toward the outside.

5.   If you have a lot of round or irregular stones, start each course by placing the worst stones down the middle of the wall, placing and shimming them so they do not wobble. Then, place rocks with at least one flat side along the sides. In this type of arrangement, each stone should touch five others: rocks to each side, two rocks beneath, and at least one core stone. If you are short of stones, you also can use this arrangement to fill the core of the wall with rubble.

6.   On any wall, you must place tie stones every 6 to 8 feet. A tie stone runs across the wall, its longest dimension perpendicular to the line of the wall. In such a manner, these rocks tie one face of the wall to the other, and add to its transverse strength.

477

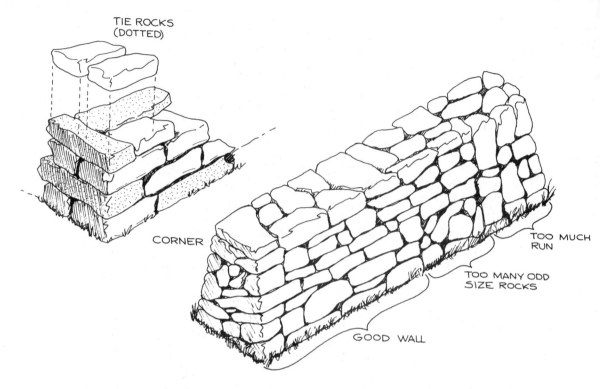

TIE ROCKS (DOTTED)

CORNER

TOO MUCH RUN

TOO MANY ODD SIZE ROCKS

GOOD WALL

7. Ends and corners demand special attention, and you will have to use your best rocks for them. The biggest, flattest rocks, and any rock with a square end should go on the ends. Ends should use as many long rocks as possible to tie the end into the wall, and the end must also use tie rocks on every other course.

8. Corners are more difficult because it is at the corner that any shifts along either wall line will meet. You will need plenty of tie rocks, and you must be especially careful that the stones in one course do not have edges atop any edges below, except, of course, along the wall's faces. Each stone should cover as many joints below it as possible. The corner will have to be tied into both lengths of wall. Ideally, each course should have tie rocks running from the corner into each wall. If you don't have enough good tie rocks to do this, alternate courses and directions.

9. You also will use these end and corner techniques in building stiles, gates, and steps. A simple stile that will turn livestock can be made by building an 18-inch-wide gap that runs through the wall on a 45-degree angle. Animals will not notice daylight through the wall on a 45-degree angle, and therefore are less inclined to try to squeeze through.

10. For stairs, begin leaving out stones as you build up toward the inside of the wall. The sides of the steps will be built like wall-ends. If your wall is only 2 or 3 feet wide, build steps going up from one face, and going down the other side a few feet down the wall.

FENCES

In the old days, homesteaders spent as much time and money on fences as they did on their home or barn. As they cleared forests for tilling, raw material for rail and pole fences was plentiful. Those primitive-style fences are seldom seen anymore. They have given way to mill-cut posts and planks, barbed wire, or portable electric fences.

But the purposes fences serve remain unchanged. They keep animals in a pasture or barnyard. They keep children off highways or away from other dangerous places, and they keep animals out of gardens.

Modern society has created other reasons for wanting fences. A white picket fence in front of the house may not function any better than a more primitive style, but it looks better in a residential area. There may be no livestock on your land, but a board fence on the perimeter establishes property lines. A board fence or hedge can block the stares of neighbors or passersby. Fences such as these may have little to do with farming or practical homesteading, but the need for them is nonetheless real.

To decide what kind of fence to build, first consider where it is to go, and what its purpose will be. These things decided, choices on material and style will be narrowed down.

For a patio, yard, or swimming pool, a privacy fence is probably what you want. This calls for either some sort of solid wood construction, which is expensive, or a "living fence" or hedge.

A garden fence can be of several types. They include the picket-style wooden fence that became popular in this country during the nineteenth century. A split rail or board fence can be attractive, and with woven wire added, can also restrict the movements of animals.

If you keep cattle, horses, or sheep, you can keep them in a pasture bounded by board and rail fence or barbed wire, woven or welded wire, or an electric fence.

For keeping animals such as hogs, goats, or fowl in a livestock yard, there is another type fence. What style you use depends on what animals you keep. For instance, woven wire will keep placid cows in place, but goats are more adventuresome (rowdy even), and soon would have the fence bent and broken.

PLANNING

Some planning should precede any fence building you do. If you are putting a simple chicken wire fence around your garden, you will at least have to measure your plot so you know how much wire and how many posts to buy. If you own a genuine farm with acres of pasture and a large barnyard to fence, your planning will be more complex.

For a simple wire or board fence around a garden, yard, patio, swimming pool, or barnyard, start by placing stakes at the corners, and mark your gates with stakes. Measure all the sides as accurately as you can. The total is the amount of wire or boards you must use. To determine how many posts you need, start with one for each corner and a pair for each gate. For the spaces between, figure on one post every 12 to 14 feet for barbed wire; one every 16 feet for woven or welded wire; and for a board or rail fence, one every 5 to 8 feet, depending on the length of your boards.

Planning for a pasture or other large enclosure requires more work. The task will be simplest if your land is flat, with no obstructions along the fence line. In such a case, you can probably sight from corner to corner, and fill in the lines with the help of an assistant.

On hilly land, or around trees, rock outcroppings, marshes, or ponds, more care must be taken. Here are some hints.

—To sight a fence line through heavy underbrush, use a 10- to 12-foot pole with a flag to mark stakes as you proceed.

—If there is a hill or valley between two points on a fence line, start by putting a stake at each end. Then, put two stakes about 10 feet apart at the top of the hill, or bottom of the valley, so they both are visible from

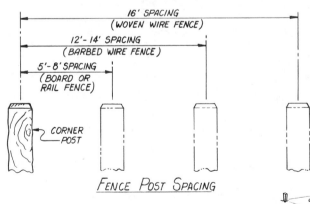

FENCE POST SPACING

16' SPACING
(WOVEN WIRE FENCE)

12'-14' SPACING
(BARBED WIRE FENCE)

5'-8' SPACING
(BOARD OR RAIL FENCE)

CORNER POST

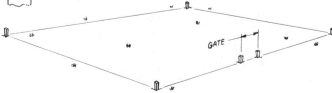

GATE

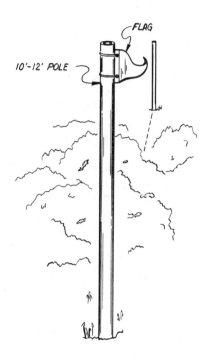

FLAG

10'-12' POLE

will have to be 8 feet apart. By reducing your post spacing and keeping the curve smooth, the fence will pull evenly on all the posts.

Your land may present other problems. If you have to set a post in a low place, it may gather water, and frost will tend to set there first. Set that post in concrete, in a hole dug below the frost line.

To set posts in a marshy area or at the edge of a pond, use 9-foot metal posts or pipe set in an oil drum filled with stone or gravel. You should use another 5-foot piece of 2-inch pipe, fastened to the bottom of the barrel with clamps. Crimp the bottom shut, as this piece will be used to anchor the barrel into the pond bed.

the end stakes. Align the two middle stakes by sighting first from one end and then the other, until all four are in line.

—To lay out a fence on a contour, start by staking out a smooth curve, with stakes about 16 feet apart. If there is a sharp curve, cut your spacing to 8 feet and put three stakes at the sharpest part of the curve. Stretch a string between the two end stakes. Measure the setback of the center stake from the string. If it is 4 inches or less, you probably can use your regular 16-foot spacing for poles around the curve. For each 2 inches over 4, decrease your post spacing by a foot. For 14 to 20 inches, your posts

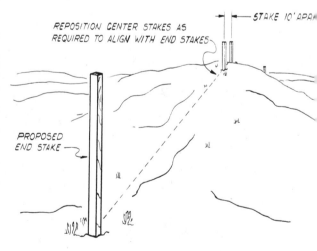

REPOSITION CENTER STAKES AS REQUIRED TO ALIGN WITH END STAKES

STAKE 10' APART

PROPOSED END STAKE

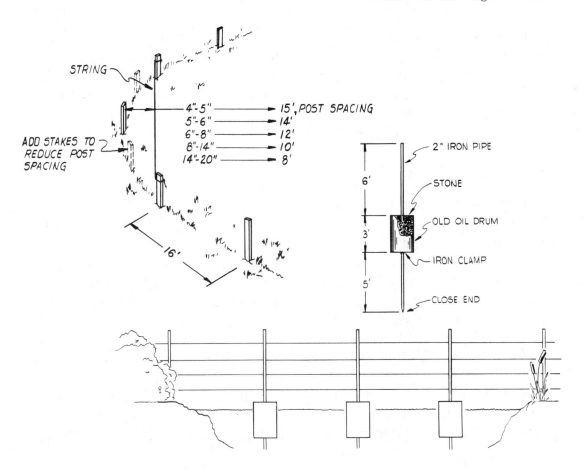

BOUNDARIES AND LEGAL MATTERS

When your fence is on your property line, its placement is very important. The most care must be taken if your home is close to neighbors, in a city or suburban setting. In rural areas, you probably will not have as many neighbor problems.

In any case, you must know where your property line is. If you have recently purchased the property, the mortgage company or bank may have required a property survey along with the title search. If not, you can look up your deed at the county courthouse and check the measurements yourself. You can also hire a surveyor.

The point is, if you erect a fence on your neighbor's property, it comes under his or her control, or, at best, it can become the topic of a legal fight. Unless you are a lawyer yourself, such confrontations are best avoided, so a survey is worthwhile.

If you are fencing a backyard or garden along the boundary line, you may want to ask your neighbor to spilt the cost and labor. If you do, it may be a good idea to add a clause to both deeds spelling out your agreement, should the fence need repairs after the property changes hands.

ECONOMICS

The truth about any fence building is that costs may be the most important factor in deciding what you build. If you can locate used material, such as pipes, concrete poles, and even wire, you can keep costs down. But beware of combining worn material with new. If your posts have only ten years of life left, it will not matter if your wire has fifty years.

It is difficult to advise specifically on what fencing materials cost. They vary from place to place and from year to year. Lay out your fence, inventory the number of posts and the amount of wire or lumber you will need, and do some comparison shopping. But in more than a few cases, you will have settled on the exact fence materials you want or need before you consider the cost.

A prudent homesteader will realize, on the other hand, that price is not the same thing as cost. If you scrimped on material and wild dogs break into your stock pen, the costs of your economy fence will be sadly increased.

CONSTRUCTION PRINCIPLES

There are some features of construction that are common to many types of fences. The most important of these probably is the post.

SETTING POSTS

Unless you have very many holes to dig, you probably can do the job by hand. Digging tools come in two styles, the auger and the clamshell digger. If your soil is rocky, the clamshell is more suitable to the job. An auger makes a neater hole and is best suited for deeper holes.

A rule of thumb is for the holes to be one third as deep as the post is

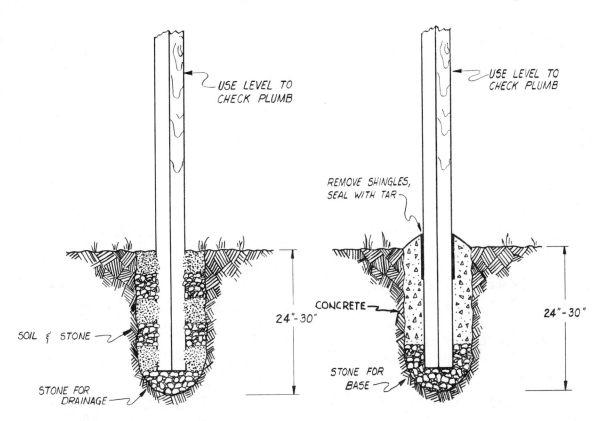

long, usually about 24 to 30 inches. At the bottom of the hole, before you put in the post or anything else, put in a few inches of stones to allow water to drain away from the post. Alternate layers of soil and stones, tamping down firmly every few inches. Recheck the plumb of your post as you go along.

You can make the post stronger by putting brick-sized rocks in the hole, or by attaching horizontal wooden cleats (1-inch by 2-inch pieces about 10 inches long are suitable).

Setting the posts in concrete will make for a strong, more permanent set. Mix your concrete on the dry side, because the mixture will absorb moisture from the soil. A mixture of one part cement, two parts sand, and three parts gravel is about right.

Make sure the post extends below the concrete. If you do not, the post will be enclosed by a water-catching concrete cup, and it will rot more quickly.

When you pour the concrete, mound it around the post so rainwater will run away. You can make a water-tight expansion seal for your posts by first cutting old shingles to fit along the sides of the post. When the concrete dries, pull the shingles out, and fill the spaces with tar.

Not all fence posts need predug holes. If the soil is sandy or loose, many posts can be driven to the needed depth. Metal posts can be driven as they are, and you can sharpen one end of a wooden post. You should do this before you treat the post with preservative.

If you drive your wooden posts with a wooden maul or sledgehammer, there is danger of splitting the posts. There are two ways to increase the odds in your favor. In the old days, farmers used a scantling, a piece of green hardwood 18 inches long and tapered on the ends, with a 3-foot broomstick handle. The scantling was held atop the post by a helper and the sledge struck it, instead of the post. You probably will need some kind of sturdy stand if you have to drive longer posts.

A better way is to make a post driver out of a piece of pipe. The pipe will have to fit loosely over the post and it should be 18 to 24 inches long. On top, a $\frac{1}{4}$-inch or $\frac{3}{8}$-inch steel plate is welded. You can also weld handles on the sides. Slip it on top of the post and you can drive without worrying about teetering atop a stepladder.

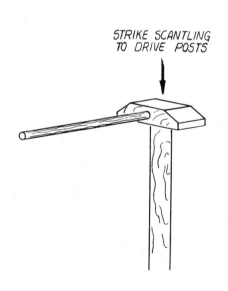

STRIKE SCANTLING
TO DRIVE POSTS

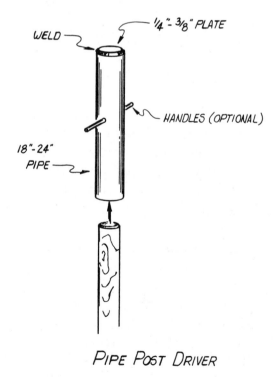

WELD

$\frac{1}{4}$"- $\frac{3}{8}$" PLATE

HANDLES (OPTIONAL)

18"- 24"
PIPE

PIPE POST DRIVER

BRACING CONSTRUCTION

Any kind of wire fence (barbed or woven), and some board fences, need special construction techniques to brace posts at ends, corners, and on both sides of gates.

Without braces, the corner and end posts will soon sag, no matter how well the post has been planted. Wire fencing exerts tremendous pull on the corners and ends. A well-constructed woven wire fence can exert a pull of 3,000 pounds, and in cold weather, when the wire contracts, the pull can increase to 4,500 pounds.

These posts should be set 3½ feet deep. You therefore may have to start with posts that are longer than your line posts.

The key to this construction is the triangle, which, as bridgebuilders and architects know, is the most stable geometric figure. Mated to this is the principle of "tensegrity," which, sim- ply stated, means that a line that is drawn tight has as much strength (in a triangle) as does a rigid line. In the case of building a fence, the corner post, a horizontal brace along the top of the fence, and a metal cable attached to a second post form the triangle.

The second post is placed to support the horizontal brace, usually 8 feet long. The cable runs from the top of it to the bottom of the corner post.

CONSTRUCTION

1. Set, plumb, and fill in the corner post.
2. Using your horizontal brace (a 2 x 4 similar piece, or a 1½-inch pipe), mark the hole for your second, or brace post.
3. Install your brace post, but fill the hole only partly.
4. Measure 8 to 12 inches from the top of the brace post, and drill a ¾-inch hole, 2 inches deep. This will hold the dowel to join the horizontal brace.
5. Bore a similar hole in the corner post, and bore holes of the same size into each end of the horizontal brace.
6. Insert one 4-inch-long dowel into the corner post. Install the brace, insert the other dowel into the other end of the brace, and work it into

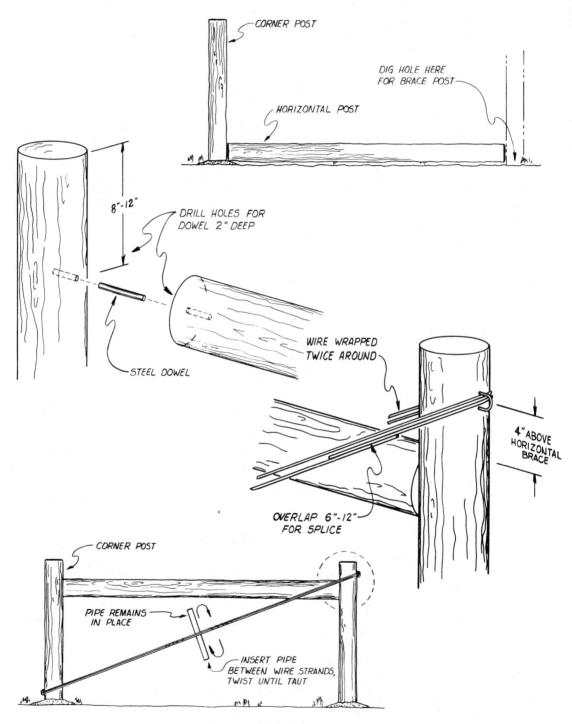

CORNER POST

DIG HOLE HERE
FOR BRACE POST

HORIZONTAL POST

8"-12"

DRILL HOLES FOR
DOWEL 2" DEEP

STEEL DOWEL

WIRE WRAPPED
TWICE AROUND

4" ABOVE
HORIZONTAL
BRACE

OVERLAP 6"-12"
FOR SPLICE

CORNER POST

PIPE REMAINS
IN PLACE

INSERT PIPE
BETWEEN WIRE STRANDS,
TWIST UNTIL TAUT

the hole in the brace post. Finish filling the brace post hole, and tamp down.

7. Drive a staple into the outside of the brace post, about 4 inches above the top of the horizontal brace. Drive a second staple into the outside of the corner post, about 4 inches above the ground. The staples should be driven in only half of their length.

8. Cut a piece of wire long enough to make two complete loops diagonally from post to post, passing through the staples. Allow 6 to 12 inches extra to make a splice.

9. Using either a wire splicer or two pliers, make your splice. Put a strong stick or pipe, 18 to 24 inches long, between the strands and tighten the cable by twisting. As you twist, tap the cables where they wrap around the posts so they lay smoothly. Leave the stick in place. If you are inclined to using hardware, you also can install turnbuckles to tighten the cable.

MATERIALS

Wood

1 pc. 2 x 4 x 8' (horizontal brace)

1 post, the length of your corner post (height of fence plus 2' to 2½') (brace post)

Hardware

2 pcs. 4" x ⅜" steel dowel
36' 12-gauge galvanized fence wire
Fencing staples
Stick or pipe 18" to 24" long

VARIATIONS

If your fence is more than 40 rods in length (660 feet), you will have to build a double brace. That is, add another brace pole, another horizontal brace and brace wire.

Long fences should also use braces on line posts every 40 rods. Build them the same as corner post braces, but run two brace wires in opposite directions to form an **X**. Make two of these brace panels side by side, so the pull is balanced in both directions. You can also install these braces where there is a sudden dip or rise in the terrain.

There are other methods of bracing corners and ends. If you use metal posts and you work with concrete, you can set the corner post and use ¼-inch by 2½-inch angle iron for

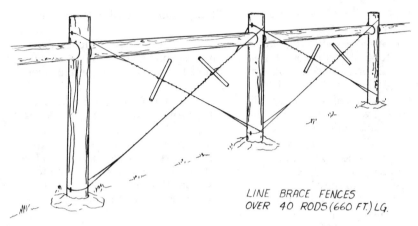

LINE BRACE FENCES
OVER 40 RODS (660 FT.) LG.

the horizontal braces. Bolt the angle irons about 4 inches from the top of the corner post. Where the brace touches the ground, dig a hole 15 inches by 18 inches by 8 inches deep. Put the brace into the hole, and mix and pour your concrete. It must cure for one week. *Note:* In areas where the ground freezes deeply, dig the holes an extra 8 inches deep to get below the frost line.

A third way to brace corners is by using a prefabricated steel post known as a "dirt-set." It consists of the post with two horizontal steel plates attached to the bottom by a pivot. The post is placed in the hole, and twisted a half turn to fan out the plates.

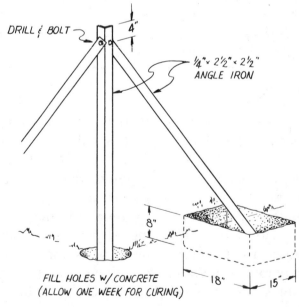

DRILL & BOLT

4"

¼" × 2½" × 2½"
ANGLE IRON

8"

FILL HOLES W/ CONCRETE
(ALLOW ONE WEEK FOR CURING)

18"   15"

490

CHOOSING AND PRESERVING POSTS

Most kinds of fences use square or rectangular wooden posts. Wire fences and a modified kind of rail fence can use concrete posts. Wire fences, including electric fences, also can use metal posts.

The most popular wood sizes are 3 x 3, 4 x 4, 4 x 5, 4 x 6, 5 x 5, and even 6 x 6. Post lengths run up to 8 feet, with the rule of thumb that posts be set 2½ feet, or a third of their total length, into the ground. (Corner posts, as mentioned, should be set deeper—3½ feet—because of the additional strains they bear.) Lower, light-duty fences which run up to 30 inches in height can use 2 x 4 or even 2 x 3 posts.

As for what variety and grade of wood to use, your choices are wide and limited only by your budget. The longest lasting wood is Osage orange, which resists rot for fifty years. However, Osage orange now is rare in most parts of the country. On the other extreme, and a poor choice for most fences, is birch, which rarely lasts more than one year in average North American climate. More reasonable choices and their life expectancies, when treated, are red cedar, 40 years; black locust, 36 years; white oak, 30 years; maples, 26 years; and hickory, 20 years.

It is almost not worth setting a wooden post that has not been treated against rotting. The best method—pressure soaking the lumber by a commercial operator—is also the most expensive. You can do almost as good a job yourself, especially since creosote and other commercial-grade preservatives are sold ready-mixed.

Ideally, the entire post should be treated, but the 2 to 3 feet in the ground is most susceptible to rot. You can put either end of a sawmill post in the ground, but if you are using saplings for a split rail or other primitive-style fence, put them in thicker end up, the opposite from the way they grew. This way, they last longer.

The oldest method of preserving the in-ground piece is charring. Put the posts in fire until a crust of black char appears all the way around.

Creosote probably is the most popular preservative. Utility companies use it to treat their poles, and railroads use it on their crossties. Creosote is toxic to animals, and it has a heavy, oily-medicine odor. Another drawback is that it is impossible to paint over.

The best method for applying creosote is with a combination hot and cold soak. You will have to get metal drums or a metal trough to hold the creosote.

If you are working with barrels, put in creosote to a depth of 30 inches or so. To heat the barrel, put it on blocks a few inches above your fire, or above a propane burner. It should be heated to 170° or 180°F. but not much hotter. A chemistry lab or even a kitchen candy thermometer can be used.

Soak the posts in the hot creosote for at least four hours. If all your posts fit into the barrel, douse the fire and allow the posts to continue soaking as the creosote cools. You should allow another two to three hours soaking in the cool creosote. If you have more than one batch of posts to soak, it will be worth your while to get another barrel and use it for the cold bath. Allow the posts to dry in the air for twenty-four hours before you install them.

Other preservatives range from salt solutions such as chromated zinc arsenate, to the older pentachlorophenol. The salt solutions are toxic to plants and animals, and must be handled with extreme caution. Pentachlorophenol is toxic to broad-leaved plants, and it even is sometimes used as an herbicide. The advantage of these preservatives is that they can easily be painted over.

Copper naphthenate is safe for use around plants, and although it stains

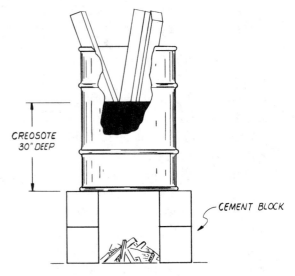

CREOSOTE 30" DEEP

CEMENT BLOCK

wood green, it can be painted over.

All of these preservatives should be soaked-in. Brushing on, no matter how many coats are applied, does not give good results. Of course, rails and boards can be painted with preserva-

BEVELED POST TOP

SHINGLE CAPPED POST

tive for good service, since they are not touching the ground.

The tops of posts deserve special care. Never leave the top of a square cut post exposed. Either cut it on an angle, or install some kind of water-repellent cap, such as a shingle, to stop this kind of end rot.

An old and novel method of preserving posts is to create a reservoir of preservative in the section that will be in the ground. Bore a 1-inch hole into the bottom end of the post, deep enough to reach above the ground level. Put a wooden plug in the bottom and plant the post. Then, bore a second hole from the side, slanting down to meet the vertical hole. Pour the preservative in until it overflows, and keep a cork or plug in the hole to stop evaporation and to keep insects out. Add more preservative as it is absorbed.

When you buy your wooden posts, you will get longer life from them if you specify that you want heartwood

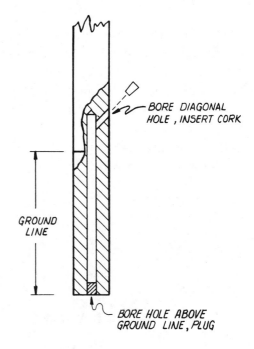

BORE DIAGONAL HOLE, INSERT CORK

GROUND LINE

BORE HOLE ABOVE GROUND LINE, PLUG

CREOSOTE RESERVOIR

posts. This is the part of the tree which contains the most natural resins. Of course, heartwood is more expensive than sapwood.

METAL POSTS

Most of the metal fence posts on the market are for stringing wire fences. Angle iron, $\frac{1}{4}$ inch by $2\frac{1}{2}$ inches by $2\frac{1}{2}$ inches, can be bought in lengths of up to 8 feet. Angle iron comes with handy lugs for holding horizontal wire strands.

These metal posts with lugs also come in **U**-bar, studded **Y**, and studded **T** styles. These metal posts are most useful for temporary fences around a garden or pasture, designed to be brought in for winter.

CONCRETE POSTS

Concrete posts last longer than any wooden posts. Making your own is not difficult. The most common size for concrete posts is about 4 inches square, and you can make them whatever length you need. Details on making concrete fence posts are in the chapter on concrete.

PRIVACY FENCES

Fences designed to block the view of neighbors or passersby are called privacy fences. They usually are built around relatively small areas, such as a backyard, patio, sun deck, or swimming pool. They can be constructed of wood, or they can be a living fence, a planting arrangement which, when properly cared for, not only gives privacy, but controls the roaming of children and some animals.

LIVING FENCES

The major advantage of a living fence is its aesthetics. A living enclosure, which shines after a rain storm, admits thin sunlight in shimmering patterns, and actually lives and grows, offers a pleasing alternative to a flat board fence.

In fact, living fences first became popular in areas where timber was scarce. Timber industrialists today claim trees are a renewable resource, a harvest such as grain. But the ecosystem of a tree farm is not very much like that of a natural forest, so the arguments against gluttony with trees remain strong.

The biggest disadvantage to a living fence is that it takes time, usually at least three years, for it to grow to a functional size.

Talk with a nursery expert before choosing your plants. You should look for a species that will tolerate heavy cutting back; that can tolerate winter weather; and that will produce thick, twiggy growth. Osage orange is one popular species. Others you may consider are black or honey locust, multiflora, Spanish bayonet, Russian olive, or Japanese quince.

The nursery will help you figure how many plants you need. Specify that you intend to plant two parallel rows of plants, staggered so that the plants in one row are in the spaces of the second row.

Let your plants grow through the first year. The next spring, cut the plants down to ground level. This will force branch shoots to grow. In midsummer, and again in September, cut the shoots back to about 4 inches. The following spring cut the plants again, but this time, to about 6 inches from the ground.

When you prune the plants, never let the tops get wider than the bases. If you do, the lower branches, whose growth is important to a full, impenetrable hedge, will not get the sunlight they need. Prune the hedge so the sides and top slope inwards, even to form a point.

Another type of living fence can be had by growing an annual or perennial vine on a wooden trellis, wire mesh, or grape stakes.

WOODEN STYLES

There are several types of wooden privacy fences. To serve their function, they must be of fairly solid construction, which raises two planning problems—frost and wind.

The problem of frost is that it flows downhill, like water. A solid fence placed at the bottom of a hill faces the biggest threat of damage from frost heaves. Any post in that position should either be planted extra deep in concrete or moved.

A solid fence is not the best protection against wind. Actually, it not only must be constructed extra strongly to resist wind pressure, but it can aggravate wind conditions on one side of the fence. An eddy is formed on the lee side of the fence, creating a low pressure area close to the ground. This causes wind blowing over the top of the fence to swoop down to ground level.

Wind tunnel tests have shown three designs seem to be the most protective—down-canted, horizontal louvers; vertical boards with spaces between them; or baffle panels mounted

495

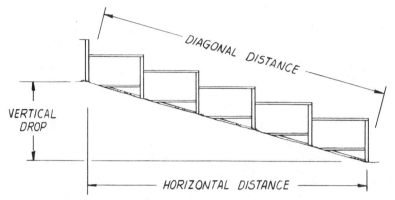

atop the fence leaning at a 45-degree angle to the inside.

While most wire, rail, and other fences can be built to follow the contour of hilly land, the privacy-style fences are best built in terraces or steps. This requires careful planning. Measure the horizontal distance from the top to the bottom of the hill and the vertical drop. Measure the diagonal distance along the slope and lay out this triangle on graph paper. If you know the height and spacing of your posts, you can work out the placement of the horizontal pieces to give a regular step pattern.

Several kinds of wooden privacy fences begin with a basic frame. In most cases, 4 x 4 posts, 8 or 9 feet long, will do the job.

You will need at least two horizontal rails, one at the top and one at the bottom. The bottom should be 4 or 5 inches off the ground, and the top can be either a like distance from the top of the posts, or mounted atop the posts.

Depending on your carpentry skills, you can choose from a variety of joints for the rails. The simplest is to toenail the 2 x 4s to the posts, but this is also the weakest method, so you should at least reinforce with a 2 x 2 or similar-sized block under the rail. Other joint methods include dado, and mortise and tenon.

For any wooden fence, it is definitely worthwhile to spend the little extra money for aluminum alloy or galvanized nails instead of common steel. Any joint held by a rusted nail is weakened, **and the rusty nails can**

leave stains on the painted surfaces.
The simplest construction is to nail
vertical planks to the rails. The most
popular-sized planks are 1-inch board,
using either random widths or 6- or 8-
inch widths. They can be butted to-

2 x 4

1 x 6 OR
1 x 8

BOARD-ON-BOARD FENCE
—ALTERNATE AS SHOWN

MATERIALS (for one 8-foot section of board-on-board fence)

Wood

2 pcs. 4 x 4 x 8' (posts)

2 pcs. 2 x 4 x 8'   or   **Top rail:** 1 pc. 2 x 4 x 8'

                               Bottom rail: 1 pc. 2 x 4 x 92½"

8 pcs. 1 x 8 x 12'   or   **Vertical boards:** 16 pcs. 1 x 8 x 6'

Hardware

Galvanized 8d nails
Galvanized 12d nails

gether for a really peep-proof enclosure. Or, you can let space between the planks in the style of a picket fence. Another alternative, to give both airiness and privacy, is to nail planks to both sides of the rails,

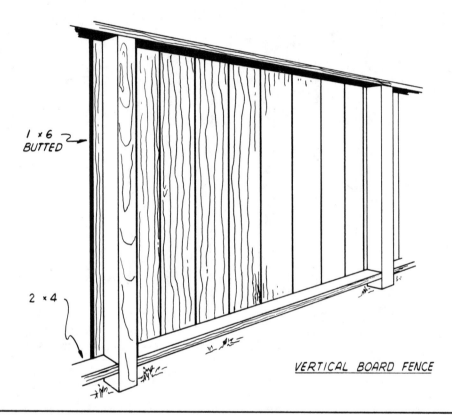

1 x 6 BUTTED

2 x 4

VERTICAL BOARD FENCE

MATERIALS (for one 8-foot section of vertical board fence)

Wood

2 pcs. 4 x 4 x 8' (posts)

2 pcs. 2 x 4 x 8'   or   **Top rail:** 1 pc. 2 x 4 x 8'

Bottom rail: 1 pc. 2 x 4 x 92½″

9 pcs. 1 x 6 x 12'   or   **Vertical boards:** 18 pcs. 1 x 6 x 6'

Hardware

Galvanized 8d nails
Galvanized 12d nails

placing them so the boards on one side are opposite the spaces on the other side.

For a louvered fence, plan on your 1 x 6 board fitting between the two rails. To space the planks evenly and

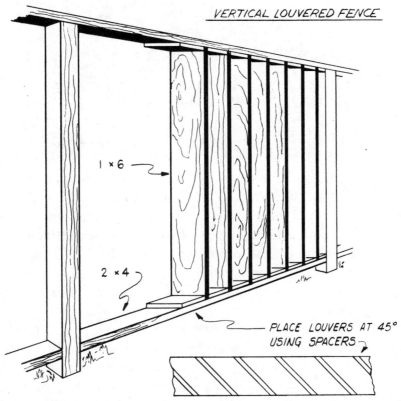

VERTICAL LOUVERED FENCE

1 x 6

2 x 4

PLACE LOUVERS AT 45°
USING SPACERS

MATERIALS (for one 8-foot section of vertical louvered fence)

Wood

2 pcs. 4 x 4 x 8′ (posts)		
2 pcs. 2 x 4 x 8′	or	**Top rail:** 1 pc. 2 x 4 x 8′
		Bottom rail: 1 pc. 2 x 4 x 92½″
11 pcs. 1 x 6 x 10′	or	**Louvers:** 22 pcs. 1 x 6 x 5′
1 pc. 1 x 4 x 10′	or	**Spacers:** 22 pcs. 1 x 4 x 5″

Hardware

Galvanized 8d nails
Galvanized 12d nails

on a regular angle, you should make spacer blocks. Cut a 1-inch strip at a 45-degree angle every 3 inches. Nail the pieces along both the top and bottom rails. It will be easiest to put on the first pair of spacer blocks, one at the top and one at the bottom, then the first louver, and so on.

You can set horizontal louvers in the same manner, with the spacers mounted on the vertical posts. You may want to use lighter wood for horizontal louvers, perhaps ½-inch instead of 1-inch stock.

There are disadvantages to louver fences. Because the louvers overlap, you will need more wood per running foot of fence than other types of fence. Also, unless you use top grade, kiln-dried lumber, vertical louvers may twist, and horizontal louvers may sag after they have been exposed to the weather for a few months.

For another type of fence, you also can nail plywood or other panels to the frame. Reinforce plywood with 1-inch laths.

Basket-weave fences are popular because they are attractive and do not require much heavy lumber.

A vertical weave is easy to make. Use 4-inch by ¼-inch strips of any length for the slats. For the horizontal spacers, use pieces about 1½ inches by 1 inch, of the length you need to go from post to post. Toenail or dado the spacers to the posts.

Paint or treat with preservative all the wood pieces before you assemble the fence. Basket-weave fences are very hard to paint when they are assembled.

Slide the slats down from the top, weaving them alternately front and back around the spacers. A wooden mallet or block of wood will be useful to tap the slats into place, and also to tap them sideways to butt against the other slats.

A horizontal weave fence can be

made by nailing each end of the slats to the posts and weaving the spacers through. A better method is to build the panels before mounting them on the posts. To do this, make a panel weaving tool. It requires two lengths of 2 x 4, 15 inches longer than the width of the panels you want; four 8-inch pieces of 1 x 4; and about 3 feet of 1 x 2 stock.

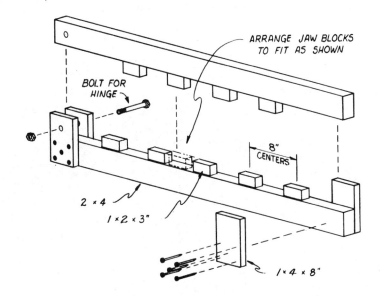

ARRANGE JAW BLOCKS TO FIT AS SHOWN

BOLT FOR HINGE

8" CENTERS

2 x 4

1 x 2 x 3"

1 x 4 x 8"

CONSTRUCTION

1. Nail the 1 x 2 by 3-inch jaw blocks along one of the 2 x 4 pieces. Space them apart exactly twice the width of the planks you are using in your weave. (If your planks are 4 inches wide, space the blocks 8 inches from center to center.)

MATERIALS

Wood

1 pc. 2 x 4 x 14'	or	**Jaws:** 2 pcs. 2 x 4 x 6½'
1 pc. 1 x 2 x 4'	or	**Jaw blocks:** 15 pcs. 1 x 2 x 3"
1 pc. 1 x 4 x 4'	or	**End pieces:** 4 pcs. 1 x 4 x 8"

Hardware

6d nails
1–4" x ¼" bolt w/nut and washer

2. At both ends of this 2 x 4 beam, nail two 1 x 4 end pieces, one on each side.

3. Using the other 2 x 4 beam, nail similar jaw blocks at the same interval as on the other beam, but stagger them so they are opposite the spaces on the other beam.

4. Place the second beam between the upright pieces of the first beam and adjust the jaw blocks so they mesh. Drill a hole through the two end pieces and the upper 2 x 4 and insert a bolt, large nail, or dowel for a hinge.

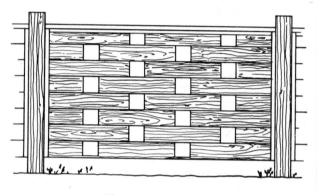

HORIZONTAL BASKET-WEAVE

USING THE TOOL

1. Lay the 4-inch by ¼-inch slats side by side on the ground, butting, but not overlapping. To make the end frames, use two 1-inch-square pieces, as long as your panel is high. Put one beneath, and one on top of the planks, and nail together.

2. Slide the started panel, joined end first, onto the jaw blocks of the

---

MATERIALS (for one 8-foot panel of basket-weave fence)

Wood

      7 pcs. 1 x 2 x 12′   or   **Spacers:** 14 pcs. 1 x 2 x 6′

      2 pcs. 1 x 1 x 12′   or   **Panel frame vertical members:** 4 pcs. 1 x 1 x 6′

      2 pcs. 1 x 1 x 16′   or   **Panel frame horizontal members:** 4 pcs. 1 x 1 x 8′

      2 shts. ¼″ ext. plywood (good two sides)   or   **Slats:** 15 pcs. 4″ x 8′

Hardware

      Galvanized 8d nails
      Galvanized 10d nails

weaving frame. While the lower blocks push up on every other slat, close the frame so the upper blocks push down on the alternate blocks.

3. At this point it will be easy to weave a spacer through the slats. Then slide the panel about 18 inches along the frame, and adjust it so the slats that were pushed down before, are now pushed up, and vice versa.

4. Continue this to the end of the slats. Then finish the panel by sandwiching that end between two more 1-inch-square strips. You may also want to nail a 1-inch-square framing strip along the top of the panel, nailing it from behind before fastening the panel to the posts using 10d nails.

GARDEN FENCES

Just as there are different types of gardens, there are different types of garden fences. For purposes of discussion, there are two groups: wire mesh, which serve to keep animals out of gardens, and those which also are ornamental, such as picket fences.

PICKET FENCES

Picket fences start with the basic frame. For a 5- or 6-foot-tall fence, use 4 x 4 posts and 2 x 4 horizontal stringers. A fence that is to be only 3 or 4 feet tall can use lighter posts, even 2 x 4s, and lighter horizontal pieces, perhaps 2 x 2s.

The size, shape, and spacing of the pickets will determine the character of the finished fence. Picket tops can be square, rounded, pointed, arrow shaped, or even more ornate ginger-bread styles. Pickets can range in width from $1\frac{1}{4}$ inches to 6 inches, and $\frac{1}{2}$ inch to 1 inch in thickness. Square pickets also can be used, in sizes such as 1-inch, $\frac{5}{4}$-inch, or even 2-inch square. In California, grape stake pickets are popular. Other possi-

bilities are bamboo or even $\frac{3}{4}$-inch or 1-inch dowels.

A variety of precut pickets are available at building supply stores or in mail-order catalogs. Your costs will be considerably less if you cut them yourself. No matter how you decide to cut the tops of the pickets, the task

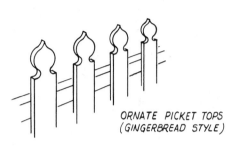

ORNATE PICKET TOPS
(GINGERBREAD STYLE)

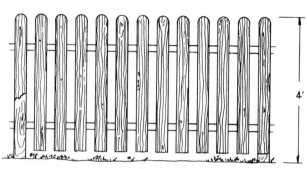

ROUND TOP PICKET

GOTHIC TOP PICKET

will be easier if you clamp a few pickets together, and cut them all at once. This also will result in more uniformity among the pickets.

Paint the pickets, posts, and horizontal stringers before you assemble the fence. This is because you will not be able to work paint into the places where pickets are nailed, and those spots will be susceptible to rot. For most thicknesses of pickets, you will need no larger than 6d or 8d nails. You can nail pickets along one side, or stagger them on both sides of the stringers. A third possibility is to use one width pickets on one side and narrower ones opposite the spaces on the other side.

If the fence is to be strictly ornamental, the spacing of the pickets is a matter of taste. If, however, the fence is to protect small children, the spacing should be no larger than 3 inches. This is the size between pieces recom-

---

MATERIALS (for one 8-foot section of picket fence)

Wood

1 pc. 2 x 4 x 12′	or	**Posts:** 2 pcs. 2 x 4 x 5½′
1 pc. 2 x 3 x 16′	or	**Rails:** 2 pcs. 2 x 3 x 8′
5 pcs. 1 x 3 x 14′	or	**Pickets:** 20 pcs. 1 x 3 x 42″

Hardware

Galvanized 8d nails

mended for manufacturers of cribs and other children's furniture. With wider spaces, there is the danger of a child getting his or her head caught between the pickets.

If your fence has to withstand the energies of children or animals, you may want to make some other structural changes. A third or even a fourth horizontal stringer can be added, either evenly spaced between the other two, or closer to the bottom.

If you want to close up the spaces between pickets and keep costs down, consider using lath strips between pickets. Actually, if your fence does not face heavy-duty use, it can be constructed entirely of laths. You can get a similar effect with snow fencing.

This consists of ½-inch by 1½-inch by 4-foot pickets held 2 inches apart by twisted strands of wire. Mail-order houses sell snow fence in 50-foot rolls, and it can be nailed directly onto your basic frame.

This leads to another picket fence which literally overlaps with the wire garden types. If you want to restrain dogs, rabbits, or fowl, staple chicken wire or a similar-sized mesh to the bottom third or so of the picket fence. To make this fence stronger, sharpen the bottom ends of the pickets, and drive them a few inches into the ground before mounting them on the stringers. Of course, they will have to be treated with the same preservative as you would use on posts.

CHICKEN WIRE FENCE

The most popular type of wire mesh for protecting gardens from rabbits or groundhogs is chicken wire. For a 3-foot-high fence, you can use 2 x 4 or 2 x 3 posts, about 5 feet long. Unless the ground is very rocky, you can probably sharpen the bottom end of the post and drive it in about 2 feet.

Before you set the posts, however, dig a trench at least 6 inches deep and 6 inches wide. Set the posts, and wrap the chicken wire down the side and across the bottom of the trench. This will deter all but the most determined groundhog.

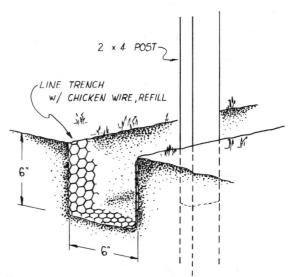

PASTURE FENCES

Pasture fences are designed to control and protect livestock over a large area. They also are suited as a boundary fence for a large area, even if there is no livestock. The best pasture fences, best suited to the most animals, are made of wood. But for large areas, only a wealthy homesteader can afford a fence built entirely of wood. Fortunately, there are wire fences which also do an efficient job.

Wire pasture fences are made from barbwire or woven wire. Smooth wire also is used for electric fences.

Choosing what wire to use depends on what animals you keep. Usually, cattle, horses, or sheep are most often kept in pasture. Only certain types of pasture fences are suitable for hogs, which can also be pastured. Likewise, goats present some special fencing challenges; a heavyweight woven fence will keep them in place.

A fence constructed of barbwire is best suited for cattle and horses. Barbs can pull the fleece off sheep. Barbs can also injure goats, which are apt to stand up on, or jump against fences.

Heavyweight and mediumweight woven wire fencing will do an excellent job with cattle, hogs, sheep, goats, and horses. Even the lightweight woven wire, which is no taller than 32 inches, will suit for all of these but horses.

Electric fences are most useful for cattle, hogs, and horses. They usually are ineffective for sheep and goats because fleece and thick hair insulate them from the shock.

Here then are some suggestions for the ideal wire fence for each kind of livestock.

Cattle: A good choice is heavyweight, 49-inch-high woven wire, made of 9- or 11-gauge wire. You can add a strand of barbwire at the top. Posts should be 5 feet tall, 16 feet apart.

Hogs: Some types of mediumweight (10- and 12-gauge wire) are called "hog-tight" fence. It is anywhere from 34 to 46 inches high, with horizontal wire 6 inches apart. If you use the 34-inch height, add a strand of barbwire at the top. You can set the mesh right on the ground or raise it a few inches, in which case, you should add a strand of barbwire to keep piglets from squeezing out. You should use at least 4-foot-tall posts, set 16 feet apart.

Sheep and goats: Medium- or heavyweight woven wire ($12\frac{1}{2}$- or 11-gauge wire either 6 or 12 inches apart) does a good job. It can range in height from 40 to 47 inches, with 4-foot-tall posts set 16 feet apart. Be sure the wire is tight against the ground to protect the sheep from dogs or coyotes.

Horses: Again, medium- and heavy-weight woven wire, with strands of barbwire added, does a good job. The fence should be at least 50 inches high, so if the mesh is only 40 or 46 inches high, you can add a 1 x 6 board or barbwire at the top. Posts should be about 5 feet tall, set 16 feet apart.

No matter what type of wire you buy, you should know something about how wire is sold and described by manufacturers. The thickness of wire is designated by gauge. The heavier the wire, the lower the gauge number. Heavyweight wire is 9 gauge. Barbwire comes from $12\frac{1}{2}$ to 14 gauge. Lightweight woven wire consists of 11 to $14\frac{1}{2}$ gauge. Electric fence can use smooth wire from $12\frac{1}{2}$ to the lightest fence wire, 18 gauge.

In a woven wire fence, stay wires are vertical and line wires are horizontal. Manufacturers catalog woven wire by design numbers. For instance, design number 1047 wire has 10 line wires and is 47 inches high. Some manufacturers add other numbers. So, 1047-12-11 wire is 10 line wires, 47 inches high. The wires are 12 inches apart and consist of 11-gauge wire.

Another feature of well-made woven wire is a **U**-shaped crimp on the line wires between stay wires. This is the tension curve, and when the fence is stretched tight, it flattens and elongates. Tension curves allow the fence to contract on cold days. In fact, wires should be installed in warm weather. If they are installed in the cold, they will sag in the summer.

Barbwire consists of either two or four pointed barbs spaced every 4 or 5 inches. If your enclosure gets a lot of pressure from animals, four-point, 12-gauge wire is best. Bigger pastures which get lighter wear can make-do with two-point, 14-gauge wire.

BARBWIRE FENCE

Barbwire is difficult to work with for exactly the reason it is effective fencing: sharp-pointed loops of wire every 4 or 5 inches. It is therefore a good idea to invest in a pair of heavy work gloves before installing barbwire.

Another preliminary preparation you should make is some means of placing the roll of barbwire on an axle to unroll it as you work. Pulling the wire off the end of the roll will put kinks and loops in the wire. You can rig an axle across the back of a pickup truck or on a tractor yoke. Using 2 x 4s, you can rig an axle and frame

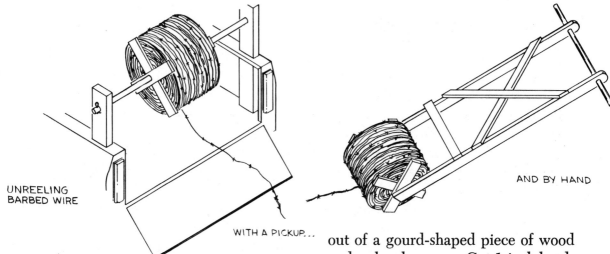

UNREELING
BARBED WIRE

WITH A PICKUP...

AND BY HAND

in a wheelbarrow. You also can make a rectangular frame with the axle at the bottom, and allow the wire to roll along the ground as it unreels.

In order to do the best job, take the time to erect a temporary dummy post on the outside of your anchor or end post, from which you will stretch the wire. Use a 4 x 4 post, the same height as your other posts. It need be sunk only 18 inches.

Set the dummy post 8 feet from the anchor post and insert a horizontal wooden brace between the two, toe-nailing it in place. You also can add diagonal 1 x 4 braces, about 10 feet long, for extra stability.

With the dummy post in place, you will need one other piece of equipment. You will need either a ratchet wire stretcher or block and tackle.

If your barbwire line is not very long, you can make a handy tightener

out of a gourd-shaped piece of wood and a claw hammer. Cut 1-inch hardwood into the shape shown, about 30 inches long, with a notch to hold the face of the hammer. Insert a $\frac{1}{4}$-inch bolt as shown to prevent splitting. Drive a series of 1-inch brads about halfway into the curve of the wood, and leave them protruding about $\frac{1}{2}$ inch. Snip off the heads to provide a nonslip face to brace against the post. You can fasten the hammer with tin or leather straps.

Be careful when stretching barbwire. Never use a tractor or truck to stretch it, because it is impossible to

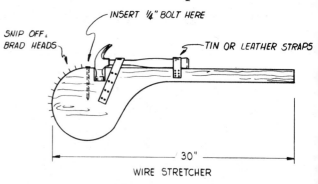

INSERT ¼" BOLT HERE

SNIP OFF
BRAD HEADS

TIN OR LEATHER STRAPS

30"

WIRE STRETCHER

safely gauge when the wire is about to break. Those barbs can make some pretty ghastly wounds. When you are stretching barbwire, keep the post between you and the wire.

CONSTRUCTION

1. Attach wire to an end post, at the far end of the line from your dummy post. Wrap the wire around the post and wrap the loose end back around itself. If you use wooden posts, secure the wire with staples; if a metal post is used, use wire clamps. *Note:* The proper way to use staples is to drive them only to hold the wire snugly, neither burying the staple in the wood nor crimping the wire. Set the staple on a slight diagonal, so both prongs do not split the same grain.

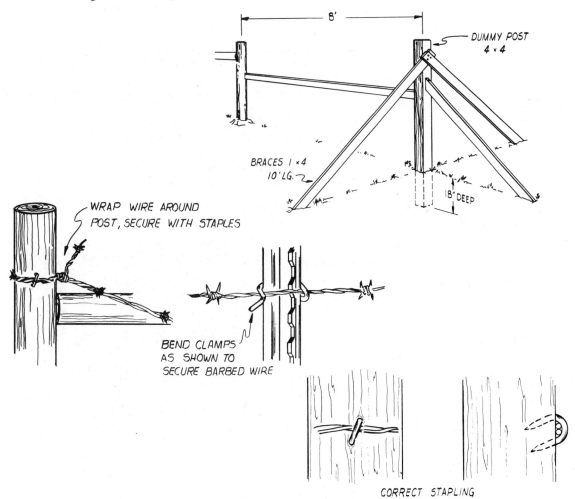

8'

DUMMY POST 4 × 4

BRACES 1 × 4
10' LG.

18" DEEP

WRAP WIRE AROUND POST, SECURE WITH STAPLES

BEND CLAMPS AS SHOWN TO SECURE BARBED WIRE

CORRECT STAPLING

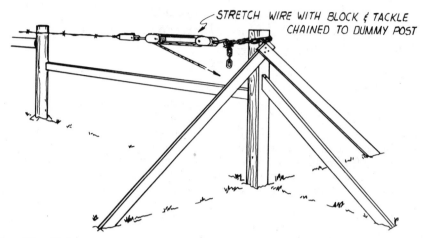

STRETCH WIRE WITH BLOCK & TACKLE CHAINED TO DUMMY POST

2. Unroll the wire until you get to the dummy post, where you attach the wire to the stretcher or block and tackle. The stretcher is attached to the dummy post with a chain.

3. Stretch the barbwire until it is fairly tight. Be sure to check that it is free of obstructions and kinks as you stretch.

4. Attach the taut wire to the end post with staples. Disconnect the stretcher, and wrap the end around the post and back around the wire itself.

5. Go back and staple the wire to the other line posts.

WOVEN WIRE FENCE

The techniques of installing woven wire are a bit different from installing barbwire. If you are working with a wide roll, the job will be easier with a helper.

Plan to put the wire on the side of the posts which will get the most pressure, that is, the inside. This way, the posts, and not just the staples, will receive the pressure.

To stretch woven wire, you again will need a dummy post. Your stretcher should be outfitted with a clamp bar, about as long as the wire

is high. If two stretchers or blocks and tackles are available, it will be easier to evenly stretch the woven wire.

510

CONSTRUCTION

1. Examine your wire roll to determine which way it unrolls, and which end is the bottom (the end with the closer line wire spacing). Lay the roll on the ground with the bottom closest to the posts, and unroll it past the first two or three posts. Allow about 2 extra feet to wrap around the first post.

2. Remove the first stay wire on the loose end. Do this by cutting the stay wire between line wires, and loosening the joints.

3. Stand the fence roll against the post, and adjust it to the proper height. (About 3 inches off the ground if you are going to use a strand of barb-wire at the bottom; about ½ inch if you are not.)

4. Fasten the fence by stapling each line wire. Be sure to leave enough of the ends free to wrap all the way around the post, and to wrap around the wire itself.

5. Complete unrolling the fence. If the fence is on a contour, the wire should be on the outside of the posts. You may have to switch from side to side as the contour changes.

6. Stand the wire against the posts, holding it in position with loops of string or props, every third or fourth post. Attach the chain for the

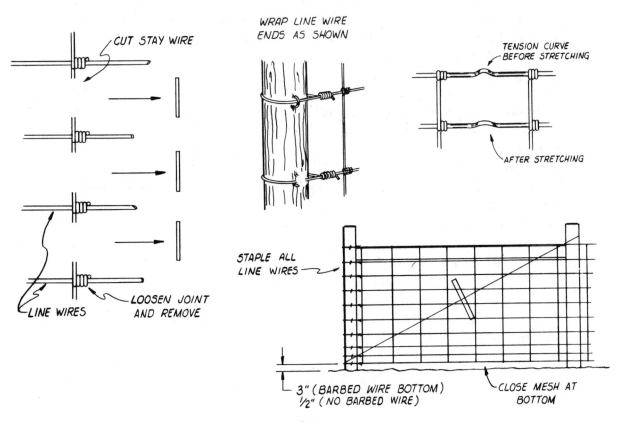

CUT STAY WIRE

WRAP LINE WIRE
ENDS AS SHOWN

TENSION CURVE
BEFORE STRETCHING

AFTER STRETCHING

LINE WIRES

LOOSEN JOINT
AND REMOVE

STAPLE ALL
LINE WIRES

3" (BARBED WIRE BOTTOM)
½" (NO BARBED WIRE)

CLOSE MESH AT
BOTTOM

stretchers to the dummy post. If you have two, one goes at the top and one at the bottom of the fence.

7. Fasten the clamp bar to the fence, which should have the last spacer wire removed. When you connect the stretchers, they should be higher on the dummy post so the pull is exerted up, and the fence will not drag.

8. Stretch slowly, working first the top and then the bottom stretcher. As you stretch, a helper should shake the wire from time to time to free it from snags. Stretch until the tension curves begin to flatten.

9. Cut loose the middle line wire from the stretcher bar, and wrap and staple it to the end post. Do the same with every other wire, working toward top and bottom, until all are fastened and the stretcher is free.

10. Go back and attach line wires to the other posts, starting from the post farthest from the stretcher.

11. Add barbwire if needed. On top, one strand should go 2 inches above the woven wire. Additional strands (on, perhaps, a 32-inch or 26-inch fence) can be spaced at 6 inches and then 8 inches.

GROUNDING THE FENCE

If your livestock are near a wire fence that is struck by lightning, they can be killed instantly. Lethal charges of electricity can carry for two miles along a wire fence. Metal poles serve as grounds, but if you use wood or cement posts, you should add a ground rod.

A ground rod simply is an 8- to 10-foot length of 1-inch or 1½-inch pipe. Drive it into the ground at a low spot on your fence line, because that is where it is most likely to remain in contact with moist soil. It should be next to a post, within 150 feet of both ends of the fence, or within 150 feet of the end and within 300 feet of the next ground rod. Drive the pipe in on the same side of the post as the fence is attached. Allow it to extend 4 to 6 inches above the post. Use 10d nails

to fasten the pipe to the post with pipe clamps.

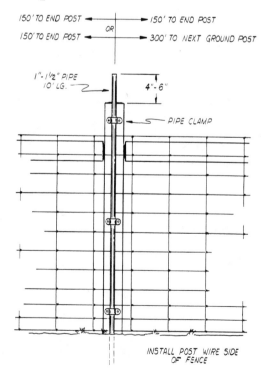

INSTALL POST WIRE SIDE OF FENCE

ELECTRIC FENCES

Electric fences are an effective means of controlling pasture animals. They call for special planning and equipment, and when in use, must be treated with caution. If children have free roam of your homestead, they must be taught what an electric fence is and why it is very dangerous to them. Most states also require that electric fences along a road or other public area be marked with large, legible signs stating that the fence is electrified.

You can use either smooth wire ($12\frac{1}{2}$ to 18 gauge) or barbwire. You also will need line post and strain-type insulators. The line post insulators attach your wire to line posts, and the strain insulators are used on end and corner posts. You can use wire clips or 12-gauge galvanized wire to fasten the fence wire to the insulators, or you can simply wrap the wire around them.

Since electric fences are considered to be temporary structures, your posts need not be as weighty as those used on permanent fences.

The posts need be no more than 1 x 2 stakes, pointed at one end. They can be 1-inch pipe, or they can be any of the patented electric fence posts, which come with an insulator loop attached. They need stand no taller than about 40 inches and can be set 10 to 14 inches deep in average soil, deeper if the soil is dry.

Spacing of posts is arbitrary and can range from 15 to 50 feet apart. The height of your wire should be two-thirds the height of the animals that are to be kept. For horses and cattle, they should be 30 to 36 inches high; for large hogs, 14 to 16 inches; for pigs, 6 to 8 inches.

Although an electric fence does not have to withstand much pressure, your fence will work better if your end posts are braced. In many cases, you may be able to use a permanent fence post as an end post. If not, construct a post with diagonal braces.

CONSTRUCTION

1. Fasten line post insulators at the height you have chosen. Insulator fasteners look like duplex head nails, or for metal posts, they have a hook on one end, and a wing nut on the other. Fasten the strain insulator with a loop of wire.

2. Fasten your wire to a strain insulator by wrapping it securely around itself. Then, work your way along the line posts. The wire can be pulled taut by hand.

3. The next step is to mount the fence controller, or charger. Chargers are

available to operate from batteries or 120-volt household current, or both. Your homestead setup will determine which you choose. If your fence is not near an electric outlet, you will have to use batteries, which can be expected to last from 1½ to three months. If your battery (either 6 or 12 volt, wet or dry cell) is protected from the weather, it will last longer.

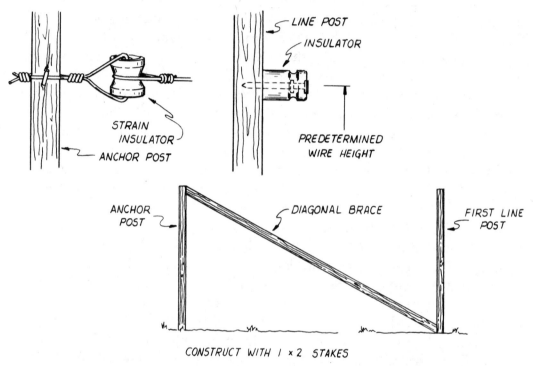

LINE POST

INSULATOR

STRAIN INSULATOR

ANCHOR POST

PREDETERMINED WIRE HEIGHT

ANCHOR POST

DIAGONAL BRACE

FIRST LINE POST

CONSTRUCT WITH 1 × 2 STAKES

MAKING THE MOST OF ELECTRIC FENCES

Things to look for in good chargers are a signal light to show when the fence is short-circuited; a switch to step up power as needed in dry spells; and good mounting fixtures. The safest type of chargers have mechanical devices so that the current actually is on only $\frac{1}{10}$ to $\frac{3}{10}$ of every second. Neither the Underwriters Laboratories Inc. nor the Industrial Commission of Wisconsin approves the type charger which has the current on continuously.

To be safe, the controller you use should have either UL or Industrial Commission of Wisconsin approval. Do not attempt to fashion your own controller. Every year, the National Safety Council reports cases of people killed by fences with homemade chargers.

Once you have chosen a place to

locate your charger, drive an 8-foot ground rod into the soil, leaving about 6 inches exposed. Connect it to the charger's ground terminal, using 6-gauge copper wire. Use the same type to attach the other charger terminal to the fence wire.

To protect your electric fence from lightning, you must use a lightning arrestor, which grounds off lethal charges from a lightning bolt, yet does not interrupt the fence's normal circuit. Attach the arrestor to a fence post with wood screws. The arrestor has two lead wires, both of which go to your fence wire. If you have two fence strands, connect one wire to each. Attach the middle (usually the white) wire to an 8-foot-long ground rod, driven in with about 6 inches exposed. You can use 6-gauge wire to reach the pipe, and a pipe clamp can be used to connect the wire to the ground rod.

You will have to carefully maintain your fence. Keep it free of weeds and windblown debris which can short-circuit the fence.

Livestock must be trained to re-

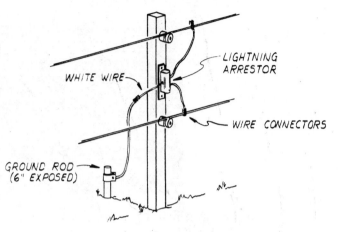

spect an electric fence. For hogs, horses, and cattle, place feed on the outside of the fence. Do not drive them to it, but let them try to reach it on their own.

Electric fencing is not usually recommended for sheep and goats because they will get a shock only if they touch the wire with their nose or ears. However, you can train them by hanging a bright object or a cob of corn on the fence, so they will try to touch the fence itself. However, sheep and goats tend to forget this lesson, and if they do not happen to touch the fence with their nose next time, they probably can walk right through it.

SPLIT RAIL FENCE

A split rail fence is useful for cattle and horse pasture and also is popular as a decorative fence. Start with 4- to 6-inch diameter posts that have been treated with preservative. Plan to

plant them about $2\frac{1}{2}$ feet deep, and figure on 6 inches above the top rail.

You can use either two or three rails. The rails can be fitted dado joints for lighter posts, or they can be

515

tapered and fitted into oval holes cut into heavier posts. Mark the posts so the rails will be evenly spaced, and using a drill and wood chisel, drill all the way through the post, shaping the hole to measure 4 or 5 inches long and 3 to 4 inches wide. On an end post, cut only halfway through. On a corner post, cut two holes at a 90-degree angle.

Prepare your rails for the dado joint, or taper about 10 inches on the ends of the rail to a thickness of 1½ to 2 inches.

Install and plumb your posts, spaced at intervals equal to the length of the rails. Place the rails in the slots, and using 16d nails, fasten the rails by driving the nails through the side of the post.

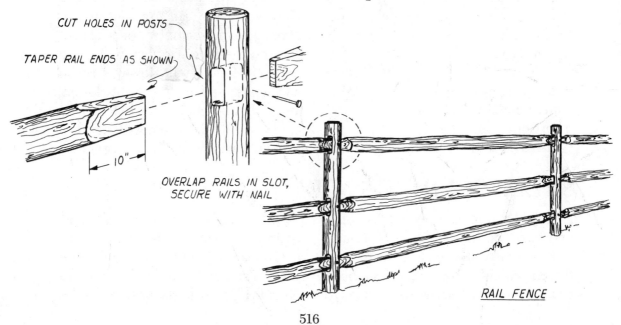

CUT HOLES IN POSTS

TAPER RAIL ENDS AS SHOWN

10"

OVERLAP RAILS IN SLOT,
SECURE WITH NAIL

RAIL FENCE

ZIGZAG RAIL FENCE

A zigzag rail fence, also known as a Virginia rail fence, was popular with East Coast settlers who had plenty of timber. It is used as a decorative fence these days, and the hardest part of building one is laying it out.

Mark your actual boundary line, and using chalk, or stakes and string, mark a parallel line one foot on the inside. To determine how wide your fence will be, take the length of your rails, say 10 feet; subtract 2 feet to allow for one foot of overhang on each end; divide this by 2, giving you 4. Therefore the width will be 4 feet, so mark a second parallel line 4 feet from your stake line.

Mark your first rail one foot from each end, and place it on a diagonal so the marks are on each stake line. Repeat this with the second rail, positioning it so one end overlaps with an end of the first rail. Repeat this sequence for the length of the fence.

Next, drive a 5-foot stake in the outside **V** formed at each overlap, to provide a guide for stacking the rails. Lay the next layer of rails on top of the bottom rails, and so on. Five or six layers of 4- or 5-inch-diameter rails will make a sturdy, 5-foot-tall fence. Note that you have used no hardware and have erected no posts.

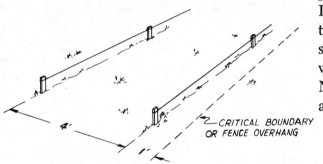

CRITICAL BOUNDARY OR FENCE OVERHANG

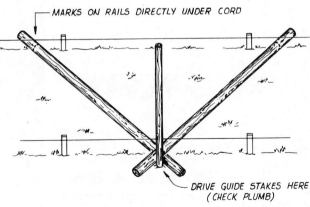

MARKS ON RAILS DIRECTLY UNDER CORD

DRIVE GUIDE STAKES HERE (CHECK PLUMB)

BARNYARDS

A sturdy board fence, built to withstand heavy use around farm buildings, is easy to build, and does not require any sophisticated carpentry skills. Basically the same fence can be used around a pasture, but because the cost of lumber is high, most homesteaders place board fences around only their smaller confinement areas. Nonetheless, they are the safest and most serviceable fence for confining almost any type of livestock.

These fences are basically 1- or 2-inch boards nailed end-to-end on sturdy posts. The most common post sizes are 4 x 4, 4 x 6, and 6 x 6. They should be 8 feet long, sunk 2 to 3 feet deep, and planted in concrete at intervals of 8 feet. *Note:* The space between your end post and the next post should be less than 8 feet to allow your boards to reach across the face of the end post and then half-way across the second post. Subtract half the width of a post from 8 feet to get this measurement, taken from post center to post center.

Build the fence in pairs of 8-foot panels, using four horizontal 1 x 6 boards per panel. Half should be 16 feet long and half 8 feet long. This will allow half the joints to go on every other post and will make a stronger fence. (Four boards means your fence will be four boards high. Actually, you will use two 16-foot and four 8-foot lengths per pair of 8-foot panels.)

Start with a 16-foot length at the

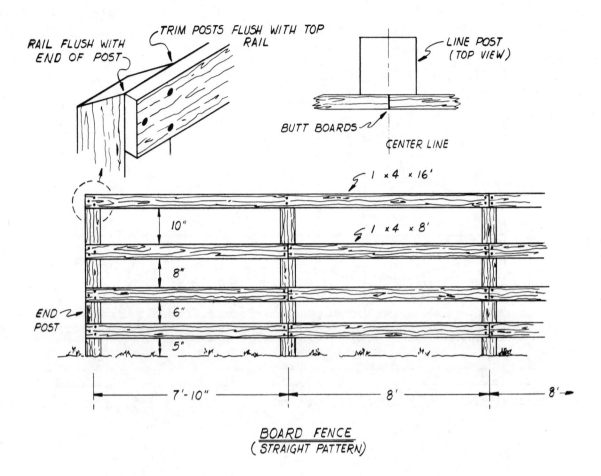

RAIL FLUSH WITH
END OF POST

TRIM POSTS FLUSH WITH TOP
RAIL

LINE POST
(TOP VIEW)

BUTT BOARDS

CENTER LINE

1 × 4 × 16'

1 × 4 × 8'

10"

8"

END
POST

6"

5"

7'-10"

8'

8'

BOARD FENCE
(STRAIGHT PATTERN)

top. Fasten the 1-inch board to each post with two or three galvanized 10d nails. Leave a space of 10 inches to your next horizontal board, which will be two 8-foot lengths butted end-to-end on the second post. *Note:* Blunt your nails a bit and position them so they are not along the same grain to avoid splitting.

The space to the third horizontal board should be 8 inches; then 6 inches to the fourth; and the space from that to the ground should be about 5 inches. The reason for the diminishing spacing is that the closer to the ground the animal is, the smaller the space through which it can squeeze.

Another good-looking barnyard fence uses a diamond or **X** pattern. Start with the same board across the top, but drop down 21 inches to the next board. The third horizontal board will be 8 inches below that,

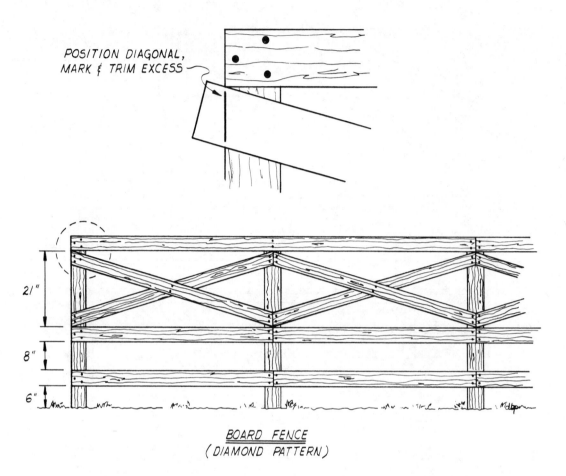

POSITION DIAGONAL, MARK & TRIM EXCESS

21"

8"

6"

BOARD FENCE
(DIAMOND PATTERN)

leaving a 6-inch gap to the ground. To form the diamond pattern, nail a 1 x 4 by 10-foot board diagonally from below the top board to above the second board on the next post. Form an **X** by nailing an identical board on the opposite slope. Trim off the triangle of overhang you will have on each end.

All your lumber should be treated against rot. Since you may have to trim some boards as you work, you can touch up the newly cut ends with preservative as you work.

In order to keep small pigs from squeezing between the bottom board and the ground, you can staple a mediumweight wire mesh 18 to 24 inches high, on the inside of your boards. Bury the wire several inches deep in a trench to keep dogs or coyotes from getting in.

WELDED FENCES

An alternative to a board fence in the barnyard is the welded panel fence. Welded panels come in 16-foot-long pieces. For hogs, they are about 34 inches high, and for cattle or horses, about 52 inches high. Welded panels are rigid and self-supporting. They usually are constructed of ¼-inch steel wire, welded to form rectangles measuring roughly 4 inches by 8 inches.

Posts for this type of fence should be no less than 5-inch square and should be 8 feet long. They should be set 2 to 3 feet in concrete.

When you lay out your fence, plan the sides to run in multiples of 16, because the panels are difficult to trim. For the same reason, you must be exact in measuring the placement of your posts.

At corners, you will have to put one panel on the inside, and one on the outside of the post, because the panels cannot be crossed. On a hill, the panels can be stepped down from post to post. Installing welded wire panels is easy if your posts are positioned properly.

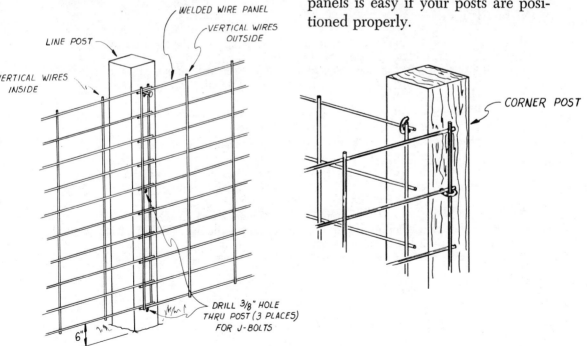

LINE POST

WELDED WIRE PANEL

VERTICAL WIRES OUTSIDE

VERTICAL WIRES INSIDE

DRILL ³⁄₈" HOLE THRU POST (3 PLACES) FOR J-BOLTS

6"

CORNER POST

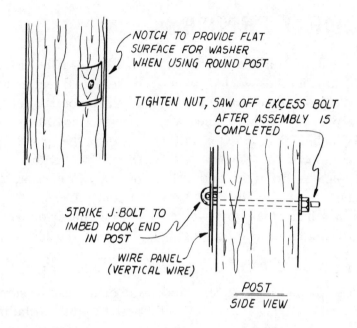

NOTCH TO PROVIDE FLAT
SURFACE FOR WASHER
WHEN USING ROUND POST

TIGHTEN NUT, SAW OFF EXCESS BOLT
AFTER ASSEMBLY IS
COMPLETED

STRIKE J-BOLT TO
IMBED HOOK END
IN POST

WIRE PANEL
(VERTICAL WIRE)

POST
SIDE VIEW

CONSTRUCTION

1. Drive a 10d nail about halfway into the posts to support the top wire in
    the panel, leaving a space of about 6 inches to the ground. Temporarily
    hang the first panel on the first two posts so the vertical wires are on the
    inside. The next panel should be hung so the horizontal wires are on
    the inside, and so on.

2. Drill ⅜-inch holes through the post at the top, center, and bottom of the
    panel. These will accommodate the J-bolt fasteners.

3. Chisel an indentation on the outside of the post to accommodate the
    flat washer which goes on the J-bolt shank.

4. Place the J-bolt through the hole. On each post, every other bolt should
    be on horizontal wires, the others on verticals. Each bolt holds the end
    of two panels, except at the ends of the fence line.

5. Rap the J-bolt with a hammer, imbedding the hook end into the wood.
    Place the flat washer on the other end and tighten the nut. Cut off the
    bolt end, using a chisel or hacksaw.

GATES

Almost any fence you build will need a gate or other passageway. Gates in fences around a garden or yard need only be big enough to admit people. If there is any need to get in with a garden cart or mower, 4 feet is a good minimum width. On the farm, machinery seems to be getting bigger every year. In most cases, a 12-foot-wide gate is big enough, but if you have large machinery or need room to make a turn along the fence line, 14 to 16 feet is a more prudent width.

Most of the gates described here are built in essentially the same way, and most swing on hinges. The key to their durability is their construction. There also are passageways called cattle guards, which consist of a trench at an open space in the fence line, covered with pipes or narrow boards: people and machines can cross, but most livestock will not trust the footing. Floodgates are installed where the fence line crosses a stream. They permit water and debris to pass, but animals are stopped. Another passageway is the stile, a ladder or stepladder arrangement, which allows people to cross a fence line without necessitating a break in the fence.

SETTING THE POSTS

Gates get the most wear and tear of any part of the fence. Since they are opened, closed, slammed, and swung on by children, they must be sturdily built, or they soon will sag and will be useless.

No matter what kind of hinged gate you build, start by installing strong posts on either side. One method to do this is to brace both posts with the brace and cable assemblies described in the chapter on fences.

Another way is with a concrete threshold. This approach will necessitate construction of the gate before the fence and the posts are in place (with other approaches, it is possible, and even desirable, to install the posts and the fence, then construct a gate to fit).

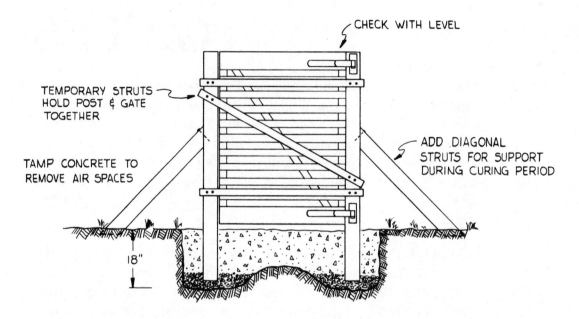

CHECK WITH LEVEL

TEMPORARY STRUTS
HOLD POST & GATE
TOGETHER

TAMP CONCRETE TO
REMOVE AIR SPACES

ADD DIAGONAL
STRUTS FOR SUPPORT
DURING CURING PERIOD

18"

CONSTRUCTION

1. Dig a 12-inch-wide trench the width of the gate and posts. The trench should be at least 18 inches deep at the outer extremities, but need only be a foot deep in the center.

2. Attach the hinge-post to the gate with hinges. Using scraps of wood, tack the latch-post and gate together as close as they must be for the gate to function properly, but do not install the latch. Remember that at least 18 inches of post should be in the ground.

3. Erect the gate and posts in position above the trench and secure it there with bracing constructed of scrap materials.

4. Pour a few inches of gravel or crushed stone in the bottom of the trench, then fill with concrete. Trowel the threshold smooth.

5. When the concrete has cured, remove the bracing and install the fence and the gate latch.

VARIATION

A third way to install strong gate posts is with a concrete strain plug.

CONSTRUCTION

1. Dig your post holes 24 to 36 inches deep and about 16 inches square.

2. Use a 4-inch-square post, about 8 feet long. At the bottom, nail two

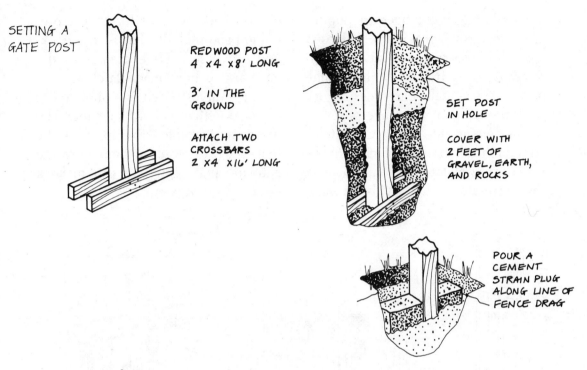

SETTING A GATE POST

REDWOOD POST
4 x4 x8' LONG

3' IN THE
GROUND

ATTACH TWO
CROSSBARS
2 x4 x16' LONG

SET POST
IN HOLE

COVER WITH
2 FEET OF
GRAVEL, EARTH,
AND ROCKS

POUR A
CEMENT
STRAIN PLUG
ALONG LINE OF
FENCE DRAG

crossbars on opposite sides. Use 16-inch (or whatever width your hole is) pieces of 2 x 4s fastened with galvanized 10d nails.

3. Fill the hole with dirt and gravel and tamp it down tightly, to within about 12 inches of the surface.

4. Using about a cubic foot of concrete, form a horizontal block on opposite sides of the post, along the drag line of the gate (parallel with the fence line). Locating the concrete on either side of the post provides the needed strength, while allowing drainage away from the concrete and the post.

HINGES AND LATCHES

You will need to know a bit about hinges. Many hinges, such as strap or **T** hinges, can be mounted with either side up. Others, such as lag-bolt hinges, loose-pin hinges, and all those which are held together by gravity and the gate's own weight, must be specified to be either left- or right-hand hinges. To determine which you need, stand so the gate will swing away from you. If it swings to the right, it takes a right-hand hinge, and vice versa.

For most gates, strap or **T** hinges

are used. Lag-bolt hinges are popular on wide farm fences. The halves of lag-bolt hinges separate, into what are referred to as the male and female parts. The female part goes on the gate, the male on the fence post.

There is a wide variety of latches manufactured for gates, but there also is a variety of latches you can make for your gates. These will—in many cases—work even better than store-bought sliding bolts, hasps, and hook-and-eye types. Here are some suggestions for homemade latches.

The simplest latch is a short piece of wood with a nail in its center. The wood strip rotates to lap onto the fence post to close, or back onto the gate to open. But you can make a more refined version.

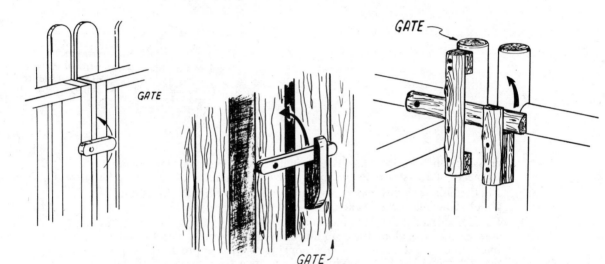

CONSTRUCTION

1. A lever-type latch is made by fastening a 1-inch-wide strip about 12 inches long about 8 inches in from the edge of the gate, using a heavy nail or bolt for a pivot.

2. Holding the latch bar horizontal, position the retainer on the fence post to accommodate it. You can make the retainer by cutting a notch into the end of a 2 x 4 or by nailing smaller blocks together.

3. Make a guide for the latch near the edge of the gate by nailing small blocks above and below the latch, far enough apart to allow the latch to swing up and out of the retainer. Bridge these two blocks with another 1-inch strip.

4. Add a short dowel or bolt to the latch bar as a handle.

VARIATION

For a heavier, farm gate version of this latch, use saw mill waste slabs or 2-inch boards instead of the 1-inch strips.

A sliding latch is made with essentially the same pieces, but the latch bar is not fastened directly to the gate. Instead, it should be held horizontal by two of the bridge-type guides on the gate, and should have a third guide on the fence post. These guides should be fairly close fitting since all the latch has to do is slide. Add a perpendicular bolt or dowel to the latch bar as a handle.

Another possibility is to cut a semicircle from ⅜-inch or ½-inch exterior plywood and attach a 1-inch strip perpendicular to the diameter, extending 2 or 3 inches past the edge of the arc. Align the diameter with the edge of the gate and fasten with a bolt or nail pivot. (This is the unlatched position.) Using drill and wood chisel, cut a mortise into the fence post to accommodate the corner of the semicircle. Rotate the semicircle a quarter-turn to the latched position.

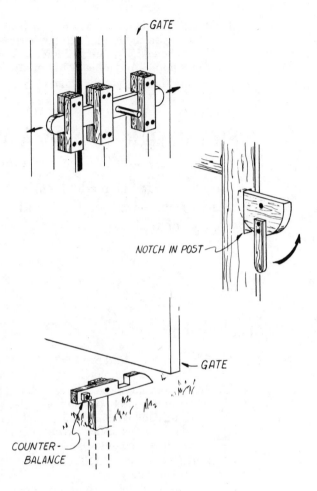

GATE

NOTCH IN POST

GATE

COUNTER-BALANCE

There also are latches which keep gates open, and they are especially useful when you have your hands full.

CONSTRUCTION

1. Swing your gate wide open, and mark the spot on the ground where you want it to be held.
2. Drive a 1-inch stake, about 12 inches long, into the ground, leaving enough protruding to almost touch the bottom of the gate.

3. Make the catch from a 6- to 8-inch similar piece of wood, but with a notch wide enough to hold the bottom of the gate cut about 2 inches from one end. Square the notch off, but taper that end of the wood to a blunt point. Add a heavy nut or other counterweight to the other end.

4. Mount the catch to the stake with a bolt, with the pointed end toward the gate.

ANOTHER VARIATION

A similar gadget is made from a scrap of furring, a 1 x 3 or 1 x 1, and a short piece of 1 x 1.

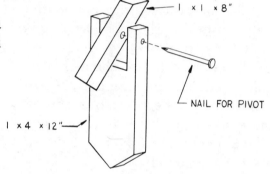

1 x 1 x 8"

NAIL FOR PIVOT

1 x 4 x 12"

CONSTRUCTION

1. The furring should be about 12 inches long. Cut a point on one end, and a 1-inch by 2-inch notch into the opposite end, as shown.
2. Bevel one end of the 1 x 1, which should be about 8 inches long, then afix it in the notch, beveled edge up, so that it will pivot freely. (In the 1 x 1, drill an oversized hole 3 inches from the beveled end, and under-sized pilot holes in the furring—to prevent splitting—and drive an 8d nail through the holes.)
3. Drive the device into the ground just short of the farthest travel of the gate. The gate will pass over the bevel, pivoting the stop to a horizontal position. But once free of the gate, the stop will drop back to its normal position and prevent the gate from completing its return swing. Flip up the lower edge with your toe to free the gate and close it.

GARDEN GATES

Most garden gates are styled to go with the rest of the fence. Therefore, the basic wire or boards used for the rest of the fence pretty much define how you will build the gate. If you are working with wood, you can use 1- or 2-inch boards for the four sides and diagonal brace. The frame will be strongest if you first bolt the corners together using 2- or 2½-inch carriage bolts. You also can nail the frame together using galvanized 10d nails, with the ends clinched over.

Another construction tip that will apply to many kinds of gates: Usually, your square or rectangular gate will be much sturdier if you add a diagonal brace to its frame, before you install boards, pickets, or wire. The lower end of the diagonal always goes on the hinge side of the gate. If you reverse it, the gate soon will sag.

Lay out and mark the ends of your diagonal brace for cutting to fit the horizontal top and bottom pieces. Fasten with nails or bolts just inside the corner joints.

A slightly different framing method is better suited to thicker boards (2 x 4 or 2-inch stock) and will allow you to build a thicker gate.

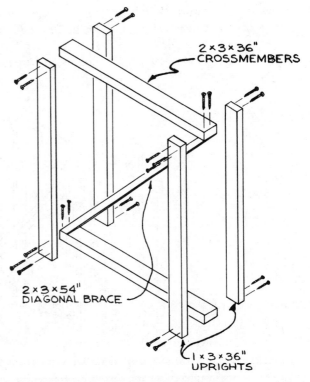

FRAMING A 3' WIDE GATE

CONSTRUCTION

1. Cut a top and a bottom crossmember from 2 x 3 stock to the width of the finished gate you want. Lay them out so they are the proper distance from each other, then measure and cut a diagonal brace from 2 x 3 stock to fit as shown.

MATERIALS (for framing a 3-foot-wide gate)

Wood

1 pc. 2 x 3 x 12′	or	**Crossmembers:** 2 pcs. 2 x 3 x 36″
		Diagonal brace: 1 pc. 2 x 3 x 54″
1 pc. 1 x 3 x 12′	or	**Uprights:** 4 pcs. 1 x 3 x 36″

Hardware

4–2½″ #10 screws
20–1½″ #10 screws

---

2. Using 2½-inch #10 screws, assemble the three pieces to form an **N**.
3. Cut four 1 x 3 uprights to the height of the gate.
4. Using 1½-inch #10 screws, fasten the uprights to the gate, as shown.
5. Fill in with pickets, boards, or wire mesh, and hang using hinges of your choice.

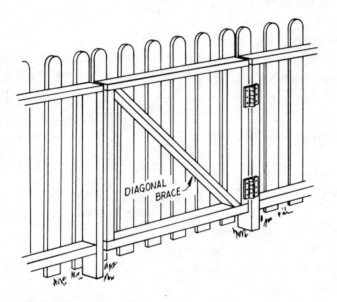

DIAGONAL BRACE

MATERIALS (for a 3-foot-wide gate)

Wood

1 pc. 2 x 3 x 16′	or	**Rails:** 2 pcs. 2 x 3 x 36″
		Uprights: 2 pcs. 2 x 3 x 33″
		Diagonal brace: 1 pc. 2 x 3 x 51″
2 pcs. 1 x 3 x 14′	or	**Pickets:** 8 pcs. 1 x 3 x 42″

Hardware

12–3″ #10 screws
Galvanized 8d nails
2–4″ butt hinges w/ screws

A ROLLING GATE

A special garden gate that wa described in OGF back in 1968 by Vollie Tripp had wheels. This design is especially well suited for wide gates across driveways, with widths in the 15-foot and up range.

You can use any wheel, ranging in diameter from 4 to 8 inches. There are two ways to mount the wheels, and which you use depends on whether your gate is to slide or swing. For a sliding gate however, the posts on either side of the gate opening will have to be offset about 6 inches. Lay a wooden track on the ground, parallel and inside one side of the fence. It will have to be equal to the width of the gate. The track can be built out of wood, or you could sink a rectangular rain gutter halfway into the ground. Mount two wheels, one on each end of the gate. You can use long bolts for axles, inserted through opposing boards on each end, as shown.

For a swinging gate, you will mount hinges on one end. On the other end, mount the wheel in the opposite direction, that is, with the axle-bolt running parallel to the fence line. Extend opposing boards a few inches below the end piece of the gate and mount the hinges on the fence post at the appropriate height.

Open the gate to trace the wheel's path, and lay out your arc-shaped track. You can build it with boards or bricks. You probably can get away with no track if your gate opens onto

531

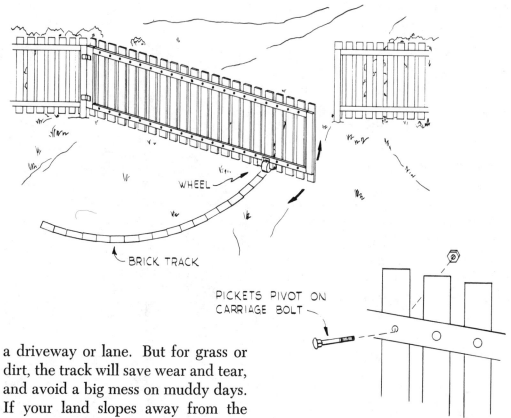

WHEEL

BRICK TRACK

PICKETS PIVOT ON
CARRIAGE BOLT

a driveway or lane. But for grass or dirt, the track will save wear and tear, and avoid a big mess on muddy days. If your land slopes away from the fence, fasten vertical pickets with $\frac{1}{4}$-inch carriage bolts, and fasten the strap hinges to the fence post with only one bolt or screw in each. This will result in a flexible gate, which will sag a bit as the gate swings down the sloping track.

FARM GATES

For pasture and livestock fences, you can construct gates from boards or pipe. There also are temporary gates, and an inexpensive gate that is constructed of split saplings, known as an English hurdle.

THE METAL GATE

A wire pasture fence is the best place to install a pipe fence. You can use $\frac{3}{4}$- or 1-inch pipe. It should be welded together, but a simple rectangular gate also can be formed by using regular pipe elbows at the corners. You also can use **T** fittings to install vertical braces. If you can weld, you can add two features. For instance, you can weld $\frac{1}{4}$-inch by 1-inch flat steel in place as a diagonal brace. You also can weld three pieces of pipe to the outside of one end vertical piece. These will serve as the female part of a lag-bolt hinge.

After this basic frame is finished, lay out and cut a section of woven

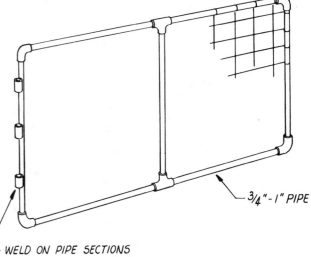

3/4"-1" PIPE

WELD ON PIPE SECTIONS
IF USING LAG BOLT HINGE

INSTALL TURNBUCKLE
& CABLE

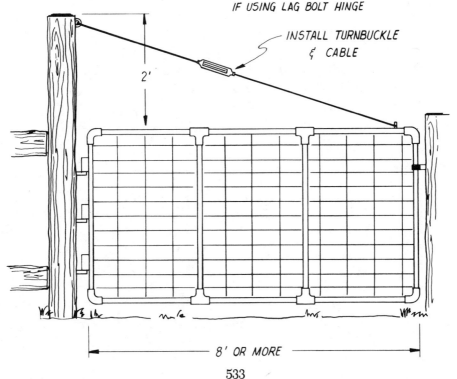

2'

8' OR MORE

533

wire big enough to fasten all strands to the pipes.

If your gate is more than 8 feet wide, it will need some extra bracing. One of the best ways is to install a post on the hinge side that is about 2 feet taller than the gate and the rest of the fence. Run a cable from the top of the post to the far top corner of the gate. Fasten it with a turnbuckle so you can tighten the cable to eliminate any sag.

MATERIALS

Hardware

> 3 pcs. 48" x ¾" galvanized pipe (uprights)
> 4 pcs. 36" x ¾" galvanized pipe (horizontal bars)
> 4 pcs. ¾" 90-degree elbows
> 2 pcs. ¾" tees
> 3 pcs. 2" x ¾" galvanized pipe
> 1 pc. 48" x 72" woven wire fencing

THE WOODEN GATE

Wooden farm gates usually are made from 1 x 6 boards, but they can be of any width board you desire. They can be assembled to suit your taste, with diagonal brace pieces forming an **X** pattern or with parallel horizontal pieces spanning as many as four uprights.

A very good-looking gate can be built using 5-inch-wide boards cut from 1-inch stock. Use five cross boards and four uprights, fastened to-

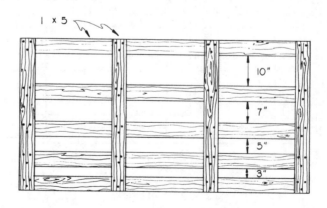

gether with 8d nails, clinched over. Spacing of the crossbars is important. We'd suggest 3 inches between the bottom and second board; 4 or 5 inches between the second and third; 7 inches between the third and fourth; and 10 inches to the top board.

What is most interesting about this gate is that it has no hinges, but swings instead on a slide bar pivot.

Next to the anchor post (where you would have mounted the hinges) set another post. It should be the same size and height as your other fence posts, but position it about 6 inches to the inside of the fence line and 6 inches inside of the gate opening. Next, set your gate in place, on a stone or other object to raise it to the height you want it mounted. The gate now should be in a closed position. Measure on the posts for a slide bar that will fit between the top crosspieces of the gate. Nail the slide bar

to the posts. Remove the rock, and the gate is supported on the slide bar. To open the gate, slide it back about a foot, and swing it open, using the slide bar as a fulcrum.

MATERIALS

Wood

    5 pcs. 1 x 6 x 8' (crossbars)

    2 pcs. 1 x 6 x 10'   or   **Uprights:** 4 pcs. 1 x 6 x 52½"

Hardware

    Galvanized 8d nails

BOARD GATE

Here is how to make a gate of very durable construction for a board pasture or stockyard fence. The key is a tall post on the end of the fence line to which the gate hinges are to be attached. A wire brace, with a turnbuckle for adjusting the tension, is strung from the top of this post to the far, upper corner of the gate to prevent sagging.

CONSTRUCTION

1. Use 1 x 6 lumber for this gate, or whatever size you have used for the rest of the fence. Lay out the measurements and cut the pieces; use 10d nails to temporarily hold the gate together. You will use, in this case, three 12-foot lengths and six 4-foot lengths to form a rectangular frame. Note that you double up the 4-foot vertical pieces (the uprights) so the horizontal boards (the rails) are sandwiched at the joints. Add four 7-foot lengths for diagonal bracing, trimming the ends to fit.

2. Drill holes for two $\frac{3}{8}$-inch carriage bolts at each joint. You will use $2\frac{3}{4}$-inch bolts where there are only two thicknesses of wood, $3\frac{1}{2}$-inch bolts where there are three thicknesses. Install the bolts and, after squaring the gate carefully, tighten them securely.

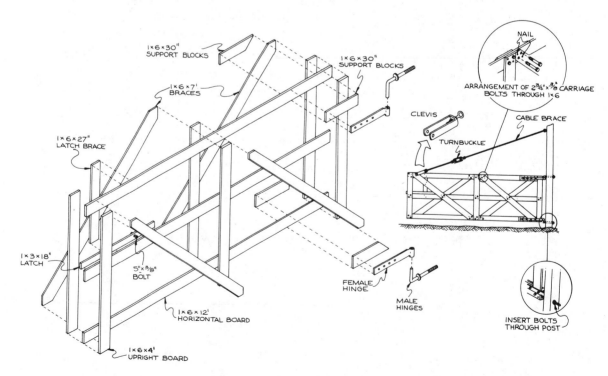

3. Mark the four 30-inch 1 x 6 hinge support blocks and cut them as necessary to fit around the diagonals. Nail the blocks on using 10d nails.

4. Cut an 18-inch-long piece of 1 x 3 for the latch. Slide it between the uprights on the end opposite the hinges. Mark a 27-inch piece of 1 x 6 for the vertical latch brace and nail it to the top horizontal piece and one of the diagonals. Drill a $\frac{3}{8}$-inch hole in the latch and install a 5-inch by $\frac{3}{8}$-inch bolt for a handle.

5. Drill four holes, evenly spaced and centered, at the end of the top and bottom horizontals to hold the female hinge halves. Bolt the hinge halves into place.

6. Measure from the upper edge of the top hinge to the lower edge of the bottom hinge. Mark the long end fence post for the male hinges so the gate will hang even with the rest of the fence. Then, drill holes all the way through the post for the male hinge halves.

MATERIALS

Wood

6 pcs. 1 x 6 x 12′	or	**Rails:** 3 pcs. 1 x 6 x 12′
		Uprights: 6 pcs. 1 x 6 x 4′
		Diagonal brace: 1 pc. 1 x 6 x 7′
		Hinge block: 1 pc. 1 x 6 x 30″
		Latch brace: 1 pc. 1 x 6 x 27″
3 pcs. 1 x 6 x 10′	or	**Diagonal braces:** 3 pcs. 1 x 6 x 7′
		Hinge blocks: 3 pcs. 1 x 6 x 30″
1 pc. 1 x 3 x 2′	or	**Latch:** 1 pc. 1 x 3 x 18″

Hardware

10d nails
16–2$\frac{3}{4}$″ x $\frac{3}{8}$″ carriage bolts w/ nuts and washers
23–3$\frac{1}{2}$″ x $\frac{3}{8}$″ carriage bolts w/ nuts and washers
1–5″ x $\frac{3}{8}$″ bolt w/ nut and 2 washers
2–2″ x $\frac{1}{4}$″ female hinge straps w/ bolts, nuts, and washers
2–15″ x $\frac{5}{8}$″ male hinge bolts w/ nuts and washers
1–12″ x $\frac{5}{8}$″ eyebolt w/ nut and washer
1 clevis
1–3$\frac{1}{2}$″ x $\frac{3}{8}$″ machine bolt w/ nut and washer
15′ x $\frac{3}{8}$″ steel cable
1 turnbuckle

7. Hold the gate in position and engage the hinge halves. You should reverse the top male half to prevent the gate from being lifted off the hinges. Slide the male hinge halves through the holes in the post, add washers and nuts, and tighten.

8. To install the cable brace, drill a ⅝-inch hole through the tall end post 8 feet from the ground and install the 12-inch by ⅝-inch eyebolt. Attach the clevis to the far top corner of the gate using a 3½-inch by ⅜-inch machine bolt.

9. Attach the 15-foot length of ⅜-inch cable to the gate post eyebolt. About two-thirds the way down its length, cut the cable and splice in the turnbuckle. Attach the shorter piece to the clevis and use the turnbuckle to adjust the tension.

THE ENGLISH HURDLE

English hurdles are good for fence openings in cattle and sheep pastures. The hurdle is a good choice for the homesteader who has saplings ranging in diameter from 3 to 5 inches. The hurdle shown is 6 feet wide and about 4½ feet tall.

Skin the bark off the saplings to forestall rotting. Use the heavier saplings for the uprights. Drill or chisel mortise holes to receive the crossbars, putting the lower crossbars closer together than the top two.

Next, taper the ends of the cross-

bars, using an axe or drawknife. Tap the crossbars into one upright, then the other. Drive a nail through each tenon to make a strong joint. Next, nail two diagonal braces from the ends of the bottom crossbar, meeting at a point above the top crossbar. Complete the hurdle by adding a vertical brace between the diagonals.

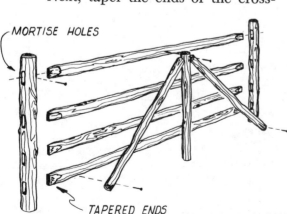

MORTISE HOLES

TAPERED ENDS

THE WIRE GATE

A good gate for a pasture ringed by barbwire is a simple wire gate. Choose the two fence posts between which you will place your gate. Put

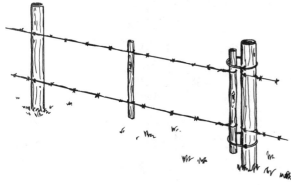

up the barbed wire fencing, treating the posts on either side of the gap as terminal posts. But leave strands on one post long enough to reach across the gap. Fasten these strands to a light pole, like a broomstick. On the opposite post attach two loops of wire, one below the bottom strand near the ground and the other near the top. Stretch the gate across and place the pole first in the bottom loop then the top. You also can staple a light piece of wood in the middle to keep the strands spread when you open the gate.

ELECTRIC FENCE GATES

To make a gate in an electric fence, you will need both the line-type insulator and a ceramic gate handle sold in hardware catalogs or building supply stores. Your gate will be electrified until you unlatch it to pass through. Do not fail to turn off the power to the fence before doing this job.

If your electric fence crosses a ditch or a drainage swale, you can build another type of "gate" to keep stock from walking under. Simply hang an extra loop of wire in slack fashion to block passage.

CONSTRUCTION

1. Attach a line insulator to one end post.
2. Use about 24-inch length of your regular line wire, or 9-gauge wire to splice from an inch or two on the hot side of your last line insulator. Clip or wrap it around the line insulator you just installed, leaving 12 inches standing free.
3. Form a 6-inch loop in the end.

4. Attach another piece of line wire, about the same length as the distance between your two open posts, by means of a screen door spring. Pull the spring so it will hold the wire fairly tight, and cut it at the right length. Form a hook in the end.

5. Run a 6-inch loop of wire around the spring, which will keep it from stretching too far.

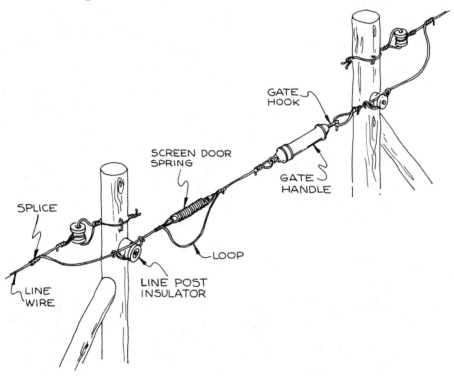

GATE HOOK

SCREEN DOOR SPRING

GATE HANDLE

SPLICE

LOOP

LINE WIRE

LINE POST INSULATOR

FLOODGATES

A structure across a stream to control livestock must be constructed to allow water and floating debris to pass through. If your water gate is not "self-cleaning," debris will collect, can cause damage, and can even cause upstream flooding. Floodgates suspended from above will swing open as the water level and pressure increase. These gates must be constructed of preservative-treated lumber, and they will need maintenance from time to time to clean the debris that does collect. Floodgates like these can be suspended from a rail added to the bottom of a fence, or from a bridge.

The floodgate can be made by

wiring 1-inch boards of any width in a parallel, loose-jointed grid with 9-gauge wire, and using the same wire to suspend the gate from the overhead beam. Floodgates also can be made of all wood construction, with three or four crosspieces nailed to uprights. You also can make a floodgate from saplings by nailing the ends to a log placed across the creek. These saplings hang diagonally, pointed downstream into the streambed.

You also can construct a durable floodgate out of pipe or welded tubing. Wire woven wire to the frame, and suspend it from the bottom of your fence.

If your hogs root into the streambed trying to squeeze beneath your floodgate, construct a baffle by placing a 2-inch board across the creekbed, held in place by 2- to 3-foot pipe stakes. This board should not be so wide as to block the flow of the stream.

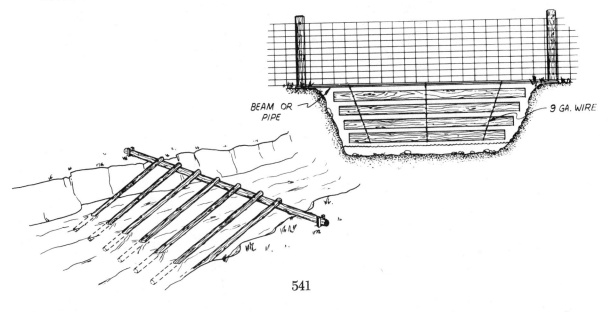

541

CATTLE GUARDS

A cattle guard will turn most livestock, but it provides passage for vehicles and persons. It consists of a grid of pipes or boards set on edge across a trench.

Start with the trench, about 2 feet deep, 6 to 8 feet wide, and 10 to 16 feet long. Lay concrete beams or 2-inch boards across the trench (perpendicular to the fence line) as supports for the deck pipes or boards. The deck can be made from $1\frac{1}{2}$- to $2\frac{1}{2}$-inch pipe, or 2-inch boards set on edge. They should be spaced 3 inches apart. Sheep and goats are the most tenacious about crossing cattle guards. They can walk on anything wider than 2 inches.

The deck pipe or boards are laid parallel with the fence line. Construct wooden triangle panels as shown, out of 1-inch boards and 2 x 4s to close the holes between the guard and the end fence posts.

A cattle guard can convert to a livestock crossing by installing solid platforms in a vertical position on either side of the guard. Hold them at the top with hooks or some other fastening arrangement, so they can be lowered on top of the guard, giving animals a solid walking surface.

A temporary cattle guard needs no trench and can be towed from place

to place. Mount the deck pipe or boards atop 8- to 10-inch wide 2-inch boards, and construct detachable ramps for either side so vehicles can cross.

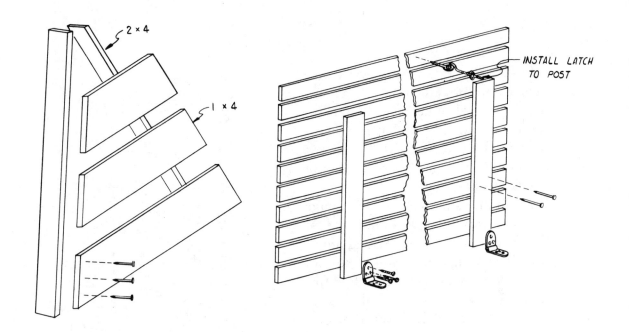

2 × 4

1 × 4

INSTALL LATCH
TO POST

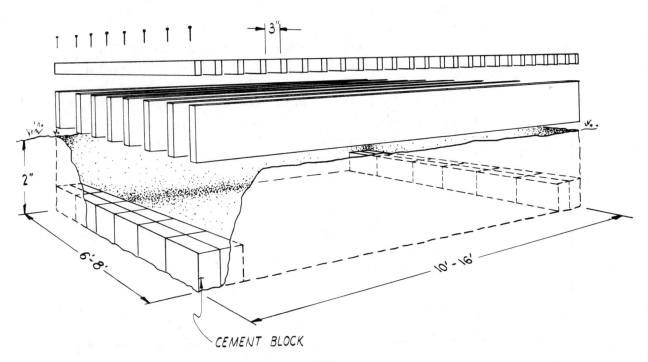

3"

2"

6'-8'

10'-16'

CEMENT BLOCK

543

STILES

Stiles provide passageways for people, but turn all kinds of livestock. Their great advantage is that an existing fence line does not have to be cut to permit access across the fence. Generally, stiles resemble ladders or stepladders.

An in-line stile has the advantage of not sticking out on either side of the fence. It uses an existing fence post for one upright. Sink a second post 2 or 3 feet away for the other upright. The second post should be the same height or higher than the original post. Use 2 x 4 or similar size wood for the rungs. If your posts are the same size, you may want to add a vertical 2 x 4 to one post as a handhold. Your top step may be wider, using a 2 x 6 board.

A rail stile consists of two long pieces no lighter than 2 x 6, one on each side of the fence, inclined from

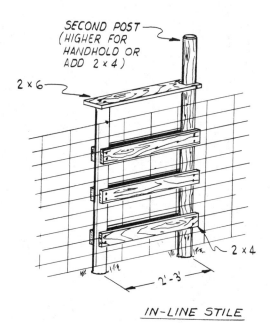

IN-LINE STILE

the ground to near the top of a fence post. Nail the 2 x 6s to the post using 16d nails. The ground, or bottom, ends of these rails should be firmly anchored with stakes. Use 2 x 4s for

MATERIALS (for in-line stile)

Wood

1 pc. 4 x 4 x 8' (post)		
1 pc. 2 x 6 x 4'	or	**Top rung:** 1 pc. 2 x 6 x 3'
1 pc. 2 x 4 x 12'	or	**Rungs:** 6 pcs. 2 x 4 x 3'
1 pc. 2 x 4 x 8'		

Hardware

16d nails

the rungs. The rungs will run through the fence, so obviously this type of stile is best suited to electric, barb-wire, or board fences. Nail the rungs in place with 10d nails. Add a piece of 2 x 4 to the top of the post to give a handhold.

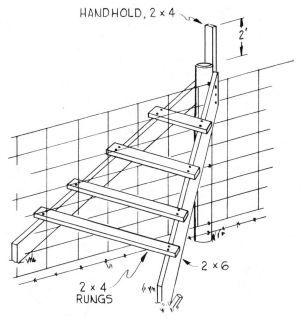

HANDHOLD, 2 x 4

2'

2 x 6

2 x 4 RUNGS

MATERIALS (for rail stile)

Wood

1 pc. 2 x 6 x 10′	or	**Rails:** 2 pcs. 2 x 6 x 5′
1 pc. 2 x 4 x 10′	or	**Rungs:** 1 pc. 2 x 4 x 6′
		1 pc. 2 x 4 x 4′
1 pc. 2 x 4 x 10′	or	**Rungs:** 1 pc. 2 x 4 x 3′
		1 pc. 2 x 4 x 2′

Handhold: 1 pc. 2 x 4 x 3′

Stakes: 2 pcs. 2 x 2 x 2′ (ripped from 2 x 4 x 2′)

Hardware

16d nails
10d nails

PORTABLE STILE

This sturdy stile has the advantage of being portable. It can bridge a fairly tall fence. It is not terribly difficult to construct, although it may provide a challenge for the beginner.

Basically, the stile is constructed of 2 x 6s. Two identical ladders are built, then hinged together at the top. A chain passes through the fence to connect the two sides and keep them from spreading open too far. It is wise to tie or wire the stile to a fence post to steady the stile.

This stile, constructed in the OGF Workshop, will bridge a fence up to 4 feet high. You can easily alter the height of the stile by changing the dimensions.

CONSTRUCTION

1. The critical parts of the stile are the ladder uprights. There are two ways to lay out these legs. The easiest involves the use of a framing square, but you can lay the legs out without the square if you don't have one.

   a. Lay a 10-foot 2 x 6 on your workbench or across two sawhorses. Hold the framing square with the tongue (the shorter, more slender leg) in your left hand and the blade (the longer, broader leg) in your right. Lay the square on the 2 x 6, lining up the 6¾-inch mark on the tongue and the 12-inch mark on the blade with the edge of the 2 x 6 farthest from you. Keeping the two marks aligned with the edge of the board, slide the frame along the board until the outer edge of the tongue intersects the inner corner of the board. Mark the board along the outer edge of the tongue. This will be the base cut. All other cuts must be made parallel to this mark.

   b. If you haven't a framing square, you will have to lay out the leg on the shop floor. Basically, you will be laying out a right triangle, with the stile leg as the hypotenuse. So measure 55 inches along a 2 x 6 and mark it. Measure 48 inches along a second 2 x 6 (or some other board of sufficient length). Butt the corners of the two boards

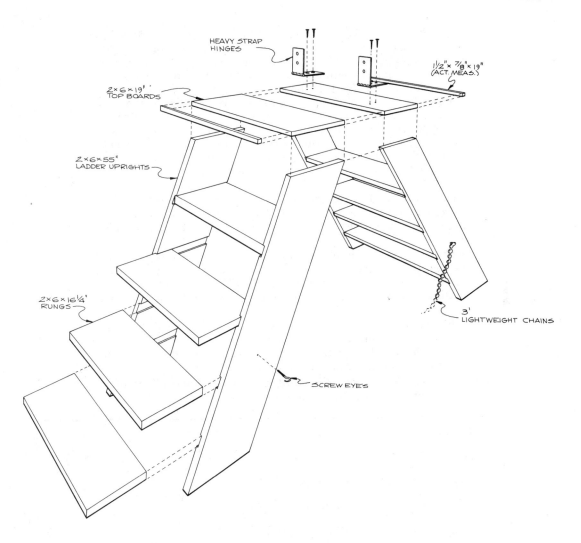

HEAVY STRAP HINGES

1½" × 7/8" × 19" (ACT. MEAS.)

2×6×19' TOP BOARDS

2×6×55" LADDER UPRIGHTS

2×6×16¼" RUNGS

3' LIGHTWEIGHT CHAINS

SCREW EYES

together and swing the opposite ends until the 48-inch mark is 27 inches from the 55-inch mark. The two corners should still be touching. With your measure stretching from the 48-inch mark to the 55-inch mark and on across the 2 x 6 leg, mark the cut along the measure.

With the angle of the steps and the base and top cuts established, mark off the remainder of the leg. The top cut and the base cut are 55 inches apart. The center lines of the steps are 11¼ inches apart. Measure along one edge of the board from your preliminary mark, be it the base or top cut, and mark the locations of the other cuts. Use the framing square or a sliding T-bevel to duplicate the proper angle. Since you should be using a 10-footer, level a space

547

the width of a saw kerf between the top cut on one leg and the base cut of the second leg and lay out a second leg on the same board. On a second board, lay out the remaining two legs, but this time work from the right with the framing square (hold the tongue in the right hand, the blade in the left; still align 6¾ inches on the tongue, 12 inches on the blade; work from right to left on the board). If you are laying out the legs on the shop floor, work on the opposite side of the plumb board. (Or you can lay out the legs all the same, but transfer the marks "around" the board on two of them.) The point is to produce matched sets of legs, one the mirror image of the other. If all exactly the same, the stile won't go together.

2. Mark and cut the dadoes for the steps. Measure ¾ inch on either side of the center lines for the steps and mark. Cut dadoes 1½ inches wide and ½ inch deep, but be sure you are cutting the dadoes on the proper sides of the legs.

3. Cut eight 16¼-inch lengths of 2 x 6 for the steps. Cut two 19-inch lengths of 2 x 6 for the two top steps. Since the legs are cut on an angle, making the width of the combined top cuts more than 11 inches, you must cut an additional 19-inch 2 x 6, then rip two ⅞-inch-wide strips to glue to the top steps.

4. Assemble the two ladders. Use waterproof glue and 16d nails to secure the steps in place. Glue up the two top steps with waterproof glue, then secure them in place with glue and 16d nails. The glued-on strip should be to the outside, rather than the inside.

5. Join the two ladder units together with heavy strap hinges. Turn four screw eyes into the stile, one on the outside of each leg between the

---

MATERIALS

Wood

3 pcs. 2 x 6 x 10'	or	**Ladder uprights:** 4 pcs. 2 x 6 x 55"
		Rungs: 7 pcs. 2 x 6 x 16¼"
1 pc. 2 x 6 x 8'	or	**Rung:** 1 pc. 2 x 6 x 16¼"
		Top boards: 2 pcs. 2 x 6 x 19"
		2 pcs. 1½" x ⅞" x 19" (act. meas., ripped from a 2 x 6 x 19")

Hardware

16d nails
Waterproof glue
1 pr. heavy strap hinges
4–1" screw eyes
6' lightweight chain   or   2 pcs. 3' long

second and third steps. Open the stile so the legs are setting flat, then measure the distance between the screw eyes on each side and cut light-weight chains to fit (they should be about 3 feet). The chains can be secured to one screw eye on each side, but at least one end should be removable.

6. For longest life, the stile should be painted with a good exterior (water-proof) finish.

BRIDGES

For the homesteader with a small creek or drainage swale on the property, a wooden bridge can make passable what otherwise would be a major barrier. People go to college for years to learn modern bridgemaking, but with a few principles of construction in mind and some stout beams, you can make a bridge that will carry pedestrians and light tractors.

The wood frame bridge described here is strong enough to support a Gravely tractor. It spans a creek about 15 feet wide, and its triangular braces reduce springiness to almost nothing, even when an adult jumps up and down in the middle of the bridge deck.

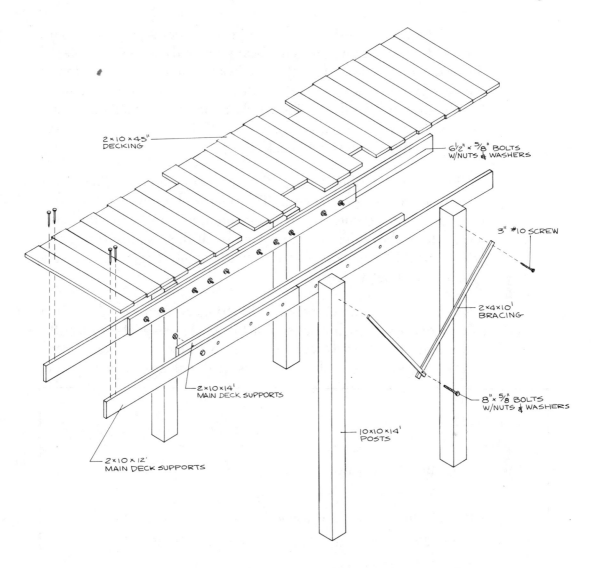

2×10×45"
DECKING

6½" × ⅝" BOLTS
W/NUTS & WASHERS

3" #10 SCREW

2×4×10'
BRACING

2×10×14'
MAIN DECK SUPPORTS

8" × ⅝" BOLTS
W/NUTS & WASHERS

10×10×14'
POSTS

2×10×12'
MAIN DECK SUPPORTS

Before you build any bridges, check with your local farm agent or municipal building officer. In some areas, you need a permit to build bridges, flood walls, or other structures along waterways.

The key to this bridge's strength is two triangles formed by the heavy upright posts, the bridge deck stringer, and the horizontal braces. Since the triangle is the most stable architectural shape, the deck will not sag as long as these joints are fastened.

In Colonial days, bridges were built with a king post truss. This consisted of a heavy, upright beam erected in the middle of the bridge deck, with diagonal brace beams running from the top of the post to the ends of the bridge deck stringers. These diagonals, like the diagonals in the bridge we describe here, actually are compression pieces, which means they can withstand tremendous downward pressure on the bridge deck.

The bridge described here used 10-inch-square posts which were taken from a dismantled barn. The length of the posts you need depends on the contour of the creek you are crossing, but the posts must extend above the bridge deck one-half the distance the bridge deck spans. In this case, the posts were about 7 feet tall and the actual span about 14 feet.

The main deck supports are 2 x 10 stringers, doubled up on each side to give 4 x 10-inch beams. For this bridge, two 14-foot lengths and four 12-foot lengths were used. Two 12-foot pieces are butted end-to-end, and the 14-foot piece is centered on the joint. Bore

---

MATERIALS

Wood

4 pcs. 10 x 10 x 14' (posts)

2 pcs. 2 x 10 x 14' (main deck supports)

4 pcs. 2 x 10 x 12' (main deck supports)

10 pcs. 2 x 10 x 12'   or   **Decking:** 30 pcs. 2 x 10 x 45"

2 pcs. 2 x 4 x 10' (bracing)

2 pcs. 2 x 4 x 8'   or   **Stakes:** 8 pcs. 2 x 4 x 24"

Hardware

18–6½" x ⅝" bolts w/ nuts and washers
2–8" x ⅝" bolts w/ nuts and washers
6–3" #10 screws
10d nails

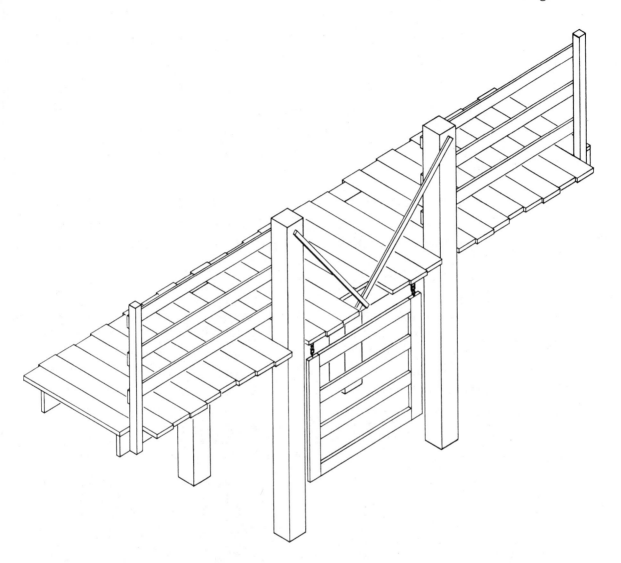

$\frac{5}{8}$-inch holes and use 6½-inch by $\frac{5}{8}$-inch bolts to fasten the 2 x 10s face-to-face. This yields an assembly that is 24 feet long, so your finished bridge deck actually will extend 5 or 6 feet onto each bank.

For the deck planking, use 2 x 10 boards cut to the width of bridge deck you want. This bridge was 45 inches wide, and some of the planks had to be trimmed to accommodate posts and diagonals. Figure you will need thirty of these boards to cover a 24-foot deck.

You also will need two 10-foot pieces of 2 x 4 or 1 x 2 for the diagonal braces.

Start building the bridge by sinking the four 10-inch-square posts into the creek banks. Site them above the normal level of the water. Posts on one side of the bridge (one on each bank) will reach only to the planking of the bridge deck. The others are taller and will be used to anchor the braces.

Lay the assembled stringers in place and hold them on both ends with 24-inch stakes. Install the diagonal braces using 8-inch by $\frac{5}{8}$-inch bolts on the stringer end and screws or dowels on the top. Nail on the deck planks, using 10d nails. Trim where necessary to accommodate the braces and posts.

If the bridge is along a fence line, you may want to construct fence panels along the deck to connect with the rest of your fence line. Use 1-inch stock, 5 or 6 inches wide. You also may want to hang a floodgate beneath the bridge. Finish the bridge by installing ramps on both ends.

FOOTBRIDGE

Besides enhancing the appearance of a small brook or pond, a simple, serviceable footbridge strategically situated can save countless extra steps on the farmstead and make accessible otherwise underutilized parts of your property.

A footbridge of this type should be at least twice as long as the width of the stream to be spanned. In this case, the three 2 x 6 lateral supports are 12 feet long. The treads are 3-foot 2 x 6s, centered on the lateral supports so that they extend $1\frac{1}{2}$ inches beyond the outer members.

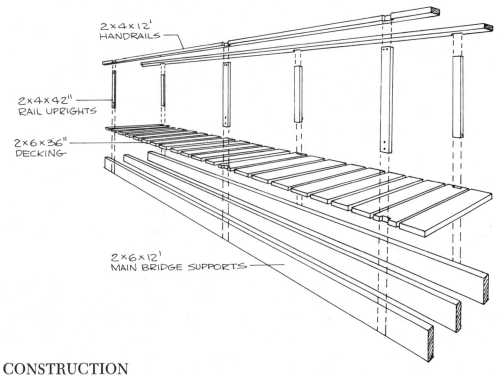

2×4×12'
HANDRAILS

2×4×42"
RAIL UPRIGHTS

2×6×36"
DECKING

2×6×12'
MAIN BRIDGE SUPPORTS

CONSTRUCTION

1. Using 16d nails, fasten one tread on each end of the three 12-foot lateral supports, making sure that supports are square with treads.

MATERIALS

Wood

3 pcs. 2 x 6 x 12' (main bridge supports)

6 pcs. 2 x 6 x 12'   or   **Decking:** 24 pcs. 2 x 6 x 36"

1 railroad tie   or   2 pcs. 3½' long

2 pcs. 2 x 4 x 12' (handrails)

3 pcs. 2 x 4 x 8'   or   **Rail uprights:** 6 pcs. 2 x 4 x 42"

Hardware

16d nails
12–2½" #10 screws
12–3½" x ⅜" carriage bolts w/ nuts and washers
Exterior stain

2. To keep supports from coming into contact with the ground, place a 3½-foot piece of railroad tie under each end of the bridge.
3. The handrails are constructed of 2 x 4s, dadoed 1½ inches deep, 6 inches from each end and at the center to accommodate 2 x 4 uprights. The uprights (42 inches long) are fastened to the rails with two 2½-inch #10 screws (drill pilot holes). The completed rails are then attached to the lateral bridge supports with two 3½-inch by ⅜-inch carriage bolts at the bottom of each upright.
4. The remainder of the treads are then nailed on, with ½-inch spaces between treads. The ends of the treads that fit between uprights must be cut to fit.
5. Sand the corners of the handrails, and apply a coat of exterior stain or paint.

STONE BRIDGE

This attractive stone bridge is built atop a 2-foot by 2-foot by 2-foot concrete foundation, the top of which extends to the bottom of the culvert pipe. Stones were then laid up with masonry to a height of 4 feet. The width narrows from 2 feet at the base to 18 inches at the top. Stretch string with line level between stakes to keep top of wall level. See the chapters on concrete and walls for more information on building with stones and mortar.

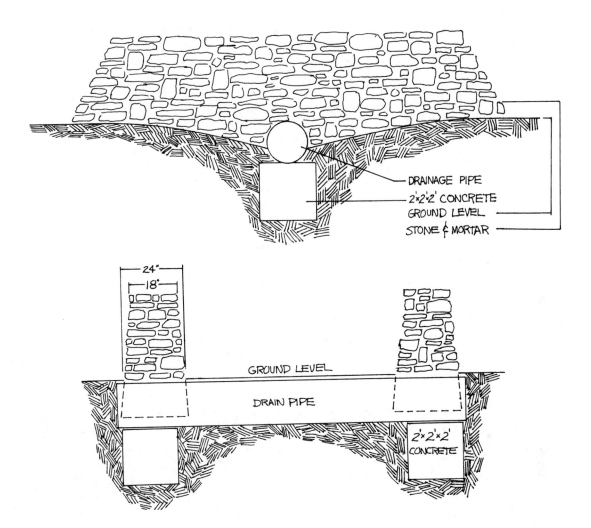

DRAINAGE PIPE
2'×2'×2' CONCRETE
GROUND LEVEL
STONE & MORTAR

24"
18"

GROUND LEVEL

DRAIN PIPE

2'×2'×2'
CONCRETE

OUTDOOR FURNITURE

The construction of furniture is usually the domain of only the most skilled woodworkers. The fine furniture woods are expensive; the joints must fit without error. It's no place for a woodbutcher.

But even the novice can successfully tackle the rough sorts of seats and tables that get parked beside the garden, on the patio, under the apple tree. Ofttimes, such furniture is made from dimension lumber, held together with ordinary bolts and nuts or with screws. There's margin for error.

The following projects all will give a reasonable challenge to the beginning carpenter, and the product will grace the homestead landscape. And give you a place to rest your chore-weary bones.

A STURDY GARDEN BENCH

How often have you longed for a shady bench to rest those weary bones after a morning's weeding, or regretted not having a flat, steady surface for some impromptu potting work, or just wished for a seat to "set a spell" and delight in the fruits of your labor? Here's a simple, rugged model that will enhance the appearance of any garden.

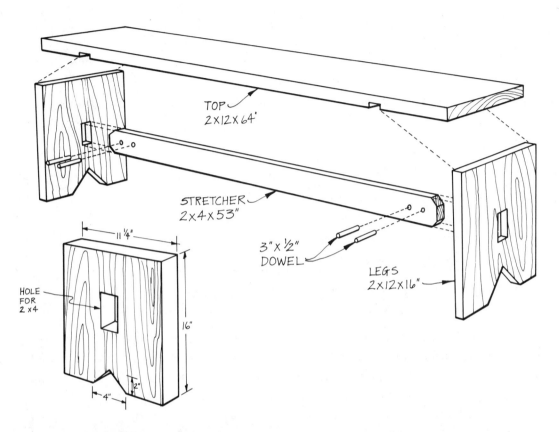

TOP
2X12X64"

STRETCHER
2x4x53"

3" x ½"
DOWEL

LEGS
2X12X16"

11 ¼"

HOLE
FOR
2 x 4

16"

2"

4"

CONSTRUCTION

1. A piece of 2 x 12 rough-cut spruce is used for the top and legs. Out of an 8-foot plank, cut one piece 64 inches for the top and two pieces 16 inches for legs. Sand all pieces lightly, especially edges and corners.

2. On the bottom of the seat plank, 8 inches from each end, cut a ½-inch-deep channel the thickness of the legs. (This can be done either with repeated cuts of the table saw or with a handsaw and a hammer and chisel.)

3. Cut a small **V** notch on the bottoms of the 16-inch legs. Cut a hole large enough to insert a 2 x 4 in the middle of each leg. (Mark the hole, drill out the bulk of the material with a brace and bit, then clean up the edges with a hammer and a chisel.)

4. Cut a 53-inch length of 2 x 4. Cut corners on 45-degree angles, as illustrated.

5. Insert legs into the channels. Glue and nail from top with 16d nails. Insert the 2 x 4 into holes in legs. Drill ½-inch holes in the 2 x 4 on each side of each leg and insert 3-inch-long ½-inch dowels. (You can fashion your own from a piece of scrap wood.) Two coats of linseed oil will help weatherproof the wood.

559

MATERIALS

Wood

  1 pc. 2 x 12 x 8′ rough-cut spruce   or   **Top:** 1 pc. 2 x 12 x 64″

                    Legs: 2 pcs. 2 x 12 x 16″

  1 pc. 2 x 4 x 8′   or   **Stretcher:** 1 pc. 2 x 4 x 53″

  1 pc. 36″ x ½″ dowel   or   4 pcs. 3″ x ½″ dowel

Hardware

  16d nails
  Waterproof glue

PICNIC TABLE

The table shown here was David Caccia's first home-building project. It served as his family's dining table and workbench when they lived in a tent as they were building their house in Sewell, New Jersey. Thanks to rugged construction, it is still serving well despite exposure to year-round weather.

About half a day should see the project through to completion. As for tools, a saw, drill, wrench, and hammer are all that are needed. The entire table is made of 2 x 6s except for two 2 x 3 cross braces. Caccia used Douglas fir lumber and found this quite satisfactory. If you have access to any of the more durable woods such as redwood, cedar, white oak, or locust, so much the better.

CONSTRUCTION

1. Cut two 2 x 3 by 12-inch cross braces. Cut ends on 45-degree angles.
2. Lay out leg assemblies on flat surface. Drive a nail into each joint to hold pieces while four ⅜-inch holes are drilled in each 40-inch leg.

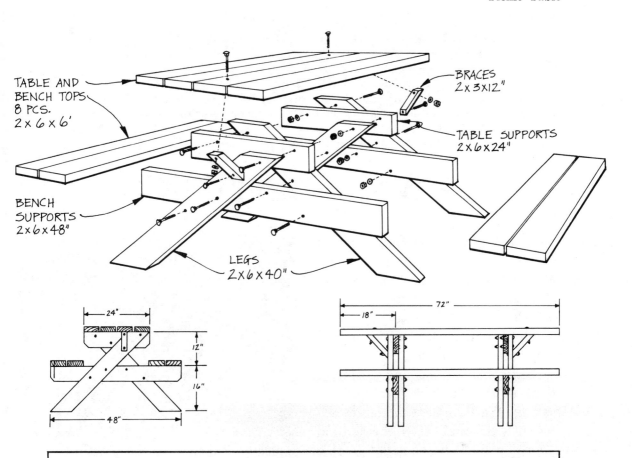

TABLE AND BENCH TOPS
8 PCS.
2 x 6 x 6'

BRACES
2 x 3 x 12"

TABLE SUPPORTS
2 x 6 x 24"

BENCH SUPPORTS
2 x 6 x 48"

LEGS
2 x 6 x 40"

24"

12"

16"

48"

72"

18"

MATERIALS

Wood

1 pc. 2 x 3 x 2'	or	**Braces:** 2 pcs. 2 x 3 x 12"
1 pc. 2 x 6 x 14'	or	**Legs:** 4 pcs. 2 x 6 x 40"
5 pcs. 2 x 6 x 12'	or	**Table and benchtops:** 8 pcs. 2 x 6 x 6'
		Table supports: 2 pcs. 2 x 6 x 24"
		Bench supports: 2 pcs. 2 x 6 x 48"

Hardware

10d nails
Wood preservative
20–4" x $\frac{3}{8}$" carriage bolts w/ nuts and washers

3. Before assembling two legs, brush on clear wood preservative. Then assemble the legs with 4-inch by ⅜-inch carriage bolts with washers.

4. Nail four 72-inch planks in place for the tabletop, leaving ½-inch space between each. Do same with four 72-inch seat planks.

5. Position the 2 x 3 top braces as shown, then drill ⅜-inch holes through the braces, leg, and top, as shown. Attach the braces with ⅜-inch carriage bolts.

6. Brush on preservative, then apply coat of exterior varnish.

LAWN FURNITURE

This is a type of lawn furniture that was once very popular, and with good reason. It is fairly simply made, it is durable, and it is surprisingly comfortable. If it has a drawback, that drawback is the amount of material used in the construction.

There are an astonishing variety of styles in this kind of furniture. In making the samples pictured, we started with some very old extension service plans, then made a few changes, principally in the cut of the seat back. We used screws to join the leg assemblies. The furniture held up to nearly a full summer of use, until an unusual bit of teenage rough-

housing dismembered one side of the chair. The assembly was rejoined using 2-inch-long ¼-inch carriage bolts. If you expect the furniture to be stressed, you may want to use the bolts in the initial assembly.

CHAIR CONSTRUCTION

1. Begin construction with the leg assemblies. Cut from 1 x 4 two of each of the following parts: 22-inch-long front legs, 25¼-inch-long upper supports, 37¼-inch-long lower supports, and 24-inch-long rear legs. Write the name or some identification on each piece so you don't get them mixed up. As you assemble these pieces into the leg assemblies, remember that you want one assembly to be the mirror image of the other, not a duplicate. (If you do goof, you can consider yourself started on the settee, which uses the same leg assemblies.) You'll probably want to construct one unit, then the other.

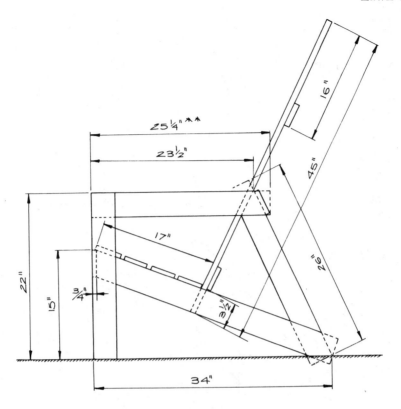

SIDE VIEW OF LEG ASSEMBLY

** OVERALL LENGTH BEFORE TRIMMED

a. Fasten the front leg to the upper support. Use a simple overlap joint, making sure, through the use of a try square or framing square, that the two pieces are at right angles to each other. Use a waterproof glue and three 1¼-inch #10 screws, countersinking the screws here and everywhere else you use them in this project.

b. The front leg is the outermost of three layers of the assembly, so the lower support is fastened to the same side of the leg as the upper support. The rear leg will be added to the inside of the supports. The assembly process is most tricky at this point. As shown, the lower support ends ¾ inch shy of the front edge of the leg (so the front crossmember will be flush with the front edge of the legs). Therefore, draw a line parallel to and ¾ inch from the front edge of the leg and mark the spot along the line that's 15 inches from the foot of the leg. Lay your assembly on the workbench with the leg down, the support up (use a scrap of wood to hold it level). Place the lower support in position, with the upper front corner on the point you've marked on the leg (and put another scrap of wood under it to hold it level too). The rear leg is placed on top, in position, and the two loose pieces slid about until they line up properly, as shown. Remember that several of the corners will be

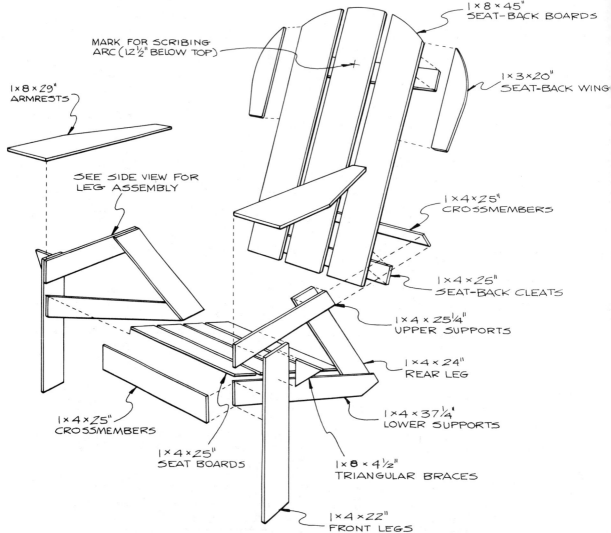

MARK FOR SCRIBING
ARC (12½" BELOW TOP)

1 × 8 × 45"
SEAT-BACK BOARDS

1 × 3 × 20"
SEAT-BACK WING

1 × 8 × 29"
ARMRESTS

SEE SIDE VIEW FOR
LEG ASSEMBLY

1 × 4 × 25"
CROSSMEMBERS

1 × 4 × 25"
SEAT-BACK CLEATS

1 × 4 × 25¼"
UPPER SUPPORTS

1 × 4 × 24"
REAR LEG

1 × 4 × 25"
CROSSMEMBERS

1 × 4 × 37¼"
LOWER SUPPORTS

1 × 4 × 25"
SEAT BOARDS

1 × 8 × 4½"
TRIANGULAR BRACES

1 × 4 × 22"
FRONT LEGS

trimmed off, so don't worry too much about them. Fasten the pieces together using waterproof glue and three 1¼-inch #10 screws at each joint. At the joint of the upper support and the rear leg especially, remember that the forward corner of the leg will be trimmed off, so be careful where you locate the screws.

c. With a backsaw, trim off the excess corners. Do this promptly if you are using a fast-setting glue. Cut the front end of the lower support, parallel with the edge of the front leg. Trim the corners of the upper and lower supports jutting beyond the rear edge of the rear leg. Trim off the forward corner of the rear leg along a line determined as follows: Mark a point 17 inches from the front upper corner of the lower support, then lay a rule extending through that point and the upper rear corner of rear leg-upper support joint. Scribe a line along the ruler and trim the rear leg along that line. The final cut is to trim the foot of the rear leg support.

    d.   The second leg assembly may be constructed using the first as a pattern, provided you remember that a mirror image, not a duplicate, is what you need. The use of a sliding T bevel will permit you to transfer the various angles onto the four leg assembly parts before fastening them together.

2.   Cut the remaining pieces of the chair. From 1 x 4 material, cut two 25-inch-long crossmembers, four 25-inch-long seat boards, and two 25-inch-long seat-back cleats. From 1 x 8 material, cut three 45-inch-long seat-back boards, two 29-inch-long armrests, and a $4\frac{1}{2}$-inch piece for the armrest braces. Finally, cut two 20-inch lengths of 1 x 3 for the seat-back wings.

3.   Using 8d finishing nails and the waterproof glue, fasten the two crossmembers to the leg assemblies as shown. Next, nail the four seat boards in place, using 6d finishing nails. The leading edge of the first seat board should just project past the front leg; the distance from front to rear should be 17 inches.

4.   Assemble the seat back. The three boards should be laid out, properly aligned, with $\frac{1}{2}$-inch gaps between them. The bottom cleat is fastened in place using the waterproof glue and two $1\frac{1}{4}$-inch #10 screws driven into each board. It should be located $3\frac{1}{2}$ inches above the bottom end of the back, with $\frac{3}{4}$ inch projecting on either side. The top cleat is attached in like manner, $12\frac{1}{2}$ inches below the top of the back. Tack the wings in place so that you can remove them for cutting after the back has been marked for the rounded shape.

5.   Turn the back over (cleats down) and mark the spot in the center of the middle back board that's $12\frac{1}{2}$ inches below the top end of the board. Take a piece of scrap wood that's at least 13 inches long and drive two nails through it, $12\frac{1}{2}$ inches apart, making a scribing tool. Push one nail of the tool into the point you've marked on the back and swing the other in an arc, scribing the line along which you will cut to shape the back's top. Pull off the wings, then cut along the line with a coping saw or a saber saw. While the wings could be shaped to carry the rounded shape below the horizontal, we shaped ours to taper from full width at the horizontal to a width of $1\frac{1}{4}$ inches at the bottom. When they are finished, nail (with 8d finishing nails) and glue them in place (nail through the edge of the wing into the edge of the back board; the wing is narrow enough to be penetrated by an 8d nail).

6.   The armrests should be shaped as shown by cutting off one corner of each. Using a rasp, round the top edges and the corners. Glue and nail, using 8d finishing nails, in place. Cut the $4\frac{1}{2}$-inch piece of 1 x 8 in half diagonally, making two triangular braces. The braces are positioned beneath the armrest, against the front leg, one to each arm, as shown. Drill pilot holes through the brace into the leg and into the armrest, then secure each brace with glue and two 3-inch #8 screws.

7.   The back is put into place last. It may be nailed or screwed in place, but leaving it unsecured will permit you to remove the back to ease moving or storing the chair.

MATERIALS (for chair)

Wood

3 pcs. 1 x 4 x 12'	or	**Front legs:** 2 pcs. 1 x 4 x 22"
		Upper supports: 2 pcs. 1 x 4 x 25¼"
		Lower supports: 2 pcs. 1 x 4 x 37¼"
		Rear legs: 2 pcs. 1 x 4 x 24"
		Crossmembers: 2 pcs. 1 x 4 x 25"
		Seat boards: 4 pcs. 1 x 4 x 25"
		Seat-back cleats: 2 pcs. 1 x 4 x 25"
1 pc. 1 x 8 x 8'	or	**Seat-back boards:** 3 pcs. 1 x 8 x 45"
1 pc. 1 x 8 x 10'		**Armrests:** 2 pcs. 1 x 8 x 29"
		Armrest braces: 1 pc. 1 x 8 x 4½" (cut diagonally in half to make two braces)
1 pc. 1 x 3 x 4'	or	**Seat-back wings:** 2 pcs. 1 x 3 x 20"

Hardware

Waterproof glue
32–1¼" #10 screws
8d finishing nails
6d finishing nails
4–3" #8 screws

SETTEE CONSTRUCTION

1. Construction of the settee is exactly the same as the construction of the chair, with the exception of the back. Begin with the leg assemblies, cutting and assembling the parts as explained in the chair construction directions.

2. The two crossmembers and four seat boards are each 45 inches long and are cut from 1 x 4 stock. They are positioned and fastened to the leg assemblies as were the matching pieces in the chair.

3. The armrests too are the same as those on the chair. Cut them and attach them to the settee, following the chair construction directions.

4. The seat back is composed of two 45-inch lengths of 1 x 4, four 45-inch lengths of 1 x 8, and two 20-inch 1 x 3 wings, all held together by two 45-inch 1 x 4 cleats. After cutting the parts, lay out the seat-back

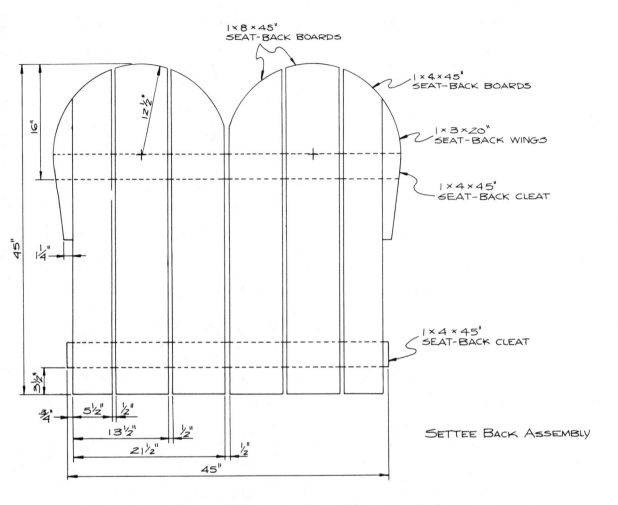

1×8×45"
SEAT-BACK BOARDS

1×4×45"
SEAT-BACK BOARDS

1×3×20"
SEAT-BACK WINGS

1×4×45"
SEAT-BACK CLEAT

1×4×45"
SEAT-BACK CLEAT

SETTEE BACK ASSEMBLY

boards with the 1x 4s on the outside. Space them a ½ inch apart. Lay the lower cleat in place, 3½ inches above the bottom of the back, with ¾ inch projecting on each side. Fasten the cleat to the back boards with waterproof glue and two 1¼-inch #10 screws driven into each board. The top cleat is attached in like manner, 16 inches below the top of the back. Tack the wings in place, so they can be removed after they are marked for cutting.

5. Use the same homemade scribing tool that you used to mark the back of the chair to mark the back of the settee. Mark a spot in the center of each of the two outermost 1 x 8s, 12½ inches below the top end. Press one nail of the scribing tool into one mark and swing the other end of the tool in an arc, marking half the top for cutting. Repeat the process using the other point to mark the other half of the back. As with the chair, you next remove the wings, cut them and the back, then reinstall the wings. The back fits the settee as the chair's back fits it.

MATERIALS (for settee)

Wood

6 pcs. 1 x 4 x 10′	or	**Front legs:** 2 pcs. 1 x 4 x 22″
		Upper supports: 2 pcs. 1 x 4 x 25¼″
		Lower supports: 2 pcs. 1 x 4 x 37¼″
		Rear legs: 2 pcs. 1 x 4 x 24″
		Crossmembers: 2 pcs. 1 x 4 x 45″
		Seat boards: 4 pcs. 1 x 4 x 45″
		Seat-back boards: 2 pcs. 1 x 4 x 45″
		Seat-back cleats: 2 pcs. 1 x 4 x 45″
1 pc. 1 x 8 x 10′	or	**Seat-back boards:** 4 pcs. 1 x 8 x 45″
1 pc. 1 x 8 x 12′		**Armrests:** 2 pcs. 1 x 8 x 29″
		Armrest braces: 1 pc. 1 x 8 x 4½″ (cut diagonally, forming 2 braces)
1 pc. 1 x 3 x 4′	or	**Seat-back wings:** 2 pcs. 1 x 3 x 20″

Hardware

Waterproof glue
48–1¼″ #10 screws
8d finishing nails
6d finishing nails
4–3″ #8 screws

PATIO FURNITURE

Redwood-framed patio furniture is very popular these days, not only for its appearance, but for its durability and comfort. There are many variations, but generally the furniture is constructed of 2 x 4 stock and it is very easily assembled.

We constructed a set of this style furniture, including a chair, a settee that is no more than a wide chair, a table, and a chaise lounge. We used common fir 2 x 4s, some plywood, and a lot of screws and bolts. The cushions we purchased, though they could

just as easily have been homemade too. For longest life, the wood used in the furniture should be liberally treated with a wood preservative and a finish of some sort applied.

CHAIR CONSTRUCTION

1. Cut the frame pieces for the chair: from 2 x 4, four 22-inch legs, two 29½-inch sides, two 27-inch arms, two 25½-inch backrest sides, and a 20-inch backrest top; from 2 x 3, two 20-inch crossmembers; from 2 x 2, two 12-inch seat cleats.

2. The basic angle in the chair is 10 degrees. It is easiest to deal with if you use a protractor and sliding T bevel to set the angle. Mark the legs, top and bottom, with the angle, making the legs 21¼ inches long. Be sure the angles are parallel, rather than converging. Then cut. Thus modified, the legs will intersect the sides at an angle 10 degrees off vertical. The bottom edge of the sides meets the leg 10¾ inches from the foot, so scribe a line on the leg at that point to aid in the layout. The front legs meet the sides at a point 2 inches from the front and ⅛ inch from the rear. Mark these points on the lower edge of the sides, then using your sliding T bevel, scribe that 10-degree angle across the face of the side, so the front legs lean toward the back and the rear legs lean toward the front. Lay the legs on the sides and drill two ¼-inch holes for the bolts that will secure them. (In drilling the holes of the rear legs, try to avoid positioning the bolts so they conflict with the rear crossmember; we had such a conflict, which was resolved by chiseling an inside corner off the crossmember.)

3. Assemble the basic frame from the sides and crossmembers. After drilling appropriate pilot holes and countersinking, drive two 3½-inch #12 screws through the sides into the butt ends of each crossmember. The front crossmember should be flush with the bottom of the sides, while the rear crossmember should be flush with the tops of the sides. Bolt the legs to the basic frame.

4. The arms can be given a more finished appearance by cutting a slight bevel around the top edge with a block plane and rasp. Then secure

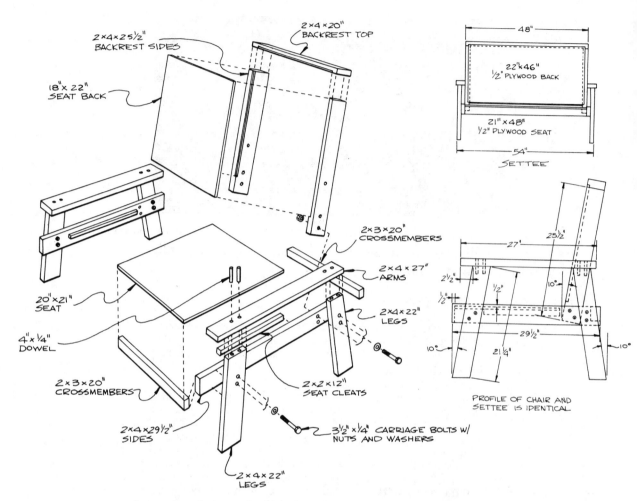

the arms to the tops of the legs with 4-inch pieces of ¼-inch dowel. The arm overhangs the front leg by 2½ inches, and the inner edge must be in the same plane as the inner edge of the sides. Position the arms, and have someone hold them in place while you drill holes for the dowels. Dab a bit of waterproof glue on each dowel and drive it home.

5. Assemble the seat back. After drilling pilot holes and countersinking, drive two 3½-inch #12 screws through each end of the top into the butt ends of the backrest sides. Router a ½-inch-deep, ⅜-inch-wide rabbet into the back assembly for the plywood seat back to set into; the rabbet extends across the lower edge of the top and 21⅝ inches down the inner edge of each side. (If you haven't the tools to cut the rabbet, cut appropriate lengths of 2 x 2 or 1 x 1 for cleats and secure them to the inside of the seat-back assembly, a ½-inch from the front edge. Then cut the plywood back a bit smaller so it will fit into the assembly and rest against the cleats.)

6. The backrest assembly tilts off vertical at the same 10-degree angle that the legs tilt. For an approximation of that angle, line up the back edge of the assembly with the front edge of the rear leg at the bottom of the side, and with the rear edge of the leg at the top of the leg. Use a try square to line up the back of the back and the back of the leg. Have a helper hold the assembly in place and drill one $\frac{1}{4}$-inch hole through each side and backrest side. Bolt the assembly in place, make final adjustments and drill a second hole, and finish bolting the back in place. Drill a pilot hole through each backrest side into the arm, countersink and drive in a $2\frac{1}{2}$-inch #12 screw.

7. Attach the seat cleats, one on each inner face of the sides, 1 inch below the top, with two $2\frac{1}{2}$-inch #12 screws each.

8. Cut a 20-inch by 21-inch piece of $\frac{1}{2}$-inch exterior plywood for the seat, and an 18-inch by 22-inch piece for the seat back. Using plywood that's good on at least one side will permit your chair to present a better appearance. Install the seat and seat back with the good side down and secure with 6d finishing nails.

MATERIALS (for chair)

Wood

2 pcs. 2 x 4 x 12'   or   **Legs:** 4 pcs. 2 x 4 x 22"

Sides: 2 pcs. 2 x 4 x 29$\frac{1}{2}$"

Arms: 2 pcs. 2 x 4 x 27"

Backrest sides: 2 pcs. 2 x 4 x 25$\frac{1}{2}$"

Backrest top: 1 pc. 2 x 4 x 20"

1 pc. 2 x 3 x 4'   or   **Crossmembers:** 2 pcs. 2 x 3 x 20"

1 pc. 36" x $\frac{1}{4}$" dowel   or   8 pcs. 4" long

1 pc. 2 x 2 x 2'   or   **Seat cleats:** 2 pcs. 2 x 2 x 12"

1–2' x 4' sht. $\frac{1}{2}$" ext. plywood   or   **Seat:** 1 pc. 20" x 21"
(good one side)

Seat back: 1 pc. 18" x 22"

Hardware

12–3$\frac{1}{2}$" #12 screws
12–3$\frac{1}{2}$" x $\frac{1}{4}$" carriage bolts w/ nuts and washers
Waterproof glue
6–2$\frac{1}{2}$" #12 screws
6d finishing nails

MATERIALS (for settee)

Wood

2 pcs. 2 x 4 x 10′	or	**Legs:** 4 pcs. 2 x 4 x 22″
1 pc. 2 x 4 x 6′		**Sides:** 2 pcs. 2 x 4 x 29½″
		Arms: 2 pcs. 2 x 4 x 27″
		Backrest sides: 2 pcs. 2 x 4 x 25½″
		Backrest top: 1 pc. 2 x 4 x 48″
1 pc. 2 x 3 x 8′	or	**Crossmembers:** 2 pcs. 2 x 3 x 48″
1 pc. 36″ x ¼″ dowel	or	8 pcs. 4″ long
1 pc. 2 x 2 x 6′	or	**Seat cleats:** 2 pcs. 2 x 2 x 16″
		Seat brace: 1 pc. 2 x 2 x 26½″
1–4′ x 4′ sht. ½″ ext. plywood (good one side)	or	**Seat:** 1 pc. 21″ x 48″
		Seat back: 1 pc. 22″ x 46″

Hardware

12–3½″ #12 screws
12–3½″ x ¼″ carriage bolts w/ nuts and washers
Waterproof glue
8–2½″ #12 screws
2–3″ #12 screws (seat brace)
6d finishing nails

SETTEE CONSTRUCTION

1. The settee is constructed in the same manner and sequence as the chair. The only difference is that the backrest top and the crossmembers, and consequently the seat and seat back panels, are longer. Cut the pieces as indicated in the materials list and assemble them in accordance with the directions for the chair.

2. Before installing the seat panel, cut and install a 26½-inch 2 x 2 seat brace extending from crossmember to crossmember, midway between the sides. Drive a 3-inch #12 screw through the crossmembers into each end of the brace. This brace will prevent the seat from sagging. Moreover, you may want to use a seat panel cut from ¾-inch plywood.

TABLE CONSTRUCTION

1. Cut the wooden pieces for the table. The top and legs are 21-inch lengths of 2 x 4. You'll need ten pieces in all. Mark and cut parallel 55-degree angles on the ends of the legs, shortening them to 19 inches. For a finished appearance, use a block plane and rasp to cut a slight bevel into the top edges of the six top pieces.

2. Measure 10¼ inches along one edge of a leg from an *acute* angled corner. Using a try square, mark a perpendicular across the face of the leg. Find the center of the face on that line, then drill a ¼-inch hole through the leg. Repeat the process on the other three legs.

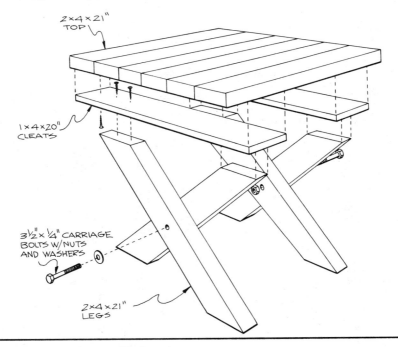

$2 \times 4 \times 21''$ TOP

$1 \times 4 \times 20''$ CLEATS

$3\frac{1}{2}'' \times \frac{1}{4}''$ CARRIAGE BOLTS W/NUTS AND WASHERS

$2 \times 4 \times 21''$ LEGS

MATERIALS (for table)

Wood

2 pcs. 2 x 4 x 12′	or	**Top:** 6 pcs. 2 x 4 x 21″
		Legs: 4 pcs. 2 x 4 x 21″
1 pc. 1 x 4 x 4′	or	**Cleats:** 2 pcs. 1 x 4 x 20″

Hardware

2–3½″ x ¼″ carriage bolts w/ nuts and washers
20–2″ #12 screws

3. Cut two 20-inch lengths of 1 x 4 for cleats. Using 3½-inch by ¼-inch carriage bolts, fasten the pairs of legs together. Set a pair on its feet, lay a cleat across the top, and drive two 2-inch #12 screws through the cleat into each leg. Repeat the process with the second pair of legs.

4. Lay out the top pieces, edge to edge, top down. Set the cleat-leg assemblies in place, cleats down, feet in the air. Drive a 2-inch #12 screw through each cleat into each of the six top pieces.

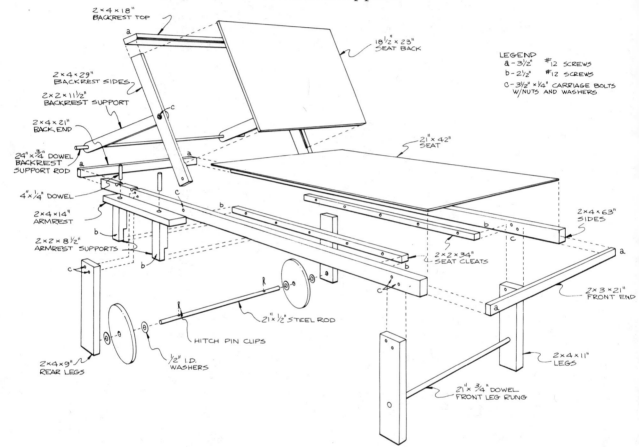

CHAISE CONSTRUCTION

1. Fabricate and assemble the basic framework first. Cut the two 63-inch-long sides and a 21-inch-long back end from 2 x 4 and the 21-inch-long front end from 2 x 3. From 2 x 2 cut two 34-inch-long seat cleats. Using two 3½-inch #12 screws at each joint, fasten the sides to the end pieces, making sure the bottom of the front end is flush with the bottoms of the sides. The seat cleats are secured to the sides with five 2½-inch #12 screws in each. The cleats are located 1 inch below the top edge of the sides and 7½ inches shy of the very front of the assembly.

2. Install the front legs. Cut two 11-inch legs from 2 x 4 and a 21-inch length of $\frac{3}{4}$-inch dowel for the rung. Drill a $\frac{3}{4}$-inch hole in the middle of each leg, 4 inches from the foot. Clamp one leg in position, butted against the seat cleat, top of the leg flush with the top of the cleat. Drill two $\frac{1}{4}$-inch holes through the side and the leg. Repeat the process with the other leg. Drive the rung into the $\frac{3}{4}$-inch hole in one leg, then force the other leg on the other end of the rung, making sure the legs are parallel. With the chaise frame upside down, slip the leg assembly in position and bolt in place with four $3\frac{1}{2}$-inch carriage bolts with nuts and washers.

3. Install the rear legs and wheels. Cut two 9-inch legs from 2 x 4, a 21-inch axle from $\frac{1}{2}$-inch steel rod, and two 6-inch-diameter wheels from 1 x 8. Drill a $\frac{1}{2}$-inch hole for the axle in the middle of each leg, 1 inch from the bottom. In succession, clamp each leg in position, $7\frac{1}{4}$ inches from the very rear of the chaise frame, 1 inch below the top edge of the sides, and drill two $\frac{1}{4}$-inch holes for the mounting bolts. Drill a $\frac{1}{8}$-inch hole $2\frac{1}{2}$ inches from each end of the axle for the hitch pin clip. Insert a clip in one of the holes, then in succession add a washer, a wheel, another washer, and a leg. Repeat the process at the other end of the axle, then position the assembly on the chaise frame and bolt in place.

4. Fabricate and assemble the backrest. Cut two 29-inch sides and an 18-inch top from 2 x 4, two $11\frac{1}{2}$-inch supports from 2 x 2, and a 24-inch support rod from $\frac{3}{4}$-inch dowel. Fasten the sides and top together, driving two $3\frac{1}{2}$-inch #12 screws through each side into the butt ends of the top. Router a $\frac{1}{2}$-inch-deep, $\frac{3}{8}$-inch-wide rabbet into the backrest for the plywood seat back to set into; extend the rabbet across the lower edge of the top and 23 inches down the inner edge of the sides. (If you haven't the tools to cut the rabbet, cut appropriate lengths of 2 x 2 or 1 x 1 for cleats and secure them to the inside of the seat back assembly, a $\frac{1}{2}$-inch from the front edge. Then cut the plywood seat back a bit smaller so it will fit into the assembly and rest against the cleats.) In the middle of the sides, 15 inches from the top, drill a $\frac{1}{4}$-inch hole. Drill a similar hole 1 inch from the bottom of the sides. In each support, drill a $\frac{1}{4}$-inch hole in the middle $\frac{3}{4}$ inch from one end and a $\frac{3}{4}$-inch hole in a similar spot at the other end. Force the supports over the ends of the support rod, so that $1\frac{1}{2}$ inches of the rod project through the support. Then bolt the support assembly to the backrest frame with a $3\frac{1}{2}$-inch carriage bolt with washer and nut in each support. Finally, bolt the backrest assembly to the chaise frame.

5. Mark the top of the chaise frame sides for the notches that hold the backrest support rod. Measure from the rear end of the frame and square a line across the top of the sides at $2\frac{1}{4}$, 5, 8, and 11 inches from the rear. These lines are at centers of the notches, which are made with an 8-inch half-round rasp.

6. Cut a 21-inch by 42-inch seat and an $18\frac{1}{2}$-inch by 23-inch seat back from $\frac{1}{2}$-inch exterior plywood. The seat back at least should be a piece of plywood with one good side, so that the chaise, viewed from the rear, has a nice appearance. Place the panels in position and secure with several 6d finishing nails.

7. Cut two 14-inch armrests from 2 x 4 and four $8\frac{1}{2}$-inch supports from

2 x 2. The supports must be notched half their thickness and the depth of the sides, so that they lap onto the sides. Secure them in place with two 2½-inch #12 screws in each. The rear supports are 20 inches from the rear of the frame, the front ones 32 inches from the front of the frame. Center the armrests on the supports and secure in place with ¼-inch dowel.

MATERIALS (for chaise)

Wood

1 pc. 2 x 4 x 12′	or	**Sides:** 2 pcs. 2 x 4 x 63″
		Back end: 1 pc. 2 x 4 x 21″
1 pc. 2 x 4 x 14′		**Front legs:** 2 pcs. 2 x 4 x 11″
		Rear legs: 2 pcs. 2 x 4 x 9″
		Backrest sides: 2 pcs. 2 x 4 x 29″
		Backrest top: 1 pc. 2 x 4 x 18″
		Armrests: 2 pcs. 2 x 4 x 14″
1 pc. 2 x 3 x 2′	or	**Front end:** 1 pc. 2 x 3 x 21″
1 pc. 2 x 2 x 8′	or	**Seat cleats:** 2 pcs. 2 x 2 x 34″
		Backrest supports: 2 pcs. 2 x 2 x 11½″
		Armrest supports: 4 pcs. 2 x 2 x 8½″
2 pcs. 36″ x ¾″ dowel	or	**Front leg rung:** 1 pc. 21″ long
		Backrest support rod: 1 pc. 24″ long
1 pc. 1 x 8 x 2′	or	**Wheels:** 2 pcs. 6″ dia.
1–4′ x 4′ sht. ½″ ext. plywood (good one side)	or	**Seat:** 1 pc. 21″ x 42″
		Seat back: 1 pc. 18½″ x 23″
1 pc. 36″ x ¼″ dowel	or	4 pcs. 4″ long

Hardware

12–3½″ #12 screws
18–2½″ #12 screws
12–3½″ x ¼″ carriage bolts w/ nuts and washers
1–36″ x ½″ steel rod   or   **Axle:** 1 pc. 21″ long
2 hitch pin clips
4–½″ washers
6d finishing nails

GARDEN PONDS

A small pond will create a new dimension in your garden no matter how big the yard. Its pleasing illusion of spaciousness— reflecting the changing sky above and nearby blossoms—draws the eye like a magnet. And the smooth surface of the water complements the protective rock borders which are so functional around a backyard pool.

If the chance to grow water lilies is not what led you to put in a pond, it won't be long before you want to give these exotic beauties a try. After you begin pond gardening you'll quickly discover the multitude of aquatic plants to try: cattails and rushes in the shallow water, and mosses and ferns on the banks. Fish will help to balance the health of the pond; choose species to control algae, insects, and tadpoles.

How large you make the pond is determined by what you want to grow in it. In no case need it be very deep. The common range is 18 inches to 24 inches. Water lilies take the most space, needing at least 6 inches of soil to grow in and 6 to 8 inches of water above the crown. They'll do best in containers 1 foot on each side, which means larger plants and blooms. A 6-square-foot pond will support three lilies and a half-dozen or more shallow water plants. For stocking fish, a good rule of thumb is 6 inches of fish for every square foot of surface (discount the shallows). For example, a 4-square-foot pond could be stocked with four 6-inch fish, two 12-inch fish, or one 24-inch fish. If you want to harvest fish for the table, allow 3 cubic feet per every mature pound.

The light a pond reflects can be a very effective accent near a wall or by a steep embankment. But it is a good idea to avoid trees and shrubbery. Although a beautiful juxtaposition, the leaves would foul the water in a small pond quite quickly and the roots disturb the foundation. Consider the possibilities of any poorly drained area. If the spot suits your taste, there is an excellent chance that soil properties there will allow pond construction with a minimum of materials.

With larger pools the hardest decision prior to construction will be whether or not to put in drainage. If you plan to build with concrete, drainage is essential to remove the alkalinity. Of course, a drain is always a helpful feature—its utility increases with the size of the pond. If flooding could be a problem, an overflow drain will aid in stabilizing conditions in the pond. But the low-lying areas that will need this the most are also the toughest to build drainage for.

Decide if it is possible in your location, and how much work and money it will involve. Your county extension or soil conservation agents can provide advice on these questions. In fact, their wide experience with farm ponds will help with everything from construction tips to sources and care for fish and plants.

TUB

This pool is fast and takes just a few dollars. All you need is a container large enough to support a water lily. This can be a galvanized wash-tub, a molded plastic form, or even a discarded bathtub. Here are plans for converting a galvanized tub which will grow just one lily.

CONSTRUCTION

1. Paint the tub to prolong the life. Inside, a blue enamel will give the water a pleasing color. Prime galvanized metal for paint by scouring it and rubbing with vinegar.
2. Dig a hole as deep as the tub. Then tamp the bottom and level it with enough gravel so the rim of the tub is about an inch higher than the surrounding ground.
3. Place a board across the rim and use a level to make sure the tub is resting flat.
4. Carefully fill around the sides, and tamp the soil gently, keeping the tub level. To top it off, line the border with rocks or bricks.
5. Place a thin layer of sand in the bottom and enough soil to plant the lily. To top if off, lay out a bed of perennials which will naturalize and complement your pool.

PLASTIC LINERS

For making a large garden pool conveniently, a flexible waterproof liner can't be beat. Brian Furner reports that digging and lining his 2-foot by 9-foot-square pond took just two hours. And if the need arises, this type is far easier to remove than a concrete pool.

Polyethylene sheets make construction economical too. But since the plastic deteriorates in the sun, you will need to shield exposed edges (a slight overhang of the flagstone border, paint, or a strip of plastic). Butyl rubber, which is shown here, is much stronger and more expensive. All plastic liners need to be handled very carefully during installation but are quite sturdy once in place.

CONSTRUCTION

1. Determine the length of the liner you will need by adding twice the maximum depth of the pool to the length. Get the width by adding twice the maximum depth to the width. Then add two feet to each of these dimensions in order to allow plenty of overlap.
2. Mark the outlines for the features of the pond with string, as shown. Notice Furner's use of a ledge 8 inches wide and 8 inches from the top of the pool for shallow water plants. This makes for easy construction and easy plant care.
3. Dig the pit and remove all small stones.
4. Lightly pack the sides and bottom. Then line it with fine sand, moist newspapers, or peat moss.
5. Put in the plastic liner. Pull it moderately taut and weight the edges.
6. Fill the pond.
7. Line the perimeter with brick or flagstone.

8. In a pond like this it is better to use baskets or tubs to contain your soil and plants. Thus maintenance of the vegetation is neat, and the water is kept clear.

BENTONITE CLAY

This kind of pool can also be sealed with bentonite. The clay swells from ten to twenty times its original volume, sealing all pores. It is easy to apply and fairly inexpensive. Perhaps the only drawback is the sticky gum it forms, which could be messy when you move your plants. You can overcome this by adding gravel or stepping stones in spots around the bottom.

Bentonite is available in 50-pound bags through some ceramic dealers. On a real sandy soil it will take 8 pounds to seal 1 square foot, or 2 to 4 pounds on a soil with more clay. Consult your extension agent for an evaluation of your soil's porosity and application rates.

If you have to establish application rates for yourself, a distributor of the clay recommends this technique. Punch holes in the bottom of a container (a coffee can or basin), then put in a couple of inches of your subsoil and compact it lightly. Add a small amount of the clay (1 teaspoon, or $\frac{1}{2}$ teaspoon, depending on the size of the container and your guess about the soil's makeup) and work it lightly into the surface. Add water to see if this amount seals. Slowly add measured amounts of clay until seepage stops. Then extrapolate your pool's requirements. Add a 15 percent safety factor to that amount, to make sure the pool will be sealed.

CONSTRUCTION

1. Dig the hole as in the preceding plans.
2. Spread the dry bentonite evenly around the bottom and sides by hand, then lightly work it into the surface with a hoe.
3. Fill the pond. If time shows that the pond leaks, let it drain to the level where the leaking stops. Then spread another thin and even layer of bentonite and refill it.

CONCRETE

Properly installed the concrete pool is the most durable and trouble-free of all. Construction, though, is a little more complicated, since this pool must have a drain.

Right after the pool is finished, it must be filled and drained at least three times at weekly intervals to flush alkalinity from the pool. Unless it's removed, plants won't grow. The drain will continue to be useful because this type of pool will last a long time. Every so often you will want to empty it to remove debris and clean the bottom.

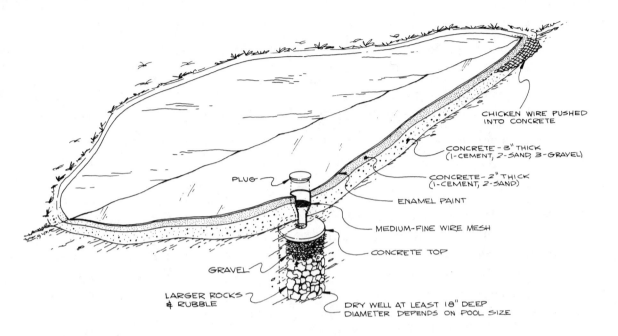

CHICKEN WIRE PUSHED
INTO CONCRETE

CONCRETE - 3" THICK
(1-CEMENT, 2-SAND, 3-GRAVEL)

CONCRETE - 2" THICK
(1-CEMENT, 2-SAND)

ENAMEL PAINT

MEDIUM-FINE WIRE MESH

CONCRETE TOP

PLUG

GRAVEL

LARGER ROCKS
& RUBBLE

DRY WELL AT LEAST 18" DEEP
DIAMETER DEPENDS ON POOL SIZE

CONSTRUCTION

1. Excavate the pond 6 inches larger in all directions than you want the
    pool, in order to accommodate the concrete. For a free-form pond, it
    may be easier to make the outline with a garden hose than with a string.

2. Put in the drainage.

    a. For smaller ponds make a small drainage field by digging a dry
        well at the deepest point, as shown. It should be about 18 inches
        deep; the diameter depends on the size of the pool. This well is
        filled with cinders or gravel. Then lay the concrete over this in the
        same way you will do for the rest of the pool, leaving a drainage
        hole that you can plug tightly in the center. Install a medium-fine
        wire mesh to keep debris from clogging the gravel bed, recessed
        enough to accommodate the plug. When you remove the plug, the
        water will seep out slowly through this French drain.

    b. For larger pools, or any in a low-lying, poorly drained soil, you will
        need to lay a drain pipe away from the pool. The alternative is to
        use a pump. The drain pipe should be threaded at the floor of the
        pool, so you can screw in a vertical section for an overflow drain.
        Dig a shallow trench to accommodate your pipe. Lay in about
        1 inch of gravel for a bed, then pack the pipe in gravel, at least
        within the pool. Now you are ready to apply the concrete over the
        bottom of the pool. Just as there is a screen over the overflow
        drain, put another one into the pipe at the bottom of the pool.

3. After the hole and drain laying are complete, ram the bottom and sides.

4. Working out from the center, lay 3 inches of concrete on the bottom with a trowel. Be careful not to incorporate any soil into this layer. The mixture should be one part cement, two parts sand, and three parts gravel.
5. Lay chicken wire over this and push it into the concrete a bit. Then let it dry for about two days.
6. The second layer of concrete is a mix of one part cement and two parts sand. Apply this 2 inches thick. After it has dried, paint it with enamel.
7. Rinse out the alkalinity as described, and landscape the borders with rocks, ferns, and grasses.

Once your pond is filled and planted, you have a unique experience in store. Getting to know aquatic ecology and how to encourage the plants you want will take some time and provide endless fascination. Watch carefully and be patient. After a few weeks, the clear water will grow green with algae. Then it may turn muddy or brown—don't panic, that's algae too. Whatever changes occur, there is no need to empty the pond and start over. The pool will come to a balance on its own.

PART V
Outbuildings

REPAIRING AN OLD OUTBUILDING

How many times have you heard ". . . and next spring I'm going to fix the barn . . ."? Better yet, how many times have you said it? Well, it can be done. It takes a lot of cursing, sweating, and pain, but it can be done. You don't just tear into it, though. Old barns are big, heavy, rugged buildings, and while they may have taken a lot of abuse over the years, you have to understand them to be able to fix them. Go into your barn and sit down at one end. Look down the whole length of the barn and notice the sections one after the other like ribs holding it up. These are called "bents." When the barn was built, the foundation was laid, the floor was framed and decked, and these bents were assembled on the floor and then raised into place and connected and braced. This was the part that took all the men from miles around.

Everything went in order, one piece on top of another, everything fitted with an unbelievable precision. The barns were built to last forever. With proper care, most of them might have made it, too. But now, too often, neglect has taken its toll. The marginal farms on the poorer land have slowly but surely been shut down or abandoned. Rising prices, rising taxes, inflation—they all played a part and the farmer just got tired of fighting it.

GETTING STARTED

If you've bought one of these old abandoned farms and plan to bring it to life again, more power to you. If the buildings are still in good repair, good fortune smiles upon you greater than anything you can imagine. If the barn is rotten and saggy you may have been sucked in by a terrible curse. It's going to take some hard decisions now whether to tear it down or repair it. Study it carefully. If the barn is bigger than anything you anticipate using, you may be able to salvage some material from one end to repair the other. This can save you a lot of money in materials. You may want to tear the whole thing down and start fresh. The advantage to this is you may be able to build a new barn that is more efficient for your own operations. Remember, these old barns were built for times when everything was done by hands, backs, and horses.

Fixing old barns or houses is some of the most miserable work you can think of. And the biggest disappointment comes when you get done and you find you have a building that is no more or less than it was when it was built. At least when you build a new barn you've created a brand new building where there was none before. When you're done, the work stands there fresh and new and everyone can stop and admire it. But you can grub around in a barn for six months and when you're done you'll have probably dug about a cord of slivers out of your hands, pinched your fingers, banged your shins, gotten dirtier and

sweatier than you'd have ever believed possible, and you'll still end up with a barn that was already there.

The first thing you should get straight is that there is a great deal of difference between the words "restoring" and "repairing."

Restoring means going to the woods and finding just the tree to do the job, cutting it down with an ax, hewing it to the proper size, then mortising and tenoning all the joints and holding them together with hardwood pegs. That sort of thing is fine for people in Old Deerfield or Colonial Williamsburg but will probably go unappreciated on cows, pigs, and chickens. Repairing means making an old building functional again, and with any luck at all, doing it with less money and effort than would go into a new barn.

EQUIPMENT

Let's talk about equipment, then. Assuming you've already got all the

temperament you'll need, you'll require all the jacks and posts you can get your hands on: hydraulic jacks, screw jacks, telescoping post jacks (tele-posts); 6 x 6 and 8 x 8 timbers in varying lengths from 8 to 16 feet; a chain saw (nice but not necessary); a ½-inch drill if you have electricity in your barn, a bit and brace if you don't; a winch or come-along or chain-fall, or maybe all three; and some rope.

Another thing that might come in handy, depending on your situation, is cribbing, which is 4- or 5-foot lengths of 8 x 8 that you stack in pairs like a tic-tac-toe game to shorten the distance from the bottom of the jack to the top of the lifting post. It also provides a very sturdy base for the jack.

LOCATING THE TROUBLE

There are any number of different types of farm building construction. There are, to name a few, pole barns with dirt floors, pole barns with cement floors, and post and pier buildings, usually with wooden floors. Whatever type you have, by the time you get it, will probably have been neglected for years and be at the crossroads of repair or ruin. Structural repairs (repairs to the main timbers that hold the building upright) are the most difficult, roof repairs the most dangerous, and windows, trim and interior facilities perhaps the most time-consuming. It's best to start first with structural problems, for without a basic structure all the other work will be for nothing.

The first step in reconditioning any old building is to spend a lot of time looking at it inside and out to decide what is really wrong. Barns and other buildings seem to be similar in most

farming areas, so try to find one at another farm built like yours, but in good shape. This is a good excuse to get to know the neighbors and take an afternoon off.

Most problems that show up in the roof, like corners sagging or a ridge that looks like a serpent, have their origins in the foundation or upright poles and timbers. So first inspect those. Climb around underneath looking for broken or rotted structural members. And then work your way up.

Take your hammer, pocketknife, and tape measure with you on trips under the building. Since you will want to make a list of needed lumber, either take a pencil and paper or have someone else keep notes.

Before you crawl under the building or begin to check it inside, hit your hammer on a piece of wood you know is sound. It will sound solid.

Rotten wood makes a dull, crunchy thud. If you aren't sure, stick the suspect wood with your pocketknife or pare off some of the surface. You'll quickly see what's rotten and what's not.

THE FIRST STEPS

The most common rotten wood in pole barns will be the bottom of the poles where they meet the ground. In post and pier buildings, posts, sills, joists, and floorboards may be rotted. Resolve at the outset that anything rotten is going to be replaced. Otherwise the termites and dry rot that did the damage in the first place will have a banquet and you'll be doing the job again in a few years.

Before you start ripping out anything, consider the consequences. If you remove part of the underpinnings of a building without first providing a temporary crutch in its place, you are asking to get squashed.

Look up. Is there some way to nail braces on the top of a pole or timber so it won't slip to the side as it is jacked? If so, put some in. Even if they aren't needed, they will give you peace of mind.

There are a couple of preparatory moves you should make before you really get into the work. The first is obvious: Empty the barn—at least the section you're going to be working in. There's no need to lift a lot of extra weight in the first place, and it gives you a lot more space to run if things start falling in the second. The next thing you should do is to open up as much of the floor or walls as necessary to give yourself plenty of room to work. This means taking off siding or taking up the flooring.

If you're planning on using this lumber over again, this is called salvaging. How much are you going to salvage? "All of it, of course." Well, maybe. Dilapidated buildings don't come apart too easily. A good nail puller is an important tool and learning to use it well is even more important, but it won't help if the nails have turned into rust. You can recognize these nails right away because as soon as you pull on them, the nailhead pops off. Depending on how much of the nail is left, you may be able to get in behind the board and gently pry it off with a wrecking bar. Easy does it. These boards are going to be old and dry and will split very easily. The amount of lumber that you eventually salvage is directly related to the length of your patience. If you've had a rotten day, you ought to find something else to do.

THE COLLAPSING FOUNDATION

The most fundamental problem you'll ever face is a collapsing foundation. David Chase of Brattleboro, Vermont, had this problem with the bank barn on his homestead, and he devised a repair method that may solve your problem too.

Chase gave up discussing the situation with foundation contractors after he'd gotten a couple prices. Instead, he studied the problem in more detail and found the solution was under the barn all the time.

Except for the two walls built into the bank, the barn was designed and built to concentrate its load on col-umns, or piers. There are six piers under the center of Chase's barn and seven around the two lower level out-side walls. Chase decided he could pour concrete piers one at a time and then pour a section of wall in between them. That way he'd only have to jack up a small portion of the barn at any one time. Since he'd be dealing with relatively small batches of con-crete each time, he could buy a cement mixer, mix his own concrete and save about $10 per yard over the delivered price. He did the whole job a little at a time and, as a bonus, he still has the cement mixer.

The depths to which Chase's barn had sunk are reflected in these photos. When the barn was jacked into proper position, a gap ranging from 3 to 8 inches existed between the foundation wall and the sill along the rear wall. The obvious problem for Chase was to reconstruct the foundation.

Here's how you can do it.

On either side of the post you're going to be working on, lay down cribbing to distribute the weight of the barn when you jack it up with the tele-posts. Get them reasonably level, put in the tele-posts, and jack up the barn enough to get the weight off the posts. Slip a length of pipe over the turning bar in the tele-post to give you more leverage. When you buy tele-posts don't buy the cheapies you can sometimes find in discount building supply places. Make sure you get good heavy ones.

CONSTRUCTING NEW FOOTINGS

The posts in Chase's barn were set on piles of stones which were buried in the ground with just a hint of mortar between them. The top stones weren't too big, and they were rolled out of the way with little trouble. But when he got into the ground a short way, Chase found what had really been holding the barn up all those years: the bottom rock was about 3 feet around. The cheapest way to move such rocks is to dig a hole next to the rock, undermine the rock a bit, and then roll the rock into the hole and out of the way, which is what Chase did. If your digging isn't too rough, this is a good solution, but be sure to dig the hole big enough. You haven't lived until you've had to dig another 6 inches of hole while the rock's in there with you.

With the rock out of the way he was ready to prepare the hole for the pad or footing. Chase planned the bottom of the pads to be about 4 feet below finish grade. With the snow cover in southern Vermont, he figured that was deep enough to avoid damage from frost. Further north you may want to go deeper, and down South you won't have to go as deep. It isn't necessary to bother with forms for the pad. Just dig the hole to the right size and dump in the concrete. To locate the

Keep the mixer close but out of the way. Chase's arrangement was to have the gravel, cement, and water on one side, the wheelbarrow on the other. The mixer is up on blocks.

pad, use a plumb bob. Hang the plumb line from the beam where the top of the old post used to be. Try to make the hole about 3 feet square, but if you can get 18 inches from the string in all directions you'll be safe enough.

You can drive a stake into the bottom of the hole and pour the concrete to the top of it. The concrete pad should be 10 to 12 inches deep.

Work the wet concrete with a shovel to get it to settle as level as possible and smooth it with a wood float. It's going to make a big difference later if you fuss to get the pad smooth and level now. When the concrete has set up a bit, put in the vertical reinforcing rods to strengthen the pier. The pier will be a foot square and as long as they're inside there somewhere you'll be all right.

CONSTRUCTING NEW PIERS

Give the concrete at least a day to set up before assembling the forms for the pier. Details for the pier forms are shown. You'll need two of each panel. The key strips and the bevel strips for the corners should be nailed on with small nails like 4d finishing nails so that they can be easily taken off and moved as the requirements for the forms change. The drawing shows how the forms would go together for an outside wall pier, for instance. For inside piers, you'll want bevels on all four corners. For an outside corner pier, you'll only want one beveled corner and one of the key strips will have to be moved to another panel and two more holes will have to be bored for the tie rods (horizontal rods running through the pier).

These bevels on the corners are not just fancy stuff. They help minimize damage to the pier should you back into one with a truck. Not only that, if you should stumble one day and drag your leg across the pier, you'll be a lot less apt to lay your leg open.

There are two things to remember when you're building forms. First, they can't be too strong. Second, when you get ready to strip them they should come apart easily. The forms shown worked very well for Chase. Using 2 x 4s, you can make the wooden brackets shown, to hold the forms together. You'll want two pairs, though only one pair is shown. If you don't make the inside dimensions of the brackets more than $\frac{1}{2}$ inch bigger than the outside dimensions of the forms you'll be able to wedge them all together with wood shingles at the points shown.

These forms will last indefinitely with a little care. Paint the inside face of the forms with crankcase oil before

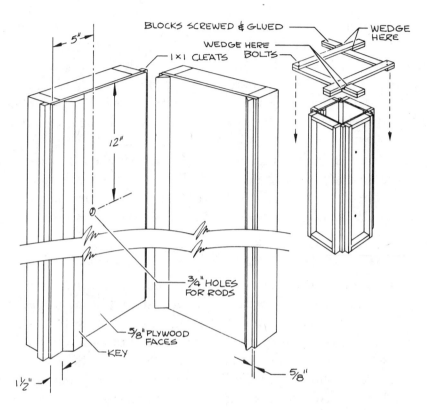

you put them together. This not only makes it easier to strip the forms from the concrete but helps prevent raising the grain on the plywood face.

When the forms are together, check the position again. This position is more critical than the pad so if the wind is blowing at all, you should set up the final position with a straight-edge and a level. Locate the forms so that the outside edge of the pier will be flush or even with the outside edge of the post. Check both outside corners so that the pier won't end up twisted out of line.

If the pad has been poured smooth and level you'll have very little trouble locating the form for the pier and it will stand by itself with no bracing. Slide the reinforcing rods into the holes in the form and check the position of the pier again. It doesn't take but a minute to check and it can save you a lot of grief later on. Pour the concrete into the form. When you've filled it, take a length of reinforcing rod or some similar object and work it up and down inside the form to help settle the concrete and work out the air bubbles. Don't work it too much. Wet concrete exerts a tremendous pressure on forms and you may find

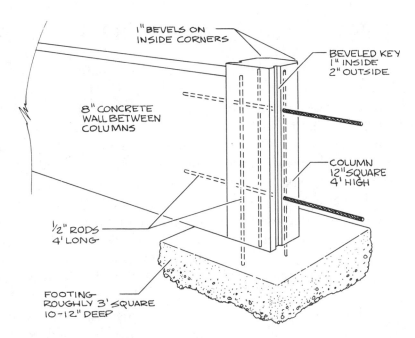

1" BEVELS ON INSIDE CORNERS

BEVELED KEY
1" INSIDE
2" OUTSIDE

8" CONCRETE
WALL BETWEEN
COLUMNS

COLUMN
12" SQUARE
4' HIGH

½" RODS
4' LONG

FOOTING
ROUGHLY 3' SQUARE
10-12" DEEP

them spreading a bit on the bottom. Work it just enough to settle it. Rapping on the outside of the form with a hammer helps settle the concrete, too, especially around the outside and in the corners. Check the position of the form again. You can still move it a little and brace it if you have to.

When the concrete is set and the forms are off you can cut the post and put it back in. Now is the time to adjust the barn to correct any heaves and sags. Some barns of half-breed framing will sag but the older brace frame barns with the braces and wooden pegs are apt to be pretty well set in their ways and if they have sagged at all they aren't going to correct too readily. You have to play

it by ear to some degree. Ofttimes it's just as well to leave a little of the sag and let people stop by to admire "the character of that fine old barn."

The finished corner post: The forms have been stripped, the concrete is cured, and the post is back in. The ditch on the right is dug ready for the wall forms.

POURING A NEW CONCRETE WALL

That, then, is the plan for the piers; one at a time until they're done. In between the piers Chase poured an 8-inch-thick wall to within an inch or two of the top of the piers. This is tied to the piers by the keyway and the rods as shown. The first section of wall will be the hardest while you get the pieces cut and get used to building forms. In constructing the

first section Chase built, he nailed everything together, then almost didn't get the forms off. After that experience, he secured the forms just enough to hold everything until he could get the wires and spacers in place and tight.

Note the 1 x 8 spacer in the forms. You'll probably need two of these in a 12-foot wall section. These prevent the forms from being squeezed together too tight by the wires and the dirt on the bottom. Chase got by quite well with just three wire ties. Use form wire, which should be available at concrete places or a good hardware store. When you have it threaded through the forms and have the ends twisted together, take a short length of pipe or a stick and twist the wires together inside the form. This will pull the forms together and hold them tight. Pull the 1 x 8 spacers out when the forms are about a third full of concrete.

If you're wary of the rock and dirt system for holding the bottom of the forms in place, you can dig the ditch a little wider and put another set of wales and wire ties in. If your walls are going to be more than 4 feet high you'd better plan on another set of wales anyway, 2 feet below the ones shown.

The wall forms will rest on the

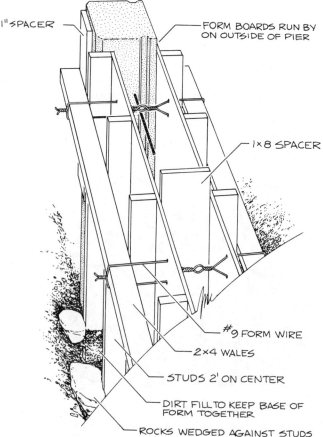

1" SPACER

FORM BOARDS RUN BY ON OUTSIDE OF PIER

1 x 8 SPACER

#9 FORM WIRE

2 x 4 WALES

STUDS 2' ON CENTER

DIRT FILL TO KEEP BASE OF FORM TOGETHER

ROCKS WEDGED AGAINST STUDS

FORMS FOR WALLS BETWEEN PIERS

pads. If the pads are all the same height and level, the wall forms will be level. If not, you can measure down from the beam overhead and snap a chalk line inside the form or drive in some nails to determine the height of the wall. The concrete doesn't have to come clear to the top of the forms. Work the concrete lightly with a rod and then float off the top with a wooden float.

POURING A NEW CONCRETE FLOOR

Under the barn Chase poured the concrete floor in 12-foot squares using the piers as the corners of the squares. The illustration shows the layout. If you've leveled the barn to within reason you can make yourself a measuring stick. Hold the stick against the bottom of the barn floor joists to see how much you have to dig or fill.

Make another one 4 inches shorter to set your forms with.

Pour the floors a little wetter than the piers and walls to make it easier to screed it off. Pour a little at a time and screed it with the straightedge as shown by the arrows. When it's all poured and screeded, pull up the form in the middle of the slab. Don't pull

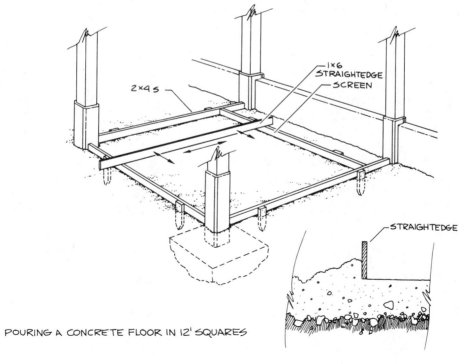

2×4 s

1×6
STRAIGHTEDGE
SCREEN

STRAIGHTEDGE

POURING A CONCRETE FLOOR IN 12' SQUARES

up the outside forms. Fill in the hole left by the form and smooth it with the wood float. Then float the entire slab to correct any bad spots left by the screeding. If you want the floor really smooth, wait until the wet glaze is gone and go over the whole thing again with a steel trowel. You can make a couple kneeling pads about 24-inch square out of old plywood to get out to the middle. It takes at least two.

Once the concrete is done and the posts are back in under the barn you can do as you please with the open spaces. Chase decided to have a lot of windows. If you're planning a door, be sure to leave an opening in the concrete wall. You'll also want to make the bottom of the wall deeper at the doorway for protection against frost. Depending on your foundation problem, this approach, or one similar to it, could solve your problem. If your trouble is in the framework, you've got a lot of work still ahead of you.

REPAIRING THE FRAME

Basically, repairing the frame means lifting the barn, holding it there, pulling out the rotten timber, putting in the new one and letting the barn back down again. No two situations are alike, but from the information that follows, you should be able to analyze and solve your own problems.

Before and after photos show best the frustration of repairing an old barn: the difference doesn't reflect the amount of work involved. Besides closing in the open bays, which was a relatively easy project, Chase reconstructed much of the barn's foundation, which wasn't easy by any standard.

THE ROTTED POST

The rotted post is likely to occur underneath or in the lower levels of barns which are built into a hillside. The problem is caused by the moisture that gets into the bottom of the post from time to time. Wood will last indefinitely if kept either completely dry or completely wet. It's the alternate wet and dry periods that do it in. Even dampness coming up through the masonry pier can provide enough moisture to rot the post.

First, determine how far up the post is rotted. Use your hammer and knife and if you still wonder, stab it with an ice pick. Then you've got to jack up the barn and remove the old post. There are two methods of lifting. The better system is the tele-post, but it can't lift very much. The other system is a hydraulic jack or a screw jack and a long post. But this system also has a weak point: If the base of the jack isn't set soundly and level the whole thing can jackknife and come tumbling down. If the tele-post won't lift the barn you can set up a dual system with a tele-post and a hydraulic jack. Do the lifting with the hydraulic jack and for every couple of pumps take up the slack on the tele-post.

The jacks have to be on some sort of pad. It can be a good thick plank or a length of 8 x 8. One thing you'll

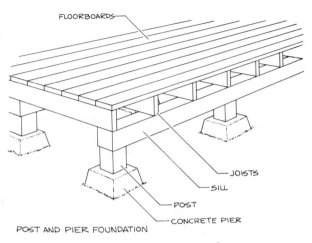

FLOORBOARDS

JOISTS

SILL

POST

CONCRETE PIER

POST AND PIER FOUNDATION

learn while working with pads is that it's a good idea to have a pad that's big enough to carry the weight of the barn for quite a while. Sometimes you just don't get back to things. If the dirt floor under your barn isn't good bearing soil, the barn may begin to sag before you get back to the work.

Where you locate the jack depends in part on your particular situation, but here's a special trick you might be able to try wherever you plan to replace only part of the post, obviously the part that's rotted.

Go up about a foot above the rot and drill three holes in an 8-inch triangle all the way through the post. Find a piece of scrap timber about the same dimension as the rotten one. Alongside the rotten timber put down your jack pad. Put the jack (in the down position) on this pad, then cut the scrap timber to fit in above it. Bolt the scrap timber to the barn timber. Then very slowly and carefully begin to elevate the jack. This should lift the rotten timber or pole off the ground and begin to raise the upper portion of your building back to level. If you are afraid something might break loose and hurt you, put in some temporary bracing so it won't.

If the timber you are raising is set in concrete, or into the ground, you must now cut it off with the chain saw.

After each few turns or pumps with the jack, take a break. Give the upper portion of the building a chance to

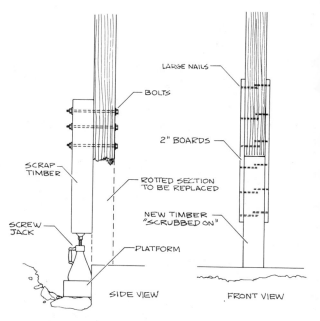

creak and squawk and readjust itself.

When you are satisfied that the roof is back to where it should be, jack a little farther. The new post will settle in the ground and this way it will settle level. There are ways to measure whether you have everything absolutely level, ranging from a simple water level to the professional's transit.

Now, cut off the original post or timber above the rotten part, but below the bolts. Cut a new timber to replace the part you cut off. Butt the two pieces together and make sure the ends meet flat. Get two pieces of 2-inch lumber 4 feet long and as wide as the pole or timber. Sandwich them on opposite sides of the joint where old and new timber butt up. This is

Here is the procedure for holding the barn while replacing one of the interior posts. Chase laid a pad of 8 x 8 timbers on the ground, then jacked up the barn with the tele-posts. The short section of plank on the underside of the carrying beam is where the post was.

600

Since the bottom of this post was rotted, it was cut away and replaced. The new section of post was scabbed in place with 2-inch planks.

called "scabbing." Nail them on with at least 40d spikes and then very slowly and carefully let the tension off the jack. When you have removed the jacking timber by taking out the bolts, you might want to scab boards to the other two sides of the joint for extra strength. And that's it.

If a whole section of the building is sagging, this procedure must be followed on all the uprights in that section at the same time. Otherwise, you will break things loose upstairs. Take your time and if in any doubt that what you are doing is safe, get some expert opinions.

If you plan to replace the entire post, you will have to jack up the beam that the rotted post supports. With the beam lifted up, the bottom of the post is free. If the braces are still in good shape you probably won't even be able to wiggle it. Now you have to decide if you're going to restore it or just fix it. If you're going to restore it, you've got to drive out the pegs (see illustration) to release all the pieces. Sometimes the pegs don't go all the way through and there's no way to drive them out. You can drill them out with a drill the same diameter as the pegs, but this

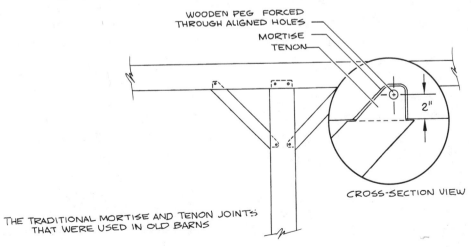

WOODEN PEG FORCED
THROUGH ALIGNED HOLES

MORTISE

TENON

2"

CROSS-SECTION VIEW

THE TRADITIONAL MORTISE AND TENON JOINTS
THAT WERE USED IN OLD BARNS

will ultimately cause problems. When they built the barns they made the hole in the tenon offset a little from the hole in the mortise so that when they drove in the peg it would draw into place. You may be able to make it work again by getting bigger pegs and relocating the holes but it's questionable.

Remember, the reason builders a century ago used the mortise and tenon joints was because hardware was unavailable or just too expensive. Labor was cheap. This is also the reason for the hand-hewn beams: they couldn't run to a sawmill to have it done for them. But you can, if you are lucky.

Many regions have small local sawmills whose operators will cut timbers any size you want. Some are limited to the length they can cut but generally if you let the operator know ahead of time, he will order an extra-long log or two from the loggers. Most localities have some species that is used primarily for framing lumber and this should do just fine.

Before you put the new post in, inspect the pier that it was sitting on. If it's loose and crumbly, better rebuild it. If it's too close to the ground, build it higher. Remember, if the post is rotted, there has to be a reason and if the reason is readily apparent, don't put in a new post without at least trying to eliminate the problem.

Rebuilding piers is not difficult and there are any number of ways to do it. One fairly simple way is to buy a few chimney blocks, lay them up, and pour the center full of concrete.

When you put the new post back in, sock a little preservative on it first. It may not stop the rot entirely but it will slow it down long enough so you won't have to replace the post again. The best way is to soak the post the way you'd soak fence posts to let the wood absorb the preservative. A couple of brush coats will help though. In some areas bugs may be a problem. Treating the post with preservative is supposed to discourage bugs, too.

When you're ready to put the post back in, it's time to correct any heaves or sags in the frame. Generally, these old brace frame buildings won't sag too much if there is nothing radically wrong with the frame. If for some reason it has sagged, don't get the idea you're going to correct it in an afternoon. Any problem that has lasted long enough to twist a hardwood 8 x 8 is going to be time-consuming to solve.

Take a couple turns on the jack in the morning and a couple more in the evening. You can tell when you've gone the limit because you can feel a lot more resistance. Just let it set for a few hours and you'll find you can jack it much easier and the barn won't

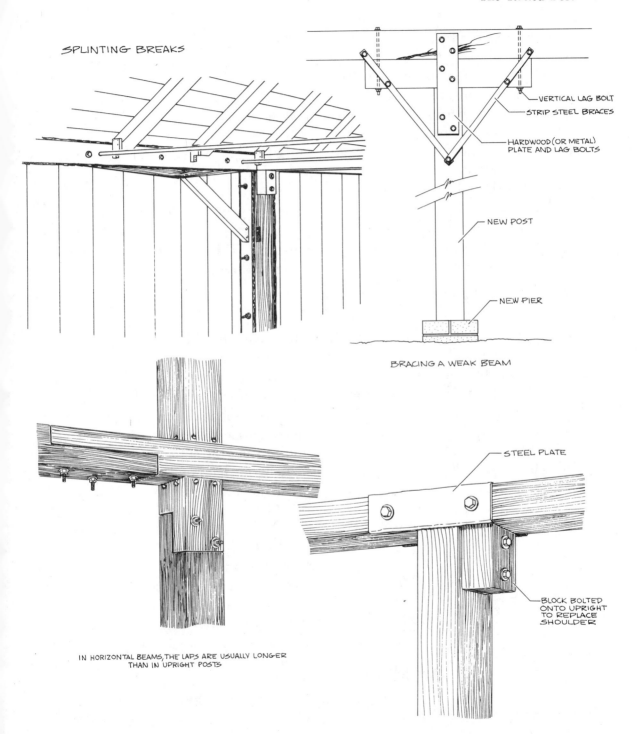

SPLINTING BREAKS

VERTICAL LAG BOLT

STRIP STEEL BRACES

HARDWOOD (OR METAL) PLATE AND LAG BOLTS

NEW POST

NEW PIER

BRACING A WEAK BEAM

STEEL PLATE

BLOCK BOLTED ONTO UPRIGHT TO REPLACE SHOULDER

IN HORIZONTAL BEAMS, THE LAPS ARE USUALLY LONGER THAN IN UPRIGHT POSTS

groan so much either. Keep an eye on the pads under the jacks. If the bearing isn't too good you may find you're just driving the pads into the ground and the barn isn't going anywhere. If this happens, you'll either have to dig down to good solid bearing like gravel, or you'll have to provide a bigger pad with more area on the ground.

If you have the barn corrected, you can put the post in. This is going to be a lot easier if you've decided not to bother with any mortise and tenon joints. The barn should be jacked up just past where you want it. This gives you a chance to slip the post into place and then ease the barn back down where it belongs. The illustrations show a few ways to reconnect some of the beams. Angle iron, sheet iron, hardwood planks, and lags and bolts can hitch just about anything together if you don't care too much about being aesthetic. They may not look too nice but they'll do the job.

THE ROTTED SILL

Let's move on to the sills. The sill is the beam that lies along the top of the foundation and locates and provides bearing for all the posts, beams, and joists. The reasons for the rot are the same: alternate wet and dry.

Occasionally someone will try to solve the rotted sill problem by pouring a concrete apron against the foundation and sill. This does just about everything wrong. The new concrete apron provides a sluice for water to run down the wall and under the sill. Once trapped there, it can't escape and rots out the sill. If you find it on your barn, the only thing to do is to break out the sledgehammer and get rid of it.

The illustration shows you the work involved. If you don't have access to a lot of jacks and can't afford to buy that many, you can replace the jacks with wooden posts and wedges as soon as you have each section jacked. This takes a lot more time though, and is quite cumbersome because you have to fit each post as you go along. The principle shown applies anywhere you're going to be working on

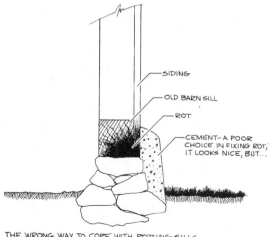

SIDING
OLD BARN SILL
ROT
CEMENT-A POOR CHOICE IN FIXING ROT, IT LOOKS NICE, BUT...

THE WRONG WAY TO COPE WITH ROTTING SILLS

DUPLICATING THE FUNCTIONS OF ROTTED BEAMS

flooring off and can lift the beam into place from above with a winch. If you don't take the floor off, you may be able to work the beam up one end at a time. However you do it, when you get the beam in the air remember to leave plenty of room to run.

With the barn and the floor supported and the siding off, you're ready to take out the beam. Just saw off the tenon on the bottom of the post. The ends of the sill may be half-lapped and pegged into the adjacent sills. If you can get a chain saw into the lap joint, you can saw off the pegs and pull out the rotten piece. If you can't do that, you can saw off the rotten sill piece just beside the post over the joint. Then you can split out the end of the beam to expose the pegs and you can then cut them off. When everything is cleaned out of the way you can cut the new sill, making all the necessary notches to take the ends of the joists, make the half-lap joints on the ends, and slide it into place. Sock some preservative on it

a section of the barn that is carrying the weight. You have to provide the bearing somewhere else and quite often this means going clear up through the barn.

If you have floor joists going into the sill you'll have to support them too, assuming of course that they're not all rotted too. A way of doing it is shown. Putting the beam into place is a lot easier if you have some of the

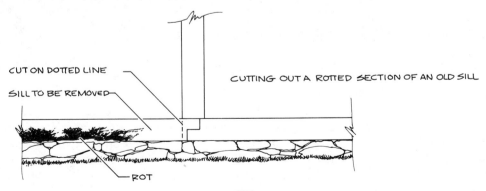

CUT ON DOTTED LINE

SILL TO BE REMOVED

CUTTING OUT A ROTTED SECTION OF AN OLD SILL

ROT

first, though. Before you put weight on the sill again, get it trued up and into place and then mix some mortar and work it in between the sill and the foundation. If the foundation is laid up dry, be very careful that you don't upset it while you're working on the beams.

ROTTED FLOOR JOISTS

Floor joists are somewhat simpler. Usually the floor is laid on the frame and you don't have to hold up the rest of the barn while you're repairing it. If the joists are rotten, check the floorboards too. The dampness may have eaten away at the whole floor. If you're going to be putting any weight at all on the floor you ought to tear it out and put in a new one. If you don't need the space under the floor you could put another carrying timber under the center of the span and run new wood to replace

Use a chain saw to cut away rotted flooring. One homesteader experienced in barn repairs of this sort recommends a sledgehammer test of flooring: A hard whack will reveal whether or not a floorboard needs replacement.

After the rotted flooring is removed, replacement planks are nailed to the joists. By leaving a narrow gap between planks, you can provide some drainage and improve air circulation, helping to prevent future rotting. The piece of plywood in the photo is a temporary spacer used to establish the gap between planks.

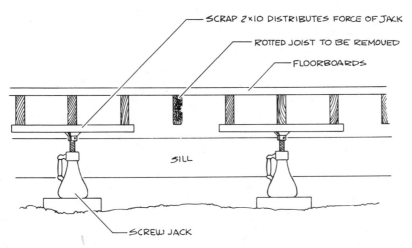

SCRAP 2×10 DISTRIBUTES FORCE OF JACK

ROTTED JOIST TO BE REMOVED

FLOORBOARDS

SILL

SCREW JACK

the rotten ends. If the joists are cracked from overloading, you may get by with doubling them up. This is a relatively simple procedure except for one thing. You have to put the joist in flatways and then twist it into place. The problem comes when you twist it. It measures longer from corner to corner across the end than it does when it's in position. Perhaps you can force it into place. If not, you can cut the ends a little bit small and then nail the new piece to the old joist as long as there is still some good wood in the old joist. The problem with this is that the new joist won't be bearing on the ends and the strength of your floor will then be dependent on nails. If one or two of the joists have sagged, jack them back into place first and then double or triple them.

If you decide to replace the floor, you can probably use the same size lumber that was used before unless you're going to be driving into the barn with a loaded truck. The oldest barns were designed for loaded wagons and horses, not trucks. The best solution to this would be to do some research first into live loads for wood frame buildings. You may be able to get good advice at your local lumberyard.

RAFTERS AND ROOFING

The illustration shows a way to support the rafters if you're unfortunate enough to have to replace the beam called the plate. The plate is the beam that runs all around the top of the barn and provides support for the rafters. The problem is keeping the supporting beam from sliding up the rafters. In the way shown the jacks are lifting straight up instead of at an

607

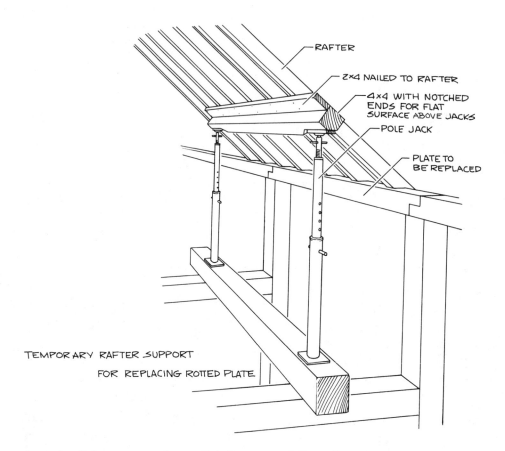

RAFTER

2×4 NAILED TO RAFTER

4×4 WITH NOTCHED ENDS FOR FLAT SURFACE ABOVE JACKS

POLE JACK

PLATE TO BE REPLACED

TEMPORARY RAFTER SUPPORT
FOR REPLACING ROTTED PLATE

angle and while not a perfect solution, it's about as safe as anything that can be rigged up in the top of a barn.

Rafters are very tricky to replace. The first problem is that they are where they are, so high above the ground. And even if it were completely safe up in the top of the barn, there are still other problems. Try to take the old rafter out: You can't do it without doing a lot of prying and yanking and damage to the roofing. If you do manage to get it out, you then have all the nails jutting from the roof boards. You can't drive them back out because they'll upset the roofing. If you leave them in you'll lay your arm open trying to put in the new rafter. Moreover, after the new rafter is in, you won't be able to nail the roof boards to the new rafter without taking all the roofing off.

The best solution is to double the rafters as necessary. The ends don't need to bear as might be desirable with the joists. Roofs, while they carry considerable weight after a snowstorm, don't support the con-

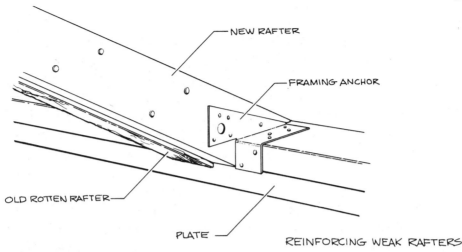

NEW RAFTER

FRAMING ANCHOR

OLD ROTTEN RAFTER

PLATE

REINFORCING WEAK RAFTERS

centrated loads involved when you drive a loaded truck onto the barn floor.

With the price of roofing materials going out of sight and the work involved, think twice or maybe three or four times before writing off a barn roof. It may be that only a part of it is bad or a shingle here and there. A good heavy shake or shingle roof should last a hundred years or more on a barn. On a house, small leaks can be much more of a problem.

On gently sloped roofs, remove the broken shingles and old nails carefully and weave the new shingles under the edges of the old ones. Work from bottom to top and use galvanized roofing nails. Anything else will rust in a few years.

Tack a 1 x 4 against the bottom end of the shingles on both sides of the hole. Use it for a straightedge to keep the new shingles in line with the old.

For small holes in steep roofs, a push pole may do a serviceable job. A ladder will get you to the edge of the roof. To a 1 x 2 long enough to reach the rest of the way, tack two pieces of ¼-inch plywood about 3 inches by 6 inches. This forms a slot into which you can fit a shingle. With the thick end of the shingle in the slot, slide the shingle onto the roof and up under the course of shingles above the hole. It isn't permanent, but it will last a good while. For a better repair, put some mastic on the shingle before pushing it into place.

Siding, flooring, roofing, doors, windows probably all need work. If you're going to repair rather than replace, pay attention when you're tearing things apart. Then carefully put good wood back to replace the bad in just the reverse order you took it apart.

Since it is expensive, you may want to do your building repairs in stages.

If so, do the important structural stuff first. It doesn't show as much, but the building won't blow down either. Next protect from rain and snow. Then do the rest of it at your leisure and as money and necessity dictate. If you are wondering whether it is worth all the hours and labor, just call a few contractors for estimates. Our guess is that you'll do it yourself.

No book can provide a step-by-step guide to repair every barn. We've tried, however, to provide some information that will help you go into this job with your eyes open (at least until you get a face full of chaff and splinters), so that you won't have too many surprises or disappointments. All barns don't rot in the same place. All barns weren't built by the same person either. When the barn went up it was with the help of a huge gang of men. You're apt to find yourself working alone with a come-along, a sledgehammer, and a bunch of jacks.

Study the situation, decide where you're going, and take a deep breath before you start. You've got your work cut out for you. Go to it—and leave plenty of room to run.

BUILDING FROM THE GROUND UP

If your homestead outbuildings are beyond repair, or if you have none to begin with, you'll need to know something about construction from the ground up to cope adequately with your building needs. Almost all buildings, from doghouses to barns, are built using the same basic techniques. The construction is much like residential construction, it just involves less finish work (fewer layers of flooring and sheathing, less fancy trim).

Once you have a basic grasp of the fundamentals involved in the basic types of construction, you'll be better able to plan the outbuilding you want to build. These construction basics, together with ideas from structures others have erected and an inventory of your needs, are three of the most vital ingredients in planning and designing your own homestead outbuildings.

There are two important things to remember in outbuilding construction. The first is that there are few hard and fast rules. As you'll see in this chapter and those that follow, homestead builders often make their own construction rules as they go, working with the materials on hand. In some instances, they "overbuild." In others, they "underbuild." But the results speak for themselves. There's no sound reason why a chicken house or toolshed must be built with a poured concrete foundation well below frost line, with multiple layers of sheathing, with double-hung windows, with studding on 16-inch centers, with 2 x 10 joists and 2 x 8 rafters. Don't be afraid to follow your own instincts, unless the second important thing to remember applies to you.

That thing is building and zoning codes. Increasingly, the government is intruding upon all kinds of construction, forcing restrictions and requirements on builders. In some cases, these rules are reasonable and valid, yet many of them *are* foolish. You'd best find out about them, however, unless you are prepared to put up with one of the hassles of your life.

If your area government does enforce a code that regulates building, it isn't all bad. The code will usually tell you—in so many words—how to construct a building that's going to be approved. You'll have to build in steps, with a building inspector reviewing and approving (or disapproving) your work all along the way. In the best of circumstances, you'll learn a lot from the inspector and the working experience. Check codes before you begin planning.

In the pages that follow, you will learn about the basics of construction. And you'll see examples of good old applied homestead construction.

There are four basic types of construction: stud frame, pole frame, rigid arch frame, and masonry. Stud framing is the type most widely used in residential construction, and it has a legitimate place in homestead building. Pole framing is increasingly popular in agricultural construction. It has been widely used in industrial construction for years, but farmers have embraced it only relatively recently. Rigid arch construction is a melding of the stud and pole framing methods. Masonry construction is durable above all else and is adaptable to almost any building you may want to construct.

The two major parts of a building are the foundation and the part above the foundation, which is called the superstructure. A frame building is one in which the skeleton of the superstructure consists of a framework of wooden structural members. This framework is called the framing of the building, and the framing is subdivided into floor framing, wall framing, and roof framing. Floor framing consists for the most part of horizontal members called joists, wall framing for the most part of vertical members called studs, and roof framing for the most part of inclined members called rafters. Even a masonry building will include some framing, at the least roof framing but quite commonly floor, partitions and roof.

In the days when lumber and labor were plentiful and nails were scarce, it was the custom to use large-dimension timbers ("4-by," "6-by," "8-by," etc.) for framing members and to join members together with mortise-and-tenon joints, fastened with wooden pins. As lumber and labor became more expensive, as nails became cheaper, and as the machinery for cutting lumber to smaller dimensions became more highly developed, the large-timber method of framing (called full framing or post and beam framing) gradually went out of use. Newer methods, in which the framing members consist of small-dimension lumber (usually "2-by") fastened together with nails, are now used.

FOUNDATIONS

Foundations vary according to their use, the bearing capacity of the soil, and the type of material available. The material may be cut stone, rock, brick, concrete, tile, or wood, depending upon the weight which the foundation is to support. Foundations may be classified as wall or column (pier) foundations.

Wall foundations are built solid, the walls of the building being of continuous heavy construction for their

total length. Solid walls are used when there are heavy loads to be carried or where the earth has low supporting strength. These walls may be made of concrete, rock, brick, or cut stone, with a footing at the bottom. The rule of thumb for determining the width or depth of a footing for a foundation is as follows: The width should be twice the thickness of the wall; the thickness (depth) of the footing should be the same as the thickness of the wall. For complete information on constructing concrete footings and masonry foundation walls, see the chapters on concrete and walls.

In homestead construction, a foundation wall is most appropriate where a dirt or concrete floor will be used in the finished building. For most outbuildings with a wood floor, masonry piers will provide an adequate foundation for the building.

But either foundation could be used in either situation.

Column or pier foundations save time and labor. They may be constructed from masonry or they could be wood posts. The piers or columns are spaced according to the weight to be carried. In most cases, the spacing is from 6 to 10 feet.

MASONRY CONSTRUCTION

Masonry construction we bring up first because it very often figures in building construction, regardless of the dominant construction technique. Pole buildings usually have their main supporting members set in concrete. Stud frame or rigid arch buildings begin, ofttimes, with a masonry foundation. Consequently, the homesteader is well advised to know a bit about working with masonry.

The place to begin is this book's chapters on concrete and walls. These chapters detail the basics of mixing concrete and mortar, laying out build-ing lines, pouring footings, laying up block, brick, and stone walls. Whether your design is to build a masonry building or merely to lay up concrete block piers as a foundation for a small shed, you'll need to know about masonry.

If you do intend to construct a masonry building, the information you may need for framing a floor plat-form (should you choose to include a wooden floor), interior partitions, and a roof will be found in subsequent pages under Stud Frame Construc-tion.

STUD FRAME CONSTRUCTION

Stud frame construction is the closest to a total construction system that exists. It is possible to con-struct an entirely wooden building using this type of construction, by erecting the framework atop wooden piers.

Even if you choose some other form of outbuilding construction, you'll want to know something about stud frame construction, since any wooden floors will be "stud framed," as will the roof.

In the pages that follow, you will see photos of the construction of two homestead out-buildings, one intended to be a chicken house, the other intended to be a combination chicken house-storage shed. Neither strictly follows all the conventions of stud frame construction. Both, however, are sturdy, weatherproof, and both serve their purposes well.

You can learn a lot by studying the photos. If nothing else, you should derive from the lot of them an understanding that there are innumerable options in construction. Every builder favors particular techniques, materials, styles. And no two builders fully agree on all these particulars.

Build to suit your purpose, your time, your materials, and especially yourself.

SILL FRAMING

Framing the superstructure generally begins with the sills. The work involved in sill construction is very important for the builder. While the foundation wall is the support upon which the whole structure rests, the sill is the real point of departure for the actual building. It is the first part of the frame to be set in place. The sills rest directly on the foundation, the piers, or the ground, and may extend all around the building; they are joined at the corners and spliced when necessary. The headers and outer joists are laid edgewise on the outside edge of the sill.

If piers are used in the foundation, heavier sills are often used. These sills are of single heavy timbers or are built up of two or more pieces of timber. Where heavy timber or built-up type sills are used, the joints should occur over piers. The size of the sill

depends upon the load to be carried and upon the spacing of the piers. Where earth floors are used, the studs are nailed directly to the sill plate.

It should be noted that sills are not absolutely necessary. Many small wood-floored structures are erected without sills. The floor frame of joists and headers rests directly on foundation piers. For any major building, however, you'll undoubtedly want to include sills in the framework.

FLOOR FRAMING

Wooden floors are supported on a series of joists, which are dimension lumber framing members lined up parallel to one another about 16 to 24 inches apart. They rest on the sills and abut header joists at their ends. The header joists are spiked to the joists with 20d nails. The joists and header joists are spiked to the sills with 16d nails. The flooring is then

nailed to this framework, as detailed below.

A variation is to nail a 1 x 3 ledger strip to the side of the header joists, then to notch each joist so it both rests on the ledger strip and butts against the strip and the header. This technique is most often used when sills are omitted.

Depending upon the length of the

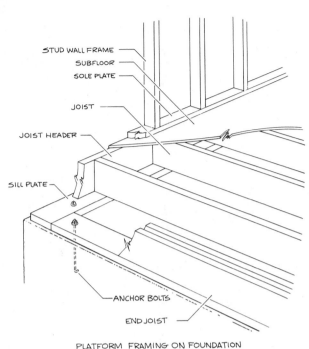

STUD WALL FRAME
SUBFLOOR
SOLE PLATE
JOIST
JOIST HEADER
SILL PLATE
ANCHOR BOLTS
END JOIST

PLATFORM FRAMING ON FOUNDATION

For a chicken house or small shed, 2 x 6 joists would undoubtedly suffice. Most residential construction features 2 x 10 joists.

On upper floors, the joists and header joists are assembled and toe-nailed to the plates. After the flooring, or subflooring, is in place, the wall framing for that story is assembled and erected. This form of stud frame construction is thus called platform framing.

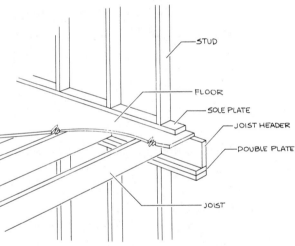

STUD
FLOOR
SOLE PLATE
JOIST HEADER
DOUBLE PLATE
JOIST

SECOND FLOOR EXTERIOR WALL PLATFORM FRAMING

span (the distance between the end supports of the joists) and the expected size of the combined live and dead load on the floor, joists may run anywhere from 2 x 4 (for a loft, for example) to 3 x 10 or even larger (in, for example, a barn floor, where a tractor, pickup, or other heavy equipment might occasionally be parked).

FRAMING JOISTS TO GIRDERS

The distance between an opposing pair of outside walls is often too great to be spanned by a single joist. When two or more joists are required to cover the span, intermediate support for the inboard joist-ends is provided by one or more girders. First floor girders are supported on piers or on basement columns; upper floor girders are supported on lower floor columns. Girders may consist of wood, either solid or laminated (built up of several wooden members spiked or bolted together), or they may consist of steel beams.

There are three common methods

617

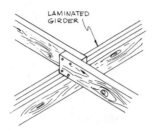
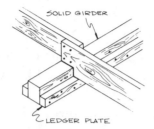
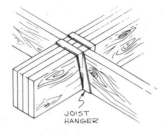

FRAMING JOISTS TO A BEAM

of framing inside ends of joists to wooden girders. In one, the joist ends are lapped on and toenailed to the girder and spiked to each other. In the second, the joist ends are notched so as to bear partly on the girder and partly on a ledger plate nailed to the side of the girder. Again the joists are toenailed to the girder and spiked to each other. Joists should not be notched to more than one-third of their depths. The joist hanger (also called a stirrup) is used when the nature of the construction requires that the upper and lower edges of the joists come flush with the top and bottom of the girder.

FRAMING AROUND FLOOR OPENINGS

Where a floor opening occurs (such as a stairway opening), the parts of the common joists which would extend across if there were no opening must be cut away. The segments remaining on either side of the opening are called cripple or tail joists. The wall-opening ends of cripples are framed against headers as shown. Headers are often doubled, sometimes tripled.

Headers are framed between the full-length joists which lie on either side of the floor openings. These joists are called trimmers, and they, too, are usually doubled or tripled. Headers up to 6 feet in length are fastened with

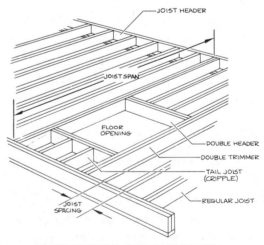

FRAMING AN OPENING IN THE FLOOR PLATFORM

618

This building is perched atop concrete block piers, which are themselves setting atop concrete footings. The building measures 12 feet by 24 feet. There is a pier every 6 feet around the perimeter of the building and one smack in the middle. A two piece girder—two railroad ties—extends along the center of the long dimension of the building. The floor platform is constructed of 2 x 6 joists covered with straight-laid common-board flooring.

20d nails, driven through the trimmers into the ends of the headers. Headers more than 6 feet in length should be fastened with joist hangers.

FLOOR FRAMING UNDER A PARTITION

A partition is a wall other than one of the outside walls of the structure. An upper story partition is not always supported by a partition located directly under it on the story below. When it is not, the floor must be strengthened to carry the load of the partition. For a partition running parallel to the lines of the joists, strengthening is accomplished by doubling the joist under the partition.

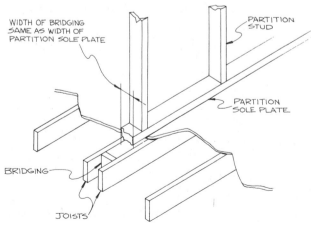

WIDTH OF BRIDGING SAME AS WIDTH OF PARTITION SOLE PLATE

PARTITION STUD

PARTITION SOLE PLATE

BRIDGING

JOISTS

619

The joist is doubled by nailing two joists to a series of solid bridges, usually placed from 14 to 20 inches on center. The bridges must separate the joists by the width of the partition sole plate, to ensure that the upper edges of the joists will be available as nailing surfaces for the flooring. Sole plate stock, cut in lengths equal to the depth of the joist, is the best material to use for the bridging.

BRIDGING

The system of bracing the joists to each other is called bridging. The avowed purpose of bridging is to hold the joists plumb and in correct alignment, and also distribute part of a concentrated heavy load over several

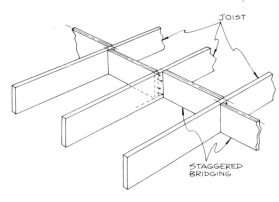

joists next to those directly under the load. The current thinking is that bridging does little of what it is said to do.

There are two types of bridging: cross bridging and solid bridging. Cross bridging consists of pairs of struts (common sizes of strut stock are 1 x 3, 1 x 4, 2 x 2, and 2 x 4) set diagonally between the joists. Solid bridging consists of pieces of joist-size stock set at right angles to the joists. This type of bridging can be staggered for easier installation. Cross bridging is seldom used in modern construction because of the amount of time it takes to install.

For joist spans of ordinary length, a row of bridging for every 5 to 8 feet of span is all that's necessary. For unusually long spans, the maximum distance between rows of bridging is about 6 feet. The bridging is installed after the joists have been set in place, but before the floor is laid.

FLOORING

Since the flooring—subflooring in home construction—helps to hold the joists plumb and rigid, it is considered to be a structural element and therefore a part of the framing.

The most common flooring is ply-wood, and depending upon the application, the thickness used ranges from $\frac{1}{2}$ inch to $\frac{3}{4}$ inch. Common boards and dimension lumber (where heavy loading will occur) can also be used.

Lumber for flooring is usually

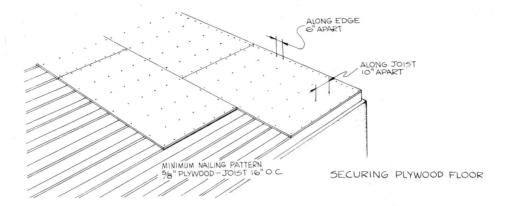

ALONG EDGE
6" APART

ALONG JOIST
10" APART

MINIMUM NAILING PATTERN
5/8" PLYWOOD - JOIST 16" O.C.

SECURING PLYWOOD FLOOR

square edged. Unless boards are end-matched (shaped on the ends to form tongue-and-groove end joints), they must be cut so as to bring end joints over joists.

Straight-laid flooring is laid at a 90-degree angle to the lines of the joists; diagonal laid flooring at a 45-degree angle. To ensure that the lines of end joints will be parallel to the lines of the joists, straight-laid boards must be cut off square, and diagonal-laid boards mitered to 45 degrees.

Straight-laid flooring is started at a wall line; diagonal-laid flooring at a corner. The first board laid is called the starter board. The starter board for diagonal-laid flooring is a small piece shaped like a 45-degree triangle.

Flooring is nailed down with two 8d nails at each joist crossing—with four nails (two in each board) at every crossing where an end joint between boards occurs.

WALL FRAMING

Wall framing is composed of regular studs, diagonal bracing, cripples, trimmers, headers, and horizontal nailer blocks and is supported by the floor sole plate. The vertical members of the wall framing are the studs, which support the top plates and all of the weight of the upper part of the building or everything above the top plate line. They provide the frame-work to which the wall sheathing is nailed on the outside and the inside.

The wall frames are generally laid out on the floor platform, nailed together, then erected and temporarily braced in position until all the exterior supporting walls are in place. The wall frame units are plumbed up, then nailed together at the corner posts and a second plate is nailed atop the

621

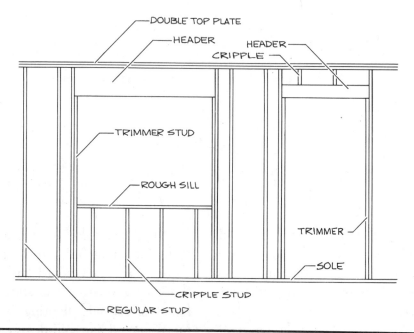

DOUBLE TOP PLATE
HEADER
HEADER
CRIPPLE
TRIMMER STUD
ROUGH SILL
TRIMMER
SOLE
CRIPPLE STUD
REGULAR STUD

This is how the framing began. The foundation, such as it is, is composed of a half-dozen concrete blocks set on the ground. An 8-foot-square floor platform composed of 2 x 6 joists nailed on 2-foot centers and two sheets of ½-inch plywood rests on the blocks. Here the framing for the 7-foot-high front wall is temporarily braced in place.

first, but in such a way that the top plate overlaps the joints between units at the corner post, thus helping to tie the walls together and strengthen the structure. Finally, some type of bracing is applied. It can be cut-in or let-in bracing or the wall sheathing itself, as explained below.

SOLE PLATE AND TOP PLATE

All partition walls and outside walls start with a 2 x 4 (or with a piece of timber corresponding to the thickness of the wall) that is laid horizontally on the floor or joists. It carries the bottom end of the studs and is called the sole or sole plate. It is nailed with two 16d nails to each stud and with two 16d or 20d nails to each joist that it crosses. If it is laid lengthwise on top of a girder or joist, it should be nailed with two nails every 2 feet.

A similar 2 x 4 nailed to the top of the studs is called the top plate. It serves two purposes: to tie the studding together at the top and form a finish for the walls, and to furnish a support for the lower ends of the rafters. The top plate serves as a connecting link between the wall and the roof, just as the sills and girders are connecting links between the floors and the walls. The plate is made up of one or two pieces of timber of the same size as the studs. (In cases where the studs at the end of the building extend to the rafters, no plate is used at the end of the building.) When it is used on top of partition walls, it is sometimes called the cap. Where the plate is doubled, the first plate or bottom section is nailed with 16d or 20d nails to the top of the corner posts and to the studs. The second plate is not added until the wall frames are erected.

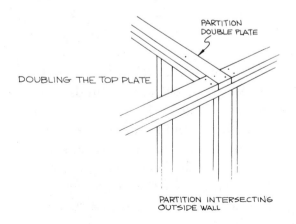

DOUBLING THE TOP PLATE

PARTITION DOUBLE PLATE

PARTITION INTERSECTING OUTSIDE WALL

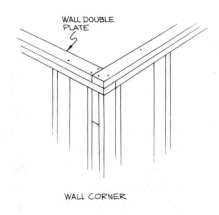

WALL DOUBLE PLATE

WALL CORNER

623

CORNER POSTS

The studs used at the corners of the frame construction are usually built up from three or more ordinary studs to provide greater strength. These built-up assemblies are corner partition posts. A corner post may consist of a 4 x 6 with a 2 x 4 nailed on the board side, flush with one edge. This type corner is for a 4-inch wall. Where walls are thicker, heavier timber is used. A 4 x 4 may be used with a 2 x 4 nailed to two of the adjoining sides. Two 2 x 4s may be nailed together with blocks between and a 2 x 4 flush with one edge. A 2 x 4 may be nailed to the edge of another 2 x 4, the edge of one flush with the side of the other. This type is used extensively where no inside finish is required.

Whenever a partition meets an outside wall, a post wide enough to extend beyond the partition on both sides—often called a **T**-post—is used; this affords a solid nailing base for the

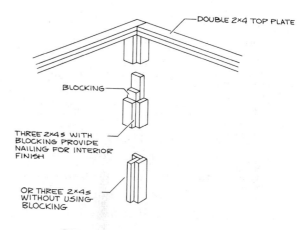

DOUBLE 2×4 TOP PLATE

BLOCKING

THREE 2×4s WITH BLOCKING PROVIDE NAILING FOR INTERIOR FINISH

OR THREE 2×4s WITHOUT USING BLOCKING

CORNER POST FRAMING TECHNIQUES

inside wall finish, and is made in several different ways.

- A 2 x 4 may be nailed and centered on the face side of a 4 x 6.
- A 2 x 4 may be nailed and centered on two 4 x 4s nailed together.
- Two 2 x 4s may be nailed together with a block between them and a 2 x 4 centered on the wide side.
- A 2 x 4 may be nailed and centered on the face side of a 2 x 6, with a horizontal bridging nailed behind them to give support and stiffness.

STUDS

After the posts and plates are in place, the studs are placed and nailed with two 16d or 20d nails through the sole and top plate. Before the studs are set in place, the window and door openings are laid out. Then the remaining or intermediate studs are laid out on the sole plates by measur-ing from one corner the distances the studs are to be set apart. Studs are normally spaced 12, 16, and 24 inches on center, depending upon the type of building and the type of outside and inside finish. Where vertical siding is used, studs are set wider apart, and horizontal blocks are nailed be-

The walls were framed using 2 x 4s and 4 x 4s, no sole plates but a doubled top plate. A 4 x 4 post was toenailed to the floor platform at each corner. Then 4 x 4 posts were toe-nailed to the platform at the center of each dimension. The long west wall has no windows, so 2 x 4 studs were toenailed to the platform on 3-foot centers, filling the space between the 4 x 4s. In the south wall, a 2 x 4 stud was added. In the other walls, studding was shifted off the 3-foot centers where necessary to accommodate windows and doors. The south wall has a 33½-inch by 43-inch window on each side of the center post. The east wall has two similar-sized windows and a 28-inch by 74-inch doorway just north of the center post. The north wall has a 60-inch by 84-inch doorway.

tween them to afford a nailing surface.

When it is desirable to double the post of the door opening, first place the outside studs into position and nail them securely. Then cut the shorter studs, or trimmer studs, the size of the opening, and nail these to the inside face of the outside studs as shown. In making a window opening, a rough sill must be framed; this sill is either single or double. When it is doubled, the bottom piece is nailed to the studs on either side of the opening at the proper height and the top piece of the rough sill is nailed into place flush with the bottom section. The door header is framed as shown. The trimmer stud rests on the sole at the bottom.

After the wall unit is framed, it must be erected in its proper location, plumbed up, and nailed to the floor platform. Temporary braces, extending from the corner post to the side of the floor platform, should be nailed in place (using duplex nails will ensure the braces are secure, while permitting them to be removed easily at the appropriate moment). With all the walls erected, the second top plate is nailed in place. In the case of the building with end walls framed with studs running from sole plate to rafters, of course, these end walls are not framed until the roof framing is erected atop the walls that support it.

PARTITIONS

Partition walls are walls that divide the inside space of a building. These walls in most cases are framed as part of the building. In cases where floors

The back wall framing was nailed together, including nailing blocks between the studs, then erected and temporarily braced in position. Then rafters were cut and set in place, spanning the distance between the front and rear walls. The two end walls were studded in by marking the stud locations on the sole plates nailed to the floor platform, then setting the studs in place, marking and cutting them to fit. The tops are notched to fit firmly around two sides of the rafters. The studs and rafters are set on 2-foot centers.

are to be installed after the outside of the building is completed, the partition walls are left unframed. There are two types of partition walls: the bearing and the nonbearing types. The bearing type supports ceiling joists. The nonbearing type supports only itself. This type may be put in at any time after the other framework is installed. Only one cap or plate is used. A sole plate should be used in every case, as it helps to distribute the load over a larger area. Partition walls are framed in the same manner as outside walls, and door openings are framed as outside openings. Where there are corners or where one partition wall joins another, corner posts or T-posts are used as in the outside walls; these posts provide nailing surfaces for the inside wall finish. Partition walls in a one story building may or may not extend to the roof. The top of the studs has a plate when the wall does not extend to the roof; but when the wall extends to the roof, the studs are joined to the rafters.

BRACES

Bracing stiffens framed construction and helps it to resist winds, storm, twist, or strain stemming from any cause. Good bracing keeps corners square and plumb and prevents warping, sagging, and shifts resulting from lateral forces that would otherwise tend to distort the frame and cause badly fitting doors and windows. Current residential construction depends upon the strength and rigidity of plywood sheathing to brace the building. Often, a single sheet of ¾-inch plywood is nailed to the studs at each corner of a building for bracing and the bulk of the building is sheathed with a cheaper less rigid composition board. Prior to plywood there were three commonly used methods of bracing frame structures.

Let-in bracing is set into the edges of studs so as to be flush with the surface. The studs are always cut to let in the braces; the braces are never cut. Usually 1 x 4s or 1 x 6s are used, set diagonally from top plates to sole plates.

Cut-in bracing is toenailed between studs. It usually consists of 2 x 4s cut

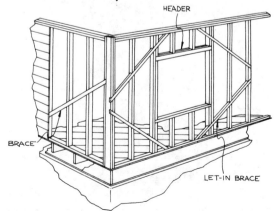

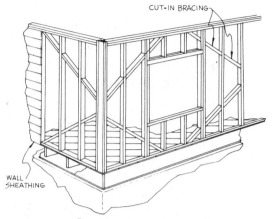

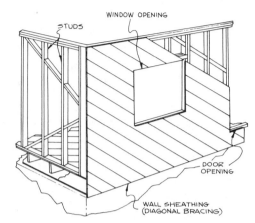

at an angle to permit toenailing, inserted in diagonal progression between studs running up and down from corner posts to sill or plates.

Diagonal sheathing is the type of bracing with the highest strength. Each board acts as a brace of the wall.

CEILING JOISTS

Ceiling joists in residential construction are used to support the ceiling and, occasionally, to support attic flooring. In homestead construction, the latter purpose dominates.

The basic construction is similar to

*Furring strips were used to brace the building. The strips were held in position, the studs marked, then notched with a circular saw and hammer and chisel. The strips were then set in the notches and nailed fast. The braces form **V**s, extending from the top of the corner studs to the sole plate at the centers of the walls.*

A modified sort of let-in bracing was used. Three-foot-long 2 x 4s were mitered at 45 degrees at both ends, then nailed between posts and floor and posts and top plate. Two rows of nailing blocks (2 x 4s) were toenailed between the various vertical framing members.

floor framing. Usually lighter members are used. No header joists are used, and often the pitch of the roof requires that the ends of the ceiling joists be trimmed so they don't project beyond the face of the rafters. The line of the cut is laid out using the framing square as illustrated.

Ordinarily, the top plate is marked for the position of both the rafters and the ceiling joists at the same time. The joists are installed by toenailing them in position using two 10d nails on each side. When the rafters are erected, they are nailed both to the plate and the joists.

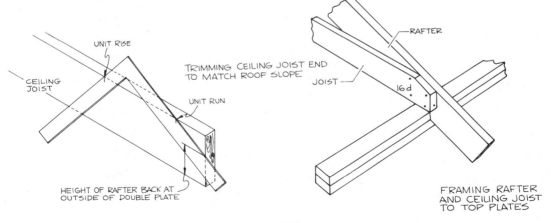

629

ROOF FRAMING

The primary object of a roof in any climate is to keep out the rain and the cold. The roof must be sloped so as to shed water. Where heavy snows cover the roofs for long periods of time, roofs must be constructed more rigidly to bear the extra weight. They must also be strong enough to withstand high winds. The most commonly used types of roof construction include the gable, the lean-to or shed, the gambrel, the hip, and the gable and valley.

The gable roof has two roof slopes meeting at the center, or ridge, to form a gable. This form of roof is simple in design, economical to construct, and may be used on any type structure.

The lean-to or shed roof is a near-flat roof and is used where large buildings are framed under one roof, where hasty or temporary construction is needed, and where sheds or additions to buildings are erected. The pitch of the roof is in one direction only. The roof is held up by the walls or posts on four sides; one wall or the posts on one side are at a higher level than those on the opposite side.

The gambrel roof has two separate slopes. This style is perhaps most traditional for barns, though it is used almost exclusively on small sheds these days. It provides a spacious attic, hence its use on livestock barns, where the attic was heaped full of hay, which could easily be thrown to the floor below at feeding time. Obviously, the gambrel roof is not easy to frame.

The hip roof consists of four sides or slopes running toward the center of the building. Rafters at the corners extend diagonally to meet at the center, or ridge. Into these rafters, other rafters are framed. This roof is strong, but it is quite difficult to lay out and construct and is not widely used in farm and homestead construction.

The gable and valley roof is a combination of two gable roofs intersecting each other. The valley is that part where the two roofs meet, each roof slanting in a different direction. This type of roof is slightly complicated and requires much time and labor to construct.

The *pitch* or *slope* is the angle that the roof surface makes with a horizontal plane. The surface may vary from absolutely flat to a steep slope. The usual way to express roof pitch is by means of numbers; for example, 8 and 12, 8 being the rise and 12 the run. It is usually written 8/12 or 8:12.

The *span* is the shortest distance between the two opposite rafter seats. Stated in another way, it is the measurement between the outside plates,

The roof is framed with 2 x 4 rafters, 2 x 6 ceiling joists, and a 1 x 4 ridge. The rafters and joists are on 2-foot centers.

measured at right angles to the direction of the ridge of the building.

The *total rise* is the vertical distance from the plate to the top of the ridge.

Total run is the level distance over which any rafter passes. For the ordinary rafter, this would be one-half the span distance.

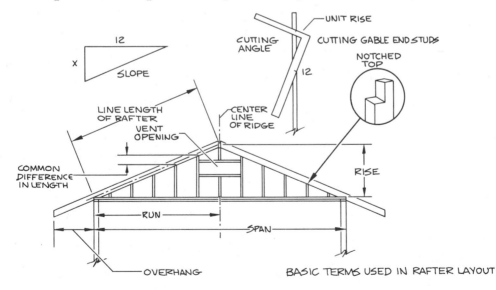

BASIC TERMS USED IN RAFTER LAYOUT

The *unit of measurement* or *unit of run,* 1 foot or 12 inches, is the same for the roof as for any other part of the building. By the use of this common unit of measurement, the framing square is employed in laying out large roofs.

The *rise in inches* is the number of inches that a roof rises for every foot of run.

RAFTERS

The pieces that make up the main body of the framework of all roofs are called rafters. They do for the roof what the joists do for the floor and what the studs do for the wall. Rafters are inclined members spaced from 16 to 48 inches apart. They vary in size, depending on their length and the distance at which they are spaced. The tops of the inclined rafters are fastened in one of the various common ways determined by the type of roof. The bottoms of the rafters rest on the plate, which provides a connecting link between wall and roof and is really a functional part of both. The structural relationship between rafters and wall is the same in all types of roofs. The rafters are not framed into the plate but are simply nailed to it, some being cut to fit the plate while others, in hasty construction, are merely laid on top of the plate and nailed in place. Rafters may extend a short distance beyond the wall to form the eaves and protect the sides of the building.

The *top* or *plumb cut* is the cut made at the end of the rafter to be placed against the ridgeboard or, if the ridgeboard is omitted, against the opposite rafter.

The *seat, bottom,* or *heel cut* is the cut made at the end of the rafter which is to rest on the plate.

The *rafter length* is the shortest distance between the outer edge of the plate and the center of the ridge line.

The *eave* or *tail* is the portion of the rafter extending beyond the outer edge of the plate.

The *measure line* is an imaginary reference line laid out down the

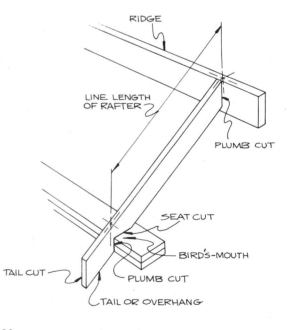

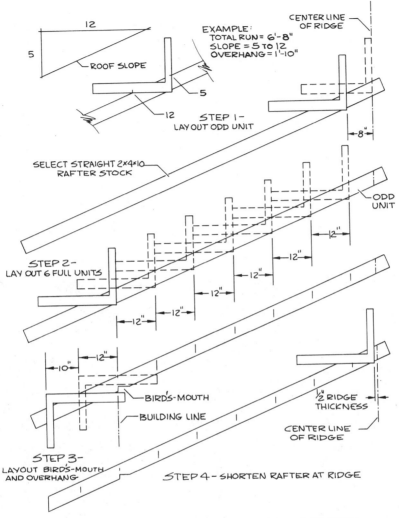

ROOF SLOPE

EXAMPLE:
TOTAL RUN = 6'-8"
SLOPE = 5 TO 12
OVERHANG = 1'-10"

CENTER LINE OF RIDGE

STEP 1 — LAY OUT ODD UNIT

SELECT STRAIGHT 2×4×10 RAFTER STOCK

ODD UNIT

STEP 2 — LAY OUT 6 FULL UNITS

BIRD'S-MOUTH

BUILDING LINE

½ RIDGE THICKNESS

CENTER LINE OF RIDGE

STEP 3 — LAYOUT BIRD'S-MOUTH AND OVERHANG

STEP 4 — SHORTEN RAFTER AT RIDGE

PROCEDURE FOR LAYING OUT A COMMON RAFTER BY THE STEP-OFF METHOD

middle of the face of a rafter. If a portion of a roof is represented by a right triangle, the measure line will correspond to the hypotenuse, the rise to the leg, and the run to the base.

This right triangle is the key to rafter layout. The most commonly used method for laying out rafters is the step-off method. Using the framing square to duplicate the base and leg of the right triangle, each foot of run is stepped off along the rafter, as shown, establishing the proper length. The proper angle for the plumb cut, the tail cut, and the bird's-mouth is also established.

633

In brief, the unit run (12 inches) is located on the blade of the framing square and the unit rise on the tongue. These points are lined up along the edge of the rafter stock. Starting at the ridge end of the rafter, the plumb cut is laid out first. Then any odd unit of run is stepped off, followed by a full step for every foot of run. With the last foot of run stepped off, the building line is scribed, and the square reversed to scribe the bird's-mouth. With the square still reversed, any overhang is stepped off. Finally, half the thickness of the ridgeboard is deducted from the rafter at the ridge end of the layout.

BIRD'S-MOUTH

A rafter with a projection has a notch in it called a bird's-mouth. The plumb cut of the bird's-mouth, which bears against the side of the rafter

The roof is sheathed with three sheets of ½-inch plywood. A 1-foot by 8-foot strip was cut from one sheet and nailed to the center rafter with full sheets flanking it. The remaining piece of the third plywood sheet was cut into three like-sized pieces, which were just the right size to sheath in the remaining open space. To provide a bit of extra support at the joints between panels, two pairs of nailing blocks were toenailed between the middle three rafters. Facsia boards were nailed across the ends of the rafters and parallel to the slope of the roof. After a drip edge was installed, roll roofing was laid.

plate is called the heel cut; the level cut, which bears on the top of the rafter plate, is called the seat cut.

The size of the bird's-mouth is usually stated in terms of the depth of the heel cut rather than in terms of the width of the seat cut. You lay out the bird's-mouth in about the same way you lay out the seat on a rafter without a projection. Measure off the depth of the heel on the heel plumb line, set the square and draw the seat line along the blade. For the roof surface, all rafters should be exact, therefore, the amount above the seat cut, rather than the bottom edge of the rafters, is the most important measurement. The amount above the seat cut should be such as to adequately support the overhang of the roof, plus anyone working on the roof. The width of the seat cut is important as a bearing surface. The maximum width of the common rafter should not exceed the width of the plate.

COLLAR TIE

Gable or double-pitch roof rafters are often reinforced by horizontal members called collar ties.

To find the line length of a collar tie divide the amount of drop of the tie in inches by the unit of rise of the common rafter. This will equal one-half the length of the tie in feet. Double the result for actual length. The formula is: Drop in inches x 2 over unit of rise equals the length in feet.

The length of the collar tie depends on whether the drop is measured to the top edge or bottom edge of the collar tie. The tie must fit the slope of the roof. To obtain this angle, use the framing square. Hold unit of run and unit of rise of the common rafter. Mark and cut on unit of run side.

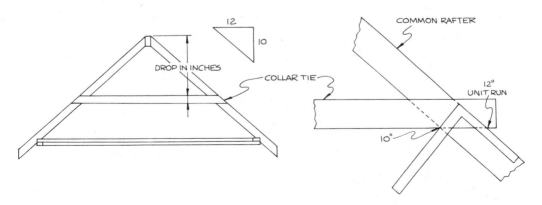

SHED ROOF FRAMING

As previously mentioned, a shed or single-pitch roof is essentially one-half of a gable or double-pitch roof. Like the full-length rafters in a gable roof, the full-length rafters in a shed roof are common rafters. Note, however, that the total run of a shed roof common rafter is equal to the span of the building *minus the width of the rafter plate on the higher rafter-end wall.* Note also, that the run of the projection on the higher wall is measured from the inner edge of the rafter plate. To this must be added the width of the plate and the length of the overhang at the top. Shed-roof common

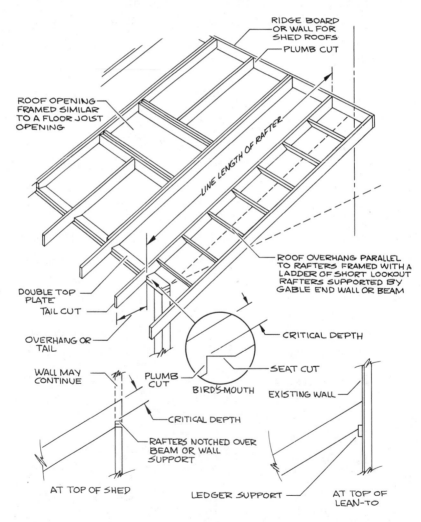

636

rafters are laid out like gable-roof common rafters. A shed-roof common rafter has two bird's-mouths, but they are laid out just like the bird's-mouth on a gable-roof common rafter.

The height of the higher rafter-end wall must exceed the height of the lower by an amount equal to the total rise of a common rafter.

ROOF TRUSSES

Much modern roof framing is done with roof trusses. The principal parts of a truss are the upper cord (con-sisting of the rafters), the lower chord (corresponding to a ceiling joist), and various diagonal and/or vertical bracing and connecting members which are known collectively as the web members.

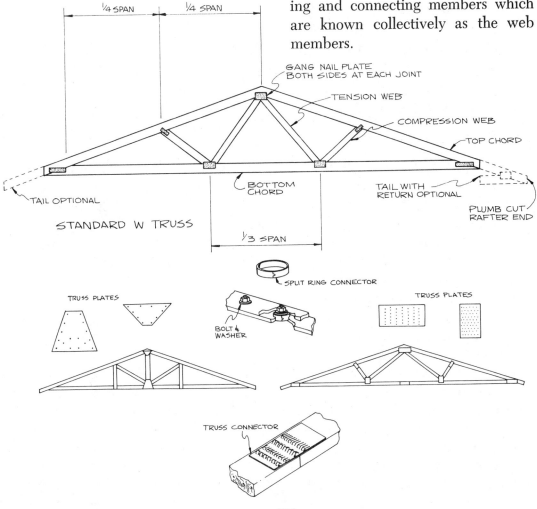

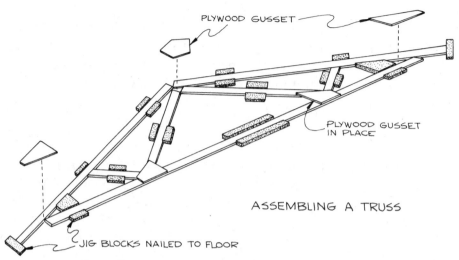

PLYWOOD GUSSET

PLYWOOD GUSSET
IN PLACE

ASSEMBLING A TRUSS

JIG BLOCKS NAILED TO FLOOR

The truss is joined at the corners with plywood gussets. Other methods of corner joining are by metal gussets or by various types of notched joints, reinforced with bolts. Construction information on trusses is usually given in detail drawings.

GAMBREL ROOF FRAMING

The purpose of the gambrel roof on the farm is to create a voluminous space in the barn above the animals for the storage of hay. To do this, a double-pitch roof is created, using what amounts to two separate gable-roof rafters.

On large structures, the gambrel roof is usually framed with a purlin located at the junction of the two rafters on each side of the ridge. The rafter ends are notched in much the same way the bird's-mouth is laid out and cut, to fit snugly about the purlin. The individual rafters are laid out and cut using the step-off technique.

A significant drawback to the gambrel roof occurs in the erection. A lot of manpower and scaffolding is necessary to hoist the rafters, collar ties, ridge, and purlins into position and nail them fast. Partly for this reason, the gambrel roof is usually restricted, these days, to small garden sheds.

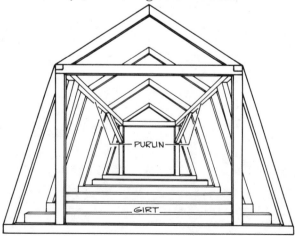

PURLIN

GIRT

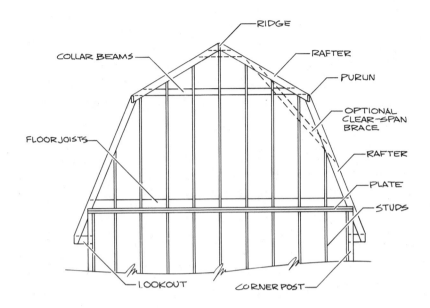

Perhaps the best technique is to erect sufficient studs to support the purlins and end-wall plate, then the lower rafters. The final step is to erect the ridge and the rafters that extend from the purlins to the ridge.

In framing a gambrel roof on a small building, it is far easier to construct the rafter units as trusses, using plywood gussets to join the rafters. Then the trusses are hoisted atop the wall framing.

SHEATHING IN THE STRUCTURE

After the entire framework is erected, plumbed and braced, the sheathing begins. The actual sequence of work isn't too significant on typical homestead construction, although ordinarily the walls are closed in before the roof is sheathed. In fact, occasionally, the wall sheathing begins before the roof is framed, especially where the wall sheathing also serves as the bracing.

WALL SHEATHING OR SIDING

In residential construction, the wall's skin is multilayered, including insulation between the studs, a covering on the inside like plasterboard or thin veneer paneling, and, on the outside, a layer of sheathing, a vapor barrier, and siding. In outbuilding, construction on the homestead, the sheathing layer is usually it: the siding. Anything more than closing out the weather is usually unnecessary.

There are a good number of sheathing/siding materials to choose from, including metal siding, plywood and tempered hardboard panels, and the old standbys, board sidings. Among the critical factors to consider in selecting a siding material are cost, durability, availability, and ease of installation. All of those listed above are durable and fairly easy to install. Availability and cost can only be determined by checking building materials dealers in your locale. In more than a few cases, the availability of free or inexpensive used siding ma-

terials influences the choice.

Plywood as a siding has a lot to recommend it: size, weight, stability, structural properties, as well as ease and speed of appilcation. Moreover, plywood manufacturers have responded to the marketplace and have made available a wide variety of exterior siding designs and textures, in addition to the old reliable exterior plywood.

Plywood adds considerably more strength to the frame than does diagonally applied boards. When plywood sheathing is used, corner bracing can be omitted. Large size panels—they come in 4-foot by 8-, 9-, and 10-foot sizes—effect a major saving in time

VERTICAL BOARD AND BATTEN SIDING   MANUFACTURED BOARD SIDING

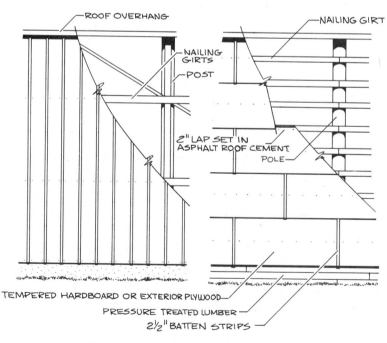

ROOF OVERHANG

NAILING GIRTS

POST

2" LAP SET IN ASPHALT ROOF CEMENT

NAILING GIRT

POLE

TEMPERED HARDBOARD OR EXTERIOR PLYWOOD

PRESSURE TREATED LUMBER

2½" BATTEN STRIPS

The siding is common boards of varying widths. Since the entire building was constructed using green lumber purchased at a sawmill, the builder is prepared to install ⅜-inch by 1½-inch battens to cover the gaps between the siding boards that will develop as the building dries. Moreover, the lumber—framing and sheathing—is full-dimension material.

required for application and still provide a tight, draft-free installation. The minimum thickness of plywood siding, where no other sheathing will be used, is usually recommended to be ⅜-inch on studs on 16-inch centers and ½-inch on studs on 24-inch centers. Those are minimums, remember. The panels should be installed with the face grain parallel to the studs. A little more stiffness can be gained by installing them across the studs, but this requires more cutting and fitting in most instances.

In applying plywood horizontally, stagger the vertical joints and be sure they occur directly over a stud. The horizontal joints should occur over nailing blocks or girts. Use 6d galvanized or aluminum nails for $\frac{5}{16}$-, ⅜-, and ½-inch panels and 8d galvanized or aluminum nails for ⅝-, ¾-, and $\frac{13}{16}$-inch panels. Space the nails every 6 inches at the edges and every 12 inches on other supports.

Tempered hardboard is similar to plywood in panel sizes, but the similarity ends there. The material is thinner—$\frac{5}{16}$ inch to $\frac{7}{16}$ inch most commonly—and requires quite a bit of backing, nailers 24 inches on center between the studs, for example, and studs no greater than 16 inches on center. Hardboard siding is applied using 6d galvanized or aluminum nails, spaced as with plywood.

Metal siding is available in galvanized steel and aluminum, in a variety of corrugations. The aluminum siding, which is not like the ersatz beveled board aluminum siding popular in residential construction, is made in 2- and 4-foot widths in several lengths from 6 feet up to 12 feet. It is applied vertically and should be secured using aluminum nails. Steel or galvanized steel nails will react with the aluminum and damage the siding. The maximum spacing for nailers is 36 inches on center. The galvanized steel material is applied horizontally or vertically.

The galvanized steel siding is made in panels similar in size to the aluminum siding. It is the same stuff used for roofing. The corrugations are overlapped to ensure a watertight seal. It is fastened using galvanized steel nails with neoprene or lead washers.

The old standby sidings are the board sidings. These include vertical board and batten or board on board siding, vertical or horizontal tongue and groove or ship-lap siding, clapboard or beveled board siding.

Board siding can be obtained in almost all widths, lengths, and grades. Generally, widths are from 6 to 12 inches, with lengths selected for economical use. Almost all solid wood

Old barn siding was used to close in the walls of the chicken house. Just enough tongue-and-groove boards were available to close in the back wall, which has no windows and faces the prevailing winds. The remaining three walls were closed in with common board siding of varying widths, cut to fit and butted edge to edge and nailed on. If the building ever proves too drafty, ⅜-inch by 1½-inch battens can be nailed over the joints between boards.

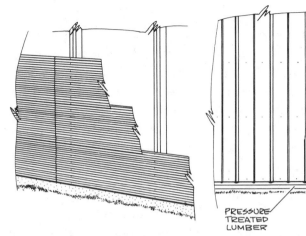

HORIZONTAL METAL SIDING

VERTICAL METAL SIDING

wall sheathing used is ¾ inch thick and either square or matched edge. Naturally, the more highly milled material is more costly, making board on board or board and batten the least expensive, since it uses common board lumber. In fact, where tightness isn't requisite, plain vertical board siding, complete with irregular gaps between the boards, is okay.

Board siding may be nailed on horizontally, vertically, or diagonally. Diagonal application contributes much greater strength to the structure, but such application is seldom seen as siding. Siding should be nailed on with three 8d galvanized or aluminum nails to each bearing if the pieces are more than 6 inches wide. Use 10d weatherproof nails to secure battens or the outer board of the board on board configuration. Board siding is laid on tight, with all joints over the studs or

nailers. If the siding is to be put on horizontally, it should be started at the foundation and worked toward the top. No nailing blocks between studs are necessary with this type of siding. If it is to be put on diagonally, it should be started at the corners of the building and worked toward the centers or middles of the walls. Nail-

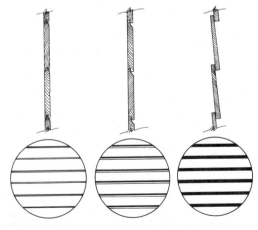

CROSS-SECTION AND FRONT VIEWS OF
3 DIFFERENT HORIZONTAL BOARD SIDING

ers are not necessary, but they are helpful in this situation. Vertical plain board siding should be started at the corners and windows, and the gaps between filled in, to avoid the need to notch boards to fit around the windows (it is far easier to rip a board than to cut a long, narrow notch in one edge of it). Tongue-and-groove vertical siding must be started at a corner and nailed up working toward the other end of the wall. With all vertical siding, at least one row of between-studs nailers is necessary.

ROOF SHEATHING

The lower layer of roof covering is called the roof sheathing; the upper layer is called the roof covering or the roofing. Roof sheathing, like wall sheathing and subflooring, may be laid either horizontally or diagonally. Horizontal sheathing may be either closed sheathing (laid with no spaces between the courses) or open sheathing (laid with spaces between the courses).

Closed sheathing is usually plywood these days, although common boards or tongue-and-groove boards are still used. It is used with the asphalt-based roofing materials that require a solid base, and in metal-roofed livestock and poultry shelters where a vapor barrier is needed to prevent condensation on the underside of the metal.

Plywood as roof sheathing is laid horizontally. The nailing requirements match those previously described for plywood siding. In addition, special clips are available for fastening the plywood panels together, spreading the load from one panel to its neighbors.

Open sheathing is used when the roofing is to be wooden shingles or metal panels. It usually consists of 1 x 3 or 1 x 4 strips. When wooden

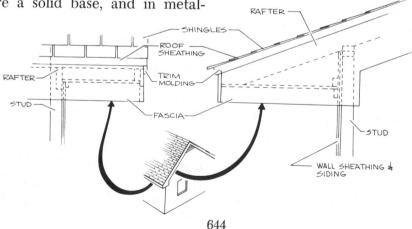

Like the floor and siding, the roof sheathing is random-width common boards, straight laid. The roofing is asphalt shingles laid over tar paper. The roof edge is finished with a drip edge and fascia boards. A frieze board, notched to accommodate the rafters, is nailed to the walls, sealing the joint between the top of the siding and the bottom of the roof sheathing.

shingles are to be used, the strips are spaced on center equal to the specified exposure of the shingles to the weather. With metal roofing panels, the spacing of the strips is that—usually ranging from 12 to 36 inches on center—recommended by the roofing manufacturer.

With some metal roofing, purlin decking is used. This consists of 2 x 4 members set on edge and spaced 12 to 24 inches on center. By setting these purlins on edge, longer nails can be used, which hold the roofing tighter to the framework. Moreover, the purlins can carry heavier loads when set on edge.

Sheathing, whether closed or open, should be nailed with two 8d nails to each rafter crossing. End-joint requirements are the same as those previously described for board siding. The sheathing should be sawed flush with the outer face of the end-wall sheathing, unless a projection of the roof sheathing over the end walls is called for. If such a projection is needed, projecting sheathing boards must be long enough to span at least three rafter spaces.

With closed sheathing, it is common to install a drip edge around the perimeter of the roof. The drip edge is a strip of galvanized metal or aluminum, roughly **L**-shaped, that fits over the top and edge of the roof sheathing. It covers about 2 or 3 inches of the sheathing, and extends below the edge of the sheathing to protect the end and edge grain from the weather. The roofing should cover the portion of the drip edge that lies on the sheathing surface.

It is also common to install fascia boards at the time the sheathing is installed. Fascia boards are nailed across the ends of the rafters to conceal and protect their ends from the weather, and they are installed parallel to the rafters to brace the sheathing that extends beyond the walls of the building, forming eaves. This latter portion of the fascia board is sometimes called the rake fascia, the rake comprising the trim pieces that run parallel to the roof slope. The fascia boards should be carefully fitted and installed.

ROOFING

Roofs are covered with many different kinds of materials, such as slate, tile, wood shingles, asbestos-cement, asphalt, and metal sheeting. The most commonly used in the homestead situation are asphalt roofing in rolls or shingles and sheet metal. With the former you use closed sheathing, with the latter, open sheathing or purlin decking.

Roofing is usually purchased by the "square," or the amount required to cover 100 square feet.

Asphalt roofing, as noted, comes in rolls and shingles of various configurations, ranging in weight from 45 to 325 pounds per square. Obviously, the heavier the material, the longer it will last. The material is a layer of felt saturated with asphalt, with the portion to be exposed to the weather coated with granite chips. Because of the nature of the material, it should be laid in warm, but not hot, weather. At 70° to 80°F. temperatures, the asphalt will seal properly, while it will be too soft and damage-prone at higher temperatures.

Roll roofing is the least expensive, but also the shortest lived. It is suitable for roofs with a pitch as low as 1/12. Installation instructions vary somewhat from manufacturer to manufacturer, but in general, the roofing must be applied to a dry deck over a thin layer of mastic. Galvanized or aluminum roof nails, $1\frac{1}{4}$ inches long, are driven through the mastic so the hole is sealed.

Asphalt shingles are made of the same material as the roll roofing. Each strip is about 36 inches long and is

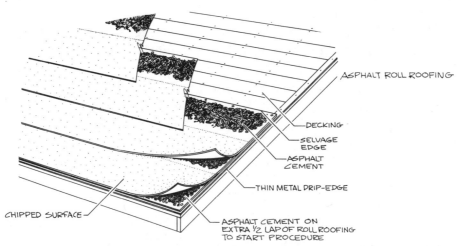

ASPHALT ROLL ROOFING

DECKING

SELVAGE EDGE

ASPHALT CEMENT

THIN METAL DRIP-EDGE

CHIPPED SURFACE

ASPHALT CEMENT ON EXTRA 1/2 LAP OF ROLL ROOFING TO START PROCEDURE

divided into three 12-inch shingle tabs along one edge. Shingles are generally used on roofs with a pitch of 1/4 or steeper. If used on a roof with less of a pitch, a double layer of roofing felt should underlie the shingles.

As with roll roofing, specific installation procedures vary. Generally, the roof sheathing is covered with a layer of roofing felt. Then the shingles are laid. The first course must have something under it besides the sheathing and roofing felt. Some roofers lay a course of shingles turned upside down, others lay a strip of roll roofing. A first course of shingles, properly applied, is then laid atop this first-course underlayment.

Use 1¼-inch galvanized or aluminum roofing nails, six to a shingle, for best results. Most asphalt shingles come with a spot of mastic on the underside of each tab, which seals the tab to the shingles in the course

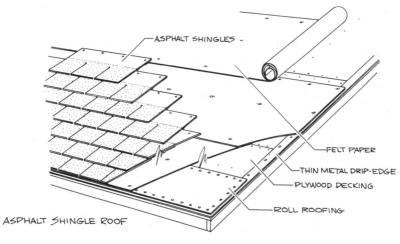

ASPHALT SHINGLES

FELT PAPER

THIN METAL DRIP-EDGE

PLYWOOD DECKING

ROLL ROOFING

ASPHALT SHINGLE ROOF

below it. You should make it a point to purchase these shingles if you live in a high wind area. The slots between tabs should be staggered from course to course.

It is important to cap the ridge. With roll roofing, coat the ridge with mastic, then lay a strip of the coated mineralized portion of the roofing along the top of the ridge and lap the edges down the slope of the roof. With shingles, cut a number of the shingles apart into tab-sized strips. Lay a strip of roofing felt, then the shingle tabs, parallel with the ridge.

Metal roofing panels normally come in 26-inch widths, which cover 24 inches on the roof with 2 inches of edge lap. Occasionally you can get 30- and 48-inch-wide panels. Lengths range from 6 to 12 feet, and on up to 30 feet in corrugated steel, although anything over 12 feet long is terribly cumbersome.

For most types of corrugated metal roofing, the sheathing strips, whether purlins or decking, should be spaced 24 inches on center. When laying the roofing, start in the bottom corner away from the strongest winds. Provide about an 8-inch end lap and 1½ corrugations of side lap. There is a "right side up" for the sheets to make this side lap possible. Use 2½-inch spiral-shank galvanized nails with a lead head or neoprene washer, putting one nail in every other corrugation and locating them in the ridges, not the troughs. Do not over drive the nails and dent the roofing. If the roofing is aluminum, use aluminum nails.

With **V**-crimp and other roofing shapes with large flat surfaces, the sheathing must be broader and more

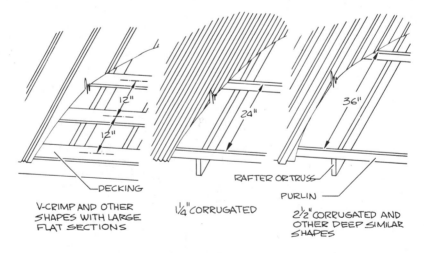

V-CRIMP AND OTHER
SHAPES WITH LARGE
FLAT SECTIONS

¼" CORRUGATED

2½" CORRUGATED AND
OTHER DEEP SIMILAR
SHAPES

METAL ROOFING

closely spaced, generally 12 inches on center.

Steel roofing is actually zinc-coated steel. The amount of zinc in the coating is the critical factor in the roof's durability. A standard coating for a roof with an estimated life of ten to twelve years would be 1¼ ounces of zinc per square foot of sheet, with half the zinc on each side. A 2-ounce coating (per square foot) will provide a roof-life of twenty-five years or longer. Any good quality steel roofing will have a zinc coating indicated on each sheet. To prolong the life of this type of roofing, it should be painted periodically with a zinc paint. The first application should be made just when rust begins to be visible on the roofing.

Wooden shingles, while pretty, are generally quite expensive. As shown, they are applied to an open-sheathed roof using galvanized shingle nails. The first course is a double layer, and subsequent courses are overlapped as much as two-thirds of the total length of the shingle.

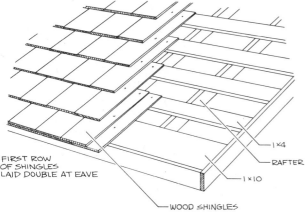

FIRST ROW
OF SHINGLES
LAID DOUBLE AT EAVE

1 x 4
RAFTER
1 x 10

WOOD SHINGLES

DECKING MEMBERS FOR WOOD SHINGLES CAN BE SPACED ACCORDING TO THE AMOUNT THE SHINGLES ARE EXPOSED.

WINDOWS AND DOORS

Locating windows and doors is one of the first planning decisions and installing them is one of the final construction steps. In residential use, windows and doors serve a variety of purposes—light, ventilation, access—and are rather complicated in construction and must be installed with precision. In homestead outbuilding construction, the same concerns do not necessarily apply.

In the case of the barn or toolshed, the door is for access. You may use a premade door, new or used, or you may construct one. The typical outbuilding door is assembled from lengths of siding joined together with two or three horizontal battens and one or more diagonal battens. Tongue-and-groove siding will produce the tightest door, but common boards will serve just as well. When nailing this sort of door together, use 8d or 10d nails, driving them through the siding and battens and clinching them across the grain of the wood.

If your carpentry is sure and neat, a functionally decorative door can be constructed by assembling a perimeter framework, which will be on the outside, and securing the siding to it. Obviously, in such a case, you will want to clinch the nails on the inside of the door.

You can construct most any size door using this technique, including one wide enough and high enough for a tractor or other vehicle. For the widest, and thus heaviest, of doors, it

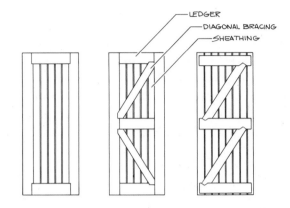

THREE ECONOMICAL BATTEN DOORS

*A doorway had been framed into the north wall, using a single stud on each side of the doorway and a single 2 x 4 header. The door itself was nailed up of pieces of the siding. Two large **T** hinges were used. A homemade latch was fabricated of three pieces of 2 x 3, a length of furring, and three pieces of dowel.*

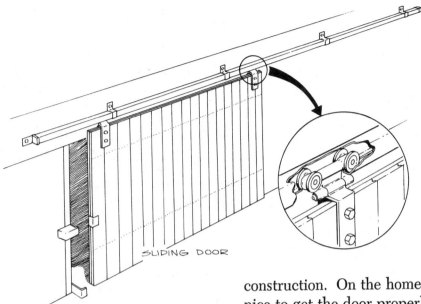

SLIDING DOOR

is wise to hang the door from a track so it slides open, rather than using hinges.

The precision part of door work in residential construction is the hanging. If the door is not properly hung, it will bind or stick, it will swing open or closed if not secured. And such are regarded as problems in residential construction. On the homestead, it is nice to get the door properly aligned, but a barn is a barn.

Moreover, the trim isn't as significant in the installation in a shed as it is in the dining room. Commonly in residential construction, the rough framing is concealed behind special jambs and stops and the joint between the sheathing and the jambs is con-

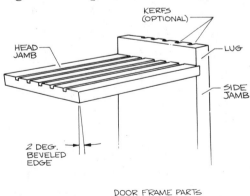

DOOR FRAME PARTS

KERFS (OPTIONAL)

HEAD JAMB

LUG

SIDE JAMB

2 DEG. BEVELED EDGE

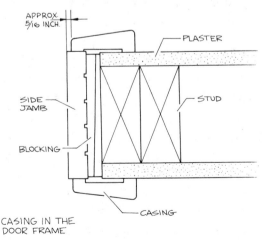

CASING IN THE DOOR FRAME

APPROX. 5/16 INCH.

PLASTER

SIDE JAMB

STUD

BLOCKING

CASING

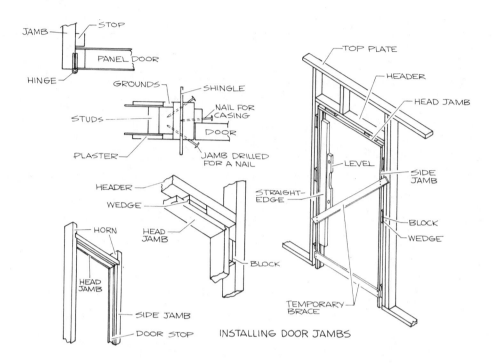

INSTALLING DOOR JAMBS

cealed behind casings. The jambs are assembled, braced, then carefully lined up within the rough framing using sets of wedges. The jambs must be plumb and level before they are fastened in place. The casings are nailed on, then the door is hung.

In the shed, the rough framing is framing enough. For a conventional door, attach the hinges securely to the door, then set up the door in the doorway. Using slivers of wood as shims or wedges, line up the door, then attach the hinges to the building. Strips of 1 x 1 can be nailed to the rough framing of the doorway to serve as a stop. There is a wide variety of latches available at building supply

stores and hardware stores. Or you can make your own.

Windows, like doors, do not need

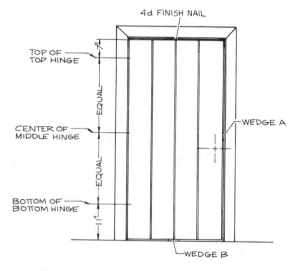

LAYING OUT HINGE LOCATIONS

The building has the two doors, noted above, as well as a small entrance for the chickens, who occupy a portion of the structure. The largest doorway is covered by a door fabricated by nailed tongue-and-groove siding to a common board framework and hung from an overhead track. This door is oversize and overlaps the doorway on all sides when fully closed. The other door is nailed up of common boards and is hung with two strap hinges. It has a store-bought latch. This door overlaps the rough-framed opening all around by about ¾ inch, and seats flush with the siding.

to be as involved in outbuilding construction as they are in residential construction. It is again a matter of eliminating the fancy trim. And it is a matter to challenge your ingenuity. Constructing sashes is not easy, and it should be a last resort for any homestead builder. But sashes can be acquired, new and used. And sashes aren't really necessary.

If the purpose of the windows is strictly to light the interior of the building, you need do no more than secure glass in the rough-framed window openings. This can be done in a variety of ways. One would be to construct a frame inside the rough opening using 1-inch stock. Nail quarter-round molding around the inside of the new frame, then set the glass in place, using glazier's points and putty or more molding to secure it. If you have sashes, you can always simply nail them into the rough openings.

If you want windows that can be opened to ventilate the building, you'll have to acquire or make sashes. Use butt hinges or T hinges, and attach them to the top or bottom, the inside or the outside, depending on the way you want the window to open.

The most involved installation would be full window assemblies. The assemblies must be temporarily braced so that the whole assembly is square and aligned so the sashes operate freely, then set in the rough opening, plumbed and leveled, then nailed in place. Finally, a casing must be nailed on.

With the exception of trim and finish, and any interior work, the windows and doors generally constitute the final construction work. With the building finally and completely

The windows are fixed. The rough openings were tailored to accommodate eight pieces of glass that the builder had on hand. The finish frames were constructed of 1 x 4 headers and sills and 1 x 3 uprights. These were nailed directly to the rough framing members. A 1½-inch strip was ripped and toenailed between header and sill in the middle of each window frame, then a 1 x 1 tacked to the back of this mullion. The glass was set on the rough sill, pushed up against the edge of the finish frame and secured with strips of quarter-round molding. A screened vent was framed directly above the front wall windows.

The builder purchased four metal window units intended for use in masonry buildings. Their construction was such that they could be sandwiched between the framing and the siding, holding them securely in place. A 1-inch board was used to fabricate an exterior sill for the windows.

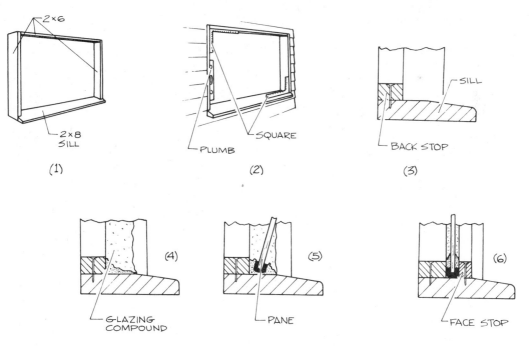

FRAMING AND GLAZING A WINDOW

closed in, you can paint the outside and prepare the inside for the building's ultimate use.

The sequence then in erecting a stud-frame building, designed to include all the elements—sills, a wooden floor, ceiling joists—and to include them in the most common order of construction follows. It assumes that you have planned your building and that the appropriate foundation exists. It is important to remember that not every homestead outbuilding need include all the elements, and that the parts of the building do not have to be assembled strictly in accordance with the following sequence.

To protect the garden from the chickens and the chickens from neighborhood pooches, a wire-enclosed run was constructed. Seven 2 x 4 posts were set into the ground marking off an 8-foot square run. To complete the run's frame 2 x 2s were run from post to post. Using aluminum staples, 4-foot-high 14-gauge welded wire fencing with 2-inch-square mesh was attached to the frame. The top of the run is covered with two 8-foot lengths of the fencing. An end of one of the lengths is free, forming a sort of trapdoor, through which the owner has access to the run. The chickens gain access by way of the traditional trapdoor and cleated ramp.

The building is a dual-purpose structure, so a partition was built in to keep the chickens out of their feed, the garden tools, and other items kept in the storage room. The partition is framed and sheathed like the exterior walls. It has a doorway and homemade door.

CONSTRUCTION

1. Lay out the sills.
   a. The sill is normally the first member to be laid out. As indicated, the edge of the sill is usually set back from the edge of the foundation a distance equal to the thickness of the sheathing. When this is the case, the length of sill stock required to cover a section of foundation wall is equal to the length of the wall section minus twice the amount of the setback.
   b. Once the required length has been made up, the next step is to lay out the locations of the bolt holes as follows: place each piece of sill stock on the foundation, inboard of the bolts, but otherwise in exactly the position it is to occupy, and square a line across the stock from the center of each bolt. To lay out the bolt-hole center on each of these lines, measure the distance from the center of each bolt to the outer edge of the foundation; subtract the amount of the sill setback from this distance, and lay off the remainder on the corresponding bolt line, measuring from what is to be the outer edge of the sill. The reason you must lay out each bolt hole separately is that the bolts may be set at slightly varying distances from the edge of the foundation and from each other.
2. Place the sills. Bore the bolt holes with an auger bit $\frac{1}{8}$ inch larger in diameter than the bolt diameter, to allow for making slight adjustments in the location of the sill. When all the holes have been bored, try the

657

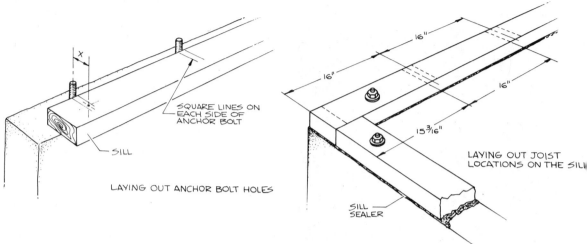

SQUARE LINES ON
EACH SIDE OF
ANCHOR BOLT

SILL

LAYING OUT ANCHOR BOLT HOLES

LAYING OUT JOIST
LOCATIONS ON THE SILL

SILL
SEALER

stock for the whole section on the bolts for a fit. If the fit is satisfactory, remove the pieces of stock and place a thin layer of mortar on top of the foundation. Replace the pieces and check the whole sill for line and level. Place small wedges, if necessary, to hold pieces level until the mortar sets. Then place the washers on the bolts, screw on the nuts, and bolt the sill down.

3. Lay out the joists. A common joist is a full-length joist, as distinguished from a cripple joist. The best way to lay out common joists for cutting is to figure the correct length of a common joist, cut a piece of stock to this length, notch for identification, and use the piece as a pattern from which to cut the other common joists. The best way to lay out cripples for cutting is to postpone the cripple layout until after the headers have been placed; then measure the spaces which are to be spanned by the cripples.

   a. In platform framing, the outer ends of the joists usually butt against a header joist which is set flush with the outer edge of the sill. In this case the length of a wall-to-wall common joist will be the distance between the outer edges of the sills, minus twice the thickness of a header joist.

   b. The length of common joist required to cover a given span between an outside wall and a girder varies with the character of the wall framing and also with the manner in which the joists are framed to the girder. The length of common joist required to cover a given span between two girders varies with the manner in which the joists are framed to the girders. Joists which lap a girder with full bearing (meaning joists which extend all the way across the top of the girder) must obviously be longer than joists which butt each other on the top of a girder. Joists in hangers, which butt against the sides of a girder, are shorter than joists which butt each other on top of a girder.

   c. The whole floor-framing situation, then, must be studied closely before a common joist pattern is cut. Whenever possible, the cutting of a pattern should be delayed until the sills, headers, and other supporting or abutting members are erected. The joist

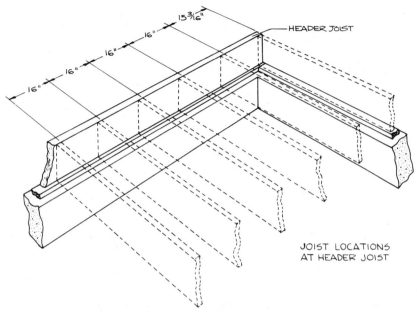

15³⁄₁₆"
16"
16"
16"
16"

HEADER JOIST

JOIST LOCATIONS
AT HEADER JOIST

length can then be determined by measurements taken on the actual structure. Whenever possible, too, the common joist pattern should be tried on the actual structure for a fit before any joists are cut from it.

4. Lay out the joist location. The location of a joist end is marked on a sill or a header joist by squaring a line across and drawing an X alongside it. The X indicates the side of the line on which the joist end-section is to be placed.

   a. The location of one of the outside joists is marked first, and the locations of the others are then measured off from this one in accordance with the specified spacing of joists on center (O.C.).

   b. Before you start laying out the joist locations you should study the floor framing plan to learn the locations of any double trimmers around floor openings. Locations of double trimmers are marked with two lines and two X's. The locations of cripples are marked the same as the locations of common joists, but with the word *crip* written in alongside.

5. Assemble the floor platform.

   a. Header joists are cut and erected first. As a general rule, the length of a platform-frame header is equal to the shortest distance between the outer edges of the sills. Header joists are toenailed to the sills with 16d nails spaced 16 inches on center.

   b. As soon as a common joist pattern has been laid out and cut as previously described, cut the common joists. As each joist is cut, carry it to its location and lay it flat across the span. With one man at each end of the span, erect the outside joists first. Each of these is toenailed down to the sill or plate with 16d nails spaced 16 inches on center, and end-nailed through the headers with two 20d nails driven into each joist end. Incidentally, many joists have a slight curve to them, and the convex edge of a joist is called the crown. A joist should always be placed with the crown up.

c. Next the joists lying between the outside joists are set on edge and the ends of each joist are toenailed down to the sill or plate with two 16d nails, one on each side of the joist. Only the inner trimmer of each pair of trimmers is erected at this time. After all the common joists, and the trimmers as mentioned, have been set on edge and toenailed, the joists are plumbed and temporarily braced.

d. The temporary brace (usually a 1 x 6) is laid across the tops of the joists at the center of the span. The outer ends of this brace are tacked down to the outside joists with 8d nails, driven only partway in to allow for extracting later when the brace is removed. Beginning with the joist next to an outside joist, the joists are plumbed consecutively, and as each joist is plumbed it is braced with an 8d nail, driven through the brace into the joist. A joist that butts against a header is plumbed by lining up the joist end with the perpendicular location line on the header. When the joist is in plumb position, it is nailed at the ends with 20d nails, two to each end, driven through the header into the joist.

e. After all the common joists, plus the inside trimmers (if there are any), have been plumbed and braced, the framing around a floor opening (if there is one) is installed. First the locations, then the lengths of the headers are determined by measurement of the shortest distance between the inside trimmers. The double headers are then cut to correct length, after which the outside header of each pair is set in place and fastened to the inside trimmers with 20d nails, three to each end, driven through the trimmers into the ends of the headers. Once the outside headers are in place, the lengths of the cripple joists can be determined by simple measurement. The cripples are cut, set in place, plumbed, fastened at the outer ends like common joists, and fastened at the floor-opening ends with 20d nails, three to each cripple, driven through the outside headers into the ends of the cripples. Next the inside headers are set in place, fastened to the outside headers with 16d nails spaced 6 inches on center, and fastened to the inside trimmers with 20d nails, three to each end, driven through the trimmers into the ends of the headers. Finally, the outside trimmers are set in place and nailed to the inside trimmers with 16d nails spaced 12 inches on center.

f. As soon as enough common joists have been erected, the installation of bridging begins. Solid bridging is usually nailed with 16d nails. It is usually staggered to ease installation. Remember the joist should be placed with the crown up, so that any settlement under the weight of the flooring will tend toward a level instead of toward a sag.

6. Lay out the studs for cutting.

a. Before you can lay out any studs for cutting, you must calculate how long the studs must be, which is not at all hard. The length of the stud is the height of the wall, less the thickness of the plates.

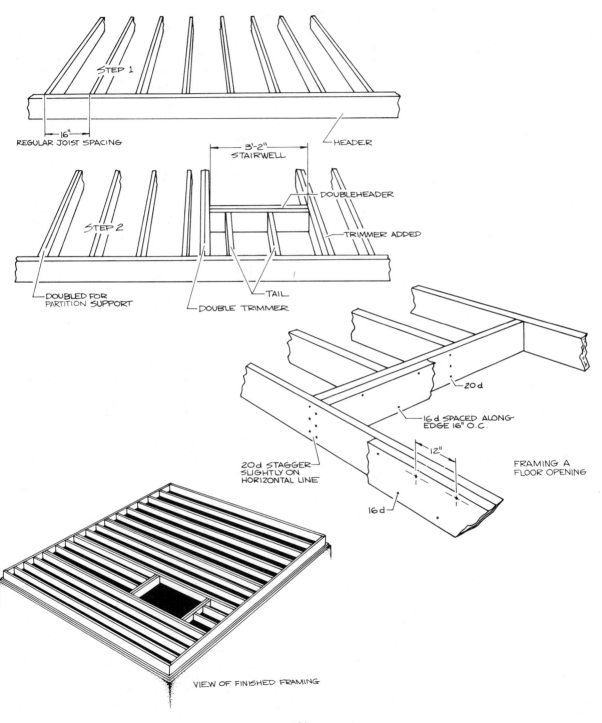

STEP 1

16"
REGULAR JOIST SPACING

HEADER

3'-2"
STAIRWELL

DOUBLEHEADER

TRIMMER ADDED

STEP 2

DOUBLED FOR
PARTITION SUPPORT

TAIL

DOUBLE TRIMMER

20d

16d SPACED ALONG
EDGE 16" O.C.

12"

FRAMING A
FLOOR OPENING

20d STAGGER
SLIGHTLY ON
HORIZONTAL LINE

16d

VIEW OF FINISHED FRAMING

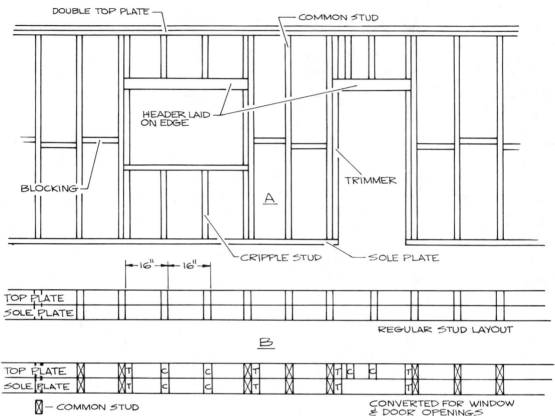

DOUBLE TOP PLATE

COMMON STUD

HEADER LAID ON EDGE

BLOCKING

TRIMMER

A

CRIPPLE STUD

SOLE PLATE

←16"→←16"→

TOP PLATE
SOLE PLATE

REGULAR STUD LAYOUT

B

TOP PLATE
SOLE PLATE

⊠ — COMMON STUD
T — TRIMMER STUD
C — CRIPPLE STUD

CONVERTED FOR WINDOW
& DOOR OPENINGS

LAYING OUT THE PLATES

b. The next step is to lay out the segments of the gable-end studs which extend above the level of the top of the rafter plate. In order to do this, you must calculate the common difference of gable-end studs. The common difference may be found by multiplying the spacing of the studs by the pitch of the roof, expressed as a fraction. Assume a stud spacing of 16 inches and a roof pitch of 8/12. The common difference in the length of the gable stud is 16 inches by 8/12 equals $10\frac{3}{4}$ inches. Expressed as a formula, stud spacing x pitch of the roof = common difference. If the rise of a right triangle for 16 inches of run is $10\frac{11}{16}$ inches, the rise for twice as much run, or 32 inches, must be twice as much, or 2 x $10\frac{11}{16}$ inches; the rise for three times as much run must be 3 x $10\frac{11}{16}$; and so on. This means that, moving inboard from the rafter plates, each gable-end stud is $10\frac{11}{16}$ inches longer than the preceding gable-end stud. Knowing this, you can lay off the lengths of the gable-end studs by laying off $10\frac{11}{16}$ inches (which is called the common difference of gable-end studs) progressively for each stud, from the shortest to the longest, in either side of

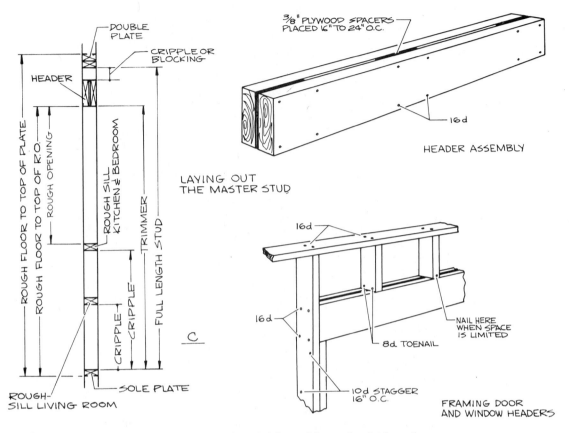

LAYING OUT
THE MASTER STUD

HEADER ASSEMBLY

FRAMING DOOR
AND WINDOW HEADERS

the end wall. The top end cut of the gable stud is laid out by
using the cut of the roof and marking on the rise side.

7. Lay out the stud locations. Stud locations are marked on sole plates
in the same manner as joist locations. The sole plate is marked first,
then the marks are transferred to the corresponding top plate, by
"matching" the top plate or rafter plate against the marked sole plate
and squaring the marks across. The studs around wall openings
require special treatment. First locate the center line of the opening.
Let's say that the opening is a door, and that the center line of this
door lies 7 feet 5 inches from one of the building corners. Measure
this off and square a line across the sill or plate at this point. Next find
the width of this door, which we'll say is 3 feet. Lay off one-half of
this, or 1 foot 6 inches, on either side of the center line and square lines
across.

8. Erect the wall framing. Erection of the wall sections may be either by
the piece-by-piece method or by the section method. In the
piece-by-piece method, the wall is erected a piece at a time, meaning
that the corner posts, then each of the studs is raised and toenailed in
place separately, after which the top plate or rafter plate is nailed on.
In the section method the entire wall section is assembled lying flat

on the subflooring. The section is then heaved up into place and fastened at the bottom and the upper member of the top plate installed. Nowadays the section method is used for almost all stud-frame walls.

a. The top plate and sole plate are laid on the floor platform parallel to each other and the full-length studs laid out between them, both the plates and studs being set on edge. Nail the plates to the studs using two 16d nails at the end of each stud. Then lay any trimmer studs in place and nail them to the full-length studs. Place headers in place against the trimmers and nail through the full-length studs into the ends of the headers using 16d nails. Cripple studs between the header and the top plate, if any, may be installed now or after the wall section is erected. The same is true of rough sills and lower cripples. Install any other necessary blocking, such as where a partition will intersect the outside wall.

b. With the section ready for erection, tack temporary braces to each end of the section near the top plate. After the section is erected and positioned properly, tack the lower end of the brace to the edge of the floor platform to hold the section. The sole plate is nailed to the floor platform with 20d nails. Check the plumb of the wall with a level or plumb line. The usual procedure is to erect the main sidewalls, then the end walls.

c. With all the sections erected, nail the end studs, which will compose the corner posts, together. Install any cripples not previously nailed in place. Braces should be added, as previously explained. Then add the second member of the top plate, being sure to lap the top member over joints between the wall sections. Use 10d nails for this, spotting two at each end and staggering the rest along the length of the plate.

9. Lay out the roof framing member locations and install the ceiling joists.

a. Lay out the ceiling joist and rafter locations on the top plate. Roughly locate the positions of the framing members, then square the marks across the plate, spotting an X to the side of the line that the rafter or joist will be placed. Use an R to designate a rafter location, a J to designate a ceiling joist.

b. Measure from outside-of-plate to outside-of-plate to get the length of the ceiling joist. After cutting a pattern joist to length, use the roof pitch and your framing square to mark the joist for trimming. After the pattern is cut, trimmed and given a test fitting, cut all the ceiling joists needed and hoist them into position. The joists are toenailed to the top plate with an 8d nail in each side.

c. Laying out the ridge for a gable roof presents no particular problem, since the line length of the ridge is equal to the length of the building. The actual length would include any overhang. To mark the ridge for rafter locations, it is matched against the plates, after they have been marked.

10. Rafter lay out is the next step. Rafters must be laid out and cut with slope, length, and overhang exactly right so that they will fit when

placed in the position they are to occupy in the finished roof.

a.   The builder first determines the length of the rafter and the length of the piece of lumber from which the rafter may be cut. To determine the rafter length, first find one-half of the distance between the outside plates. This distance is the horizontal distance which the rafter will cover. The amount of rise per foot has yet to be considered. If the building to be roofed is 20 feet wide, half the span will be 10 feet. For example, the rise per foot is to be 8 inches. To determine the approximate overall length of a rafter, measure on the steel carpenter square the distance between 8 on the tongue and 12 on the blade, because 8 is the rise and 12 is the unit of run. This distance is $14\frac{5}{12}$ inches, and represents the line length of a rafter with a total run of 1 foot and a rise of 8 inches. Since the run of the rafter is 10 feet, multiply the line length for 1 foot by 10. The answer is $144\frac{2}{12}$ inches or 12 feet $\frac{1}{6}$ inch. The amount of overhang, normally 1 foot, must be added if an overhang is to be used. This makes a total of 13 feet for the length of the rafter, but since 13 feet is an odd length, a 14-foot board is used.

b.   After the length has been determined, the timber is laid on sawhorses, with the crown or bow (if any) at the top side of the rafter. If possible, select a straight piece for the pattern rafter. If a straight piece is not available, have the crown toward the person laying off the rafter. Hold the square with the tongue in the right hand, the blade in the left, the heel away from the body, and place the square as near the upper end of the rafter as possible. In this case, the figure 8 on the tongue and 12 on the blade are placed along the edge of timber which is to be the top edge of the rafter. Mark along the tongue edge of the square, which will be the plumb cut at the ridge. Since the length of the rafter is known to be 12 feet $\frac{1}{6}$ inch, measure the distance from the top of the plumb cut and mark it on the timber. Hold the square in the same manner with the 8 mark on the tongue directly over the 12-foot $\frac{1}{6}$-inch mark. Mark along the tongue of the square to give the plumb cut for the seat. Next measure off, perpendicular to this mark, the length of overhang along the timber and make a plumb cut mark in the same manner, keeping the square on the same edge of the timber. This will be the tail cut of the rafter; often the tail cut is made square across the timber.

c.   Instead of using the above method, the rafter length may be determined by "stepping it off" by successive steps with the square. Thus, if your building has a span of 13 feet 4 inches, or a run of 6 feet 8 inches, you take the same number of steps as there are feet in the run, which leaves 8 inches over a foot. This 8 inches is taken care of in the same manner as the full-foot run; that is, with the square at the last step position, make a mark on the rafters at the 4-inch mark on the blade, then move the square along the rafter until the tongue rests at the 4-inch mark. With the square held for the same cut as before, make a mark along the tongue. This is the line length of the rafter. The seat cut and overhang are made as described above. When laying off rafters by any method, be sure to recheck the work carefully. When two rafters have been cut, it is best to put them in place to see if they fit. Minor adjustments may be made at this time without serious damage or waste of material.

11. Erect the roof framing. For a gable roof the two pairs of gable-end rafters and the ridge are usually erected first. Two workers hold the ridge in position, while a third sets the gable-end rafters in place, nails them to the ceiling joist, and toenails them to the rafter plate with 8d nails, one to each side of a rafter. Each "ridge-holder" then end-nails the ridge to one of the rafters with two 10d nails, driven through the ridge into the end of the rafter, and toenails the other rafter to the ridge, and to the first rafter with two 10d nails, one on each side of the rafter. If you are short of manpower, suspend the ridge in position between two temporary 2 x 4 uprights, which are removed after the rafters are in place. Temporary braces like those for a wall should be set up at the ridge ends to hold the rafters approximately plumb, after which the rafters between the end-rafters should be erected. The braces should then be released, and the pair of rafters at one end should be plumbed with a plumb line, fastened to a stick extended from the end of the ridge. The braces should then be reset, and they should be left in place until enough sheathing has been installed to hold the rafters plumb. Collar ties, if any, are nailed to common rafters with 8d nails, two to each end of a tie. Ceiling-joist ends are nailed to adjacent rafters with 10d nails, two to each end.

12. As soon as all the wall openings have been framed, the application of the sheathing begins. Board sheathing should be nailed on with three 8d nails to each bearing if the pieces are over 6 inches wide. Wooden sheathing is laid on tight, with all joints made over the studs. If the sheathing is to be on horizontally, it should be started at the foundation and worked toward the top. If it is to be put on diagonally, it should be started at the corners of the building and worked toward the center or middle of the building. Plywood sheathing should be installed with the face grain parallel to the studs. However, a little more stiffness can be gained by installing them across the studs, but this requires more cutting and fitting. Use 6d nails for $\frac{5}{16}$-, $\frac{3}{8}$-, and $\frac{1}{2}$-inch panels and 8d nails for $\frac{5}{8}$- and $\frac{13}{16}$-inch panels. Space the nails not more than 6 inches on center at the edges of the panels and not more than 12 inches on center elsewhere.

13. Sheath the roof. Roof sheathing, like wall sheathing and subflooring, may be laid either horizontally or diagonally. Horizontal sheathing may be either closed sheathing (laid with no spaces between courses) or open sheathing (laid with spaces between courses). As previously noted, open sheathing is when the roof covering is to be wooden shingles or any of the many varieties of panel roofing materials. Closed sheathing is usually plywood, although common boards of a nominal 8-inch width are still used.

   a. Sheathing should be nailed with two 8d nails to each rafter crossing. End-joint requirements are the same as those previously described for wall sheathing. The sheathing ends should be sawed flush with the outer face of the end-wall sheathing, unless a projection of the roof sheathing over the end walls is called for. If such a projection is needed, projecting sheathing boards must be long enough to span at least three rafter spaces.

    b. Plywood, usually in 8-foot by 4-foot sheets, is laid horizontally. Nailing requirements are the same as those previously described for plywood wall sheathing.

    c. After the sheathing is nailed down, cut fascia boards and nail them in place. If closed sheathing has been used, install a drip edge around the perimeter of the roof sheathing.

14. The roofing is applied next, in accordance with the directions noted above.

15. The final construction step is the installation of the window units and the hanging of doors. The specifics of these tasks will vary in accordance with the design and function of the units chosen. New window units invariably have installation instructions provided with the unit by the manufacturer. Suggestions for constructing windows and doors, as well as installing them, have been included above.

POLE CONSTRUCTION

Clear-span construction is quite new in farm buildings, although this principle has been recognized and used in industry for some time. Rural contractors and farmers generally know how to use this construction, which is easier than conventional construction and which can be done with unskilled labor.

If you plan to construct this type of building, you can save time by doing the operations in a certain order, as outlined here.

Choose poles that have been commercially pressure-treated with a permanent type preservative. You can use good native lumber if it is properly cut and dried. Where strength is important, do not use boards with large knots or other defects, or those which are warped and twisted. Select the best lumber for joists, rafters, girders, and trusses. You can use the poorer material for roof girts and bracing.

For glued construction, use planed lumber. The ends of the boards at a glued joint must be the same thickness. Do not use warped or twisted lumber.

The joints are usually the weak points in farm buildings. Make the joints as strong as the wooden members. If you use poor or too few fasteners, you reduce the strength of the whole building.

Pole construction has just a few joints, so each joint must be strong. The common nail or spike is not strong enough for pole buildings. Nails used in pressure-treated material are even weaker because of the

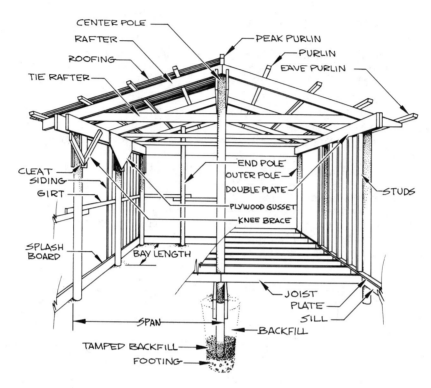

CENTER POLE
RAFTER
ROOFING
TIE RAFTER
PEAK PURLIN
PURLIN
EAVE PURLIN
CLEAT
SIDING
GIRT
END POLE
OUTER POLE
DOUBLE PLATE
STUDS
PLYWOOD GUSSET
KNEE BRACE
SPLASH
BOARD
BAY LENGTH
JOIST
PLATE
SILL
SPAN
BACKFILL
TAMPED BACKFILL
FOOTING

POLE BUILDING TERMINOLOGY

lubricating effect of the preservative. Deformed nails (ring shank or screw shank) are recommended. Oil-hardened nails are harder than regular steel nails, so you can use a thinner shank to reduce the chance of splitting. Oil-hardened nails cost more per pound, but there are more nails in a pound, so the cost per nail is about the same. Use two nail sizes: 40d for purlins, braces; 60d for rafter plates, scabs.

Use machine bolts with a 2-inch steel washer on both ends. When fastening rafter supports, keep the head of the bolt to the outside so it will not interfere with putting on the siding. With full-dimension native lumber, use longer bolts so you won't have to countersink the head.

Split-ring connectors provide top strength truss construction. With them, you can use minimum-sized members. One split-ring connector with a ½-inch bolt is as strong as six ½-inch bolts or thirty 16d nails. Installation of slit-rim connectors, however, requires rather expensive and specialized tools. If you are only building one structure and you can't borrow or rent the tools, stick with the more conventional fasteners.

Some homesteaders have used glue-nail trusses successfully. Use exterior plywood and a water-resistant or waterproof glue for the gusset plates. Type I aircraft casein glue is water resistant and suitable for buildings with low-moisture conditions, such as a machinery storage.

Truss members are connected by $\frac{5}{8}$-inch plywood gusset plates. Put glue on both the truss members and on the plywood. Then nail the gusset plates in place with 6d box nails 3 to 4 inches apart on all members. This provides pressure for the initial glue set. Nail one gusset plate to each joint. Then remove the truss from the jig and glue and nail the gusset plates to the other side. Let the glue set for twenty-four hours before placing the truss on the building.

In regular frame construction, continuous concrete footings 12 to 18 inches wide and 8 inches thick are used to provide enough contact area on the ground. In pole construction, this size of contact area between each pole and the ground is too small. To carry the heavy pole loads, always use concrete pads 18 to 24 inches in diameter and 8 to 12 inches deep. Clean the bottom of the hole of all loose soil and make it flat, not ball shaped. Use a good dry mixture of concrete (one part cement to five parts pit-run gravel and six gallons of water per sack of cement). Place it in the hole at least twelve hours before setting the poles. Use about 1 cubic foot for a hole of the size mentioned above. Dip or pump out all water in the holes before pouring the concrete. If water seeps into the bottom of the holes during the drilling operation, consider relocating the building.

Once the pole framework is erected, sheathing in the building generally follows the approaches outlined above under stud frame construction. Exterior siding can be metal, vertical wood siding, or exterior plywood. You can use any of the roof sheathing and roofing variations detailed under stud frame construction.

CONSTRUCTION

1. The first step is to lay out the building.
    a. Locate and set corner stake A. Drive a nail in the top of the stake to locate the exact corner.
    b. Stake out a line in relation to roads, buildings, fence lines, etc. Measure the length of the building with a steel tape along this line. This becomes the base line for the building.
    c. Set second corner stake B with a nail in the top at the exact distance from A.

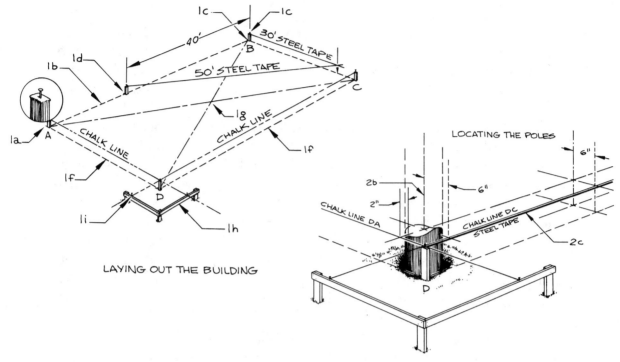

LAYING OUT THE BUILDING

LOCATING THE POLES

d. Measure back exactly 40 feet along line BA, set a stake, drive a nail in the top, and hook one steel tape to the nail.

e. Hook a second steel tape on the nail at stake B, cross tapes at 30 and 50 feet, and establish line BC. Locate third corner stake C on line BC at the desired width of the building. (A right angle is formed with sides of a triangle in the ratio 3-4-5.)

f. From corner stake A, measure the width of the building; from corner stake C measure the length of the building; and set fourth corner stake D.

g. Recheck all four sides for correct length, then check diagonals. The distance from A to C must equal B to D and they should cross each other at the middle.

h. Place batter boards at all four corners. Locate batter boards far enough away from the corner stakes to operate hole-digging equipment. This distance may vary 5 to 10 feet. All four sets of batter boards should be level.

i. Stretch a chalk line from the batter board at D to the batter at A exactly over the nails in stakes D and A. Put a nail on each batter board to locate permanent reference points. Repeat this procedure for the other three sides.

2. Locate the poles.

a. Determine the four corner-pole locations first.

b. Locate the center of the corner pole by measuring in from the chalk line one-half the diameter of the pole plus 2 inches for nailing girts.

   c.   Hook a steel tape over the nail at D and measure along chalk line DC, the distance to the first pole. Locate pole center 6 inches in from chalk line.

   d.   Leave the tape hooked to the nail at A and measure to the second pole. Repeat for all poles.

   e.   Take down the chalk line and remove corner stakes.

3.   Prepare the holes.

   a.   Drill holes 8 inches deeper than the set of the pole about 5 to 6 feet deep and 18 to 24 inches in diameter.

   b.   Place 8 inches of concrete in the bottom of each hole. (An 18-inch hole takes about 1 cubic foot of concrete.)

   c.   Do not place concrete in water-filled holes. Pump or bail water out of the holes first.

   d.   Allow the concrete to set for twelve hours before placing poles in the holes. Do not set poles in fresh concrete.

   e.   Reset the chalk lines.

4.   With the holes ready, it is time to set the poles.

   a.   Select four straight poles for the corners.

   b.   Set the poles in the corner holes the thickness of a nailing girt (2 inches) from the chalk line. At the same time, plumb the pole on two sides by placing a straight board with a carpenter's level on the outward side of the pole.

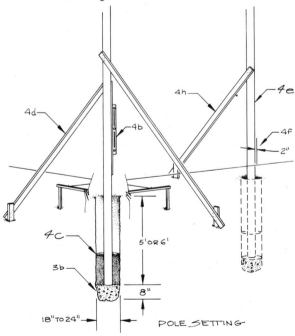

POLE SETTING

    c.   Fill and tamp to only one-third depth.

    d.   Brace corner poles from two directions. Put the top of the braces below the bottom of the plate location, and so they will not be in the way of nailing girts.

    e.   Place the rest of the poles in the holes with the straightest side outward. Small bumps and curves on the inside will not alter the shape of the building.

    f.   Set the pole plumb 2 inches (the thickness of a nailing girt) from the chalk line. Be sure the pole spacing agrees with the plan.

    g.   See that the side poles are in line by sighting from corner pole to corner pole.

    h.   Brace the poles from the inside—every third or fourth pole along the side.

5.   With all the poles set up, you must next determine floor and plate level.

    a.   Find a level point on all four corner poles; also on other poles if distance between corner poles is more than 50 or 60 feet. Use an engineer's level for this. If you don't have an engineer's level, use a water-filled hose to find the level points. A transparent hose is good for this.

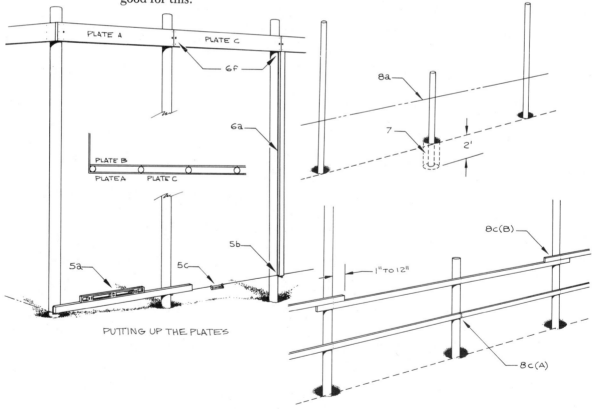

PUTTING UP THE PLATES

    b.   Drive a nail halfway into the poles to mark the level points on corner poles and on each fourth pole between.

    c.   Set the level point on other poles with taut chalk line and a line level from corner pole to corner pole. Mark level points on poles with a nail. Be sure the chalk line is taut and the wind is not blowing it out of line.

    d.   Measure up or down from level points to establish plate and/or floor lines.

6.   Install the plates.

    a.   From the plan, determine the distance from level points on poles to the bottom of plates. Cut a 2 x 4 to this dimension to use as a measuring stick. Use it to measure exact plate height.

    b.   Cut plates squarely and to the exact length.

    c.   Plate A length is from the center line of pole 2 to the outside of pole 1, plus the thickness of a 2-inch nailing girt.

    d.   Plate C length is from the center line of pole 2 to center line of pole 3.

    e.   Plate B length is plate A length minus the thickness of a 2-inch nailing girt or a 2-inch plate.

    f.   The length of plate A equals the length of plate C.

    g.   Start one 60d ring-shank nail in the center of the plate, $1\frac{1}{2}$ inches from the end. Set the plate on the 2 x 4 measuring stick held against the pole, and rest it on the nail driven near the bottom of the poles. Center the end of the plate on the pole. Drive a 60d nail into the pole. Drive the nail in the other end of the plate. Put up the inside plate, the top level with the top of the outside plate. Continue installing plates on one side of the building. If bolts are needed, use a 16-inch tree surgeon bit for drilling through plates and poles. Repeat for plates on the opposite side of the building.

7.   If your plan calls for intermediate posts, now is the time to locate and set them. Drill holes about 2 feet deep. Intermediate posts are used to provide support for the nailing girts when the poles are more than 8 feet apart.

8.   Install the siding girts next.

    a.   Place post in the hole, sight along the outside of the framing poles, or use a chalk line stretched along the outside of the poles to make sure they are even.

    b.   Backfill one-third and tamp all intermediate poles.

    c.   Apply siding girts by using (A) butt joints or (B) lap joints, depending on the length of the siding girt.

    d.   You can use both butt and lap joints on the same building. Using both may save some time in putting on the girts.

    e.   Use two 60d ring-shank nails in each end of the girt.

9.   The framework is now ready for the trusses.

    a.   Install vertical bridging before the truss is set on the plate.

    b.   With truss upside down, place one end over the plate. Next, set the opposite end of truss over the opposite plate.

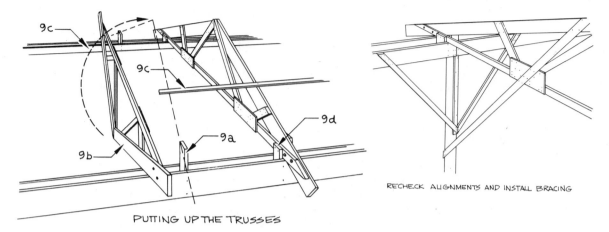

9c

9c

9d

9a

9b

PUTTING UP THE TRUSSES

RECHECK ALIGNMENTS AND INSTALL BRACING

    c.   The truss is now supported upside down over the plates. Pivot the truss into an upright position and hold it steady with a roof girt extending from the last truss; also nail the heel to the vertical bridging. Before nailing, be sure the truss is in the correct position on the plate, and that the width from outside of the rafter plate to outside the opposite rafter plate is the width called for on the plan.

    d.   Install second piece of vertical bridging after all trusses are nailed or bolted in place.

10.   Recheck the alignments.

    a.   Recheck building for plumb. Sight along plates on the front of the building to be sure they are straight. It is possible that the plate on the back side of the building can be slightly out of line. There are two choices: leave as is or split the difference on the two sides.

    b.   Fill all holes and tamp.

    c.   Install bracing as shown on the plan.

11.   Plan the roof.

    a.   Measure the distance from the ridge to the eave along the rafter and add 2 inches for metal overhang. This is the length to use when figuring the length of the sheets.

    b.   Choose roofing sheet lengths that overlap at least 8 inches at each joint. Consult your dealer to find out the available lengths.

    c.   You can sometimes get the right overlap using a different width ridge roll, which allows the top sheet to start farther down from the ridge. Extend lower sheet 2 inches below the first nailing girt.

    d.   Measure the distance along the ridge from the outer edge of the end rafters and add 1 foot (6 inches on each end for finishing).

    e.   Since most sheets normally cover 2 feet wide, divide the total (from step 11d) by 2 feet for the number of rows you need. Roofing is sold by the square (10 feet by 10 feet), or 100 square feet. A square will not cover 100 square feet, because it does not allow overlaps. Ask your local dealer about roof coverage other than the 2 feet.

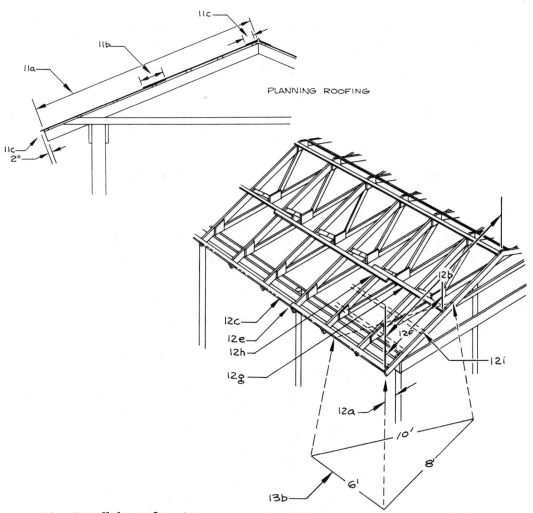

PLANNING ROOFING

12. Install the roofing girts.

    a.   Measure the plate-to-eave distance of the end rafters on one side of the building.

    b.   If the distance varies, mark a point (measuring from the ridge down) that is equal to the shorter of the two. Mark each rafter.

    c.   Place a taut chalk line between these two points.

    d.   If the rafters between vary less than 1 inch, you can correct the differences when putting on the first eave roofing girt. (Let the roof girt overhang the short rafters.) If there is a difference of more than 1 inch, remake the chalk line to the length of the shortest rafter and cut the others off to match.

    e.   Choose a straight 2 x 4 for the first (eave) roof girt. Use the taut chalk line or corrected rafter overhang as a guide. Use butt joints on the first roof girt.

675

f. Measure up from the eave along the end rafters. Measure the length of the first sheet less the 2-inch metal overhang and half of the end lap. Mark this point.

g. Again, place a taut chalk line between these two new points on the end rafters.

h. Place 2 x 4 roof girts above and below this chalk line using a lap joint. Nail each 2 x 4 roof girt with two 40d ring-shank nails.

i. Locate the other roof girts, spacing them 24 to 30 inches on center between the roof girts already placed.

13. Install the roofing itself.

a. Start putting the roofing on at the east end of an east-west building, or at the north end of a north-south building. The side laps then will be away from the prevailing winds.

b. Make a line on the nailing girt at the eave girt. With a 6-foot by 8-foot by 10-foot triangle, as shown, make a line at right angles to the eave as a guide for placing the first sheet of roofing. If this line is not parallel to the rafter, let the metal overhang vary at the end of the building.

c. Continue, putting on the lower row of sheets lapping $1\frac{1}{2}$ corrugations, nailing with $2\frac{1}{2}$-inch screw-shank nails.

d. Put on the other rows of roofing, starting at the same end of the roof.

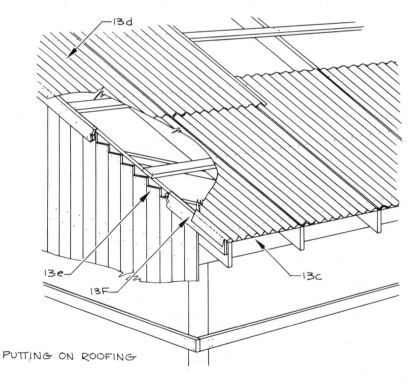

PUTTING ON ROOFING

e. Install the siding on the ends and butt it up to the roofing on the gable ends.

f. Nail the 2 x 8 trim board over the siding to the ends of the roof girts. Then bend the metal overhang over the 2 x 8 trim and nail with galvanized roofing nails.

g. Install eave troughs and downspouts. Where buildings are more than 40 feet long, provide downspouts at both ends.

h. Finish putting on siding, installing braces, and adding other accessories.

RIGID ARCH CONSTRUCTION

Rigid arch construction, as noted previously, is something of a combination of pole and stud frame construction. The wall and roof frame members are joined together, using plywood or metal gussets, into huge, angular arches, which are erected, tied together and sheathed in. In addition to wood, steel and concrete are also used to make rigid arch framing units, but invariably in prefabricated buildings.

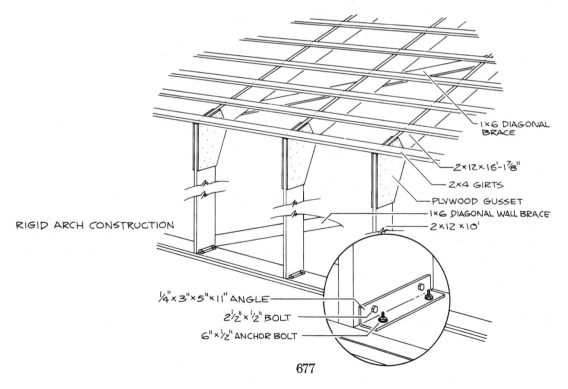

RIGID ARCH CONSTRUCTION

1×6 DIAGONAL BRACE

2×12×16'-1⅞"

2×4 GIRTS

PLYWOOD GUSSET

1×6 DIAGONAL WALL BRACE

2×12×10'

¼"×3"×5"×11" ANGLE

2½"×½" BOLT

6"×½" ANCHOR BOLT

677

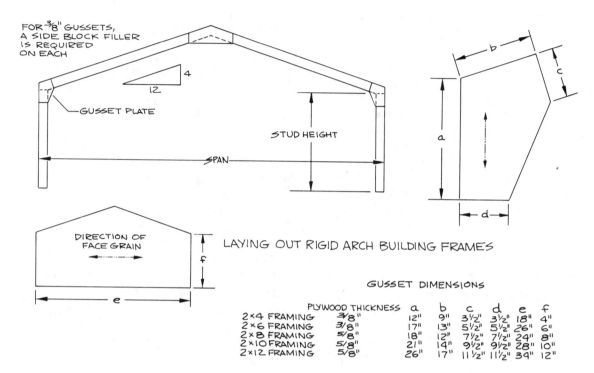

FOR ⅜" GUSSETS, A SIDE BLOCK FILLER IS REQUIRED ON EACH

GUSSET PLATE

STUD HEIGHT

SPAN

DIRECTION OF FACE GRAIN

LAYING OUT RIGID ARCH BUILDING FRAMES

GUSSET DIMENSIONS

	PLYWOOD THICKNESS	a	b	c	d	e	f
2×4 FRAMING	⅜"	12"	9"	3½"	3½"	18"	4"
2×6 FRAMING	⅜"	17"	13"	5½"	5½"	26"	6"
2×8 FRAMING	⅝"	18"	12"	7½"	7½"	24"	8"
2×10 FRAMING	⅝"	21"	14"	9½"	9½"	28"	10"
2×12 FRAMING	⅝"	26"	17"	11½"	11½"	34"	12"

Rigid arch construction is little used on the homestead. Fabrication of the arch units themselves is not difficult, but erection of them without some heavy equipment, scaffolding, and ingenuity is, unless they are small. Since the advantage of the rigid arch, like the pole building and the gambrel-roofed stud frame building, is the vast area enclosed, small rigid arch buildings are rarities. The rigid arch building has a high ceiling and a clear span, making it useful for storing large volumes of hay or bedding and for housing large farm machinery. Most farmstead examples are prefabs, trucked to the site and assembled by building contractors.

The illustrations depict the basics of rigid arch construction. The four elements of the arch are cut to size, laid out, then joined with plywood gussets attached to each broad face of the framing members, using glue and lots of threaded nails. Each size of framing material will require a different shape of gusset. The shape of the gusset is also determined by the slope of the roof.

While rigid arch construction isn't used much—if at all—in chicken houses and toolsheds, there's no reason why it couldn't be. It would certainly yield an interesting, serviceable, and unique homestead outbuilding.

SHEDS AND BARNS

The first step, of course, in any homestead construction project is the planning step. You've got to decide what you want, how it is to be framed and sheathed, and where you want to locate it. These three decisions are important whether you are building a garden shed or a barn.

Ask yourself the question: "Why do I want this building?" List the uses it will have: will it house livestock or just your garden tools? Be specific, and be ranging, putting down every conceivable use you might have for the building. Then jot down space requirements: so many square feet for chickens, so many for power garden tools or the homestead tractor, so many for the workshop.

Ask yourself about other expectations you have about the building. How about the appearance? Cost? Flexibility (you might put a building to one use now and another ten years from now)? Ease of construction (do you want to build it yourself or do you have lots of friends you can count on for help)?

Read through this part of the book. Note the types of construction—dirt floor, wooden floor, stud wall, pole, shed roofed, gambrel roofed—and the advantages and disadvantages of each. Look at the specific buildings others have constructed. Check with your county farm agent, the U. S. Department of Agriculture, your state's agriculture department, land grant college or extension service. These government agencies make available for nominal cost a wide variety of building plans, for structures ranging from the most elaborate and modern agribusiness facilities down to single-stall horse barns and garden tool sheds. Then take a tour of your own area, noting the types of buildings that prevail. If you live in Mississippi, there's no need to frame for snow loads, but if you live in Minnesota, you better.

Now sift through your lists, allocating space, assigning priorities. Cost is almost invariably a major factor in any building project, and building materials are *not* cheap. You won't want to build a barn when a garden shed will satisfy your needs. Be honest with yourself, and be prepared for a rude shock at the lumberyard (if you have to buy much or all of the materials new).

The fellow at the lumberyard will be a big help to you when it comes to materials. If you give him accurate plans—they don't have to be blueprints, but they should be specific and accurate—he will work out a materials list, because he expects to sell you those materials, and a price. He can often give you a choice of woods or types of woods (panels or boards, for example) at different prices, depending on the current market. This information will help you weigh your priorities; utility vs. cost vs. appearance is probably the most agonizing.

Of course, if you are using recycled lumber—you've torn down an old barn on your own or a neighbor's property—you should inventory the materials available and design your structure around them.

In either case, arm yourself with ruler, pencil, eraser, and graph paper and start designing. First you have to decide the overall size of your building. Then make a plan of it drawn to scale. You don't have to be an architect to make workable plans. All you have to do is know how to measure. Use a scale, say $\frac{1}{4}$ inch to 1 foot, or a $\frac{1}{2}$ inch to 1 foot. Draw the outline of your building to scale. Mark in doors and windows to scale. Walls should be 8 feet tall ordinarily, but perhaps you want to economize with a 6-foot wall on small buildings. Whatever, draw in your walls to scale. Decide on your roof slant, and draw that in over your end walls. Then with your ruler, you can easily measure all dimensions.

Try to design efficiently around panels. Plywood comes in 4 x 8 sheets, and plywood can be used for flooring, sheathing, and siding. Metal panels for roofing siding are similarly sized. If you plan properly, you can save yourself a lot of sawing.

GARDEN TOOLHOUSE

In a week of spare-time carpentry evenings, Walter Masson of Needham, Massachusetts, built a 4-foot by 8-foot garden toolhouse against a blank wall of his house.

This is a convenience that saves endless time lugging the lawn mower, garden cart, tools, and fertilizer from cellar or garage to various parts of the yard.

You can build a similar house and regulate its size according to your needs. If you do not have a blank wall, you can build a four-sided house in a corner of your yard.

The foundation of the shed was set on cement blocks. After several years of weathering through New England winters, it has hardly budged an inch.

To aid drainage and prevent frost heave, Masson dug a trench in the soil around the outline of the foundation for the shed. Then he collected small stones from the surrounding area and set them in a 3-inch layer over the bottom of the trench. The cement blocks went on top of these with open ends up and were extended 2 inches above soil level to keep the wooden framework from touching the ground.

The framework of 2 x 3 wooden studs was built on top of the blocks. Three studs were used at the sides and two at the front. All but the studs against the house were 6½ feet high

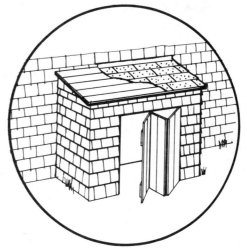

(Masson wanted the house to be high enough to take rakes and other long garden tools with ease). Studs on each side that were nailed to the wall of the house were 7 feet tall to allow for a pitch in the roof.

Bottom and top joists were held together with a frame. To give slant to the roof, side studs were run from the 6½-foot joist to the 7-foot joists.

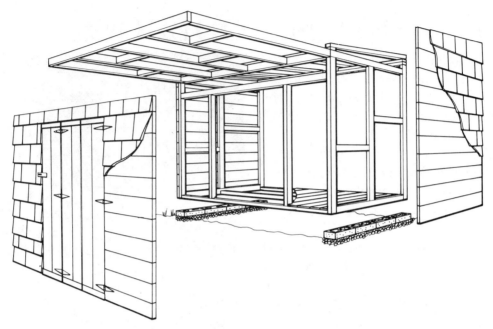

Similar studs were nailed to the roof frame and a center stud was added to give the floor frame added strength.

Studs at the front were adjusted and carefully measured so a folding door could be added.

For a modern touch, five studs, 8 feet long, were nailed to the top framework so they would project over the front. They were spaced equidistantly apart and filled in with 2 x 3s to form a lattice. The facing end was tailored off with a 2 x 3 stud and finished with a 1 x 4.

The floor framing was covered with 1 x 12 pine boards with $\frac{1}{4}$-inch spacing to allow for ventilation. Pine boards also were used to fill in sides and roof.

Each door was made of two 1 x 8 boards, cut to $5\frac{1}{2}$ feet long and cleated at top and bottom, using countersunk wood screws. The three doors were attached with strap hinges and hung to the house so they folded neatly against its side when open. This provided plenty of room to get equipment in and out.

Roofing paper was attached to the outside and top of the house and covered with cedar shingles on the side (to match the house) and asphalt shingles on the roof. A piece of flashing was run between the side of the house and the roof of the toolhouse before the shingles were nailed on.

To avoid drip, Masson attached a metal gutter (with drainpipe) to the front of the house. Painting to match the trim of the house completed the project.

A MINIBARN

A garage full of garden tools can give the family car a bad case of rusty nuts and bolts. Or is it the other with you—the car's inside where it belongs, but the garden tools are all covered with rust?

In either case, it's time to think of building a toolshed which can pay for itself by protecting your tools and power equipment and keeping them in good working order. David Caccia built a 6-foot by 7-foot shed, about 8 feet high, with a roof that slopes from front to rear and with a cinder block base and wooden top structure. In the decade since its construction, Caccia has found this small building a useful working addition to the homestead— it provides his goats with a snug home.

Caccia chose durable materials. Hastily scraped-up farm buildings cost little but soon fall apart and are poor investments in the long run.

He decided on a 4-foot-high cinder block foundation to keep the wood well off the ground, safe from dampness and termites. The frame was made of 2 x 6s and 2 x 4s with a ½-inch exterior plywood roof, covered with asphalt shingles leftover from the house. The sides were also leftover— cedar siding used both vertically and horizontally.

The door is flanked by a pair of win-

dows—glassless because of the goats. Instead, Caccia stapled window screening over the openings and then covered everything with ½-inch wire mesh. In cold weather he latches plywood panels over the openings. He would have used glass if he were making a toolshed. The overall size was determined by construction convenience—two 4 x 8 plywood sheets form the roof and give plenty of headroom.

The first step is to lay out the footings. Level the ground and then drive in eight stakes for your guidelines. Dig a ditch 8 inches deep and wide around the four sides. Next mix concrete and fill the ditch 4 to 6 inches, adding a few reinforcing bars or iron pipes to the footing.

When the concrete has set, lay the cinder blocks. The chapter on walls gives specific directions. Imbed an-

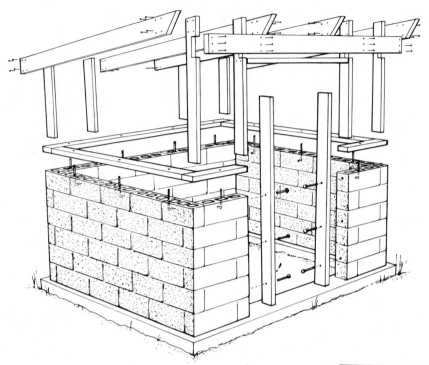

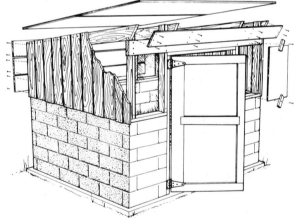

chor bolts in the mortar as the top row of blocks is laid to hold the 2 x 4 sill in place, so the wooden frame will in turn be secured to the sill.

The four roof rafters are 2 x 6s supported at each end by a vertical 2 x 4 which is toenailed to the sill. The roof is simply two sheets of $\frac{1}{2}$-inch plywood laid across the rafters. Asphalt shingles are nailed down over the plywood.

To close the sides in, Caccia used some rough cedar boards and ran them vertically from the sill to the roof rafters. A few lengths of leftover horizontal siding closed the rear.

The door consists of one 2 x 8—a 2 x 6 will do—on the hinge side, and a 2 x 4 on the latch side, tied together on the top, bottom, and in the middle by three horizontal 2 x 4s. Use a lap joint at the four corners, then glue and nail them together. The bottom half of the door is covered with ¼-inch exterior plywood, while the top is covered with window screening. Two heavyweight garage-door hinges give it ample support and ease in handling, while a simple bolt keeps it shut. If you want to be fancy, a padlock will give you extra security and a coat of white paint will give you a bright interior.

THE ANY-PURPOSE SHED

This small shed in old homesteader Wes Smith's backyard is beginning to get a bit swaybacked in its old age, but it still houses a small flock of hens as well as any building could. There's nothing about its construction you haven't met in discussions of other small buildings in this book, but it suggests, better than any of them, a model for a shed that could be used for a variety of purposes. It's fine for chickens, but could house any kind of small animal, or be used to store tools, or as a repair shop, or as a craft or carpentry shop, or even a studio, office, or vacation cabin.

For shop or office use, you'd add insulation of course, and perhaps more windows, especially in the north side (the photos show the south windowed side and the east entrance side). If you wanted a chicken coop, you'd put hinged, flap-down doors on the north side to take manure out of the catching frames (see design of traditional chicken coop elsewhere in this book). For rabbits, you'd definitely want screened windows and. screened doors and more screened

vents for optimum air circulation without flies. For tool storage, you'd need a larger door, perhaps a double door, with a ramp leading up to it for ease of entrance and exit with lawn mower and garden tractor.

The only fault with this structure is that its dimensions do not apply

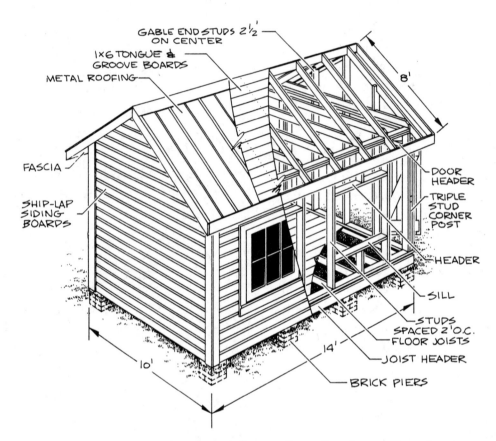

GABLE END STUDS 2½' ON CENTER

1×6 TONGUE & GROOVE BOARDS

METAL ROOFING

8'

FASCIA

SHIP-LAP SIDING BOARDS

DOOR HEADER

TRIPLE STUD CORNER POST

HEADER

SILL

STUDS SPACED 2' O.C.

FLOOR JOISTS

JOIST HEADER

BRICK PIERS

10'

14'

themselves to economic use of standard-sized paneling. The roof slopes are only 7 feet. Better to widen the building or increase the roof slope, so that the slope measures 8 feet, the length of standard metal roof panels and plywood panels.

The building is erected following the procedure described for other small sheds built above ground on piers. First set concrete, brick, or stone piers in the ground and level with each other. Then frame up the floor platform and set it on the piers. Nail down the flooring. Then the sole plate and studs. Ceiling joists, rafters, and roofing follow in that order, then siding, and lastly, doors and windows. It's all basic construction and the secret of good work is using the measuring tape and level with assiduous care and attention. Building is just like football: it's not the fancy play but firm adherence to basics that wins.

A GAMBREL-ROOFED SHED

Here is a gem of a storage building, which will contain a lawn tractor, tiller, rotary mower, trailer, and numerous hand tools. While there are numerous small barns available, none had the proportions P. G. Howerton was searching for. After many plans he decided on the one shown as having the best proportions and taking maximum advantage of standard lumber

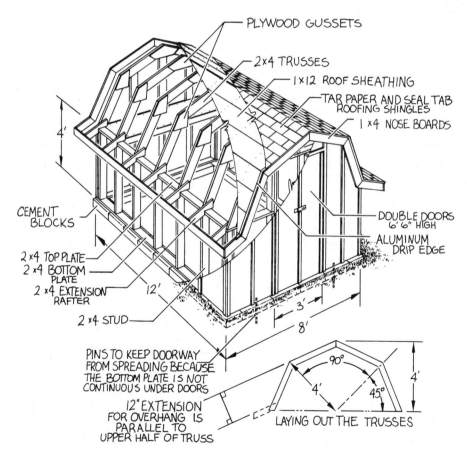

PLYWOOD GUSSETS

2×4 TRUSSES

1×12 ROOF SHEATHING

TAR PAPER AND SEAL TAB ROOFING SHINGLES

1×4 NOSE BOARDS

DOUBLE DOORS 6'6" HIGH

ALUMINUM DRIP EDGE

CEMENT BLOCKS

2×4 TOP PLATE

2×4 BOTTOM PLATE

2×4 EXTENSION RAFTER

2×4 STUD

4'

12'

3'

8'

PINS TO KEEP DOORWAY FROM SPREADING BECAUSE THE BOTTOM PLATE IS NOT CONTINUOUS UNDER DOORS

12" EXTENSION FOR OVERHANG IS PARALLEL TO UPPER HALF OF TRUSS

90°

4'

4'

45°

LAYING OUT THE TRUSSES

sizes. Construction took the better part of a week and the cost was surprisingly low. Howerton set the shed on blocks instead of a concrete slab. A slab would be preferable but he was mainly interested in economy.

The side and rear walls can be built inside, along with the trusses, and carried to the site if desired. The tricky part is building the roof trusses. Howerton was unsuccessful in trying to cut the parts with a framing square and used an alternate method.

It is necessary to have a smooth level concrete or wood surface and chalk or pencil for laying out the pattern for the trusses. Start with a straight line 8 feet long and then find the half or 4-foot point on this line. From this 4-foot point make another line 4 feet long and perpendicular to the first line. This locates the peak of the roof. Now draw lines which bisect (45°) the two right angles

formed previously, and mark 4 feet on each of these lines. Now you have located the peak and the first "bend" in the roof and all that remains is to connect the points you have just located.

The final piece of rafter for the overhang is not attached to the trusses but is nailed to the top plate of side-walls. To look right, this must be parallel to the uppermost roof slope. From the pattern drawn, boards can be cut and matched to the lines drawn.

The barn was sided with $\frac{1}{4}$-inch hardboard and trimmed with $1\frac{1}{4}$-inch by $\frac{3}{8}$-inch lattice used as battens. Roof sheathing was 1 x 12 by 14-foot lumber, while framing was 2 x 4s. A 1 x 4 nose board was placed around the entire building and trimmed with an aluminum drip edge. Felt tar paper and regular 240-pound seal tab roofing shingles were used.

A PRACTICAL SMALL BARN

Call it toolshed, garden shed, or barn—a small storage building of some kind is a must for the space-conscious gardener. With a 96-square-foot floor area and two 4 x 8 loft shelves, this minibarn provides an attractive, useful structure for proper garden and lawn care.

The double-doored, 4-foot-wide entrance is handy for taking bulky items

such as bales of straw and tillers in and out. The owner's garden tractor is easily put away by the use of a ramp; otherwise, there is an 8-inch step into the structure.

The building is based on six cement block piers (corners being double block and center piers single block), with 2 x 6 header joists and 2 x 6 joists 16 inches on center. Flooring is ¾-inch exterior plywood.

From flooring up, basic construction techniques were used, including 2 x 4 framed walls with sole plates and double rafter plates. Studs are 24 inches on center with horizontal blocking—a technique that was used because of the 12-inch-wide vertical aluminum siding. Alternating siding panels are anchored all the way along the stud; the in-between siding is

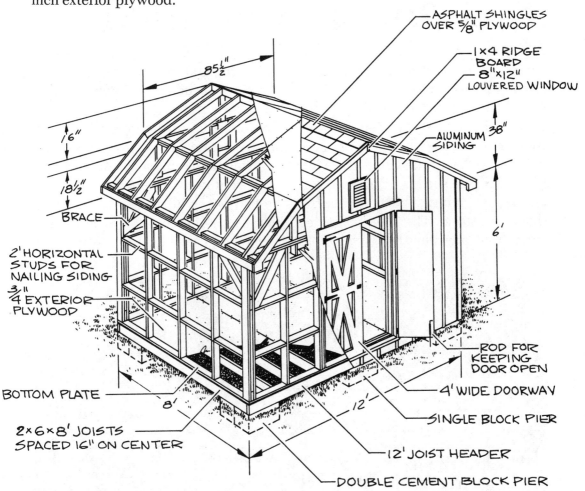

ASPHALT SHINGLES OVER ⅝" PLYWOOD

1×4 RIDGE BOARD

8"×12" LOUVERED WINDOW

ALUMINUM SIDING

38"

85½"

6"

18½"

BRACE

2' HORIZONTAL STUDS FOR NAILING SIDING

¾" EXTERIOR PLYWOOD

6'

ROD FOR KEEPING DOOR OPEN

BOTTOM PLATE

8'

4' WIDE DOORWAY

SINGLE BLOCK PIER

2×6×8' JOISTS SPACED 16" ON CENTER

12'

12' JOIST HEADER

DOUBLE CEMENT BLOCK PIER

anchored at sole plate, rafter plate, and horizontal blockings.

The roof is gambrel style, constructed with 2 x 4 roof rafters 16 inches on center. A double rafter supports the hip of the roof, leaving the ceiling area open for easy access to loft shelves. The roof rafters are covered with ⅝-inch exterior plywood with roofing felt and shingles. An aluminum drip edge and molding were used to finish off the eaves.

The trim work around the corners of the building, the ventilation windows, and the crossbuck type of double doors give the structure character. The barn was topped off with a cast-iron weather vane.

A SMALL POLE SHED

This barn is a typical example of modern pole construction. You can't cover ground with less cost per square foot. You pay for the economy by having the ugliest building in the country but that's what progress and technology have done for us. This particular pole shed is being used for machinery storage, but could also shelter livestock. The open east side, away from prevailing winds, doesn't hurt cattle even in very cold weather. Cold temperatures do not hurt livestock; wet bedding and windy drafts do. Since it rarely blows or snows from the east in the area where this shed is located (Midwest), the open east side represents smart savings.

The outline of a pole building must be laid out with string and stakes so that the corner posts are positioned squarely. Then dig the postholes at

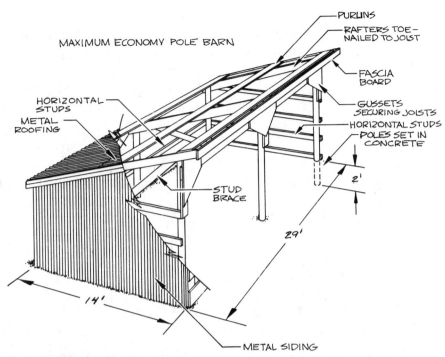

MAXIMUM ECONOMY POLE BARN

PURLINS

RAFTERS TOE-
NAILED TO JOIST

FASCIA
BOARD

GUSSETS
SECURING JOISTS

HORIZONTAL STUDS

POLES SET IN
CONCRETE

HORIZONTAL
STUDS

METAL
ROOFING

STUD
BRACE

2'

29'

14'

METAL SIDING

least 2 feet deep and wide enough to pour 2 to 3 inches of concrete around the poles.

With the poles set, nail on the front and rear joists just below the top of the poles, and brace them with gussets, as shown. Use spikes that go into the poles at least one-and-a-half times the thickness of the joists. Install the joists just far enough below the top of the poles to allow the rafters to sit on the joists even with the top of the poles.

Next, nail on the horizontal framing studs and stud braces on the rear wall and end walls as shown. The corrugated metal panels will be nailed to these boards. When you put up the vertical panels later, curl the panels

adjacent to the front corner posts around the posts a little.

If you intend to house cattle in the building, *by all means* build a solid wall from the ground up to about 3 feet—or in other words, fill in between the bottom stud and the next one solidly with planking. If you don't, the livestock will trample manure up against the wall and push the metal exterior panels out. Another way to protect the walls is to line the whole inside wall with wooden gates such as those across the front of the building.

Next toenail the rafters onto the joists front and rear and to the poles wherever possible. Then nail on the purlins to which the metal roofing will be nailed, spaced about 3 feet apart.

The 15½-foot roof slope counting overhang will take two 8-foot panels lapped over the center purlin. With only a 6-inch lap, you would do well to sandwich a layer of roofing tar between the two panels at the lap, to seal them together. Since the roof is 30 feet long, counting 6 inches overhang on each end, you'll need thirty such panels to cover the entire roof. There is no reason you couldn't use plywood sheathing and asphalt roofing instead of purlins and metal roofing.

Lastly nail on the exterior metal panels. In the rear, fifteen 8-foot panels will cover the whole wall. On the sides you will have to use 12-footers and cut them to fit up against the roof. Seven panels on each side will do it. All metal panels for barn roofs and exterior walls are 2 feet wide plus lap.

A BOARD AND BATTEN BARN

This particular small shed or garden house was built by Dennis Barnes and serves both as storage for garden and lawn tools and as shelter for a few chickens. The board and batten is cedar for long life. The roof is asphalt shingles over plywood sheathing. The floor of plywood rests on 2 x 10 plank framing, which in turn rests on brick tiers at each corner and midway between the corners on the long sides. The bricks are imbedded in the soil about a foot. The floors are ½-inch plywood, wall framing 2 x 4s, joists 2 x 8s, and rafters 2 x 6s. The overall size is 10 feet by 16 feet.

Construction went strictly according to the book in most details. Having laid out square corners and built up the brick tiers to surface level, Barnes nailed together the 2 x 10s

with 16d spikes, framing them 2 feet apart inside 2 x 10 joist headers.

Since the brick tiers are less than a foot in the earth, the building rises and falls ever so slightly with the freezing and thawing of the soil. But in ten years, no harm has befallen the little shed because of it.

After the floor platform is framed,

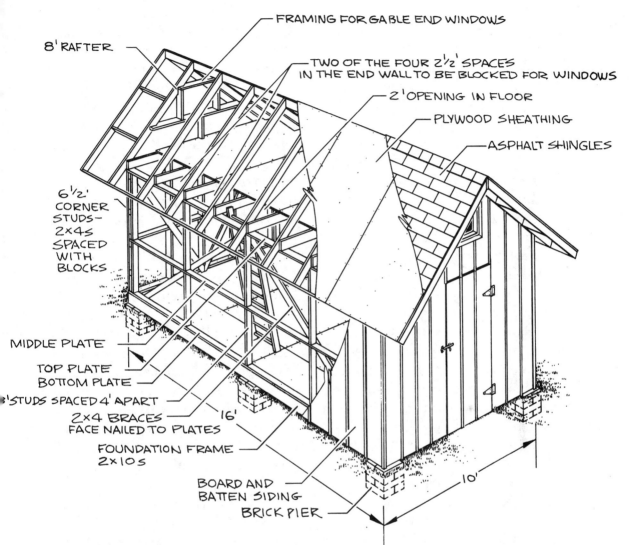

FRAMING FOR GABLE END WINDOWS

8' RAFTER

TWO OF THE FOUR 2½' SPACES
IN THE END WALL TO BE BLOCKED FOR WINDOWS

2' OPENING IN FLOOR

PLYWOOD SHEATHING

ASPHALT SHINGLES

6½' CORNER STUDS— 2×4S SPACED WITH BLOCKS

MIDDLE PLATE

TOP PLATE

BOTTOM PLATE

3' STUDS SPACED 4' APART

2×4 BRACES FACE NAILED TO PLATES

16'

FOUNDATION FRAME 2×10S

BOARD AND BATTEN SIDING

BRICK PIER

10'

lay the flooring. If you use plywood, as in this particular barn, you will have to cut one panel in two lengthwise, which, along with four whole panels, will cover the 10-foot by 16-foot area.

Next the walls were framed up. Here 2 x 4s were used and spaced very precisely. At the corners, triple 2 x 4s were used, exactly as they are used in a regular stud wall. Unlike conventional framing practice, Barnes located a middle plate (a 2 x 4) between the sill and the plate and used 3-foot studs located on 4-foot centers. Thus the corner studs are $73\frac{1}{2}$ inches long. A stud runs from sill to middle plate, and another from middle plate to plate. Finally, Barnes located diagonal braces (2 x 4s) running from the sill at the corners to the center stud at the plate, as shown. These braces are face-nailed to the framing on the inside of the wall.

The end walls are constructed basically like the sidewalls, except that the studs are on 2½-foot centers, and the diagonal braces run from the plate at the corners to the sill at the center stud. There are windows blocked in where planned for. Next, 2 x 8 ceiling joists are toenailed to the top plate (you could probably get by with 2 x 6s) and then the rafters go up. Rafters can be 2 x 6s or 2 x 4s. With the rafters up, you better put the loft flooring down if you are going to use paneling, as 4 x 8 panels may be a little difficult to hoist up there after the barn's closed in. The floor space in the loft of this barn is 10 feet by 16 feet, but you can use four 4 x 8 panels, leaving a foot of space open along the outside edge of the floor next to the roof. Or you can shove the panels over against one side, and leave a 2-foot opening on the other where you can put a ladder from the first to second floor and get things up and down easier. In any event, you will have to provide some kind of opening and a ladder to get to the second floor.

With a width of 10 feet and desiring headroom under the peak of about 6 feet, your roof works out to having a pitch of 14½/12. Counting a bit of overhang at the bottom on each side, your rafters can be 8 feet long, or slightly less if you use a ridge pole as Barnes did. That's what you want if you are using plywood sheathing for the roof. If you want some overhang on the gable ends, as was desired in this building, you will need 18 feet of paneling the long way, or four panels and a half. This means you have to cut one panel lengthwise.

Trim in your roof edges with fascia board and frame and close the gable end walls. The gable end walls on so small a building do not amount to much. A horizontal stud halfway between peak and top plate is about all you need unless you are putting windows in. Then you will need to frame in the window opening. The more traditional approach will be to install three vertical studs as explained in the previous chapter.

The front door of the barn is, literally, the siding cut out of the door space. With inch board frames nailed on the inside, the three 1-inch by 12-inch-wide pieces of siding board make a neat door. When closed it is hardly noticeable. Grapes grow up the south wall of the building, adding a homey touch. In back, on the west wall, a small 1-foot-square door lets the chickens out into an enclosed run on sunny days. Inside, a chicken fence partition divides the rear third of the floor off for the chickens. Only about four hens are kept, and so they stay quite clean and odorless in their 6-foot by 10-foot pen.

A SMALL BANK BARN

The ideal barn for cold climates is the bank barn—forerunner of the split-level house. The bottom floor of a bank barn is built into a hillside in such a way that the farmer can enter it at ground level on the second floor from the uphill side of the barn while livestock can enter and exit the first floor at ground level from the other side. The bank barn should always be built into a hill that faces east or southeast so that the lower floor opens away from the prevailing winds. A bank barn with the lower floor facing west would lose much of the advantage gained by this type of structure.

The soil surrounding the lower floor on three sides acts as insulation and keeps that area cool in summer, and in winter holds in the heat given off by livestock. Even on the coldest days, livestock can keep the lower floor fairly warm. The farmer can enter and exit the barn on the second floor, and store grain and hay there for easy feeding to the cattle below.

Remembering the bank barns of his native Wisconsin, Dennis Barnes decided to model his small homestead barn in Ohio on them—more for the

beauty of the stone walls than for the convenience a commercial livestock or dairy farmer would build a bank barn for. "I always wanted to try to lay up a stone wall anyway," he says.

The barn measures only 12 feet by 14 feet with stone walls about 8 inches thick. The rear wall and the sidewalls near the rear wall have no footings below floor level because the wall already sits into the hill well below frost line. In the front of the building, the walls rest on a concrete footer sunk over a foot into the ground—below frost line. (Two-foot-deep foundations are considered safe from frost heaving in the Barnes's part of the country.)

With the dirt excavated from the barn site—a backhoe can do a job this small in a couple of hours—Barnes proceeded to lay up his stone wall. He used rocks from a nearby quarry, trying to pick out the flattest and/or most square-sided rocks for easier wall building. "The more experience you gain, the easier it becomes to fit the rocks together," says Barnes. "You sort of get a feel for it after awhile." The limestone rocks he used can be cut with hammer and stone chisel but more often than not they will break the wrong way.

To construct the walls, Barnes relied on that never failing trial and error method. He didn't use forms— just laid up a course or two everyday chinked with mortar. When that much hardened, he'd lay another course or two the next day. The typical homesteader will do well to get that much done in his spare time each day. But where flat rocks are not available and the art of laying up round ones has not been learned, you may want to build up your stone walls with forms, the way farmers in Minnesota and Wisconsin did for a century. (And as detailed in the chapter on walls.)

The top floor or loft of the bank barn is composed of 2 x 6 joists, spaced 2 feet apart, overlaid with ½-inch plywood. Front and rear gable end walls are cedar 1 x 12 boards, battens are 1 x 2s, and the roof is ⅜-inch plywood covered with aluminum roofing.

Very little framing was necessary for the end walls. The vertical boards and battens could be nailed to the end rafters and joists, and studding was necessary only to frame in the small front window and the rear door.

The first step in erecting the top floor was to install the 2 x 8 plate on top of the stone wall. Bolts, inserted down through the plate into the mortar between the top rocks before it is dry, hold the plank down securely. While many builders will put a double plank down for the plate so that it will accept longer nails, among other reasons, here a double plate was not deemed necessary. Then the joists were toenailed to the plate, followed by the rafters face-nailed to the joists and to each other at the ridgeboard. The slope of the rafters was dictated by the width of the building—12 feet—and the desired amount of headroom under the peak of 6 feet. That makes a steep roof—a pitch of 12/12 or about an 80-degree peak angle—but gives you a surprising amount of storage space for so small a building.

The dimensions of this building—as the builder knew and so planned—are perfect for putting on a roof that makes the best economical use of today's standard panel sizes. A floor 12 feet wide and 14 feet long with a 6-foot perpendicular to the roof peak, takes four standard plywood panels on each side without any cutting, if you allow for a roof overhang of 1 foot at each gable end. That roof can then be covered with sixteen standard width aluminum roof panels, each 8 feet long. Because the metal roof panels do not extend completely to the peak of the roof (the metal roof cap extends down a couple of inches on either side), you can allow the panels to extend an inch beyond the plywood sheathing at the bottom edge of the roof, and by that simple procedure, prevent rain from getting into the edge of the plywood.

Interlocking aluminum panels now available allow you to nail down a panel at the edge, then cover the nails with the overlapping, interlocking edge of the next panel. Your finished roof has no exposed nailheads where leaks might possibly develop. This particular barn does not have that type of roof, but you might want to consider it.

Hay and straw bales can be put into the loft through the door on the uphill end of the barn. The door is 4½ feet tall and 2 feet wide, equipped with a wooden drawbolt latch. Latch construction is clear from the photo. Two short pieces of 2 x 4 are cut out so they will accept the sliding bolt and then screwed to the door next to and in line with a similar cut-out piece of 2 x 4 on the wall, into which the bolt is slid when the door is closed.

A peg on the sliding bar (not visible) keeps the bar from sliding too far and falling out of the holders.

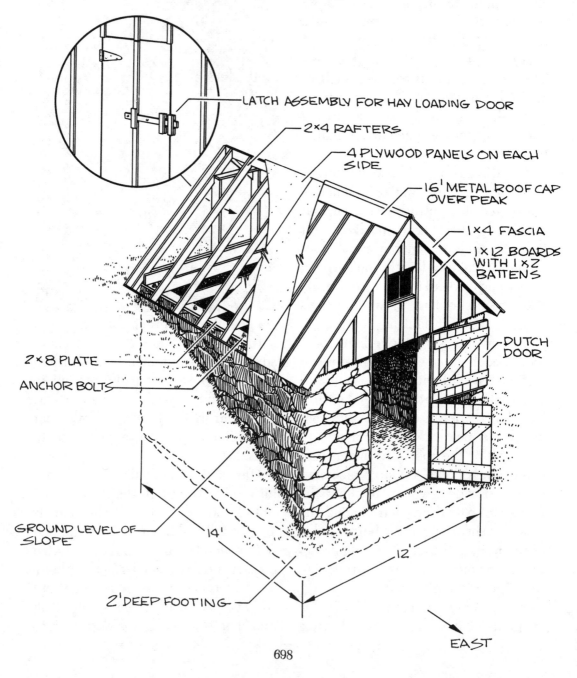

LATCH ASSEMBLY FOR HAY LOADING DOOR

2×4 RAFTERS

4 PLYWOOD PANELS ON EACH SIDE

16' METAL ROOF CAP OVER PEAK

1×4 FASCIA

1×12 BOARDS WITH 1×2 BATTENS

DUTCH DOOR

2×8 PLATE

ANCHOR BOLTS

GROUND LEVEL OF SLOPE

14'

12'

2' DEEP FOOTING

EAST

The door itself is made of the part of exterior siding board and batten cut from the wall for the door opening. These are nailed to 1 x 6s on the inside to hold the door together.

The front Dutch door is made of inch boards 6 inches wide nailed to Z braces of 2 x 4 and 2 x 6 plank ends.

The barn has been used more or less continuously for two horses, but the owners have found that the 12 feet by 14 feet of space is really only comfortably adequate for one horse. The other problem they experienced was that the horses gnawed on every bit of wood they could reach inside the barn, chewing some of the joists halfway through. No matter how well fed or not fed, the horses persisted on chewing the wood. None of the treatments sold to protect wood from horses worked for them. Finally, they tried creosote. That did the trick, but only if they repainted the boards once a month.

Other than its uses for any kind of livestock, the small bank barn could be converted into a root cellar with a minimum of effort. All that would be required would be to partition the lower room in half. The back half would then be a room totally underground except on the front side which would be enclosed by the well-insulated partition wall. With the ceiling well insulated and the floor above covered thickly with straw or hay: instant root cellar.

AN IMPROVISED BARN

The barn pictured is a good example of the need to *improvise* when building homestead barns. Jim Barnes's Ohio barn is built of lumber taken from an old, larger barn. He found that when using recycled lumber that way, he couldn't follow a neat set of standardized plans with joists and studs and rafters and whatever spaced just so-so and precisely this way and that. The material available dictated to some extent what kind of structure he would build, and everything in it does not agree with the bible according to professional car-

penters. The homesteader must sometimes make do or do without.

Barnes decided, after he had torn

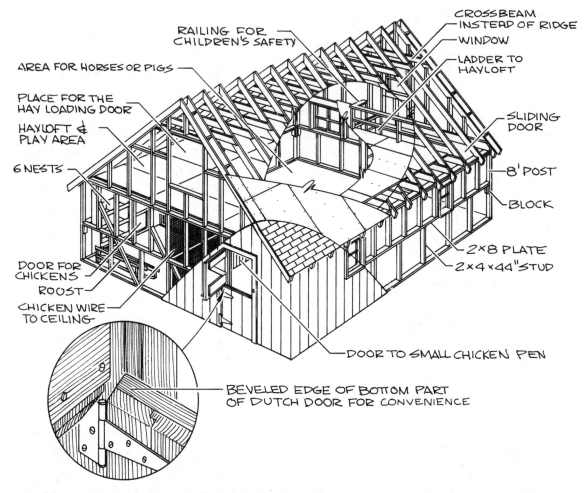

RAILING FOR CHILDREN'S SAFETY

CROSSBEAM INSTEAD OF RIDGE

WINDOW

LADDER TO HAYLOFT

AREA FOR HORSES OR PIGS

PLACE FOR THE HAY LOADING DOOR

HAYLOFT & PLAY AREA

6 NESTS

DOOR FOR CHICKENS

ROOST

CHICKEN WIRE TO CEILING

SLIDING DOOR

8' POST

BLOCK

2×8 PLATE

2×4×44" STUD

DOOR TO SMALL CHICKEN PEN

BEVELED EDGE OF BOTTOM PART OF DUTCH DOOR FOR CONVENIENCE

down the old barn, that he had enough good lumber to build a structure about 30 feet by 20 feet. He settled on a size of about 26 feet by 20 feet however, mostly because the long beams he wanted to use for the sills were 26 feet in length. He also decided to frame the barn with the beam and post method rather than with vertical 2 x 4 studs every 2 feet as is commonly done in buildings now,

because that's the way the old barn was built.

None of the lumber from the old barn was of the standard sizes used today. And being rough sawed on a farm sawmill years ago, boards of the same size were not always exactly the same size—an inch board might vary from $\frac{7}{8}$ inch to $1\frac{1}{8}$ inches in thickness. A 2 x 4 might be as large as $2\frac{1}{4}$ inches by $4\frac{1}{2}$ inches, but never as small as the measly 1½-inch by 3½-inch size they measure today. Therefore, if you intend to follow this barn plan, you will have to *improvise* and *use your head* just like the builder did. Exact detailed plans aren't going to help you all the time, especially since the dimensions were not planned to take advantage of today's standard panel sizes. The economy in this kind of a barn comes from using recycled lumber and the quaintness of appearance that can be more rewarding than brand new (and expensive) barns.

As mentioned earlier, the first consideration you must give your barn is its purpose. They may seem utterly obvious, but many homesteaders in their planning often fail to answer this question *completely* before they start construction: "Why do I really want this building?"

For the barn being discussed, the purposes, *in order of priority*, were as follows. 1. The structure had to be, and look like, a real barn, and since it was to be visible from the road, it had to be attractive and match the design of the homesteader's house. 2. It had to adequately shelter six chickens and perhaps in the future, a horse or steer, and provide food storage for these animals. 3. There had to be room enough for lawn and garden equipment storage. 4. It had to accomplish all these purposes at lowest possible cash cost.

Using recycled barn lumber, the owner could automatically accomplish the first and fourth purposes. With a steep roof he insured himself of a second story or loft large enough to hold a fair quantity of hay and straw necessary for housed animals. By planning a large sliding door (11 feet wide) on the south end of the barn, he made it easy and convenient to take equipment in and out of the barn. And lastly, by deciding on a barn with 520 feet of floor space, he assured himself of *ample* room for chickens plus horse or cow stalls.

Windows add expense to a barn and give amateur builders fits in getting them blocked into walls properly. But they are necessary for light and air circulation. This barn has them where they count most: three on the south side and two on the west.

On the north side, there are doors— a Dutch barn door on the bottom floor and a side swinging door into the hay storage area upstairs. Hay and straw bales can be conveniently unloaded from a truck directly into the loft.

The first thing you do in building any structure is to lay out the outline of it and establish square corners. This particular barn was built according to the beam and post method, so commonly used for barns because it dispenses with the need for digging a foundation. At the corners, stone or cement rests are set firmly in the ground. For this small barn, two cement blocks sunk into the ground at each corner and the four corners leveled with each other sufficed. On the blocks were laid large heavy beams from the old barn foundation— 12 inches by 8 inches thick of ancient and virtually indestructible white oak.

These beams butt against each other. You can drive 50d or 60d spikes on angles from one beam into the other. In the old days, the beams were mortised and tenoned to each other as was all the structural framing.

Next you put up the wall framing, which consists in this case of smaller beams and posts from the old barn. The first row of posts was spaced about 3 feet apart and toenailed into the bottom beam. The posts were 44 inches long except the corner posts which extended the full wall (8 feet tall) and were 4 inches by 6 inches thick. Then a 2 x 8 plate was nailed over the tops of the first row of posts and a second row of 44-inch-long posts was toenailed to that plate. The second row of posts was spaced about 2 feet apart, and a second or top plate was nailed over them. The posts are oddball $2\frac{1}{2}$ inches by 5 inches and some are 4 inches by 6 inches. Since no inside paneling of any kind was planned, the posts did not need to be even on the inside. But the outside edges must be, so that the exterior siding can be nailed to it to form an even outside wall.

As you put up these outside "bones" of your building, the frame will be very shaky for awhile. You will find it useful to angle a few boards from one upright to another, just to steady and plumb the wall until there's enough structure there to hold itself solid. You will wonder if the walls ever will get solid. Don't worry, they will.

To repeat, the important thing to remember is that the top plate, middle plate, and sill (or bottom beam or sole plate) are as perfectly even on the outside as possible and that none of the upright posts stick out beyond the outer edge of the plates. When you nail the exterior siding onto the plates, you don't want the posts sticking out to hinder you.

Notice that there are two windows in the west wall of this barn. Blocking a window into a wall frame is a fairly simple, standard procedure. Depending upon window size, the opening needs a header or top frame, a sill or bottom frame, and perhaps a cripple or door buck stud on either side running up to the header, to close in the proper amount of space to accept the window. In this barn, windows were of the narrowest standard size, 2 feet wide, and were slipped between the posts (which we could refer to as studs). No stud (post) had to be cut and blocked, as would be necessary in normal buildings.

Next, you have to frame the second-story gable walls at each end of the barn. Proceed in the same manner as you framed the lower walls, your studs or posts cut at the top to fit the slope of the roofline. In this barn, a rather large opening was blocked into the framing studs on the north side to accommodate the swinging door that was planned there to bring hay into the barn.

But before you put up the roof rafters and ceiling joists, you need a beam or load bearing wall *inside* the barn for the joists to rest on. The joists in this barn had to stretch 20 feet from sidewall to sidewall, much too long for the 2 x 4 available. The builder ran a double 2 x 4 beam the length of the building (26 feet), supported by two pillars or posts about 6 feet apart. That gave the joists more than enough support for all the hay or whatever might be stored on the upper

floor. The beam does not run down the middle of the lower floor however, but divides the space 9 feet on one side, 11 on the other. In case the owner ever wants to partition the main floor with a wall, the wall would leave a wide enough lane (11 feet) for driving a tractor and manure spreader into the barn.

This barn was built without a ridgeboard, which enabled the owner to put two opposed rafters together with a ceiling joist on the ground. Two rafters and a joist, angles properly cut, nailed together with a gusset just below the peak, can then be installed like a premade truss. This is a good technique for small farm buildings, and certainly faster.

The first end rafter must be put on first. Then the next "truss unit" can be hoisted up on the top plates, positioned properly, toenailed to the top plate, then tacked to the end rafter temporarily with any scrap inch board available. Then proceed to the next truss unit. When all are in place and toenailed to the top plates, roof sheathing boards can be nailed onto the rafters and the temporary holding boards taken off.

Before the rafters are cut, you must give some thought to how much roof overhang you want. This barn has an overhang of about 10 inches. The overhang adds to the attractiveness of the barn, and is in any event, advisable, because an ample overhang protects exterior walls from rain much more than you might realize.

The proper way to finish an overhang is with a frieze board closing the space between rafters and top plate, and fascia board out covering the butt ends of the rafters. A soffit to close in the overhang is rarely necessary on a barn, but you should nail on the fascia board for good looks. This barn, you note, does not have fascia boards. The rafter ends are left exposed and detract a little from the appearance of the barn. Frieze boards are absolutely necessary, however, if you intend to keep chickens or cats in a barn, and keep wild birds, weasels, skunks, coons, and squirrels out. Amateur barn builders sometimes overlook that space left between roof and top plate until something gets into the barn and kills some chickens.

If you are using plywood it is important to get your rafters up very straight and spaced precisely 2 feet apart, so that the edge of the panels meets at a rafter for nailing. If you are using inch boards for sheathing— no matter what width—that precise spacing is not so critical. On this particular barn, one side of the roof has inch board sheathing, the other plywood. The builder simply miscalculated—didn't have enough boards from the old barn to do the whole roof. The plywood was, how-

ever, the only lumber he had to buy.

Once your sheathing is on, you should try to get the roof covered as soon as possible since rain never does wood any good. At least roll on your tar paper (if you are going to finish with shingles) right away. Install your roof according to manufacturer's instructions, and if none are available, don't be too proud to ask your building supply dealer any questions that puzzle you.

This barn is covered with asphalt shingles over tar paper. Because of the steepness of the roof, it should last about forever.

Next proceed to nailing on the exterior siding. With post and beam framing, as against regular stud framing, the siding can be put on vertically, which is the main reason for using this type framing. The siding for this barn is boards 12 inches wide, 1 inch thick. As you can see, they are nailed up vertically, as close together as it was humanly possible to fit them. Small cracks still exist between the boards, enough to allow some circulation of air, but not enough to let in rain or much snow. Battens would have to be nailed over the cracks in the boards if any kind of interior wall and insulation was contemplated, or if used in the far North where too much finely powdered snow would certainly sift through during blizzards.

The boards are nailed to the sill,

middle plate, and top plate with 8d nails. Be sure that you use *galvanized* nails that won't rust for exterior wall work like this. Otherwise, common steel nails will rust and make unsightly rust marks running down the wall.

The Dutch door's construction details can be easily ascertained from the photo. The only critical part of the Dutch door is the slanted edges where top and bottom sections of the door meet. There are several reasons for the slant. For one thing, wind, rain, and snow cannot come through the break in the doors nearly so easily as if they butted up to each other square. Secondly, the upper part of the door can be opened independently, but the lower part can only come open by pushing the top along with it. In other words, you can't have the bottom open and the top closed.

Can you guess why? Bent down with the weight of a sack of feed or a forkful of hay on his back, yesterday's farmer was apt to walk right into a closed top half of a Dutch door if the bottom were open. Also, and more importantly, the Dutch door could enclose animals and still allow a breeze or light into a building. If you had the bottom open, however, you better have the top open too, or a cow or horse might go through and take the top section right along into the barnyard, hinges and all! But of course, the main reason for the slant is simply convenience. If you want to push or pull the door open entirely to walk through, it certainly is easier to shove or pull with one hand on the door latch instead of having to use both hands, one on the bottom and one on the top section.

The dimensions of this door are about 40 inches wide and 6½ feet high, but you can make one any reasonable size you desire. Hardware—hinges and latches—is the kind commonly available at hardware stores.

The inside floor plan of the barn is quite simple at this stage since the only animals the owner houses at present are chickens and cats. The chicken pen occupies the northeast corner of the floor. A pen in the southeast corner is for a pig though the owner has since built a separate pigpen to fatten the one hog he raises every year. The barn pen is used only when the pig is small and the weather still cold in the spring. There is space that will become horse or cow stalls when necessary. The rest of the barn is machine and tool storage.

Entrance to the second floor is gained by climbing a simple, permanent barn ladder at the south wall, near the sliding door. A balustrade up in the loft around the ladder hole protects against children falling from the second floor. Though the main purpose of the upstairs room is hay and straw storage, it has become the owner's children's playhouse—hay bales and all. The kids, including the neighbors, enjoy playing there so much that the owner considers the building justified for that reason alone.

The bottom floor in this barn is dirt which is all that's necessary. If and when a horse stall is added, flooring might be advisable in that area. Better that a horse stand on wood than on concrete, but a cow can tolerate concrete just fine.

The top floor is inch boards nailed to the joists. If you don't have recycled boards from an old barn, you may find some boards much cheaper than good flooring boards. You don't really need the latter in a barn like this. In fact just about any inch board will work. A few cracks in the floor won't hurt at all. And plywood may be cheaper than boards.

In building a barn, even a small one, you should order a little more wood than you think you are going to need. There are always gates and braces you don't think about beforehand, and if there is any wood left after that, the scraps can be utilized to make nests for the chickens, feed troughs, ladder hangers, shelves, and who knows what all.

Notice the chicken nests in the photo. And the roost to the left of the

nests. Both were made with leftover scraps. The four nearly vertical boards above the nests are there to discourage the chickens from roosting on top of the nest boxes and fouling them with droppings. Note also that the roost has no catching frame under it. In this case, no more than four or five hens are ever kept in a space of about 70 square feet. There are more than 10 square feet per chicken. Such spaciousness is unheard of in commercial flocks where you simply cannot afford that much room per bird. But it's the only way to go when you want to keep just enough hens for

your own eggs. The pen stays clean and rarely smells because there is ample bedding to absorb and compost the wastes from the few chickens.

The small exit door allows the chickens to go outside. The chickens can exit into the wire cage for a bit of sunlight on warm days. In summer, towards evening, the cage can be pulled away from the door, and the chickens can roam around the barnyard or into a nearby woodlot or field occasionally.

In summing up, here are a few words of wisdom from the men who built the barn, Jim Barnes and his dad, Ed. You do save money, lots of it, by tearing down an old barn if you can get it for nothing. But you pay for it in labor, as the tearing down can be quite a job. That's why owners of old barns are sometimes willing to

"give" you a barn if you agree to clean it up completely. You might be wiser to make this agreement only on smaller buildings, as the tearing down and cleaning up of very large, old barns can be a major operation. Sometimes you can sell hand-hewn beams and weathered siding for a good price and help pay for the labor of tearing down and cleaning up.

If you do agree to tear down and clean up a building, make sure you allow yourself ample time and put that ample time in the agreement. It's going to take longer than you think, like maybe a half-year of spare time on weekends. But with the high price of lumber today, the time is well spent. There's nothing you will find handier on your homestead than a stack of lumber at your disposal.

LIVESTOCK HOUSING

More often than not, the first outbuildings erected on a homestead are homes for animals. In the previous chapter, for example, several of the sheds and barns were built for animals, several for tools, and several for both. Regardless of the intended use of the buildings, none were unsuited to livestock, but perhaps, for light and ventilation.

As a general rule, homesteaders tend to overhouse their animals more often than underhouse them. Most animals are surprisingly hardy, although their housing needs are not always what you expect. Hogs and sheep, for example, need shelter from the hot summer sun more than they need shelter from winter's cold blasts. Invariably, housing recommendations can be boiled down to: clean, dry, draft-free shelter. If you provide that, you'll not go wrong.

Most animals, especially in the homestead situation, will fair best if given some freedom. Sheep, goats, cattle, and horses will do well in a spacious, well-bedded box stall offering free-choice access to the outdoors. Chickens can be allowed to roam, scratching for food where they can find it, roosting at night indoors.

In the end, if you want to invite animals to your homestead, but you need a roof over their heads, turn to "Sheds and Barns" for housing ideas. In the pages that follow, you will find projects for special shelters, feeders, brooders, milking stands and the like. Many of them will serve more than one kind of animal. The stalls included in the section on cows and horses, for example, will be useful for confining goats and hogs, just as well as cows and horses. So don't confine your browsing to one section of this chapter, regardless of your livestock inclinations.

POULTRY

There's no more practical livestock for the small homestead than chickens—if you house them properly. It makes little difference whether the coop is round or square, flat roofed or hip roofed, plain or fancy. The crucial question is how much room you give your hens—how many square feet of floor space you provide for each one. You'll not have one speck of disease trouble with the chickens if you allow the hens much more floor space than commercially designed poultry houses call for.

The experts will tell you a chicken needs no more than 2 square feet of floor space, and you can get by with less. If you are going to build a 50,000-bird house, you simply can't afford not to follow that advice. But as a homesteader who wants to raise only a few chickens for your own meat and eggs, ignore the experts completely on this point. Provide your hens with at least 8 to 10 square feet of floor space each. That may sound extravagant, but a 10-foot by 20-foot building can be built very reasonably for twenty hens. It won't stink enough to bother even the most cranky neighbor, won't create a fly problem, won't draw rats, and will not need cleaning out more than once a year, if that much. But it works only because each hen has at least 10 square feet of floor space.

Here's how Gene Logsdon built a chicken coop to meet those requirements.

Choose a high spot of ground, from

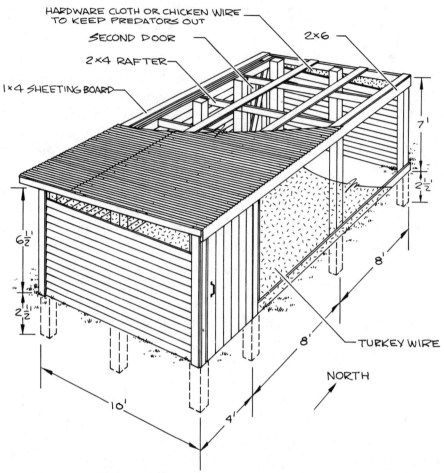

HARDWARE CLOTH OR CHICKEN WIRE
TO KEEP PREDATORS OUT

SECOND DOOR

2×4 RAFTER

1×4 SHEETING BOARD

2×6

7'

2½'

6½'

2½'

8'

8'

TURKEY WIRE

NORTH

10'

4'

which runoff water flows away, not toward or through it. Mark off a 10-foot by 20-foot rectangle so that one of the long sides faces southeast, away from prevailing westerly winds but turned enough southward to catch some of the winter sun. Old traditional coops have one long side with windows facing directly south. But Logsdon's coop has translucent roof panels to let sunlight in, and doesn't need windows, so the build-ing is faced more easterly to give better wind protection. On that side is stretched strong, finely meshed tur-key wire for a wall rather than boards. In winter corn shocks are set against the wire for insulation.

The design calls for a flat, slant-roof shed. Logsdon's building has two doors, one in the rear wall at a corner, the other in the front wall at the corner at the opposite end of the building. You don't absolutely need two doors, but they come in very handy.

The 10-foot span between corner posts on the ends of the coop may be too wide for the type of siding you intend to use. For more wall strength, another post can be placed midway between the corner posts. If you foresee keeping a pig, sheep, or cow in your coop, by all means set more posts along the front and back sides too.

Logsdon chose pole-type construction because, as he put it, "even a simple-minded noncarpenter like me can master the skill of setting posts in the ground and nailing boards on them." He set the four corner posts, sinking them $2\frac{1}{2}$ feet into the ground and leaving $6\frac{1}{2}$ feet exposed at the rear corners, 7 feet at the front corners.

Set four more posts, two in the front wall, two in the back wall. Set one midwall post in each wall 4 feet from a corner post, and the other midwall post 8 feet from the other corner post. The 4-foot space will be the doorway. Since the doors are at opposite ends of the building, set the posts that way.

Nail 2 x 6 boards on the outside top of the posts along both long sides, as shown. Nail 2 x 4 rafters to the 2 x 6 supports, as shown. Allow about a foot overhang on back wall. Nail 1 x 4 sheathing boards on 2 x 4 studs.

Nail corrugated roof panels to sheeting. You'll need seven 12-foot

panels, four metal and three fiberglass, the latter either clear or translucent green. For the metal panels, galvanized steel is better than aluminum. Cheaper too. Use roofing nails that have lead seal washers under the nailheads. Nail through the corrugation ridges, not the troughs, and pound the nails snug against the ridge without denting the panel in.

Now nail up boards or barn siding or whatever material you can get for the walls to the back and end walls. Make doors out of any wood material at hand and fasten them to the corner posts with large T or strap hinges. Set doors should open out.

Stretch turkey wire across the framing for the front wall. If you don't have corn shocks to set along the turkey wire walls in winter, you can put plastic curtains over them to keep out the cold.

Along the top side of the building between roof and walls, stretch and nail chicken wire over any openings large enough for coons, opossums, etc., to squeeze through. If you want or need to keep out sparrows, use hardware cloth.

Keep two steel 55-gallon barrels right outside the door, properly covered from rain and rodents, to store the chicken feed in.

Inside the building, along the higher front wall near the roof, make some kind of shelf and bed for a cat. Feed the cat there at all times so it becomes accustomed to staying there. It will keep birds and mice away. (Birds, especially sparrows and starlings, carry lice.)

Cats can be very independent animals, like humans, and are inclined to do as they please. They can be very difficult to keep in a barn if they don't want to be there. If you allow them in the house part of the time, they are not going to want to stay in the barn the rest of the time. It helps if the cat is born in the barn and plays there throughout its kitten life.

Leave a hole somewhere between roof and wall for the cat to enter and exit according to its own whims. If you don't, the cat will undoubtedly find or make its own hole anyway.

Along the back between the doorway and the end wall, about 3 feet above the floor and at least 18 inches away from the wall, install a single 2 x 4. That's all the roost you'll need for twenty hens. Be sure the roost is 18 inches from the wall. If closer,

droppings will slide down the wall sometimes instead of falling directly to the bedding, and that looks very unappealing to say the least.

On the floor of the coop you need a foot of straw for bedding initially. In two weeks add another foot. After that, add a few inches of fresh bedding (dry grass clippings, dried leaves, hay, fodder, sawdust, and peat moss work almost as well as straw) about once a month.

When you feed the chickens, scatter their grain on the floor, so they have to scratch for it. The hens' constant scratching in the bedding keeps mixing the manure and bedding together, turning all into a rich compost. The compost contains vitamins that keep hens healthier without medicine than hens in cages or on clean cement or

wood floors. That's scientific fact. The hens also eat any fly eggs that might get laid in the manure, and no fly problem develops. And you have a source of compost for the garden anytime you want to use it. The only requirement is that the bedding remain dry—which you insure by providing each hen with 10 square feet of floor space.

Even the droppings under the roost will get worked into the bedding and be composted without much odor. There may be a small buildup of manure in the morning, but the scratching chickens soon bury it in the bedding.

In a conventional, crowded coop, droppings from the roost fall on catch boards rather than on the floor. The manure is supposed to be raked from the catch boards into a manure spreader and hauled away regularly, but that rarely happens. The droppings lie on the catch boards, build up, stink, harbor millions of fly eggs, and lead to a sordid, disease-breeding mess. But if you crowd hens into 2 square feet of space per bird or less, you have to have catch boards under the roost because the bedding couldn't compost all that manure.

Along the inside of the end walls, you can put two or three nests on bracketed shelves. Three old 5-gallon buckets turned on their sides make very good nests that hens like to sit in. An extra block of wood across the bottom lip of the bucket will prevent the hen from dragging nesting material or eggs out of the nest when she exits.

Close management of the flock is necessary to keep from overcrowding the 10-foot by 20-foot building in late summer when the new pullets are growing but have not yet replaced the older hens.

Should you build a fenced run for your chickens outside the coop? Up to you. A run soon becomes a strip of bare ground. Logsdon keeps his chickens penned inside and leaves them out only on nice days towards evening. They don't stray too far and as soon as darkness falls, they go back into the coop of their own accord. If, however, you have little area for the chickens to roam in, better fence their yard.

THE TRADITIONAL AMERICAN CHICKEN COOP

This hen house comes close to being the perfect example of the kind of building the farm flocks of yesterday were housed in. Hundreds of farm and ex-farm boys, maybe thousands, share none too pleasant memories of cleaning coops like this Saturday after Saturday. They had to be cleaned out nearly every week because their mothers, in an effort to make a little more money from the eggs they sold, crammed as many chickens as possible into them. A coop of this size, 22 feet by 12 feet, might house two hundred chickens when one hundred would have been comfortable and fifty far safer in terms of hen health.

Notice the important features that make this a good hen house. No wood was wasted with unnecessary headroom. The simple-to-build slant roof goes from about 9 feet in height at the front wall to 6 feet at the rear. No wasted space, but you won't hit your head on the ceiling either. Where the ceiling is low, on the north side, the roosts are located and you can't walk there.

Appreciate the position of the hen house. The door is on the east side, away from prevailing winds. It is a sliding door rather than a swinging door, and therefore easier to open when the snow is deep. The windows are on the south side, where they belong to allow in the winter sun. Window space is ample too. But the small roof extension above them sticks out just far enough to act like a sun visor in summer—shading some of the hot sun rays out. Note too, the vertical 1-inch by 1-inch boards under that roof extension. That's a sort of wood vent to let in some air. It should have wire screening over it to keep out insects. On the north side, the hinged vent boards can be opened in hot weather to allow better air circulation.

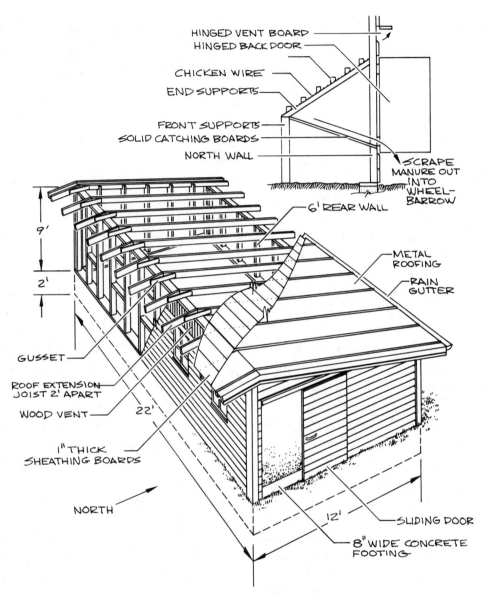

HINGED VENT BOARD
HINGED BACK DOOR
CHICKEN WIRE
END SUPPORTS
FRONT SUPPORTS
SOLID CATCHING BOARDS
NORTH WALL
SCRAPE MANURE OUT INTO WHEEL-BARROW
6' REAR WALL
METAL ROOFING
RAIN GUTTER
9'
2'
GUSSET
ROOF EXTENSION JOIST 2' APART
WOOD VENT
22'
1" THICK SHEATHING BOARDS
NORTH
12'
SLIDING DOOR
8" WIDE CONCRETE FOOTING

The vent boards are right above the catching frames and vent off some of the odors arising from there.

About the only way this coop differs from most traditional coops is that it lacks large hinged doors on that north side, from which, when opened, a farmer could clean out the catching frames inside directly into wheelbarrow or manure spreader—rather than having to carry the manure out through the door.

Inside, the nest boxes are made of old orange crate lumber. The tin sheets above the nests are to discourage hens from roosting on top of the nests and fouling them. Waterers and feed troughs hang suspended from wires, giving chickens more floor space and keeping them from scratching bedding into the troughs. Roosts, with catching frames underneath, are to the right, out of the picture.

In construction, there is no need to go through the basic steps common to all wooden buildings. Refer to methods described in previous pages, while we point out the differences in this one.

In this case, the foundation is concrete, about 2 feet deep in the ground and 8 inches wide. Two by eight-inch planks on top of this footer, screwed tight to bolts running down into the concrete, make the sole plate. (The floor is dirt, so there is no floor framing.) The studs are toenailed to the sole plate. Studs are 2 feet apart on the long walls, though you will notice in the photos that the studs on the end walls are not so exactly spaced. Notice how the 2-foot-wide windows fit nicely between every other stud spacing on the south wall. All the builder had to do was block in the headers and rough sills between the studs to make his window openings.

In the shed roof construction used

here, rafter and ceiling board become one and the same board. They're spaced 2 feet apart too. The south roof projection—the sun visor—can be connected to the main rafters in several ways. You can overlap them and face-nail a visor joist to each rafter, toenailing both into the wall they rest on. Or you can butt them up against each other after sawing the proper angle on both ends and nail together with a gusset or scab.

The roof is built up of sheathing boards (inch boards of varying widths) overlaid with tar paper and asphalt. You could use corrugated metal too. Notice that eave troughs have been installed to carry the water away rather than let it drip directly off the roof all along the north side of the building. Guttering may not be absolutely necessary on a small barn, but it certainly is nice not to have mud and puddles around it during rainy weather.

Regular wood siding finishes off the exterior. The siding is nailed directly to the studs. On the end walls, the top siding boards are cut to butt up neatly

against the sloping end rafter-joist. All outside corners are trimmed with 1 x 4 vertical boards to cover the edges of the siding boards that would otherwise show on the corners. Trimming gives the building a neater appearance.

If you are going to put quite a few chickens in a coop of this size (more than twenty year-round) you probably need a catching frame under the roosts. Otherwise that many chickens will deposit so much manure on the floor while they roost during the night that you won't be able to keep the floor dry and neat, even with lots of bedding. There's no particular right way to build a catching frame under

the roosts. It needs to be screened off so the chickens can't get into it, but constructed so that you can scrape it out easily.

Therefore, you'd be smart to make hinged doors in the north side of the barn which you can open to scrape out the catching frame (a hoe is the best tool for that job) directly into a wheelbarrow or manure spreader. Inside, the roosts should be built in gradually ascending tiers from about waist high 4 feet out from the wall back to the wall just under the roof. Roost boards can be 1 x 2s or 2 x 2s or poles 2 inches or so in diameter. Under the roost boards, chicken wire is stretched. Manure drops through it (usually) but the chickens can't.

The catching frame of solid boards starts right under the first or lowest roost board 4 feet out from the wall, and slopes slightly downward to the back wall, but still high enough off the ground so you can scrape into a wheelbarrow or other vehicle. This kind of roost and catching frame does not take up any floor space either—a decided advantage in a crowded coop.

A SMALL HEN HOUSE

If you don't have enough room to build a large structure on your place but would still like to have housing for a few chickens, this small hen house, designed and constructed by

Billy R. Tyler of Otis, Oregon, might be just what you need. It can be constructed of scrap lumber in whole or part. Its size makes it fairly inexpensive to build new and facilitates mov-

717

ing the building to provide new grass for the chickens if this is desired. You can put as many as ten chickens and a rooster in here if you wish—that's enough eggs for an average family—but housing this many birds in so small a space will create disease problems unless the hen house is cleaned out frequently and well. Attaching a run, as shown, will alleviate these problems somewhat and allow chickens to supplement their grain rations with greens.

The hen house is easy to build. The rear wall consists of two plates 2 x 4 by 6 feet with 5-foot 2 x 4s nailed at each end on 18-inch centers. For the front wall, nail a 6-foot 2 x 4 at each end of two 6-foot plates and nail a 6-foot upright to the plates 18 inches (outside to inside) from each end. The 36-inch gap between these uprights will be used for framing a window and a door for the chickens to enter the run—if you're building the run.

For the window, nail a 36-inch 2 x 4 horizontally, 15 inches down from the top plate. Measure 18 inches from one of the studs, and nail an upright from the bottom plate to the horizontal portion of the window. Frame an 18-inch-square opening for the door by nailing a horizontal piece between this upright and the stud.

The front and rear walls are tied into each other by two 4-foot 2 x 4s toenailed into the front and rear bottom plates. Or, for a more permanent joint, you may want to cut lap joints at the corners of the front plates before you begin framing the walls. Cut the top part of the lap on the front and rear walls, and frame the walls. When you want to tie in the front and rear walls, slip the side plates with the underneath part of the lap joint into place and nail.

Rafters are 6-foot 2 x 4s. Allow an 18-inch overhang in the front of the building, cut the bird's-mouths, and nail the rafters 2 feet on center.

Frame a 20-inch-wide doorway on the left end wall as shown. The upright can be toenailed into the bottom plate and end-nailed into the rafter. Nail an upright in the middle of the opposite end wall, toenailing it into the plate and end-nailing it into the rafter as when framing the door.

Nail two 5-foot 2 x 4s diagonally against the front and rear walls as shown. These will support the roosts:

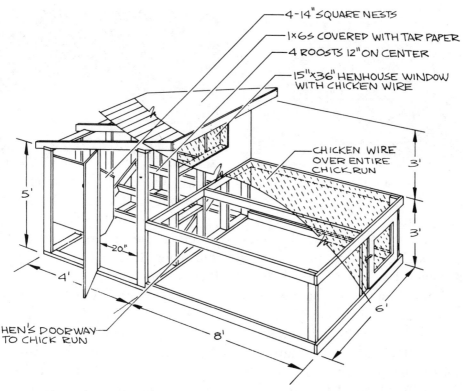

4-14" SQUARE NESTS

1×6S COVERED WITH TAR PAPER

4 ROOSTS 12" ON CENTER

15"×36" HENHOUSE WINDOW WITH CHICKEN WIRE

CHICKEN WIRE OVER ENTIRE CHICK RUN

HEN'S DOORWAY TO CHICK RUN

2 x 4s nailed to these diagonals, 12 inches on center. A nesting box is mounted beside the door, as shown.

Cover the roof with 1 x 6s nailed perpendicularly to the rafters. Staple or nail tar paper on the 1 x 6s.

The sides of the coop may be covered with scrap lumber and tar papered, or covered with plywood. A single sheet of plywood cut to fit can serve as a door. Mount with scrap hinges. Cover the window with chicken wire.

The run is simply constructed of 1 x 3s covered with chicken wire.

TURKEY SHELTER

This structure is designed to serve as an on-range shelter for turkeys, but can be used for chickens or other poultry. It is easily constructed, and, since it is built on skids, is easily portable.

The basic frame is constructed from 2 x 4s. The length for the side pieces is 10 feet; crossmembers are 9 feet long, spaced at 29½ inches on center. Nail these pieces together (use 16d nails for frame construction) and

square the frame using temporary braces.

Cut six pieces of 2 x 4s 23 inches in length. These will be nailed as uprights in each corner and in the center of the long sides flush with the bottom of the frame. Cut two 12-foot pieces of 1 x 3 and fasten to the top outside of the uprights (you may, if you wish, notch the tops of the uprights to accept the 1 x 3), allowing 1 foot of the 1 x 3 to extend in the front and back of the shelter.

At the center of both short ends of the frame, temporarily nail a 50-inch piece of 1 x 3 flush with the bottom of the frame, making sure that the 1 x 3s are square with the frame. At the top center of these uprights attach a 12-foot length of 1 x 3, toenailing it temporarily into the uprights, and allowing 1 foot to extend past each end of the structure. This piece will serve as a guide for cutting rafters and as a ridgepole.

Rafters are 1 x 3s 6 feet in length and spaced on 1-foot centers. Cut the upper angle to fit against the ridge-pole, and cut bird's-mouths on the underside of the rafters where they join the sides of the shelter. Nail the rafters to the ridgepole and the sides, and when the roof is framed, remove the uprights.

The opening for the door is approximately 31 inches wide and centered. Uprights are nailed from inside the 2 x 4 frame to the inside of the rafter, with a crosspiece nailed between them as shown. The same type of frame is also built in the back of the shelter. This makes the shelter sturdier and gives extra area for attaching chicken wire.

To cover the shelter, nail a cheap insulation board on the rafters. Then nail the tin in place using galvanized roofing nails.

Next, install the floor. We used 1-inch rough-cut lumber, nailed to the 2 x 4 frame with 8d nails. You could use scrap lumber, plywood, or tongue and groove. If using plywood, you may want to install the floor *before* the roof is framed and the front and rear framing is in place. Nail 1 x 3

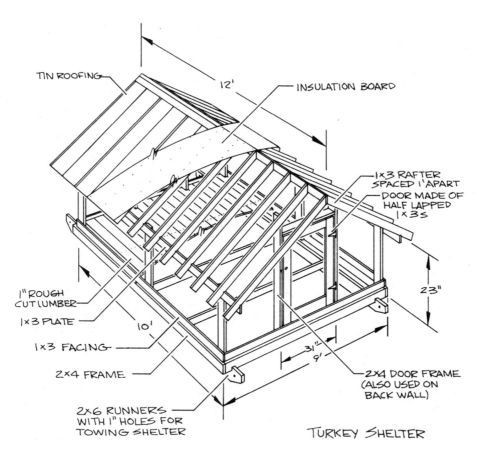

TIN ROOFING

12'

INSULATION BOARD

1×3 RAFTER SPACED 1' APART

DOOR MADE OF HALF LAPPED 1×3s

23"

1" ROUGH CUT LUMBER

1×3 PLATE

1×3 FACING

10'

2×4 FRAME

31"

9'

2×4 DOOR FRAME (ALSO USED ON BACK WALL)

2×6 RUNNERS WITH 1" HOLES FOR TOWING SHELTER

TURKEY SHELTER

facing around the bottom perimeter of the shelter.

The door is made of 1 x 3s with half-lap end joints, assembled with screws and glue, and mounted with **T** hinges.

Runners were fastened under our shelter to facilitate moving, and are simply two 2 x 6s 12 feet long, tapered at both ends and notched out 1 foot from each end $1\frac{1}{2}$ inches deep so that the 2 x 4 frame will fit over and inside them. One foot should protrude from either end. Drill a 1-inch hole 6 inches from both ends of the runners for attaching a towrope.

Staple chicken wire over the entire outside area.

CHICKEN FEEDERS

The very simplest chicken feeder is the ground: just toss scratch feed there and let them eat. That's what the farmer did in the old days. But by

721

feeding chickens on the ground, you often end up feeding the local birds and, all too often, rats. Using feeders can save a lot of feed over a year's time, and they are so quickly and inexpensively made, it's silly not to.

Three of the feeders shown here are of the same basic design; they differ only in size. The fourth feeder is designed around a large capacity, allowing you to fill the feeder and forget it for a week or more at a time. That's a nice feature if you want to be able to get away from the homestead for a weekend or more at a time.

The first feeder is for chicks. It is built low to the ground so the little peepers can get at the feed. If you are planning on raising more than sixty or seventy chicks, you may find it advisable to make the feeder 4 feet long.

Before making it longer than that, however, you may find it more practical to make a second feeder. The same holds true for the larger feeders.

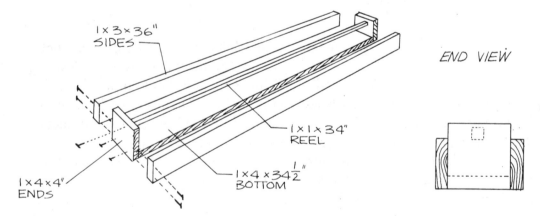

CONSTRUCTION

1. Cut two 36-inch lengths of 1 x 3 for the sides. Cut a 34½-inch length of 1 x 4 for the bottom, and two 4-inch lengths of 1 x 4 for the ends.
2. Butt the ends against the bottom and nail with two 6d nails in each end.

3. Nail one side, then the other.
4. Drill a hole in each end, near the top. Insert a nail through each hole and drive it into an end of the 1 x 1. When properly done, the 1 x 1 will spin, preventing a bird from roosting above the feeder and fouling the feed.

MATERIALS

Wood

1 pc. 1 x 3 x 6′	or	**Sides:** 2 pcs. 1 x 3 x 36″
1 pc. 1 x 4 x 4′	or	**Bottom:** 1 pc. 1 x 4 x 34½″
		Ends: 2 pcs. 1 x 4 x 4″
1 pc. 1 x 1 x 4′	or	**Reel:** 1 pc. 1 x 1 x 34″

Hardware

6d nails

MEDIUM-SIZED FEEDER

The intermediate feeder is designed for intermediate-sized fowl. It is eminently suited for pullets and banties, and will even serve full-size birds.

CONSTRUCTION

1. Cut two 8-inch ends and a 34½-inch bottom from the 1 x 6. Clamp the ends together and cut the top corners off on a diagonal, as shown. Cut two 36-inch sides from the 1 x 4.
2. Butt the ends against the bottom and nail in place.

723

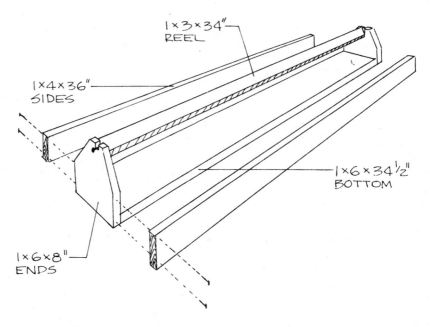

1 × 3 × 34"
REEL

1 × 4 × 36"
SIDES

1 × 6 × 34½"
BOTTOM

1 × 6 × 8"
ENDS

3. Nail the sides in place.
4. Saw a ½-inch notch in the top center of each end. Drive a nail into each end of the 1 x 3, leaving enough nail protruding to permit the resulting reel to be set in the notches and have it spin freely.

MATERIALS

Wood

1 pc. 1 x 6 x 6′	or	**Ends:** 2 pcs. 1 x 6 x 8″
		Bottom: 1 pc. 1 x 6 x 34½″
1 pc. 1 x 4 x 8′	or	**Sides:** 2 pcs. 1 x 4 x 36″
1 pc. 1 x 3 x 4′	or	**Reel:** 1 pc. 1 x 3 x 34″

Hardware

6d nails

FEEDER AND STAND

Here's your large economy size feeder, complete with a stand to keep the trough up out of the bedding (keeps the chickens from scratching litter in their food). This feeder has a built-in compartment for grit.

As with the previous feeders, the more birds you have, the longer you may want to make the feeder (and its stand). But length does become self-defeating, and the feeder can become very unwieldy to move when it comes time to clean out the chicken house. Four feet may be the optimum length, but, of course, suit yourself.

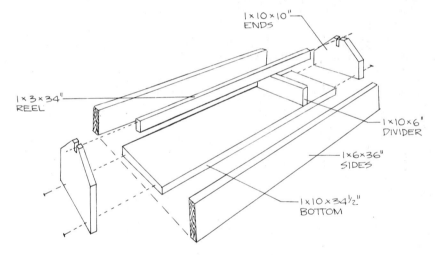

CHICKEN FEEDER

CONSTRUCTION

1. Cut two 36-inch lengths of 1 x 6 for the sides; one 34½-inch length of 1 x 10 for the bottom; two 10-inch 1 x 10s for the ends; and a 6-inch 1 x 10 for the compartment divider. Cut the two corners off the ends, as shown.
2. Nail the feeder together. Nail the ends to the bottom. Then nail the sides in place. Position the divider and drive nails through the side into the divider, then drive one or two through the bottom into the divider.
3. Notch the tops of the ends (or drill a hole through the tops of the ends) and install the 1 x 3 reel. It should spin freely.

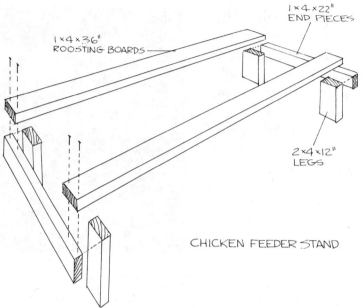

1×4×22" END PIECES

1×4×36" ROOSTING BOARDS

2×4×12" LEGS

CHICKEN FEEDER STAND

4. Cut the parts for the stand: four 1-foot 2 x 4 legs, two 36-inch 1 x 4 roosting boards, and two 22-inch 1 x 4 end pieces.

5. Nail the end pieces to the legs, as shown. Attach the roosts, making sure they overlap the legs and the end pieces.

MATERIALS

Wood

1 pc. 1 x 6 x 6'	or	**Sides:** 2 pcs. 1 x 6 x 36"
1 pc. 1 x 10 x 6'	or	**Bottom:** 1 pc. 1 x 10 x 34½"
		Ends: 2 pcs. 1 x 10 x 10"
		Divider: 1 pc. 1 x 10 x 6"
1 pc. 1 x 3 x 4'	or	**Reel:** 1 pc. 1 x 3 x 34"
1 pc. 2 x 4 x 4'	or	**Legs:** 4 pcs. 2 x 4 x 12"
1 pc. 1 x 4 x 10'	or	**Roosting boards:** 2 pcs. 1 x 4 x 36"
		End pieces: 2 pcs. 1 x 4 x 22"

Hardware

6d nails

SELF-SUPPLYING CHICKEN FEEDER

Here is a chicken feeder, that for the amount of time, about three hours, and the few dollars invested can be a real asset and time-saver for keeping just a few chickens or a large flock.

The feeder can be built to any length desired, depending upon the number of birds in your flock. Approximately 2 running feet of double feeder are adequate for twelve chickens. In large flocks, cut this to 2 feet for every eight birds.

The hopper is filled with feed and as the chickens consume it from the trough below, the feed flows downward, keeping the trough filled. This eliminates the need for continual checking during the day, especially appreciated when you must be gone all day. Or when you want to be away for a weekend. Mash, finely ground feed, works fairly well, but pelleted feed works the best. If mash is or must be used, then adding a little cracked grain will aid in the flow of feed to the trough.

Where floor space in the chicken house is limited, the single feeder against a wall is advantageous. To prevent the chickens from perching on top of the feeder and soiling the feed, nail vertical strips of 1-inch material upright to the ends of the lid with white string laced back and

forth the length of the feeder. Or adapt the reels of the trough feeders to the lid, supporting a reel with two short furring strips nailed to the lid ends.

Should the chickens develop the practice of raking the feed out of the trough, a narrow strip can be tacked along the lip of the trough. Where more than 2 running feet of feeder are built in one long section, then spacers or dividers should be provided every 2 feet to create better distribution of feed and stiffen the front and back of the hopper. Cleats can be nailed to the bottom of the feeder to accommodate its height to the size of the chickens.

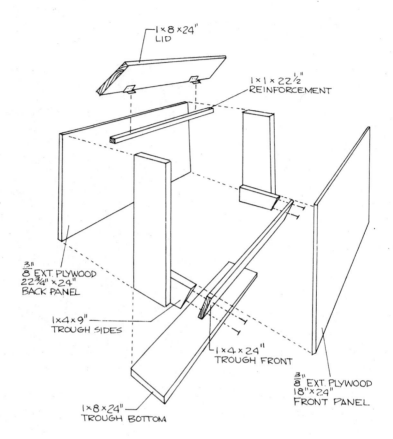

1 x 8 x 24"
LID

1 x 1 x 22½"
REINFORCEMENT

3/8" EXT. PLYWOOD
22¾" x 24"
BACK PANEL

1 x 4 x 9"
TROUGH SIDES

1 x 4 x 24"
TROUGH FRONT

3/8" EXT. PLYWOOD
18" x 24"
FRONT PANEL

1 x 8 x 24"
TROUGH BOTTOM

CONSTRUCTION

1. Cut the following parts to the feeder: two 9-inch trough sides from 1 x 4, two 22-inch bin sides from 1 x 6, one 24-inch trough bottom from 1 x 8, one 24-inch trough front from 1 x 4, a 22½-inch reinforcement from 1 x 1, and one 24-inch lid from 1 x 8. From ⅜-inch exterior plywood, cut an 18-inch by 24-inch front panel and a 22¾-inch by 24-inch back panel.

2. Clamp the trough sides together and cut them on a diagonal on one end, so the top edge measures the full 9 inches and the bottom edge measures 7¼ inches.

3. Fasten the trough sides to the bin sides, as shown, using glue and brads. Be sure the trough sides will be on the inside when the feeder is assembled.

4. Nail the trough bottom and front to the sides, using 6d nails. Drilling pilot holes will prevent splitting. Nail the reinforcing 1 x 1 into place at the top rear, between the bin sides.

5. Nail the plywood front and back panels in place, again using 6d nails.

6. Fasten the lid to the reinforcement with the two butt hinges.

MATERIALS

Wood

1 pc. 1 x 4 x 4′	or	**Trough sides:** 2 pcs. 1 x 4 x 9″
		Trough front: 1 pc. 1 x 4 x 24″
1 pc. 1 x 6 x 4′	or	**Bin sides:** 2 pcs. 1 x 6 x 22″
1 pc. 1 x 8 x 4′	or	**Trough bottom:** 1 pc. 1 x 8 x 24″
		Lid: 1 pc. 1 x 8 x 24″
1 pc. 1 x 1 x 2′	or	**Reinforcement:** 1 pc. 1 x 1 x 22½″
1–2′ x 4′ sht. ⅜″ ext. plywood	or	**Front panel:** 1 pc. 18″ x 24″
		Back panel: 1 pc. 22¾″ x 24″

Hardware

Glue
1¼″ brads
6d nails
2 small butt hinges

VARIATIONS

This feeder is easily made into a double-troughed feeder, if you need the feeding space and can use it as a freestanding feeder. Simply use a 24-inch length of 1 x 12 for the bottom, 13-inch lengths of 1 x 4 for the trough sides, cut an additional 24-inch trough front and for the second trough pare the back panel to 18 inches by 24 inches. Cut both ends of the trough sides on a diagonal running from top edge corner to a point ⅞ inch in from the bottom edge corner. Assemble with a trough on either side of the feeder bin.

As already mentioned, the feeder can also be made longer, to increase the feeding space, if you have more birds. The lid, bottom, trough fronts, and plywood panels will necessarily be longer, and 1 x 6 spacers should be added, as mentioned, to help keep the feeder rigid. Just remember that the longer the feeder is, the more cumbersome it is; it may be best to limit the length to 4 feet, building double-troughed feeders and additional feeders for very large flocks.

WATERER STAND

There's probably nothing more infuriating than the speed with which chickens foul up a waterer. If set on the chicken house floor, they'll have the trough clogged with litter in no time. By setting the waterer up off the floor and somewhat removed from the bedding, the trough will stay clean longer.

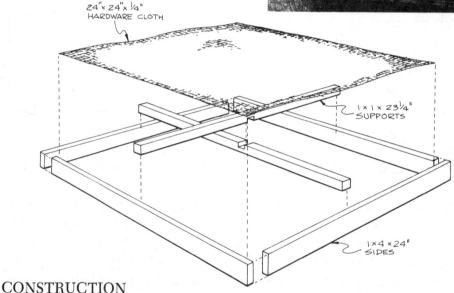

24" x 24" x ¼"
HARDWARE CLOTH

1 x 1 x 23¼"
SUPPORTS

1 x 4 x 24"
SIDES

CONSTRUCTION

1. Cut four 24-inch lengths of 1 x 4 and two 23¼-inch lengths of 1 x 1.
2. Nail the sides together with 8d nails, forming a 24¾-inch square frame. Each side overlaps one neighbor and is overlapped by the other.
3. Lay out the two 1 x 1s so they cross each other at their centers and at right angles. Mark and cut a lap joint in them, then secure in place inside the frame. Drive an 8d nail through the frame side into the ends of this waterer support.
4. Cut a 24-inch square piece of ¼-inch hardware cloth and staple it in place.

MATERIALS

Wood

1 pc. 1 x 4 x 8′	or	**Sides:** 4 pcs. 1 x 4 x 24″
1 pc. 1 x 1 x 4′	or	**Supports:** 2 pcs. 1 x 1 x 23¼″

Hardware

8d nails
1 pc. 24″ sq. hardware cloth, ¼″ mesh
Staples

NEST BOXES

Nest boxes can be as simple a contrivance as a bucket on its side or as elaborate as the racks of galvanized metal bins available through farm supply firms.

The nest boxes here can be constructed easily and quickly from common dimension lumber. The design is such that you can construct one or two, or you can construct hundreds. The directions below are for a three-nest unit.

CONSTRUCTION

1. Cut out the various pieces as indicated in the materials list.
2. The partitions must have the tops cut on a slope to support the roof (so the chickens won't roost on the nests and foul them with droppings). Since the end pieces overlap the bottom, they must be ¾ inch taller than the inner partitions. Cut them so the rear edge measures 20 inches and the front edge 12 inches. Cut all the inner partitions so the rear is 19¼ inches and the front 11¼ inches.
3. Butt the two outer partitions against the edge of the bottom board and nail them in place, using 8d nails.
4. Nail the roof in place atop the partitions, again using 8d nails.
5. Position the inner partitions and nail them fast.
6. Nail the 1 x 4s to the front and back of the unit, as shown.

Nest Boxes

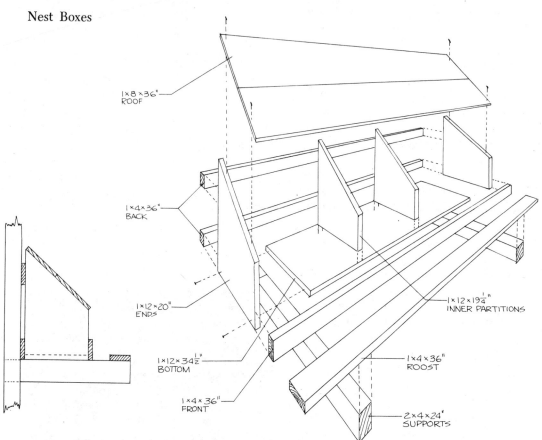

1×8×36"
ROOF

1×4×36"
BACK

1×12×20"
ENDS

1×12×34½"
BOTTOM

1×4×36"
FRONT

1×12×19¼"
INNER PARTITIONS

1×4×36"
ROOST

2×4×24"
SUPPORTS

MATERIALS

Wood

1 pc. 1 x 12 x 10′	or	**Ends:** 2 pcs. 1 x 12 x 20″
		Inner partitions: 2 pcs. 1 x 12 x 19¼″
		Bottom: 1 pc. 1 x 12 x 34½″
1 pc. 1 x 8 x 6′	or	**Roof:** 2 pcs. 1 x 8 x 36″
1 pc. 1 x 4 x 12′	or	**Front:** 1 pc. 1 x 4 x 36″
		Back: 2 pcs. 1 x 4 x 36″
		Roost: 1 pc. 1 x 4 x 36″
1 pc. 2 x 4 x 4′	or	**Supports:** 2 pcs. 2 x 4 x 24″

Hardware

8d nails

7. Nail the 2 x 4 supports to the wall studs in your chicken house, 12 to 18 inches above the floor. Set the nest box unit atop the supports and nail it fast. Finally, nail the roost board to the end of the supports in front of the nest boxes.

BROODER

Unless you plan to purchase started pullets or fully grown birds, you will need a brooder of some sort to keep chicks warm for their first weeks of life. This brooder is easily made, inexpensively operated—a 60-watt light bulb will provide sufficient heat—and very durable. It is large enough for up to one hundred chicks.

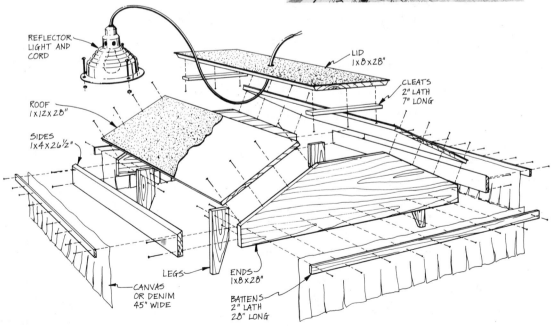

REFLECTOR LIGHT AND CORD

LID 1x8x28"

CLEATS 2" LATH 7" LONG

ROOF 1x12x28"

SIDES 1x4x26½"

LEGS

ENDS 1x8x28"

CANVAS OR DENIM 45" WIDE

BATTENS 2" LATH 28" LONG

733

CONSTRUCTION

1. Cut two pieces, 28 inches long, of 1 x 8. Cut each to have sloped side sections 11¼ inches long, a center section 7 inches wide, and edges 3¼ inches high, as shown. Save the cut-off triangles to make legs.
2. Cut two 28-inch 1 x 12s, two 26½-inch 1 x 4s, and a single 28-inch 1 x 8.
3. Trim the 1 x 4s down to an actual 3¼ inches, then bevel to 3 inches on one edge and 3¼ inches on the other.
4. Take the triangles and cut to make the legs. Cut off one point to make them 10 inches long. Cut off the other point to make them 3 inches wide.
5. Attach the legs to the ends with three 1¼-inch #10 screws each. Have 2½ inches against the end, 7½ inches extending below.
6. Attach the beveled sides, nailing into the legs and also nailing through the ends into the beveled sides.
7. Nail the roof on with 6d nails. The two 1 x 12s cover the sloped sides being nailed into the sides. Bevel the edges of the 1 x 8 lid so it fits snugly in the opening left. Cut and nail with brads two short cleats to each end of the 1 x 8 to locate it securely in position. Drill a hole through the center of this movable lid to run the lamp cord through.
8. Using ¾-inch galvanized roofing nails, attach pieces of roll roofing to the top of the brooder. The roofing may lap over the sides of the

MATERIALS

Wood

1 pc. 1 x 8 x 8′	or	**Ends:** 2 pcs. 1 x 8 x 28″ (use excess for legs)
		Lid: 1 pc. 1 x 8 x 28″
1 pc. 1 x 12 x 6′	or	**Roof:** 2 pcs. 1 x 12 x 28″
1 pc. 1 x 4 x 6′	or	**Sides:** 2 pcs. 1 x 4 x 26½″
10′–2″ lath	or	**Cleats:** 2 pcs. 7″ long
		Battens: 4 pcs. 28″ long

Hardware

12–1¼″ #10 screws
6d nails
¾″ brads
¾″ galvanized roofing nails
1 reflector light and cord (for outside use)
4–2″ x ¼″ stove bolts w/ nuts

Miscellaneous

1 roll of roll roofing   or   3 pcs. 28″ long
1 yd. canvas or denim (45″ wide)

brooder, and the piece applied to the lid should have a bit extending over the sides to overlap the joint between the lid and the two sides of the roof. Slit a hole in the roofing for the light cord.

9. Cut the canvas or denim skirt into 10-inch by 45-inch strips. Use lath as battens to secure the skirt. Vertical slits in the skirt will ease access for the chicks.

10. Punch three holes, evenly spaced around the rim, into the lip of the reflector. Install 2-inch stove bolts with nuts so the reflector will be held up off the floor, as shown. Run the cord through the hole in the lid and install the plug.

AN OLD-FASHIONED BROODER HOUSE

Brooder houses like this were turned out en masse by lumberyards in years past. The design was generally hexagonal, though this particular one is not *evenly* six-sided. Most were. The brooders were movable, sort of, and seem to be virtually indestructible. The one Gene Logsdon's mother raised chicks in became his gang's playhouse over thirty years ago. Much later it was moved back into the woods and converted into a summer cabin. Now Logsdon's son and his cronies have further transformed it into their clubhouse.

The structure is definitely a project for an advanced builder, since it demands so many tricky angle cuts to fit it together. A square brooder house would be just about as effective. The hexagonal shape was used because it fitted well around the brooder stove inside so that there were no cold corners for the chicks to huddle in and chill. The hexagonal shape also gave more strength to a little building that was going to be moved around some. But as much as anything, the shape was a bit of bravura on the part of the lumberyard, since it had the fancy equipment to make all those odd angle cuts. The brooder was something it could build that a farmer couldn't duplicate too easily.

The illustration depicts a brooder with uniform sides and uniform windows. The brooder in the photo has a longer south side, the better to put two windows in, so that at the peak or point of the roof, where the chim-

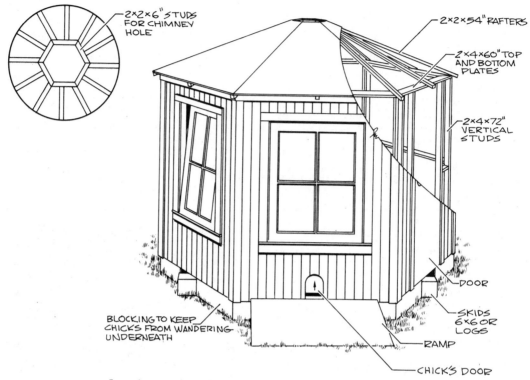

2×2×6" STUDS
FOR CHIMNEY
HOLE

2×2×54" RAFTERS

2×4×60" TOP
AND BOTTOM
PLATES

2×4×72"
VERTICAL
STUDS

DOOR

SKIDS
6×6 OR
LOGS

RAMP

CHICK'S DOOR

BLOCKING TO KEEP
CHICKS FROM WANDERING
UNDERNEATH

ney comes out, there's a bit of a ridge. In many hexagonal brooders, there is just a hexagonal hole, as shown. And, of course, you must always remember to put nonflammable insulation between the chimney flue and the wood.

Windows on a brooder, of whatever kind, should open easily. The kind illustrated are the best as they cannot stick and hardly any rain would get in if you left them open by mistake during a sudden shower.

The brooders of this design always sat up on something—logs, skids, poles, bricks, cement blocks. That meant space under the brooder. Such space should be blocked off as in the photo so cold air will not get under and chill the floor too much. Also rats and cats like to get under brooders and lay in wait for naive chicks. Or the chicks will run under the brooder when you let them outside on mild days and you have a devil of a time getting them out and back inside in the evening when the air gets chilly. They will sit under there and cheep but avail themselves not a bit to walking out and going in their little door. They think they are inside and can't figure out why it isn't warm.

RABBITS

One of the attractions of raising rabbits for food or for fun is that they require a minimum of costly special equipment. There are just a few design features that should be present in all rabbit housing.

The major consideration is space. A doe with a litter should have a minimum of 10 square feet of floor space, with a height of at least 18 inches to permit stretching up on their hind legs. In addition to this space, there should be a nesting box of at least 2 square feet.

When designing a hutch, try to keep the door at waist height for your convenience, and leave enough room under the cages to clean up the droppings. When making wire cages, always use $\frac{1}{2}$-inch by $\frac{1}{2}$-inch or $\frac{1}{2}$-inch by 1-inch mesh, galvanized after welding, placed rough side down.

Build your hutch with at least one solid wall to block the wind and a slight overhang of the roof to keep rain and direct sun out of the cage. If protected from dampness and the wind, rabbits can tolerate subzero temperatures, but extreme heat is their worst enemy. In the outdoor hutch, the roof should be inclined to shed rain and snow.

A RAISED OUTDOOR HUTCH

This raised outdoor hutch is designed to accommodate three does and their litters. The unit has two hay mangers with access from the front and three nest boxes that are removable from the rear.

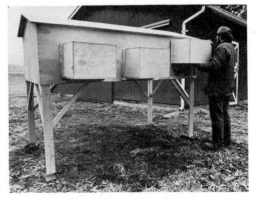

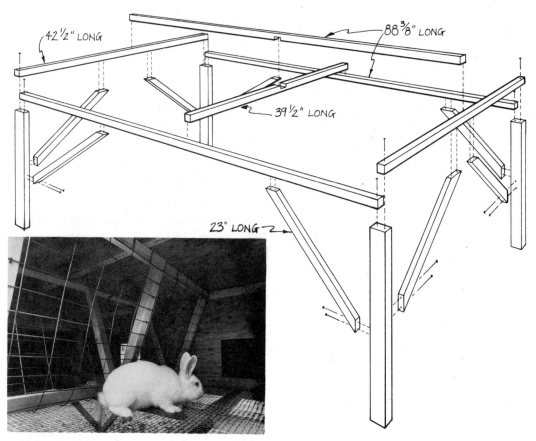

42½" LONG

88⅜" LONG

39½" LONG

23" LONG

CONSTRUCTION

1. Begin construction by cutting four 36-inch 2 x 4s for legs. Then, from
    10-foot lengths of 2 x 2, cut the following pieces: three pieces 88⅜
    inches, two pieces 42½ inches, one piece 39½ inches, and eight pieces
    23 inches. Cut 45-degree angles on each end of the 23-inch pieces,
    which will be used as braces. Assemble the base frame as shown. The
    1½-inch by 1½-inch by ¾-inch cross-lap notch can be made with a router
    or by making multiple cuts ¾ inch deep and then chiseling out the wood.

2. From a sheet of ½-inch exterior plywood, cut a piece 22⅜ inches wide
    and 91½ inches long for the rear of the hutch. From another sheet, cut
    two identical end pieces, as shown. Begin each end as a 42½-inch by
    29-inch panel. Mark the gable by measuring 22½ inches up each side,
    then extending a line from that point to the center of the top edge.
    Cut both panels.

3. Nail the ends and back to the frame (keep the bottom flush). Cut a
    90⅜-inch piece of 2 x 4 to be used for the roof support. Rip or plane the
    edges of the 2 x 4 at an angle corresponding to the pitch of the roof.
    To attach the roof support to the plywood end pieces, nail from outside
    plywood with two 10d nails on each end.

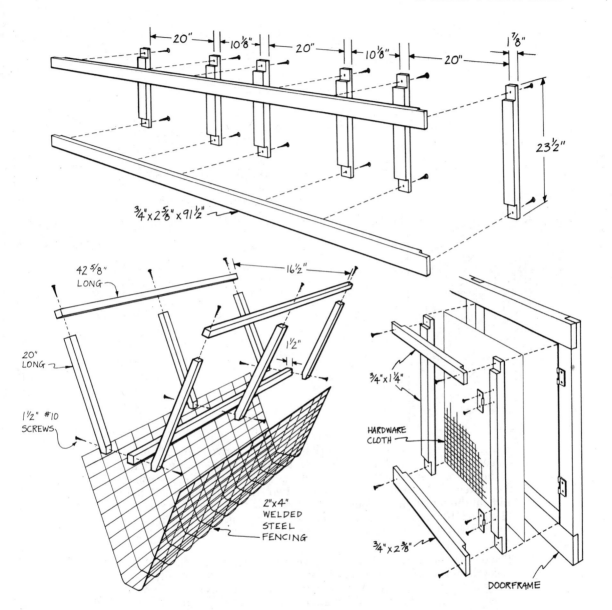

4. You will need 21 feet of 24-inch-wide ½-inch mesh hardware cloth for the floor and doors. Attach the hardware cloth to the floor with ½-inch staples. To prevent gnawing, many rabbit raisers like to cover the sides, back, and all other exposed wood in the hutch with either chicken wire or ⅝-inch wire mesh. Chewing the wood fiber is not harmful to rabbits, but they can demolish a cage in surprisingly short order.

5. Construct the two hay mangers as shown. For each manger, cut three 42⅝-inch lengths and six 20-inch lengths from 2 x 2. The bottoms of the 20-inch lengths must be cut on two angles that can be determined by

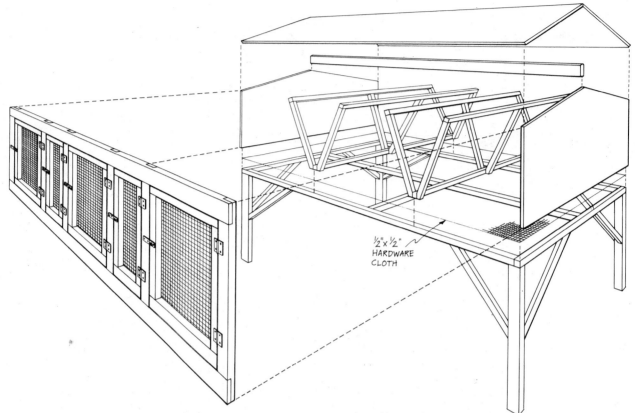

½" x ½"
HARDWARE
CLOTH

laying out the pieces. On your workbench, lay out two of the 20-inch pieces so they form a **V**, 16½ inches apart at the top and nearly touching at the bottom. Butt another 2 x 2 to them, and scribe the angles, using the butted 2 x 2 as a guide. Use the first two sides as patterns and mark and cut the remaining 20-inch 2 x 2s. Assemble the mangers, using a 1½-inch #10 screw at each joint. Finally, wrap a piece of 2-inch by 4-inch mesh welded steel fencing around the manger frame and staple it in place.

6.   The doorframe is assembled from pieces ripped from 1 x 6 stock. To make the top and bottom members, rip a 91½-inch length in half. The uprights, six of them, are 1⅞ inches wide and 23½ inches long. They can be ripped from a single 6-foot length of 1 x 6. Put the doorframe together with lap joints, as illustrated. Use one ¾-inch #10 screw and glue on all joints. To facilitate anchoring the doorframe to the hutch, glue a 23½-inch-long 1 x 1 (ripped from a 1 x 3; see step 9) nailer flush to the inside edge of each plywood side. Then attach the doorframe with 1-inch #10 screws, taking care to keep the top edge of the bottom of the doorframe flush with the floor of the hutch.

7.   The doors are assembled from pieces ripped and cut from 1 x 6 stock. Begin with a 10-foot length of 1 x 6. Rip it into a 2⅜-inch-wide strip and two 1¼-inch-wide strips. From the 2⅜-inch-wide strip, cut three

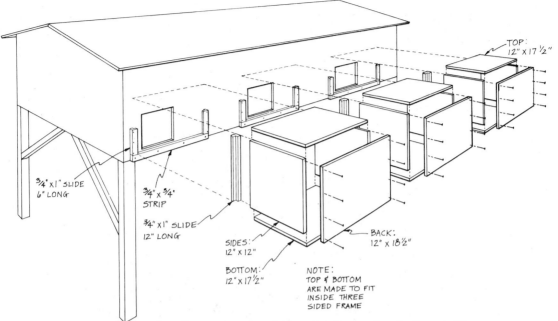

TOP:
12" X 17½"

¾" X 1" SLIDE
6" LONG

¾" X ¾"
STRIP

¾" X 1" SLIDE
12" LONG

SIDES:
12" X 12"

BACK:
12" X 18½"

BOTTOM:
12" X 17½"

NOTE:
TOP & BOTTOM
ARE MADE TO FIT
INSIDE THREE
SIDED FRAME

19¾-inch cage door bottoms and two 9⅞-inch manger door bottoms. Rip the remaining 2⅜-inch-wide piece down to a 1¼-inch-wide strip. Then, from the 1¼-inch-wide material, cut three 19¾-inch-wide cage door tops, two 9⅞-inch manger door tops, and ten 18-inch uprights. The doors are assembled with corner lap joints, using glue and a ¾-inch #10 screw at each joint. The doors should be a ¼-inch smaller than the openings to prevent binding. Staple ½-inch mesh hardware cloth to each door, then hang each in place with two 1½-inch hinges. A small hasp and staple are used to secure the doors.

8. Cut the roof by ripping a sheet of ½-inch exterior plywood in half lengthwise. Leave the excess as overhang on all sides, and cover with roll roofing.

9. The nest boxes are made to mount on the outside back of the hutch. Each is assembled from ½-inch exterior plywood: two pieces, 17½ inches by 12 inches; two pieces, 12 inches square; and one piece, 18½ inches by 12 inches. The boxes are mounted on the hutch by slides fabricated from stock measuring an actual 1 inch wide. Rip a 1-inch strip and a ¾-inch strip from a 10-foot 1 x 3. Along one end of the 1-inch-wide strip, cut a $\frac{7}{16}$-inch-wide and $\frac{7}{16}$-inch-deep rabbet. Cut six 6-inch pieces and six 12-inch pieces. Using glue and 6d nails, attach the 12-inch pieces to the edges of the sides of the nest boxes. Next, cut three 20¾-inch lengths of the ¾-inch-wide strip and glue and nail one to the bottom edge of the back behind each rabbit cage, as shown. Hold the nest boxes in place and locate the 6-inch slides that will be attached to the back of the hutch. These slides are attached with glue and 2d nails. Finally, using a keyhole or saber saw, cut a hole, about 8 inches square, through the back into each cage, to give the doe access from the cage to the nest box. (A panel of plywood may be cut and slipped into the slides, covering the access hole when the nest boxes are not in place.)

MATERIALS

Wood

1 pc. 2 x 4 x 12′	or	**Legs:** 4 pcs. 2 x 4 x 36″
10 pcs. 2 x 2 x 10′	or	**Frame rails:** 3 pcs. 2 x 2 x 88$\frac{3}{8}$″
		Frame crossmembers: 2 pcs. 2 x 2 x 42$\frac{1}{2}$″
		Center crossmember: 1 pc. 2 x 2 x 39$\frac{1}{2}$″
		Braces: 8 pcs. 2 x 2 x 23″
		Manger horizontals: 6 pcs. 2 x 2 x 42$\frac{5}{8}$″
		Manger uprights: 12 pcs. 2 x 2 x 20″
3 shts. $\frac{1}{2}$″ ext. plywood	or	**Back:** 1 pc. 22$\frac{3}{8}$″ x 91$\frac{1}{2}$″
		Ends: 2 pcs. 42$\frac{1}{2}$″ x 29″
		Roof: 2 pcs. 24″ x 96″
		Nest box tops and bottoms: 6 pcs. 12″ x 17$\frac{1}{2}$″
		Nest box sides: 6 pcs. 12″ sq.
		Nest box backs: 3 pcs. 12″ x 18$\frac{1}{2}$″
1 pc. 2 x 4 x 8′	or	**Roof support:** 1 pc. 2 x 4 x 90$\frac{3}{8}$″
1 pc. 1 x 6 x 8′	or	**Doorframe top and bottom:** 2 pcs. $\frac{3}{4}$″ x 2$\frac{5}{8}$″ x 91$\frac{1}{2}$″ (act. meas.)
1 pc. 1 x 6 x 6′	or	**Doorframe uprights:** 6 pcs. $\frac{3}{4}$″ x 1$\frac{7}{8}$″ x 23$\frac{1}{2}$″ (act. meas.)
1 pc. 1 x 3 x 10′	or	**Doorframe nailers:** 2 pcs. $\frac{3}{4}$″ x $\frac{3}{4}$″ x 23$\frac{1}{2}$″ (act. meas.)
		Nest box slides: 6 pcs. $\frac{3}{4}$″ x 1″ x 6″ (act. meas.)
		Nest box slides: 6 pcs. $\frac{3}{4}$″ x 1″ x 12″ (act. meas.)
		Stops: 3 pcs. $\frac{3}{4}$″ x $\frac{3}{4}$″ x 20$\frac{3}{4}$″ (act. meas.)
1 pc. 1 x 6 x 10′	or	**Cage door bottoms:** 3 pcs. $\frac{3}{4}$″ x 2$\frac{3}{8}$″ x 19$\frac{3}{4}$″ (act. meas.)

Manger door bottoms:
  2 pcs. $\frac{3}{4}''$ x $2\frac{3}{8}''$ x $9\frac{7}{8}''$ (act. meas.)

Cage door tops: 3 pcs. $\frac{3}{4}''$ x $1\frac{1}{4}''$ x $19\frac{3}{4}''$
  (act. meas.)

Manger door tops: 2 pcs. $\frac{3}{4}''$ x $1\frac{1}{4}''$ x $9\frac{7}{8}''$
  (act. meas.)

Door uprights: 10 pcs. $\frac{3}{4}''$ x $1\frac{1}{4}''$ x $18''$
  (act. meas.)

Hardware

10d nails
1 pc. 21' x 24" hardware cloth, $\frac{1}{2}''$ mesh
$\frac{1}{2}''$ staples
24–$1\frac{1}{2}''$ #10 screws
2 pcs. 4' sq. welded wire fencing, 2" x 4" mesh
Glue
32–$\frac{3}{4}''$ #10 screws
10–1" #10 screws
10–$1\frac{1}{2}''$ hinges w/ screws
5 small hasps and staples w/ screws
1 roll of roll roofing
$\frac{1}{2}''$ roofing nails
6d nails
2d nails

THE ALL-WIRE HUTCH

Wire hutches for domestic rabbits are very easy to construct and very easy to clean. Rabbits like clean, light living quarters. They can endure plenty of cold, but need protection from winds, drafts, and high temperatures. Damp floors or leaky roofs soon bring sickness.

The photos show a raised outdoor hutch consisting of eight $2\frac{1}{2}$-foot by 3-foot cages, wired and clipped together and hung from a sheltered framework. The structure faces south, away from the prevailing winds. It is basically an open-sided pole building, using 4 x 4 posts, 6 feet high (above ground) in the front and 5 feet high in the rear. The individual cages are hung from the 2 x 6 roof rafters with heavy-gauge wire.

Plywood, sheet metal, or some other type of facing should be nailed to the rear 4 x 4 posts for protection from the elements.

The individual 2½-foot by 3-foot cages are easily constructed with nothing fancier than a pliers and wire cutter. Wire cages of this type are easily removable—an important feature when it comes time for a periodic hosing and disinfection. The best wire for the front, back, and sides of the hutch is 1-inch by 2-inch welded 14-gauge galvanized wire fencing. The wire should be 18 inches wide (to allow rabbits to stretch up on their hind legs) and 11 feet long for a cage with a floor area of 2½ feet by 3 feet.

To bend the wire, lay it flat on the floor and form four corners by hammering it around a piece of 2 x 4. Don't bend at the weld points. When you have formed a rectangle, fasten the ends either with hog rings or by twisting the cut ends of the wire with pliers.

For the floor, use ½-inch by 1-inch mesh, 14-gauge welded, galvanized wire; each 2½-foot by 3-foot hutch will take a piece 30 inches by 36 inches. Fasten this to the bottom with clips or by twisting wire around the sections. For the top, use the same 1-inch by 2-inch wire as on the sides, and attach in the same manner.

The door opening should be a foot square. Leave ½-inch stubs when cutting the wire, then bend back the stubs. Using the 1-inch by 2-inch welded wire mesh, cut a door large enough to overlap at least an inch all the way around. Hinge the door at the top with clips or rings so that it swings up and into the cage. This way, the door is inside the hutch when open, not sticking out into the aisle between hutches. Various types of automatic feeders and waterers can be used to make daily opening and closing of the hutch doors unnecessary.

To conquer the manure problem—

in fact, to turn it into an asset—lay concrete blocks around the droppings area beneath the hutch, then spread lime and peat moss over the droppings from time to time to prevent any disagreeable odor. To this mixture add material from the nest boxes and, occasionally, leaves.

When the bedding material reaches a depth of about a foot, it could be taken from under the hutches and spread on the garden, but many raisers put it to another use first—they raise worms in it. A small trench is opened up down the middle of the manure bed and the earthworms— 100 per square foot—are placed in the trench. The trench is then covered lightly with bedding, sprinkled thoroughly and left alone for the worms to multiply. The worms do an amazing job of converting the rabbit droppings into a rich, black humus, ready to be mixed directly into the garden soil, where it is mild enough to sow seeds into directly.

RABBIT FEEDER

The simplest way to feed a pet rabbit is to set out a dish made from a coffee can. A more expensive way is to buy an elaborate metal feeder available commercially. The best compromise is to build a wood and metal feeder that attaches to the outside of the pen. The trough portion protrudes through a hole cut in the wire. The bottom is screened to permit the dusty portion of the feed—the part rabbits won't eat—to sift through.

CONSTRUCTION

1. Cut two 12-inch lengths and one 10½-inch length of 1 x 8. Then make the 12-inch pieces into L-shapes as shown by cutting a 9-inch by 4-inch rectangle from them.
2. From the sheet metal, cut a 12-inch square, a 5-inch by 12-inch rectangle, a 9-inch by 12-inch rectangle, and two ¾-inch by 4-inch strips.
3. Assemble the feeder, as shown. Attach the wooden deflector to the sides with glue and 6d nails. Then tack the sheet metal and screening in place.

Rabbit Feeder

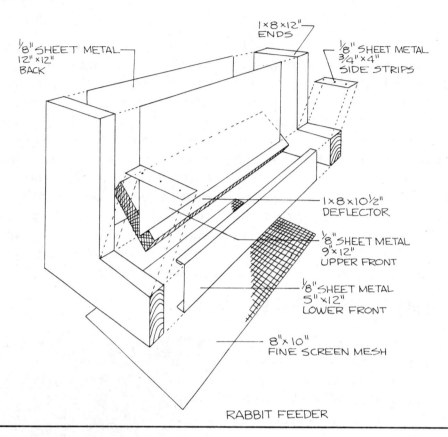

1×8×12"
ENDS

⅛"SHEET METAL
12"×12"
BACK

⅛" SHEET METAL
¾"×4"
SIDE STRIPS

1×8×10½"
DEFLECTOR

⅛"SHEET METAL
9"×12"
UPPER FRONT

⅛"SHEET METAL
5"×12"
LOWER FRONT

8"×10"
FINE SCREEN MESH

RABBIT FEEDER

MATERIALS		
Wood		
1 pc. 1 x 8 x 4′	or	**Ends:** 2 pcs. 1 x 8 x 12″
		Deflector: 1 pc. 1 x 8 x 10½″
Hardware		
1 pc. 3′ sq., ⅛″ sheet metal	or	**Back:** 1 pc. 12″ sq.
		Lower front: 1 pc. 5″ x 12″
		Upper front: 1 pc. 9″ x 12″
		Side strips: 2 pcs. ¾″ x 4″
Glue		
6d nails		
1 pc. 8″ x 10″ fine screen mesh (bottom)		
Tacks		

RABBIT NEST BOX

The standard rabbit box is generally 12 inches by 24 inches and 12 inches high for breeds such as New Zealand. It can be made of wood or sheet metal. In summer, some large rabbitries use wire nest boxes lined with paper. The nest ought to have a partial roof. Mother rabbits enjoy the security such cover provides.

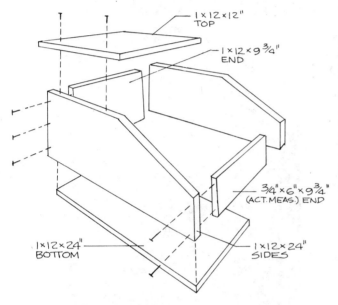

+---

MATERIALS

Wood

1 pc. 1 x 12 x 10'   or   **Top:** 1 pc. 1 x 12 x 12"

Bottom: 1 pc. 1 x 12 x 24"

Sides: 2 pcs. 1 x 12 x 24"

End: 1 pc. 1 x 12 x 9¾"

End: 1 pc. ¾" x 6" x 9¾" (act. meas.)

Hardware

Glue
6d nails

CONSTRUCTION

1. Cut 1 x 12 stock as follows: one 12-inch top, one 24-inch bottom, two 24-inch sides, and two 9¾-inch ends. Rip one end to a width of 6 inches.
2. Clamp the sides together and cut along a diagonal from a point midway along the top edge to a point on the end 6 inches from the bottom.
3. Assemble the box. The sides butt (and overlap) the ends top and bottom. Glue and nail using 6d nails.

SMALL ANIMAL CARRYING CAGE

The principal feature of this easy-to-make cage is the removable animal droppings tray made from an old cookie sheet. Thus, the dimensions of your cage depend on two things— the sizes of your animal and cookie sheet. Here we have a 17-inch by 14-inch sheet. When a cage is built around it there is enough room for a rabbit is to set out a dish made from a small dog.

CONSTRUCTION

1. From 1 x 3, cut two 17¾-inch and one 13½-inch lengths. Cut a ⅜-inch-deep kerf into the two longer pieces, ½ inch from one edge, for the droppings tray.
2. Cut a 13½-inch and four 14¾-inch lengths of 1 x 1. Cut two 17¾-inch, two 13½-inch, and four 12½-inch lengths of 1 x 2.
3. Assemble the cage frame using glue and 4d nails. Butt the two 17¾-inch 1 x 2s against the 13½-inch 1 x 2s and fasten them. Butt the slotted 1 x 3s against the 13½-inch 1 x 3 and the 13½-inch 1 x 1 and fasten. Be sure the 1 x 1 is flush with the edge furthest away from the two slots for the droppings tray. Fasten the four uprights to the top and bottom frames. Nail the remaining 1 x 1s to the frame as shown.
4. Cut a piece of ½-inch hardware cloth to fit inside the bottom of the cage (so it will be between the animal and the droppings tray). Staple it in place. Cut hardware cloth to cover the sides and staple in place.

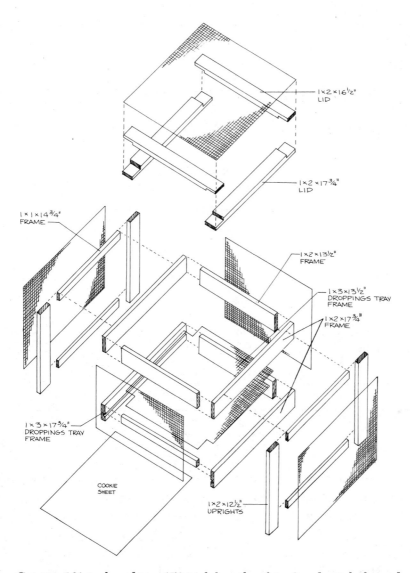

1×2×16½"
LID

1×2×17¾"
LID

1×1×14¾"
FRAME

1×2×13½"
FRAME

1×3×13½"
DROPPINGS TRAY
FRAME

1×2×17¾"
FRAME

1×3×17¾"
DROPPINGS TRAY
FRAME

COOKIE
SHEET

1×2×12½"
UPRIGHTS

5. Cut two 16½-inch and two 17¾-inch lengths of 1 x 2 and notch the ends for half-lap joints. Assemble the lid, using glue and nails. Install two butt hinges along one side of the lid frame and a hasp in the center of the opposite side. Attach the lid frame to the cage. Position the hasp staple on the cage and attach it to the cage. Finally, cut a section of hardware cloth to cover the lid and staple it in place.

MATERIALS

Wood

1 pc. 1 x 3 x 6'	or	**Droppings tray frame:** 2 pcs. 1 x 3 x 17¾"
		1 pc. 1 x 3 x 13½"
1 pc. 1 x 1 x 6'	or	**Frame:** 1 pc. 1 x 1 x 13½"
		4 pcs. 1 x 1 x 14¾"
2 pcs. 1 x 2 x 8'	or	**Frame:** 2 pcs. 1 x 2 x 17¾"
		2 pcs. 1 x 2 x 13½"

Uprights: 4 pcs. 1 x 2 x 12½"

Lid: 2 pcs. 1 x 2 x 16½"
2 pcs. 1 x 2 x 17¾"

Hardware

Glue
4d nails
1 pc. 48" x 36" hardware cloth, ½" mesh
Staples
2 small butt hinges
1 small hasp and staple
1 cookie sheet (14" x 17")

SWINE

The place where sows give birth to pigs and nurse them those first tender days of life is called a farrowing house. If you don't provide her with a farrowing house, your sow will wander off to the woods, should one be available, and build herself a nest of brush and sticks and leaves and do quite splendidly with her family if the weather is not too cold. She and her young will certainly be happier in the woods, or in a small house in the pasture than in the modern confinement buildings now commonly in use.

Many farmers think so too, because they go on raising their hogs out "on pasture" rather than in confinement.

There is no one right way to build a small farrowing house. The two shown here indicate there are at least a couple of ways to raise a pig. In fact, you can build from any number of ideas, so long as you stick to a few rules applicable to all.

1. The shelter must keep out moisture and drafts.

2. The shelter should be small enough so that the body heat of the

mother sow will keep the space comfortably warm in cool weather.

3. The shelter, if to be used in summer, must be vented so that it doesn't get too hot inside.

4. The shelter ought somehow to allow you to examine, even pick up, the pigs (for clipping needle teeth, giving iron shots, castrating male pigs) without getting into the pen. The sow does not take kindly to human intervention in her affairs. If a pig is squealing because it is caught, or because the mother is unknowingly lying on it, as sometimes happens, you want to free the pig. In the process, the mother might charge you and take a hunk out of your leg because she thinks you are the cause of her squealing pig.

5. The shelter should have some contrivance to protect nursing pigs from being rolled on and/or crushed by the mother. Some sows are more careful than others, but very small pigs are often killed accidentally by being suffocated under a distraught mother.

A SMALL FARROWING HOUSE

The small building shown fits these five conditions very well. The walls and roof are weathertight. At one time, there was even a door over the sow entrance, which is unusual and would be necessary only for pigs born in the coldest part of winter—a situation you as a homesteader would be wise to avoid. Also, the farrowing house has a floor in it to keep pigs off the cold, damp ground.

The shelter has only about 4 by 6 feet of floor space, which the sow's body heat can keep warm enough except in the coldest part of winter. In that case, if you are so unfortunate as to be in that case, you should have the pen close enough to an electric outlet so you can put a heat lamp inside.

If the mother is having pigs in hot

weather, the shelter's tip-up roof will allow a cooling breeze through the shed. Also, you can stand outside and reach in through the opening provided by the tip-up roof and handle the pigs without getting your leg bitten by the mother. The lower, swing-out door makes cleaning out the shelter easy.

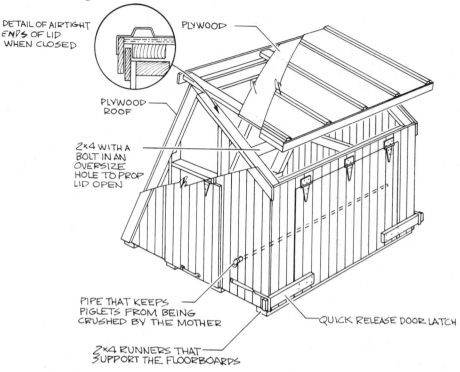

DETAIL OF AIRTIGHT ENDS OF LID WHEN CLOSED

PLYWOOD

PLYWOOD ROOF

2×4 WITH A BOLT IN AN OVERSIZE HOLE TO PROP LID OPEN

PIPE THAT KEEPS PIGLETS FROM BEING CRUSHED BY THE MOTHER

QUICK RELEASE DOOR LATCH

2×4 RUNNERS THAT SUPPORT THE FLOORBOARDS

The pipe sticking out of the front wall runs through the shed about 8 inches off the ground and a foot out from the wall. Its purpose is to keep the sow from rolling on the pigs or crushing them against the wall. She can roll up against the pipe, but that stops her, while the pigs scoot under to safety. There are other ways to give pigs some protection. In fact, the reason the traditional sow house was an **A**-frame affair was not just because that design was simple to build, but because the slant of the walls gave the pigs a place of safety. The mother couldn't crush them against the side walls.

In a pen, some protection for a pig can be provided by leaving about 8 inches of space between the gate and the floor. Or by installing a wooden bumper all around the pen 8 inches off the ground and extending 8 inches out from the sides.

The drawings detail how to frame up the little shed. The exterior walls are tongue-and-groove siding and the plywood roof is covered with aluminum paneling. Two steel hooks hold the side door in place, as shown. The skids underneath make it possible to pull the shed with a tractor to different locations, but these have deteriorated after many years of resting on the ground.

The door on the entrance has also been taken off. It is seldom necessary anyway, except during farrowing in very cold weather. However, with the entrance open like that, be sure to face it away from the prevailing winds, which usually means facing it eastwards.

A LARGE FARROWING HOUSE

The larger house can be used for farrowing, for older pigs that are still running with the mother, or for a few fattening hogs. With the partition down the middle, it becomes a two-sow garage or a two-patient room in the maternity ward. The building was designed for summer use as well as cooler weather, since the entire front

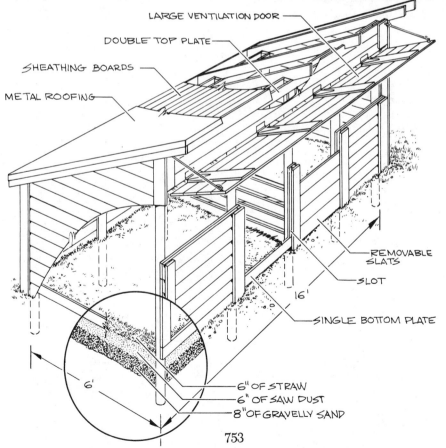

LARGE VENTILATION DOOR

DOUBLE TOP PLATE

SHEATHING BOARDS

METAL ROOFING

REMOVABLE SLATS

SLOT

16'

SINGLE BOTTOM PLATE

6'

6" OF STRAW
6" OF SAW DUST
8" OF GRAVELLY SAND

wall has been remodeled so that a large section can be opened for good air circulation in warm weather.

The construction of this shed is apparent from the photo. The floor might better be concrete here, since the building is not portable anyway. Concrete may be more expensive as an initial investment but certainly would last longer than wood. Or if it is left as a dirt floor, you might over the years spend more time and money keeping it built up with dry litter than the extra you spend to have a concrete floor. It is best when installing a concrete floor to pour deep footings all around. The footing not only prevents the floor from cracking so fast, but can discourage rats from tunneling under the concrete. Better a dirt floor than a rat-infested concrete floor.

If you choose to have a dirt floor, build it up with 8 inches of gravelly sand, top it with 6 inches of sawdust, and replenish periodically with 6 inches of straw or clean sawdust. You will have a perfectly dry floor—drier, indeed, than most concrete floors stay.

If you decide to build a shed like this one, any of the typical construction methods already described will be suitable. Pen space measures 6 feet by 8 feet in both halves of the building.

FIELD SHELTER FOR HOGS OR SHEEP

Simple sheds like this one dotted pastures of American farms in years past. They were not so often used for sheep which actually require little shelter except during lambing time and extremely severe weather. Rather these small barns were used only for the rams during the winter when they were kept separated from the flock or for a few late fattening lambs during real hot weather if no other shade were available. More often than not, though, sheds of this type were built for hogs, which do need weather protection on wet and chilly days or extremely hot days.

The main advantage of this type of

shed is that it is extremely simple to build. Also it is efficient, covering the greatest amount of space for the least amount of lumber used. The walls are posts set 2 feet into the ground with siding nailed to them. The roof is corrugated tin nailed to a few widely

spaced purlins, which are in turn nailed to randomly spaced rafters spiked to the top of the posts. The floor is dirt. You can get in the shed by crawling through the low doors, but obviously builders of such sheds do not envisage having to go inside very often. And that's another advantage of this type of building, or rather another reason why they were built this way: cattle which might be running in the same field, couldn't get inside to bother the smaller animals.

The first step in construction is to set your posts in the ground, making sure the sidewall posts are at right angles with the front and back wall posts. You want a rectangle, not a parallelogram. If you don't lay out the outline of your building with stakes and string, you can easily get one corner out of line, even though the corners all measure the correct distance from each other.

Posts ought to be burr oak, black locust, catalpa, cedar (if available in large diameter sizes), or white oak, which make the longest lasting wood in the ground. You will probably have

to settle for creosoted or otherwise treated posts from the lumberyard, though some claim such posts do not last as long as untreated posts of the woods mentioned above. If you have a woodlot with any of those woods in it, you will definitely save yourself money by making use of it. Old telephone poles are excellent if you are lucky enough to be able to get some. Railroad ties too, if not too badly deteriorated. An 8-inch-diameter post size is best, but for a small shed like this, 6-inch diameter posts will suffice in a pinch. Use the straightest posts you can get because you will be nailing the siding right to them and crooked posts could mean a crooked wall. If you *have* to use a crooked post nail a 2 x 4 along the side of it so the edge of the 2 x 4 sticks out to make an even, straight line to nail the siding to.

When the posts are all in place, put up the rafters. Often, in this type of construction, a plate is nailed on the inner top side of the posts along the two long walls, for the rafters to rest on. That way you can space the rafters out evenly and toenail them to that plate. In this building however, the builder simply nailed the rafters to the posts, resulting in a somewhat random spacing between rafters. Use 16d spikes. A good 3-foot level will assure getting the rafters up *even with each other*, so the roof does not look humped or swaybacked.

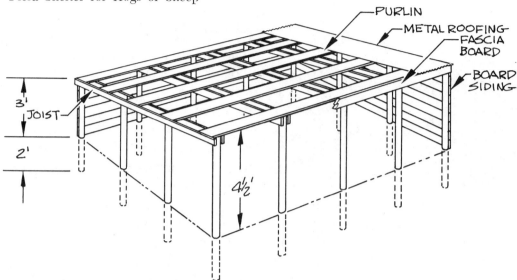

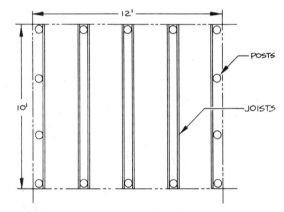

Purlins—lengths of 1 x 8—were then nailed to the rafters, and the roofing nailed to the purlins.

The roof extends a little beyond the walls on all four sides, you will notice. There's fascia trim only on the ends of the roof. The building would look nicer if there was a fascia board across the front.

Lastly nail on the siding with 7d galvanized nails. With the type of siding used here, two boards, counting the lap between them, cover a foot in width. Use the dimensions of this building and the boards will come out even on the height. On the ends, the top siding boards have to be cut to fit snugly against the roofline.

This type of building can be built with plates and studs instead of posts, with or without a floor in it, but with 4-inch-thick (or doubled 2 x 8s) skids under it. With a tractor and log chain, the shed can then be moved to different locations as desired.

GOATS

Goats do not need elaborate or expensive housing. Most any of the small structures detailed in "Sheds and Barns" would be adequate to house two or three goats.

Only a few essentials must be

remembered: House them in a clean, dry place, free from drafts but well ventilated. If this is done, they will stand almost unlimited cold or heat in any climate. Where the animals are kept stanchioned, a minimum of about 2½ feet by 5 feet is required for each animal, plus whatever alleyways, feedways, and the like may be desired or required. This presupposes that the goats will receive some exercise in an outside pen or on a tether. If goats are shut in the barn during part of the day or night, but not confined to stanchions, a minimum floor space of 3 square yards (a space 3 feet by 9 feet) should be provided for each goat.

GOAT MANGER

Goats are notoriously wasteful eaters. One way to minimize wasted hay is to feed just a pound or so per animal three times a day rather than the entire portion all at once. The other way is to build the kind of hay manger that prevents them from tossing so much hay to the floor. The rack shown here has slats spaced 3 inches apart to keep waste to a minimum. The top of the manger should be about 3½ feet high.

CONSTRUCTION

1. From 2 x 4 stock, cut two 41½-inch pieces, two 29-inch pieces, and two 24-inch pieces. Cut also a 45½-inch 2 x 6 and rip one edge to a 35-degree angle.

2. Cut a 1½-inch by 1½-inch notch in one end of each 24-inch-long 2 x 4 and a 1½-inch by 3½-inch notch in the other end. Be sure the notches are made into the same side of the 2 x 4s, as shown.

3. Lay out the two 2 x 4s, notches up, then place one of the 41½-inch 2 x 4s into the notches, as shown, and nail it in place with 12d nails. Lay the 2 x 6 bottom in place, square edge in the notches, and nail it fast.

4. Butt a 29-inch 2 x 4 against the beveled edge of the 2 x 6 at one end, so the butt edge of the 2 x 4 is flush with the bottom of the 2 x 6, and nail it in place. Nail the second 29-incher to the other end of the 2 x 6. Nail the 41½-inch-long 2 x 4 top rail in place.

5. Cut two pieces of 2 x 4 approximately 22 inches long. Nail one to each

end of the manger, butting it against the ends of the top rail and the rear crossmember. Using a backsaw, trim the manger end pieces flush with the front uprights and the front uprights flush with the bottom and the top rail.

6. Cut six 29-inch lengths of 1 x 2 hardwood and nail them to the front of the manger, as shown, using 8d nails. Space them about 3 inches apart. Trim the tops and bottoms with the backsaw.

7. Cut two 19-inch lengths and two 16-inch lengths of the 1 x 2 hardwood. Nail them to the ends of the manger as shown, then trim flush with the front uprights.

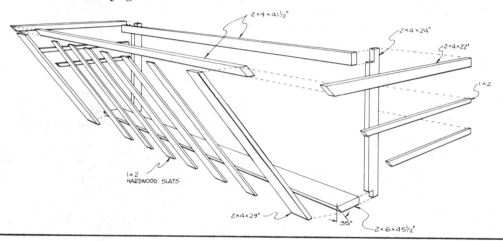

MATERIALS

Wood

2 pcs. 2 x 4 x 10'	or	**Top rails:** 2 pcs. 2 x 4 x 41½"
		Front uprights: 2 pcs. 2 x 4 x 29"
		Rear uprights: 2 pcs. 2 x 4 x 24"
		Manger ends: 2 pcs. 2 x 4 x 22"
1 pc. 2 x 6 x 4'	or	**Bottom:** 1 pc. 2 x 6 x 45½"
1 pc. 1 x 2 x 12' hardwood	or	**Front slats:** 6 pcs. 1 x 2 x 29"
1 pc. 1 x 2 x 10' hardwood		**End slats:** 2 pcs. 1 x 2 x 19" 2 pcs. 1 x 2 x 16"

Hardware

12d nails
8d nails

GOAT-MILKING PLATFORM

Milking goats can be a pain in the neck—or, more exactly, the back—if you're tall. A solid goat-milking platform is perhaps the most basic piece of equipment for the goat keeper. You can make your own milking platform, complete with feed trough and stanchion. All you need are hammer, saw, nails, glue, and wood. You can add a ramp if you want, but your goat can easily mount the platform at milking time.

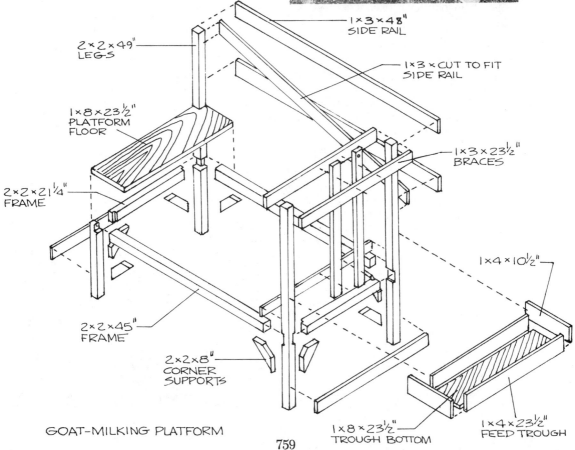

1×3×48" SIDE RAIL

2×2×49" LEGS

1×3× CUT TO FIT SIDE RAIL

1×8×23½" PLATFORM FLOOR

1×3×23½" BRACES

2×2×21¼" FRAME

2×2×45" FRAME

1×4×10½"

2×2×8" CORNER SUPPORTS

1×8×23½" TROUGH BOTTOM

1×4×23½" FEED TROUGH

GOAT-MILKING PLATFORM

Goat-Milking Platform

CONSTRUCTION

1. From four 10-foot 2 x 2s cut the following pieces: three legs 49 inches, one leg 17½ inches, two frame members 21¼ inches, two frame members 45 inches, two stanchion pieces 36 inches, and eight 8-inch-long braces with opposing 45-degree angles on the ends, as shown.

2. Cut ⅜-inch-deep, 1½-inch-wide dadoes on two adjoining sides 16 inches from the bottom on each of the four legs to accommodate the frame members. The front and rear frame members must consequently be rabbeted at either end. Cut the rabbet ⅜ inch by ⅜ inch in one face (the same face on either end). The dadoes and rabbets are most easily made with a router or power saw with the appropriate dado, but they can be made with a saw and hammer and chisel.

3. Glue and nail frame members to legs, using 8d nails. Nail 8-inch angled corner supports to bottom sides of legs and frame, using 6d nails. Drilling pilot holes will forestall splitting.

4. Cut 1 x 8 boards to size for the platform floor. The length should be 23½ inches; you will need seven boards, with one being ripped to the proper size to fill the final gap. The boards at either end of the platform will have to be notched to fit tightly around the three legs that project above the platform floor. (You can use only six boards, spacing them out ¾ inch apart. Moreover, it isn't necessary to use 1 x 8 lumber for the floor; any dimension lumber or combination of dimension lumbers will do.) Attach the flooring with 6d nails.

5. Cut five 23½-inch lengths of 1 x 3. Attach one brace to the outside of the rear legs, and a second to the outside of the front legs, both about 4 inches from the bottom. Attach a third to the inside of the front legs against the top of the platform floor. The last two 1 x 3s are attached to the top of the front legs, one on the outside, one on the inside. Use 6d nails at all these joints.

6. Cut a 47¼-inch length and a 48-inch length of 1 x 3. These are the side rails; the longer piece is the top rail and is attached to the top of the front and rear legs, while the slightly shorter piece is attached to the legs a foot above the platform floor. Again, 6d nails are used. Measure the distance between the inside of the front leg at the lower rail to the

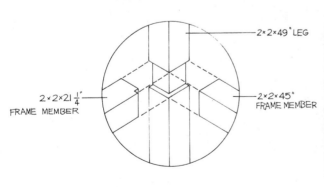

2 × 2 × 21¼" FRAME MEMBER

2×2×49" LEG

2×2×45" FRAME MEMBER

inside of the rear leg at the upper rail, cut a 1 x 3 brace to fit and nail in place (driving 6d nails through the edge of the brace into the legs).

7. Install the stanchion. The fixed member is the one closer to the side rails. Position it so the inner edge is 9¾ inches from the outer edge of the leg. Drill a hole for a ¼-inch stove bolt through the member and the upper 1 x 3 braces and through the member and the lower 1 x 3 braces. Bolt the member in place. Position the movable stanchion member so there is a 4-inch opening between it and the fixed member. Drill a hole for a ¼-inch stove bolt through the member and the lower 1 x 3 brace, then install the bolt. Finally, drill a small hole through the top of the fixed stanchion member to accept a rawhide or string loop to hold the stanchion closed.

8. Cut and assemble the feed trough. Cut two 23½-inch sides from 1 x 4,

MATERIALS

Wood

4 pcs. 2 x 2 x 10′	or	**Legs:** 3 pcs. 2 x 2 x 49″
		1 pc. 2 x 2 x 17½″
		Frame: 2 pcs. 2 x 2 x 21¼″
		2 pcs. 2 x 2 x 45″
		Stanchion: 2 pcs. 2 x 2 x 36″
		Corner supports: 8 pcs. 2 x 2 x 8″
2 pcs. 1 x 8 x 8′	or	**Platform floor:** 7 pcs. 1 x 8 x 23½″
		Trough bottom: 1 pc. 1 x 8 x 23½″
1 pc. 1 x 3 x 10′	or	**Braces:** 5 pcs. 1 x 3 x 23½″
1 pc. 1 x 3 x 14′	or	**Side rails:** 1 pc. 1 x 3 x 47¼″
		1 pc. 1 x 3 x 48″
		1 pc. 1 x 3 x cut to fit
1 pc. 1 x 4 x 6′	or	**Feed trough:** 2 pcs. 1 x 4 x 23½″
		2 pcs. 1 x 4 x 10½″

Hardware

Glue
8d nails
6d nails
3–6″ x ¼″ stove bolts w/ washers

Miscellaneous

14″ of rawhide

two 10¼-inch ends from 1 x 4, and a 23½-inch bottom from 1 x 8. Nail the sides to the bottom, driving 6d nails through the sides into the edges of the bottom. Butt the ends in place, so 1½ inches of each end overlap the same side, and nail in place. Position the trough about 5 inches above the platform floor, as shown, and nail through the overlapping ends into the legs.

VARIATIONS

A somewhat more simple construction approach would be to eliminate the dadoed joints in the frame in favor of butt joints. To do this, cut the frame members ¾ inch shorter (44¼ inches for the sides, 20½ inches for the ends) or figure on expanding the length and width of the platform by ¾ inch, in which case you would assemble the frame and cut the floor, stanchion supports, side rails, and the trough to fit. The latter is a wise approach in any case, since dimensions of lumber do vary slightly.

A further variation would be to use ¾-inch exterior plywood for the flooring, and—even—the rails, supports, and the trough.

A seat is quite easily included in the design, and a ramp can be constructed to supplement the platform.

COWS AND HORSES

There are a surprising number of people who keep a cow or two around, 13,000 in Texas alone, according to *Dairyman's Digest*. If you are considering joining these folks, don't let worries about housing hold you back.

A cow will do all right in any kind of shed or barn that is not too drafty and that is kept dry underfoot. Hopefully, the cow will have a pasture to graze and exercise in. Cows *will* adapt to living almost full time in a pen, stall, or stanchion, but they'll be better off with a bit of room to roam.

Horses are much less likely to be confined than cows. There's nothing a horse can do for you in confinement. Like most other animals, horses should be housed in a clean, dry, draft-free shelter. For the homesteader, the horse will be happiest and least troublesome in a box stall and with free access to the outdoors. Feeding and adding bedding will be the only daily chores if the horse is so housed The box stall will need to be cleaned no more than three times a week if bedding is added daily. A tie stall will have to be cleaned daily.

STALLS

Obviously, the loafing barn is the easiest to outfit, since you are not allocating particular areas for particular animals. The individual animals can come and go at will and can move freely within the confines of the barn when indoors.

A box stall requires that a particular area, one about 14 feet square for a horse, for example, be fenced off and a gate installed for access. Ordinarily, 2-inch planks are used, arranged horizontally and without spaces between them. Hardwood is recommended for constructing stalls because of the additional strength it affords. Block, brick, or stone could conceivably be used to partition off stalls, provided, of course, the masonry units are mortared together.

In any case, the sides of the stall should reach higher than the underside of the animal's belly.

The popular conception of a tie stall is probably something on the order of a narrow box stall with the back end open: a partitioned parking place just wide enough for one cow or horse. A manger, like the one described in the goat section above, should be installed in the stall, together with a grain box. These should be at the head of the stall, and the stall should be arranged so that you have access to the feedbox and manger without having to go through the stall. The traditional dairy barn is arranged with a central aisle into which the cows face.

A tie stall can usually be converted to a stanchion stall without too much work. You can buy stanchions, but you can make wooden ones on the

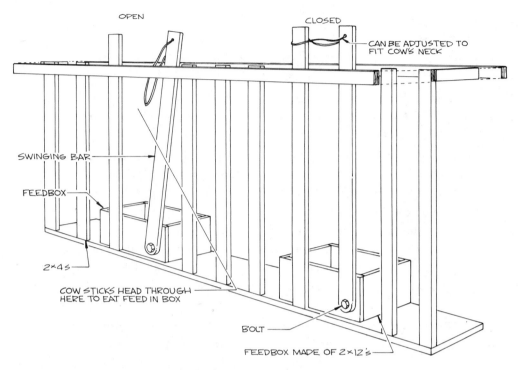

OPEN

CLOSED

CAN BE ADJUSTED TO FIT COW'S NECK

SWINGING BAR

FEEDBOX

2×4s

COW STICKS HEAD THROUGH HERE TO EAT FEED IN BOX

BOLT

FEEDBOX MADE OF 2×12's

HOMEMADE DOUBLE STANCHIONS

order of the stanchion used on the goat-milking platform.

First, build a feedbox about 10 inches by 20 inches, with straight sides and about a foot deep. Locate it at the end or head of the pen or stall. The feedbox ought to set right on the floor, so that you can pile hay for the cow on top of it when she is not eating grain from it.

Separating the box or feeding trough from the stall should be bars or boards so the cow cannot get herself or even her hooves into the feeding area. All she should be able to do is get her head through the opening directly in front of the feedbox. Consequently, as the illustration shows,

you must install two horizontal bars, one at the floor level and one above the cow's head. Vertical bars are fastened to these. Two particularly stout bars are needed to form the stanchion itself. One is fixed to the upper and lower horizontals at one end of the feedbox, while the other is bolted to the lower horizontal at the other end of the feedbox; it remains free at the top. You must work up some system for fastening it once the cow has put her head through the stanchion, be it a loop of wire or some sort of latch.

When locked in the stanchion, the cow cannot move forward or backward, though she can swing her hindquarters around and she can lie down if she wants to.

Any stall can be provided with a concrete floor or a wooden floor or a dirt floor. All have their advantages and their drawbacks. Your best bet is to avoid the elaborate. If you are building, it is unwise to install a wooden floor. But if you are using an existing, wooden-floored building, don't worry, the wooden floor will serve well. Again, if you are building, pouring a concrete floor is just unnecessary work. Your cow or horse, even your goats, hog, or sheep, will do just as well, if not better, on a gravel floor deeply bedded with straw. But don't try to break up a concrete floor if you already have one.

A TIE STALL WITH WOODEN FLOORING

Moving on to a new (or old) homestead brings its dilemmas, not the least of which is how to best house animals in an old rattletrap barn until getting around to building a new one. The homesteader's program is often a juggling act with time, materials, economics, and know-how; the decision must be made of how to best use what one has.

In the mountains of North Carolina, Drew and Louise Langsner had to deal with a "burley barn," designed for curing tobacco and made even more airy with old age. They began by making a box stall for their Jersey heifer and bedding her with straw. As she grew, so did the amount of bedding required, and the situation was not helped by the deep hole worn in the dirt floor of her stall. To compound the problem, a Brown Swiss heifer joined the first, and the Langsners ran out of bedding straw.

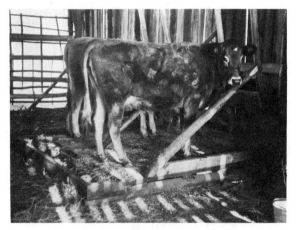

At that point, they decided their heifers needed a wooden floor. The chosen design was based on the tie stalls of small barns they had seen in the Swiss Alps. This involves a wooden platform with a hayrack in front and a gutter for collecting manure behind. A light sprinkling of sawdust, or better, plane shavings, is sufficient bedding. Both are free for the taking at many lumberyards and sawmills.

In practice, cows are tied to the center support of each stall by a rope of minimum length to allow them to comfortably lie down as well as reach into the hayrack. The Langsners use snap links hooked onto the halters. Floor length should be calculated to fit the inhabitant, no longer. Wood shavings or sawdust are spread on the floor for bedding. Manure is hoed into the gutter, then shoveled out with a square-blade spade. A more ideal system would extend the gutter out the barn into a tank.

The Langsners' heifers quickly learned to come to their stalls. They are out every day so don't "mind" being tied. It is much easier to keep them clean with this system. Additional advantages are that the animals become accustomed to being handled a great deal, and the setup is fine for milking. Finally, manure (including urine) is very easy to collect and handle without the messy difficulties of dealing with long lengths of matted and soiled straw.

Since the Langsner's are surrounded by woods, they made use of this natural source of building materials. The sills, joists, hayrack support, and other elements of the tie stall were made of various size logs and poles cut and hauled in from the woods. Rough sawn—and thus full dimension—1-inch stock was used for flooring, hayrack, and gutter. Some 2 x 4s were used also.

The homesteader without a woodlot should be able to adapt the Langsner's tie stall design for construction using lumberyard materials. Two 2 x 8s or 2 x 10s could be spiked together for each sill, 2 x 8s or 2 x 10s would serve as joists, 2 x 2s or 2 x 3s could replace the poles used to support the hayrack.

CONSTRUCTION

1. Prepare your building site by scraping the dirt floor to reach a solid foundation. Have rocks available for further leveling. Place the first outside sill (6- to 8-inch-diameter, 8-foot-long logs) on rocks, allowing a 3-inch slope from head to tail end. This and all horizontal logs should be positioned crown up. The other outside sill is placed next, using a level to line it up with the first. (An inexpensive line level makes this easy.) Locate the middle sill.

2. Hew out saddle notches on each joist (4- to 5-inch-diameter, 8-foot-long logs) at the intersection with sills. Set end joists, then middle joists, preserving the 3-inch flooring slope. With brace and bit, drill one ½-inch hole through the joist and sill at each intersection. Camfer both ends of the 6- to 8-inch-long ½-inch dowel sections and tap into place.

3. Level all curves and bumps on the joist poles so that the flooring will lie flat. Use an adze, if available. Otherwise, the logs may be scored with

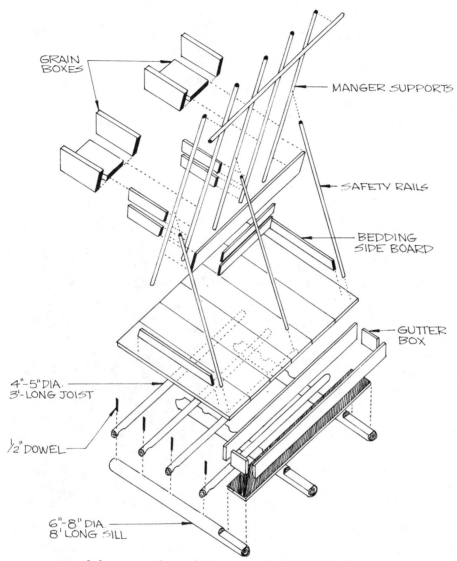

GRAIN
BOXES

MANGER SUPPORTS

SAFETY RAILS

BEDDING
SIDE BOARD

GUTTER
BOX

4"-5" DIA.
3'-LONG JOIST

½" DOWEL

6"-8" DIA.
8' LONG SILL

a saw and the pieces chipped out using a wide chisel or hatchet. Use of
the wooden pegs allows leveling without danger of running into nails.

4. Hew a 4-inch-deep section off the last 18 to 24 inches of the sills to make
a support for the manure gutter. Saw the gutter pieces and coat with
creosote. Also, creosote the substructure at this time. Assemble the
gutter, sealing all seams with roofing cement.

5. Flooring must be rough lumber, *not* creosoted on the surface as this
would cause it to become slippery and dangerous. Nail on the boards
to pass over the gutter edge at each sill. In between stalls use boards
of sufficient length to overlap the front wall of the gutter.

6. The manger is designed for one large, central hayrack and two individual grain troughs (which may also hold water pails). If no ceiling beam is available, install a pole for the attachment of the manger supports. Nail supports from ceiling to floor 1 foot out from the end of the platform. Nail cleat strips to the wall for side board attachment. Align cleats to inner edges of supports, as the grain racks are boxed in with side boards nailed to insides of supports for sturdiness and simplicity of fitting the bottoms. Box in sides and bottoms.

7. Install safety rails (3-inch-diameter poles) running from floor to manger supports at sides and center. A bedding side board at each side of the platform will hold in bedding.

CALF MANGER

Anyone can build this calf manger and feeder. It is plain as the nose on your face, has no critical measurements. There are angled slats above to hold the hay and a solid floor underneath for grain, minerals, and to catch the leaves of the hay as they fall between the slats when the calves pull the hay through.

The manger is 5 feet high, 2 feet wide, and 4 feet long. The corner posts are 2-inch stock, while the rest is 1-inch material. The directions that follow suggest a specific way to construct such a manger-feeder, but you can use any materials on hand. The one shown reflects the secondhand materials approach.

Moreover, the dimensions and amount of material used in the manger-feeder can be altered too. Such a manger could be used to feed goats or sheep or even full-size cattle.

The manger-feeder shown is located in an outdoor pen for calves, and that's where yours could go. But it could also be used indoors, in tie stalls, box stalls, or loafing pens. It can be made much much longer to serve a whole herd, or shortened to serve a single animal. The choice is really yours.

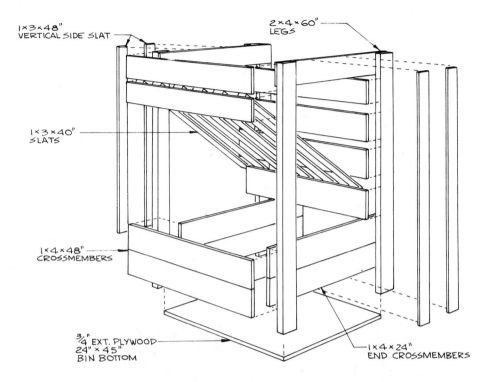

1×3×48"
VERTICAL SIDE SLAT

2×4×60"
LEGS

1×3×40"
SLATS

1×4×48"
CROSSMEMBERS

3/4" EXT. PLYWOOD
24" × 45"
BIN BOTTOM

1×4×24"
END CROSSMEMBERS

CALF MANGER

CONSTRUCTION

1. Cut four 60-inch 2 x 4 legs, six 24-inch 1 x 4 end crossmembers, and six 48-inch crossmembers for the front and back.

2. Lay out two of the legs and join them together with the end crossmembers, one at the top and two laid edge to edge, beginning about 12 inches above the bottom. Use 8d nails. Join the other two legs in like manner.

3. With one leg assembly laying crossmembers up, butt the longer crossmembers in place, one at a time, and nail them fast. These crossmembers should abut the legs at the same place the end crossmembers do. Set up the framework and nail the second leg assembly in place.

4. From 1 x 4 stock, cut five more 48-inch crossmembers. Nail one to the insides of the back legs, abutting the top of the lower end crossmembers. Nail another inside the back legs abutting the top end crossmembers. Two more should be nailed to the inside of the back legs, evenly spaced between these two. The last one is nailed to the front legs, about $1\frac{1}{2}$ inches below the top crossmembers.

5. Cut six 40-inch lengths of furring (1 x 3) and place them, evenly spaced, so that they angle between the bottom of the top front

769

crossmember and the top of the bottom inner rear crossmember, as shown. Nail them fast.

6. Cut a piece of ¾-inch exterior plywood 24 inches by 45 inches, or cut seven 45-inch lengths of 1 x 4. Turn the manger upside down and nail the plywood or the 1 x 4s to the bottoms of the crossmembers, forming the floor of the mineral bin.

7. Finally, cut four 48-inch lengths of furring and nail two to each end, extending from the mineral bin to the top of the manger, as shown.

MATERIALS

Wood

2 pcs. 2 x 4 x 10′	or	**Legs:** 4 pcs. 2 x 4 x 60″
4 pcs. 1 x 4 x 12′	or	**End crossmembers:** 6 pcs. 1 x 4 x 24″
1 pc. 1 x 4 x 8′		**Front and back crossmembers:** 11 pcs. 1 x 4 x 48″
5 pcs. 1 x 3 x 8′ furring	or	**Slats:** 6 pcs. 1 x 3 x 40″
		Vertical side slats: 4 pcs. 1 x 3 x 48″
1–2′ x 4′ sht. ¾″ ext. plywood	or	**Mineral bin bottom:** 1 pc. 24″ x 45″

Hardware

8d nails

BEES

Getting started in beekeeping, even on a small scale, can be an expensive proposition. The bees themselves aren't that costly, but there is a lot of equipment, ranging from hives to veils and smokers to extractors, that is necessary.

We're not going to tell you how to keep bees; there are lots of books on the subject. But we are going to tell you how to cut some of the start-up and expansion costs by making much of your own equipment.

BEEHIVES

The modern beehive consists of a brood body, with a removable top and a separate bottom. The brood body is a 9½-inch-deep frame without top or bottom, which holds ten comb frames. The beekeeper stacks additional hive

make the frames. There's money to be saved on each item you make for yourself.

What's so tough about it? The exacting dimensions. The hive—regardless of manufacturer—is a standard device. Over the years, beekeepers have settled on particular dimensions for the various components. The deep super or brood chamber has interior measurements ranging from $18\frac{1}{4}$ inches by $14\frac{5}{8}$ inches by $9\frac{1}{2}$ inches all the way up to $18\frac{3}{8}$ inches by $14\frac{3}{4}$ inches by $9\frac{5}{8}$ inches. An $\frac{1}{8}$ inch is all the leeway there is in any one dimension. The shallow super has the same width and length dimensions, but is only $5\frac{11}{16}$ inches in depth, give or take a $\frac{1}{16}$ inch. The frames are made to fit these sizes of hive bodies with a particular, fixed amount of elbowroom. The tops and bottoms are made to support and cover these size bodies.

The dimensions are critical because of what is known as bee space. The commonly accepted bee space is $\frac{5}{16}$ inch, though it ranges from $\frac{1}{4}$ inch to $\frac{3}{8}$ inch. Bees will plug up any space or hole smaller than $\frac{3}{16}$ inch with a tough, sticky substance called propolis. In a space larger than $\frac{3}{8}$ inch, the bees will build comb. Before the proper size of the bee space was figured out, beekeeping was a sticky proposition, because the bees would weld all the comb frames together and

bodies—either deep supers of the same size as the brood body or smaller ones called shallow supers—atop the brood chamber, filling these bodies with ten frames each. The queen will fill the brood chamber's combs with eggs, the worker bees will fill the supers' combs with honey. A certain amount of honey will be needed by the bees to see them through the winter, but most years, they'll make and store far more than they need; the beekeeper harvests this excess.

The biggest single expense in beekeeping is the hive. Although good hives are constructed to very exacting standards, there's no good reason why a reasonably competent homestead handyman can't make all the hive components but the frames. And if he's really competent and has the woodworking equipment, he can even

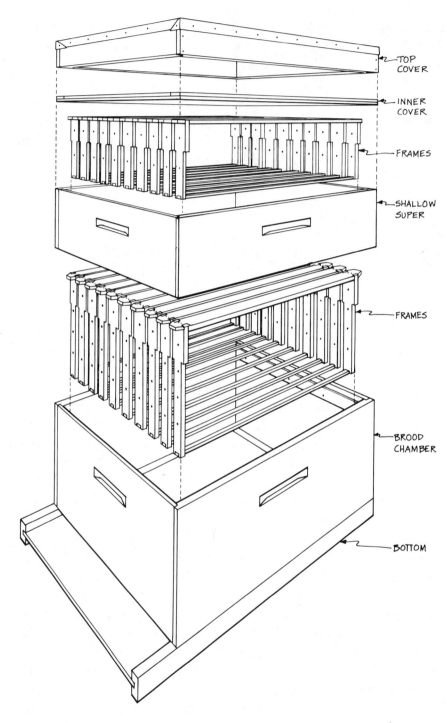

TOP COVER

INNER COVER

FRAMES

SHALLOW SUPER

FRAMES

BROOD CHAMBER

BOTTOM

to the body with propolis and comb. The individually movable frame is a vital—more than convenient—part of modern beekeeping.

Consequently, the homesteader contemplating the construction of hives should weigh his skills candidly. Every time you fudge a dimension a bit, you are going to create potential trouble when you try to execute an incident-free parting of the bees from the honey. Be candid, but don't be afraid to test your skills. Constructing the hive bodies, bottom, and top is not all that difficult if you are careful. It is in constructing these items, too, that the biggest saving is realized. The frames are not all that expensive, though at ten frames per super, their cost does mount up.

In the following directions, instructions are given for building a brood chamber (which is the same as a deep super), a shallow super, the bottom, the inner cover, and the top cover. As previously explained, you will need only one bottom, one brood chamber, one inner cover, and one top cover per hive. The number of supers, shallow and/or deep, will vary according to the honeyflow. Build what you need.

A circular saw, a hammer, and a paintbrush are the only tools necessary to make your own supers and hive bodies. You'll also need some cement-coated or galvanized 7d nails and a quart of acrylic exterior paint for ten to twelve supers. Different colors of paint are best for a large number of hives to help the bees distinguish their hive from others, but if you have only a few hives, one color, usually white, will do fine.

Each hive body (or deep super) requires a 6-foot length of 1 x 12 lumber. This length is sufficient for one deep super plus some useful leftovers. Knots are all right in bee super lumber if they are strongly attached. It's good practice to buy enough lumber for at least four supers per colony to start.

BROOD CHAMBER (DEEP SUPER) CONSTRUCTION

1. Rip a 6-foot 1 x 12 to an actual width of $9\frac{5}{8}$ inches. Cut the board into four pieces: two side pieces $19\frac{7}{8}$ inches long and two end pieces $15\frac{1}{2}$ inches long.

2. The body will be assembled using a rabbet joint, with the rabbets cut in the butt ends of the sides. The rabbet should be half the thickness of the stock deep, $\frac{3}{8}$ inch, and the width of the stock wide, $\frac{3}{4}$ inch. For the best finish, the rabbets should be partially stopped, since the top edge of the ends must be rabbeted to accept the comb frames. Since this latter rabbet will be the same size—$\frac{3}{8}$ inch wide and $\frac{3}{4}$ inch deep— stop the former rabbets $\frac{3}{4}$ inch from the top edge of the sides and rabbet that small portion only $\frac{3}{8}$ inch wide.

3. Cut a $\frac{3}{4}$-inch-wide by $\frac{3}{8}$-inch-deep rabbet along the top edge of the end pieces.

4. Cut a $\frac{1}{2}$-inch-deep finger grip into each piece of the body. The grips should be about 5 inches long and should be centered in each piece, about 3 inches below and parallel to the top edge. An option would be to nail a 5-inch length of 1 x 1 in the same position for a grip.

5. Using five 8d cement-coated or galvanized box nails and a bit of waterproof glue at each joint, fasten the sides and ends together.

6. Cut two $14\frac{3}{4}$-inch lengths of 1-inch-wide galvanized sheet metal or aluminum and tack them to the ends along the rabbets for the comb frames. These strips should project $\frac{1}{8}$ inch above the bottom of the rabbet. Their purpose is to make the removal of the frames much easier. Remember that the amount the strips project above the bottom surface of the rabbet is critical, because if it projects less than $\frac{1}{8}$ inch, the bee space will be too big, and if it projects more than $\frac{1}{4}$ inch, the bee space will be too small.

7. Paint the entire outside of the body with two or more heavy coats of acrylic paint. A light color will help keep the hive cooler in summer. It is not necessary to paint the inside of the body.

MATERIALS (for brood chamber)

Wood

1 pc. 1 x 12 x 6′	or	**Sides:** 2 pcs. $\frac{3}{4}''$ x $9\frac{5}{8}''$ x $19\frac{7}{8}''$ (act. meas.)
		Ends: 2 pcs. $\frac{3}{4}''$ x $9\frac{5}{8}''$ x $15\frac{1}{2}''$ (act. meas.)

Hardware

8d cement-coated box nails
Waterproof glue
1 pc. 1″ x $29\frac{1}{2}''$, $\frac{1}{32}''$ galvanized sheet metal or **Frame support strips:** 2 pcs. 1″ x $14\frac{3}{4}''$

Tacks
Acrylic paint

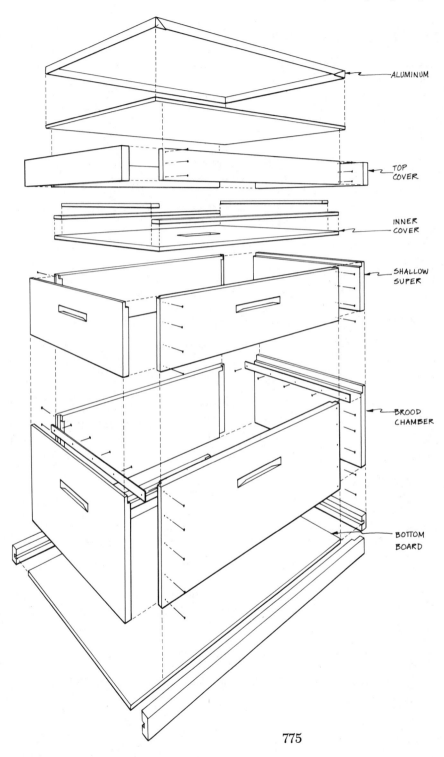

ALUMINUM

TOP
COVER

INNER
COVER

SHALLOW
SUPER

BROOD
CHAMBER

BOTTOM
BOARD

BOTTOM BOARD CONSTRUCTION

1. Cut a piece of $\frac{3}{8}$-inch exterior plywood $15\frac{1}{2}$ inches by $21\frac{3}{4}$ inches.
2. Rip nominal 1-inch material to an actual width of $1\frac{5}{8}$ inches. If you have made a super, use the strips ripped from the 1 x 12 or 1 x 8 used to make the super for this purpose. Cut the $\frac{3}{4}$-inch by $1\frac{5}{8}$-inch strip into two pieces $22\frac{1}{8}$ inches long and one piece $15\frac{1}{2}$ inches long.
3. Rip a $\frac{3}{8}$-inch-wide by $\frac{3}{8}$-inch-deep dado the full length of each piece in a board face, locating its center $\frac{9}{16}$ inch from the bottom edge. Cut a $\frac{3}{4}$-inch-wide by $\frac{3}{8}$-inch-deep rabbet in one butt end of each of the long pieces. The rabbet should be in the same face as the dado.
4. Slip the frame pieces over the edges of the plywood, as shown, and secure with a bit of waterproof glue and 6d cement-coated box nails.
5. Paint the assembled bottom board with acrylic paint.

MATERIALS (for bottom board)

Wood

1–2′ sq. sht. $\frac{3}{8}$″ ext. plywood   or   **Bottom:** 1 pc. $15\frac{1}{2}$″ x $21\frac{3}{4}$″

Side frames: 2 pcs. $\frac{3}{4}$″ x $1\frac{5}{8}$″ x $22\frac{1}{8}$″ (use waste strips ripped in making supers)

End frame: 1 pc. $\frac{3}{4}$″ x $1\frac{5}{8}$″ x $15\frac{1}{2}$″ (use waste strips ripped in making supers)

Hardware

Waterproof glue
6d cement-coated box nails
Acrylic paint

INNER COVER CONSTRUCTION

1. Cut a $19\frac{7}{8}$-inch by $16\frac{1}{4}$-inch piece of $\frac{3}{8}$-inch exterior plywood.
2. Rip a 6-foot strip of the waste from construction of a super to an actual width of $\frac{5}{16}$ inch. Cut this strip into two pieces $19\frac{7}{8}$ inches long and two strips $14\frac{3}{4}$ inches long.
3. Using waterproof glue, attach the strips around the top of the plywood cover, flush with the edges.
4. Using a keyhole saw, cut a hole $1\frac{1}{8}$ inches wide and $3\frac{3}{4}$ inches long in the center of the cover.

MATERIALS (for inner cover)

Wood

1–2′ sq. sht $\frac{3}{8}$″ ext. plywood   or   **Cover:** 1 pc. 19$\frac{7}{8}$″ x 16$\frac{1}{4}$″

Frame sides: 2 pcs. $\frac{3}{4}$″ x $\frac{5}{16}$″ x 19$\frac{7}{8}$″
(act. meas.)

Frame ends: 2 pcs. $\frac{3}{4}$″ x $\frac{5}{16}$″ x 14$\frac{3}{4}$″
(act. meas.) (use waste strips from
super construction)

Hardware

Waterproof glue

TOP COVER CONSTRUCTION

1. From 1 x 2 material, cut two 21$\frac{3}{4}$-inch lengths and two 16$\frac{1}{2}$-inch lengths. From $\frac{1}{2}$-inch exterior plywood, cut a piece 18 inches by 21$\frac{3}{4}$ inches.
2. Using 8d cement-coated box nails, nail the 1 x 2s together, forming a frame 18 inches by 21$\frac{3}{4}$ inches. Using 6d cement-coated box nails, nail the plywood to the top of the frame.
3. Cut a piece of galvanized sheet metal or aluminum 19$\frac{1}{2}$ inches by 23$\frac{1}{4}$ inches. Use this metal to cover the wooden top cover, lapping the metal over the sides and ends of the cover at least $\frac{5}{8}$ inch to $\frac{3}{4}$ inch to provide a watertight seal. Use $\frac{1}{2}$-inch tacks to attach the metal to the cover.
4. Paint the cover with acrylic paint.

MATERIALS (for top cover)

Wood

1 pc. 1 x 2 x 8′   or   **Frame sides:** 2 pcs. 1 x 2 x 21$\frac{3}{4}$″

Frame ends: 2 pcs. 1 x 2 x 16$\frac{1}{2}$″

1–2′ sq. sht. $\frac{1}{2}$″ ext. plywood   or   **Top:** 1 pc. 18″ x 21$\frac{3}{4}$″

Hardware

8d cement-coated box nails
6d cement-coated box nails
1 pc. 19$\frac{1}{2}$″ x 23$\frac{1}{4}$″, $\frac{1}{32}$″ galvanized sheet metal
$\frac{1}{2}$″ tacks
Acrylic paint

SHALLOW SUPER CONSTRUCTION

The shallow super is constructed in the same fashion as the brood chamber. However, use a 1 x 8 instead of a 1 x 12, and rip it to an actual width of $5\frac{11}{16}$ inches. Cut it into the same length pieces, rabbet them in the same fashion, assemble them, install the frame support strips, and paint.

MATERIALS (for shallow super)

Wood

    1 pc. 1 x 8 x 6'   or   **Sides:** 2 pcs. $\frac{3}{4}''$ x $5\frac{11}{16}''$ x $19\frac{7}{8}''$ (act. meas.)

                    Ends: 2 pcs. $\frac{3}{4}''$ x $5\frac{11}{16}''$ x $15\frac{1}{2}''$ (act. meas.)

Hardware

    8d cement-coated box nails
    Waterproof glue
    1 pc. 1" x $29\frac{1}{2}''$, $\frac{1}{32}''$ galvanized sheet metal or **Frame support strips:**
                                              2 pcs. 1" x $14\frac{3}{4}''$

    Tacks
    Acrylic paint

FRAMES

There is really no practical reason for making your own frames for the honeycomb. The frames are surprisingly inexpensive to purchase, though the cost does mount when you consider the large number—ten per super —that are required. If you value your time, you'll not be able to make them for less than you can buy them.

There is, however, that pleasure of making your own, of learning something new about woodworking, and you may want to try your hand at the project for that reason.

Unlike the construction of the hive body, the construction of frames for

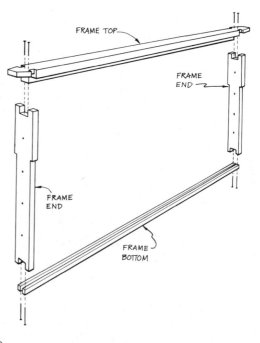

FRAME TOP

FRAME END

FRAME END

FRAME END

FRAME BOTTOM

the comb requires some fairly sophisticated woodworking skills. Moreover, the frames require you to use $1\frac{3}{8}$-inch-thick stock, which is nonstandard. If you don't have a jointer, you will either have to have nominal 2-inch stock planed at a lumberyard or cabinet shop that does custom millwork. Or you'll have to try your hand at planing the material with a hand wood plane. Be sure to use the best quality clear material for this work.

CONSTRUCTION

1. The frame ends are shaped as shown in the illustration. The basic approach to their fabrication will be to form a block of wood to the configuration of the frame pieces, then cut off $\frac{5}{16}$-inch slices.

2. The frame ends are constructed from stock measuring an actual $1\frac{3}{8}$ inches thick. Plane a length of 2 x 10 to the required thickness, then cut off a $9\frac{1}{4}$-inch length for deep super/brood chamber frames or a $5\frac{5}{8}$-inch length for shallow supers.

3. The notch in the top is $\frac{3}{4}$ inch wide and $\frac{3}{8}$ inch deep. To make it, use a router or dado head in a circular saw to cut the proper-sized dado through the center of the butt end. The notch in the bottom is the same width, but it is only $\frac{5}{16}$ inch deep. Cut it in the same manner as the first dado.

4. The lower portion of the frame is clearly narrower than the upper portion. The deep super frame end has a $1\frac{3}{8}$-inch width in the top $2\frac{3}{4}$ inches and a $1\frac{1}{8}$-inch width in the bottom $6\frac{3}{8}$ inches. The shallow super frame end is $1\frac{3}{8}$ inches wide at the top $2\frac{1}{4}$ inches and $1\frac{1}{8}$ inches wide at the bottom $3\frac{1}{8}$ inches. To reduce the width of the frames, you must measure the requisite distance from the bottom and scribe a line on both sides of the block. One-eighth inch of material must be routered or dadoed from the block on each side from the line to the bottom of the block. It is possible that the process will split or splinter the edges of the dado in the butt end, so a support block fabricated from a scrap of wood must be tightly, but temporarily, secured to the bottom of the frame end block. Rip a scrap of wood to a width of $1\frac{3}{8}$ inches. Cut it to a length of $9\frac{1}{4}$ inches (the width of the frame end block). Form a tongue on this support block to fit into the dado in the bottom of the frame end block by cutting a $\frac{5}{16}$-inch-wide by $\frac{5}{16}$-inch-deep rabbet in each edge of the support block. Fit the support block and the frame end block together, secure with brads and proceed to trim away the excess stock.

5. Remove the support block and rip the frame end block into $\frac{5}{16}$-inch-thick slices. You should get about twenty-one frame end pieces—enough for all the frames in one super—from a single such block.

6. Holes for the wires that secure the comb foundation in the frame must be drilled in each frame end piece. Each hole is $\frac{1}{8}$ inch in diameter and is located on the center line of the piece. The topmost hole is $1\frac{3}{8}$ inches below the bottom of the notch ($1\frac{3}{4}$ inches below the topmost

edge) and three more are located on 1¾-inch centers below this first hole.

7. The frame tops are formed from 19-inch lengths of stock measuring ⅞ inch by 1 inch. This stock can be made by ripping 2 x 10 material into ⅞-inch-thick strips, then re-ripping each strip to a 1-inch width. Each 19-inch piece of 2 x 10 should yield nine such strips.
8. Cut a 1-inch-wide by ½-inch-deep rabbet through the 1-inch width and into the ⅞-inch thickness of each butt end of each frame top piece.
9. To accommodate the tops of the frame ends, $\frac{5}{16}$-inch-wide by ⅛-inch-deep notches must be cut into the sides of the projection formed by the rabbet made in step 8. Form these carefully, cutting and fitting so they aren't made too big, causing the frames to fit only loosely together.
10. The final step in the fabrication of the frame tops is to cut a $\frac{9}{16}$-inch-wide and ⅜-inch-deep rabbet into the bottom edge of the frame tops. DO NOT use a router to cut this rabbet. Use a saw, so that the strip of material removed can be used as a tacking strip to help secure the comb foundation in the frame.
11. The bottom frame pieces are fabricated from $\frac{5}{16}$-inch-wide strips ripped from nominal 1-inch stock. Cut the strips into 17⅝-inch lengths. Using a saw creating the thinnest kerf possible, rip through the ¾-inch width, cutting the strips into pieces approximately $\frac{5}{16}$ inch by $\frac{5}{16}$ inch.
12. Assemble the frame ends with the frame top and the two-strip frame bottom, using ½-inch brads. The comb foundation is installed by feeding it through the narrow slit in the frame bottom and tacking it to the frame top with the strip of material removed from the rabbet. Feed the foundation wires through the holes in the frame ends and secure.

MATERIALS (for ten deep and ten shallow frames)

Wood

1 pc. 2 x 10 x 6′	or	**Shallow frame ends:** 20 pcs. $\frac{5}{16}$″ x 1⅜″ x 5⅜″ (act. meas.)
		Deep frame ends: 20 pcs. $\frac{5}{16}$″ x 1⅜″ x 9⅛″ (act. meas.)
		Frame tops: 20 pcs. ⅞″ x 1″ x 19″ (act. meas.)
1 pc. 1 x 12 x 4′	or	**Frame bottoms:** 20 pcs. $\frac{5}{16}$″ x ¾″ x 17⅝″ (act. meas.)

Hardware

½″ brads

A HONEY EXTRACTOR

The honey extractor has revolutionized beekeeping since the turn of this century. With its use, honeycomb can be emptied and then put back with the bees to be used over again. That brings a considerable saving in time and labor, since the bees do not have to build new comb each time.

Most honey extractors operate on the concept of centrifugal force. The machine whirls combs of honey around and around at a high rate of speed. The honey is thrown out and away from the comb.

There are many extractor designs; most are available from beekeeping supply houses. They normally range from $100 upwards to about $500.

Probably the most efficient design is the radial extractor. The frames of honeycomb are placed vertically into holders or "baskets" which radiate out from a central axle, much like the spokes of a wheel. The advantage of this system is that both sides of the comb are emptied without having to stop the machine and turn the comb around. Also, very few combs break or are deformed with this design.

The comb must be uncapped before being put into the extractor. A hot knife will easily slice through the thin wax cappings.

Terry Domico built the very ser-

viceable extractor pictured here from an old wooden barrel, a few lengths of wood, and a ¼-inch power hand drill. The drill turns the shaft and "baskets" of the extractor. Its speed must be regulated and increased slowly. For this purpose, a common dimmer switch or rheostat must be used, or you must use a variable-speed drill.

If a barrel is not available, a large wooden box can be made to serve in its place. Basically it acts as a shield for the flying honey and as a foundation to mount the other parts. The liquid honey will run down the side of this "tank" and should flow out of a hole near the bottom and into a waiting bucket.

Domico's extractor is a four-frame model. The baskets which hold the honeycomb frames are attached to a rotating shaft. The shaft's lower bearing is simply a hardwood block with a hole the same diameter of the shaft drilled partway through. This wooden block is nailed into the bottom-center of the barrel. The shaft rests in this socket.

The drill is mounted on a 2 x 4 crosspiece. The shaft passes up through a hole bored in this crosspiece and is coupled securely to the chuck on the drill.

A hinged cover will protect the room from flying droplets of honey. After the machine is loaded with honeycombs, care must be made not to start the extractor spinning too quickly. A slow increase in speed will result in fewer, if any, broken combs.

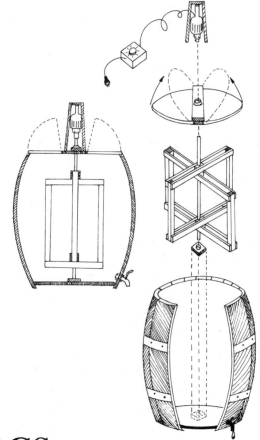

DOGS

As often as not, the homestead hound is an outside dog. And any outside dog needs shelter from the wind, rain, and snow, and from the blistering sun. Hence, the doghouse.

While the doghouse should be sturdily constructed, it should not be insulated except in the coldest climates. The insulation will promote condensation inside the house from the dog's body heat. The condensation could give the dog a thorough chill.

The size of the doghouse should be closely related to the size of the dog. It should be only slightly larger than the dog, making it something like a den or cave. In cold weather, an ample supply of bedding will allow the dog to satisfy its instinct to burrow in and curl up.

Always face the house south, and move it periodically to allow vegetation to regrow and to control parasites.

ROVER'S PALACE

For the homestead with a big dog to house, Rover's Palace is just the ticket. Designed and constructed by Jim Schneck of Allentown, Pennsylvania, for his big dog, the house is very sturdy and weathertight.

Schneck chose to construct the house like a miniature house, using what amounts to stud frame construction. The floor is supported by joists, the walls by studs, the roof by trusses. Changing the dimensions to tailor the house to suit a different sized dog would be no problem.

CONSTRUCTION

1. The floor platform is framed of 2 x 3s. Use two 42-inch lengths for header joists and three 27-inch lengths for joists. Use 12d box nails to assemble the frame. Cut a 30-inch by 42-inch piece of ½-inch exterior plywood for the floor and nail it to the frame with 7d box nails.

2. The two sidewalls are framed with six 19-inch 2 x 3 studs and four 42-inch 2 x 3 plates. Use two plates and three studs to frame each wall, fastening the pieces together with 12d box nails. Cut two 25½-inch by 42-inch pieces of ½-inch exterior plywood to sheath the sides. The sheathing should be nailed to the wall frames, using 7d nails, so that the sheathing is flush with the top edge of the top plate and overhang the bottom plate by 3½ inches.

3. The roof is supported by three trusses, assembled from 2 x 3s and plywood gussets. The outer trusses are assembled using two 18¼-inch 2 x 3s, a 30-inch 2 x 3, and a triangle of the ½-inch exterior plywood measuring 21 inches on two sides and 30 inches on the third side (make the necessary two triangles by cutting a 21-inch square of the plywood in half on the diagonal). The ends of the 2 x 3s should be mitered, as shown, on 45-degree angles. Lay out the 2 x 3s and nail the plywood to them with 7d box nails. The center truss is formed of two 21¾-inch 2 x 3s, mitered on the ends and secured with a triangular gusset cut from plywood scrap and 7d box nails.

4. Using the 12d nails, fasten the sides to the floor platform, then nail the roof trusses in place. Cut a 25½-inch by 31-inch piece of plywood for the back and nail it in place. Cut two 25½-inch by 9-inch pieces of plywood and nail them to the front, forming a doorway. The roof sheathing is two 24-inch by 48-inch pieces of plywood.

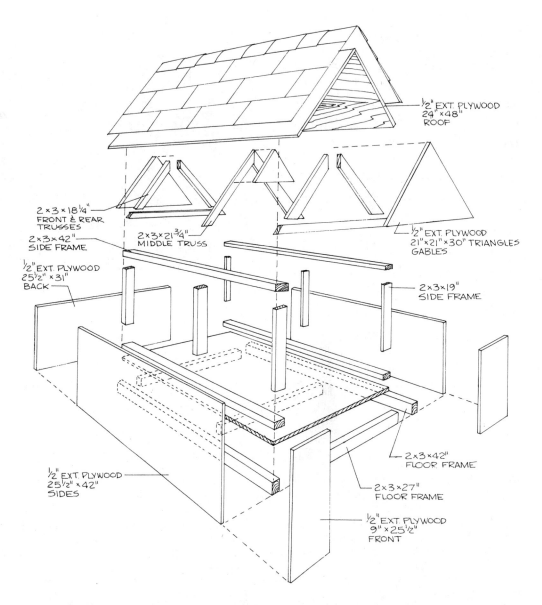

½" EXT. PLYWOOD
24"×48"
ROOF

2×3×18¼"
FRONT & REAR
TRUSSES

2×3×42"
SIDE FRAME

½" EXT. PLYWOOD
25½"×31"
BACK

2×3×21¾"
MIDDLE TRUSS

½" EXT. PLYWOOD
21"×21"×30" TRIANGLES
GABLES

2×3×19"
SIDE FRAME

½" EXT. PLYWOOD
25½"×42"
SIDES

2×3×42"
FLOOR FRAME

2×3×27"
FLOOR FRAME

½" EXT. PLYWOOD
9"×25½"
FRONT

5. The house is now ready for shingles. (Roll roofing could also be used.) The shingles are laid from the bottom edge of the roof to the peak, with a ridge cap of shingle pieces.

    a. Begin by inverting one course of shingles, so the slits are toward the peak, and nailed to the roof sheathing using $\frac{7}{16}$-inch roofing nails. Cut off any excess with a sharp knife and a straightedge.

b. Place a second course of shingles, correctly oriented—the slits away from the peak—directly over the first course and projecting beyond the sheathing just slightly.

c. Third and successive courses are placed, alternating the location of the shingles so that no slit is in line with one in a previous course of shingles.

d. After both slopes are shingled, cut about eight shingles into thirds by cutting them at the slits, and attaching them along the ridge. These are placed at 90 degrees to the others, centered on the ridgeline and bent down over both slopes. The second short shingle laps over the first, covering the nails; the third laps over the fourth and so on, until the ridge is sealed.

6. A finishing touch, after painting, is the installation of a door drape, made of a piece of towel or an old throw rug. Wrap a portion of the drape over a length of furring and nail in place.

MATERIALS

Wood

8 pcs. 2 x 3 x 8'   or   **Floor frame:** 2 pcs. 2 x 3 x 42"
3 pcs. 2 x 3 x 27"

Side frames: 6 pcs. 2 x 3 x 19"
4 pcs. 2 x 3 x 42"

Front and rear trusses: 4 pcs. 2 x 3 x 18$\frac{1}{4}$"
2 pcs. 2 x 3 x 30"

Middle truss: 2 pcs. 2 x 3 x 21$\frac{3}{4}$"

2 shts. $\frac{1}{2}$" ext. plywood   or   **Floor:** 1 pc. 30" x 42"

Sides: 2 pcs. 25$\frac{1}{2}$" x 42"

Gables: 2 pcs. 21" x 21" x 30" triangles

Back: 1 pc. 25$\frac{1}{2}$" x 31"

Front: 2 pcs. 25$\frac{1}{2}$" x 9"

Roof: 2 pcs. 24" x 48"

Hardware

12d box nails
7d box nails
1 bdl. #240 shingles
$\frac{7}{16}$" galvanized roofing nails

DOGHOUSE WITH A REMOVABLE ROOF

This doghouse is constructed largely of plywood. Its most interesting feature, perhaps, is that the roof removes completely for full access to the inside of the house. The house was designed and constructed by Robert Branch of Waterbury, Connecticut.

MATERIALS

Wood

1 sht. $\frac{5}{8}$" ext. plywood or

Sides: 2 pcs. 16" x 26$\frac{3}{4}$"

Front and back: 2 pcs. 16" x 25$\frac{1}{2}$"

Bottom: 1 pc. 26$\frac{3}{4}$" x 23$\frac{3}{4}$"

Trusses: 2 pcs. 25$\frac{1}{2}$" x 7$\frac{5}{16}$"

Braces: 2 pcs. 3" x 23$\frac{3}{4}$"

Roof: 2 pcs. 17" x 34"

Fascia: 2 pcs. 3" x 17"

Hardware

Glue
4d nails
1 bdl. shingles
$\frac{3}{4}$" roofing nails

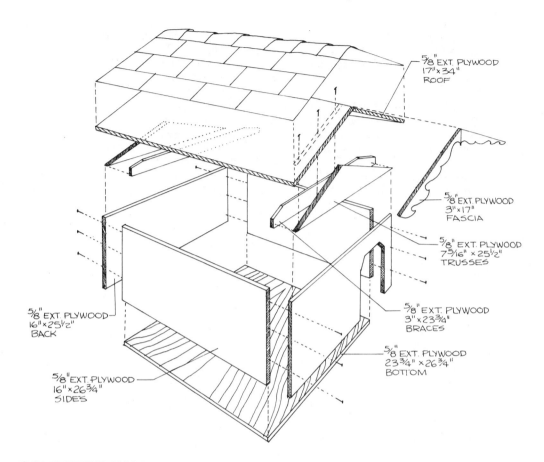

5/8" EXT. PLYWOOD
17" x 34"
ROOF

5/8" EXT. PLYWOOD
3" x 17"
FASCIA

5/8" EXT. PLYWOOD
7 5/16" x 25 1/2"
TRUSSES

5/8" EXT. PLYWOOD
16" x 25 1/2"
BACK

5/8" EXT. PLYWOOD
3" x 23 3/4"
BRACES

5/8" EXT. PLYWOOD
23 3/4" x 26 3/4"
BOTTOM

5/8" EXT. PLYWOOD
16" x 26 3/4"
SIDES

CONSTRUCTION

1. From $\frac{5}{8}$-inch exterior plywood, cut two 16-inch by 26$\frac{3}{4}$-inch side panels, a 16-inch by 25$\frac{1}{2}$-inch front and a like-sized back, and a 26$\frac{3}{4}$-inch by 23$\frac{3}{4}$-inch bottom. In the front panel, cut a door hole. The door hole should be as small as possible, and it should be located off-center, as in the illustration. Using glue and 4d nails, fasten the front and back to the sides. Then drop the bottom into place and drive nails through the sides and front and back into the bottom.

2. The roof trusses are cut from two 25$\frac{1}{2}$-inch by 7$\frac{5}{16}$-inch pieces of the plywood. Tack the two pieces together, then mark them for cutting and cut both at the same time. Locate the peak of the truss or gable, which is the center of the top edge. Scribe a line from that point to each of the bottom corners, and cut along the line.

3. Cut two 3-inch by 23$\frac{3}{4}$-inch strips of plywood and fasten one to the inside of each roof truss, so that it projects an inch below the bottom edge of the truss. Cut off the corners of this brace that project beyond the slope of the truss.

787

4. Cut two 17-inch by 34-inch roof panels from the plywood. Nail them to the trusses so that they meet at the peak, are flush with the back truss, and project about 5½ inches beyond the face of the front truss. The trusses should be 26¾ inches apart (inside face to inside face) so that the roof assembly will set squarely upon the house sides. The braces attached to the trusses will position the assembly.

5. The fancy scrollwork fascia boards aren't necessary, but they are interesting. Cut two 3-inch by 17-inch pieces of the plywood, clamp them together, then mark and cut the scallop design into both at the same time. Make plumb cuts on the ends that will join at the roof peak, then glue and nail in place.

6. Apply shingles using ¾-inch roofing nails.

7. To finish the doghouse, use an exterior paint.

CROP STORAGE

Some means of storing field crops is a necessity on any working homestead. Hay will naturally be stored in the shed or barn that houses the livestock. But feed corn, wheat, oats, and other grains require special structures; corncribs, grain sheds, and feed bins to hold sacks of grain.

CORNCRIBS

The corncribs described here have in common two features: they allow for air ventilation by being no more than 4 feet in width, and while they may permit some windblown rain to get to the corn, they allow the water to drain away. This drainage is assured by having the walls slope outward.

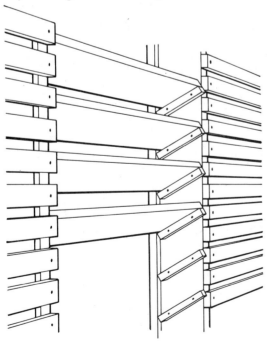

In planning your corncrib, figure a cubic foot of storage space will hold about four-fifths of a bushel. How much corn you store depends on how many animals you have to feed or what your fields have produced. Gene Logsdon says he uses fifteen bushels to fatten a hog; twenty-five bushels to feed five ewes and their lambs; and twenty-five bushels to feed thirty chickens for a year.

A construction trick that will serve for several types of corncribs is a kind of door that allows you to remove the amount you need without an avalanche of corn pouring out.

After you have framed your door, nail 3½-inch-long 1 x 1 strips to the inside of both vertical frames. These will look like shelf supports, but don't set them horizontally level. Instead, pitch them about 30 degrees downward toward the inside of the crib, as shown. The strips should be matched in pairs on either sides of the doorframe, because they will hold the boards that will control your corn or grain.

Nail a vertical 1-inch strip along the inside ends of your slanted strips to keep your door boards from sliding through. Cut 1 x 4 boards to fit across the door and slide them into place.

When the crib is full, your shelf-door will work in this way: Just start at the top and pull out one, two, or as many shelves as you must to get the corn you need.

SAPLING CORNCRIB

The homesteader who has a supply of saplings can build a serviceable corncrib without any major money investments. Saplings 2 or 3 inches in diameter simply are stacked in log cabin fashion to make a corncrib which will measure about 4 feet by 8 feet, standing about 6 feet tall.

Obviously, because saplings are not saw-milled timber, they have crooks

and bumps in them, and the spaces between them may be somewhat irregular. A cob of corn may fall out now and then, but the spaces are not a problem as far as keeping the corn goes, because stored corn requires free air circulation. Likewise, the outer layer of corn will not be damaged by the rain.

One problem you may want to correct for in the basic design is for protection against birds, squirrels, and other animals, including rats. Whether rats are a problem depends partly on your location. If the area around the crib is free of convenient and secure burrowing places you may have no problems. (Keep a barnyard cat or two: they will police any rats.) Birds and squirrels still may dine at the crib. You can probably live with losing an ear or two a day to your animal neighbors. If, however, you'd rather not lose the corn, line the interior of the crib with hardware cloth or a fine wire mesh.

This corncrib will hold between seventy-five and one hundred bushels of corn, depending on what your specific dimensions are. Since it has no doors, you can fill it by shoveling the corn in from the top. If you have no truck or other platform from which to shovel, you may want to leave off the roof and the last few layers of saplings, and fill as you go. To empty, you can shovel from the top, taking down the walls as you go. You can also shovel from the bottom by cutting through the first two logs on one end and slide them out. You will have to replace the saplings you cut with others or use a board to keep the corn from tumbling out.

CONSTRUCTION

1. Start building your corncrib by staking out the four corners, where posts will be sunk. Since you will be using a sheet of plywood for a floor, locate the posts at the corners of a 4-foot by 8-foot rectangle. Position the crib so a narrow end faces the prevailing winds. The posts should be about 5 inches square, and about 9 feet long, sunk about 2 feet deep. You should treat these posts with preservative. (Check the chapter on fences for details, as well as information on how to plant the posts.)

2. Plant the four posts, but don't finish tamping them down. Place six cement blocks, one at each corner and two in the middle, to support your floor. The floor is a $\frac{5}{8}$-inch sheet of exterior plywood.

3. Putting the floor into place will give your posts the necessary outward slant. Using 10d nails, fasten lengths of 2 x 4 ($4\frac{1}{2}$-foot pieces for the ends, 9-foot pieces for the sides) to the tops of the saplings. Fit the shorter right under the longer ones.

4. Start laying in the saplings, layer by layer, just as you would build a log cabin. You may as well not bother to trim the lengths of the saplings at this point. They will have to be continually longer as you build up, because of the outward slanting walls. When you finish, you can trim off all the ends evenly with a chain saw. Ideally, the space between the saplings should be about 2 inches. You can notch off-size or crooked saplings where they overlap to narrow the spaces, if necessary. Also, as you build the sides, alternate top and bottom ends of the saplings on each side so the layers stack evenly.

5. For the roof, you can nail tin, corrugated metal, or wood to the 2 x 4 frame. The roof is not a critical point of construction. Old-timers often simply laid a layer of corn stalks on top to channel away the worst of a downpour.

791

TRADITIONAL CORNCRIB

This is the traditional wood frame corncrib, narrow at the bottom and wider at the top, the kind you see in rural areas wherever corn has been a basic feed crop. The boards are spaced fairly wide apart and the walls are lined with hardware cloth or wire mesh to allow good air circulation and to keep rodents out.

Pick a high, level spot for your corncrib. Again, position it so the narrow end faces the prevailing winds.

CONSTRUCTION

1. Start construction by pouring a concrete pad 3 feet by 8 feet by 5 inches deep. (See masonry chapter for details.) Before the concrete has set, place four 8-inch by $\frac{1}{2}$-inch bolts evenly spaced along each 8-foot side, 2 inches in from the edges. Don't put them where a post or brace will conflict with them. Leave $4\frac{1}{2}$ inches of each bolt protruding. Allow the concrete to cure.

2. Assemble the side frames as shown before you bolt them into the concrete pad. Use 4 x 4 stock for the frame. For each side you will need two horizontal pieces 8 feet long for the top and bottom, and three pieces 6 feet long for the end and center supports. Toenail the corners and center support with 20d nails. Use 12-inch pieces of 2 x 4, mitered at a 45-degree angle at each end, for braces, two at the top of the center upright, and one in each bottom corner. At the center of each post, on the outside, cut a $\frac{3}{4}$-inch-deep by $7\frac{1}{2}$-inch-wide dado. Cut a similar dado in the back side of the rear post. Lay an 8-foot 1 x 8 running from post to post in the dadoes and nail it in place with 8d nails. This board will be a nailing strip for the hardware cloth.

3. Drill $\frac{1}{2}$-inch holes through the bottom piece for the anchor bolts. Place the frame on the anchor bolts, add washers on top, and snug down the nuts, but don't tighten them. Set up a temporary brace to support the frame until the whole works is securely nailed together and the sill bolts are given their final tightening. Use a scrap length of wood, like a 5-foot furring strip. Drive a single nail through one end into the 4 x 4 end post, leaving the head protruding so you can easily remove the nail when you don't need the brace anymore. Nail the other end to a foot-long stake, which you drive into the ground. To align the frame, pull the brace nail out of the 4 x 4, jockey the frame into position, then

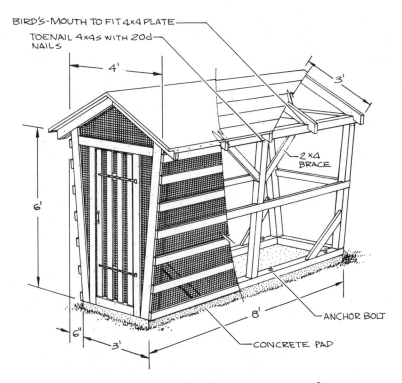

BIRD'S-MOUTH TO FIT 4x4 PLATE

TOENAIL 4x4s WITH 20d NAILS

4'

3'

2x4 BRACE

6'

ANCHOR BOLT

8'

6"

3'

CONCRETE PAD

drive the nail back into the post. The frame is in proper alignment when it is 6 inches out of plumb. Attach a plumb line to the top of the post. When it hangs 6 inches away from the bottom of the post, the post is properly aligned; nail that brace in place. To avoid frame flex, check the plumb—and brace the frame—at both the front and rear posts.

4. Measure the distance between the two frame assemblies at the sills and the plates. Then cut 4 x 4 pieces to fit at these locations. For the best fit, you'll want to cut these pieces on the proper angle. To do this, hold a board so it runs from post to post, making sure it is level. With a pencil, scribe a line on the board using the post as a guide. Using a sliding T bevel, transfer the angle to the several 4 x 4s you must cut. Toenail the 4 x 4 pieces in place with 20d nails. The crib should be self-supporting by this time, and the temporary braces may be removed.

5. At the rear of the crib, cut a 1 x 8 to bridge from post to post midway between the sill and plate. Nail it in place in the dadoes with 8d nails.

6. At the door end, measure the vertical distance from the 4 x 4 sill to the 4 x 4 plate, and cut two 4 x 4s to fit on a vertical plumb. These will form the doorframe. Toenail them in place with 20d nails.

7. Lay out the rafters. Start with a 40-inch length of 2 x 4 for each rafter, there being ten in all. The pitch is 9/12, meaning the roofline rises 9 inches for each 12 inches of run. Using the framing square as

explained in "Building From the Ground Up," lay out the rafters, marking each for the bird's-mouth and plumb cuts. You want 6 inches of overhang. After the rafters are cut, nail pairs of them together and toenail them in place atop the plates, locating them on 2-foot centers.

8. To fill the crib, you will want a rooftop door. Cut four $20\frac{1}{2}$-inch lengths of 1 x 8. Assemble a frame for the door, by butting ends against sides and nailing with 6d nails. Slip the frame between the rafters just rear of the center of the crib and nail in place, locating the frame so it projects 4 inches above the rafters. Construct a lid for the door using 1 x 4: cut five $20\frac{3}{4}$-inch lengths and two $22\frac{1}{4}$-inch lengths. Butt two of the longer pieces against the two short pieces, making a frame. Evenly space the other three pieces inside the frame, as a top, and nail in place. Cover the lid frame with the roofing material.

9. Install the roofing, in accordance with the directions given in "Building From the Ground Up." Remember to lap the roofing up the sides of the rooftop doorframe.

10. Staple $\frac{1}{2}$-inch hardware cloth (or its equivalent) to the crib, covering any and all openings except the doorway. The point is to prevent vermin from getting into the crib. Hardware cloth is available in a 3-foot width, so you will need two 8-foot lengths for each side (one for the space between the sill and the nailer, one for the space between the nailer and the plate) and a $3\frac{1}{2}$-foot and a 4-foot length for the back

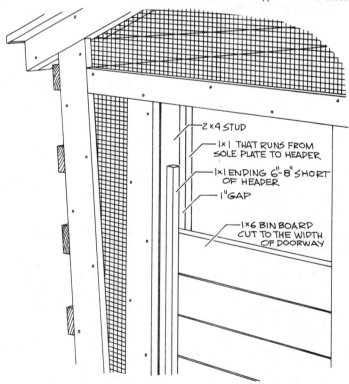

2 x 4 STUD

1 x 1 THAT RUNS FROM SOLE PLATE TO HEADER

1 x 1 ENDING 6"-8" SHORT OF HEADER

1" GAP

1 x 6 BIN BOARD CUT TO THE WIDTH OF DOORWAY

end. You will also need odd-sized pieces for the space between the plates and the rafters both front and rear and for the spaces between the posts and the doorframe.

11. Cut fourteen 8-foot lengths of 1 x 4 and nail them to the sides of the crib, as shown, using 8d nails. Cover the sills, the plates, and the nailer to cover the joints between the hardware cloth and the crib, then space the remaining boards over the sides of the crib. Cut 1 x 4s to fit corresponding spots on the back of the crib, and nail them in place. Lastly, cut 1 x 4s to cover the sill, plate, posts, doorposts and gable end-rafters on the front of the crib and nail them in place.

12. Measure the dimensions of the doorway and construct a door to fit. Cut four 1 x 4s the length of the doorway, and two 1 x 4s and two 1 x 2s the width of the doorway. Tack the 1 x 2s to the tall 1 x 4s, evenly spacing the 1 x 4s the width of the door. Turn the assembly over and staple hardware cloth to the 1 x 4s. Then nail the shorter 1 x 4s over top of the hardware cloth, about 6 to 8 inches in from the ends. Remove the 1 x 2s from the front of the door and nail them to the inner side flush with the top and bottom. Measure for a diagonal brace between the horizontal 1 x 4s, cut it from a 1 x 4, and nail in place. Finally, attach the hardware—hinges, door pull, and latch—to the door and hang the door.

13. To prevent the corn from flooding out when the door is opened, install bin boards in the doorway. Nail a 1 x 1 to both sides of the doorframe, extending the full height of the doorway. Leaving an inch gap, nail a second 1 x 1 to the doorframe, but have this one end about 6 inches short of the header. Slip bin boards—board lumber cut the width of the doorway—into these tracks at the top and slide them down, closing up the doorway board by board. As you empty the crib, you remove the boards.

14. Paint the corncrib.

VARIATIONS

This size crib is nice for the homestead. But if more capacity is needed, the crib can be made longer, witness the length of corncribs on larger farms.

There are a lot of things that can be done differently in constructing a corncrib. It can be constructed on posts and have a wooden floor. If you choose this approach, nail a metal cap that extends down the sides of the posts to prevent rodents from scaling the posts and gaining access to the crib (they won't have footing on the metal), position the side slats closer together, and eliminate the hardware cloth liner.

You can build a shed-type roof, which is easier to construct than the gable type. Use a door like that described earlier in this chapter. Or redesign to take advantage of materials you have at hand.

SELF-EMPTYING CORNCRIB

Most corncribs—no matter what kind of handy access doors you have made for them—require lots of shoveling and the eventual crawl inside as you near the end of your stores. Robert Frey of Upper Sandusky, Ohio, designed his own unique solution to all that work: an almost self-emptying corncrib.

The key is a floor constructed to slant toward the emptying doors. Gravity does the rest.

Frey's corncrib is practically rodent proof, owing to the tin plates on the bottom and siding where the crib is supported by posts.

The crib measures 4 feet wide by 10 feet 2 inches long. It is 6 feet high on the low, or emptying side, and 7½ feet, ground to roof, on the high side. If you follow Frey's example, you can vary the dimensions to suit yourself, but remember that experienced farmers don't like to build cribs that are much wider than 4 feet, to assure that air circulates through the corn to prevent spoilage.

CONSTRUCTION

1. You will need eight posts, about 8 inches square. They should be planted 2 feet into the ground. The four on the low side should extend 1½ feet above the ground, and those on the high side should extend 3 feet. (See the chapter on fences for instructions on how to treat your posts with preservative and how to plant them in post holes.) The posts should be set 2½ feet apart along the 10-foot 2-inch length, and the two rows should be 4 feet apart.

2. Nail a piece of tin, at least 12 inches square, flat on the top of each post. You can use short roofing nails, and you will wrap and fasten the tin to the sides after the siding is in place.

3. Construct the framing for the two long walls. The sill should be a 2 x 8, 10 feet 2 inches long. Cut six 51-inch-long 2 x 4 studs for each wall, and a 10-foot-2-inch-long 2 x 4 sole plate. Drive 16d nails through the sill and plate into the studs, which are located on 2-foot centers. On the frame for the low side wall, install two headers for the unloading doors. The header need be nothing more than a 22-inch length of 2 x 4 nailed between the studs parallel to and 22½ inches above the bottom edge of the sill.

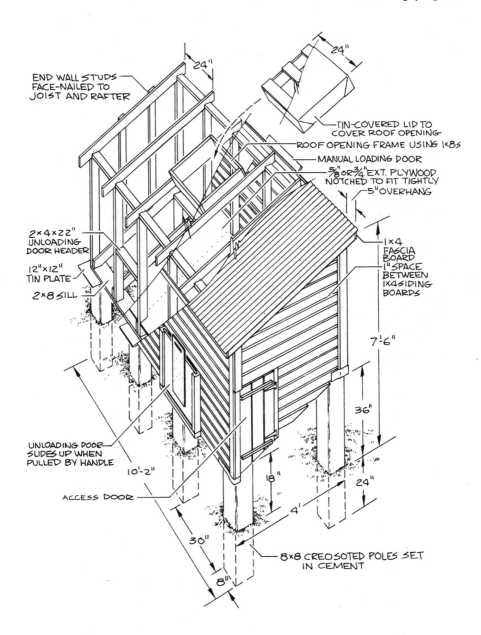

END WALL STUDS
FACE-NAILED TO
JOIST AND RAFTER

24"

24"

TIN-COVERED LID TO
COVER ROOF OPENING

ROOF OPENING FRAME USING 1×8s

MANUAL LOADING DOOR

⅝" OR ¾" EXT. PLYWOOD
NOTCHED TO FIT TIGHTLY

5" OVERHANG

2×4×22"
UNLOADING
DOOR HEADER

12"×12"
TIN PLATE

2×8 SILL

1×4
FASCIA
BOARD

1" SPACE
BETWEEN
1×4 SIDING
BOARDS

7'6"

36"

UNLOADING DOOR
SLIDES UP WHEN
PULLED BY HANDLE

18"

24"

ACCESS DOOR

10'2"

4'

30"

8"

8×8 CREOSOTED POLES SET
IN CEMENT

4. Erect the wall frames, making sure they are plumb and securing them
    in place with temporary braces. Cut six 54-inch lengths of 2 x 6 for
    joists. You want the joists to seat securely on the sills, so you will have
    to notch the high end and cut the corner off the low end, as well as
    cut the butt ends so that they are plumb. Consequently, lay out the
    joists as rafters (see "Building From the Ground Up"). The pitch of

the joists is $4\frac{1}{2}/12$. Use the first joist as a pattern for cutting the remaining five. Then nail the joists in place. The joists at each end are positioned *inside* the corner studs. Toenail the joists to the sill and face-nail them to the studs.

5. Use a 4 x 10 sheet of $\frac{5}{8}$-inch or $\frac{3}{4}$-inch exterior plywood for the floor. You will have to notch it to fit tightly around the studs. Mark the dimensions and locations of the studs on the edges of the plywood, cut them out, and install the floor.

6. Cut six 60-inch rafters from 2 x 4. Cut two bird's-mouths so the rafter will seat firmly on the plate, and cut the ends so they will be plumb. Nail them in place, directly above the studs except the outer rafters, which should be directly above the joists.

7. Cut four 54-inch 2 x 4 studs for the front and back walls and face-nail them to the end joists and rafters. To prevent the studs from blocking the flow of ear corn to the doors, be sure to position these studs broadside against joist and rafter. These studs will be on 16-inch centers. Nail a header for the access door in place, about 36 inches above the sill on the low side. The door doesn't need to be very large, since it will undoubtedly be little used.

8. Make provision for a loading door. It can either be on the roof at the high side or in the high-side wall. The door in the wall is easier to load through if you will be doing the work by hand.

    a. For a rooftop door: cut four $22\frac{1}{2}$-inch lengths of 1 x 8. Assemble a frame for the door between the rafters in the middle of the roof, as shown, positioning it between the rafters so it is flush with the bottoms of the rafters and projects 4 inches above them. Construct a lid for this roof hole from 1 x 4: cut five $24\frac{1}{4}$-inch lengths and two $24\frac{1}{4}$-inch lengths, assembling them as shown. The lid will be covered with the same material used to cover the roof.

    b. For a door in the wall: rough sill between the studs in the center of the high-side wall, $22\frac{1}{2}$ inches below the top of the plate. After the siding is installed, make a door by nailing five 2-foot lengths of 1 x 4 to two $20\frac{1}{2}$-inch-long 1 x 4 battens. Attach the door to the crib with two hinges at the rough sill. Two knobs on nails at the studs will keep this door closed.

9. Cut the siding from 1 x 4 and nail it in place. Begin on the sides, installing the siding boards so they are flush with the bottom of the sill and the top of the plate, and are spaced 1 inch apart. You will need twelve boards for each side. You will need to leave open the spaces allocated for doors. After the sides are closed in, cut and fasten the siding to the front and back ends. Cut 1 x 4 board to cover, as shown, the corners where the siding boards meet and nail them in place. Finally, wrap the metal rodent guards up around the siding and nail it in place.

10. Make up and install the doors. If you have opted for a loading door in the wall, attach it as previously explained.

    a. The access door is made up of any combination of 1-inch stock, such as three lengths of 1 x 6, nailed to two or three cleats, as shown. Measure and cut the door to fit, attaching it with strap or butt hinges and wood screws. Keep it closed with a hasp or a simple block-of-wood-on-a-nail closure.

b. The unloading doors should be made of ⅝-inch exterior plywood panels. Cut two 22-inch-square doors and two 24-inch by 8-inch pull panels from the plywood. Cut out a 5-inch by 2-inch hole in one end of each pull panel as shown to make a grip: drill a hole in each inside corner of the grip hole and cut it out with a keyhole saw or saber saw. Nail the pull panel to the door panel with the grip jutting above the door. Drive 8d nails through the panels and clinch on the inside of the door. Nail 24-inch 2 x 2 to the sill at the door opening to serve as a bottom stop for the sliding door. Make tracks for the door by cutting a ¾-inch-deep by 1-inch-wide rabbet the length of a 2 x 3 and securely nailing 22-inch lengths of it to the studs on either side of the door, spacing the inner faces of the rabbet 22½ inches apart, and butting the ends of the tracks against the bottom stop. Use 10d nails. (You can make up tracks from 22-inch lengths of 1 x 1 and 1 x 2, or 1 x 2 and 1 x 3, nailing them together so you have what in effect is a rabbet along one edge.) Slide the door into place. You will need four tracks to mount the two doors.

11. Install the roof. Cut two 11-foot fascia from 1 x 4 boards and nail them across the ends of the rafters, leaving an equal amount extending beyond the two end rafters. Measure the distance from fascia board to fascia board at the front and back of the crib, cut 1 x 4 boards to fit, and nail them in place. (You can cut 2 x 4 blocks to fit between the end rafters and fascia to brace it.) If you are using metal roofing, cut four 1 x 4 boards and nail them, evenly spaced, to the rafters to serve as nailers. Nail the roofing to the nailers. If you will be using shingles or roll roofing, sheath the rafters with plywood or tongue-and-groove roofers instead of nails, then install the roofing. In either case, if you've opted for the rooftop loading door, run the roofing material up the sides of the doorframe and install roofing on the door lid.

GRAIN STORAGE CRIB

This grain storage building is built to be rodent and bird proof, not to win any beautiful farm contests. Its corrugated metal or tin sides resist moisture penetration and frustrate birds and rodents. Your construction must be tight: leave no holes for sparrows to get in. Since wheat runs through holes and cracks almost as readily as water does, your floor and sides should be as tightly made as you know how. The floors and walls should be tongue and groove or plywood.

The grain crib is covered tightly with metal sheathing, in the case of this crib, corrugated metal. Aluminum siding can be used. Some farmers contend that bird droppings will corrode the aluminum, resulting eventually in breaches in your grain's armor, but the manufacturers contend, on the other hand, that this problem has been solved.

Some air circulation is desirable, especially if the grain has not quite dried to 12 percent moisture as it should. This can be provided by installing wire mesh on vents cut in frieze boards under the roof.

The granary described here is 5 feet wide, 8 feet long, and 6 feet high on the high side, 4½ feet high on the low side.

CONSTRUCTION

1. Start your grain crib by setting 8-inch square posts (or the equivalent) about 1½ feet deep, or below the frost line whichever is greater. These should be 1½ feet above ground. Set one at each corner and space the other posts evenly, 2 or 3 feet apart. You will need twelve posts for this grain crib. Nail 12-inch square tin sheets to the top of each post, to be wrapped up the sides later for rodent protection.

2. Construction of floor joists and wall studs is the same as that described in "Building From the Ground Up." Cut the joists and joist headers from 2 x 6, making the headers 8 feet long and the joists (five of them) 57 inches long. Spike them together with 16d nails. Position the floor frame atop the posts and toenail in place. Then lay the flooring, using ¾-inch exterior plywood or tongue-and-groove boards. Frame the two long walls, using five 69-inch studs on 2-foot centers for the higher wall, five 51-inch studs for the shorter wall. Erect the two walls, set them in plumb, nail to the floor, and fix them in position with temporary braces.

3. Lay out the rafters. Start with a 6-foot 2 x 4 for each rafter (there are five). The pitch is 3/10, that is, the roofline rises 3 inches for every 10 inches of run. Using the framing square as explained in "Building From the Ground Up," lay out the rafters, marking for bird's-mouth and plumb cuts (you'll want about 6 inches of overhang on either side of the building). Nail the rafters in place.

4. It is best to install a rooftop door for the filling of the grain crib (you can

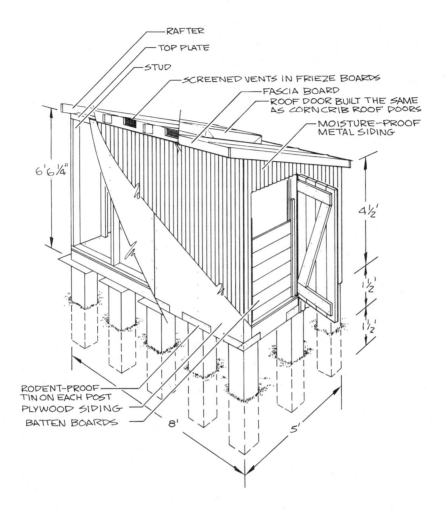

RAFTER
TOP PLATE
STUD
SCREENED VENTS IN FRIEZE BOARDS
FASCIA BOARD
ROOF DOOR BUILT THE SAME AS CORNCRIB ROOF DOORS
MOISTURE-PROOF METAL SIDING

6' 6 1/4"

4 1/2'

1/2'

1/2'

RODENT-PROOF TIN ON EACH POST
PLYWOOD SIDING
BATTEN BOARDS

8'

5'

get more grain in). Frame in such a door, as described in the construction directions for the traditional corncrib, using 1 x 8s. Frame a lid with 1 x 4s and cover it with the roof material you will use for the roof.

5. Frame the end walls, cutting sole plates and studs to fit, notching the stud ends to fit securely at the rafters. Cut three studs for the back wall, locating them on 15-inch centers. For the front wall, locate studs on 15-inch centers, but omit the stud closest to the tall corner stud, since it would interfere with the access door. Locate a header 4½ feet above the sole plate and run a cripple stud between the header and the rafter.

6. Install the sheathing, either ⅝-inch or ¾-inch exterior plywood or tongue-and-groove sheathing, to the outside of the grain crib. Fold the rodent shields up around the building above the posts and nail them in place.

7. Install your roofing.

8. Install the metal siding. DO NOT penetrate the sheathing with nails.

The nail will provide an access for moisture, which could lead to spoilage. In nailing up the metal siding, be very sure your nails are driven only into the studs. If using corrugated siding, as shown, be sure to start at the bottom, lapping upper panels over lower panels so the joints shed water. If you want a tight grain crib and are handy with tin snips, notch the top siding panels to fit around the rafters and allow the siding to fit tightly against the underside of the roofing. If you think it advisable to have a ventilated grain crib, cut frieze boards to fit between the rafters, roof, and top plate and cut holes, which you cover with screening or hardware cloth, in the boards before nailing them in place.

9. Fabricate a door and hang it. The most easily constructed door is assembled from board lumber fastened to two battens and a diagonal brace, as shown. Use 8d nails, and clinch them over the cleats and brace. Hang the door using two or three strap hinges, and secure it with a hasp or homemade closure. To keep the grain from flooding out when the access door is opened, you must install bin boards, as described in the construction directions for the traditional corncrib.

FEED BIN

If you have a few chickens, rabbits, goats, or other animals, you know about the hassle of storing sacks of feed. You don't want to visit the grain crib daily, but you don't want feed spilling in a corner of the barn or shed. This feed bin is designed to store those sacks of grain. It will give longest service if you keep it inside a barn or otherwise protect it from the weather. It is not intended for outside storage.

The bin was made from standard tongue-and-groove siding. The vagaries of milling the tongues and groove on the boards and the tightness with which individual carpenters will lay them up makes it difficult to provide exact numbers and widths of boards needed. Inevitably, you will have to rip several, but don't rip them until you are sure, by measurement, of the widths to which you must rip them.

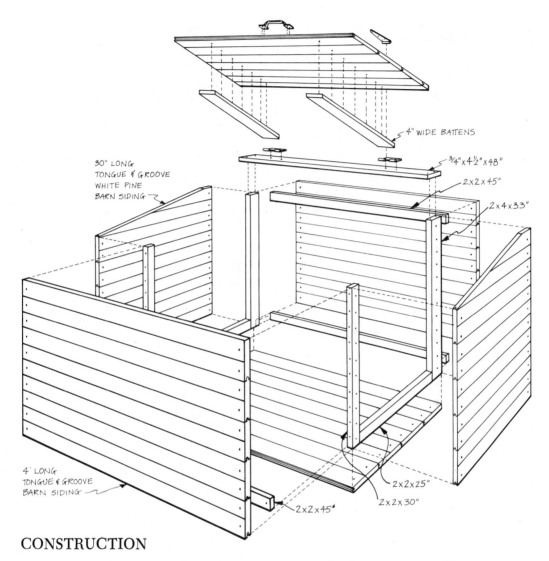

30" LONG
TONGUE & GROOVE
WHITE PINE
BARN SIDING

4" WIDE BATTENS

¾"x4½"x48"

2x2x45"

2x4x33"

4' LONG
TONGUE & GROOVE
BARN SIDING

2x2x45"

2x2x30"

2x2x25"

CONSTRUCTION

1. Start by cutting 2 x 2 stock: two pieces 25 inches long, two pieces 30 inches long, and three pieces 45 inches long. Cut two 33-inch lengths of 2 x 4. These are the nailers, or frame on the inside of the box.

2. Use tongue-and-groove white pine barn siding or comparable material (plywood, for example) for the sides, front, back, top, and bottom of the bin, using 6d nails to fasten the boards to the frame pieces. Assemble the sides first. Cut seven 30-inch lengths of the siding and nail them together, using a 33-inch 2 x 4 and a 30-inch 2 x 2 as nailers, as shown. Rip the groove from the board that will be the bottom of the side. Lay up the boards, nailing them to the frame. One of the 25-inch lengths of 2 x 2 is nailed inside the bottom edge of the side. Before nailing the

top board or two to the frame, set them in place and mark them for the angle that must be ripped. After cutting the boards, nail them in place. Construct the second side in the same fashion.

3. Next, nail 4-foot tongue-and-groove pieces to join the two sides and form the front. Nail one of the 45-inch 2 x 2 nailers at the bottom. Make the back in the same way, but put a second nailer at the top to support your lid hinges. Remember too that the back is taller than the front. Rip the grooves off the siding lengths that will be the bottom boards, and the tongue off the pieces that will be the top boards.

4. Turn the four-sided frame over and nail 4-foot lengths of tongue-and-groove boards on for the bottom. Turn it right-side up. Rip the tongue and groove off another 4-foot piece and nail it to the top of the back of the bin. This will anchor your hinges.

5. To make the lid, measure from the front edge of the box to the trimmed hinge anchor board you installed at the top of the back. This gives the total width for the lid. The two battens will be 1 inch shorter. Cut the battens from the tongue and groove, or any 1-inch stock. Nail the lid together, using nails that are long enough to clinch.

6. Fasten the lid with two **T** hinges. It's best to use stove bolts that go completely through the lid and battens. Finish the box by adding a handle or knob in front. Set your bin on blocks or a shipping pallet.

MATERIALS

Wood

1 pc. 2 x 2 x 10'	or	**Frame:** 2 pcs. 2 x 2 x 25"
1 pc. 2 x 2 x 12'		2 pcs. 2 x 2 x 30"
		3 pcs. 2 x 2 x 45"
1 pc. 2 x 4 x 8'	or	**Frame:** 2 pcs. 2 x 4 x 33"
19 pcs. 1 x 6 x 8' t & g siding	or	**Sides:** 14 pcs. 1 x 6 x 30"
		Front: 6 pcs. 1 x 6 x 48"
		Back: 7 pcs. 1 x 6 x 48"
		Bottom: 6 pcs. 1 x 6 x 48"
		Top: 1 pc. $\frac{3}{4}$" x $4\frac{1}{2}$" x 48"
		Lid: 7 pcs. 1 x 6 x 48"
		Battens: 2 pcs. $\frac{3}{4}$" x 4" x 30"

Hardware

6d nails
2 **T** hinges w/ stove bolts
1 door pull w/ screws

FEED SCOOP

To go with any small livestock operation, here's a feed scoop. It takes
the spills out of filling feeders and will
offer a rough measure of the amount
of feed scooped up.

TIN

WOOD

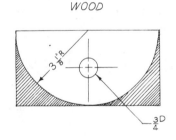

CONSTRUCTION

1. Plane the 1 x 4 to an actual width of 3 inches.
2. Drill a ¾-inch hole in the center of the board for the dowel-handle. If you want the handle to be at an angle, drill the hole at the desired angle.
3. Using a compass or other technique, mark off two corners at a 3⅛-inch radius from the center-point of the opposite side, as shown. Cut along the curved line with a coping saw.
4. Mark the tin, as shown, and cut. Punch four holes for screws. Then bend the tin into the scoop shape and attach to the wood with small screws.
5. Drive the handle into place and secure it by hammering a finishing nail through the edge of the scoop back into the dowel.

MATERIALS

Wood

      1 pc. 1 x 4 x 2'   or   **Back:** 1 pc. ¾" x 3" x 6¼" (act. meas.)

      1 pc. 36" x ¾" dowel   or   **Handle:** 1 pc. 6" x ¾" dowel

Hardware

      1 pc. 9¾" x 8" tin or sheet metal
      4 small screws
      1–4d finishing nail

HAY BALER

Hay is easier to handle and store if it has been baled. This homemade baler is easy to build from plywood and 2 x 4s. It's obviously no way to bale large amounts of hay. But if you enjoy occasional strenuous work, and you have a small amount of hay to be stored, this little baler makes pretty good sense.

You can tailor your baler to make any size bale. Stewart Coffin, who described this baler to OGF back in 1968, said he got 25-pound bales from a 16-inch-square by 34-inch-long box.

Here is how the baler works. Lay two lengths of twine, about 7 feet long, in the slots, fitting it down the sides and across the bottom of the baler. Let the ends hang through the slots, and fasten them to the cleats so they don't slip. Load the straw in, stamping it down as you go. When it's full, tie a regular sailor's bow in one end, which gives you a loop. Pass the other end of the twine through the loop, and pull the bale tight. Tie the end securely and lift the bale out of the frame.

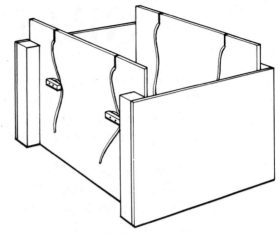

CONSTRUCTION

1. Cut four pieces of 2 x 4 to 16-inch lengths. From ½-inch exterior plywood, cut two 16-inch-square pieces, one 16-inch by 34-inch piece, and two 20-inch by 34-inch pieces.
2. Nail posts, sides, ends, and bottom together, with the posts on the outside, using 6d nails.
3. Cut two slots about 4 inches deep into the top of each side, measuring in about 8 inches from each end. Finish the baler by attaching a cleat a few inches below the bottom of each slot, four cleats in all. You can use hardware cleats or you can substitute 1-inch strips of wood.

MATERIALS

Wood

1 pc. 2 x 4 x 6′   or   **Frame posts:** 4 pcs. 2 x 4 x 16″

1 sht. ½″ ext. plywood   or   **Ends:** 2 pcs. 16″ sq.

Bottom: 1 pc. 16″ x 34″

Sides: 2 pcs. 20″ x 34″

Cleats: 4 pcs. 1″ x 4″

Hardware

6d nails

GREENHOUSES

Indoor gardening with greenhouses is now one of the largest hobbies in America. The inflationary economy and spiraling food prices have helped convince people that greenhouse gardening can be economical as well as enjoyable.

There are several advantages that all-year gardening greenhouses afford. Summer and fall crop yields can be stretched one season longer, often through the otherwise deadly winter season. Gardeners also use their greenhouses to gain a head start on springtime planting.

Another important plus to greenhouse gardening comes with the opportunity to control the growing environment. Frosts, blizzards, rainstorms, heat waves, and other weather nuisances can virtually be ignored behind the protection of greenhouse windows and walls.

Further, there is the therapeutic value of home gardening. Tending fresh fruits, vegetables, and ornamental flowers throughout the year is considered by many doctors to be a tranquilizer for daily stress and work tension.

Putting up a greenhouse is a bit expensive, but it really expands the realm of home gardening, from fresh vegetables all winter to a little extra income propagating house and vegetable plants. With energy costs so high, though, the expense of building one will be quickly overshadowed by the expense of keeping it warm in winter. And what do you want a greenhouse for but winter?

With cheap fuels following the path of the dinosaur, greenhouse design has to consider energy conservation every bit as much as maximizing sunlight. The plans here will give you some hints on how to put that compromise into action.

Greenhouses today fall into two general categories: *freestanding* (full-sized units separate from the house) or *attached* (units ad-

808

joining the house). The latter variety includes window box, basement, patio, or sun porch greenhouses.

Before selecting either the freestanding or attached variety, the greenhouse gardener must carefully assess his needs. Common considerations are construction costs, available yard space, durability, time limitations, and expected yield. Both types offer several advantages of their own in these respects.

For example, the gardener seeking to minimize expenses may find an attached greenhouse most suitable. Heating, maintenance, and construction costs are usually lower with this type of structure. The trade-off is that there is less growing space and no privacy from the adjoining house.

When space and finances allow, a freestanding greenhouse is recommended, since this type offers the most room for growing plants as well as work space for the gardener.

When durability is a major priority, certain construction materials are recommended over others, such as glass rather than polyethylene film. In making any decisions as to the type of greenhouse, construction materials, location and maintenance, the gardener must always keep his goals and plant-growing needs in mind.

Choosing the best greenhouse site is an important step requiring several considerations. Convenience, accessibility, yard space, and general land conditions are such variables to consider. Attached greenhouses enable the gardener to enter his greenhouse quickly and easily through adjoining, enclosed entrances. They best suit gardeners with little yard space but available sunlit basements, large windows and sills suitable for a small greenhouse "box," or enclosed porches. Freestanding greenhouses should be located in more spacious environments, and where they can be exposed to sunlight from all directions.

Exposure to sunlight is an important consideration. All greenhouses should be situated so that the maximum dosage of sunlight is utilized, especially in winter when it is most needed. A three-hour exposure of sunlight is considered the minimum daily requirement for most plants during winter.

The most basic step to take is to orient the clear face favorably to the sun. The largest wall *should* face due south. The face *should be* sloped at an angle perpendicular to the sun's rays at noon on the winter solstice, so the house will receive the most possible radiation at the time of year when the least is available. (And the most possible energy is deflected in the summer when there is a great surplus in a greenhouse.)

These are the ideals, and not every homeplace has a suitable site with a southern exposure. Thus it is comforting to know that contrary to popular belief, the precise direction in which a greenhouse faces is usually not the crucial consideration. If the ends face east and west, plants on the greenhouse's north side may get more shade, but this is not a shortcoming. Many plants thrive on shade. Some plants in attached greenhouses grow best in a southern, southeastern, or southwestern exposure, in that order. Western exposures provide ample sunlight but lack shade needed in the summer.

A more important consideration is the direction of prevailing winds. If you shield the greenhouse from biting winter winds, you'll cut down on the need for expensive heating. This is where the benefit of attached greenhouses show up. The fact that the greenhouse is attached to another building, preferably one that is heated, cuts down considerably on materials (the entire back wall) and provides excellent insulation at the same time. If it's the wall of the home, the greenhouse also benefits from the heat the wall radiates at night, capitalizing on what ordinarily is lost.

Construction itself is not unusually difficult. In a sense, constructing a greenhouse is less difficult than constructing a building, although the two projects are much akin. Any of the framing techniques explained in "Building From the Ground Up" will serve. The frame need not be as heavy for a greenhouse as for a barn, simply because the skin of a greenhouse isn't as heavy as the skin of a barn. However, because the skin of a greenhouse lacks the rigidity of plywood or board siding, the greenhouse frame must be well braced.

One framing method that seems particularly well suited to traditional greenhouse design, whether freestanding or attached, is the rigid arch. In brief, one need only assemble a series of half or full arches of 2 x 4 material, swing them into place, brace them, and attach the skin of your choice. More specific information on foundations and framing can be found in previous chapters, as noted.

GREENHOUSE COVERINGS

Obviously, the element that differentiates the greenhouse from the shed is its covering. There are several factors to be weighed in selecting the covering you will use, and compromises have to be made on a basis of priorities. Here are the factors you should weigh when making your decision.

1. Initial cost
2. Maintenance and replacement cost
3. Heat efficiency
4. Light transmission
5. Durability
6. Safety
7. Clarity
8. Beauty
9. Ease of installation
10. Structural flexibility

With these factors in mind, here's a look at what's available today for covering your greenhouse, hotbed, or cold frame.

POLYETHYLENE

This is the "cheapy" greenhouse covering material, but don't let the low price fool you. Many commercial growers are using one or two layers of polyethylene as the sole covering for their houses. Others use a single layer, either inside or outside the main glazing material, to help keep heat inside. A roll of 6-mil polyethylene 2 feet by 100 feet will cover a 14-foot by 14-foot freestanding greenhouse of conventional design twice. While most polyethylene only lasts a year, there are some special polyethylene films good for two years and maybe three, but the initial cost is about double.

Since polyethylene is replaced every season or two, there is obviously some extra work involved, but greenhouses properly designed for this covering are easy to re-cover. The major maintenance tool is a 2-inch-wide tape used to repair rips, but unless you're hosting the pitchfork throwers convention this year, you won't use much of it.

Heat efficiency is competitive with other popular coverings when all factors are considered. A single layer of polyethylene film loses considerable heat by radiation through the film. However, this heat loss is cut in half by a layer of condensation on the film which commonly occurs in greenhouses. The big heat retention advantage of polyethylene is that it comes in large, wide sheets. (Try to find it in wide rolls. The folded sheets usually available at building supply houses are weakened where they've been folded.) These large sheets mean a very "tight" house can be achieved with polyethylene. Other materials which lose less heat through radiation than polyethylene lose significant amounts of heat through tiny cracks where pieces of covering are joined.

Still, a single-layer polyethylene house is probably not very good from a heat conservation standpoint, and if you live in an area of cold winters, it would be best to adopt the double-layering system. This can be done in a number of ways and is simplest when a greenhouse is designed with it in mind. Almost any house, no matter what the covering materials, can be improved with a second layer of polyethylene. However, before you do this to an existing greenhouse, make sure the structure can stand the added snow load that will result when there isn't enough heat escaping through the roof to melt snow. If there is a significant problem, and the house can't be easily strengthened, use double layering on vertical walls and ends, but not the roof.

Depending on climate and the design of the individual greenhouse involved, a second layer of polyethylene can result in a heat saving of 25 to 40 percent. If you're burned up about heating prices, that's a big plus.

A system many growers are turning to employs a tight-fitting, 4-mil polyethylene sheet on the outside frame, covered by a second layer of 6-mil polyethylene put on looser. At night, or on cloudy days, a small fan is used to blow air between these two layers.

Light transmission is comparable with other materials. Studies at the University of Kentucky rated solar transmission of a single layer of polyethylene at 89 percent. Ironically, the

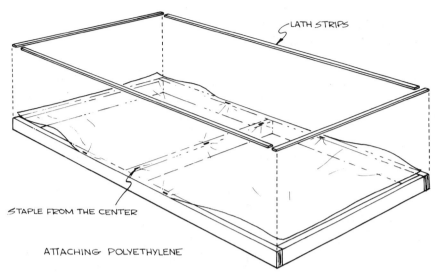

LATH STRIPS

STAPLE FROM THE CENTER

ATTACHING POLYETHYLENE

worst enemy of polyethylene is the one thing it can't be sheltered from—the sun. Ultraviolet radiation from the sun destroys the average film in a single season. Films specially protected from ultraviolet will last twice as long.

But don't get the idea that just because polyethylene sunburns easily it's the 97-pound weakling of the greenhouse set. It isn't. Researchers at the University of Kentucky say that strength of new 4-mil and 6-mil film is one to two times that of $\frac{1}{8}$-inch standard glass.

If the neighborhood baseball players and rock throwers worry you, polyethylene is a good choice. Being greeted some day while puttering in your greenhouse by a hard ball and a shower of glass splinters is a shattering experience. On the other hand, polyethylene burns rapidly and extra

precautions must be taken with heating systems and anything that might start a fire.

Although there are some clear films, most greenhouse polyethylene is clouded. This destroys that dream image (seldom achieved in practice with any covering) of a home greenhouse filled with beautiful flowering plants while snow piles up outside. While beauty may be in the eye of the beholder, many persons who behold a polyethylene-covered house feel it isn't beautiful. It has a makeshift look about it.

As with all greenhouse coverings, there is a wide variety of ways to install polyethylene. However, in general, it is probably the easiest of covering materials to install, and for structural flexibility, it's hard to beat. It can be bent to fit many odd-shaped houses and cuts easily with ordinary scissors to fit any shape you like. Small greenhouses using it need only be anchored against high winds. A foundation below frost isn't needed because heaving of the ground may twist the frame a little, but it won't break the covering. This may also lead to a tax bonus, for such greenhouses are not considered permanent structures by tax assessors in many communities. One commercial grower with more than a dozen large polyethylene houses saves enough on taxes to pay for recovering his houses every other year.

VINYLS

Various vinyl films are showing up more and more, especially on small, hobby greenhouses. Their cost is generally three or four times that of polyethylene, but this is in line with their longer life span. They require regular cleaning because they tend to be electrostatic and collect dust. The heat transmittance is far less than polyethylene, while light transmittance is slightly better. They have the same safety advantages and disadvantages of polyethylene, and if anything are stronger, since they usually come in 8- to 12-mil thicknesses. Life span is two to six years, depending on the individual product and local climate conditions. As with polyethylene, different manufacturers produce products with varying degrees of resistance to ultraviolet deterioration.

Since they are clear, vinyls offer advantages similar to glass in respect to beauty and ease of seeing in and out of the greenhouse. However, they are usually available in relatively narrow widths (5 to 7 feet), with wider pieces heat-seamed together by manufacturers.

Because it is a little heavier, you may find polyvinyl a bit more difficult to work with; the narrower widths mean a cover must be attached at more points on the structure. However, the clear vinyls allow you much the same flexibility in structure and design as polyethylene.

FIBERGLASS

The cost of fiberglass greenhouse coverings depends on the weight and quality you buy. It is competitive with glass. Look for panels made for greenhouse use. Cheaper panels may look the same as the expensive ones, but they'll deteriorate quickly with exposure to sun, and their light transmission will drop off.

Maintenance is a key to fiberglass.

It should be washed down with a hose at least once a year, and more often if you live in an area where there's a lot of dust or other particles in the air. Not only do such particles lower light transmission, but they speed up general deterioration of the panel caused by ultraviolet radiation. If panels start showing signs of dullness and exposed fiber after several years, they can be improved considerably by a thorough cleaning with fine steel wool and water. They are then coated with a clear refinisher supplied by the manufacturer.

Fiberglass is tops in terms of minimizing heat loss. Since it comes in rolls and wide panels (2 to 5 feet) and lengths of anywhere from 6 to 50 feet, there also are relatively few joints in a fiberglass house for heat to escape through, and it is easy to make these quite tight by using a sealant between overlapping panels. Light transmission of newer panels now on the market is said to be better than 90 percent.

The real question about fiberglass is its durability. Most manufacturers say you'll get ten to fifteen years from their acrylic modified panels. (The acrylic modification reduces the deteriorating effects of ultraviolet radiation, so look for panels which have between 10 and 15 percent acrylic content.)

The best panels are coated with a

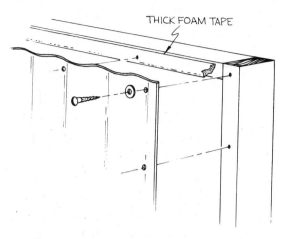

THICK FOAM TAPE

INSTALLING FIBERGLASS PANELS

product called Tedlar. These should last twenty years or more, and at least one manufacturer is guaranteeing them for twenty-five years. However, many manufacturers hedge their guarantees, especially when dealing with amateur growers; if the panels aren't properly cared for and periodically restored they don't last. The heavier-weight panels, 5 and 6 ounces per square foot, last longer. Fiberglass is two to four times more resistant to impact than glass. Ice and hail present no problems. Sometimes a panel will craze when something strikes it, but unless the surface cracks, this causes no problem, and the panel can still be used. One school superintendent said they put fiberglass in the school greenhouse after suffering severe damage from vandalism. So far it has resisted stones and even one brick.

Some folks like the frosted view,

diffused light, and color patterns of plants seen through fiberglass, but it certainly isn't clear, and many persons find this objectionable. As with the films, it will burn rapidly.

Corrugated panels are stronger and generally used on roofs. Flat sections are usually reserved for vertical walls. (Special corrugated strips give a tight fit along structural members.) Panels should be stored out of the sun and on edge, or else heat and moisture build up and cause damage.

Fiberglass is easy to work with.

ACRYLIC

Acrylic is great, if you can afford it. It is stronger than glass, has a comparable life span, can be bent in curved panels, is clear, and has good light transmission. But it costs appreciably more than glass and has been seldom used as a greenhouse covering for that reason. If you are making a small home greenhouse, particularly a window greenhouse, the extra cost may not be a problem. If you do use acrylic, don't nail or screw it down. It expands and contracts with temperature and should be held in a channel with soft sealer to allow movement.

GLASS

Cost is high, but certainly not out of line with its permanence. Double-strength tempered glass should be

The 4-ounce size can be cut with ordinary scissors, while the heavier stuff can be cut with tin snips or a saw. (Use a saber saw with an old, fine-toothed blade to cut corrugated panels.)

Fiberglass has many of the advantages of polyethylene, requiring less attention to structure and foundations than glass. Its diffused light eliminates shadow areas and "hot spots" sometimes found in glass greenhouses.

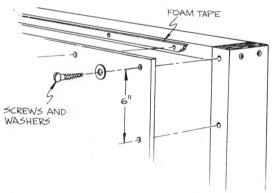

ATTACHING RIGID PLASTIC TO GREENHOUSE FRAME

Also, it is softer than glass, is easily scratched, and some cleaning solvents can damage it.

used in greenhouses, especially in roofs. While heat transmittance is not high, relatively small panes mean that there are plenty of places where a glass house can "leak" heat. This can be solved with a layer of polyethylene on the inside, although in some houses this is difficult to install. Light transmission is excellent, clarity is unchallenged, and most homeowners find glass greenhouses complement the architecture of their homes.

Maintenance problems are not severe, but glass should be washed and caulked between panes and checked annually for signs of deterioration. Glass demands more structural members. Small aluminum and glass greenhouses are frequently advertised as not needing permanent foundations, but such foundations are needed for larger units. The question of whether to use glass or not usually boils down to one of durability and looks. Many homeowners want a hassle-free greenhouse that doesn't need re-covering every year, or even every fifteen years. They feel more comfortable with glass, especially if the greenhouse is to be attached to their home.

Finally, don't overlook various combination possibilities which take advantage of the best qualities of each of the covering materials.

There's no reason why you can't mix materials to give you the best of all worlds. For example, a home hobby house may have a corrugated

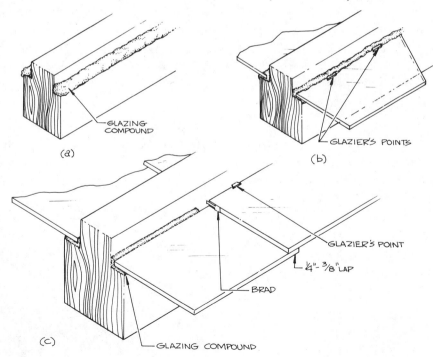

817

fiberglass roof for strength and good light diffusion, glass sides for beauty and clarity, and an inner shell of polyethylene put on for the harshest winter months when heating is at a maximum. It's your choice.

In the pages that follow are depicted a number of greenhouses. They range from the simple to the elaborate. Each represents one owner's solution to the problem of building the greenhouse that would best serve his needs, within his ability to finance and construct it. There are traditional designs, as well as more experimental ones. Read about them all. Then choose the design and construction that suits you best.

THE LOW-COST, PLASTIC-COVERED TRADITIONAL GREENHOUSE

The design that undoubtedly comes to the most minds at the mention of "greenhouse" is the long gable-roofed structure. Most commercial greenhouses are of this design, and while they used to be glassed in, the ones being constructed these days generally are covered with a layer or two of polyethylene film or fiberglass. The relative low cost and the ease of construction are their positive features.

A typical example of this approach to greenhouse construction on a homestead is the one Frank Romano and his son Tom built on their 6-acre place near Ambler, Pennsylvania.

The project began when Tom worked up a 15-square-foot patch of ground in the sunniest, most protected spot in the pasture. Then he put about 6 inches of horse manure on the patch and tilled that into the soil. Over the plot, the Romanos then built a makeshift tent of plastic film (6- to 9-mil thickness) using 2 x 4s for a supporting frame. The small building would win no architectural awards—there isn't even a door. To get in or out, you have to lift the plastic on one wall and hunker in under it. The roof is steep enough that snow won't accumulate on the

film and collapse it, though in areas where heavy snows are the rule, you would probably want to put the 2 x 4s closer together under the plastic. But the Romanos were building with economy and simplicity in mind.

The plastic serves to hold in moisture as well as heat. The Romanos never water their plants. And even on the coldest nights—10°F. above zero —the temperature inside the plastic tent does not drop below freezing.

The Romanos' goals and experiences with the "plastic tent" greenhouse follow those of commercial growers across the country. Cyrus Hyde, of Port Murray, New Jersey, for example, is an herb and flower grower. To get an early start on spring, he uses a plastic-covered greenhouse, perhaps the quintessential commercial hothouse. Most people would associate the shape with a "true" greenhouse, but it originated in a time when heating fuel was very cheap. It lets in the maximum amount of light and utilizes familiar construction techniques. But it's very heat inefficient. Unless you already have a suitable heater, don't plan to operate this structure in the winter. It's fine as a giant cold frame for starting garden plants, though, and could make you enough money to get going.

In subsequent years, the framework could easily be re-covered with a more durable material, such as fiber-

glass. Or after the structure has served its purpose, the wood can be used again in a more durable and efficient greenhouse.

A greenhouse, much like Hyde's, is depicted in the illustration. It is 10 feet wide and 24 feet long, framed of 2 x 4s and 4 x 4s, and covered with polyethylene film.

To build such a greenhouse, begin with a brick or block foundation, set on footings poured below the frost line. The sills are 12-foot lengths of 2 x 4, jointed at the four corners with half-lap joints. Three-foot 4 x 4 studs or posts are toenailed to the sills, one at each corner and on 6-foot centers along the sidewalls. The top plate, also 2 x 4 material, is dadoed to lap over the 4 x 4 posts.

With the two sidewalls framed and temporarily braced in position, turn to the rafters. You want at least 8 feet of headroom at the center of the building. The sidewalls are just over 3 feet high. The run is 5 feet. Figure on a total rise of 5 feet, giving you round numbers to work with: a pitch of

12/12. Plan to use a 1 x 4 for the ridge. Obviously there is no overhang. With these facts in mind, lay out two rafters using 2 x 4 stock.

After these rafters are cut out, set up the ridge, supporting it between two 2 x 4s set up temporarily for the purpose. Position the first two rafters and check the fit. Make any adjustments that are necessary, then mark out and cut out the remaining twenty-four rafters. Nail them in place.

Collar ties are used on every other pair of rafters. Measure for these, lay them out, cut and nail in place.

The end walls each have two 4 x 4 posts. The end wall with the door has these two posts located $32\frac{1}{4}$ inches apart. Mark their positions on the sill, then set the posts in position and mark for cutting and notching so they set securely against the rafters. After they are cut, nail them in place. By so locating the posts, you may put a door in each end of the structure. Cut a 2 x 4 header for each doorway and toenail them in place $6\frac{1}{2}$ feet from the base of the uprights. On the outside edge of each of the uprights, nail a couple of 1-inch blocks to make ledges at the 3-foot level. This will make it a lot easier to attach the crosspieces between the uprights and the corner 4 x 4s. Finally, measure and cut four pieces of 2 x 4 to fit between the end wall uprights and the sidewalls (about 3 feet 3 inches each) and nail them in place.

A vent should be installed at each end near the peak, in the area between the ridge and the crosspiece between the uprights. This can be a removable panel held in place with pins, a set of louvered panels on the venetian blind principle, or a hinged window (elbow hinges will hold it open or just use a prop with a hook and eye to close it). There should be a screen over it to keep birds out.

Each face—roof, sidewalls, end walls—should be covered as a separate unit.

The roof is the hardest, so do it first. Start at the lowest level and lay down a strip of plastic from the roll from one end wall to the other. Leave just an inch or two of overlap down the sidewall. Pull the covering fairly taut between each rafter and staple it near the top and bottom edge of the sheet.

Then do the next level up, overlapping the layer below it like shingling, for several inches. In this manner proceed to lay plastic strips up to the ridge. The plastic should lap generously over the ridge. After one side is finished, go back and tack strips of lath over each rafter; this holds the polyethylene (or other covering) strongly in place.

Repeat the process on the other side. Don't succumb to the temptation to use the staples liberally to hold down the plastic. Use the lath and nails for a firm bond. The staples have such fine edges that the plastic tears

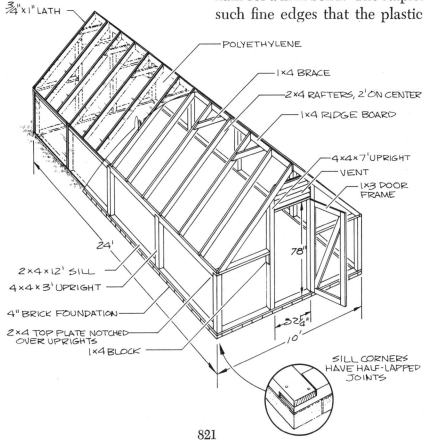

¾"x1" LATH

POLYETHYLENE

1x4 BRACE

2x4 RAFTERS, 2' ON CENTER

1x4 RIDGE BOARD

4x4x7' UPRIGHT

VENT

1x3 DOOR FRAME

24'

2x4x12' SILL

4x4x3' UPRIGHT

4" BRICK FOUNDATION

2x4 TOP PLATE NOTCHED OVER UPRIGHTS

1x4 BLOCK

78"

32½"

10'

SILL CORNERS HAVE HALF-LAPPED JOINTS

away easily. Moreover, you will need to replace the plastic every two years, and removing those staples is a bothersome chore.

Do essentially the same thing for the sides and end walls, again using lath to hold the plastic firmly in place. In the warmer months you likely will want to roll up the plastic on the sides to allow plenty of ventilation. Use screen to keep out the birds.

In the coldest weather, you should put up a second layer of plastic on the inside of the house. This cuts down on the light a little, but greatly reduces the heat losses due to drafts and air flow. (In fact two layers in the roof can be permanent—the extra one acts as a shading in the summer.)

If you install a small heater and air circulating system, the heater is best placed in the center so that the chimney stack has to pass horizontally through most of the house before going out the end. That means more material for the metal chimney, but much greater heat efficiency. Increase the efficiency even more by putting a reflective layer of aluminum foil over the top half of the stovepipe's full length.

The door(s) is made by constructing a frame of 1 x 3s and covering it with polyethylene. Since the door takes the hardest use, a layer of chicken wire makes it more durable. When hanging the door, put a ¼-inch piece of scrap wood between the bottom of the door and the sill, and attach the hinges.

A DOME GREENHOUSE

The dome, a popular modern design, is a very strong structure that allows lighter framing materials to be used than in traditional designs— saving considerable expense. If your winters are mild, this is an excellent greenhouse.

The shape admits the maximum amount of sunlight, it is slightly more heat efficient than the typical plastic-covered greenhouse, and since the peak area is relatively small, more heat is concentrated at plant level. It also has a smaller surface area for its volume. Still the dome requires a lot of heat to be warm enough for plants in the winter.

This one is covered with polyethylene. For a longer life, consider glass or a semirigid fiberglass. Fiberglass won't hold in the heat any better than polyethylene, but it will make a stronger building and should last twenty years without need for repair. Glass is the best covering of all. Only slightly more expensive than fiberglass, it traps infrared (heat) radiation inside the house—the famous greenhouse effect, lacking in plastic greenhouses.

This dome is about 12 feet in diameter and 8 feet high. The ceiling is made up of twelve 5-foot struts. The others are all 3 feet long, except for the top horizontal ring (see illustration) which is made of 28-inch boards. The doorframe is made of 2 x 4s with the vertical members running down to the ground where they are held rigid by diagonals and rocks.

The dome is supported by twelve 2 x 4 blocks set under the bottom horizontal ring. A small fan may be placed in one of the windows for ventilation, and a small smudge pot or heater helps fight frost. Leave a small hole in the center of the ceiling for a removable stovepipe chimney. Circular racks in the interior support flats or pots and make for effortless watering by a standard radial garden sprinkler.

To construct the ceiling, cut twelve 5-foot lengths of 1 x 2s, and twelve more 28-inch lengths of the same. Use a miter box or table saw to cut all wood with 60-degree ends which makes for tight joints. Paint all wood before you start construction. Use 6-inch-wide aluminum sheet metal discs cut from roofing material to join the struts. Holes in the discs are drilled before assembling—screws are used

in the ceiling, threaded nails in the walls.

First join the 28-inch pieces in a line and then attach the 5-foot lengths, and then bring the assembly into a ring. It's a good idea to get a friend or neighbor to lend a hand here—you'll need it. Secure the 5-foot boards in the center of the ceiling by joining two boards at a time with a sheet metal plate, then joining another pair by using another overlapping plate, and thus continuing all the way around, leaving the hole in the center for the chimney.

Cut seventy-two 3-foot struts for the middle ring (or wall), paint them, and then give them 60-degree ends. Next cut the sheet metal discs for the twelve vertices or meeting places on the middle ring where six supports

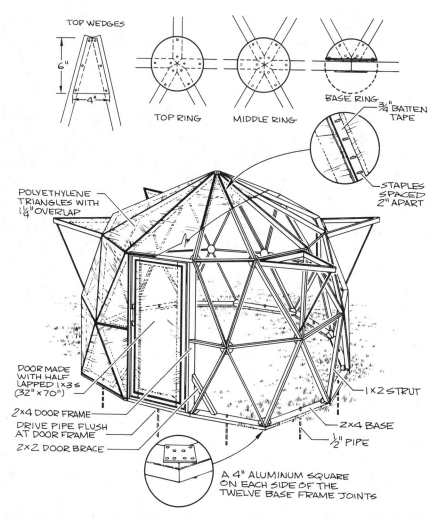

TOP WEDGES

6"

4"

TOP RING

MIDDLE RING

BASE RING

¾" BATTEN TAPE

STAPLES SPACED 2" APART

POLYETHYLENE TRIANGLES WITH 1¼" OVERLAP

DOOR MADE WITH HALF LAPPED 1x3s (32"x70")

2x4 DOOR FRAME

DRIVE PIPE FLUSH AT DOOR FRAME

2x2 DOOR BRACE

1x2 STRUT

2x4 BASE

½" PIPE

A 4" ALUMINUM SQUARE ON EACH SIDE OF THE TWELVE BASE FRAME JOINTS

meet, and twelve for the bottom ring where four boards meet. Cut the holes in the discs in advance, two holes for each wood support. When lining the struts with the discs, mark the wood exactly to fit the holes in the discs and then drill holes to avoid splitting.

Lay out the entire wall on the lawn and assemble. Then, with the welcome help from friends, raise the completed ceiling assembly and support its center about 5 feet above the ground on a ladder. Then, bring the wall upright, and circle it around so you can connect it to the ceiling with screws to create the dome. The door-frame is installed last after you have placed your greenhouse on its permanent site.

A 6-foot by 100-foot roll of 6-mil

polyethylene is enough to cover this size dome. Use tar paper to make an exact outline of each triangle and use the pattern to cut out the plastic with a razor and straightedge. Allow overlap to compensate for errors and to cover the vertices. Double the ceiling layers if snow and severe weather conditions prevail in your area. Laying the plastic on stretched chicken wire will make an even more durable ceiling. A staple gun will secure the sheeting to the wire, while ¼-inch staples will secure it to the struts. Finally, leave a little extra plastic for the bottom triangles so it will cover the ground and keep the cool air out.

A PIT GREENHOUSE

Anyone interested in moving his gardening indoors should consider building an insulated pit greenhouse. Pit greenhouses are partially sunk below grade level, with glass in the south-facing side only. The remaining walls or roof are insulated. The greenhouse can be freestanding or attached to the south side of another building as a lean-to; regardless of the design, because it is partially underground, this kind of greenhouse stores heat better and, with the insulated walls, loses the stored heat more slowly than does a standard greenhouse. With some kind of insulation (burlap bags filled with leaves, for instance) covering the glazed south wall during nights and cloudy days, it is possible to keep the pit heated throughout the winter entirely by solar radiation for cool weather plants or with slight supplemental heat for plants with higher temperature requirements.

When Judy Yaeger ran across a book describing pit greenhouses, she was so intrigued with the idea that when her family's vegetable operation developed to the point where they needed a greenhouse to raise enough transplants, there was no question about style: they would dig a greenhouse. They decided to make theirs L-shaped, with the long leg of the L a lean-to along the south side of their house for transplants and the short leg against the west side of the house for a potting area. This exact location was chosen with reference to basement windows; using the selected site, two basement windows would open into the pit and make it even more easy to regulate the temperature in the greenhouse.

Building the greenhouse took several weeks. First they dug a hole a little more than 4 feet deep, 4½ feet wide by 21 feet long, along the south house wall and 9 feet wide by 4½ feet

long on the west house corner. (Measurements given are the final inside dimensions they were aiming for.) After pouring footings, they laid a cement block wall six courses high, ending a little above grade level, and set 2 x 8 wooden sills on top of the blocks.

They next milled out 2 x 2s with a rabbet on two edges, into which the glass would be laid, and cut them to length so that they formed a 45-degree angle with the sills and the house. This angle is important for getting the maximum sun in winter. They put these rafters on 19-inch centers, after considering costs of glass and sizes available, cost of wood, and strength needed. Next came the studding for the end walls on the east and west walls and for the roof needed to cover the short leg of the **L**. Leaving space for a door on the west wall and a small window on the east, they nailed ¼-inch tempered hardboard to the studding on the inside and the outside, with 3-inch fiberglass

roll insulation sandwiched between. Roll roofing was put on over the roof, and for added class and insulation, they nailed some scrap aluminum siding to the side walls.

They built the door and window by making frames of 2 x 4s and covering them with hardboard, again with insulation in between. A screen door was made and fitted, and screening was also tacked over the window opening to keep out unwanted insects.

Next they ordered enough pea gravel to cover the pit floor about 3 inches deep. Although their soil is sandy, the gravel was still necessary to prevent the greenhouse from becoming a hog wallow after watering the plants.

Finally it was time to set the glass in place. Using glass rather than plastic seemed overly luxurious at first, but after careful discussion the Yaegers concluded that with reasonable care, over the years the cost of using glass would be equalled by that of replacing plastic; furthermore, tearing down and replacing the plastic every year didn't excite them too much. Setting the glass was quite easy. Starting from the bottom, each pane was laid in the rabbets between the rafters, with each course overlapping the lower one by about an inch. To keep each pane from sliding down, two small brads were nailed into the rafters at the point where the bottom edge of the pane should rest. Lapping the glass like shingles is one standard way of glazing greenhouses, and there are even special greenhouse glazing points for holding the panes in place, but brads work just as well. The advantage of this method is that pane replacement, should some tragedy (hail, winds, or baseballs) occur, is very easy. The brads are simply pulled out, the broken pane slipped down and out, the new pane slipped in and up, and the brads replaced.

After laying the top course of glass, the Yaegers laid a horizontal board across the length of the top, fitted as close to the wall of the house as possible. Finally, they caulked all cracks where water or air might leak in.

Now they could turn to the inside of the pit. First steps down were necessary. They temporarily stacked some cement blocks in a stairlike arrangement; four years later they are still using the temporary stairs. Benches were necessary since the seed flats should be at about ground level. They simply made columns of cement blocks, crossed with 2 x 4s to make trestles, and then laid 2 x 4s across these for the benchtop. Although no

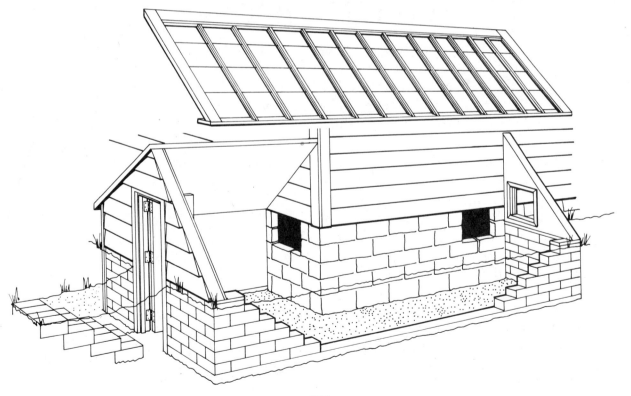

parts of the bench were fastened together, the result was quite sturdy. Shelves for supplies were added to the north wall of the potting area, with a table underneath. The pit was complete.

How useful is the greenhouse? With about 50 square feet of bench space, Judy Yaeger can raise 2,000 to 3,000 transplants at a time, depending on the size of the containers used, and each spring she raises twice that number by starting cabbage, broccoli, and lettuce early enough so that they are being hardened off by the time tomatoes, peppers, and eggplant are ready to be transplanted from germination flats.

The greenhouse is almost cost free to operate. If it becomes too hot, the Yaegers simply open the door and/or the window. This works especially well because they are oriented with the prevailing winds. With the two basement windows opening into the pit, Mrs. Yaeger needs no supplemental heat unless there is an unusually cold night.

A SOLAR LEAN-TO GREENHOUSE

While some gardeners are spending money to heat their greenhouses each winter, Christopher and Melissa Fried are using their greenhouse to help them hold their total winter heating bill down.

Besides producing a quarter of the heat required to warm their nine-room farm home near Elysburg, Pennsylvania, the Frieds' homemade "sun structure" keeps them in fresh vegetables year-round and serves as a pleasant place to relax in a light summery atmosphere in the dead of winter.

When Fried packed in his aerospace engineering job in Long Island for an uncertain future on a nine-acre farmstead two years ago, one of his primary objectives was to liberate his family from dependence on the oil companies and utility giants, along with the air and water pollution they help create. His other goal was to acquire the means of producing a steady, year-round supply of inexpensive, high-quality food for the family.

The attractive 24-foot by 14-foot lean-to greenhouse that now graces the south side of his two-story house answers both requirements admirably.

By plugging into free energy from the sun—primarily in the form of solar radiation captured and put to work in the greenhouse and second-

arily in the form of stored solar energy (wood) burned in a high-efficiency wood heater that serves as backup to the greenhouse—Fried's net outlay is for the electricity to run the ½-h.p. blower and the gasoline for his chain saw.

The operation of the system is simplicity itself. As solar radiation enters the 350-square-foot fiberglass sun wall, it strikes the ground and walls inside and quickly warms the sun room. When the temperature reaches 95°F. (around 11 A.M. on a clear day in winter, when the sun's rays strike the earth at their lowest angle), Fried opens the kitchen and living room windows (both contained inside the solar system) and a thermostatically controlled fan blows the hot, moist air inside. Late in the afternoon, or when cloud cover develops and the inside temperature drops below 75°F., the blower goes off and windows are closed.

The wall of the lean-to, extending 12 feet out from the house at its base

and slanted at an angle of 56 degrees (optimal for the collection of solar radiation at Fried's latitude), consists of two layers of Kalwall Sunlite fiberglass (.025 inch thick) fastened to 1 x 6 rafters on 2-foot centers. The upper two-thirds of the wall (250 square feet) covers aluminum, air-type absorbers, while the lower third remains unblocked so that light will strike the plants on the ground. The house cellar door and two windows are included inside the structure for an entrance and air circulation. Double-glazed windows on each end of the structure allow for the entrance of compost, rotary tiller, summer ventilation, and early and late sunlight.

The absorbers Fried made from recycled printing-press plates are inexpensive yet remarkably efficient. Fabrication involved bending them so that fins to enhance hot-air movement protrude on the back side, then painting them flat black. Air is circulated throughout the system with a ½-h.p.

fan that blows it through 1-foot by 2-foot ducts.

Heat storage, when completed, will be by rocks in the cellar. In the area previously occupied by the coal bin, Fried is building an insulated bin that will hold about 25 tons of rocks.

By using his cabinet-making skills to keep waste to a minimum, and scavenging for used materials where possible, Fried has kept the cost of the entire system down. Several solar devices that could have improved the performance of the unit were considered but ultimately rejected as adding too much to the cost and complexity of the intentionally simple design.

THE SOLAR GREENHOUSE

The solar greenhouse may not look like a greenhouse, but it is the oldest shape of all, dating back to the late 1700s. It is the most heat-efficient design known. Reducing the transparent surface area means trimming the heat-losing material. This in turn allows all the rest of the walls to be as well insulated as the builder desires. But doesn't that sacrifice too much solar energy for the plants? Not really.

This house still admits nearly all of the direct radiation that will fall on the walls and roof of a building. In clear winter climates, there is so much direct sunlight that losing the indirect light scarcely matters. Remember that the heat-inefficient, all-glass commercial greenhouses often have to let out excess heat that builds up during a winter day, or the plants will cook. Even in cloudy climates, like the northeastern United States, only a third of the available winter sunlight is indirect. So by eliminating half of the greenhouse's clear surface, the available light is reduced only by about one-sixth.

Long cloudy stretches and cold nights mean that the walls and ceiling must be insulated well. If possible, invest in glass for its heat efficiency and long life. Still, the house will need some extra heat at night, from a heater of some sort or from solar collectors such as black-painted cans or barrels filled with water and lined up along the back wall. Aluminized blankets or insulated panels can be put up over the glass at night. This is very effective, but doing it is time-consuming.

One version of this type of greenhouse was constructed by Rodale Press's Research and Development Group at the new Organic Gardening Experimental Farm near Maxatawny, Pennsylvania. The greenhouse design was worked out by Dr. Dave McKinnon, a physicist with the Museum of Northern Arizona and the

Atmospheric Sciences Research Center of the State University of New York at Albany. The theory is, according to Dr. McKinnon, that in winter the sun rises and sets fairly far south on the horizon. That's why there is so little light to work with. But it's also why clear end walls wouldn't give much extra light. By the time the sun is strong enough for plant growth—9 A.M. to 3 P.M. in the dead of winter—it's high enough to shine right in the clear wall. The only light the design cuts out is indirect, like under a shade tree. Even if the other three-quarters of the surface area were clear, the greenhouse would gain only one-third more light. But this way, the rest can be insulated.

In 1975, the time seemed right to sort through the wealth of information on solar collecting and heating, and to apply it to greenhouses. The R & D researchers came to share Dr. McKinnon's conviction that greenhouses that would operate on the sun's energy alone could be designed for more temperate climates. With the cost of heating a small greenhouse being what it is, McKinnon's greenhouse, if it worked, could pay for itself with the fuel savings alone in just a few years. They decided to build one to see how well the greenhouse would work.

That's how the 16-foot-square salt-box structure came to stand at the new farm. Devices to record the daily maximum and minimum temperatures inside and out were immediately installed. Other instruments recorded the amount of solar energy entering the structure. And just as fast as that, the energy efficiency of the structure began to prove itself.

For the initial testing period, the researchers didn't put any plants in. There were too many other things they wanted to watch. For the novices to solar technology among them, feeling the temperatures soar into the high eighties—sometimes the nineties —on any bright November morning was a quick lesson in sun power. When a few of the nights dipped below freezing, the air inside the greenhouse held at 50°F., fine for most vegetable plants.

The design of the greenhouse was letting in almost all useful light. And just a month before its annual low point, the sun was delivering more than enough heat to warm the daytime air to the 70°F. ideal for plant growth. The relatively warm nighttime temperatures inside showed that the solar greenhouse was capable of holding a lot of the energy in, although a long stretch of severe winter weather hadn't been seen yet.

Being able to insulate three-quarters of the building was the key. The walls and roof all held $7\frac{1}{2}$ inches of cellulose fiber insulation. For an idea of what that can do, imagine a long night of 20°F. outside, but 50°F. inside; the combined insulated wall space of this greenhouse was losing only half an energy unit (1,000 Btu's) each hour. By contrast, the one-quarter of the surface area that is

clear was passing nearly six energy units an hour.

One of the first things worked on was a way to cut those heat losses through the clear face of the greenhouse. The researchers were using Kalwall Sunlite, a very clear fiberglass-reinforced plastic. It has about the same good qualities for a greenhouse covering as glass does, including the ability to hold in heat rays. A layer of polyethylene, on the other hand, lets heat out extremely fast. By wrapping wooden frames with polyethylene, clear removable panels were made to fit behind the Kalwall on the rafters. They are light and inexpensive.

The air spaces they create make a big difference. One set of panels installed behind the clear wall cuts its heat losses in half, while retaining most of its transparency. Two sets of the panels cut losses down to just 1.4 energy units per hour with 30° separating the inside and outside temperatures.

The best part of this tactic is the way the transparent face now can be matched to the weather. On a clear, cold morning, the panels can be taken down to charge up the house. But when it's cloudy, they help the greenhouse coast through to fairer weather on its reserve heat. That option puts the operator in control of a greater share of the energy that the greenhouse absorbs.

The biggest problem is modulating the heating-cooling cycle. The greenhouse can take in so much energy that it becomes too hot inside for healthy plant growth. Potentially, though, all the surplus can be stored. The problem is that plants must cover most of the sunlit areas, so the storage material cannot get much energy directly. The converse is that, especially in cloudy winters, every bit of heat sooner or later becomes valuable to tide the little world in the greenhouse over a series of dim days. The structure does have a built-in reservoir: 2 feet of sun-warmed earth in the floor. No matter how cold the night, this reliable holdover from a bright day reveals itself in the morning.

The greenhouse loses almost no heat through the ground. Even though the earth—as in a sun pit—moderates the temperature, it is relatively cool and will steadily drain off a lot of heat. So sheets of 2-inch plastic foam insulation line the foundation.

Still, not enough energy was going into storage; the too-high daytime temperatures were a definite sign. Though the earth floor had the same storage capacity as 2,000 gallons of water, it was taking in heat very slowly. This was useful over a long term, but to moderate daily temperatures the greenhouse needed added storage.

Through late January and February, the researchers gathered metal con-

tainers, painted them black, and stacked them against the back wall. These were filled with water, which would absorb the heat much faster than earth. Positioning them higher put them in closer contact with the heat in the air. The researchers are quite sure that this will help capture more of the available heat, even though the black containers don't receive much direct radiation.

A few inventive people have already benefited from a slightly different approach to the knotty problem of heat storage. They vent it off, but into their homes. Any greenhouse is, after all, a large solar collector. This is the approach in Christopher Fried's solar greenhouse (see previous pages),

*R & D's solar greenhouse was **erected** upon a 16-foot-square foundation of concrete blocks. Inside the foundation, a base of sand was laid and leveled, then covered with 2-inch-thick panels of plastic foam insulation. The foundation walls themselves were also insulated, plastered, and coated with pitch (fir waterproofing). The insulation in the floor was covered with 2 feet of earth. Insulated panels were constructed of 2 x 8 framing material, plywood, and cellulose fiber insulation. These were set up to form the end and back walls, then a framework for the roof and the clear front wall constructed. The roof is heavily insulated, sheathed, and covered with asphalt roofing. A fiberglass greenhouse covering was attached to the clear wall framing, and removable panels (wood frames covered with polyethylene film) constructed to create insulating air spaces in the clear wall.*

which actually uses three-quarters of its solar face directly as a hot-air collector. Bill Yanda of the Solar Sustenance Project in New Mexico has built several attached structures that function primarily as winter vegetable plots. All excess heat flows into the home through a window or doorway. The beauty of this system is its simplicity; there's no need to remove heat from the air. And at night the home feeds heat back to the greenhouse.

Yet another possibility, especially when the greenhouse can't be attached to the home's south wall, is to use an outside heat source. Bill and Marsha Mackie of Oregon have attached a small flat plate collector to one side of their solar greenhouse. This way they can tap into direct radiation without sacrificing space inside. The hot water is stored along the bank wall in a large tank that also grows fish.

A freestanding solar greenhouse in cold climates will likely need some auxiliary system like this to boost the crops past the occasional frigid and cloudy stretches. When their water-storage system was in its infancy, R & D's researchers installed a small heater (something they don't plan to rely on) just to keep temperatures above freezing. They dearly wanted to see how well vegetables would grow in the light quality.

Bob Hofstetter, head gardener at the farm, was frankly skeptical. His prediction was that with only one clear wall, the plants would stretch up to get the sunlight and fall over. In the end, however, he gave rave reviews, reporting all the plants had perfect color and shape. Everyone was surprised when he claimed superior plant growth in the solar greenhouse. He believes that constant warm temperatures encourage weak, spindly growth, and that cool nights hold insect pests in check. The solar greenhouse has produced excellent lettuce, excellent chard, and even early spring tomatoes.

Dr. McKinnon has since built a sister greenhouse in Arizona, taking into account the things learned in constructing and using the Pennsylvania solar greenhouse. One interesting feature is a steeply sloped rear wall. Painted white on the inside, it should reflect substantially more light to the plants.

McKinnon's greenhouse in Arizona is more easily duplicated than R & D's greenhouse. It certainly uses a better system of framing, requiring less materials. But it also was designed with the benefit of experience.

In brief, the R & D greenhouse was framed using 4-foot by 8-foot insulated panels, framed with 2 x 8s, and sheathed with exterior plywood. Dr. McKinnon used standard stud-framing techniques. He used 2 x 6 material for framing, thus allowing less thickness for insulation. The photos below show McKinnon's greenhouse, while the illustration depicts the construction of a similar greenhouse framed of 2 x 4 material. Obviously, the latter approach would provide even less insulation space (though a more efficient insulating material than cellulose fiber could yield the same insulating effect of 5½ or 7½ inches of cellulose fiber), and probably would mean you'd have to provide some backup heating system.

Since the optimum slope of the large clear face varies with the latitude of the location, precise dimensions—especially the critical pitch information for laying out the rafters—can't be prescribed. To find the slope for your greenhouse, you need to determine the angle of the sun's rays at solar noon of the winter solstice. This is easy to do, as shown.

The degree of your latitude is related to the angle of the sun at the summer solstice. At winter solstice the sun is 23 degrees lower in the sky. Draw a line to represent the horizon and another perpendicular to it. Put a protractor along the perpendicular line, and mark the center point of the protractor's straightedge along the line. Next find your latitude along the curve of the protractor—then continue 23 degrees further and mark that point. Draw a line from it to your mark on the perpendicular line. That

shows the angle of the winter solstice rays. Again using the protractor, make a slope that is perpendicular to the rays of the winter sun. Where that slope strikes the horizontal line, it shows the angle for the front of the greenhouse.

To plan the greenhouse, draw a scale model of the end wall. Let ½ inch equal 1 foot. The base is 12 feet long, the front wall 1 foot high, and the back wall 5 feet high. In the center of the base, draw a perpendicular line which extends indefinitely. Next draw a horizontal line between the top of the 1-foot front wall and the perpendicular line. Then at the front wall and that horizontal, mark the angle of slope for the front face of the house. Draw the slope; where it intersects the

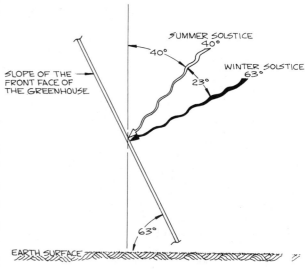

AT 40° LATITUDE (PHILADELPHIA, INDIANAPOLIS, DENVER) LOCATING THE ANGLE OF THE NOON SUN ON DECEMBER 21 AND DETERMINING THE SLOPE OF THE CLEAR FRONT FACE

central perpendicular, there is the apex. Use the scale to determine the height of the ridge, and estimate the materials needed.

Begin construction by laying out the perimeter of the structure with batter boards and string. Dig below the frost line and pour concrete footings. Lay a block foundation to slightly above ground level. Seal the outside of the foundation with cement plaster and pitch. Excavate the floor inside the foundation and cover it with several inches of sand. After leveling the sand, lay out 2-inch panels of polystyrene foam insulation to cover the floor and the inside of the foundation walls. Shovel 2 feet of earth over the insulation.

The choice of framing material depends in large measure upon the amount and type of insulation you plan to use. Cost is also a factor. If you can manage it financially, you'd be best off using 2 x 6s.

Bolt a 2 x 6 sill to the foundation. Atop it, erect a front (south facing) and rear (north facing) wall, studded on 2-foot centers using 2 x 6 material. The front wall should be 1 foot tall, the rear wall 5 feet tall. Cut studs 3 inches shorter than the height of the wall, then toenail them to the sill. Nail a 2 x 6 plate to the tops of the studs.

In the center of the east and west walls, put up 2 x 4s to support the ridge. When they are square, brace them temporarily in place. Likewise, erect the center support—a 4 x 4, which can be made by spiking two 2 x 4s together—extending from a concrete block sunk into the floor to

McKinnon's greenhouse was erected using traditional stud framing. In the walls and rear roof 2 x 6 material was used. The rafters supporting the clear wall were 2 x 4s. The rafters have bird's-mouths at both ends, so that they seat firmly on the top plates and the 4 x 4 ridge. Because of the angles involved, the front rafters project above the rear rafters at the ridge, but this presented no special problem and was easily capped when the roofing was applied.

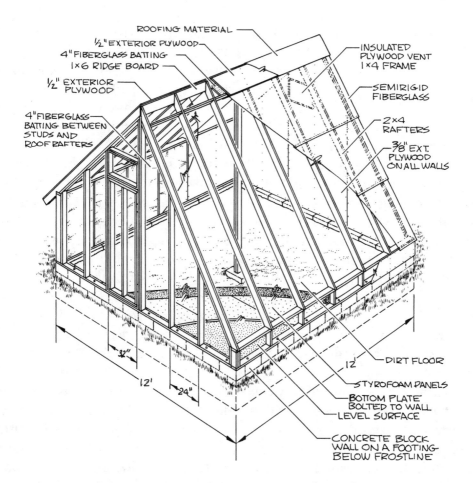

ROOFING MATERIAL
½" EXTERIOR PLYWOOD
4" FIBERGLASS BATTING
1×6 RIDGE BOARD
½" EXTERIOR PLYWOOD
4" FIBERGLASS BATTING BETWEEN STUDS AND ROOF RAFTERS
INSULATED PLYWOOD VENT 1×4 FRAME
SEMIRIGID FIBERGLASS
2×4 RAFTERS
⅜" EXT. PLYWOOD ON ALL WALLS
32"
12'
24"
12
DIRT FLOOR
STYROFOAM PANELS
BOTTOM PLATE BOLTED TO WALL
LEVEL SURFACE
CONCRETE BLOCK WALL ON A FOOTING BELOW FROSTLINE

the center of the ridge. Use a 12-foot length of 1 x 6 for the ridge. Nail it to the end wall uprights and the center support.

Lay out and cut two rafters as described in "Building From the Ground Up." The rear slope rafters should be 2 x 6s, the front slope rafters, 2 x 4s. It is unlikely that the two rafters will be alike, so don't expect them to be. Set the two sample rafters in place atop the plates and

against the ridge. Make any alterations necessary for a proper fit, then use these rafters to mark and cut the remaining number needed.

Erect the four end rafters and nail them fast. Then cut the end wall studs to fit and nail them in place. Toward the rear half of the greenhouse on the end wall facing away from the prevailing winds, frame a doorway about 32 inches wide and 78 inches high. Also install rough framing for a vent in both end walls. One can be located above the door, in all probability, while the other can be opposite the first.

The rafters on the rear roof are on 2-foot centers. The centering for the front rafters is determined by the transparent material to be used. Rigid fiberglass comes in sheets or rolls, which are put on horizontally, so 2-foot centers are fine. If glass is being used, the center for 2 x 4s should be twice the width of the glass panes. For glass, cut rabbets in the rafters (2 x 4s, and later 1 x 4s) to receive the panes.

Finish the roof in the rear of the greenhouse. On the underside of the rafters, put up $\frac{3}{8}$-inch plywood. Next lay 6-inch fiberglass batting between the rafters. Sheath the roof with $\frac{1}{2}$-inch exterior plywood. In the same fashion, sheath and insulate the walls of the greenhouse. Nail up $\frac{3}{8}$-inch plywood on the interior, install insulation, and sheath the exterior with $\frac{1}{2}$-inch exterior plywood.

Next put on the transparent surface. Lay the strips of rigid fiberglass across the rafters horizontally, starting at the bottom of the roof and nailing it securely to each rafter as you move across. Each layer should overlap the

one below it about an inch. With glass, put rabbeted 1 x 4 rafters between the 2 x 4s. Start at the bottom and lay the panes up one vertical channel to within a foot of the peak. The panes should overlap the one below by 1 inch. Hold them in place with glazier's points, then cover the seam next to the wood with putty. When one channel is finished from wall to roof, move to the next one, working horizontally across the roof. The glazing should end about a foot shy of the roof peak.

Cut a piece of $\frac{1}{2}$-inch plywood to finish off the front roof, filling the gap between the glazing and the ridge and forming a peak with the plywood overlapping from the back roof. The plywood should overlap the glazing at least 1 inch. Then cut a piece of $\frac{3}{8}$-inch plywood to fit under the rafters. Nail this piece to the bottom of the rafters, put fiberglass insulation in between rafters and in the peak, and nail the plywood strip onto the roof. Cover all plywood on the roof with tar paper, then lay shingles or roll roofing.

Build a doorframe from 2 x 6 or 2 x 4 material and plywood and insulate it. The vents can be built from 1 x 4, but also should be insulated. Attach them with hinges.

PROPAGATION BED

A handy device to have in a working greenhouse is a propagation bed. This bed, currently in use in the greenhouse at the original Organic Gardening Experimental Farm, serves much the same purpose as a propagation flat, a misting device, or a mist house.

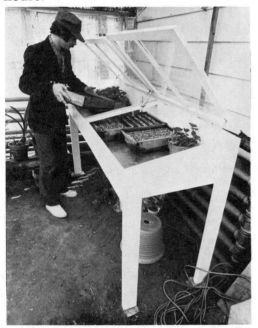

The bed provides a warm, moist environment ideal for starting seeds and bulbs, rooting cuttings and the like. The bottom of the bed is covered with a layer of sand. In the sand is placed a standard hotbed cable. Atop this is a sheet metal pan in which the pots and flats are placed. Water can be poured right into the pan to keep the developing plants well supplied with moisture.

In determining the size of your propagation bed, consider your materials. If you have some used window sashes available, design the rest of the bed to accommodate these. Building your own sashes is a time-consuming project. If you don't have any used sashes, then maybe you'll want to make the bed to fit that pan you've scavenged to use for bottom watering. There's nothing sacred about the dimensions outlined here; they just fit our own needs at the Rodale greenhouse.

CONSTRUCTION

1. Start with the bed itself first after you've determined what size best fits your materials and location. Using ⅝-inch plywood, cut the following pieces (refer to diagram for pattern to get all cuts from one 4 x 8 sheet): one 8¼-inch by 73½-inch front, one 12¼-inch by 73½-inch back, one 20⅝-inch by 25-inch side, and one 23¾-inch by 72-inch bottom. The bottom need not be in one piece—good chance to use up some scraps, though they must be at least 23¾ inches wide. On the side piece you've cut out, make a mark 8¼ inches up the left edge and 12¼ inches up the right. Draw a line from mark to mark and cut along the line to yield two identical side pieces. Glue and screw front, back, and sides

together with 1½-inch #10 screws. Insert screws through the front and back into sides so no overlapping joints are visible from a front view. Fit the bottom piece(s) in place with glue applied to edges, and screw from the outside.

2. The legs are made of 2 x 4s and are attached with screws from the inside of the bed. The front legs are 37¾ inches long, the back ones 41¼ inches long. To keep it looking nice, cut the top of the leg to match the angle on the side of the bed. When attaching the fourth leg, have someone give you a hand. One of you hold the bed steady on three legs while the other puts the fourth leg in position so the bed doesn't rock.

3. If you don't have windows suitable for this application, you will have to make them. Cut the following pieces out of 1-inch stock: four pieces 2¼ inches by 36¾ inches, tops and bottoms; four pieces 2¾ inches by 7¼ inches, sides; two pieces 2 inches by 27¼ inches, mullions.

    a. Cut rabbet grooves ⅜ inch wide and ⅜ inch deep along one edge of all pieces and two edges (same side) of the two mullions.

    b. All sash pieces are joined with shiplap joints (front and back members cut to the proper shape for joining). First cut ⅜-inch-deep shiplaps on the front sides (same side as the rabbets) of short pieces (B). These should be 1⅞ inches wide instead of the 2¼-inch width of piece A—remember ⅜ inch was removed for the rabbet so it will not be part of the joint. Now cut ⅜-inch-deep shiplaps on the back side (side opposite to rabbet) of long pieces (A). The rabbet will not effect this joint so make the cut the full width of B, 2¾ inches.

    c. Make ⅜-inch-deep inlet cuts for the mullions on the back side of the sash frame the width of the full mullion. Cut ⅜-inch-deep laps into the mullions 1⅞ inches wide.

    d. Assemble sash pieces and glue, screw, and clamp all joints. Use ⅜-inch #10 screws.

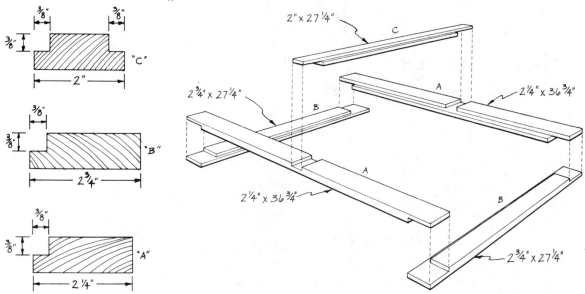

e. Insert appropriate size glass and fasten with ¼-inch quarter-round molding cut at 45-degree angles. Attach molding with ½-inch brads.

4. Paint the bed at this point.

5. Before installing the heating cable, fill the bed with either sand or perlite. Perlite is lighter and should be used if you plan to move the propagation bed much. Now coil the cable in the sand according to the directions on the package. Clothespins tacked to the bottom of the bed hold the cable in place without having it touch metal. Drill a hole in the side of the bed to let the cord out and cover the cable with sand.

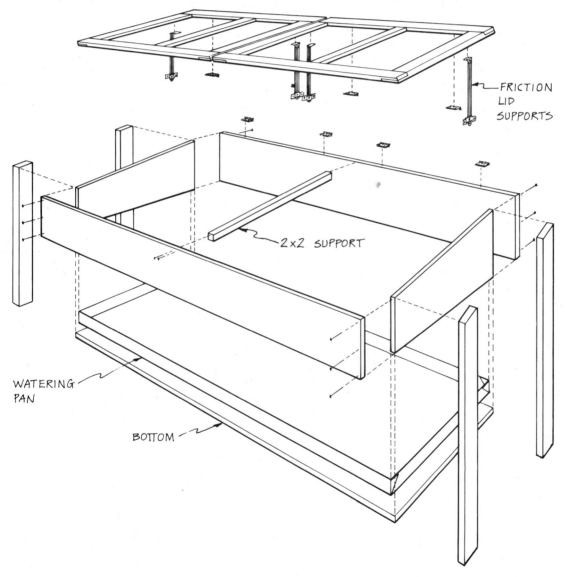

FRICTION LID SUPPORTS

2x2 SUPPORT

WATERING PAN

BOTTOM

6. If you can't scrounge some nice watering pans, you can make your own very simply out of galvanized sheet metal. For a 2-inch depth cut the sheet 3 inches wider and 3 inches longer than the bottom of the bed. Chalk lines 2 inches deep on sides and ends and cut a triangular section out of each corner as illustrated. Hammer the 2-inch marked strips into right angles to form the sides of the pan. It will be helpful to hammer the edges straight against a 2 x 4. Now fold the ends in to make corners, square them off with the hammer and 2 x 4, and solder the joint together. Remember, this thing has to hold water so solder the entire joint inside and out. Set the pan in place in the bed.

7. For added support for the sashes, cut a 2 x 2 to fit inside the bed at the top edge in the middle. Screw in place from the outside with 1¼-inch #10 screws.

8. Hinge the windows in place with sturdy 2½-inch hinges. Two friction lid supports to each window, fastened, according to directions, to the inside of the bed and to the 2 x 2 support, let you leave the windows open just where you want them.

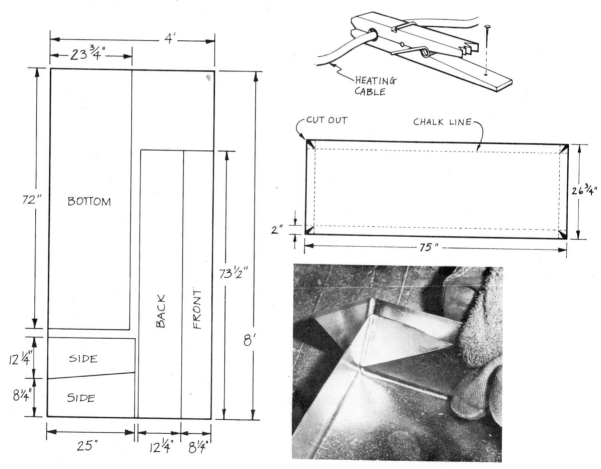

9. For finishing touches, put handles on the windows for easy opening and closing, touch up the paint, and tack up a thermometer where you can keep a close eye on temperature.

MATERIALS

Wood

1 sht. $\frac{5}{8}$" ext. plywood   or   **Front:** 1 pc. $8\frac{1}{4}$" x $73\frac{1}{2}$"

Back: 1 pc. $12\frac{1}{4}$" x $73\frac{1}{2}$"

Sides: 1 pc. $20\frac{5}{8}$" x 25" (cut as directed)

Bottom: 1 pc. $23\frac{3}{4}$" x 72"

2 pcs. 2 x 4 x 8'   or   **Front legs:** 2 pcs. 2 x 4 x $37\frac{3}{4}$"

Back legs: 2 pcs. 2 x 4 x $41\frac{1}{4}$"

1 pc. 1 x 8 x 12'   or   **Sash tops and bottoms:** 4 pcs. 1 x $2\frac{1}{4}$" x $36\frac{3}{4}$"

Sash sides: 4 pcs. 1 x $2\frac{3}{4}$" x $27\frac{1}{4}$"

Mullions: 2 pcs. 1 x 2" x $27\frac{1}{4}$"

2 pcs. 10'–$\frac{1}{4}$" quarter-round molding

1 pc. 2 x 2 x 4'   or   **Support:** 1 pc. 2 x 2 x 26" (trim to fit)

Hardware

Glue
20–$1\frac{1}{2}$" #10 screws
16–$\frac{5}{8}$" #10 screws
4 pcs. $22\frac{7}{8}$" x $33\frac{5}{16}$" window glass
$\frac{1}{2}$" brads
Paint
1 heating cable 12' long
1 pc. $26\frac{3}{4}$" x 75", $\frac{1}{32}$" galvanized sheet metal
2–$1\frac{1}{4}$" #10 screws
4–$2\frac{1}{2}$" hinges
4 friction lid supports
2 door pulls
1 thermometer

Miscellaneous

Sand or perlite
20 spring-clamp clothespins

THE LATHHOUSE

Gardeners in the Southwest and Southern California have long known how to shield their plants from the combined effects of searing sunlight and drying winds—with a lathhouse. Some years ago Victor A. Croley decided to let that idea take better root in the Midwest, and built an 8-foot by 20-foot lathhouse on his Berryville, Arkansas, homestead. His simple plans make sense for any area where there is little rain, where the summer sun nears 100°F., and where moisture-stealing winds drop humidity to 30 percent or less.

A shed made of $\frac{3}{8}$-inch redwood lath works like mulch does for plant roots; it holds moisture and keeps the ground cooler. By occasionally sprinkling the floors, you can help your humidity-producer along. The shed floor is carpeted with a 6-inch layer of mulch, in this case milled oak leaves peppered with some handfuls of cornmeal to keep the earthworms working.

The house serves a winter purpose, too, protecting camelias and azaleas, which survive in temperatures down to 10°F. so long as they're shaded. Lathhouses also make excellent protection for tuberous begonias. Started indoors in early April, these sensitive plants will get the right exposure to wind and sun if they are not moved

directly into the elements about four or five weeks later, but into a lathhouse.

Croley suggests that, with a 10- or 12-foot-wide house, you could add table and chairs to enjoy warm weather meals in the midst of your garden. In its most basic form, the lathhouse is nothing more than a framework covered with lath strips. The lathhouse can be constructed on 2 x 4 or 2 x 6 sills resting on the ground, on concrete blocks, or on a permanent, masonry foundation.

Use 2 x 3s, or 2 x 4s to frame the structure. Since sum and substance of building is the frame and lath strips, studding can be set on 3- or 4-foot centers, as can the rafters. The lath strips can be made by ripping $\frac{3}{8}$-inch-wide strips from 2-inch lumber. Nail the lath to the frame with brads leaving an inch between each slat.

THE HOMESTEAD SHOP

No homestead is complete without a shop, a corner or room or building set aside for building gardening and livestock handling equipment, for puttering and repairing, for storing tools and materials.

The ideal shop, of course, is seldom achieved. Even the person with an elaborate and spacious setup has ideas for alterations and improvements. But many of the best woodworkers and most independent homesteaders work out of the most spartan of shops. A workbench, a neat arrangement of tools and materials, adequate light: these are the basic goals. An old table, or even a sawhorse, can serve as a workbench. A shelf can hold tools, nails, glue, and screws. A toolbox is even better, for many homestead jobs can't be completed in the shop anyway. Mobility's important.

The projects that follow are intended chiefly as guides to setting up a first shop. Every situation is different, everyone's skills and desires are different. Build to suit yourself.

WORKBENCHES

While not everyone will agree that a workbench is a necessity, most everyone will build and use one, given the time, materials, and, especially, the place to put one. A lot of the struggles of carpentry and the irritations of little repair jobs are eliminated simply by having a suitable place to work, together with a few simple appliances to ease the use of the tools.

Freedom of movement around the bench is important, as is good lighting, whether natural lighting from a fortuitously located window or from light fixtures installed specifically to light the shop area. But most important, perhaps, is a firm foundation. You need a bench heavy enough to withstand pounding, pushing, and pulling without wobbling or collapsing entirely. Moreover, you need a device anchored securely, so that it doesn't slide or hop across the shop when what you need most is an immovable work surface. The best bench then, if you can manage it, is one that's attached to the building that houses it.

ATTACHED WORKBENCH

This workbench is the focal point of a garage workshop. It is securely attached to one wall of the large masonry garage. Portions of two windows and an overhead fluorescent light illuminate the work surface, and wall-mounted boards hold an array of tools within easy reach. Four-receptacle outlets provide electricity at each end of the bench. A shelf and several drawers beneath the work surface provide handy storage for fasteners, materials, and tools.

The bench is basically two 2 x 10 oak planks set atop four 2 x 4 leg assemblies. The rear legs are attached to the wall with masonry nails, the front legs angle toward the wall slightly, allowing the user to stand close to the bench without the legs being in the way.

CONSTRUCTION

1. Cut the parts of the leg assemblies from 2 x 4. Needed are four 36-inch rear legs, four 20-inch top crossmembers, four 13-inch lower crossmembers, and four 37-inch front legs.
2. Lay out the positions of the leg assemblies on the wall where the bench will be located. The bench will be 12 feet long, with the leg assemblies

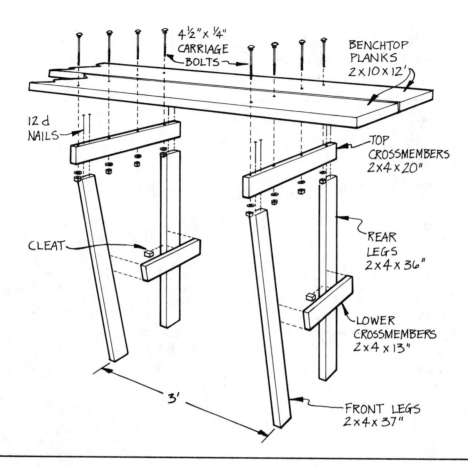

4½" x ¼"
CARRIAGE
BOLTS

BENCHTOP
PLANKS
2 X 10 X 12'

12 d
NAILS

TOP
CROSSMEMBERS
2 X 4 X 20"

CLEAT

REAR
LEGS
2 X 4 X 36"

LOWER
CROSSMEMBERS
2 X 4 X 13"

3'

FRONT LEGS
2 X 4 X 37"

MATERIALS

Wood

3 pcs. 2 x 4 x 12'   or   **Rear legs:** 4 pcs. 2 x 4 x 36"

Top crossmembers: 4 pcs. 2 x 4 x 20"

Lower crossmembers: 4 pcs. 2 x 4 x 13"

Front legs: 4 pcs. 2 x 4 x 37"

2 pcs. 2 x 10 x 12' (benchtop planks)

Hardware

12d nails
16–4½" x ¼" carriage bolts w/ nuts and washers

on 3-foot centers. At each leg location, use a plumb bob and chalk line to mark a line that is plumb on the wall. Working from these plumb lines, establish a line perpendicular to them all, indicating the line of the bench surface. It should be level, since you'll want a level work surface.

3. Work out the angles that must be cut at the tops and bottoms of the front legs, as well as the front ends of the lower crossmembers, by laying out the assembly on the shop floor. Position the rear leg and the top crossmember butting against it. Position the lower crossmember, about 18 inches above the foot of the rear leg. Finally, position the front leg, so that it is about 15 inches from the rear leg at the top and 10 inches from it at the bottom. Determine the angle of the miter that must be cut so that each front leg sets squarely upon the floor, and the top crossmember sets squarely upon the top of the leg. Cut the miters on the first leg, then assemble the unit to be sure you've got it right.

4. Nail the rear leg to the wall at one of the indicated locations. Butt the top crossmember atop the leg and nail it in place with 12d nails. Toenail the lower crossmember in place with 12d nails (a cleat of scrap material may be nailed to the rear leg first, then the crossmember to strengthen the joint and help hold the crossmember in place while you are toenailing). Finally, position the front leg and nail it in place with 12d nails.

5. With a level, check to be sure the top crossmember is level from front to back and from side to side. If all is well, transfer the front leg angles to the remaining three front leg pieces and miter them. Then assemble the units as in step 4. A 12-foot length of wood can be temporarily nailed to the front ends of the leg units to keep them properly aligned with one another until the top is secured in place.

6. Lay the two top planks in place and drill and countersink two $\frac{1}{4}$-inch holes through each plank and top crossmember, sixteen holes in all. Bolt the planks to the leg assemblies with a $4\frac{1}{2}$-inch by $\frac{1}{4}$-inch carriage bolt with nut and washer. Remove the temporary brace.

7. If desired, boards can be laid atop the lower crossmembers, forming a shelf for materials storage.

FREESTANDING WORKBENCH

There are situations in which an attached workbench is impractical or unfeasible. The obvious answer is to construct a freestanding workbench. Moreover, there are situations in which a freestanding workbench, offering access from four sides, is more desirable than an attached workbench, which allows access from, at most, three sides, and often only two or one.

The freestanding workbench shown here is constructed of 2 x 4s, 2 x 6s, and plywood. While it does have a 1 x 12 backboard attached to the back of the benchtop, the backboard could easily be left off, giving that four-sided access.

The benchtop is covered with a sheet of ¼-inch interior plywood, which provides a clean, smooth working surface. The idea is that the plywood can be replaced should the ravages of time and many projects pock its surface with holes, cuts, and gouges.

The length of the legs specified in the directions is 40 inches, which happens to be the comfortable working height of the owner, who is over 6 feet tall. A somewhat shorter handyman might find a lower workbench—with shorter legs—more comfortable. The best bet in any event is to cut the legs longer than you think you'll want and experiment until you find a comfortable working height. Don't make the mistake of cutting the legs too short. Spliced up legs aren't going to make a firm workbench. (The way to shorten legs evenly, and to level a wobbly bench or table, is: Level the bench using shims or wedges under the legs. Scribe around each leg with a dividers, resting one leg of the dividers on the floor, the other in the leg of the bench. Cut along the scribed lines.)

The entire bench is assembled using screws and glue to fasten the parts together. It could easily be joined together with glue and nails, saving a fair amount of money.

The bench shown has a commercially made vise attached in the traditional location at the front left corner. Another could be attached to the right end of the bench, a second traditional location. A short length of 2 x 4 was nailed to the right end of the frame, jutting beyond the front edge of the benchtop, to support long boards clamped in the vise.

CONSTRUCTION

1. From 2 x 4 stock, cut the following parts: four 40-inch legs, two 52-inch top frame side members, four 23½-inch top frame crossmembers, and two 48¾-inch bottom frame side members.
2. Lay out the top frame, butting the sides against the ends of the crossmembers. Secure the pieces using glue and three 3½-inch #12 screws in each joint.

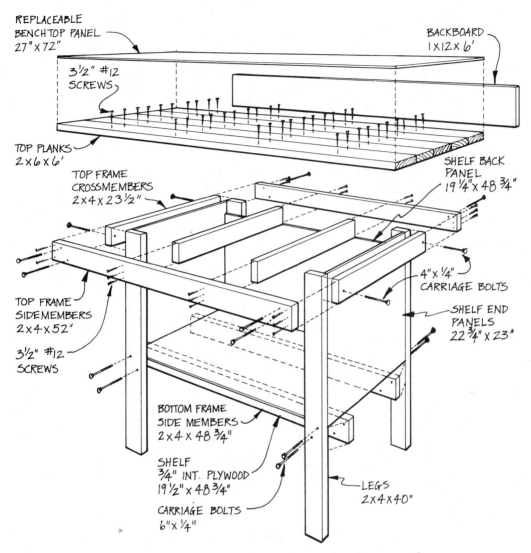

REPLACEABLE
BENCHTOP PANEL
27" X 72"

BACKBOARD
1 X 12 X 6'

3½" #12
SCREWS

TOP PLANKS
2 X 6 X 6'

SHELF BACK
PANEL
19¼" X 48¾"

TOP FRAME
CROSSMEMBERS
2 X 4 X 23½"

4" X ¼"
CARRIAGE BOLTS

TOP FRAME
SIDE MEMBERS
2 X 4 X 52"

SHELF END
PANELS
22¾" X 23"

3½" #12
SCREWS

BOTTOM FRAME
SIDE MEMBERS
2 X 4 X 48¾"

SHELF
¾" INT. PLYWOOD
19½" X 48¾"

LEGS
2 X 4 X 40"

CARRIAGE BOLTS
6" X ¼"

3. Set the legs inside the corners of the top frame, their bottom ends jutting in the air. Drill two ¼-inch holes through the frame sides and the legs, and a single ¼-inch hole through the frame ends and the legs. Bolt the legs in place, using 4-inch by ¼-inch carriage bolts with nuts and washers in the hole penetrating the side members and 6-inch by ¼-inch carriage bolts with nuts and washers in the holes penetrating the crossmembers.

4. Measure 23 inches from the top of the legs and mark a line across the inside broad face to indicate the location of the bottom frame side members. Position these side members and clamp them in place while you drill two ¼-inch holes through both them and the legs. Then bolt

them in place with 4-inch by $\frac{1}{4}$-inch carriage bolts with nuts and washers.

5. Right the bench. Cut five 72-inch lengths of 2 x 6 material and glue and screw them to the top of the bench frame. Be sure to examine the end grain of these top planks as you fasten them in place and be sure the direction of the grain alternates, that is, if the end grain of the first plank arcs upward, the next plank should be laid so its end grain arcs downward, the third one should arc upward again, and so on. This will keep the surface level and warp free. Use two $3\frac{1}{2}$-inch #12 screws to attach each plank to each of the four top frame crossmembers.

6. Cut a $19\frac{1}{2}$-inch by $48\frac{3}{4}$-inch piece of $\frac{3}{4}$-inch interior plywood for the shelf. Cut, from $\frac{1}{4}$-inch interior plywood, two $22\frac{3}{4}$-inch by 23-inch end panels, a $19\frac{1}{4}$-inch by $48\frac{3}{4}$-inch shelf back panel, and a 27-inch by 72-inch benchtop panel.

7. Position the shelf back panel against the insides of the rear legs and

---

MATERIALS

Wood

5 pcs. 2 x 4 x 8'	or	**Legs:** 4 pcs. 2 x 4 x 40"
		Top frame side members: 2 pcs. 2 x 4 x 52"
		Top frame crossmembers: 4 pcs. 2 x 4 x $23\frac{1}{2}$"
		Bottom frame side members: 2 pcs. 2 x 4 x $48\frac{3}{4}$"

5 pcs. 2 x 6 x 6' (top planks)

1–2' x 8' sht. $\frac{3}{4}$" int. plywood	or	**Shelf:** 1 pc. $19\frac{1}{2}$" x $48\frac{3}{4}$"
1 sht. $\frac{1}{4}$" int. plywood	or	**Shelf end panels:** 2 pcs. $22\frac{3}{4}$" x 23"
		Shelf back panel: 1 pc. $19\frac{1}{4}$" x $48\frac{3}{4}$"
		Benchtop panel: 1 pc. 27" x 72"

1 pc. 1 x 12 x 6' (backboard) *optional*

Hardware

Glue
64–$3\frac{1}{2}$" #12 screws
16–4" x $\frac{1}{4}$" carriage bolts w/ nuts and washers
4–6" x $\frac{1}{4}$" carriage bolts w/ nuts and washers
64–$\frac{3}{4}$" #8 screws
22–$1\frac{1}{2}$" #10 screws
11–2" #10 screws *optional*

butt against the length of the rear bottom frame side member. Screw it to each of the rear legs with four ¾-inch #8 screws.

8. Slide the shelf itself into place. Drill eleven 1½-inch #10 screws through the shelf into the bottom frame side members. Drive nine ¾-inch #8 screws through the bottom side of the back panel into the edge of the shelf.

9. Attach each of the end panels to the legs with ¾-inch #8 screws, using sixteen screws to secure each panel.

10. Lay the removable benchtop panel in place and secure it with fifteen ¾-inch #8 screws. Do not use glue in attaching this panel to the bench.

11. The final step—an optional one—is to attach a 72-inch length of 1 x 12 to the back edge of the benchtop, forming a backboard. Use eleven 2-inch #10 screws.

BENCH HOOK

A bench hook is a handy accessory for the shop that, surprisingly, a lot of handymen have never heard of. It is, basically, a board with a cleat on one side at one end and a cleat on the other side at the opposite end. In use, it is laid atop a work surface with the bottom cleat butted against the work surface edge. The work—a dowel to be sawed, for example—is pressed against the top cleat; the work thus won't twist or slide out of your grasp, so there's no need to clamp it and secure it in a vise for a brief operation.

The bench hook is a commercially made item, available from a number

of specialty tool suppliers. But there's no need to pay the high price for a bench hook when you can make one yourself from scraps of wood in five minutes.

CONSTRUCTION

Cut a 12-inch length of 1 x 12 and two 10-inch lengths of 1 x 1. Secure a 1 x 1 to each end of the 1 x 12 with two or three 1-inch #8 screws or two or three pieces of ¼-inch dowel.

MATERIALS

Wood

      1 pc. 1 x 12 x 2'   or   **Base:** 1 pc. 1 x 12 x 12"

      1 pc. 1 x 1 x 2'   or   **Cleats:** 2 pcs. 1 x 1 x 10"

Hardware

      6–1" #8 screws

MITER BOX

A miter box is a device for guiding a saw in making angle cuts. There are very expensive tools—iron miter boxes—available that are adjustable to any angle. Much less expensive ones are also available that, like the one shown here, guide the saw through 90-degree and 45-degree cuts. Usually, the box is used when cutting moldings and other items of finish trim, where accurate cuts are important.

The box shown was fabricated from

three pieces of hardwood and several screws. You can buy one just like it, but why buy when you can make.

CONSTRUCTION

1. Cut two 24-inch lengths of 1 x 10 hardwood. One will be the base. Rip the second in half, forming the two sides.
2. Using ten 1½-inch #10 screws, attach the sides to the edges of the base.
3. Using a combination square, mark the sides for cutting the slots that will serve as saw guides. First, find the middle of the channel and mark across the top edges of the sides, extending the line down the sides: this is the mark for the 90-degree saw guide. Make a mark about 1½ inches on each side of this 90-degree guideline on the outside edge of one side. Mark across the top edge of the side at a 45-degree angle pointing away from the center guideline. Extend the 45-degree lines all the way across the channel to the other side of the miter box. Extend perpendiculars down the outer sides of the miter box from these lines. These mark the positions of the 45-degree saw guidelines.

4. Using a fine-tooth backsaw, very carefully cut through the sides along the lines. Be sure to keep the saw perpendicular to the base, and to accurately follow the marked guidelines. The more carefully you make these initial cuts, the more accurate will be the subsequent cuts you make.

MATERIALS

Wood

1 pc. 1 x 10 x 4' hardwood   or   **Base:** 1 pc. 1 x 10 x 24″

                                       Sides: 2 pcs. $\frac{3}{4}$″ x $4\frac{5}{8}$″ x 24″ (act. meas., ripped from a 1 x 10 x 24″)

Hardware

10–$1\frac{1}{2}$″ #10 screws

TOOLBOX

Even if you like to have all your tools hung on the wall or laid out on a shelf, it is good to have a sturdy toolbox for carting tools for repairs and construction projects at various spots around the homeplace. Not every job, after all, is done in the workshop.

This toolbox is easily constructed. It includes a special slot for a saw or two, as well as a compartmented tray for fasteners.

CONSTRUCTION

1. Cut two $11\frac{1}{2}$-inch end pieces of 1 x 10. Using a compass set to a radius of $4\frac{5}{8}$ inches, mark off the rounded tops on the end pieces and cut, using a coping saw. Drill a 1-inch hole in the center of each piece, $1\frac{1}{2}$ inches below the top.

2. Cut a $30\frac{1}{2}$-inch bottom from 1 x 10. Also cut a 32-inch length of 1-inch dowel. Butt the ends against the bottom, inserting the dowel into the holes in the ends. Nail the ends to the bottom with 6d finishing nails. Drive a nail through the top edge of each end into the dowel.

3. Cut two 32-inch 1 x 6 sides. Nail them to the bottom and ends with 6d finishing nails.

4. Cut a $30\frac{1}{2}$-inch piece and a $6\frac{3}{4}$-inch piece of 1 x 6. Rip both to an actual width of $4\frac{3}{4}$ inches. Using the scraps, cut two $6\frac{3}{4}$-inch lengths to use as cleats to support the nail tray. Nail one to the inside of one end of the box, butted against one side, 2 inches above the bottom. The second cleat is nailed to the $6\frac{3}{4}$-inch piece of $4\frac{3}{4}$-inch material, 2 inches from one edge. Mark a line across the face of the $30\frac{1}{2}$-inch length of $4\frac{3}{4}$-inch

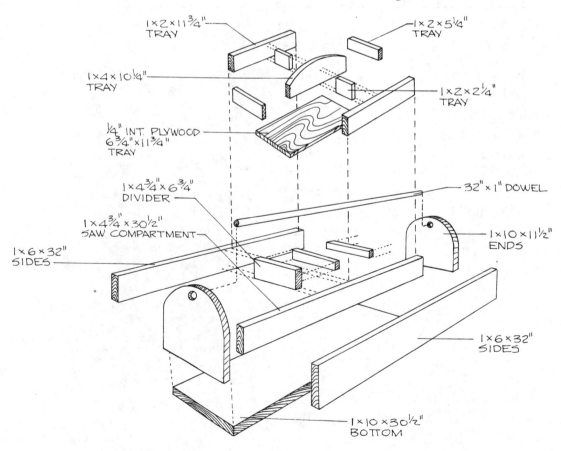

1 x 2 x $11\frac{3}{4}$" TRAY

1 x 2 x $5\frac{1}{4}$" TRAY

1 x 4 x $10\frac{1}{4}$" TRAY

1 x 2 x $2\frac{1}{4}$" TRAY

$\frac{1}{4}$" INT. PLYWOOD $6\frac{3}{4}$" x $11\frac{3}{4}$" TRAY

1 x $4\frac{3}{4}$ x $6\frac{3}{4}$" DIVIDER

32" x 1" DOWEL

1 x $4\frac{3}{4}$ x $30\frac{1}{2}$" SAW COMPARTMENT

1 x 10 x $11\frac{1}{2}$" ENDS

1 x 6 x 32" SIDES

1 x 6 x 32" SIDES

1 x 10 x $30\frac{1}{2}$" BOTTOM

material 12 inches from one end. Butt the $6\frac{3}{4}$-inch piece against the longer piece at that line and nail it fast.

5. Slip this divider unit into the toolbox. Drive nails through the ends, side, and bottom of the toolbox into the dividers.

6. Construct the nail tray. Cut two $5\frac{1}{4}$-inch pieces and two $11\frac{3}{4}$-inch pieces of 1 x 2. Butt the sides against the ends and nail with 4d finishing nails. Cut a $6\frac{3}{4}$-inch by $11\frac{3}{4}$-inch piece of $\frac{1}{4}$-inch interior plywood and nail to the tray frame. Cut a $10\frac{1}{4}$-inch length of 1 x 4 and taper the width from the full $3\frac{1}{4}$ inches in the middle of the piece to $1\frac{1}{2}$ inches at each end. Then cut two $2\frac{1}{4}$-inch pieces of 1 x 2. Slip these three pieces into the nail tray, dividing it into four compartments. Drive 4d finishing nails through the sides, end, and bottom to secure these dividers. The finished tray should rest atop the cleats nailed in the proper compartment in the toolbox.

MATERIALS

Wood

1 pc. 1 x 10 x 6′	or	**Ends:** 2 pcs. 1 x 10 x $11\frac{1}{2}''$
		Bottom: 1 pc. 1 x 10 x $30\frac{1}{2}''$
1 pc. 36″ x 1″ dowel	or	**Handle:** 1 pc. 32″ x 1″ dowel
1 pc. 1 x 6 x 10′	or	**Sides:** 2 pcs. 1 x 6 x 32″
		Saw compartment: 1 pc. 1 x $4\frac{3}{4}''$ x $30\frac{1}{2}''$
		Divider: 1 pc. 1 x $4\frac{3}{4}''$ x $6\frac{3}{4}''$
1 pc. 1 x 2 x 4′	or	**Tray:** 2 pcs. 1 x 2 x $5\frac{1}{4}''$
		2 pcs. 1 x 2 x $11\frac{3}{4}''$
		2 pcs. 1 x 2 x $2\frac{1}{4}''$
1–2′ x 4′ sht. $\frac{1}{4}''$ int. plywood	or	**Tray:** 1 pc. $6\frac{3}{4}''$ x $11\frac{3}{4}''$
1 pc. 1 x 4 x 2′	or	**Tray:** 1 pc. 1 x 4 x $10\frac{1}{4}''$

Hardware

6d finishing nails
4d finishing nails

WOOD RACK

A woeful situation in any shop is the clutter of usable scraps that seem to accumulate overnight. In too many cases, they get piled in corners or leaned against the walls or edges of the workbench. The result is a safety

Wood Rack

hazard and an inventory problem: when you need a certain size scrap, you can't locate it in the pile.

This wood rack is designed to solve the problem. Short and long remnants can be stored in it in such a way that they are flat—thus won't warp or twist—and they can be easily sorted when you need a particular piece.

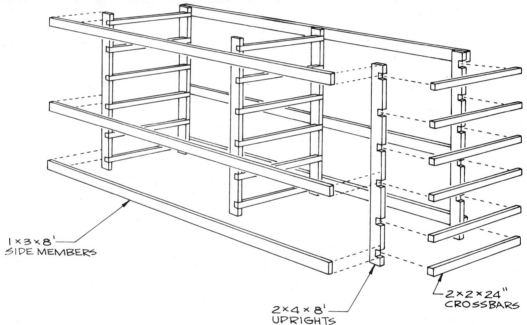

1 × 3 × 8'
SIDE MEMBERS

2 × 4 × 8'
UPRIGHTS

2 × 2 × 24"
CROSSBARS

CONSTRUCTION

1. The uprights (or legs) are 8-foot 2 x 4s. Clamp the uprights together in pairs. Mark one edge of each pair for 1½-inch by 1½-inch dadoes, six in each upright, 16 inches apart.
2. After cutting the dadoes, assemble each of the three leg assemblies. The legs are joined with six 24-inch lengths of 2 x 2 placed in the dadoes and nailed fast. Use 8d nails.
3. Link the three leg assemblies together with three 8-foot furring strips on each side. The leg units should be 4 feet apart, the furring strips located at the top and near the bottom, with the third roughly in-between.

MATERIALS

Wood

6 pcs. 2 x 4 x 8′ (uprights)

3 pcs. 2 x 2 x 12′   or   **Crossbars:** 18 pcs. 2 x 2 x 24″

6 pcs. 1 x 3 x 8′ furring (side members)

Hardware

8d nails

SAWHORSE

The sawhorse might be called the carpenter's portable workbench and scaffold. It is such a useful and easily made tool that no homesteader should be without at least one.

If you don't have one, here's a durable model, complete with a shelf for tools and materials.

CONSTRUCTION

1.   Begin by laying out the legs. Cut four 26-inch lengths of 1 x 4. Since the legs extend from the top at a compound angle, a framing square is used to mark lines for cutting the legs on both the face and edge of these 1 x 4s.

    a.   Lay out each leg, placing the framing square atop it. Line up the 24-inch mark on the blade and the 4-inch mark on the tongue with the edge of the leg, then scribe along the tongue. Reverse the framing square, lining up the same mark on the other edge of the leg, and scribe along the blade. You should have parallel lines at opposite ends of the leg, as shown.

    b.   Now lay out the cutting angle on the edges of the legs. Clamp a

Sawhorse

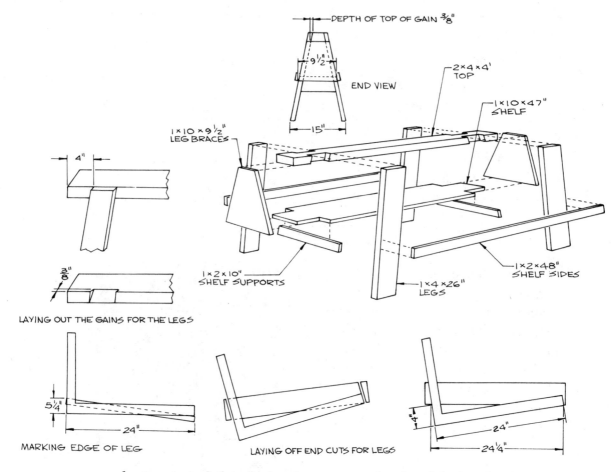

DEPTH OF TOP OF GAIN ⅜"

9½"

END VIEW

15"

2×4×4' TOP

1×10×47" SHELF

1×10×9½" LEG BRACES

4"

⅜"

LAYING OUT THE GAINS FOR THE LEGS

1×2×10" SHELF SUPPORTS

1×2×48" SHELF SIDES

1×4×26" LEGS

5¼"

24"

MARKING EDGE OF LEG

LAYING OFF END CUTS FOR LEGS

4"

24"

24¼"

leg in a vise and place the framing square on the edge of the board. Line up the 24-inch mark on the blade and the 5¼-inch mark on the tongue with the two lines scribed on the face of the leg, then scribe along the tongue across the edge of the leg. Reverse the square and mark the other end. Turn the leg over and mark the two angles on the other edge.

c. Before cutting, scribe lines across the unmarked face of the leg, joining the points on the edges. When each of the legs is thus marked, cut at the angles marked.

2. The next step is to chisel notches in the top for the legs. Cut a 48-inch length of 2 x 4 for the top. Use one leg for a template to lay out the notches on the edge of the top. Set the top on edge and butt the leg against it, so the leg slopes away from the center of the top. The tops of the two pieces should be flush, and the top outside corner of the leg should be 4 inches from the end of the top outside corner of the top, as shown. Scribe along both sides of the leg. Repeat at the other end of the top, then turn the top over and repeat at both ends. This is a

tapered notch, called a gain, that will be $\frac{3}{8}$ inch deep at the top and flush at the bottom. Mark a line on the top, $\frac{3}{8}$ inch from and parallel to the edge, connecting the two sides of each gain. Using a backsaw, cut the sides of the gain, then chisel out the material to be removed.

3. Set the legs into the gains and nail them fast with 8d nails.

4. Cut two 9½-inch lengths of 1 x 10. These will be the end leg braces. Butt them against the outer edges of the legs and the bottom of the top. Scribe along the legs and cut off the excess. Then nail the braces in place.

5. Measure the distance between the bottom edges of the two braces and cut a 1 x 10 shelf to that length. Turn the sawhorse upside down and set the shelf in place. Mark for notching out the corners so the shelf bottom will be flush with the bottoms of the leg braces. Cut out the corners, set the shelf in place, and drive 8d nails through the braces into the ends of the shelf.

6. Measure and cut two 1 x 2 shelf sides and nail them in place. Then measure and cut two shelf supports. Nail them to the legs, beneath the shelf as shown.

MATERIALS

Wood

1 pc. 1 x 4 x 10′	or	**Legs:** 4 pcs. 1 x 4 x 26″
1 pc. 2 x 4 x 4′ (top)		
1 pc. 1 x 10 x 6′	or	**Leg braces:** 2 pcs. 1 x 10 x 9½″
		Shelf: 1 pc. 1 x 10 x 47″
1 pc. 1 x 2 x 10′	or	**Shelf sides:** 2 pcs. 1 x 2 x 48″
		Shelf supports: 2 pcs. 1 x 2 x 10″

Hardware

8d nails

NONTIP SAWHORSE

A good sawhorse is an essential component of every workshop. This particular style has the advantage of not tipping over when you stand on the ends, because of the extreme angle at which the legs extend from the top.

This particular project features 22-inch legs, which means the finished sawhorse is only 19 inches high, just about knee height. If you want your sawhorse to be taller, be sure to cut the legs longer than 22 inches.

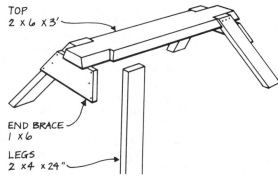

TOP
2 x 6 x 3'

END BRACE
1 x 6

LEGS
2 x 4 x 24"

CONSTRUCTION

1. Cut a 36-inch top from a 2 x 6.
2. Lay out the gains in the top for the legs. Begin by setting a sliding **T** bevel to an 18-degree angle using a protractor. This is the basic angle for the gains.

   a. On the top of the 2 x 6, measure in from each edge 1½ inches at both ends. At each of these four points set the bevel and scribe the angle on the butt end, so the line extends from the point out toward the bottom edge of the 2 x 6.

   b. Set a try square against the butt end of the 2 x 6 and scribe a line parallel to the edge, beginning where the angled line on the butt end intersects the top face of the 2 x 6. This new line should be 6¾ inches long. There should be four such lines on the top. Turn the top over and mark four similar lines on the bottom; these lines, remember, will be somewhat closer to the edge.

   c. Turn the top right side up. Using the try square, draw a line across the top of the 2 x 6, 6¾ inches from each end. Next, set the bevel, still with the 18-degree angle, against the edge of the top at each of the intersections of these two lines with the edges of the top, and

MATERIALS

Wood

1 pc. 2 x 6 x 4'	or	**Top:** 1 pc. 2 x 6 x 36"
1 pc. 2 x 4 x 8'	or	**Legs:** 4 pcs. 2 x 4 x 24"
1 pc. 1 x 6 x 2'	or	**End braces:** 2 pcs. 1 x 6 x 11"

Hardware

8d nails
6d nails

scribe the 18-degree angle across the edge of the top, sloping out from top to bottom.

    d. With the try square once again, mark across the bottom of the 2 x 6, connecting the bottom ends of the 18-degree angles marked on the edges.

3. Cut out the corners of the top, sawing carefully along the lines you have marked. Probably the easiest approach is to use a crosscut saw to cut through the edge to the marks on top and bottom, then rip along the 2 x 6 with a rip saw to these first four cuts.

4. Cut four 24-inch lengths of 2 x 4 for legs. Using 8d nails, fasten the legs to the top. Using a backsaw, cut off the portions of the legs that project above the top surface.

5. Cut two 11-inch lengths of 1 x 6 for leg braces. Butt them in place and scribe on the brace along the outer faces of the legs. After trimming the brace along the lines, nail them in place with 6d nails.

6. Level up the sawhorse, by sliding shims under short legs, if necessary. Using a dividers, scribe a line around the bottom of each leg; one leg of the dividers rides on the floor, the other marks the sawhorse leg. Cut along the mark lines and the sawhorse should be level and each leg should seat firmly on the ground.

SHAVING HORSE

Books and articles on pioneer life often mention the woodsman's use of a shaving horse for dressing shingles or other jobs. This primitive, foot-operated clamp was the common workbench before modern benches, with factory-made vises, became available. But, have you ever used one?

Drew Langsner hadn't. Not, at least, until several years ago, when he was traveling in the Swiss Alps and actually saw a shaving horse in the shop of a master cooper. He was so impressed, he decided to ask if it would be possible to serve an apprenticeship.

"For ten weeks I worked with the old man, learning the rudiments of the

ancient craft of making buckets and other containers used by the Alpine dairy farmer. Every workday, almost all day long, I straddled a shaving horse, shaping the staves, bottom, and wooden hoops of a handmade bucket," he says.

When he returned to the United States, one of the first things he did was to make a shaving horse. "As homesteaders, we (Drew and his wife, Louise) constantly use this useful device for work ranging from making tool handles and wooden hay rakes and hay forks to dressing white oak splits for basket weaving," he says. "We are always inventing new jobs for our shaving horse. (For instance, I discovered that it is ideal for holding a polled ax head for sharpening.) Use a shaving horse, and you will not want to be without one."

Traditionally, shaving horses are made of materials selected from the woodlot. This necessitates having appropriate local woods. And there are problems in seasoning green timber, besides a considerable time factor. For this book, Langsner designed and built a shaving horse using wood from a lumber company and store-bought hardware. The horse has thus been "modernized," but dimensions are patterned from the one he used in Switzerland.

The plan calls for a "jaw" bolted up from three pieces of 2 x 8 hardwood. (Although you could be ambitious and carve it from a single timber, or even a log.) Legs used are similar to the nontip sawhorse described previously. Feel free to improvise construction methods. But we strongly recommend following the given dimensions.

In addition to the lumber and hardware listed, you will need a drawknife, and probably a spokeshave, to get good use of your shaving horse. These tools are becoming hard to find, but some hardware stores and several mail-order companies sell them. It is the use of the drawknife and spokeshave with a shaving horse that makes the magic combination.

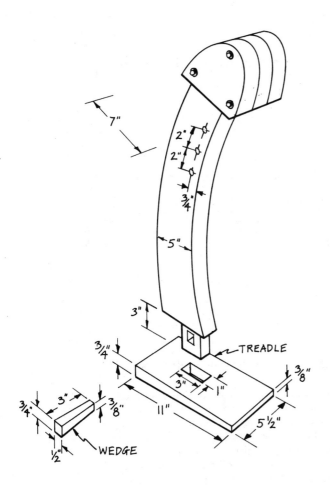

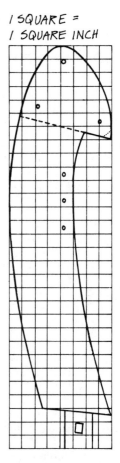

I SQUARE =
I SQUARE INCH

CONSTRUCTION

1. Lay out the curved central member on a 30-inch section of 2 x 8. The proportions are not critical. (The unit can be straight, but the balance would be inferior.) Shape with a saw and drawknife. On the remaining 2 x 8, pattern and shape the two jaw sides based on the head of the central member. Saw and chisel out the lower tenon (upon which the treadle is attached). Don't make the small mortise for securing the holding wedge at this time.

2. Make the 11-inch treadle. The foot end is tapered to help weight the leading edge (so that the jaw will open automatically when released). This taper is roughed out with a drawknife and spokeshave, then planed smooth. Beat out a mortise to match the tenon on the jaw bottom end.

3. Put the treadle in place and scribe the location of the small mortise used for the holding wedge. Now make the mortise, tapered depth

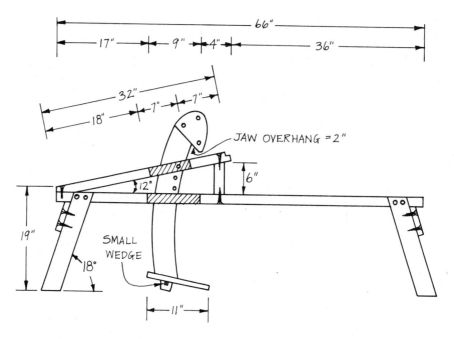

$\frac{9}{16}$ inch to $\frac{7}{16}$ inch, $\frac{1}{2}$ inch wide. Make the holding wedge from a scrap of hardwood.

4. Bolt and/or laminate the jaw sides in place. (For a nicely sculpted jaw, first glue the parts together, shape using a drawknife and spokeshave, then add the bolts.) Cut a slight bevel at the base of the jaw so it comes down flat on the work support.

5. Saw out the compound angles for the leg fittings on the 72-inch 2 x 8 at 18 degrees. These are laid out using a bevel gauge. (Or use a different leg style than outlined in steps 7 and 8. One alternative would be carving round legs with the drawknife. Shape round 1-inch tenons and mortise into angled 1-inch sockets augered through crossrails screwed below the bench. Or as a temporary setup, a legless shaving horse can be clamped onto wooden crates or set on log stumps.)

6. Beat out the large mortise for the swinging jaw. Optionally, shape the seat to fit yours. This is fun and easily accomplished by roughing out with a drawknife and finishing with a spokeshave.

7. Saw the 2 x 4 legs 19 inches long at the compound angle of 18 degrees. Attach legs. Due to the compound angle, drilling accurate lag screw holes for the legs is rather tricky. Setting the bench on boxes on the floor, at just the right height, seems easiest. First drill an angled $\frac{7}{8}$-inch seat, then the $\frac{5}{16}$-inch hole so that the lag screws will be parallel to the 2 x 8 bench. When the lag screw is turned into the hole and tightened, it is relatively easy to drill the hole for the second lag screw.

8. Cut end braces from the 1 x 6 to match angle of legs. (The compound

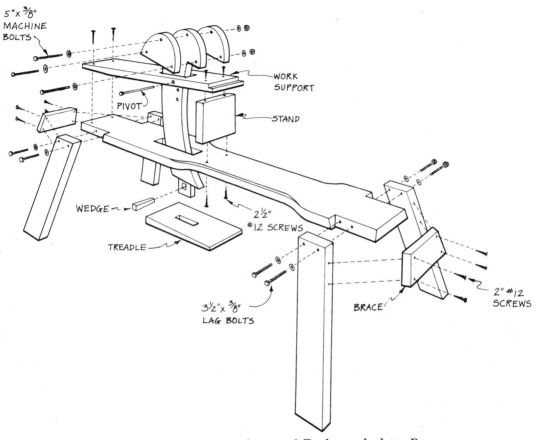

5"x ⅜" MACHINE BOLTS

WORK SUPPORT

PIVOT

STAND

WEDGE

2½" #12 SCREWS

TREADLE

3½"x ⅜" LAG BOLTS

BRACE

2" #12 SCREWS

18-degree angle forms a new angle, very difficult to calculate. Because of variables in execution, cut these braces to fit the legs as bolted in place.) It is also necessary to make a slight bevel on the outside edges of the legs where the braces cross. Attach with 2-inch #12 screws.

9. Rip the 32-inch work support to a width of 5½ inches. Saw out the end ledge and notch as shown. (These will come in handy for propping work against during some shaving horse operations.) Beat out the large mortise. Saw and bevel the bench end to 12 degrees.

10. Saw out and shape the work support stand. The top angle is also 12 degrees. Attach the work support and stand to the bench with 2½-inch #12 screws.

11. Drill $\frac{9}{16}$-inch holes through the work support and jaw. Note that jaw holes are centered ¾ inch from the trailing edge. This puts the jaw off-balance so that it automatically opens. Hack saw threads off the ½-inch machine bolt to use as a pivot. Apply a few drops of light oil to all the holes.

12. *Option:* Drill one or more ⅝-inch holes in the jaw's head to hold small tools during use of the shaving horse.

MATERIALS

Wood

1 pc. 2 x 8 x 10′ hardwood	or	**Jaw central member:** 1 pc. 2 x 8 x 30″
		Jaw sides: 2 pcs. 2 x 8 x 7″
		Bench: 1 pc. 2 x 8 x 72″
1 pc. 1 x 6 x 6′ hardwood	or	**Treadle:** 1 pc. 1 x 6 x 11″
		Braces: 2 pcs. 1 x 6 x 11″
		Work support: 1 pc. 1 x 6 x 32″
		Work support stand: 1 pc. 1 x 6 x 6″
1 pc. 2 x 4 x 8′	or	**Legs:** 4 pcs. 2 x 4 x 22″

Hardware

3–5″ x $\frac{3}{8}$″ machine bolts w/ nuts and 2 washers each
8–3$\frac{1}{2}$″ x $\frac{3}{8}$″ hex-head lag screws w/ washers
8–2″ #12 screws
8–2$\frac{1}{2}$″ #12 screws
1–8″ x $\frac{1}{2}$″ machine bolt w/ washer

A Build-It-Yourselfer's Encyclopedia of Terms, Tools, and Techniques

adhesive: A substance capable of holding materials together by surface attachment, adhesive is a general term and includes cement, mucilage, and paste as well as glue. There are many kinds of glues and adhesives for all types of porous surface. Since glues and adhesives are available under many different trade names, it is advisable to read descriptions and directions on the packaged product before you buy.

animal glue: This glue is made from the hides, bones, hoofs, and trimmings of animals. It may be purchased in a variety of forms—sheets, flakes, powder, or liquid. Animal glue is not waterproof, nor does it create as strong a bond as modern synthetic glues.

casein glue: This is a glue made from the curd of milk. Available in a powdered form, it is used as a paste through the addition of water. It is highly resistant to humidity and is chiefly used in furniture and boat construction. Be sure to carefully read the directions before using.

contact cement: A transparent, odorless, nonstaining glue, contact cement resists heat after it has aged and is water and moisture resistant. Contact cement bonds immediately and permanently without clamps. It is therefore ideal for bonding laminates. Be sure to read the instructions on the glue before proceeding.

epoxy-resin glue: This glue is made by mixing two liquids together, a white epoxy resin and a catalyst. The mixture will bond various materials, including wood, metals, china, and plastics. It is a waterproof glue and available with varying curing times. Carefully read the instructions before proceeding.

mastic adhesive: This type of adhesive creates a fairly strong water-resistant bond. Mastic adhesives are used primarily for gluing ceiling, floor, and ceramic tiles, plywood wall panels, and similar materials to wood products, concrete, or brick.

plastic cement: This glue is a very useful household glue. It creates a strong bond and is moisture resistant. It works best with wood, plastics, and glass.

plastic-resin glue: This glue is made from urea-formaldehyde powder. When mixed with water it forms a strong waterproof bond. It is extensively used in laminating plywoods but is not very weather resistant. Be sure to carefully read the directions before using.

polyvinyl-resin glue: A white, fast-setting, strong, and easy to use liquid glue, this type is generally applied with a plastic squeeze bottle. These glues, applied properly, create a joint stronger than the wood itself. All white glues are water soluble.

resorcinol-resin glue: This type of glue is made by mixing liquids from two separate tubes together. The glue is waterproof and is excellent for exposed surfaces in furniture and cabinet work. Be sure to carefully read the directions on the package before using.

rubber base cement: This glue does not create a very strong bond, but it is moisture resistant and can be used on wood products, concrete, and pottery.

aggregate: Coarse material such as gravel or sand with which cement and water is mixed to form concrete. Crushed stone is generally designed as coarse aggregate and sand as fine aggregate.

allen wrench: *See* **hex wrench.**

aluminum oxide: An abrasive used in grinding wheels, sharpening stones, and sandpaper, aluminum oxide is made by fusing bauxite clay in an electric furnace. *See also* **sandpaper.**

anchor bolts: These bolts are used to secure a wooden sill plate to concrete or masonry walls or floors. Most any bolt will serve as an anchor bolt. It must be mortared in place or placed in the setting concrete. *See also* **bolts.**

angle braces, irons, and plates: These standard hardware items come in a variety of sizes and shapes, as shown. Most are

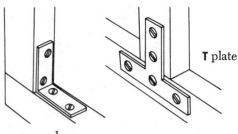

T plate

corner brace

perforated so that they can readily be used to join, reinforce, or splice wooden objects.

arbor: A short shaft or spindle on which another rotating part is mounted. The saw blade in a table saw is usually mounted on an arbor, leading some to call this tool an arbor saw.

awl: An ice pick-like tool used to scribe lines on metal or wood and for starting holes to be drilled in wood.

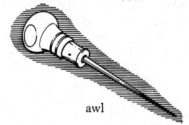

awl

backfill: The filling in of an excavation trench around a pier or foundation.

bare-faced tenon: A tenon shouldered on only one side. *See also* **joints.**

barrel bolt: A type of sliding door fastener, usually mounted to lock doors from the inside.

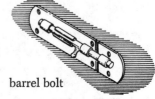

barrel bolt

base course: In masonry, the bottom row or course of brick or masonry block.

battens: Narrow strips of wood that are used to cover joints or that are used vertically for decoration on plywood siding. Battens are most easily made by ripping ⅜-inch-wide strips from nominal 2-inch-thick stock.

batter board: A temporary framework used to assist in laying out a building. Batter boards are set up outside the corners of the planned structure, and strings are stretched between them, locating the corners and demarking the perimeters of the walls.

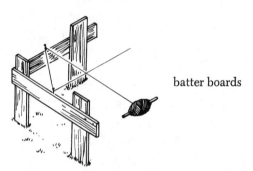

batter boards

beam: A horizontal structural member that supports loads along its length.

beam pocket: A notch that is formed at or near the top of a foundation wall to receive and support the end of a beam or girder.

bearing wall or partition: A wall or partition that supports a load.

bed: In masonry, the horizontal layer of mortar on which each row or course of masonry is laid.

berm: A narrow ledge along a ditch; a berm may be used to support beams.

bevel: To cut or plane a piece of stock to an angle other than a right angle. *See also* **chamfer.**

bevel, sliding T: This measuring tool has a slotted blade that can be clamped at any desired angle in the head or handle. The slotted blade allows the measuring of inside corners. *Use:* It is used as a try square would be except the blade length and angle are adjustable. *See also* **square, try.**

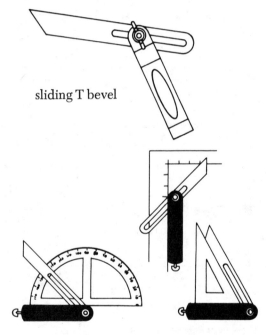

sliding T bevel

Alternative ways of setting angles on the sliding T bevel.

bit depth gauges: These come in a variety of different shapes, but they perform the same function, namely, to stop the bit at a desired depth. Most bit gauges are clamped to auger bits, but a very inexpensive one can be made from a length of dowel with the center bored out.

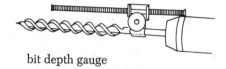

bit depth gauge

bits and drills: These are the cutting instruments used with electric and hand drills and with braces to bore holes. There is a wide variety of bits and drills.

auger bits: For wood boring with a bit brace.

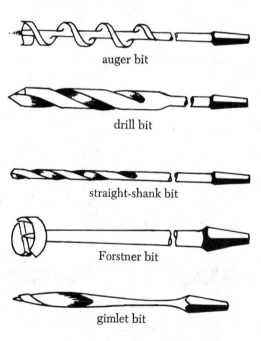

auger bit

drill bit

straight-shank bit

Forstner bit

gimlet bit

fluted bit

screwdriver bit

combination drill and countersink bit: Drills and countersinks in one operation for hand and power drills.

countersink bit: Seats screws flush with the surface of the wood for brace, hand and power drills.

fluted bit: For wood boring with hand or power drill.

Forstner bit: Used for boring wood with a bit brace, the Forstner bit has several special functions.

1. It is capable of drilling holes partway through stock where the spur of an auger bit would puncture the opposite side of the wood.

2. It can be used for boring a larger hole where there already is a smaller one, without having to plug the smaller one.

3. It can be used on end grain or where auger bit might split the wood.

gimlet bit: For wood or metal when making small bores with a bit brace.

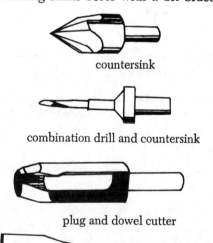

countersink

combination drill and countersink

plug and dowel cutter

spade bit

iron drill: For boring metal with a bit brace.

masonry bit: A drill bit fitted with a tungsten-carbide tip, used for drilling holes in masonry. Available in different diameters and lengths.

plug and dowel cutters: For boring plugs from wood with power drill.

screwdriver bit: For driving screws with a bit brace.

spade bit: Wood boring with power drill. Not recommended for doweling because it doesn't provide the necessary accuracy.

straight-shank twist drill: For wood and metal boring with a bit brace.

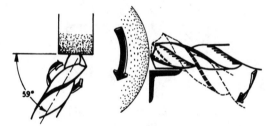

Sharpening a drill bit on a grinding wheel.

Sharpening an auger bit with an auger bit file.

black pipe: Black pipe is galvanized pipe without a zinc coating and, consequently, is cheaper. It is generally used for heating lines leading to and from radiators. Sizes and fittings are the same as for galvanized pipe.

blind-nailing: Nailing in such a manner that the nailheads are not visible on the face of the work.

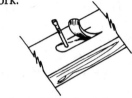

Nailing under a chiseled-up sliver.

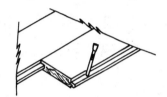

Nailing through shoulder and tongue.

board: *See* **common boards.**

board foot: A unit of measurement of lumber represented by a board 1 foot long, 1 foot wide, and 1 inch thick, or its cubic equivalent (144 cubic inches).

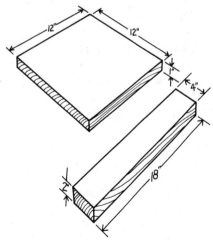

Two different pieces of wood: both a board foot.

bolts: There are many types of bolts available for all types of needs. They include machine bolts with square or hex nuts; carriage bolts which have a shoulder to hold bolt fast as the nut is tightened; stove bolts which have the entire shank threaded and come with slotted round, flat, or oval heads; and turnbuckle bolts, **U**-bolts, **J** bolts, and eyebolts. There are also a wide variety of nuts and washers available.

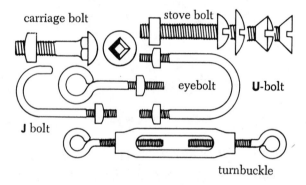

brace: An inclined piece of framing lumber used to make a wall or floor structure more rigid. Often braces are used temporarily in the construction of walls.

brace, bit: A type of hand boring tool which has a cranked shaft. It has a two jaw chuck and can only accept bits which are flat ground or square on the shank. Many bit braces are ratchet types and can be locked or operated in either direction. Bit braces come in different sizes. The size represents the diameter of the circle made when the handle is revolved. A 10-inch brace is a good size for most carpentry work. *Use:* Open the chuck and insert the bit. Tighten the chuck by holding it firmly and turning the handle. Make sure the bit is seated and revolves on center. Use a center punch to locate the

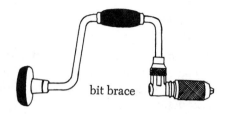

bit brace

hole and set the drill. When drilling, rotate the handle at a moderate speed and keep the drill perpendicular to the plane of the work, otherwise the hole will be slightly oversized. Do not drill straight through a piece without backing stock. Once the tip of the bit appears, stop and drill in from the other side to avoid splintering the wood. *See also* **bits and drills.**

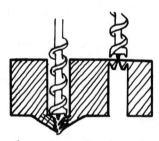

Boring from one side, then the other prevents splintering wood.

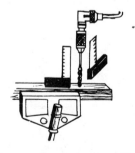

Using a try square to gauge alignment while boring.

bridging: Pieces of wood fitted between joists to distribute the floor loads. Bridging cut from joist stock is easiest to install, though crossed bridging of 2 x 2 stock is more traditional. Crossed bridging is pieces fitted in crossed pairs from the bottom of one joist to the top of the adjacent joist.

casement frames and sash: Wooden or metal frames which are hinged on a vertical edge and enclose a sash.

casing: Molding which is used to trim the jambs of window and door openings.

caster: A small swiveled wheel for supporting and moving furniture or other heavy articles.

cement: A mixture of alumina, silica, lime, iron oxide, and magnesia that is burned in a kiln, then pulverized to a fine powder. Cement is an ingredient in concrete and mortar. It is sold in 94-pound bags. Cement must be carefully stored since it is easily ruined by moisture. *See also* **concrete; mortar.**

center punch: A hardened metal shaft, squared at one end and tapered to a sharp point at the other, used to provide a starting point for drilling holes in metal. The center punch is carefully set at the spot for the hole, then tapped sharply with a hammer, denting the metal.

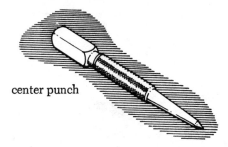

center punch

chalk line: There are many types of chalk lines; some are self-chalking, others

are not. The basic principle is that a cord is dusted with chalk and tensed over the area to be marked. The cord is then plucked and a straight mark is left on the surface from the chalk. It is best utilized in laying out lines on subfloors, roofs, or walls.

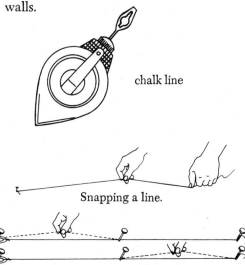

chalk line

Snapping a line.

Snapping a line in stages, using nails to secure ends and center.

chamfer: A groove or channel in a piece of wood; a beveled edge.

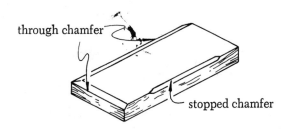

chamfer   bevel

Comparing a chamfer and a bevel.

through chamfer

stopped chamfer

checks: Small splits or cracks in the ends of boards caused by improper seasoning. Checks run parallel to the grain. *See also* **lumber.**

chisel, cold: Designed for heavy-duty use, cold chisels can cut through nails, concrete, and most other materials.

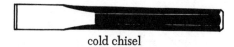

cold chisel

chisel, wood: Made from tempered steel, chisels come generally in two different types, straight and bevel edged. The most versatile ones are the beveled edge chisels. Basically there are four styles of chisels: the paring chisel is for hand chiseling and has a thin, light blade; the firmer chisel can be used for both heavy and light work and is thicker and longer than the paring chisel; the butt chisel has a very short blade and is used for heavy cutting; finally, the mortise chisel is thick and long being designed for mortising operations. *Use:* In making rough cuts, the chisel is usually tapped with a mallet or hammer. The bevel should be down, since a greater degree of control may be exercised over the depth of the cut with the bevel down. In making finishing cuts, often called paring, the chisel is driven by hand pressure alone and the bevel is usually placed up. To work properly, a chisel must be kept extremely sharp. To avoid accidents —the chisel is the hand tool that causes the greatest number of accidents—the chisel should be used with care (chisel away from yourself, for example) and the work should be securely clamped.

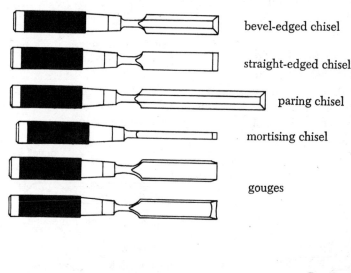

bevel-edged chisel

straight-edged chisel

paring chisel

mortising chisel

gouges

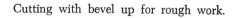

Cutting with bevel up for rough work.

Cutting with the bevel down for best control over depth of cut.

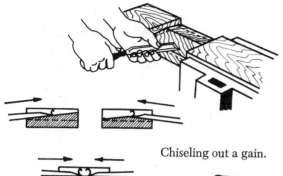

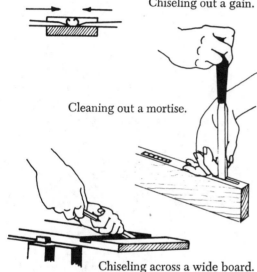

Chiseling out a gain.

Cleaning out a mortise.

Chiseling across a wide board.

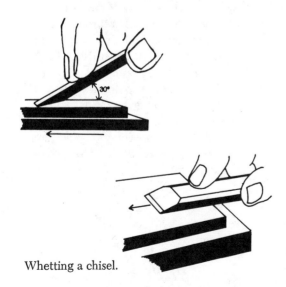

Whetting a chisel.

chuck: A broad term applied to any device that holds a rotating tool or work during an operation. Perhaps the most familiar one is the chuck on a drill, which holds the drill bits.

clamping tools: There are a wide variety of clamps available for all types of jobs.

band clamp: A canvas or cloth band or strip is drawn tight through an iron buckle. Band clamps are useful for clamping large, irregular, and round shapes. These clamps also come generally with four steel "corners" to position the band accurately on mitered work.

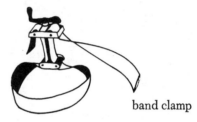

band clamp

bar clamp: These consist of a long bar with a stationary adjustable clamp at one end and a slide-lock clamp at the other. Bar clamps are most useful for edge gluing wide or narrow boards; however, they may also be used for many other gluing operations. *Use:* If possible use scrap wood to keep the clamp faces from marking the wood. When edge gluing, use a block of wood and a mallet to level the board surfaces. Alternate the clamps (above and below) and space them 12 to 15 inches apart.

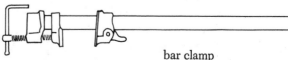

bar clamp

bench clamp: There are many types of bench clamps including vises, bench hooks, stops, dogs, and hold-fasts. Each kind is suited to a particular job, so purchase these bench clamps according to your needs. A vise serves most bench operations.

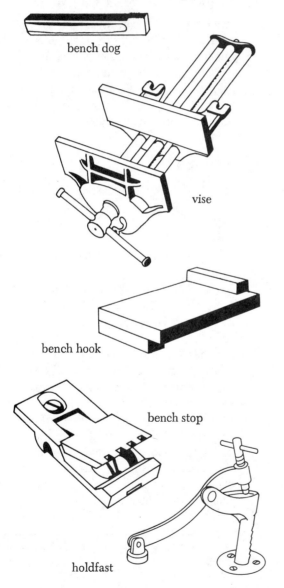

bench dog

vise

bench hook

bench stop

holdfast

C-clamp (cabinet or *carriage clamp):* A C-clamp is most useful for narrow or small work. Because the clamping surfaces are small, wooden blocks should be used to protect the work.

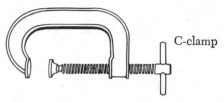

C-clamp

corner clamp: Made of steel with two adjustable jaws, corner clamps are used to make accurate and precise miter joints. The capacity of these clamps varies from 1 to 5 inches.

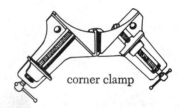

corner clamp

parallel jaw hand-screw clamp: These clamps are generally made with two wooden jaws having steel threaded rods running through them. They are most useful for gluing planks or boards surface to surface to increase the thickness of the stock, but they are useful also for a variety of different clamping operations. When using screw clamps, be sure the jaws are adjusted properly and make contact with the wood along the entire surface.

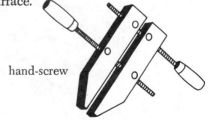

hand-screw

pinch dog: Steel **U**-shaped nails which are reusable and are driven into the end grain of boards to draw them up tight for gluing.

pinch dogs

cleat: A strip of wood fastened to another piece to provide a holding or bracing effect. Cleats may be fastened to walls or uprights of some kind to support shelves. Or they may be used to join several boards together to form a door or lid.

clinch: To turn over or bend down the protruding end of a driven nail. Clinching nails yields a strong bond, but also makes the nails very difficult to extract.

collar beam: A framing member which is used to connect opposite roof rafters in order to make the roof more rigid.

common boards: Lumber less than 2 inches thick. *See also* **lumber.**

concrete: A mixture of cement, aggregates, and water. The aggregates usually include a portion of fine aggregate (sand) and coarse aggregate (gravel or crushed stone). Depending upon the use of the concrete, the proportions of the ingredients vary, but a good all purpose mixture is: one part cement, three parts sand, and four parts crushed stone. Relatively small quantities of concrete mixture can be purchased in bags; just add water.

condensation: Drops of water which accumulate on the inside of exterior siding or walls. It is caused by moist warm interior air reaching a temperature where it can no longer hold all its moisture. Ventilation reduces attic condensation, and vapor barriers will reduce condensation in walls.

conduit, electrical: Metal pipe in which wire is installed.

construction, frame: A type of construction in which the framing or structural parts are of wood.

coped joint: A joint in which woodwork or trim is fit to an irregular surface. In molding, cutting the end of one piece to fit the molded face of the other at an interior angle to replace a miter joint.

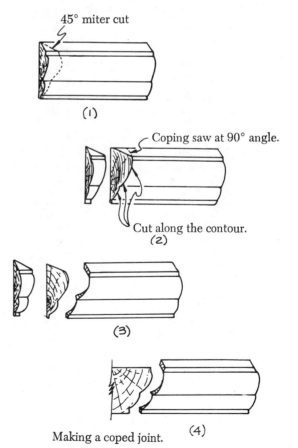

45° miter cut

(1)

Coping saw at 90° angle.

Cut along the contour.

(2)

(3)

Making a coped joint. (4)

copper naphthenate: A wood preservative that does not harm plants (although it does contain a fungicide/insecticide). The most widely available brand is Cuprinol.

core: The center of a plywood or other laminated panel. Plywood cores are either sawn lumber (lumber-core plywood) or crisscrossing layers of veneer (veneer-core plywood). *See also* **plywood.**

corner braces: Diagonal structural members used in corners to make the frame more rigid.

cornice: The overhang of a pitched roof at the eave line. It usually consists of a fascia board, a soffit for a closed cornice, and other moldings.

cotter pin: A split pin whose ends can be flared after it is inserted in holes or slots in two or more pieces to fasten them together or prevent excessive sliding or rotation. *See also* **hitch pin clip.**

cotter pin

counterboring: To enlarge a hole through part of its length by boring. Counterboring offers a technique for countersinking a roundhead screw or machine bolt. *See also* **countersink; countersinking.**

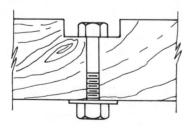

Counterbore hole to countersink machine bolt.

counterflashing: A metal flashing usually used on chimneys to cover shingle flashing and to prevent moisture entry.

countersink: A recess drilled in the top of a hole so that the head of a screw or bolt will be set flush with the surface. A nail set is used to drive finishing or casing nails below the surface of the wood so that the hole can be puttied or finished.

countersinking: To bore a shallow, conical hole for the head of a screw.

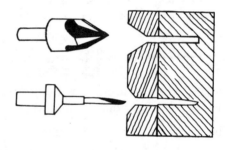

combination drill and countersink

course: A continuous row or layer of bricks, masonry, or shingles.

creosote: An oily liquid which is distilled from wood tar and is used as a preservative on wood. Creosote has a disagreeable smell and is not recommended for interior use. *See also* **finishes; preservative.**

d: *See* **penny.**

dado: A groove cut across the grain of a board. A dado can be most easily cut with a dado attachment for a power saw or with a router. Hand tools can be used: a backsaw or dovetail saw is used to cut the sides of the groove, a chisel to remove the excess material, and a router plane to smooth the bottom of the dado. *See also* **joints.**

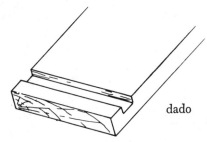

dado

dampproofing: The process of coating the outside of a foundation wall with special preparations to resist the passage of moisture through the wall.

dead load: The weight of permanent, stationary construction in a building. *See also* **live load.**

dimension lumber: Lumber ranging from 2 to 5 inches in thickness and up to 12 inches in width. *See also* **lumber.**

divider, angle: A measuring tool whose primary function is the bisecting of angles. It is well suited to measuring simple and complicated angles. It consists of three blades, one which is at right angles (90°) to the body or head, and two which are adjustable to the desired angle.

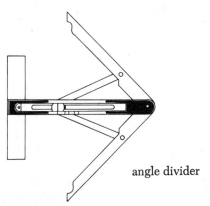

angle divider

dividers: Made of pressed steel, a dividers has two adjustable legs. Either both legs are pointed, or one is pointed and the other is shaped to hold a pencil. The tool is primarily used for scribing circles, small arcs, or marking off equal spaces.

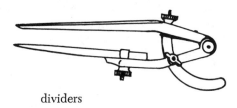

dividers

doorjamb: The surrounding case into and out of which a door closes and opens. It consists of two vertical members called side jambs and a horizontal head jamb.

doweling jig: A device which is used to guide bits when boring dowel holes or mortising. It is fully adjustable and can handle stock up to 3 inches in diameter. Bit guides are selected to conform to the size of the bit and dowel rod to be used. The major advantage of this accessory is that holes may be bored on the face or edge by simply moving the jig. *Use:* Follow the directions which come with the doweling jig.

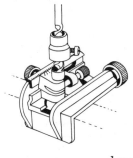

doweling jig

downspout: A metal or wooden pipe for carrying water from roof gutters.

drawknife: A tool which has two handles joined to a frame and blade. It is a type of plane used for shaping and removing large amounts of wood from curves or edges. *Use:* Clamp board securely, grasp handles and draw the knife over the work. Be careful, however, because the knife is drawn toward the operator.

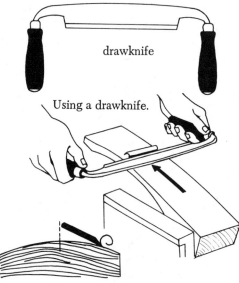

drawknife

Using a drawknife.

Keep bevel up on convex work.

Keep bevel down on concave work.

dressed and matched boards: *See* **matched lumber.**

drill, hand: Consisting of a frame handle, crank, and chuck, a hand drill imparts the turning motion of the crank to the chuck through gears. Because of this, they are used to drill holes up to a maximum of $\frac{1}{4}$ to $\frac{3}{8}$ inch in most materials. Most drill bits can be used in this type of drill; however, the most common types used are straight-shank twist drill bits. Most hand drills have a $\frac{1}{4}$- to $\frac{3}{8}$-inch chuck. The handle on many hand drills is hollow for drill storage. *Use:* Open the chuck and insert the drill bit. Tighten the chuck by holding it tightly and turning the crank. Make sure the bit is held in the middle of the three jaws. To remove bit, hold chuck and turn crank backwards. Before drilling, it is a good practice to use a center punch to locate the hole and set the drill. When drilling, rotate the crank at a moderate speed and keep the drill straight, otherwise the hole will be slightly oversized. Use a backing material and caution when the drill is exiting from the work. *See also* **bits and drills.**

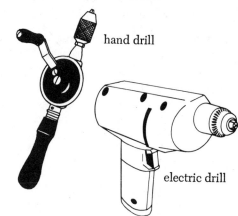

hand drill

electric drill

drill, power hand: One of the most useful power tools available, the $\frac{1}{4}$-inch drill is an extremely versatile tool. Besides being able to bore holes in wood, metal, or masonry, it can be used to saw, grind, hone and polish, sand, drive screws, and wire brush. The many accessories available allow it to become a drill press, disc sander or drum sander, grinding wheel, hedge clipper, lathe, circular saw, hacksaw, and more. *Use:* Thoroughly read operator's manual before commencing operation. *See also* **bits and drills.**

drill press: A drill press consists of a shaft and chuck or drill mounted on a column above a table. On some, the table rotates to accommodate angle bores; on others, such as the radial-arm drill press, the whole head adjusts to handle angle bores. Drill presses have a variety of different uses in woodworking including mortising, routing, and dovetailing. They also can be used for grinding, polishing, sanding, and shaping. *Use:* Thoroughly read the operator's manual before commencing operation. *See also* **bits and drills.**

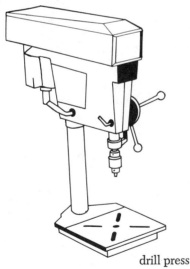

drill press

drip cap: An exterior molding which is located on the top of a window or door frame to cause water to drip beyond the outside of the frame.

drip edge: A lightweight aluminum or galvanized metal molding, roughly **L**-shaped in cross section, secured around the perimeter of a roof to protect the edges of the roof sheathing from excessive weathering.

drip edge

eaves: The overhang of a roof which projects out over the walls.

emery cloth: *See* **sandpaper.**

expansion plug: A fiber or plastic sheath which, when inserted into a pre-drilled hole, provides purchase for a screw. When the screw is turned into the plug, it expands and grips the sides of the hole. *See also* **fasteners, solid surface.**

face nailing: Nailing perpendicular to the joint or initial surface.

fasteners, hollow surface: This category of fasteners includes anchor bolts and toggle bolts or screws. Anchor or Molly bolts have grips of metal which open behind the wall when screwed or bolted tight. Toggle bolts have swivel toggles or spring-loaded arms which hold the bolt or screw tight. *See also* **bolts; nails; screws.**

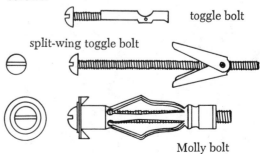

toggle bolt

split-wing toggle bolt

Molly bolt

fasteners, solid surface: This category of fasteners includes wall plugs and masonry bolts. Wall plugs are plastic or nylon sheaths which are inserted into a pre-drilled hole to provide a base for screws. Masonry bolts also use a plastic or nylon plug into which a bolt is threaded. *See also* **bolts; nails; screws.**

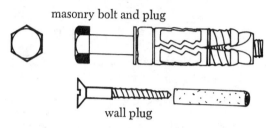

masonry bolt and plug

wall plug

fence: An adjustable metal or wooden strip mounted on a table or machine to guide the work in cutting, milling, or sanding operations.

fiberboard: A broad term used to refer to sheet materials of varying densities manufactured of refined or partially refined wood fibers. Bonding agents and other materials may be added to increase strength or resistance to moisture, fire, or decay, or to improve some other quality.

files and rasps: Files come in a variety of different types to fit the particular job at hand. The most common shapes of files are flat, half-round, round, square, and triangular. They come in many different lengths, generally from 4 to 14 inches. Every file should have a handle and should be stored so they don't rub against each other or other tools. The cutting surface of files consists of rows of teeth. On a single-cut file, the teeth run in parallel lines diagonally across the surface. On a double-cut file, a second set of teeth cross the first set at an angle. A rasp has tri-angular teeth, rather than serrations, and is used where a lot of material must be removed. The closer together the teeth, the smoother the cut of the file. Files must be kept clean, and for this job a file card is indispensible. *Use:* Clamp work and push cutting teeth over work.

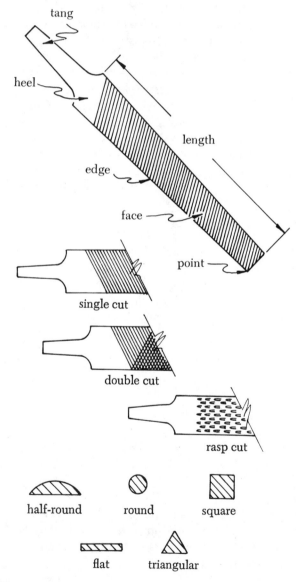

tang

heel

length

edge

face

point

single cut

double cut

rasp cut

half-round   round   square

flat   triangular

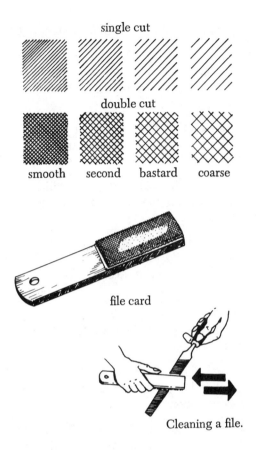

single cut

double cut

smooth   second   bastard   coarse

file card

Cleaning a file.

filler: In woodworking, any substance which can be used to fill holes and irregularities in planed or sanded surfaces. Also fillers are used to decrease the porosity of the surface before applying a finish coat.

finishes: There are innumerable ways to finish wood products, ranging from oils designed to develop and enhance the grain of the wood itself, through paints designed to cover and seal the wood. Four categories of finish materials are listed below; the materials can be used alone or in combination with others, to wit, a piece of wood can be treated with a preserva-tive, then painted, or it can be stained, then sealed with a clear coating.

clear coatings: These finishes are used to protect and enhance natural or stained wood. Included are varnishes (interior as well as exterior), shellacs, and lacquers. Shellacs and lacquers are difficult to apply properly; however, varnish, if put on in thin coats and spread well, will give a professional and durable finish. Be sure to follow manufacturer's recommendations concerning use and application. When using varnish be sure the area is dust free and follow the three step approach:

1. Apply varnish thinly beginning in the corners and at the edges of the piece.
2. Once the piece is covered, brush evenly across the grain with overlapping strokes.
3. To finish the coat, brush with the grain again using overlapping strokes.

paints: There are many different types of paints available today to suit the needs of a particular job or project. Some paints are designed to resist deterioration from weather; others are designed to make surfaces bright and clean. Most are available in flat, semigloss, and glossy finishes. Flat paint finishes tend to reflect light. Paints are formulated to meet specific application and use requirements; it is therefore recommended that one follows the manufacturer's recommendations concerning use and application. If you need a paint for a specific job, see your local paint salesman or hardware store.

preservatives: Chemical concoctions designed to extend the life of wood products by preventing or delaying decay. Most preservatives are not finishes per se; wood treated with such preservatives may subsequently be stained, painted, or varnished. Creosote is a preservative and finish, since no other finish will adhere to creosoted wood. Many wood preservatives —copper naphthenate is the notable exception—are harmful to plants.

stains: These are nonprotective finishes which are used to add or enhance the color of wood surfaces. Some also serve to seal the wood.

fire stop: A horizontal block nailed between studs of a building to deter the spread of fire and smoke through the air space. A fire stop will also provide a horizontal nailing surface between the sole and top plates, and as a consequence, it is sometimes called a nailer or nailing block.

five-quarter stock: A special lumber that measures an actual 1¼ inches in thickness. Five-quarter stock is used in stair treads and window sashes.

flashing: Sheet metal or other materials used in roof, wall, and chimney construction to protect a building from water and moisture seepage.

float: A wooden or metal tool with a broad, flat blade and a short handle used to finish concrete when a smooth surface is desired. When finishing a large slab, a long-handled float is used.

footing: A rectangular masonry form which is wider than the wall or pier it supports.

foundation: The supporting portion of a structure. The foundation includes the footings.

frieze: A horizontal member which connects the top of the siding with the soffit or cornice.

frost line: The depth of frost penetration into the soil. Footings should be placed below this depth to avoid movement.

furring strips: Strips of wood which are used on a wall or other surface to even it and to serve as a fastening base for finish material.

gable: The triangular vertical end of a building formed by the eaves and ridge of a sloped roof.

gain: A notch or mortise cut to receive the end of another structural member or a hinge or other hardware. *See also* **chisel, wood; joints.**

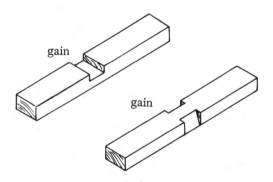

float

galvanizing: Coating metal with a thin layer of zinc to inhibit rust.

girder: A principal beam of wood or steel which supports concentrated loads at isolated points along its length.

glass: There are many varieties of this familiar substance used in windows.

double-strength glass: It is available generally in three strengths, $\frac{1}{8}$ inch, $\frac{3}{16}$ inch, and $\frac{7}{32}$ inch, and is much stronger than single-strength which breaks easily.

heat-absorbing glass: Glass which screens out infrared rays or radiant heat while allowing the light to penetrate.

insulating glass: Factory-sealed, double-paned glass with an air space in the middle. It ranges in thickness from $\frac{1}{2}$ inch through 1 inch.

plate glass (float glass): A clear quality glass that can range in thickness from $\frac{1}{8}$ inch up to 1 inch.

Plexiglas: This is a clear plastic that causes it to be less breakable but not quite as durable as glass.

sheet glass: An economy grade of glass; sheet glass has slight distortions in large sheets.

tempered glass: The glass is heat treated for greater strength. When breakage occurs, with tempered glass there is little danger of being cut because the broken pieces do not have jagged edges.

tinted glass: A glass which screens out radiant heat or infrared rays as well as visible light.

wired glass: A glass which has a wire mesh embedded within it for safety.

glass cutter: This inexpensive tool is used to score glass so that pieces can be snapped off. The cutter has a tungsten steel or tungsten carbide wheel that does the scoring, notches for breaking off narrow pieces of glass, and a ball tip for tapping the underside of the scored line to break the glass.

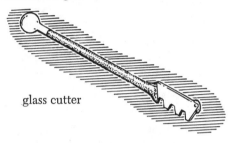

glass cutter

glazing: This term refers both to the panes fitted into doors and windows and the process of fitting the panes in place. Glazing is also the filling of pores of an abrasive stone with metal cuttings; when the stone is glazed heavily, it loses its abrasive quality and must be dressed (the glazing removed) with a grinding wheel dresser.

glazing (glazier's) **compound:** A putty-like substance that tends to retain its plasticity even when exposed to weathering. It is used to seal the joint between windowpanes and sashes and doors.

glue: *See* **adhesive.**

grade: The designation of the quality of a manufactured piece of wood. *See also* **lumber.**

grain: The direction, size, arrangement, and appearance of fibers in wood.

grout: A thin mortar mix which can be poured into narrow cavities or masonry joints.

gusset: A flat wooden member used to connect the intersection of wooden members. It is fastened by nails, screws, bolts, or adhesives.

gutter: A shallow channel of metal or wood which runs along the eaves of a house and is used to catch or carry off rainwater from the roof.

hammers: One of the most basic hand tools is the hammer. There is a hammer designed for every striking job. Three of the most useful are:

ball peen hammer: This hammer has a square face at one end and a round or ball face at the other. A ball peen hammer is primarily used for metal work such as spreading rivets or bending and shaping metal.

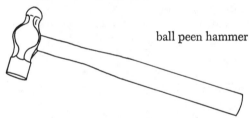

ball peen hammer

claw hammer: These are the most common types of hammers. One end is flattened or slightly convex for striking, the other has an open claw for prying or pulling nails. Chiefly there are two types of claw hammers, the curved or octagonal claw, for pulling nails, and the ripping claw, for pulling pieces apart. A hammer should be chosen for the job you are doing. Longer handles provide more leverage when striking a blow and are best used for framing and heavy construction. Shorter handles are more useful for finish work. Hammer heads also vary in weight as well as the type of

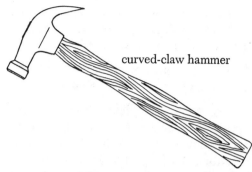

curved-claw hammer

claw. Most are between five and twenty ounces. The weight one chooses should be based on what is comfortable. *Use:* Start nail by holding it near the head and give it a few light taps until it is set. When driving the nail in, try to drive it in on an angle so that it holds better. Use a nail set to tap nail below the wood's surface. When nailing, hold hammer near its butt and swing it with a full stroke. To pull a nail out use the **V** of the claw. Rock the hammer back and forth prying the nail out. In order

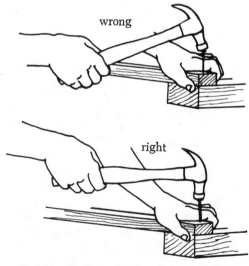

wrong

right

Keeping the hammer handle parallel to the work prevents bending nails.

not to mar the wood, put a small block of wood or a putty knife under the hammer head when extracting nails.

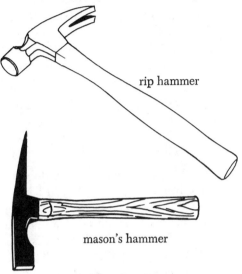

rip hammer

mason's hammer

mason's hammer: This hammer has a square face on one end and a long chisel peen on the other. Its weight varies from 1½ to 3½ pounds, and it is used for splitting or breaking blocks and bricks. *Use:* The chisel peen is used to etch the line of the cut. A sharp blow to the waste side of the line will split the brick. The chisel peen can then be used to smooth the surface.

hardboard: This versatile material is made from softwood pulp that is formed into sheets under pressure and heat. It is available in a wide variety of forms. *See also* **fiberboard.**

hardware cloth: Multipurpose, heavy-woven steel mesh.

hardwoods: Comprised of trees which have true flowers, broad leaves, and seeds enclosed in a fruit, most hardwoods lose their leaves in the fall and during the winter. Principal hardwoods would include ash, basswood, birch, cherry, hickory, mahogany, maple, oak, and walnut. The term hardwood has no relation to the firmness or density of the wood. Hardwoods are most commonly used for furniture, tools, fencing, and girder beams in barn construction. Hardwoods also cost more than softwoods but they are generally stronger. *See also* **lumber; softwoods.**

hasp: A slotted, hinged plate that fits over a loop, called a staple.

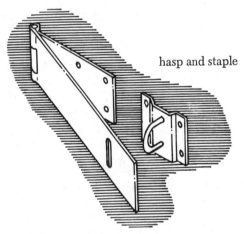

hasp and staple

header: A beam which runs perpendicular to joists and to which joists are nailed in framing chimneys, stairs, and other openings. Also header refers to wooden lintels.

heartwood: The wood that extends from the pith to the sapwood. The cells of this wood are dead and no longer participate in the life process of the tree. The heartwood is often infiltrated with resins and other substances that make it darker and more decay resistant than the sapwood that surrounds it.

hex wrench: An **L**-shaped hexagonal shaft used to fit into and turn setscrews used to secure pulleys, handles, and knobs. The wrenches, sometimes called allen wrenches, come in $\frac{5}{64}$-inch through $\frac{1}{4}$-inch dimensions. A set is inexpensive.

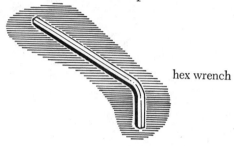

hex wrench

hinges: While most cabinet hinges are reversible (they can be mounted upside down, as well as right side up), this is not the case with many door hinges. Door hinges are therefore marked as "right hand" or "left hand." To determine this, stand so that the door opens away from you. If the hinges are to be on the left from this position, it needs "left hand" hinges, on the right, "right hand."

butt hinges: Hinges which have two pieces of rectangular metal joined by a pin. Butt hinges come in a variety of sizes and types. These include the simple butt hinge with a nonremovable pin, a loose-pin butt hinge, a loose-joint butt hinge, and a rising butt hinge. The size of a hinge is determined by its length. *Installation:* Place your door in its frame and place wedges to regulate the height and opening. Mark the hinge location on the door and the frame and chisel out the area to the depth of the hinge.

dogleg hinges (commonly referred to as a folding leg bracket): A spring-action, self-locking hinge that is used when mounting the legs of folding tables or fold-down shelves that are not required to support heavy loads.

strap hinges: Hinges which have two pieces of triangular metal joined by a pin. They vary in size and are primarily used for heavy folding doors.

T *hinges:* A combination hinge, consisting of one strap hinge leaf and one butt hinge leaf, joined by a pin. **T** hinges are useful for hanging heavy doors and gates.

other hinges: There are a wide variety of hinges available. If you have a specialty job, go to a good hardware store and explain your need, and more than likely they'll be able to outfit you with the proper hinge.

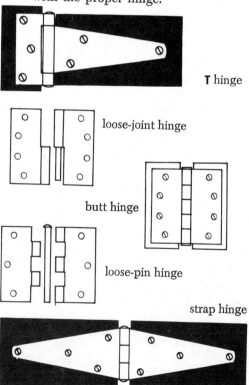

T hinge

loose-joint hinge

butt hinge

loose-pin hinge

strap hinge

hip roof: A roof which rises by inclined planes from all four sides of a building.

hitch pin clip: Commonly known as a keeper pin. A pin similar in function to a cotter pin but used where frequent removal is necessary.

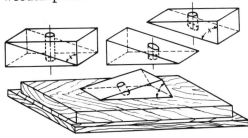

hitch pin clip

housed joint: A joint formed by a recess that receives the entire end of the mating part. It is similar to a mortise-and-tenon joint, except that the tenon has no shoulders. *See also* **joints.**

insulation, thermal: A material which has a high resistance to heat transmission when placed in walls, ceilings, or floors.

insulation board: A structural building board made of wood or cane fiber in $\frac{1}{2}$-inch to $\frac{25}{32}$-inch thicknesses. It can be obtained in various size sheets, in various densities, and with several treatments.

jamb: The side and head lining of a doorway, window, or other opening.

jig: A device used for holding work or guiding a tool in forming or assembling wooden parts.

Making a jig to guide the boring of an angled hole.

joinery: A term, used by woodworkers, that refers to the various types of joints used in a structure.

jointer: A machine with a rotating shaft faced with cutting knives, which does the work of a hand plane. In addition to performing straight planing operations, a jointer may be used for rabbet cuts, tapers, bevels, chamfers, and molding. Jointers are available in varying widths from 4 through 16 inches. Most cutting heads have three or four knives. The cutting heads and table are adjustable for depth and the fence is adjustable for angle bevels. *Use:* As with all power tools, carefully read the operator's manual before commencing operation. If you need a few pieces of wood jointed, see your local lumberyard.

joints: The space between two adjacent surfaces joined and held together by nails, screws, glues, mortar, or other means. In woodworking there are many types of joints:

> *butt joint:* An end joint where two pieces of lumber or timber meet in a square-cut joint.

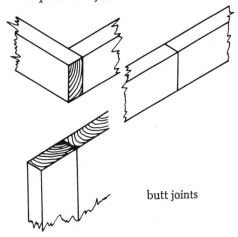

butt joints

893

dado joint: A joint in which one board fits into a rectangular groove cut across the width of the surface of a second board or plank. *Method:* Use a backsaw and chisel or a router or dado attachment on a power saw to cut a dado in one piece. Fit the other piece into the dado and secure with glues, nails, screws, or other fasteners.

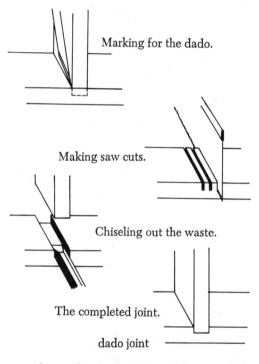

Marking for the dado.

Making saw cuts.

Chiseling out the waste.

The completed joint.

dado joint

dovetail joint: A dovetail joint is a mechanically strong joint in which a tapered pin fits snuggly into a tapered slot. *Method:* Mark and cut a tapered pin with a dovetail saw or backsaw. The angle of the taper should be slight. On the other frame piece, transfer the pin shape and mark carefully. Then using a dovetail saw or a fine-toothed backsaw cut down the shoul-

ders of the slot being careful to maintain the proper angle. Make a third cut down the middle of the slot to aid in chiseling, and chisel out the wood. The most important step in making a good dovetail joint is following your lines.

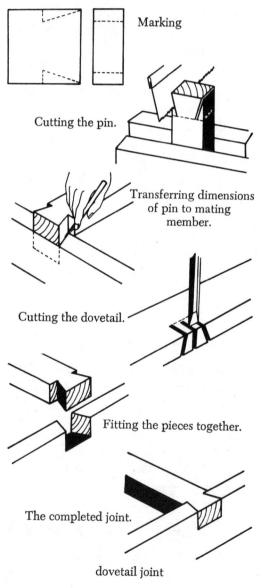

Marking

Cutting the pin.

Transferring dimensions of pin to mating member.

Cutting the dovetail.

Fitting the pieces together.

The completed joint.

dovetail joint

edge joint: The strongest method for joining long grain edges is to glue and butt them together using bar clamps; however, other methods include doweled butt joints, batten joints, lap joints, spline joints, and tongue-and-groove joints. If you are joining long grain to end grain a tongue-and-groove or lap joint is best.

lap joint: There are a number of variations on this joint, referred to as overlap joints, cross lap joints, full lap joints, and half lap joints. The most

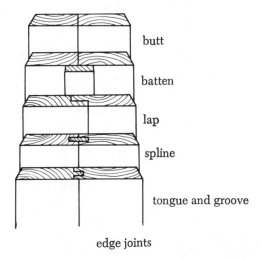

edge joints

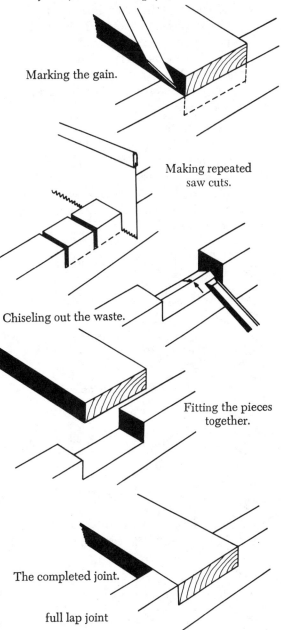

Marking the gain.

Making repeated saw cuts.

Chiseling out the waste.

Fitting the pieces together.

The completed joint.

full lap joint

end joint: The simplest method for making end joints is a butt joint with joining plates attached on both sides of the mated timbers or boards. The strongest structural end joint is obtained from a supported lap joint.

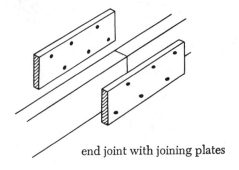

end joint with joining plates

simple is the overlap joint, in which two pieces are lapped one atop the other and secured that way. A full lap is when one piece is notched out to accept the full dimension of the second piece, as shown. In a half lap joint, both pieces are notched so that they lap and fit flush. A cross lap joint is a lap joint that occurs somewhere along crisscrossing points other than the ends.

miter joint: This joint can be made many ways, but by far the easiest is the butt joint with corrugated fasteners or blocks used for support. Other common methods would include tongue-and-groove, spline, and lap joints.

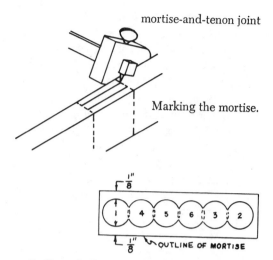

mortise-and-tenon joint

Marking the mortise.

Drill out bulk of material to be removed, then clean up mortise with chisel.

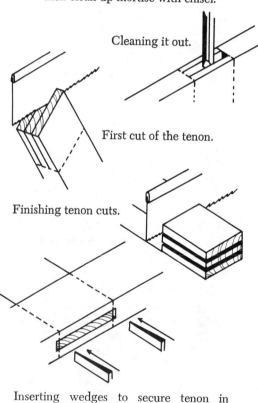

Cleaning it out.

First cut of the tenon.

Finishing tenon cuts.

Inserting wedges to secure tenon in mortise.

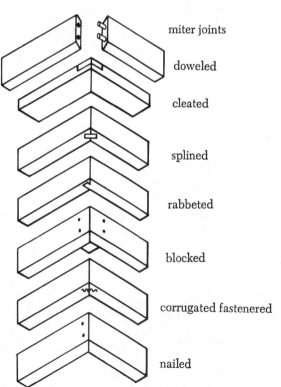

miter joints

doweled

cleated

splined

rabbeted

blocked

corrugated fastenered

nailed

mortise-and-tenon joint: The strongest type of **T** joint, the mortise-and-tenon joint is used in heavy framing and construction. It consists of a square or rectangular pin (tenon) which fits into a matched slot (mortise). The tenon should be no larger than one-third the thickness of the mortised member, otherwise the joint will be weak. *Method:* Mark the mortise, bore it out, and then chisel it smooth. (If you like, the mortise can be made slightly larger than the tenon and wedges can be used to snug the fit.) If you have a drill press with a mortising attachment, this becomes very easy. Next draw the width, length, and thickness on the tenon. Using a backsaw, cut down the lines on either side of the length of the tenon using a sloping cut. Clamp the work upright, and use the backsaw to cut squarely down the length of the tenon to the shoulder line (the sloping cuts made first will guide the saw through the work). Finally cut across the shoulder lines to complete the tenon. With a power saw, successive cuts can be made or a dado can be used to obtain the same result.

rabbet joint: A continuous slot or groove cut into the surface on the end or edge of a board, plank, or timber. *Method:* Cut a groove with a backsaw and if necessary use a chisel to finish the cut. With a power saw make continuous cuts and chisel smooth or use a dado attachment. Once the joint is made, bond it with glue and either screws or nails.

right angle joint: The simplest method for making a right angle joint

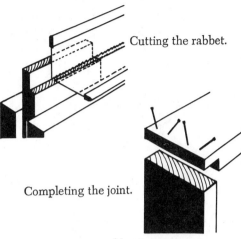

Cutting the rabbet.

Completing the joint.

rabbet joint

is with a butt joint and the use of angle brackets or blocks for support. However, doweled butt joints, rabbet joints, dado joints, multiple or single joints, open mortise-and-tenon joints, and combination joints may also be used.

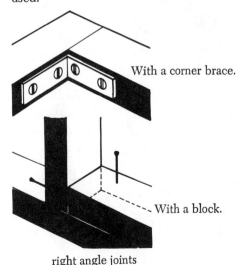

With a corner brace.

With a block.

right angle joints

T *joint:* The strongest type of **T** joint is a mortise and tenon; however, it can also be a supported butt joint, doweled butt joint, lap joint, dovetail joint, or dado joint.

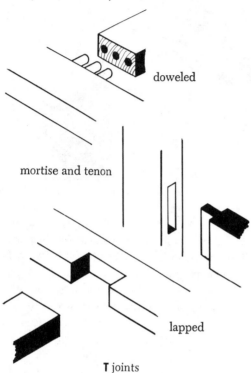

doweled

mortise and tenon

lapped

T joints

joists: Parallel beams which are used to support floor and ceiling loads. Joists in turn are supported by large beams, girders, or bearing walls.

keeper pin: *See* **hitch pin clip.**

kerf: The slit made by the blade of a saw in a material.

knot: The portion of a branch or limb of a tree which appears on the face of a piece of wood.

lacquer: A finishing material made of nitrocellulose that dries by evaporation of the solvents. *See also* **finishes.**

lag bolt (or **screw**): Large, square-headed screw made for heavy-duty applications. It functions like a screw but is turned with a wrench.

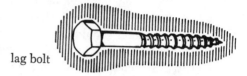

lag bolt

laminate: To build up wood in layers. Each layer is called a laminate or ply. The grains of the layers may run parallel or crisscross. Layers of veneers, as in plywood, are not usually included in the laminates, although strictly speaking they are laminates.

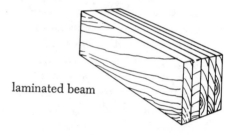

laminated beam

lathe: One of the oldest kinds of power equipment, lathes are used for fashioning many types of wooden-formed pieces, from bowls to round tabletops and decora-

lathe

tive legs. More so than other power equipment, a lathe is capable of producing finished work. A lathe consists of a motor mounted on a bed which is used to turn a piece of wood between two spindles. There are many types of lathes available. They differ according to the length of the bed and the type of motor employed. There are many types of attachments available and necessary for the proper operation of this tool. A general rule to remember: the larger the stock to be turned, the slower the speed required.

ledger: A strip of lumber which is nailed along the bottom of the side of a girder on which joists rest.

level (spirit level): An instrument for determining a true horizontal, vertical, or angular direction by centering a bubble in a glass tube filled with alcohol or ether. There are many types of levels from a couple of inches in length to over 6 feet. Some have only horizontal and vertical vials, while others have 45-degree vials or 360-degree protractor vials.

level

line level

lineal: *See* **linear.**

linear: Of or pertaining to a line. Linear measure is a measurement of a single dimension, as opposed to measurement of area or volume. Although the board foot, a volume measure, is the classic lumberman's measure, most structural materials sold by lumberyards are sold on a linear measure basis. For example, common boards and dimension lumber are sold by the linear foot.

linseed oil: A vegetable oil made from flax plants. It is used in the manufacture of oil base paints and finishes. When blended with special drying agents to hasten the drying process, linseed oil is called boiled linseed oil. This substance is an excellent finish when cut with turpentine in mixtures ranging from half and half to two parts oil to one part turpentine. The application is tiring, however, since the secret of success is a vigorous rubbing as the oil is applied with a cloth.

lintel: A horizontal structural member which supports a load over an opening such as a door or window.

live load: The total of all movable and variable loads that may be placed upon a building. *See also* **dead load.**

lock washer: A washer that has a broken rather than solid rim and is used to secure a nut when vibrations may cause it to loosen.

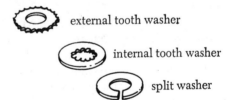

external tooth washer

internal tooth washer

split washer

louver: An opening with a series of horizontal slats so arranged as to permit ventilation but to exclude rain, sunlight, or vision.

lumber: In a technical sense, lumber is the product of the sawmill. It is the unplaned, unmilled boards of varying widths and lengths. Since relatively few handymen have access to a sawmill, they will consider lumber to be the wood products they purchase at a lumberyard, the basic building material.

Lumber can be roughly categorized as either softwood or hardwood. These designations have nothing to do with the density and firmness of the woods, but rather they are based on the nature of the tree that yielded the wood. The softwoods are conifers (needle-bearing trees) and the hardwoods are deciduous (broad-leaved trees). Thus, some softwoods are hard, and some hardwoods are soft.

In processing a sawlog, the sawmill will cut off slabs with the bark, shaping the log into a square or rectangular beam, which is then cut into lumber. Most lumberyard wood is heavily processed, being ripped into standard dimension pieces, kiln dried, planed and cut to standard lengths, generally ranging in 2-foot increments from 8 feet to 18 feet in length. The dimensions of the lumber are reduced by both the drying and the planing. Consequently, the dimensions commonly given for building lumber are nominal dimensions; a 2 x 4 *does* measure 2 inches by 4 inches when it passes from the saw, but by the time it reaches the lumberyard, it has shrunk to about 1½ inches by 3½ inches. Lineal dimensions are accurate, however.

There are a lot of defects that afflict lumber: splits and checks, shakes, warp, knots, wane. Boards, if improperly dried or stored, will cup, twist, crook, and bow,

all four conditions being variations of warp. Most of these defects concern cabinetmakers, more than rough carpenters, since only severe examples of the defects will affect the structural strength of the lumber as much as they will affect the appearance.

Lumber is graded, but there are two different systems, one for softwoods, the other for hardwoods. The softwood grading system is based on the structural usefulness of the wood. Thus dimension lumber (lumber 2 to 5 inches thick) is graded in descending order of quality: select, construction, standard, utility, economy. Common boards (lumber 1 inch thick) are graded numbers 1 through 4, with number 1 the best quality. The hardwood grading system relates to the usable lumber in a board with one face clear of knots or other imperfections. The highest cutting grade is termed Firsts and the next grade is Seconds. These two top grades are almost always combined into one grade and referred to as FAS. The third grade is termed Selects, followed by #1 Common, #2 Common, Sound Wormy, #3A Common, #3B Common.

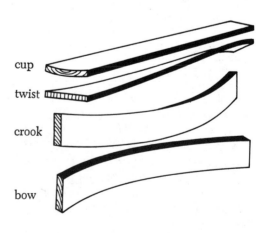

cup

twist

crook

bow

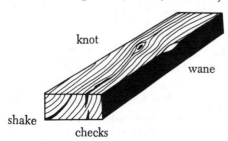

knot

wane

shake

checks

mallet: Any of various clubs made of hardwoods, rubber, or plastic, for use principally with wood chisels and carving tools. Mallets are also used when driving metal objects which might be damaged or marred if struck with a steel hammer.

mallet

marking gauge: Made from either wood or metal this marking tool is used for scribing lines parallel to the grain or face of the wood. A calibrated beam with a scribing pin is slotted through a head with a flat face plate, which rides along the face of the wood. A thumbscrew holds the beam tight in the head. *Use:* Adjust the beam through the head to the required distance and tighten the thumbscrew. Be sure when scribing the line to hold the head firmly against the face of the wood.

marking gauge

masonry: Brick, stone, cement block, tile, or other similar materials bonded together with mortar to form a wall, pier, or similar mass.

matched lumber: Lumber that has edges shaped to make close-fitting joints, such as tongue-and-groove or shiplap (rabbet) joints. Some matched lumber, such as finish flooring, has ends shaped as well as edges.

measure, folding: Made of wood, folding measures perform the same functions as tape measures, but are useful for specialized functions due to their rigidity. They are useful for measuring around corners, and folding measures may be used for gauging lines by butting the rule against the face of the work and holding a pencil or scribe at the end of the rule as it is moved along the stock. This latter function is best performed with a butt spacing folding rule.

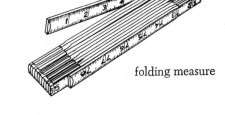

folding measure

measure, tape: Any of various metal or cloth tapes with calibrations for multipurpose measurements.

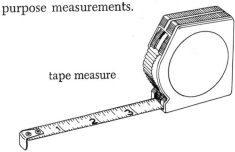

tape measure

metal shears: A plierlike tool for cutting sheet metal, wire, and heavy cardboard. Metal shears come in a surprising range of special purpose designs, including models for cutting right and left turns. A medium-metal shears

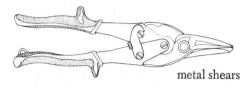

metal shears

sized straight-cutting shears is a handy general purpose cutting tool.

millwork: Wood products planed or milled from lumber in a factory. The term millwork covers such items as door and window jambs, casings, molding of all kinds, matched lumber, stair treads, and similar products.

mineral spirits: A petroleum solvent used as a substitute for turpentine.

miter (or **mitre**): A cut made at an angle, usually 45 degrees. The term also refers to the joining of two pieces at an evenly divided angle. *See also* **joints.**

molding: A wood strip having a curved or projecting surface, used for decorative purposes.

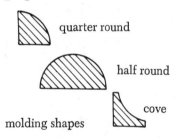

quarter round

half round

cove

molding shapes

mortar: A mixture of an aggregate, a binder, and water that is used to bond stones, concrete blocks, and bricks together. The aggregate is invariably sand, the binder either cement or lime and often a mixture of both. A good recipe for mortar is one part binder to three parts sand. Sufficient water should be added to create a plastic batter; too much water will cause the mortar mix to be too runny—experience is the best teacher here. Prepared mortar mixes are available; just add water.

mullion: A thin vertical or horizontal bar dividing the panes in a window, units of a screen, or the components of similar frames.

nails: A nail consists of a metal shaft, formed or attached at one end to a head and pointed at the other. Nails are made of many different materials and should be matched with the material being fastened to avoid staining and loss of holding power. The basic types of nails are the following:

Common nails are for general construction (2d to 60d) and are strong and have large flat heads.

Box nails are for lighter construction (2d to 40d) and have thinner shafts than common nails.

Casing nails are used for interior trim (2d to 40d) and have tapered heads that can be concealed.

Finishing nails have cupped heads for concealment (2d to 20d) and are used for interior trim, cabinet work, and furniture.

Wire brad nails (or *brads*) are for light interior trim and have thin shafts with tapered heads.

Cut nails are used for flooring and are rectangular with flat heads (2d to 20d).

Spiral nails have flat heads and are spiraled to make a tight joint.

Double-headed nails are for temporary construction and can be easily pulled, since they have two flat heads.

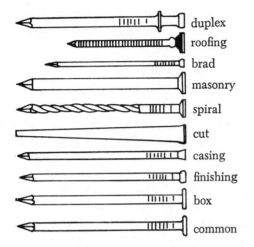

duplex
roofing
brad
masonry
spiral
cut
casing
finishing
box
common

Masonry nails can be driven into stone, masonry, and concrete and can be purchased with round, squared, or fluted shafts.

Roofing nails are made of rust-resistant materials (aluminum or galvanized steel) and have broad, flat heads.

As a rule, the nail's length should be three times the thickness of the stock being secured.

nail set: A tool for countersinking finishing and casing nails, the nail set is a hardened steel shaft, squared at one end, knurled in the center, and tapered at the other end. Several sizes of nail sets are available, ranging from 1/32 inch through 4/32 inch.

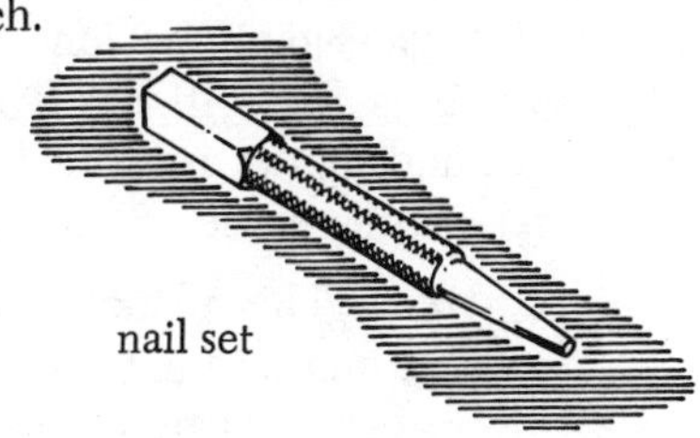

nail set

nominal size: The size by which lumber is commonly known and sold, which is not the actual size. Lumber is ordinarily full dimensioned when cut, but shrinkage resulting from drying and removal of material in planing alters the dimensions of the lumber. Largely for the sake of simplicity, woodworkers refer to lumber by nominal sizes.

nominal size (inches)	actual size (inches)
1 x 2	¾ x 1½
1 x 3	¾ x 2½
1 x 4	¾ x 3½
1 x 6	¾ x 5½
1 x 8	¾ x 7¼
1 x 10	¾ x 9¼
1 x 12	¾ x 11¼
2 x 2	1½ x 1½
2 x 3	1½ x 2½
2 x 4	1½ x 3½
2 x 6	1½ x 5½
2 x 8	1½ x 7¼
2 x 10	1½ x 9¼
2 x 12	1½ x 11¼
3 x 4	2½ x 3½
3 x 6	2½ x 5½
3 x 8	2½ x 7¼
3 x 10	2½ x 9¼
3 x 12	2½ x 11¼
4 x 4	3½ x 3½
4 x 6	3½ x 5½
4 x 8	3½ x 7¼
4 x 10	3½ x 9¼
4 x 12	3½ x 11¼
6 x 6	5½ x 5½
6 x 8	5½ x 7¼
6 x 10	5½ x 9¼
6 x 12	5½ x 11¼
8 x 8	7¼ x 7¼
8 x 10	7¼ x 9¼
8 x 12	7¼ x 11¼
10 x 10	9¼ x 9¼
10 x 12	9¼ x 11¼
12 x 12	11¼ x 11¼

on center: The measurement of spacing for studs, rafters, joists, and the like in a building from the center of one member to the center of the next. Usually abbreviated **OC.**

paint: A combination of pigments with suitable thinners or oils to provide decorative and protective coatings. *See also* **finishes.**

panel: In house construction, a thin flat piece of wood, plywood, or similar material framed as in a door or fitted into grooves of thicker material with molded edges for decorative walls.

paper, sheathing or building: A building material made generally of paper or felt and used in wall and roof constructions as a protection against the passage of air and moisture.

particle board: A manufactured building material composed of wood chips held together with an adhesive. Particle board is available in 4-foot by 8-foot sheets in a number of different thicknesses.

partition: A wall that subdivides spaces within any story of a building.

penny: As applied to nails, the term now serves as a measure of nail length and is abbreviated by the letter **d.** *See also* **nails.**

petcock: Small faucet or valve.

piano wire: Thin wire sold for hobby and workshop use.

pier: A column of masonry, usually rectangular, used to support other structural members.

pilot hole: A hole drilled in stock to be joined by screws and used as a guide for the screw. The pilot hole is narrower than the screw and approximately half the length.

pitch: The incline slope of a roof. Roof slope is generally expressed in inches of rise per 12 inches of run.

planes: These are tools for leveling, smoothing, and shaping boards. While most handymen are familiar with the smoothing plane, there is a startling range of specialized planes that he may never have heard of. The two major categories of planes are the bench planes, used for smoothing and leveling rough surfaces, and the special planes, used for cutting grooves and shaping the edges of boards. The bench planes include:

block plane: This is one of the smallest planes, only 5½ to 6 inches in length and its blade is set at a lower angle than other planes. It is principally for planing end grain and small pieces of wood. Unlike other planes, it is held in one hand when used.

block plane

fore plane: This plane is used for making glue joints on long pieces of wood. It is from 10 to 18 inches in length and lighter in weight than the larger jointer plane.

jack plane: This plane is useful for smoothing and jointing. It is from 12 to 14 inches in length and is considered to be a general purpose plane.

jointer plane: This plane is primarily used for making glue joints on long pieces of wood. It is from 20 to 24 inches in length.

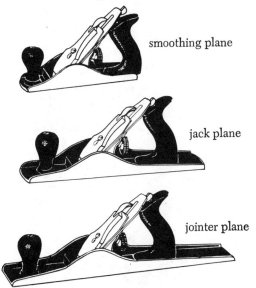

smoothing plane

jack plane

jointer plane

smoothing plane: This plane is used for extremely fine smoothing work. It is from 7 to 10 inches in length and light in weight.

A short-soled plane rides board's waves.

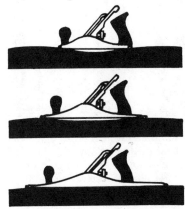

A long-soled plane bridges waves and levels them.

The depth adjusting mechanism regulates the depth of cut: sight along the sole of the plane to see how much the cutting edge projects.

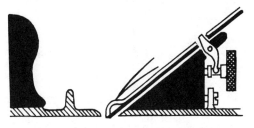

On quality planes, the width of the throat may be adjusted to regulate the amount of material shaved off the board: a wide throat setting is used for rough planing and soft woods, a narrow setting for fine smoothing and hard woods.

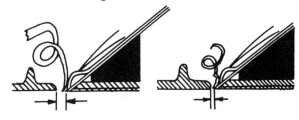

With the exception of the block plane, the bench planes are similar in construction and in the three adjustments that regulate the cutting action of the tool. The most significant difference amongst the types of bench planes is the length of the sole: the short plane will ride the unlevel board's undulations, the long plane will

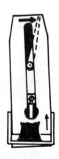

The lateral adjustment level regulates the alignment of the cutting edge in relation to the sole: sight along the sole to judge the uniformity of projection, from side to side, of the cutting edge.

Planing butt end of a board: stroke toward center to avoid splitting off edges.

Planing the edge of a board: apply pressure at knob when beginning stroke, at handle when ending stroke.

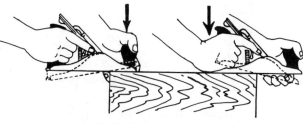

Plane with the grain to smooth and level surface.

Plane across a broad board.

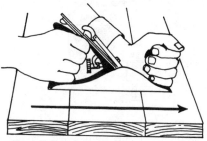

bridge them and level the board. The special planes include:

combination plane: The combination plane is used for making all types of cuts and moldings including dadoes, beads, flutes, and tongue-and-groove joints. The plane is designed to receive and be adjusted to a large variety of different blades.

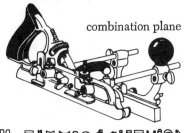

combination plane

A selection of hundreds of available irons: each yields a slightly different edge or groove shape.

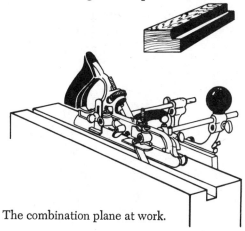

The combination plane at work.

rabbet plane: This plane is designed to cut rabbet or rectangular grooves on the faces and ends of boards. There are several varieties of rabbet planes, including modified rabbet planes, the cabinetmaker's rabbet plane, and the bench rabbet plane. Each type has slightly different features.

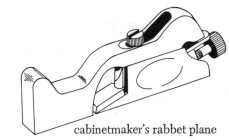

cabinetmaker's rabbet plane

Cutting an edge rabbet with the aid of a guide strip.

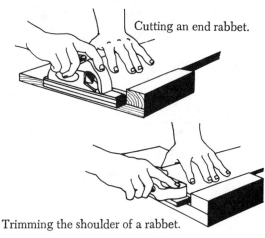

Cutting an end rabbet.

Trimming the shoulder of a rabbet.

Cutting a stopped rabbet.

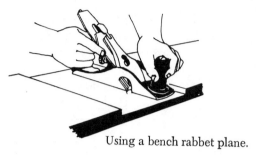

Using a bench rabbet plane.

A guide strip tacked or clamped to the
work ensures straight cuts.

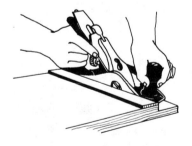

router plane: This plane is designed
to remove wood from between two
sawed or chiseled edges. It is also useful for smoothing chisel work or depressions cut with a power saw. A

small router plane is used for inlays
and locks.

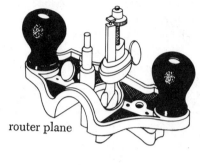

router plane

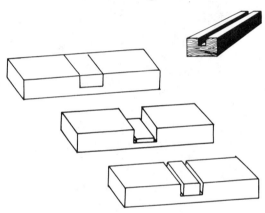

After a dado is roughed out with saw and
chisel, the router plane is used to clean
it up.

To function properly, any plane must
have a keen cutting edge. Sharpening the
blade involves grinding the proper bevel
on the cutting edge, then whetting it to the
final perfection. A 20- to 25-degree bevel
is appropriate for planing soft woods, a
25- to 30-degree bevel for hard woods,
and a 25-degree bevel a happy medium.

A jig is available to hold plane irons and chisels in proper alignment for whetting.

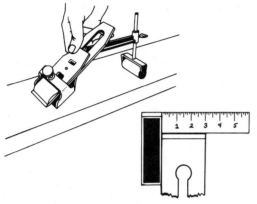

Check the squareness of the cutting edge with a try square.

A good general purpose edge.

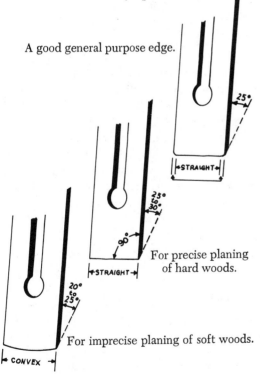

For precise planing of hard woods.

For imprecise planing of soft woods.

For the most precise work, the cutting edge should be straight and square, as determined with a try square, while a slightly convex cutting edge is suitable for less precise work. A good general purpose edge is straight with slightly rounded corners.

plate: This is a principal horizontal structural member. There are three varieties of plates:

sill plate: A horizontal member anchored to a masonry wall.

sole plate: The bottom horizontal member of a frame wall.

top plate: The top horizontal member of a frame wall supporting ceiling joists, rafters, or other members.

pliers: A pincherlike tool used for gripping and cutting pipes, bolts, wires, or other objects. Pliers come in a surprisingly wide variety of designs.

slip-joint pliers: Two pieces of steel joined with a rivet, slip-joint pliers are adjustable for large or small bolts or nuts and are an indispensable tool for fastening. Most pliers have combination jaws consisting of a flat-toothed surface, a larger surface cut with points for gripping hex nuts and bolts, and a flat cutter near the joint or rivet.

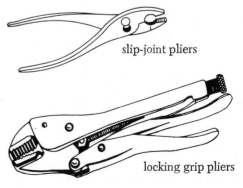

slip-joint pliers

locking grip pliers

locking grip pliers: These pliers are adjustable with a screw located in the handle of the pliers. They also are equipped with a spring-loaded locking mechanism, so that once adjusted they may be locked onto the head of a bolt, nut, or pipe.

channel-joint pliers: Called battery pliers by mechanics, these pliers are also useful in plumbing work. On the largest size pliers, the jaws expand to a maximum opening of nearly 2 inches while keeping the jaws nearly parallel.

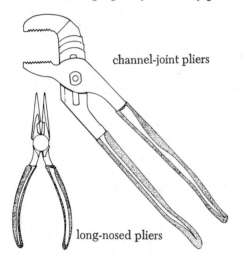

channel-joint pliers

long-nosed pliers

long-nosed pliers: These are useful in electrical work. The long tapered nose is well suited to looping wire, and a wire cutting jaw is located near the pivot point. These pliers come in various sizes and in a variety of nose shapes.

plumb: Exactly perpendicular or vertical.

plumb bob: A conical weight that is suspended on the end of a string to establish or test vertical lines. Any weight so suspended will drop at an angle of 90 degrees from the horizontal, which is known as plumb. The more elaborate plumb bobs have an internal cavity containing both string and chalk, much like a chalk line. *See also* **chalk line.**

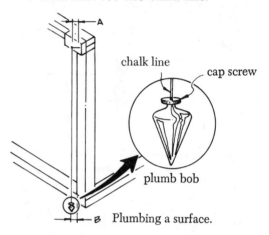

chalk line

cap screw

plumb bob

Plumbing a surface.

plywood: A piece of wood made from an odd number of glued layers of veneer. The grain of adjoining plies or layers is placed at right angles for greater strength. Plywood is usually sold in 4 x 8-foot sheets and in ¼- to 1-inch thicknesses, although other sheet sizes are available. Some lumberyards will sell a portion of a sheet. There are several grades of plywood available: N, free from defects, suitable for a natural finish; A, smooth and free from defects, suitable for painting or natural finish; B, some circular repair plugs and tight knots allowed; C, knotholes and small splits common; D, knotholes and slightly larger splits common. *Exterior* plywood has been bonded with waterproof glue and is suitable for use outside; *interior* ply is bonded with water-resistant glue, and exposed outdoor use is not recommended. In common parlance, the grading system is usually reduced to a choice between sheathing, which has knot-holes and unsanded surfaces, and panels good on one or both sides, meaning the knotholes are filled and one or both surfaces are sanded.

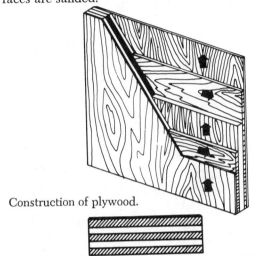

Construction of plywood.

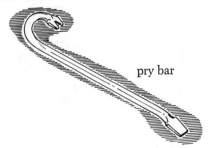

preservative: Any substance that for a reasonable length of time will prevent the action of wood-destroying fungi, borers of various kinds, and similar destructive life when the wood has been properly coated or impregnated with it. *See also* **copper naphthenate; creosote; finishes.**

primer: The first coat of paint in a paint job that consists of two or more coats.

pry bar: A **J**-shaped tool made of hardened steel. The ends are flattened and

pry bar

shaped for prying into joints. The goose-necked end has a split edge for extracting nails. The tool is used primarily for tearing things apart.

purlins: Horizontal roof members used to support the rafters between the top plate and ridge.

putty: A type of cement usually made of whiting (calcium carbonate) and boiled linseed oil, beaten or kneaded to the consistency of dough, and used in sealing glass, filling in holes in wood, and for similar purposes.

quarter-round molding: A small molding which has the cross section of a quarter circle.

rabbet: A cut made in the edge of a board, forming an open-sided groove. A rabbet is usually made in constructing a joint. A router, a dado attachment on a power saw, a rabbet plane, and a backsaw can be used to make a rabbet. *See also* **joints; planes.**

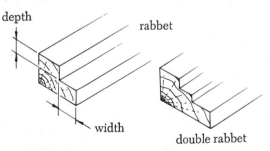

rafters: A series of structural members which are designed to support roof loads.

rasps: *See* **files and rasps.**

rebar: Steel reinforcements that are placed in concrete footings and walls.

repointing: The process of removing dry,

old mortar and replacing it with an application of cement **grout**.

retaining wall: A wall subject to lateral pressures other than from the wind. A garden wall, built to support a bank of earth, is a retaining wall.

ridge: The horizontal line at the junction of the top edges of two sloping roof surfaces.

ridge board: A board which is placed on edge at a roof's ridge and into which roof joists or rafters are fastened.

rip: To cut a board along the length of the grain.

roll roofing: Roofing material, composed of fiber and saturated with asphalt. It is generally supplied in 108-square-foot rolls of 36-inch widths. It weighs between 45 and 90 pounds per roll.

roofing: The materials—wooden, metal, asphaltic, or whatever—attached to the structure of the roof or the roof sheathing to waterproof it.

roof sheathing: The boards or material fastened to the roof joists or rafters and to which the shingles or other roof covering are attached.

router: A high speed portable machine which is used to cut and shape wood and other materials. The router cuts to a desired depth and thickness. Attachments and accessories such as templates make it

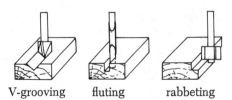

V-grooving   fluting   rabbeting

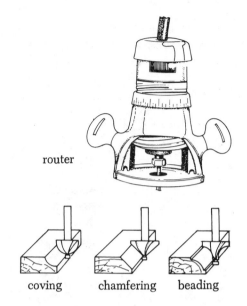

router

coving   chamfering   beading

possible to produce intricate joints, decorative cuts for trim, and inlays. It can also be used to shape edges and cut recesses as well as narrow dadoes. A router may be used freehand or clamped in a vise.

sanders: Sanding a finished product can be a long and wearying chore, but an important one. To speed and ease the sanding process, a number of different power tools are available.

> *belt sander:* A circular sanding or abrasive belt is run on rollers. Belt sanders can be either portable hand-

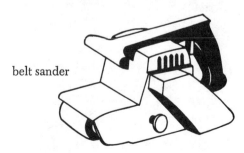

belt sander

912

operated types or mounted on tables. They are most useful for removing a large quantity of surface wood quickly; however, they may also be used for mitered, beveled, and compound angles.

disc sander: A large metal disc to which sandpaper is glued. Disc sanders can be attached to table saws and radial arm saws, or they can be purchased as a separate unit or in combination with a belt sander. They are useful for sanding mitered, beveled, and compound angles, as well as end grain, straight and convex edges.

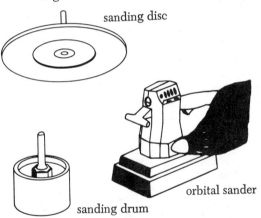

sanding disc

sanding drum

orbital sander

drum (spindle) sander: A round metal cylinder to which sandpaper is glued. Drum sanders can be attached to radial arm saws and drill presses. A drum sander is particularly useful for sanding contoured edges, inside edges, and long narrow straight edges.

orbital and vibrator sanders: Sandpaper is attached to a flat plate which vibrates in a forward-backward fashion, or in the case of an orbital sander, this vibrating motion is accompanied by a circular motion. Orbital sanders are for sanding wood down rapidly; whereas vibrator sanders are for finish work. Many portable sanders are available today which offer both orbital and vibrating motions. These sanders are primarily for surface work.

sanding blocks: Blocks of wood, metal, or plastic to which sandpaper is attached. Sanding blocks make the job of hand sanding easier and provide a flat sanding surface so that the work remains true. The sandpaper will last longer, resist buildup of cuttings, and generally do better work if the block has a rubber or felt cushion.

sanding block

sandpaper: Sandpaper is not made of sand, but rather consists of various kinds of abrasive materials which are glued or applied to paper or cloth and made into sheets, discs, drums, belts, and other forms. There are six principal kinds of abrasives used generally for woodwork and metalwork; iron oxide, emery, flint, and garnet are natural (mined or quarried) materials; and aluminum oxide and silicon carbide are artificial (manufactured) materials. (See chart.) Sandpapers are generally graded from 12 to 600. The grade of abrasive paper you select will affect the speed and quality of your sanding. When sanding, do not move more than two grades at a time. Also, only use coarse grits when absolutely necessary for removing gouge marks or for shaping operations. Wet and dry or waterproof sand-

Grades

Extra coarse	12, 16, 20
Very coarse	24, 30, 36
Coarse	40, 50
Medium	60, 80, 100
Fine	120, 150, 180
Very fine	220, 240, 280
Extra fine	320, 360, 400, 500, 600

Chart of Abrasive Coatings And Uses

Mineral or Coating	Mineral Color	Backing Available	General Use
iron oxide	reddish brown	cloth	metal polishing
emery	black	cloth	metal polishing
flint	off-white	paper	general household use
garnet	red	paper/cloth	general wood sanding
aluminum oxide	brown	paper/cloth	machine sanding hardwoods hand sanding metals
silicon	black	paper/cloth	soft metals paint, plastics, glass, leather

Note to chart: Most sandpapers are available with "open" or "closed" coats. Open coats have spaces between the grains, while closed have the grains packed tightly together. The open spaces allow cuttings to drop from the backing. Closed coats are for heavy machine sanding operations. Open coats are for hand sanding.

paper is a special type designed for use with a lubricant when hand sanding wood finishes such as varnishes, enamels, and lacquers, or machine sanding glass, metal, or plastics.

sapwood: The wood of a pale color near the outside of a log or the edges of a board. Under most conditions sapwood is more susceptible to decay than heartwood.

sash: A light frame containing one or more panes of glass.

saws: The primary cutting tool in carpentry is the saw. Many carpenters work exclusively with handsaws, and there is a handsaw specially designed for most every job. Among them are:

backsaw: Generally this saw is used in conjunction with a miter box for making precision angle and square crosscuts. *Use:* Clamp marked work in miter box or on bench and cut with

backsaw

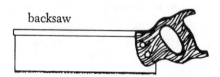

long even strokes. When using a miter box, allow the weight of the saw to carry it through the stock.

coping saw: A saw which is generally used for cutting fine detailed work in thin or soft materials. Its 6- to 8-inch blade is suspended under tension

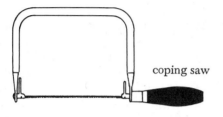

coping saw

An L-shaped sawing table with a V-cut in the top surface is handy for coping saw cuts.

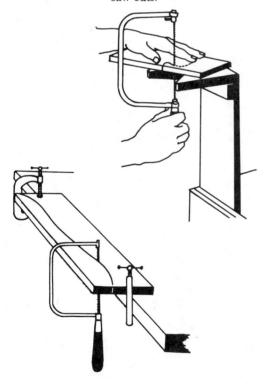

Clamp the work to the workbench edge when making long coping saw cuts.

on a steel frame. The blade may be positioned at any angle to the frame for convenience in cutting. *Use:* Clamp marked work and begin cutting with light, short strokes. The blade cuts most accurately near its ends. When using a coping saw, cut with light even pressure and never force the blade.

crosscut saws: All handsaws can generally be classified as either crosscut or rip, based on the cutting action of the teeth. Crosscut saws are designed to be used when cutting across the grain of the wood. A crosscut saw with 8 to 10 points, or teeth, per inch will cut easily. The more points per inch the finer the cut. The number of points per inch is usually stamped on the blade near the handle of the saw.

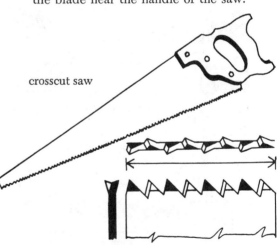

crosscut saw

Shape and set of crosscut saw's teeth.

Use: Clamp marked board and crosscut with saw held at about 45 degrees from the work. Always cut on the waste side of the marked line. To test for the angle of the cut, use a try square. With the crosscut saw, as with every saw, be sure to mark and cut your work carefully. Always cut on the waste side of the line, as in drawings 1 and 3. Failure to heed this caveat will result in pieces that are too short, as in 2, and openings that are too large, as in 4.

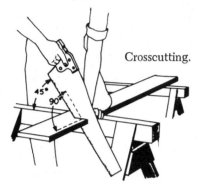
Crosscutting.

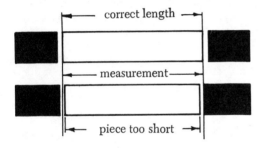
Saw carefully to ensure accurate results.

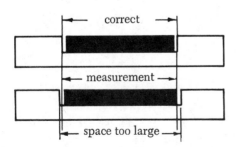

dovetail saw: A backsaw with a shorter and narrower blade and more

teeth per inch than a backsaw for finer and more accurate cuts.

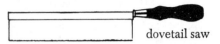
dovetail saw

hacksaw: A saw used generally for cutting metal with its blade suspended under tension on a steel frame of from 12 to 19 inches. An 18-tooth blade is best for general use. *Use:* Clamp marked work. Start cut with a file and cut with long even strokes using the entire blade. A hacksaw only cuts on the forward stroke and this is the only stroke on which pressure should be applied.

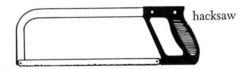
hacksaw

keyhole or compass saw: The saw blades on these handsaws are generally around 12 inches in length and taper from the handle to a point at the toe of the blade. Keyhole or compass saws are used for cutting

keyhole saw

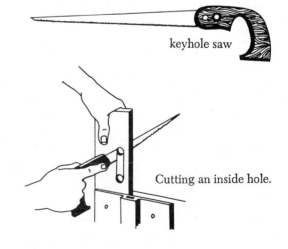
Cutting an inside hole.

curves and openings in wood. *Use:* Mark and clamp work. Interior cuts should first be bored so the saw blade can be started. Use the narrow part of the blade for small curves and starting the cut.

rip saw: All handsaws can generally be classified as either crosscut or rip, based upon the cutting action of the teeth. Rip saws are designed to be used when cutting with or along the grain of the wood. A rip saw with 5 to 7 teeth per inch will cut easily. The number of points per inch is usually stamped on the blade near the handle of the saw. *Use:* Clamp marked board and rip with saw held at about 60 degrees from the work. If saw bends, use a small wedge to spread the wood.

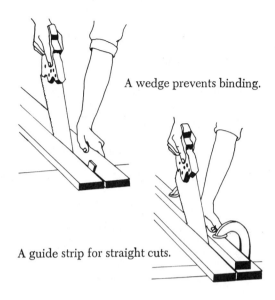

A wedge prevents binding.

A guide strip for straight cuts.

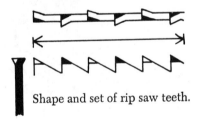

Shape and set of rip saw teeth.

Obviously, any saw will cut best when properly sharpened. This condition involves having the teeth set at the proper angle to each other and properly filed. A small triangular file is used to file the teeth, and a special plierlike tool called a saw set is used to adjust the angle of the individual teeth. The job is not difficult, but it is tedious. The saw is clamped between two boards in a vise. The shape and cutting edge of each tooth is filed. Then the angle is set using a saw set.

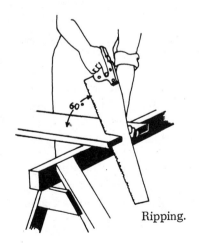

Ripping.

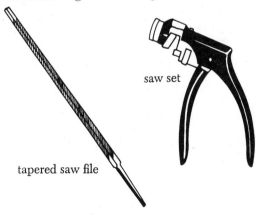

saw set

tapered saw file

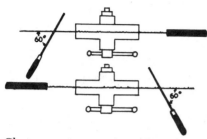

Clamp saw in vise, then file every other tooth; turn the saw around, then do teeth not touched in first filing (crosscut filing shown).

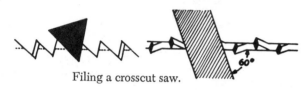

Filing a crosscut saw.

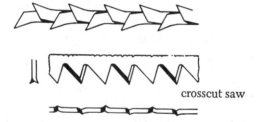

crosscut saw

Comparing the teeth of rip and crosscut saws.

rip saw

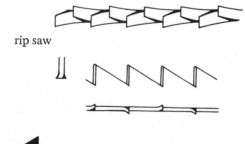

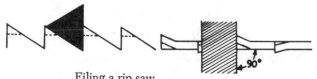

Filing a rip saw.

Since not everyone is devoted to muscle power, a number of different power saws are available. These include:

band saw: The blade is a long continuous band mounted on pulleys. Its cutting action is smooth and the saw is excellent for cutting delicate and accurate curves in stock up to 18 inches depending on the throat of the saw. It cuts wood, plastics, and other materials. The table can be adjusted for angle cuts and many come equipped with a miter gauge for crosscut operations.

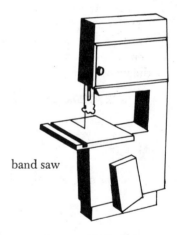

band saw

circular saw: A portable power saw with a circular blade measuring 4 to 10 inches in diameter. Interchangeable blades allow one to choose the blade suited to the particular job. Circular saws are ideal for heavy-duty use and are adjustable for compound angle or miter cuts. *Use:* Clamp marked work. Using the wing nuts, adjust the blade depth and angle desired. In order to avoid bending the saw, the blade should be set to just cut through the stock. Be sure the cord is well out of the way of the cut.

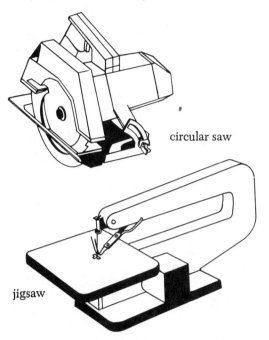

circular saw

jigsaw

jigsaw: A 6- to 8-inch blade is mounted on a motor in a steel frame and cuts with up-down action. Although a wide variety of blades is available, they all are thin and take a very fine cut. The jigsaw is ideal for delicate and fine work on curves or straight cuts. The table is adjustable for angle or miter cuts. Jigsaws are of many different types; some can be turned into a saber saw by removing the overarm; some can be used with various attachments for filing and sanding operations; some can cut wood up to 2 inches.

radial arm saw: A circular saw that is mounted on a movable head on an arm above the work surface. The head and arm rotate so that rip and crosscut operations may be performed as well as compound angle cuts. Because a radial arm saw cuts from the top down, the cutting surface is always visible for greater accuracy. In addition to being able to mount dadoes, molding heads, sanding discs, and various saw blades on the motor, a radial arm saw can also be adapted to a variety of spinning operations including drum sanding, routing, and drilling. The radial arm saw is the most versatile power saw available. The disadvantages of the saw are that it can only crosscut the length of the arm, generally about 14 to 16½ inches, and it can only rip boards 24 to 26½ inches wide. Also, for many of its operations, alternate tables must be constructed or purchased and mounted on the saw's bed.

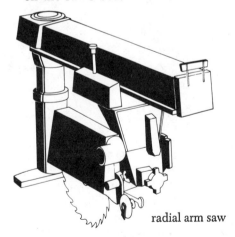

radial arm saw

saber saw (also known as a *scroll face* or *portable jigsaw*): This portable power saw has a wide variety of inexpensive blades which allow it to handle various materials including metal, plastic, and wood. The saw can perform straight or curved cuts, and the blade can be positioned at different angles for compound miter cuts. The saw can handle up to 2-inch stock. *Use:* Clamp marked work, and be sure power cord is away from cutting area.

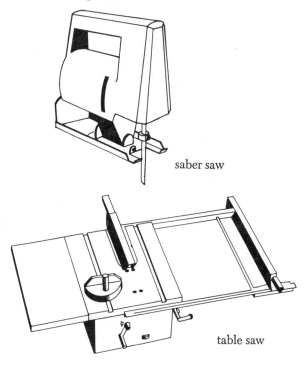

saber saw

table saw

table saw: A circular saw mounted below a table or bed with the blade protruding above the work surface. The blade is adjustable to angle and depth. The table itself has a fully adjustable fence and miter gauge for crosscutting. A table saw is ideal for accurate miter cuts and perfectly straight lines. With a variety of different blades available, a table saw can cut dadoes, grooves, bevels, and moldings. The one big disadvantage of a

table saw is that when cutting only partway through the stock one is unable to see the line of the cut.

scab: A short piece of wood or plywood which is fastened to two abutting timbers to splice them together.

screwdrivers: There are many types of screwdrivers available, the two basic types being Phillips head and plain head. When using screwdrivers one rule of thumb is to use a screwdriver which fits the slot of the screw. If the blade is too big or small it will tear the screwhead. Also, wood screws require a wider blade than do sheet metal screws, so buy the type of screwdriver suited to the job.

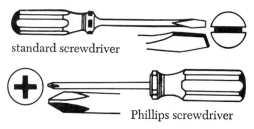

standard screwdriver

Phillips screwdriver

screw hook: A hook with threads and a sharp point on one end for easy insertion.

screws: Most screws can be classified as either plain-slotted type head or Phillips head and are available with three different types of head shapes—flathead, roundhead, and ovalhead. Flatheads should be used when the head of the screw is to be flush with the surface. Roundhead screws are useful for fastening thin materials and work that is to be disassembled. Ovalhead screws are best for countersinking. Screws vary in length from ¼ inch to 6 inches and are graded from 0 to 24 based on the diameter of the shank. Screws are obtainable with a variety of finishes and while most are made from mild steel, brass screws and coated screws are available where rusting is a problem. There are also a wide variety of special types of screws for unique jobs. *Installation:* Be sure the blade of the screwdriver fits snugly in the head of the screw. Also prebore a pilot hole smaller than the shank of the screw, and if the head is to show, you should consider countersinking the screw. If you want to put a wooden plug or screw button over the screw be sure to bore this hole first.

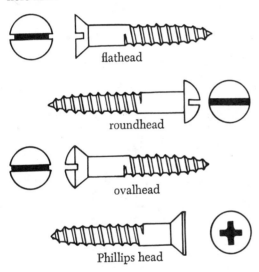

flathead

roundhead

ovalhead

Phillips head

sealer: A finishing material which can be either clear or pigmented and is used on uncoated wood to seal its surface. *See also* **finishes.**

setscrew: A machine screw fitted with a socket for an allen wrench rather than a regular slotted head. Designed for use where it must be screwed through one part to jam tightly against another to prevent movement of one part relative to the other, as when fastening a pulley to a shaft.

shake: In construction, a type of shingle usually hand split and used for roofing or weatherboarding. Shake is also the term applied to a defect in lumber caused by a separation of the spring and summer growth rings. *See also* **lumber.**

sheathing: The structural covering, usually of boards, fiberboards, or plywood, placed over exterior studding or rafters.

shellac: *See* **finishes.**

shim: A thin strip or wedge of wood used for plumbing and leveling wood members.

shingles: Used for roof or sidewall coverings, shingles are made from various materials cut to stock lengths, widths, and thicknesses.

shiplap lumber: Boards that have their edges rabbeted to form a lap joint between adjacent pieces. This is one type of matched lumber.

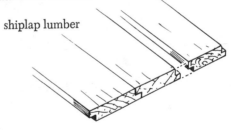

shiplap lumber

siding: The finish covering of the outside wall of a frame building including horizontal weatherboard, vertical boards with battens, shingles, or other materials.

sill: The lowest member of a frame structure. The sill rests on the foundation and supports the floor joists or the uprights of the wall. The member forming the lower side of an opening as in a doorsill or windowsill.

soffit: The underside covering of an overhanging cornice.

softwoods: These trees generally have needlelike or scalelike leaves that remain on the tree throughout the year. Principal softwoods include cedar, fir, juniper, pines, redwood, and spruce. Softwoods are used in construction for both framing and finish work.

span: The distance between structural supports, such as walls, piers, girders, and so on. For the purposes of calculating rafter specifications, the span is defined as the distance between the outside edges of the top plates on opposite sides of the structure.

spline: A thin strip of wood that is fitted into matching grooves cut in the joining faces of a joint. *See also* **joints.**

spokeshave: A short-bottomed plane with winglike handles whose principal function is smoothing curved surfaces. It

Cut with the grain always.

spokeshave

Work edge to center on concave shape, center to edge on convex shape.

is adjusted similarly to a plane and operated not unlike a drawknife. It should be used so that it cuts with the grain.

square: A unit of measure of 100 square feet which is usually applied to roofing material and sometimes sidewall coverings.

square, combination: This measuring tool has a calibrated blade 12 inches long which can be adjusted to different lengths through the head for gauging. The head has one edge at right angles (90°) to the blade and the other at 45 degrees. In addition, the combination square has a spirit level and a scriber built into the head. While the square can perform the functions of a try square including 45-degree miters, it can also be used as a marking gauge and level and the steel blade can be removed from the head and used as a straightedge.

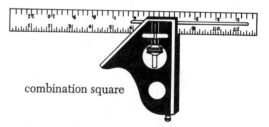

combination square

square, framing (or **steel**): This simple tool is one of the most important layout tools. The problems that can be solved with the framing square are so many and varied that entire books have been written explaining its use. Among the most common uses of the framing square are rafter layout, stairway layout, and miter layout. The tool is an **L**-shaped metal item, with a 24-inch-long, 2-inch-wide member called the body or blade and a 16- or 18-inch-long, 1½-inch-wide member called the

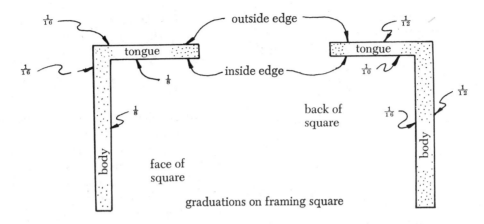

graduations on framing square

tongue. The edges of the tool are engraved with graduations of inches. The graduations on the face, which is the side with a manufacturer's stamp (or the side that is visible when the blade is held in the left hand and the tongue in the right), are of sixteenths on the outside edges, eighths on the inside edges. The back of the square has graduations of sixteenths on the inside edge of the blade, tenths on the inside edge of the tongue, and twelfths on both outside edges. In addition to these markings, the framing square usually has several tables to speed layout calculations, and the square comes with detailed instructions of making best use of these tables.

square, try: This **L**-shaped measuring tool is most commonly used for laying out or checking right (90°) angles. The tool generally has a scale on its steel blade and can also be used, depending on the type, in measuring or laying out 45-degree miters or angles. The handles of the try square are made from either wood or metal. *Use:* Place the handle along the edge or face of the wood using the metal blade for layout or checking the squareness of the work piece.

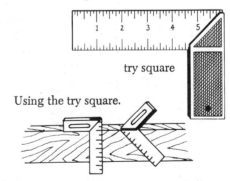

try square

Using the try square.

stain: Materials used to impart color to wood. *See also* **finishes.**

staple gun: An inexpensive and useful tool for the homestead. This spring-powered mechanical staple driver has a

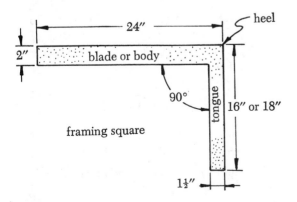

framing square

variety of accessories that permit it to use different shapes and sizes of staples to secure everything from fiberboard panels to fencing to electrical wiring.

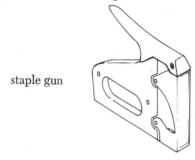

staple gun

star drill: A hand-held drill with an end fashioned into a four-cornered star, used for drilling holes in masonry. The drill is tapped with a heavy hammer and is rotated after each blow.

storm sash or storm window: An extra window placed on the outside of a window as an additional protection against cold weather.

story: That part of a building between any floor and the floor or roof next above.

story board (or **story pole**): A rod or board marked and used to lay out and transfer measurements for door and window openings, siding, shingle and masonry courses, and the like.

straightedge: A straight length of metal or strip of wood, having opposite faces parallel, used to lay out and check the accuracy of work.

street elbow: An elbow pipe fitting with outside thread on one end.

stringer: A support for crossmembers in floors or ceilings. In stairs, stringers are the support on which the stair treads rest.

stud: One of a series of vertical supports used in walls and partitions.

subfloor: Boards or plywood which are attached to joists and on which a finish floor is laid.

Surform tools: These tools are effective for removing wood, plastic, or soft metals quickly. They can be used for shaping, trimming, or forming. They are available in different shapes and sizes depending on the job to be done: round file, pocket plane, file, and plane.

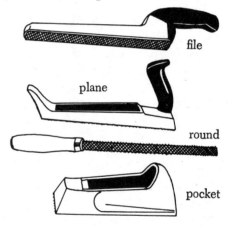

file

plane

round

pocket

taper: A gradual and uniform decrease in the size of a rectangular piece, a hole, or a cylinder.

template: A pattern or guide used to check dimensions, contours, or locations of nuts, bolts, screws, fittings, or joints on work that will be replicated.

thinners: Volatile liquids that are used to regulate the consistency of finishing materials.

threaded hook: *See* **screw hook.**

threshold: A strip of wood or metal with

beveled edges which is used over the finished floor and sill of exterior doors.

thumbscrew: A screw made with a single large ear rather than a slotted head so that it can be easily tightened or removed by hand.

timber: Lumber having both a thickness and width of at least 5 inches.

toenailing: Driving a nail at a slant to the initial surface so that it can penetrate into a second member.

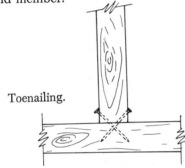

Toenailing.

tongue: A projecting bead of wood on the edge of a board which is cut to fit into a groove on another piece. (Generally tongue and grooving is done with a wood shaper or planer.)

tongue and groove: Boards which are cut or planed in such a manner that there is a groove on one edge and a corresponding tongue on the other.

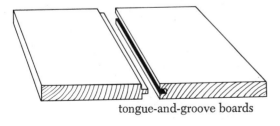

tongue-and-groove boards

trim: This is a general term applied to the various strips of wood and moldings used to finish door and window openings, as well as corners where walls intersect the floor and ceiling. The term also applies to such moldings and strips added to the exterior of buildings.

trimmer: A beam or joist to which a header is nailed in framing chimneys, stairways, or other openings.

trowels: These are the principal tools of the mason. There is a variety of trowels. The pointed trowels used in laying up bricks and concrete blocks are made in several sizes, with the smallest sizes called pointing trowels, the largest sizes called simply mason's trowels. A completely different style of trowel, called a steel finishing trowel, is used to put the smooth finished surface on poured concrete slabs. This trowel is basically a rectangular piece of sheet metal with a handle attached; the trowel is available in various sizes.

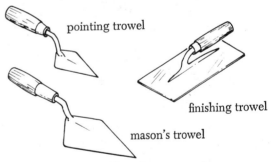

pointing trowel

finishing trowel

mason's trowel

truss: An assembly of structural members that are joined to form a rigid framework. Generally structural members are interconnected to form triangles.

turpentine: A volatile oil which is used as a thinner in paints and as a solvent in varnishes.

undercoat: In finishing, it refers to the coats applied prior to the top or finish coat.

vapor barrier: A material with a high resistance to the movement of water vapor into walls, such as foil, plastic film, or specially coated paper. Generally it is used in combination with insulation to control condensation.

varnish: A preparation of drying oil or drying oil and resin suitable for spreading on surfaces to form continuous, transparent coatings. It is also used for mixing with pigments to make enamels. Basically there are two types of varnish, marine or exterior and interior. *See also* **finishes.**

veneer: A thin sheet of wood. Veneers can be sliced, cut, sawed. Veneers are crisscrossed in glued-up layers to make plywood. Veneers of expensive woods valued for their appearance are bonded to inexpensive backing boards to yield decorative paneling and cabinetmaking material.

vent: Anything which allows air to flow as an inlet or outlet.

vise: *See* **clamping tools.**

waler (or whaler): A horizontal member used in constructing and setting up forms for concrete.

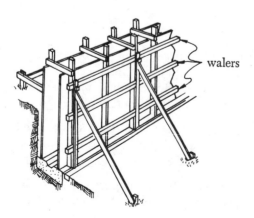

walers

wane: A defect in lumber in which either bark is present or wood is lacking on an edge or corner for any reason. *See also* **lumber.**

warp: Any variation from a true or plane surface. Warp includes crooking, bowing, cupping, and twisting or any combination of them. Proper storage of lumber can help prevent, and to some degree eliminate, warping. *See also* **lumber.**

water-repellent preservative: A liquid designed to penetrate into wood and impart water repellency and moderate preservative protection. This type of preservative is usually applied by dipping.

weatherstrip: Narrow sections of thin metal, felt, rubber, or other material to prevent air and moisture from penetrating around windows and doors.

weephole: A small hole built into a wall to drain water from one side to the other. They are commonly used in masonry walls, especially retaining walls. Water that collects inside a wall cavity or on the backfilled side of a retaining wall can damage, even collapse, the wall in time.

whetstone: An abrasive stone used to sharpen cutting tools. Some whetstones are man-made and have a coarse face and a fine face. Slipstones are simply whetstones with rounded or curved faces to

Using a whetstone.

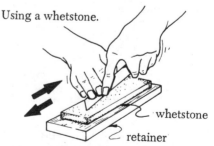

whetstone

retainer

926

ease the task of sharpening a curved cutting edge. A coating of light oil should be poured on the whetstone at the beginning of each use to help float away steel particles ground from the tool. The sharpening process often begins at a grindstone, where the cutting edge is formed. It then turns to the whetstone where the edge is honed.

wing nut: A nut with large wings or ears attached that enable it to be installed or removed very quickly by hand.

wing nut

wrenches: Any number of tools that are used for holding or turning nuts, bolts, and pipes are called wrenches. There are several types designed specifically for nuts and bolts, to wit:

adjustable wrenches: These wrenches have a stationary jaw and an adjustable jaw. When purchasing an adjustable wrench be sure of two things: first, that the wrench, when closed around a nut or bolt, forms a hex shape for a firm contact; and second, that the adjustable spring mechanism does not slip when tension or torque is applied.

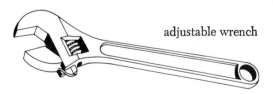

adjustable wrench

box-end wrenches: These wrenches completely surround the head or nut of a bolt. A circular steel band with generally twelve points to grip the

bolt or nut is the most common type of box-end wrench.

combination wrenches: These are wrenches which have an open-end wrench at one end and a box-end wrench at the other.

open-end wrenches: A **U**-shaped steel head is used to grip the head or nut of a bolt. Open-end wrenches are less likely to slip than box-end wrenches if the face of the bolt or nut is marred or burred.

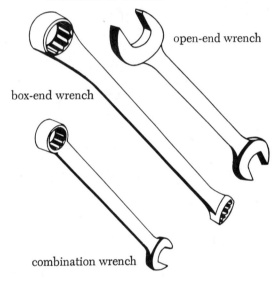

open-end wrench

box-end wrench

combination wrench

pipe wrench: A relative of the familiar monkey wrench, the pipe wrench has a loosely adjustable opening with nearly parallel, serrated jaws.

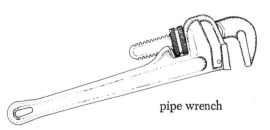

pipe wrench

The jaws are placed around a pipe; pulling on the handle toward the jaw opening tightens the grip on the pipe. Usually pipe wrenches are worked in pairs, one wrench on the pipe, another on the fitting. Many sizes are available.

socket wrench: This is actually a wrench system. Socket wrenches—often called socket sets—are the principal tools of mechanics, but they are of use to the homestead handyman too. The basis for the system is a handle that will take interchangeable sockets that fit over bolt heads and nuts. Screwdriver tips, universal joint fittings, extension bars, and other accessories expand the usefulness and run up the price of socket wrenches.

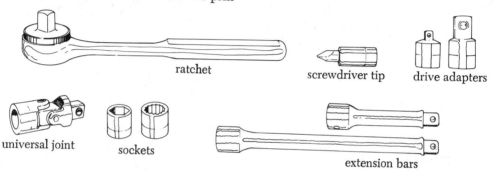

ratchet

screwdriver tip

drive adapters

universal joint

sockets

extension bars

Index

Index

Metric Conversion Chart

WHEN YOU KNOW	MULTIPLY BY	TO FIND
	length	
inches	2.54	centimeters (cm)
feet	30	centimeters (cm)
yards	.9	meters (m)
	area	
square inches	6.5	square centimeters
square feet	.09	square meters
square yards	.8	square meters
	weight	
ounces	28	grams (g)
pounds	.45	kilograms (kg)
	volume	
fluid ounces	30	milliliters (mL)
pints	.47	milliliters (mL)
quarts	.95	liters (L)
gallons	3.8	liters (L)
cubic feet	.03	cubic meters
cubic yards	.76	cubic meters